The Routledge Companion to Artificial Intelligence in Architecture

Providing the most comprehensive source available, this book surveys the state of the art in artificial intelligence (AI) as it relates to architecture. This book is organized in four parts: theoretical foundations, tools and techniques, AI in research, and AI in architectural practice. It provides a framework for the issues surrounding AI and offers a variety of perspectives. It contains 24 consistently illustrated contributions examining seminal work on AI from around the world, including the United States, Europe, and Asia. It articulates current theoretical and practical methods, offers critical views on tools and techniques, and suggests future directions for meaningful uses of AI technology. Architects and educators who are concerned with the advent of AI and its ramifications for the design industry will find this book an essential reference.

Imdat As is the recipient of the prestigious International Fellowship for Outstanding Researchers and a grant from the Scientific and Technological Research Council of Turkey (TUBITAK). He researches and teaches at the Istanbul Technical University (ITU). Imdat received his BArch from the Middle East Technical University (METU), his MSc in architecture from the Massachusetts Institute of Technology (MIT), and his doctorate from the Harvard University Graduate School of Design. He has coauthored *Dynamic Digital Representations in Architecture: Visions in Motion* (Taylor & Francis, 2008). In 2011, he founded Arcbazar.com, a first-of-its-kind crowdsourcing platform for architectural design, which has been featured as one of the "Top 100 Most Brilliant Companies" by the *Entrepreneur* magazine. In 2017, he used Arcbazar's design data through a DARPA-funded research project to generate conceptual designs via artificial intelligence (AI). Imdat is currently heading the City Development through Design Intelligence (CIDDI) lab at ITU and investigates the impact of emerging technologies on urban morphology and the future of the city.

Prithwish Basu is a principal scientist at Raytheon BBN Technologies (BBN). He has a PhD in computer engineering from Boston University (2003) and a BTech in computer science and engineering from the Indian Institute of Technology (IIT), Delhi (1996). Prithwish has been the Principal Investigator of several U.S. government-funded research projects on networking and network science during his 17-year tenure at BBN. He was the Program

Director for the U.S. Army Research Laboratory's Network Science Collaborative Technology Alliance (NS CTA) program, which ran from 2009 until early 2020, and made fundamental contributions to advancing the state-of-the-art for the science of dynamic intertwined multigenre networks. Prithwish also led the DARPA-funded Fundamental Design (FUN Design) in 2017–2018, which explored the application of state-of-the-art AI/ML algorithms for graphs encoding architectural design data. Currently, he is leading the development of algorithms in the DARPA-funded FastNICs program for speeding up a deep neural network (DNN) training by automatically parallelizing DNN workloads on fast network hardware. Prithwish recently served as an associate editor for the *IEEE Transactions of Mobile Computing* and was the lead guest editor for the *IEEE Journal of Selected Areas in Communications (JSAC)* special issue on network science. He has coauthored over 120 peer-reviewed articles (in conferences, journals, and book chapters) and has won the best paper award at the IEEE NetSciCom 2014 and PAKDD 2014. He was also a recipient of the *MIT Technology Review*'s TR35 (Top 35 Innovators Under 35) award in 2006.

The Routledge Companion to Artificial Intelligence in Architecture

Edited by Imdat As and Prithwish Basu

Routledge
Taylor & Francis Group

LONDON AND NEW YORK

First published 2021
by Routledge
2 Park Square, Milton Park, Abingdon, Oxon OX14 4RN

and by Routledge
605 Third Avenue, New York, NY 10158

Routledge is an imprint of the Taylor & Francis Group, an informa business

British Library Cataloguing-in-Publication Data
A catalog record for this book is available from the British Library

Library of Congress Cataloging-in-Publication Data
Names: As, Imdat, editor. | Basu, Prithwish, editor.
Title: The Routledge companion to artificial intelligence in architecture /
edited by Imdat As and Prithwish Basu.
Description: Abington, Oxon; New York: Routledge, 2021. |
Includes bibliographical references and index.
Identifiers: LCCN 2020047524 (print) | LCCN 2020047525 (ebook) |
ISBN 9780367424589 (hardback) | ISBN 9780367824259 (ebook)
Subjects: LCSH: Architecture and technology. | Artificial intelligence.
Classification: LCC NA2543.T43 R68 2021 (print) |
LCC NA2543.T43 (ebook) | DDC 720/.47—dc23
LC record available at https://lccn.loc.gov/2020047524
LC ebook record available at https://lccn.loc.gov/2020047525

ISBN: 978-0-367-42458-9 (hbk)
ISBN: 978-0-367-74959-0 (pbk)
ISBN: 978-0-367-82425-9 (ebk)

Typeset in Bembo
by codeMantra

Contents

Contents

Contributors

Imdat As is the recipient of the prestigious International Fellowship for Outstanding Researchers and a grant from the Scientific and Technological Research Council of Turkey (TUBITAK). He researches and teaches at the Istanbul Technical University (ITU). Imdat received his BArch from the Middle East Technical University (METU), his MSc in architecture from the Massachusetts Institute of Technology (MIT), and his doctorate from the Harvard University Graduate School of Design. He has coauthored *Dynamic Digital Representations in Architecture: Visions in Motion* (Taylor & Francis, 2008). In 2011, he founded Arcbazar.com, a first-of-its-kind crowdsourcing platform for architectural design, which has been featured as one of the "Top 100 Most Brilliant Companies" by the *Entrepreneur* magazine. In 2017, he used Arcbazar's design data through a DARPA-funded research project to generate conceptual designs via artificial intelligence (AI). Imdat is currently heading the City Development through Design Intelligence (CIDDI) lab at ITU and investigates the impact of emerging technologies on urban morphology and the future of the city.

Özgün Balaban is currently a postdoctoral researcher at TU Delft, the Faculty of Architecture and the Built Environment, Architectural Engineering + Technology Department, Design Informatics group. He was an adjunct lecturer at the Istanbul Technical University (ITU) and the MEF University. He was a PhD researcher at Future Cities Laboratories, Singapore. He has a doctoral degree from the Singapore University of Technology and Design (SUTD) and an MSc in architectural design computing from the ITU. He has a BSc in electrical engineering and A.A. in interior architecture, both from the Bilkent University. His research interests include data analytics and ML for architecture and urban planning, the use of game environments in design, and building information modeling.

Prithwish Basu is a principal scientist at Raytheon BBN Technologies (BBN). He has a PhD in computer engineering from the Boston University (2003) and a BTech in computer science and engineering from the Indian Institute of Technology (IIT), Delhi (1996). Prithwish has been the Principal Investigator of several U.S. government-funded research projects on networking and network science during his 17-year tenure at BBN. He was the Program Director for the U.S. Army Research Laboratory's Network Science Collaborative Technology Alliance (NS CTA) program, which ran from 2009 until early 2020, and made fundamental contributions to advancing the state-of-the art for the science of dynamic intertwined multigenre networks. Prithwish also led the DARPA-funded Fundamental Design (FUN Design) in 2017–2018, which explored the application of state-of-the-art AI/ML algorithms for graphs encoding architectural design data. Currently, he is leading the development of algorithms in the DARPA-funded FastNICs program for speeding up a deep neural network

(DNN) training by automatically parallelizing DNN workloads on fast network hardware. Prithwish recently served as an associate editor for the *IEEE Transactions of Mobile Computing* and was the lead guest editor for the *IEEE Journal of Selected Areas in Communications* (*JSAC*) special issue on network science. He has coauthored over 110 peer-reviewed articles (in conferences, journals, and book chapters) and has won the best paper award at the IEEE NetSciCom 2014 and PAKDD 2014. He was also a recipient of the *MIT Technology Review*'s TR35 (Top 35 Innovators Under 35) award in 2006.

Mathias Bernhard holds a doctor of science from the ETH Zurich and is currently a post-doctoral researcher in the Digital Building Technologies (DBT) group at ETH Zurich. He is an architect with profound specialization in computational design, digital fabrication, and information technology. In particular, he is interested in how artifacts can be encoded, made machine-readable, and digitally operational. His research focuses on how the increasingly ubiquitous availability of data and computational power influence the design process and how different methods of AI, ML, or evolutionary strategies can be employed in the development of our built environment.

He has more than ten years of experience in researching and teaching at the intersection of architecture, computer science, and digital fabrication. He worked on numerous projects of international renown, in interdisciplinary teams, and at a broad range of scales. His work has been published in the recognized field-relevant conference proceedings and peer-reviewed journals and exhibited internationally.

Sven G. Bilén (BS, Penn State, 1991; MSE, 1993; and PhD, University of Michigan, 1998) is the Professor of Engineering Design, Electrical Engineering, and Aerospace Engineering at Penn State and the Head of the School of Engineering Design, Technology, and Professional Programs. Bilén's research interests, coordinated through his direction of the Systems Design Lab, include the areas of space systems design; electrodynamic tethers; spacecraft–plasma interactions; plasma diagnostics for space plasmas, plasma electric thrusters, and low-temperature plasmas; software-defined radio techniques and systems; wireless sensor systems; concrete 3d printing; innovative engineering design, systems design, and new product design; engineering entrepreneurship; and global and virtual engineering design. Dr. Bilén is a member of IEEE, AIAA, AGU, ASEE, INCOSE, and Sigma Xi.

Sergey Burukin (BSE (CS), DipEng, MIA) is the Head of Decision Intelligence at Greenice. net, a web development company. He provides professional full-stack data analysis, selects the optimal solution, and supervises the development process. By architecting and developing AI (ML) systems, he enforces a decision-making process.

Bradley Cantrell is a landscape architect and scholar whose work focuses on the role of computation and media in environmental and ecological design. He has held academic appointments at the Harvard Graduate School of Design, the Rhode Island School of Design, and the Louisiana State University—Robert Reich School of Landscape Architecture. His work in Louisiana over the past decade points to a series of methodologies that develop modes of modeling, simulation, and embedded computation that express and engage the complexity of overlapping physical, cultural, and economic systems. Cantrell's work has been presented and published in a range of peer-reviewed venues internationally including ACADIA, CELA, EDRA, ASAH, and ARCC.

Stanislas Chaillou was born in Paris and received his Bachelor of Architecture degree from the Ecole Polytechnique Fédérale de Lausanne (EPFL, 2015) and his master's degree from the Harvard University (2019). His work focuses on the theoretical and applicative aspects of AI in architecture. Stanislas now works as an architect and data scientist at Spacemaker's R&D Department. He is in charge of developing research projects around AI to assist architectural design. Stanislas Chaillou is also a curator of the "Artificial Intelligence & Architecture" exhibition, which took place at the Pavillon de l'Arsenal in 2020. He also won two "American Architecture Prizes" (2017) and the "Architecture Masterprize" (2018). He has been awarded the ZGF grant for his past work. He is a Fulbright scholar and holder of the Arthur Sachs and Jean Gaillard Fellowships awarded by the Harvard University.

Angelos Chronis is the head of the City Intelligence Lab at the Austrian Institute of Technology in Vienna and he teaches at the Institute for Advanced Architecture of Catalonia. He has previously worked as an associate at Foster + Partners and has been teaching at the Bartlett, UCL, the IUAV in Venice, and the TU Graz. His research focuses on performance-driven design and simulation, but he has worked in various fields, including AI and ML, AR/VR, 3D scanning, digital fabrication, and interactive installations. He has developed various design systems and simulation interfaces, including InFraReD, an AI-based design framework for urban planning.

Zack Xuereb Conti is a registered architect and multidisciplinary researcher whose interests lie at the intersection of architecture, engineering, statistics, and AI. He is currently a research associate at the Alan Turing Institute in London and has previously conducted research at the Singapore University of Technology and Design (SUTD) and at the Harvard Graduate School of Design. Zack holds a PhD from SUTD and an MPhil in digital architectonics from the University of Bath.

Benjamin Dillenburger is an architect who explores computational design methods and digital fabrication to broaden the design freedom for architecture and to develop performative building solutions. Recent works include the design of two full-scale 3D printed rooms for the FRAC Centre, Orleans, and the permanent collection of Centre Pompidou, Paris. Benjamin Dillenburger holds a PhD degree from the ETH Zurich and is the Assistant Professor for Digital Building Technologies (DBT) at the Institute of Technology in Architecture at ETH Zurich after having taught as the Assistant Professor at the John H. Daniels Faculty of Architecture at the University of Toronto. He is the Principal Investigator of the Swiss National Competence Centre of Research in Digital Fabrication (NCCR DFAB).

José P. Duarte (Lic Arch, UT Lisbon, 1987; SMArchS, 1993; and PhD, MIT, 2001) is the Stuckeman Chair in Design Innovation and director of the Stuckeman Center for Design Computing at Penn State, where he is the Professor of Architecture and Landscape Architecture, and Affiliate Professor of Architectural Engineering and Engineering Design. Dr. Duarte was the Dean of the Lisbon School of Architecture and the President of eCAADe. He was a cofounder of the Penn State Additive Construction Laboratory (AddCon Lab), and his research interests are in the use of computation to support context-sensitive design at different scales. Recently, he has coedited (with Branko Kolarevic) the book *Mass Customization and Design Democracy* (Routledge, NY, 2019), and his team was awarded the second place in the finals of the "NASA 3D Printed Mars Habitat Challenge."

Theodoros Galanos is a leader in the use of advanced computational technologies in design for the built environment always working at the intersections between design, data, and intelligence. He seeks to create innovative, data-driven solutions within the field of computational environmental design (CED) while breaking the boundaries between disciplines, integrating technology and automation as driving factors of effective, efficient, and innovative design solutions.

Sam Conrad Joyce is an Assistant Professor and Director of the Master of Architecture course in the Architecture and Sustainable Design Pillar at the Singapore University of Technology and Design. He explores the intersection of technology-driven research and design practice, previously having worked at Foster + Partners and Buro Happold working on the computational design for a wide range of projects such as the 2014 Olympic Stadium, Louvé Abu Dhabi, UAE Pavilion Expo 2015, Apple Campus, Bloomberg London HQ, and Mexico City Airport. At the same time he completed a joint Engineering Doctorate from the Bath and Bristol Universities. Sam heads the Meta Design Lab, an interdisciplinary research group based in Singapore combining architects, engineers, cognitive-scientists, UX experts, and programmers. It seeks out conceiving, developing, and testing new interfaces to design processes; specifically, how AI and big data can help decision-making and find novel solutions with the aim to enable humans and computers to be collaborative cocreators. The lab works with companies, governments, and individuals in new ways to understand and design the built environment using these techniques.

Sawako Kaijima is an Assistant Professor of Architecture at the Harvard Graduate School of Design and the Shutzer Assistant Professor at Harvard's Radcliffe Institute. Her work investigates the integration of architectural, structural, and environmental knowledge to create unique, efficient, and previously unattainable designs. Before Harvard, Sawako held an appointment at the Singapore University of Technology and Design. In addition, she was involved in various architectural projects in collaboration with practices such as ZHA, Thomas Heatherwick, Fosters + Partners, Future Systems, and others at the London-based structural engineering consultancy, AKT. She holds a Master of Architecture from the Massachusetts Institute of Technology and a Bachelor of Arts in environmental information from Keio University, Japan.

Anatolii Kotov is an architect and technology enthusiast. Currently, he is doing PhD research as well as teaching a course for Digital Design Methods at the Faculty of Architecture at the BTU Cottbus. He is a winner of several academic competitions in both fields of architecture and programming. His particular interest lies in an efficient merging of technology with art in architecture and design. This also includes using advanced approaches such as AI/ML.

Ramesh Krishnamurti has degrees in Electrical Engineering, Computer Science, and a PhD in Systems Design. A Professor at Carnegie Mellon University, he currently directs the doctoral program in computational design in the School of Architecture. His research focuses on the formal, semantic, generative, and algorithmic issues in computational design. His research activities have had a multidisciplinary flavor and include shape grammars, generative designs, spatial topologies, spatial algorithms, geometrical and parametric modeling, sensor-based modeling and recognition, agent-based design, analyses of design styles, knowledge-based design systems, integration of graphical and natural language, interactivity and user interfaces, graphic environments, computer simulation, "green" CAD, and war games.

Tyler Kvochick received his MArch from the Princeton University in 2017, where he completed his thesis on the topic of applying deep neural networks to generating architectural drawings. He has contributed to and published work in NeurIPS AI Art Online, ACADIA, and IBPSA. He has presented his work privately and publicly at top architecture firms and industry conferences. He currently works as a computer vision engineer at 1build applying deep learning to analyzing construction documents. He lives in the Bay Area where he hikes as often as he can.

Longtai Liao is an architectural designer who received his Master of Architecture degree from the University of Michigan in 2019. Currently, he is a designer in Steinberg Hart, San Francisco. He has worked for Stanley Saitowitz and Mark Cavagnero. His design work engages the building environment with novel methods of digital design.

Henan Liu received his MArch from the University of Michigan and BArch from the Shenyang Jianzhu University. He currently works as an architectural designer at Populous in Kansas City.

Xun Liu is a PhD student at the University of Virginia. Her research focuses on the integration of physical and digital simulations, data analysis and visualization, and generative design in landscape architecture. She received a Master in Landscape Architecture with Jacob Weidenmann Prize from the Harvard Graduate School of Design, and a Bachelor of Architecture with distinction in technology from the Tongji University. Before joining the PhD program, she has worked as a research associate in the Office for Urbanization, Irving Innovation Fellow at Harvard GSD, landscape designer at Stoss Landscape Urbanism, and computational designer at New York City Department of City Planning.

Daniel Cardoso Llach brings together methods from computation, science and technology studies, and history to investigate how digital technologies restructure architectural work and the notion of the design itself. He is an associate professor in the School of Architecture at Carnegie Mellon University, where he chairs the Master of Science in Computational Design and codirects the Computational Design Laboratory (CodeLab). With his graduate students at CodeLab, Professor Cardoso investigates the nexus of AI and robotics, the material and sensual history of design technologies, and computational approaches to architectural tectonics. Their research is frequently featured in *IJAC*, *Leonardo*, *ACADIA*, among others, and in international exhibitions including SIGGRAPH Art Gallery and the forthcoming "The Architecture Machine" exhibition in Munich, Germany.

Ali Memari (BS CE, University of Houston, 1979; ME CE, University of California at Berkeley, 1981; PhD, Penn State, 1989) has over 30 years of teaching and research experience. He has taught various courses related to structural engineering. His current teaching includes earthquake-resistant design of buildings and building enclosure science and design. Dr. Memari's research has concentrated on the experimental and analytical evaluation of building envelope systems and residential and commercial light-frame and masonry structural systems under multihazard conditions as well as environmental effects. He is the author of over 280 publications. He is the Editor-in-Chief of the *ASCE Journal of Architectural Engineering* and the Chair of the Biennial Conference series on *Residential Building Design and Construction*.

Elizabeth Munch is an assistant professor at the Department of Computational Mathematics at Michigan State University. She received her PhD from the Department of Mathematics at Duke University in May 2013. She was a postdoctoral fellow at the Institute for Mathematics and its Applications at the University of Minnesota for the 2013–2014 thematic year on applications of topology. She also holds a Master of Arts in mathematics from the Duke University, a Bachelor of Science in mathematics from the University of Rochester, and a Bachelor of Music in harp performance from the Eastman School of Music. Before joining CMSE, Liz was an assistant professor in the Department of Mathematics and Statistics at the University at Albany—SUNY from 2014–2017.

Naveen K. Muthumanickam (BArch, Anna University, 2014; SMArchS, University of Michigan, 2015) is a PhD candidate in architecture at Penn State University specializing in using advanced ML-based optimization technologies to design better and efficient buildings. He was also a part of the Penn State team at the finals of the NASA 3D printed Mars Habitat Centennial Challenge where he worked on the BIM-based optimization and digital twin simulation for robotic concrete 3D printing. He is also a concurrent ME candidate in architectural engineering at Penn State along with an MS in architectural science and building technology from the University of Michigan, Ann Arbor. He is originally from Chennai, India, and holds a BArch from Anna University. He has worked at architectural practices such as Sameep Padora and Associates and Studio Daniel Libeskind and has also worked for Autodesk in the recent past.

Danil Nagy is a designer, programmer, and entrepreneur creating technology to transform the building industries. Trained as an architect, Danil has developed expertise across a diverse set of fields including professional practice, research, and software development. Danil teaches architecture and technology at Columbia University and Pratt Institute. He founded Colidescope, a consultancy focused on bringing automation and digital transformation to the AEC industry. As CTO of Deluxe Modular, he oversees the development of groundbreaking technologies to change the way buildings are designed, built, and managed.

Shadi Nazarian (BArch and BED, University of Minnesota, 1983; March, Cornell University, 1989) is a member of Penn State University's award-winning team in NASA 3D Printed Habitat Challenge Competition and an associate professor at the Stuckeman School of Architecture and Landscape Architecture. He holds a postprofessional degree from the Cornell University in architectural design and theory and a professional degree in architecture and environmental design from the University of Minnesota. Nazarian's research interests in the advancement of the discipline of architecture and the construction industry include innovations in seamless and/or sequential transition from advanced structural geopolymer-based ceramics to transparent glass, executing the concept of seamless architecture, and making possible novel sustainable practices during construction and in the building's performance.

David Newton is an assistant professor at the University of Nebraska–Lincoln where he leads the Computational Architecture Research Lab (CARL). CARL is dedicated to the research and development of next-generation computational design technologies that will make for a more environmentally and socially sustainable built environment. Professor Newton holds degrees in both architecture and computer science. This background informs a research and teaching agenda that is transdisciplinary—creating a unity of intellectual frameworks between the disciplines of computer science and architecture.

Paul Nicholas is an associate professor at the Centre for Information Technology and Architecture (CITA), KADK Copenhagen, Denmark, and head of the international master's program Computation in Architecture. He holds a PhD in architecture from the RMIT University, Melbourne, Australia, and has practiced with Arup consulting engineers and AECOM. Paul's research centers on new opportunities for interdependency across traditional boundaries between design, fabrication, and materiality. His recent research investigates the idea that new material practices necessitate new relationships between simulation and making and is explored through sensitized robotic fabrication, biomateriality, complex modeling, and AI.

Skidmore, Owings & Merrill (SOM) is a global architectural, urban planning, and engineering firm. It was founded in Chicago in 1936 by Louis Skidmore and Nathaniel Owings. The urban development predictor research was conducted as part of SOM's inaugural year one accelerator program for recent graduates in 2018. The group consisted of a wide-reaching and interdisciplinary collection of San Francisco year one participants, including Jaskanwal Chhabra and Bryan Ong from SOM's Structural studio, Wehnaho Wu from SOM's City Planning studio, Lu Wang from SOM's Open Space studio, and Daniel Lee from SOM's Architecture studio. The research was supervised by the Design Associate Grant Cogan and Senior Designer Stephanie Tabb from SOM's Architecture studio and Digital Design Group.

Maria Smigielska is an architect and researcher exploring new potentials for creation in architecture offered by digital technologies. Through computational design, material encoding, and its modulation combined with alternative robotic fabrication and assembly methods, she constructs architectural objects and installations of varied scales. Among her most recent appearances are the collective exhibitions during *Error* of *Ars Electronica Festival* (Linz 2018), *Biennale for Arts and Technology MetaMorf X: Digital Wild* (Trondheim 2020), *Tallinn Architecture Biennale* (Tallinn, 2017), and the duo show *Bits, Bots, Brains* of *Tetem gallery* (Enschede 2018). Maria cooperated with Baierbischofberger Architects on multiple complex architectural facades, Art[n+1] gallery and ABB Cergy France for the development of *bendilicious. com* project, Creative Robotics Lab at UfG Linz, and many other academic, industrial, and artistic institutions for research and teaching. Currently, affiliated with the Institute Integrative Design FHNW HGK Basel for an applied research project on customized wood façades (*codefa.ch*), Maria holds an MSc from TU Poznan and a Master of Advanced Studies degree from CAAD, ETH Zürich.

Aldo Sollazzo is a technologist, with expertise in robotics, manufacturing, and computational design. Since 2011, Aldo is the Director of Noumena, leading a multidisciplinary team toward the definition of new design strategies informed by tech-driven applications. He is also the Director of Reshape—a digital craft community, a distributed platform promoting cutting-edge ideas merging design and manufacturing. At the Institute for Advanced Architecture of Catalonia (IAAC) he is directing the Master in Robotics and Advanced Construction focused on the emerging design and market opportunities arising from novel robotic and advanced manufacturing systems. In the same institution, Aldo is also directing the Global Summer School since 2015. Aldo has been part of the Fab Academy program as a mentor of Fab Academy Paris and Frosinone from 2015 to 2017. In 2019, Aldo received, from the President of the Italian Republic, the title of Knight of the Order of the Star of Italy for the promotion of national prestige abroad as a recognition of his scientific and technological activities.

Akshay Srivastava is an architect with a keen interest in design strategy and user experience. He worked on the redevelopment and design of New Delhi International Airport and Aero City in India before moving to the United States. He is a graduate of the University of Michigan with a master's degree in architecture. He currently works as an architectural designer at Solomon Cordwell Buenz in Chicago while pursuing his interest in exploring novel ways of integrating AI/ML with the conventional design process.

Kyle Steinfeld is an architect who works with code and lives in Oakland. Through a hybrid practice of creative work, scholarly research, and software development, he seeks to reveal overlooked capacities of computational design; he finds no disharmony between the rational and whimsical, the analytical and uncanny, and the lucid and bizarre. His work cuts across media and is expressed through a combination of visual and spatial material. Across these, we find a consistent theme of undermining the imperative voice so often bestowed upon the results of computational processes and find in its place a range of alternative voices.

Oliver Tessmann is an architect and professor at the Technical University of Darmstadt where he is heading the Digital Design Unit (DDU). His teaching and research revolve around computational design, digital manufacturing, and robotics in architecture. From 2012 to 2015, he has been an assistant professor in the School of Architecture of the Royal Institute of Technology (KTH) in Stockholm. From 2008 to2011, he has been a guest professor at Staedelschule Architecture Class (SAC) and worked with the engineering office Bollinger + Grohmann in Frankfurt. In 2008, Oliver Tessmann received a doctoral degree at the University of Kassel. He conducted research in the field of "Collaborative Design Procedures for Architects and Engineers." His work has been published and exhibited in Europe, Asia, and the United States.

Can Uzun is currently a PhD student at Istanbul Technical University, Graduate School of Science Engineering and Technology, Department of Informatics, Architectural Design Computing Graduate Program. After completing his undergraduate degree in the Architecture Department of ITU (2012), he received his graduate degree in Architectural Design Department in ITU (2014). He presented his master's thesis with the title of "Form Information as a Field of Possibilities." He worked in various architectural design offices for three years during his graduate education (2012–2015). In offices, he took on the executive role in projects at different scales as the architectural scale and urban scale. During his doctorate education, he carried out research projects on virtual reality, augmented reality, design cognition, and AI. His doctoral dissertation study has been a generative adversarial network (GAN)-focused study in the interaction between architecture and AI. Currently, he has been working on generative adversarial networks for autonomous architectural plan layout generation tasks.

Guzden Varinlioglu currently works as an associate professor at the Department of Architecture at the Izmir University of Economics. Through the course of Varinlioglu's undergraduate education in architecture at the Middle East Technical University and her graduate education in graphic design at the Bilkent University, she became interested in digital technology and its contribution to the preservation and presentation of cultural heritage. Her research period at Texas A&M University in 2010 was followed by a PhD from the Program of Art, Design, and Architecture at the Bilkent University. Her research responded to the lack of systematic methodology for the collection, preservation, and dissemination of data in underwater cultural heritage studies. In 2011, Guzden received a postdoctoral position in architectural design computing at Istanbul Technical University. In 2013–2014, she did her postdoctoral studies at the Center of Digital Humanities at the University of California Los Angeles (UCLA).

Pedro Veloso is a computational designer with vast experience in research, architectural education, design technology consulting, and generative design. His interdisciplinary perspective is based on the integration of design with ideas from cybernetics, AI, deep learning, and reinforcement learning. As a practitioner, he has worked on a wide range of projects, from interactive installations to the customization of building layouts. Currently, his teaching and research interests concern generative strategies for the creative exploration of designs, with a particular focus on models that rely on data and experience. He has a Bachelor of Architecture and Urbanism from the University of Brasilia (2006) and a Master of Architectural Design from the University of Sao Paulo (2011), and he is a PhD candidate in computational design at Carnegie Mellon University, developing intelligent and interactive agents for architectural composition.

Ilija Vukorep is a professor for Digital Design methods at the BTU Cottbus and a practicing architect at LOMA architecture.landscape.urbanism. His research covers automatization methods in architecture from robotic fabrication to digital planning tools. At his university, he is organizing the annual AIAAF (AI Aided Architectural Fabrication), an international symposium with an emphasis on diverse AI-related topics.

Bastian Wibranek joined the Digital Design Unit at the Faculty of Architecture at TU Darmstadt in 2015, where he is currently a PhD candidate and a research assistant, teaching in the area of computational design and robotic fabrication. Bastian's research focuses on how we will share our future buildings with intelligent machines. He proposes that the practice of architecture must define modes of coexistence and man–machine collaborations for design and production. He taught computer-based architectural design and robotic fabrication techniques at the ITE at TU Braunschweig (2012–2015). He holds a diploma in architecture from the University of Applied Sciences and Arts, Dortmund, and a master's in advanced architectural design from the Städelschule, Frankfurt am Main.

Andrzej Zarzycki is an associate professor of Architecture at the New Jersey Institute of Technology (NJIT) and a founding member of *Technology | Architecture + Design* (TAD). His research focuses on media-based environments with applications in gaming and mobile augmented reality as well as interactive and adaptive designs integrating embedded systems with distributed sensing (smart buildings and cities) in the context of high-performance buildings. Andrzej has taught previously at the Rhode Island School of Design (RISD) and is a former visiting professor at the Korea Advanced Institute of Science and Technology (KAIST) and the Massachusetts Institute of Technology (MIT).

Zihao Zhang is a PhD candidate in the constructed environment at the University of Virginia (UVA). He teaches design computation in the landscape architecture department at UVA. His research is a transdisciplinary undertaking at the intersection of cybernetics, posthumanism, science and technology studies (STS), and landscape architecture. His dissertation seeks to map out an alternative way of thinking to engage with the environment beyond means-end reasoning and model-making paradigm. He is recently interested in cross-cultural dialogues between Chinese thinking and Western philosophy regarding efficacy, uncertainty, and potentiality.

Preface

Over the last few years, research in AI has exploded thanks to fast developments in deep learning systems—a branch of AI, which uses neural networks that loosely mimic the inner workings of the human brain. Deep learning has been utilized on a wide range of every-day applications, from voice recognition systems, such as Siri and Alexa, to self-driving cars, to online recommendation systems, language translation, and pricing algorithms. Deep learning algorithms discover latent patterns and relationships in large amounts of data, which may not be apparent to humans looking at it independently. For example, one can train a neural network to recognize dogs by training it with millions of dog images. Once the system knows what an image of a dog entails—by means of a discovered internal representation—it correctly predicts and classifies a dog in new images, even if the training data did not contain any samples of dogs looking like the one in the test sample. In 2015, the accuracy of neural networks identifying objects in images has surpassed that of human vision (He, Zhang, Ren & Sun, 2016). This is important, for example, for autonomous cars, where the instant discrimination of objects in real-time video feeds is essential to the success of steering cars safely on the road.

More broadly, the field of *AI and ML* consists of *unsupervised learning*, where algorithms work toward detecting patterns in unlabeled data; *supervised learning*, where algorithms *train* on labeled data and perform classification or prediction tasks on new *test* data; *generative algorithms*, which attempt to generate new samples given some input parameters; and *reinforcement learning*, where algorithms interact with a stochastic environment and interact with it to make utility-optimizing decisions. Not surprisingly, besides deep learning, AI—and ML in general—has a rich ensemble of other branches that researchers have extensively explored and are still actively exploring. Some of these branches are classified under symbolic or rule-based AI, e.g., expert systems, genetic algorithms, swarm intelligence, and so on; others make heavy use of statistical reasoning, e.g., support vector machines, Bayesian reasoning, and of course artificial neural networks; and, yet others are a hybrid of these two approaches, e.g., robotics.

However, using AI in architecture is complicated. Architecture is not a two-dimensional labeling problem but presents us with a three-dimensional spatial problem that is shaped by a broad set of interdependent issues. In his treatise *De Architectura*, written in 80 BC, Vitruvius wrote that any successful architecture should provide for function, beauty, and structure. And, Walter Gropius in *Scope of Total Architecture* claimed that "good architecture should be a projection of life itself that implies an intimate knowledge of biological, social, technical and artistic problems" (Gropius, 1970). Architecture thus needs to respond to (im)material and contextual conditions as well. As Gropius (1970) says, architecture has to "satisfy the human soul" and has to inevitably respond to aesthetic questions and structural efficiency and deal with contextual, ideological, sociocultural, and economic constraints and opportunities.

Therefore, AI has to be able to deal with three-dimensional space and at the same time respond to questions dealing with the wider scope of architecture.

Throughout history, architects developed various tools and techniques to describe the three-dimensional space and communicate their design intentions, e.g., drawing conventions, design templates, pattern books, and so on. In 1979, Lothar Haselberger, an architectural historian at the University of Pennsylvania, discovered one of the earliest templates used in architecture—at the Temple of Apollo, 334 BC, in Didyma, Turkey. Various geometric diagrams were incised onto the temple's inner cell depicting scaled-down blueprints that masons were using while building the columns. Similarly, researchers at Stanford University, at the Digital Forma Urbis Romae Project (formaurbis.stanford.edu), discovered pieces of an entire plan drawing of the city of ancient Rome, chiseled on an 18-m to 13-m marble wall at the Templum Pacis, dating back to 203 BC. Other graphic conventions emerged piecemeal over centuries, e.g., section cuts in the 13th century, perspective views in the 15th century, and axonometric drawings in the 17th century (Ackerman, 2000). These graphic conventions make up the drafting toolkit architects are still using today to communicate and execute their design work. Early computer-aided design (CAD) applications have translated them into digital media, mainly replacing paper and pencils with a monitor and mouse.

However, the use of computers in a more substantive manner has been a popular topic of research since the early 1960s, e.g., shape grammars, expert systems, and fractals, and later in the 1990s, agent-based modeling, L-systems, simulations, and animations. From the early 2000s onward, CAD software moved gradually to smarter parametric and building information modeling (BIM), which captures additional data beyond geometry, such as materials, scheduling, cost, and so on. BIM and software plug-ins such as Grasshopper and Dynamo offer visual programming interfaces for architects to formulate and generate rule-based parametric designs.

Recent developments in AI are furthermore shaping the next generation of computer-aided design tools. AI offers immense opportunities, and it may not only produce another novel toolkit for architects but also has the potential to cause a deeper disruption in the profession. If effective, AI will have an impact on architecture that can be compared to the invention of perspective drawing in the Renaissance. Ackerman (2000) argues that the latter was as important as the introduction of the paper to the world. It will fundamentally challenge how we conceive and produce architecture. What if, for example, AI could automatically generate multiple design solutions to a given architectural problem? For an architect, it could be similar to sourcing solutions from a team of colleagues working simultaneously on a given problem set. The architect could review the results, pick a particular solution, and tweak it further. Or, more interestingly, what if another AI system could tailor solutions directly to the client? In this scenario, a client could input various constraints and receive a fit solution that a local contractor could implement, perhaps even 3D print on the site. Although these scenarios are still elusive—at least end-to-end—current work in the field suggests a big leap forward toward automated design, deviating radically from traditional design approaches—a development that unavoidably poses important questions for architectural theory and raises puzzling issues for those who are concerned with the future of architectural practice and education.

In this book, we explore how AI is currently used by architectural researchers and practitioners. In four parts: (1) theoretical and historical background; (2) AI-based tools, methods, and technologies; (3) AI in architectural research; and (4) case studies of AI used in real-world projects—this book gives a broad overview of AI in architecture and offers a variety of perspectives. It contains 24 illustrated contributions examining illustrative work on AI from around the world, including the United States, Europe, and the Far East.

Content

In Part 1 of the book, we give an overview of the history of computation and situate AI within the overall context of computer-aided design in architecture. We discuss how AI differs and relates to traditional means of architectural design and production. Kyle Steinfeld discusses how AI/ML can be used in the architectural field to generate controlled new designs (as an *actor*), to help human designers to tap into prior architecture/design knowledge (as the *material*), or to even act as a *provocateur* to stimulate creative action directly at the start of the design process. Daniel Cordoso gives an overview of the history of ML as it relates to architecture. In particular, he shows how the experimental tradition of computational aesthetics and design underpins present-day approaches to architecture and AI. Pedro Veloso and Ramesh Krishnamurti map the scope of generative design tools. Can Uzun analyzes the "social" network of outstanding contributors to the AI field and how different fields of study "interacted" with each other to shape the emerging field of "artificial architectural intelligence."

In Part 2, we survey state-of-the-art AI-based tools, methods, and technologies. We highlight the ones that have been particularly explored in architecture—with examples of where and how they have been used. We introduce various branches of AI, e.g., ML, evolutionary algorithms, fuzzy logic, and so on—and examine their applicability in architectural design. Ilija Vukurep and Anatolii Kotov give an overview and evaluation of the existing ML tools, e.g., ones that perform multi-objective optimization, via concrete design examples. Tyler Kvochick provides a general overview of AI and how its components can be useful for classifying common structures found in architectural design. Sam Joyce shows us how AI has been used as a collaborative tool in the early stages of the design process, i.e., the conceptual design phase, which he breaks down into the site analysis, creative design ideation, and iteration with user feedback. Danil Nagy investigates the use of AI and optimization algorithms in space planning, e.g., assigning programs to available spaces. And the editors discuss how succinct graph-based and topology-based representations of building information enable one to run cutting-edge graph-AI algorithms to discover patterns and generate novel designs.

In Part 3, we explore the application of AI in architectural research. Gulden Varinlioglu and Özgün Balaban present a case study where they use AI to predict and identify long-lost caravanserais along the historic silk road in Anatolia. Theodore Galanos and Chronis Angelos present their work on using AI in real-time solar radiation prediction, and Bradley Cantrell et al. discuss how AI has been used in landscape architecture and debate how it differs from AI applications in other fields of research.

In Part 4, we present the best practice models showcasing the use of AI at various phases of a building's life cycle, from conceptual design to fabrication. We structured this part into three categories of AI use-cases, loosely adjusted from Kyle Steinfeld's introduction, i.e., the discussion of AI/ML as an *actor*, *material*, and *provocateur*. The first set of articles examine AI as an *aid* in the design and/or production processes, for example, in optimizing various aspects of design, fabrication, structure, and so on; the second set of articles present AI as controlled *coauthors*, where it works hand in hand with architects in probing architectural solution spaces. And, the last set of articles explore AI as a *disruptor*, for example, in generating unprecedented designs in a freer manner.

Naveen K. Muthumanickam et al. demonstrate the use of AI to 3D print a series of enclosed spaces developed for NASA's Mars Habitat Centennial Challenge. David Newton elaborates on multiobjective optimization and presents us with two stimulating case studies where AI has been used in housing projects and in the development of intelligent façade systems. Andrzej Zarzycki discusses how continuous data analytics can enable smart building technologies. Zach Xuereb Conti and Sawako Kaijima offer an overview of explainable AI, whose goal is to explain the relationship between the human-understandable structural features and functions of designs. Aldo Salazzo presents AI in urban image analytics and strategic planning processes for Barcelona. SOM (Skidmore, Owings & Merrill) describe their work on an AI-based future urban development predictor they used for San Francisco—from a plethora of currently measurable features. And, the editors discuss online crowdsourcing, and how AI has been utilized in its modus operandi. The next three articles focus on AI-enabled robotics applied to architectural production. Bastian Wibranek and Oliver Tessman explore modular design processes, concepts for autonomous robots, and man–machine collaboration that challenges the classical separation between design and construction, and demonstrate these through inspiring case studies. Paul Nichols investigates the application of AI algorithms in robotic fabrication of structures such as metallic "stressed skins." Mathias Berhard et al. show how AI has been used in encoding ideas and matter in robotic fabrication as well as for generating compliant designs—by using topology optimization and GANs hand in hand. Stanislas Chaillou showcases thought-provoking AI-generated architectural layouts obtained by training GANs on images of architectural floor plans, and Akshay Srivastava et al. illustrate how "form-finding" optimization algorithms from AI have been integrated in design generation and evaluations.

In this book, we give an overview of AI, situate it within the broader architectural technologies discourse, and showcase its current use-cases in architectural research and practice. We offer critical views on the prevailing tools and techniques and suggest future directions for meaningful uses of this nascent technology. Architects and educators who are concerned with the advent of AI and its ramifications for the architectural design space can take this book as an essential reference. It is the most comprehensive source available that surveys the state of the art of AI as it relates to architecture and discusses major questions around this fascinating topic. AI is a fast-moving field of research and many more articles will undoubtedly be written on topics related to this book by the time it is published. We hope the reader will find this particular collection of articles as a useful starting point to their journey in research on AI in architecture.

Imdat As and Prithwish Basu

References

Ackerman, J. (2000). Introduction: The Conventions and Rhetoric of Architectural Drawing. In *Conventions of Architectural Drawing: Representation and Misrepresentation*. Edited by James Ackerman and Wolfgang Jung. Cambridge: Harvard University, Graduate School of Design, 7–36.

Gropius, W. (1970). *Scope of Total Architecture*. New York, NY: Collier Books.

He, K., Zhang, X., Ren, S., & Sun, J. (2016). Deep residual learning for image recognition. In *Proceedings of the IEEE Conference on Computer Vision and Pattern Recognition* (pp. 770–778). Las Vegas, NV.

Acknowledgments

We are indebted to many people and institutions, who generously gave their time, offered encouragement, and provided support. We are grateful to Raytheon BBN Technologies and the University of Hartford for their support during the execution of the DARPA (U.S. Defense Advanced Research Projects Agency) funded Fundamental Design (FUN Design) program, which helped shape our thinking about the specific topics of AI in architecture. We want to thank Siddharth Pal of Raytheon BBN Technologies for working with us early on this exciting topic, and Vladimir Kumelsky of Arcbazar.com for sharing valuable design data to develop our research. We want to thank the Scientific and Technological Research Council of Turkey (TUBITAK) for supporting research in this field of investigation and sponsoring our doctoral students at Istanbul Technical University, Ozlem Cavus and Ayse Dede, who painstakingly helped us during the process of putting this book together. We also want to thank Fran Ford and Trudy Varcianna, our publishers at Taylor & Francis, for their patience and attentive help in these difficult times of covid-19 hitting the world, and lastly, we want to thank Anna Lukavska for consistently unifying all figures throughout the book.

Imdat As and Prithwish Basu

Part 1

Background, history, and theory of AI

Significant others

Machine learning as actor, material, and provocateur in art and design

Kyle Steinfeld

Artificial intelligence is a famously slippery concept, not because it is difficult to grasp, but rather because we hold a dynamic understanding of intelligence. It has been long observed (McCorduck, 1979) that once a capacity previously thought of as uniquely human is replicated by a machine, this capacity is redefined as an act of computation rather than one of true intelligence. In what has become known as the "AI effect," chasing the constantly moving target of mimicking human "intelligence" is a problem acutely felt in research, as major successes in AI are "soon assimilated into whatever application domain they [are] found to be useful in" (McCorduck, 1979). This shifting of goalposts may present frustration for AI researchers, but it also offers those of us in domains that benefit from advances in AI, such as architectural design, a different sort of opportunity.

The "AI effect" observes that, with each advancement in AI, the learned capacity – playing chess, identifying objects in images, composing a sonnet – is devalued as a mechanistic act: an act of calculation rather than a unique product of a creative mind. While this re-framing may blunt the significance of the achievement for those researchers who seek the advancement of AI, it simultaneously requires that intelligence itself be reconsidered by the rest of us. It is through this process that, in the service of maintaining the gilded position of human consciousness, the inability to precisely define intelligence is laid bare, reduced to "whatever machines haven't done yet" (Tesler, 1970). While such a challenge to the preeminence of human intelligence suggests that we might adopt a defensive posture, a posture that may explain some portion of the anxiety surrounding architectural applications of AI that may be observed today, we might instead focus on the benefits of the self-reflection latent in the AI effect. A clear-eyed examination of the nature of the newly learned abilities of machines may offer us new insight into, and renewed appreciation of, related human capacities. The AI effect cuts two ways: devaluing the significance of advancement in the science of the artificial, while simultaneously mobilizing a reconsideration of the human.

It is for this reason that, despite legitimate concerns regarding the broad and potentially negative social impacts of automation in design, I remain optimistic that the "assimilation" of recent advances in AI holds promise for the advancement of architectural design. It is this optimism that leads me to expect that we may look back at this time, not as the moment when the creative intelligence of a human designer had been effectively supplanted by some artifice, but rather as a moment of opportunity to reconsider what it means to act as a creative author in the first place. And so, rather than marking this time with a defense of those many aspects of design that have not yet (and may never) be threatened by automation, let us instead consider the ways in which this moment might, as similar proceeding moments have done, catalyze a reconsideration of the relationship between the tools of design and the culture of architectural production.

In this spirit, we may observe that the introduction of tools based upon machine learning (ML) represents one moment in an established history of adjustments of our engagement with descriptions of form and space. To the graphical and mathematical descriptions that characterized CAD in the early 2000s, we added procedural and logical descriptions with the advent of scripting and parametric modeling, and now have begun to take seriously descriptions based on data and generative statistics. For clarity, while I refer to previous models as "computer-aided design" to disambiguate emerging models as "machine-augmented design," I leave it to the reader to determine for themselves the gravity of this difference. As each of these previous shifts has reconfigured our position as authors, as well as our relationship with our work and the way we work with others, we may apply a set of lenses here similar to those that have been applied in the past. Following these previous efforts, to fully account for any pivot from one model of computer assistance to another, we are obligated to take stock of at least three broad categories of change:

- How a new model might facilitate different forms of subjectivity in design; to position us differently as individual authors in relation to our work.
- How a new model might upend existing networks of power; to support a new division of labor or engender a redistribution of design authorship.
- How a new model might necessitate different forms of knowledge; to require new competencies of designers or encourage new alliances between architects and other disciplines.

Such a project, however urgent, demands more than the constraints of this chapter allow. For now, while there are good reasons to look at how machine-augmented design tools will organize design activity differently at social and societal levels, let's adopt a more modest focus. Seeking a position within the long-studied history of the relationship between technologies of design and an architect's subjectivity, here I'll consider the narrow question of how ML tools might impact design activity at the individual level – the level of a sole human author in collaboration with a machine "partner."

In the sections that follow, I offer a sketch of a number of models that may be observed based on emerging trends in machine-augmented design practice. Each may be defined in terms of how it situates the use of ML in design differently. Speaking in such terms, and in summary, these models are ML as actor, ML as material, and ML as provocateur.

I'll begin with an account of those who see ML as an "actor" in design that is usefully regraded as on a par with human actors. Here, I'll mention a number of designers and fine artists who seek to uncover and instrumentalize the way a neural network "sees," and who set their work in relation to the essential qualities of neural networks in a manner that recalls certain aspects of the Modernist project. Next, we acknowledge those who take the position that ML is more like a new form of design "material." This work may be seen as holding to a well-established model for the integration of digital techniques into design culture, one that draws from a long craft tradition that predates the profession itself. Finally, we present a model for the use of ML in design as a "provocateur" and, in the spirit of the surrealist concept of automatism, draw from the capacity for ML as an instrument of the associative and imaginary rather than the rational.

In our account of each of these models, we draw from creative practices in the fine arts and architecture alike and seek to identify those past thinkers that appear to hold sway over approaches taken by current adherents. Further, we seek to address a number of practical questions:

- Is it possible to discern any new authorial roles or new domains of action for a creative author? Where are the new loci of authorship?
- What decisions would be left to the machine (indirect, differed authorship) and which would be claimed by a human author closer to the execution of a design?
- By what qualities would we recognize a practice that follows this model? What are the related tools, methods and procedures?
- What are the currencies of this new practice? Which performances of a design would an author value?

ML as actor

Among the designers and artists working with ML, there are those who seek to establish an authorial position in relationship to a nominal "machine intelligence" that operates as a co-creator on a par with, or acting as a surrogate for, a human counterpart. Here, authors operate in a necessarily indirect way, as orchestrators of formal systems of training, generation and selection that effectively serve as "a machine that makes the art."[1] Often in this context, efforts are made to uncover some essential quality or predilection associated with the underlying technology, an effort which we may observe in claims of revealing the way a machine "sees" or "understands space" differently than humans do.

Recalling recently developed approaches in architecture, such as generative design and emergent design [see Nervous System (Rosenkrantz, 2011) and Casey Reas (Reas, 2006)], and less proximate practices that originate in the art world [see Sol LeWitt and Joan Truckenbrod (Paul, 2018)], the role of a creative author working in this way is decidedly hands-off and is often limited to the establishment of a system that facilitates the emergence of forms and patterns. Authors typically refrain from guiding this process of generation and, at times, even forgo selecting from among the iterations that are produced. This position of "deferred authorship" (Steinfeld, Fox, and Spatzier, 2014) is not a new form of subjectivity in the arts and design, but may be seen as a radical extension of a form that extends at least as far back as the 1960s.

We may recognize a practitioner of this model by the degree to which an ML process is personified as an independent actor in the creative process. Particularly devoted adherents to this approach may at times invoke the "posthuman," a term that acknowledges that "the boundaries between human and computational cognition are increasingly blurred" (del Campo, Manninger, and Carlson, 2019). For those adopting such a position, the limited nature of today's decidedly narrow (Jajal, 2020) AI tools does not appear to diminish the utility of regrading them as a form cognition on a par with human thinking. No matter the degree of devotion of an author, we may observe that the performances and properties valued in the artifacts produced by such a model are often left unspoken or are related to the revelation of some essential quality of ML itself. Because authors necessarily operate at a meta-level, as composers of a system rather than participants in it, they often avoid claims or justifications that center themselves, and tend to step aside as an objective presenter of what their machine counterpart has produced. Since, at times, the system for producing artifacts (rather than the artifacts themselves) is seen as the authored work, in place of value claims related to artifacts, we find more elaborate observations on what "it," the system, did.

As an extension of previous trends – such as generative design, procedural design, and a passing interest in theories of complexity and emergence in design[2] – the rhetoric surrounding this model of creative practice in architectural circles tends toward the grandiloquent. In contrast to these relatively breathless accounts, it is notable that those who work more closely with the underlying technologies tend to be more direct in articulating that the personification of an ML "partner" in creative production is a contrivance, but a useful one.

A clear exemplar of this directness is the artist Tom White, whose works "The Treachery of ImageNet" and "Perception Engines" employ image classification models to produce abstract ink prints that reveal the visual concepts latent in a number of widely used computer vision processes. Speaking of this work in 2018, White outlines his position as a refreshingly nuanced expression of "machine intelligence" without negating his own subjectivity. Speaking in 2018, White states:

> I think of the computer as a tool or – if I'm being gracious – as a collaborator… I'm setting up a system where the computer can express itself, but the intent is my own. I want people to understand how the machine sees the world.
>
> *(Kazmin, 2018)*

Mario Klingemann, another AI art practitioner exhibiting work in the same 2018 exhibition, adopts a starker position, more forcefully asserting: "I am the artist, there is no question at all. Would you consider a piano the artist?" (Kazmin, 2018).

The forthrightness of Klingemann and White stands in stark contrast to the way that similarly positioned architectural designers describe their work. In the project "Imaginary Plans," architects Matias del Campo and Sandra Manninger collaborate with computer vision specialist Alexandra Carlson to propose ML systems that "learn, recognize, and generate novel plan solutions for a variety of architectural features, styles, and aspects" (del Campo, Manninger, and Carlson, 2019). While, at the time of writing, the work remains at a nascent stage, the stated ambition is a clear illustration of the desire for an autonomous "machine intelligence" in design. We can see this reflected in the range of claims surrounding new forms of architectural authorship that operate systemically rather than compositionally, for example, the notion that we might design through a process of style transfer, such that "iconic buildings in architecture can have their styles 'quantified' and transferred to other iconic buildings" (p. 415); or that we might design through a curation and mixing of imagistic influences, such that "floor plans [may] emulate aesthetic elements from the other nonfloor-plan images" or "be fused with other buildings to generate novel architectural types" (p. 416). While the underlying technologies are still in development, the "Imaginary Plans" project demonstrates how some designers are interested in uncovering radical new subjectivities "that question the sole authorship of human ingenuity" (p. 417).

Whereas "Imaginary Plans" seeks an autonomous generative tool to architectural design, we might also consider the possibility of an autonomous analytical tool. The generative adversarial network (GAN) Loci project (Steinfeld, 2019) proposes just this. Here, a GAN is trained to produce synthetic images intended to capture the predominant visual properties of urban places. Imaging cities in this manner represents the first computational approach to documenting the forms, textures, colors, and qualities of light that exemplify a particular urban location and that set it apart from similar places. The conceit of the project is that something like the genius loci of a city may be captured not as seen through the eyes of a human inhabitant, but rather from the viewpoint of a "machine intelligence." We might observe that the resulting images evoke GAN-ness just as much as they suggest the cities from which they are drawn.

This criticism, that a work speaks more of the process by which it was produced than it does to any external subject, may be fairly applied to much of the work produced under the ML-as-"author" model. Indeed, reflecting on the examples discussed in this section, we could reasonably argue that what has been captured is speaks more to the essential qualities of the underlying ML model than it does any inherent features of the world, which is both the strength of the "actor" approach and its failing.

ML as material

There are those who regard ML as a new form of design material, and, evoking the long tradition of developing tacit knowledge through the accumulation of direct experience, seek to cultivate a mastery of this new form in combination with well-established practices. As discussed above, when regarded as an "actor," we might seek out the tendencies and predilections of a constructed machine intelligence, just as we might with a human co-creator. In contrast, when regarded as a "material," we would be more interested in the properties and capacities of this medium in their active application, just as we might with any other expressive mode. This is to say that there are designers who seek to master the affordances of ML by engaging in a material practice similar to those employed by a craftsperson. This position is well summarized by the adage "we shape our tools, and thereafter our tools shape us."[3]

Adopting such a position relative to digital media is in no sense new. Writing in the mid-1990s, Malcolm McCullough argued that the actions and mind-sets supported by digital design media are not so different than those supported by traditional media. Where traditional media enables us to act in a visual and tactile way, computers "let us operate on abstractions as if they were things" (McCullough, 1996). McCullough draws out the continuities between traditional and digital crafts by describing the evolving notion of "type" across paradigms: In a craft context, a "type" refers to a particular material tradition; in an industrial production context, a "type" refers to a particular process of formation; and in software, a "type" refers to a particular conceptual abstraction. We might speculate that ML would occupy an interesting place in McCullough's account. In one sense, a "type" in ML operates as a conceptual abstraction, and may be seen as an extension of the general software type. In another sense, and in contrast to the explicit Object-Oriented-Programming construction of types in software (Ko and Steinfeld, 2018), because ML allows for implicit definition – either "by example" in a supervised learning context or discovered in an unsupervised learning context – an ML "type" may be better understood to recall certain aspects of traditional craft practices.

Following McCullough, we would recognize a practitioner of the "material" model of creative ML by the balance of attention paid to the situational curation of a training set in the service of creating a unique generative tool, and the brandishing of this tool in the crafting of a creative product. Whereas others find subjective positions at the meta-level – through the authoring of systems – those adopting a craft's mind-set operate at the meso-level – through direct engagement. While, as in the previous model, the development of a system is a central part of the creative process, the "system" in a material context is regarded more as a custom-built tool to be wielded by a master craftsperson.

Such an approach is widespread among early adopters of AI in the visual arts. In a spirit that recalls a number of craft traditions, Sougwen Chung, an artist who works with ML systems trained on images of her own drawings, claims to seek to uncover the "inherent, shared fallibility" of human and machine systems alike (Chung, 2019). Similarly, Helena Sarin, a visual artist and software engineer, notes that "neural art can still be personal and original, especially when generative models are trained on your own datasets" (Sarin, 2019). Finally, I would highlight the striking work of Scott Eaton, a mechanical engineer and anatomical artist who uses custom-trained image-to-image translation models as a "creative collaborator" in his figurative drawings (Eaton, 2020). Like Chung and Sarin, Eaton invests time in both shaping his tool, through the meticulous construction of a dataset of his own figure drawings, and allowing his tool to shape him, mastering the craft of augmented drawing through hours of daily sketching.

The Sketch2Pix drawing tool was largely inspired by Eaton's work, both in its technical approach and in its position as a tool of machine-augmented creativity. Sketch2Pix is an augmented architectural drawing tool developed to support sketching with automated image-to-image translation processes (Isola et al., 2016). The tool encompasses a "full stack" of processes required for novice users to conceptualize, train, and apply their own custom-trained AI "brushes." This holistic approach is critical to supporting the ML-as-"material" approach: First, a designer defines an indexical relationship between a hand-drawn mark and the qualities of an image it is mapped to, and only then identifies the "reason" for these images through the active composition of a drawing.

ML as provocateur

Disruption has long been shown to be a powerful tactic in stimulating creative action (de Bono, 2015). As such, it is perhaps no surprise that the notable capacity of AI for "weirdness" (Shane, 2019) should find application among artists and designers as an upender of stale practices, an instigator of new ideas and an agent of chaos. We may recognize a practitioner of ML as "provocateur" by their acceptance of a machine-generated artifact as a point of departure that mobilizes, or a catalyst that propels, a larger creative process.

The use of creative prompts in such a way is not a new tactic in the arts and design. Writing in the 1960s and extending the work of the surrealists, Pierre Boulez used the term "aleatorism" (Riley, 1966) to describe compositions resulting from actions made by chance. Later, in the mid-1970s, Brian Eno and Peter Schmidt published their well-known "Oblique Strategies" project (Eno and Schmidt, 1975), a series of prompts, printed on cards and randomly selected, in order to overcome creative blocks. Edward de Bono wrote exhaustively on the subject of the role provocation plays in creative process, coining the term "po" to describe an intentionally disruptive stimulus that is used to facilitate creative thinking (de Bono, 2015).

In contrast to the embrace of randomness found in some of these examples, ML offers a variation on creative provocation that has not been previously instrumentalized in quite the same way. To refine the well-described phenomenon of "AI weirdness" (Shane, 2019), I would suggest that, when employed as a creative prompt, a more productive quality might be termed the "AI uncanny." This distinction, separating the unrecognizably foreign from the disquietingly familiar, draws attention once more to the central locus of authorship critical to any application of ML in design: the dataset. To be specific, we can see that creative authors might willfully curate a dataset to produce ML systems that are "primed" to generate creative prompts with a particular character. This suggests the application of "directed" chance as a creative prompt, in contrast to the surrealist use of random chance. In this way, while the inner workings of an ML system are largely beside the point, certain affordances may be introduced to influence the properties of the artifacts they produce. For example, a neural net might be trained on a dataset that describes a particular genre of music, or a particular style of painting, not in order to faithfully reproduce these forms, but rather to provide an auspicious point of departure for an author who wishes to be so influenced. In this way, the ML system is not assigned any meaningful agency, nor is it regarded as a material to be mastered, but rather functions as an externalized or collectivized "association engine" to kick-start the creative process.

A clear example of the use of ML as a creative prompt may be found in the work of the dance punk band YACHT, most visibly in their album "Chain Tripping," which was nominated for Best Immersive Audio Album in 2020. Described as an AI "concept album," ML played a role at nearly every step of the production of this work, from the music itself, to the machine generation of lyrics and song titles from the band's previous albums, to a collaboration with AI artists (such as Tom White and Mario Klingemann, mentioned above) in the design of the album cover and promotional materials. Most relevant here is YACHT's approach to the composition of melodies and beats. In order to train a model called MusicVAE (Roberts et al., 2018a, 2018b) developed by the Magenta team at Google, YACHT compiled a dataset of the band's previous recordings. Once trained, MusicVAE allows for the blending of melodies, like the blending of colors on a painter's palette, in the resulting latent space of the band's own musical history. This process "allowed the band to find melodies 'hidden in between songs' in their back catalog" (Mattise, 2019). For our purposes, "Chain Tripping" is notable not only for this uniquely positioned generative tool, but for how YACHT deployed this tool in a larger creative process that clearly demonstrates the use of ML as a catalyst that propels creative action. Initially faced with a "massive body of melodic information" generated by machine (and expressed as MIDI data), the band treated this information only as point of departure. From there, "it became the humans' turn" (Mattise, 2019) to interpret, adapt, and compose the final work.

A similar example of the use of ML as a provocative starting point is the short film Sunspring (Sharp, 2016). Like "Chain Tripping," the originating document for this creative work, the film's screenplay, was generated by an AI based on a corpus of relevant historical material. Here, director Oscar Sharp and AI researcher Ross Goodwin collaborated to create a recurrent neural network dubbed "Benjamin," trained on a corpus of sci-fi screenplays from the 1980s and 1990s (Newitz, 2016). Just as MIDI data is not music, a textual screenplay is not a film. As such, the artifacts produced by Benjamin became fodder for the creative action of all the downstream parties responsible for interpreting and translating this screenplay into a film, including the actors, directors, set designers, and costume designers. In describing the value of Benjamin, a literal automaton, in their creative process Goodwin and Sharp echo sentiments found in mid-20th-century manifestoes on surrealism (Breton, 1969): "machines can help us be more classical, more personal, and more original" (Goodwin and Sharp, 2017).

In a final example that both hews closer to architectural design and precisely demonstrates the use of ML as an automatism to stimulate human imagination, we would present the work of Philipp Schmitt and Steffen Weiß. Here, as with the above examples, ML is positioned as a provocateur or "mind-bender" to catalyze a design process, in this case for the design of chairs. In 2018, Schmitt and Weiß trained an ML model, the widely used GAN DCGAN, on a corpus of images of iconic 20th-century chairs, and then allowed this model to generate hundreds of new images. These synthetic images were intentionally imperfect representations of chairs – some were blurry, some were nonsensical, and many were barely recognizable as objects at all. Perfect depictions of new chair designs were not the aim; rather, the authors sought to generate compelling "visual prompts for a human designer who used them as a starting point for actual chair design concepts" (Schmitt and Weiß, 2018). For this purpose, clear images are less desirable than those images that flicker between the suggestion of an object and the presentation of impediments to direct interpretation. For Schmitt and Weiß, "'seeing the chair' in an image is an imaginative and associative process. It pushes designers away from usual threads of thinking toward unusual ideas that they might not have had otherwise" (Schmitt and Weiß, 2018).

It was precisely this activation of an associative faculty that was sought by an undergraduate design studio at UC Berkeley in the Spring of 2020. The studio sought to understand how ML tools might function as tools of creative provocation in particular, and tools of early-stage design more broadly. In one exercise, students employed two separate ML models – one for the generation of text, and a second that generates images from textual captions – to create scenographic storyboards that were read as depictions of site and program, and that animated the beginning of a larger design project. By introducing novice students to experimental ML tools and processes, this studio illustrates the broad utility of these tools as design provocations.

Conclusion

The sections above outline three emerging models for machine-augmented design, detail how these are beginning to be applied in practice, and take stock of the emerging subjectivities. Understood as an "actor," at times imagined as a surrogate for or a coequal participant alongside a human actor, we find authors exploring new ways of "viewing the world" through the eyes of a machine intelligence, as well as the emergence of an important new locus of design authorship: the training dataset. Understood as a "material," we find efforts to leverage the unique capacity for ML to capture tacit knowledge through the accumulation of direct experience, efforts that further the project of bringing digital practices into closer harmony with craft practices. Finally, understood as a "provocateur," we find ML practices that seek to stimulate creative action at the start of a design process by supporting the associative over the deductive (Steinfeld, 2017), the "imaginary rather than the rational" (Schmitt and Weiß, 2018).

We might speculate that the examples presented here, however anecdotal, not only indicate a coming shift in the way design tools operate, but also suggest that this shift might accompany a broader reconsideration of the relationship between the tools of design and the culture of architectural production.

Notes

1 Adapted from "The idea becomes a machine that makes the art," attributed to Sol LeWitt in 1965 (Kosuth, 1966).
2 See Andrasek (2015), Snooks and Jahn (2016) and others of the time that offer unqualified and eager personifications of computational processes.
3 Attributed to Churchill or McLuhan or Maeda.

References

Andrasek, Alisa. 2015. "Indeterminacy & Contingency: The Seroussi Pavilion and Bloom by Alisa Andrasek." *Architectural Design* 85 (3): 106–111. https://doi.org/10.1002/ad.1908.
Bono, Edward de. 2015. *The Mechanism of Mind: Understand How Your Mind Works to Maximise Memory and Creative Potential.* London: Random House.
Breton, André. 1969. *Manifestoes of Surrealism.* Vol. 182. Ann Arbor, MI: University of Michigan Press.

Campo, Matias del, Sandra Manninger, and Alexandra Carlson. 2019. "Imaginary Plans." In *Proceedings of the 39th Annual Conference of the Association for Computer Aided Design in Architecture (ACADIA)*, 412–418. Austin, TX: Association for Computer Aided Design in Architecture.

Chung, Sougwen. 2019. "Why I Draw with Robots." Presented at the TED Institute, Mumbai, September. https://www.ted.com/talks/sougwen_chung_why_i_draw_with_robots.

Eaton, Scott. n.d. "Creative AI by Scott Eaton." Accessed May 26, 2020. http://www.scott-eaton.com/category/creativeai.

Eno, Brian, and Peter Schmidt. 1975. "Oblique Strategies." *Opal*. Limited Edition, Boxed Set of Cards.

Goodwin, Ross, and Oscar Sharp. 2017. "Machines Making Movies." Presented at the TEDx Boston. https://tedxboston.org/speaker/goodwin.

Isola, Phillip, Jun-Yan Zhu, Tinghui Zhou, and Alexei A. Efros. 2016. "Image-to-Image Translation with Conditional Adversarial Networks." *CoRR*, November 21, 2016. abs/1611.07004.

Jajal, Tannya D. 2020. "Distinguishing between Narrow AI, General AI and Super AI." *Medium* (blog), February 13, 2020. https://medium.com/@tjajal/distinguishing-between-narrow-ai-general-ai-and-super-ai-a4bc44172e22.

Kazmin, Amy. 2018. "An AI Genre in Its Infancy Questions the Nature of Art." *Financial Times*, August 27, 2018.

Ko, Joy, and Kyle Steinfeld. 2018. *Geometric Computation*. London: Routledge.

Kosuth, Joseph. 1993. *Art After Philosophy and After: Collected Writings, 1966–1990*. London: MIT Press.

Mattise, Nathan. 2019. "How YACHT Used Machine Learning to Create Their New Album." *Wired*, September 5, 2019. https://arstechnica.com/gaming/2019/08/yachts-chain-tripping-is-a-new-landmark-for-ai-music-an-album-that-doesnt-suck/.

McCorduck, Pamela. 1979. *Machines Who Think: A Personal Inquiry into the History and Prospects of Artificial Intelligence*. San Francisco, CA: W. H. Freeman.

McCullough, Malcolm. 1996. *Abstracting Craft: The Practiced Digital Hand*. Cambridge, MA: MIT Press.

Newitz, Annalee. 2016. "Movie Written by Algorithm Turns out to Be Hilarious and Intense." *Ars Technica*, June 9, 2016. https://arstechnica.com/gaming/2016/06/an-ai-wrote-this-movie-and-its-strangely-moving/.

Paul, Christiane. 2018. "Histories of the Digital Now." *Programmed: Rules, Codes, and Choreographies in Art, 1965–2018*. New York: Whitney Museum of American Art. https://whitney.org/essays/histories-of-the-digital-now.

Reas, Casey. 2006. "Process/Drawing." *Architectural Design* 76 (4): 26–33.

Riley, Howard. 1966. "Aleatoric Procedures in Contemporary Piano Music." *The Musical Times* 107 (1478): 311–312.

Roberts, Adam, Jesse Engel, Colin Raffel, Curtis Hawthorne, and Douglas Eck. 2018a. "A Hierarchical Latent Vector Model for Learning Long-Term Structure in Music." ArXiv Preprint ArXiv:1803.05428.

Roberts, Adam, Jesse Engel, Colin Raffel, Ian Simon, and Curtis Hawthorne. 2018b. "MusicVAE: Creating a Palette for Musical Scores with Machine Learning." *Magenta* (blog), March 15, 2018. https://magenta.tensorflow.org/music-vae.

Rosenkrantz, Jessica. 2011. *Hele-Shaw Cell Experiments*. Video. https://www.flickr.com/photos/jrosenk/5607488831/.

Sarin, Helena. 2019. "Playing a Game of GANstruction." Presented at the Eyeo Festival, St Louis, MI, August 16. https://vimeo.com/354276365.

Schmitt, Philipp, and Steffen Weiß. 2018. "The Chair Project: A Case-Study for Using Generative Machine Learning as Automatism." 32nd Conference on Neural Information Processing Systems (NIPS'18), December 3–8, 2018, Montréal, Canada.

Shane, Janelle. 2019. *You Look Like a Thing and I Love You*. New York: Little, Brown & Company.

Sharp, Oscar (Dir.). 2016. *Sunspring*. Short, Sci-Fi. Culver City, CA: End Cue.

Snooks, Roland, and Gwyllim Jahn. 2016. "Stigmergic Accretion." In *Robotic Fabrication in Architecture, Art and Design 2016*, edited by Dagmar Reinhardt, Rob Saunders, and Jane Burry, 398–409. Cham: Springer International Publishing. https://doi.org/10.1007/978-3-319-26378-6_32.

Steinfeld, Kyle. 2017. "Dreams May Come." In *Proceedings of the 37th Annual Conference of the Association for Computer Aided Design in Architecture (ACADIA)*, 590–599. Cambridge, MA: Association for Computer Aided Design in Architecture.

————. 2019. "GAN Loci." In *Proceedings of the 39th Annual Conference of the Association for Computer Aided Design in Architecture (ACADIA)*, 392–403. Austin, TX: Association for Computer Aided Design in Architecture.

Steinfeld, Kyle, Levon Fox, and Alex Spatzier. 2014. "The Data Made Me Do It: Direct, Deferred, and Dissolved Authorship and the Architecture of the Crowd." In *Paradigms in Computing: Making, Machines, and Models for Design Agency in Architecture*, edited by David Gerber and Mariana Ibanez, 65–91. New York: eVolo.

Tesler, Larry. 1970. "Curriculum Vitae." http://www.nomodes.com/Larry_Tesler_Consulting/Ad-ages_and_Coinages.html.

White, Tom. 2018a. "Perception Engines." *Artists and Machine Intelligence* (blog), September 3, 2018. https://medium.com/artists-and-machine-intelligence/perception-engines-8a46bc598d57.

————. 2018b. "Synthetic Abstractions." *Medium* (blog), September 3, 2018. https://medium.com/@tom_25234/synthetic-abstractions-8f0e8f69f390.

2

Sculpting spaces of possibility

Brief history and prospects of artificial intelligence in design*

Daniel Cardoso Llach

This chapter offers a brief history of, and new directions for, artificial intelligence (AI) in design. Drawing together examples from architecture, music, and the visual arts, it shows how an experimental tradition of computational aesthetics and design underpins present-day approaches to architecture and AI. In exploring this history, the chapter calls attention to two aspects that have frequently been overlooked: first, the materially specific acts of codification that structure these experiments, and second, the reconfigurations of author and user roles that they entail. With these as points of reference, the chapter identifies new directions for creative research on AI and design that eschew simplistic approaches to style transfer or machine autonomy. As illustrations, three recent projects developed at the Computational Design Laboratory at Carnegie Mellon University are discussed. These explore new drawing interfaces that enable users to manually control the weights of a neural network; new approaches to computational urban analysis that reveal morphological gradients at the urban scale; and "distant readings" of architectural data that open up new approaches to design description, analysis, and generation.

Despite the aura of novelty that still accompanies artificial intelligence (AI) methods in popular and academic discourses about design, dreams of adaptive design machines and autonomous creativity have long populated the imagination of computationally minded architects, designers, and artists—and that of artistically inclined mathematicians, scientists, and engineers. Take for example computer scientist Frederick Brooks and his collaborators at the Harvard Computation Laboratory, who developed in 1957 a method for generating musical tunes automatically by numerically encoding and analyzing the structure of 37 sample melodies. Aided by a digital computer, the team counted the number of occurrences of specific melodic sequences, creating frequency tables that described this dataset probabilistically (see Figure 2.1, left). For example, a 0.2 probability of the note A following the musical sequence C-E-G meant that the note A follows two in ten occurrences of the C-E-G pattern in the set. So, if a computer program generates a pseudorandom number, and it falls within the 0 and 0.2 range, it could compose the sequence C-E-G-<u>A</u> (Brooks et al., 1957). Brooks and collaborators created such a program and generated new melodies that fit with the musical pieces in the original dataset. This quintessentially inductive process is nicely illustrated in Figure 2.1, right. By putting frequency tables and rudimentary statistical analysis in the

TABLE I
SORTED OCTOGRAMS, ILLUSTRATING THE FORMATION OF THE
CUMULATIVE PROBABILITY TABLES

Cell 1 2 3 4 5 6 7 8	Octo-gram Count	Hepta-gram Count	Relative Fre-quency	Cumula-tive Probability
36 37 26 27 32 33 26 22	1			
*36 37 26 27 32 33 26 22	2		2/8	2/8
36 37 26 27 32 33 26 27	1			
36 37 26 27 32 33 26 27	2			
36 37 26 27 32 33 26 27	3			
36 37 26 27 32 33 26 27	4			
*36 37 26 27 32 33 26 27	5		5/8	7/8
*36 37 26 27 32 33 26 28	1	8	1/8	8/8
36 37 26 27 32 33 32 33	1			
*36 37 26 27 32 33 32 33	2	2	2/2	2/2
*36 37 32 33 32 33 32 33	1	1	1/1	1/1
36 37 32 33 32 33 36 37	1			
*36 37 32 33 32 33 36 37	2		2/3	2/3
*36 37 32 33 32 33 36 42	1	3	1/3	3/3

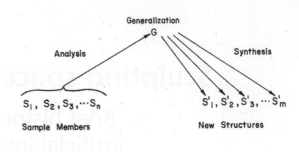

Figure 2.1 Left: Frequency table counting the occurrences of melodic patterns in a dataset of musical compositions. Right: A process diagram explaining the inductive nature of the process (Brooks et al., 1957).

service of generative inference with the intent of producing an artistic result, Brooks and his collaborators anticipated present-day applications of AI—and more specifically machine learning—in art and design. The term "machine learning" was not coined until 1959, and thus it was not available to Brooks and his coauthors. However, invoking computer scientist Claude Shannon, they used a language that unequivocally anticipated this paradigm of computation: "[m]any interesting computer experiments in game playing, 'learning,' theorem proving, etc., have been aimed at discovering methods of simulating rudimentary inductive processes with a computing machine" (Brooks et al., 1957, p. 175).

Another early explorer of computer music, US chemist-turned-composer Lejaren Hiller, helps illustrate how the aspiration to simulate inductive reasoning was central to some early expressions of computational art and design. In the late 1950s, Hiller and his collaborators at the University of Illinois modified a computer program used in chemistry for calculating the geometry of molecular bonds, adapting it to generate melodic lines by transposing the structure of tetrahedral carbon bonds into the structure of musical counterpoints (Bewley, 2004). The program generated melodic samples using the Monte Carlo method, a stochastic process weighed to select results conforming to predefined attributes (Hiller & Isaacson, 1959; Zaripov & Russel, 1969). In theory, these attributes could be derived from the statistical analysis of music by other composers—not unlike Brook's experiment. However, these researchers followed a different approach. They encoded style rules in smaller pieces of code called subroutines, which specified musical characteristics concerning the melody, harmony, and structure of the piece. Random note sequences generated by the program would be checked for compliance with rules specifying, for example, that "no tritones are permitted," or that "the melody must start and end on middle C," or that "the range of the melody from its highest to lowest note must not exceed one octave" (Hiller & Isaacson, 1959, p. 75). If the sequence conflicted with any of the rules, it was rejected, and a new sequence was automatically generated.

At first glance, it is difficult to reconcile Hiller's work with present-day approaches to machine learning, which tend to relishin enormous datasets and seemingly obscure algorithms. After all, instead of generalizing from examples, it appears to rely on a fixed set of predefined style rules (Figure 2.2). However, if we look closely, it becomes clear that the rules themselves result from a process of observation and analysis of examples—which are just other words for "learning." For example, the rules of strict counterpoint encoded in the program were

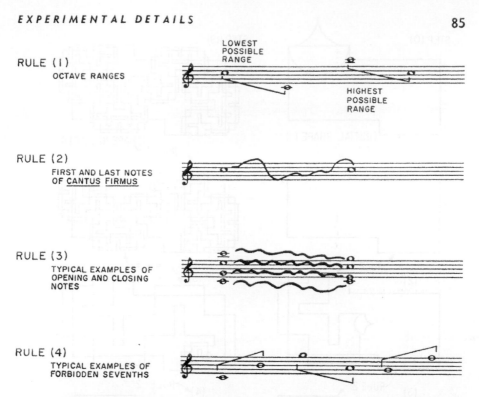

Figure 2.2 Early experiments in rule-based musical composition sought to reproduce stylistic traits identified in a set of melodic samples (Image credit: Hiller & Isaacson, 1959, p. 85).

derived from methods of composition created by 18th-century Italian composer Palestrina (Hiller & Isaacson, 1959). In this precedent from the Renaissance, the US researchers found "a logical abstraction of many important elements of musical structure and form a fundamental basis for handling linear melodic flow" (Hiller & Isaacson, 1959, p. 83). If Brooks used a probabilistic description of a curated set of sample melodies to shape the melodic outcomes of a computer program, Hiller used stylistic rules derived from the work of a composer to constrain brute-force algorithms to the same effect.

Researchers in architecture and the visual arts confronted a similar question: How to shape, or sculpt, the vast spaces of possibility afforded by computational methods and generate meaningful outcomes? However, they dealt with a different material. While musical scores could be represented as one-dimensional sequences of numbers, shapes, colors, and volumes, architecture and the visual arts seemed to demand a different approach. Some of the best-known examples of early computer art and design rely on the codification of the cartesian plane and the exploration of constrained randomness and pen plotters as aesthetic devices (Caplan, 2020). Other theorists and researchers imagined visual and architectural designs as language structures comprising vocabularies of elements and sets of grammatical rules for their combination. US mathematicians and design theorists George Stiny and the late James Gips, for example, defined design computationally as a visual algebra where shapes themselves are the units of calculation (see Figure 2.3)—a theory and a praxis they called

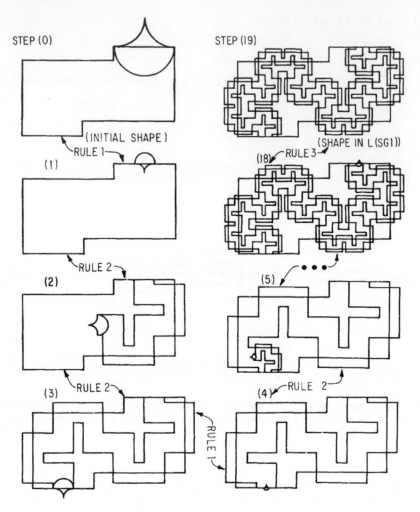

Figure 2.3 United States mathematicians and design theorists George Stiny and James Gips imagined design as a visual form of computation with elements called "shapes," structured by grammatical rules (Image credit: Stiny & Gips, 1972).

shape grammars (Stiny & Gips, 1972). Like Hiller and Isaacson, Stiny and Gips were familiar not only with earlier experiments in computer art (Bense, 1971) but also (and perhaps more crucially) with earlier developments in mathematics and generative linguistics (Birkhoff, 1933; Chomsky, 2015).

One important difference between shape grammars and the experiments in musical composition considered above is that shapes are themselves the units of calculation. In other words, rather than computing with numerical representations of shapes, as both Hiller and Brooks had done with music, shape grammars compute directly with shapes via spatial relations and transformations (Knight, 1994). Hence, they redefine design as a visual form of computation and, in consequence, as an activity inseparable from perception and interpretation—that is to say, from human experience.

A canonical example of a shape grammar helps reveal their capacity to elicit design inductively from examples. In the late 1970s, Stiny and the late Australian architectural theorist

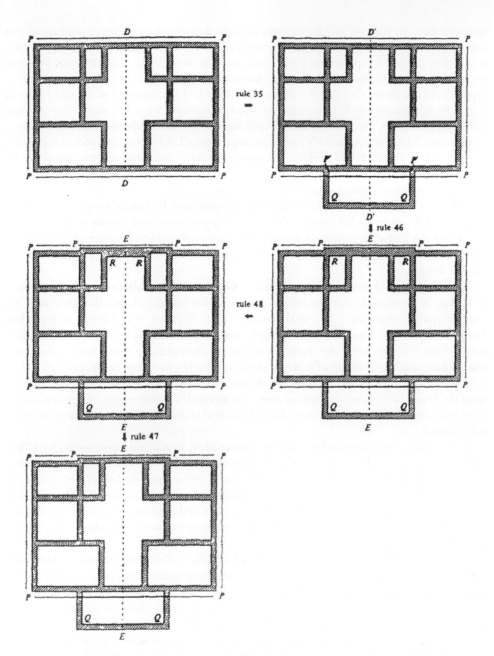

Figure 2.4 The Palladian grammar by George Stiny and William Mitchell is a generative description of all of Andrea Palladio's villas (Image credit: Stiny & Mitchell, 1978).

William J. Mitchell set out to codify the design principles of Italian Renaissance architect Andrea Palladio into a shape grammar. They noted that, while Palladio made many of his design principles explicit in his writings, many remained implicit. So, to recast Palladio "in a modern, generative form," they examined both Palladio's writings and his built work and created a set of rules (see, for example, Figure 2.4). Unlike Brooks' experiments in musical composition, the rules were not the result of statistical analysis but from a careful and judicious study by the two computationally inclined design and architecture scholars. In that sense, Stiny and Mitchell's Palladian grammar is closer to Hiller and Isaacson's experiment—in that they abstract compositional principles from a particular body of work. In the language of symbolic AI, Stiny and Mitchell were "knowledge engineers"—laboriously "extracting" expertise, to the extent that this is possible, from Palladio's documented works and encoding it in a formal system. Both buildings and words comprised what in present-day machine learning parlance we may refer to as the "training set" for their Palladian grammar.

However, Stiny and Mitchell's ambitions went beyond mere style transfer. An effective grammar, they wrote, should perform descriptive, analytic, and synthetic functions (Stiny & Mitchell, 1978). In other words, it should (a) characterize the traits shared by all Palladian buildings, (b) assess whether a given design, real or invented, fits within the constraints of the Palladian style, and (c) be able to generate entirely new Palladian designs (Ibid.). They emphasized the open-ended nature of the resulting grammar, and on the extent to which it codified the Palladian style, and not so much on its potential to be automated. For these reasons, the resulting grammar is a work of architectural history as much as one of computational design.

An important difference between Stiny and Gips' work and Hiller's experiments in music is that, as mentioned, shape grammar units were not numerical, and thus they were not conventionally computable. As visual elements, their pliability was difficult to reproduce digitally. As many a shape grammarian would attest, the structured nature of computational descriptions contrasts with the plasticity of visual perception. In this sense, shape grammars can be seen as a critique of numerocentric approaches to computational design and, in fact, as a provocative redefinition of *both* design and computation. Stiny and the late Gips spent the better part of their academic careers clarifying this point—decoupling computation from computers—and investigating a fascinating (and difficult) question: How to compute with shapes?

Despite these important differences, the experiments in musical composition by Hiller, Brooks and their collaborators, and the mathematically tractable visual computations envisioned by Stiny and Gips, share the same ambition: to define open-ended and yet stylistically consistent aesthetic systems. Their authors sought to ensure this consistency by imposing restrictions through statistical, probabilistic, or rule-based methods. Crucially, by selecting stylistic traits and curating a set of precedents, these authors set the boundaries of a space of possibilities: a *design space*.

While architects have been using rules for a long time—think of Vitruvius or Durand—open-ended design worlds such as those described through grammatical rules or probabilistic descriptions express a distinctive 20th-century imaginary of design linked to information theory and mathematical abstraction. They express a desire to codify design knowledge to make it computable and malleable in new ways. Crucially, they inscribe new conceptualizations of the design process and, in particular, new modes of authorial agency in design. These sensibilities remain at the core of present-day efforts to harness AI and machine learning methods in design. In what follows, we will examine transitions and overlaps between rule-based and data-intensive design systems, pondering what kind of design "knowledge" these systems encode—and what different kinds of "learning" they rely upon and facilitate.

From rule-making to data-wrangling

The origins of today's machine learning techniques are often traced to the convergence of AI research and statistics in the 1980s (Park, 2015). More recently, a series of technological shifts such as the availability of increasingly large datasets and processing power, and the resurgence of neural networks, has infused new life into the promise of using statistical analyses to inform computational reasoning. Machine learning researchers, however, do not conform to a unitary voice, and different schools of thought, each with their guiding theories and preferred algorithmic tools, converge in a diverse (and rapidly evolving) field. What seems to best unite this community and their tools is the notion that computational methods might help automate something akin to inductive reasoning: to draw generalizations, to infer patterns, and to predict future outcomes based on prior experience encoded as data. But data are never neutral—they are cultural artifacts situated in social and material settings (Drucker, 2011; Boyd & Crawford, 2012; Paglen, 2016; Crawford & Paglen, 2019; Loukissas, 2019; D'Ignazio & Klein, 2020). This means that data themselves are not inherently truthful but *constructed*, and thus their production and the processes for collecting, curating, and visualizing them are acts of design.

A closer look at some machine learning techniques helps illustrate this. US psychologist Frank Rosenblatt's formulated artificial neural networks in 1958. Based on a loose analogy of the human brain, neural networks use a combination of simple calculating units, each able to compute a very simple output from a very simple input. Trained on a sufficiently large number of examples, a neuron can, for example, react to particular details or features in pictures, such as edges, shadows, or colors. Convolutional neural networks (CNNs), one of the most commonly used techniques for visual recognition, are multilayered neural networks able to detect patterns in images at different scales and levels of complexity. CNNs were first demonstrated in the 1990s to be able to interpret handwriting in a computationally efficient way (LeCun et al., 1998). Their first major application was to interpret handwriting in checks (LeCun, 2014). Today, a common use of CNNs is the classification of images based on resemblance—for example, they are the backbone of Google's image search feature. Groups of neurons can recognize (or represent) images with shared features or infer those features on any given image (Mordvinstev, 2015). A neural network trained on, for example, the work of an expressionist painter can transfer this particular style into any image. However, unlike its stochastic and grammar-based predecessors, this type of work resembles a Photoshop filter more than a generative device.

Projects exploring the aesthetic potential of CNNs include experiments in style transfer (Gatys et al., 2015; Kogan, 2015): a search engine that finds places on satellite photographs based on visual likeness (Levin et al., 2016); and the at-times disturbing imagery produced by Deep Dream, a CNN developed at Google that can be directed to recursively infer and emphasize a variety of patterns in images—such as faces, colors, or edges (Mordvinstev, 2015; Mordvinstev et al., n.d.). Recent work on recurrent neural networks (RNNs) suggests a different type of production system. RNNs are a type of neural network that computes its own output. US computational artist and author Kyle McDonald shows that RNNs can be used to classify images by similarity (Figure 2.5) or to generate new text that resembles the style of a set of examples (McDonald, 2016). For example, an RNN trained on the written works of author Zadie Smith can produce text that maintains a stylistic resemblance with her works—despite being mostly nonsensical (Karpathy, 2015a, 2015b). Unlike CNNs, which are designed to work on image maps, RNNs are designed to process sequential inputs of arbitrary length, which makes them suitable for processing text.

Compared with the Cold-War era experiments in music and design we discussed at the beginning of the chapter, the training sets for these experiments are larger—in some cases millions of examples versus a few dozen—and their computational techniques more sophisticated—distributed, multiple "neural" processes vs. stochastic or rule-based ones.

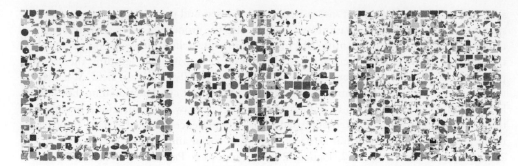

Figure 2.5   In Innards, US computational artist Kyle McDonald uses a recurrent neural network to generate emoji from vectorial graphics using a character-level recurrent framework. The result evokes Allison Parrish's work "smiling face withface" (Image credit: McDonald, 2016).

And yet, despite a well-engrained cultural fascination with "big data," not all approaches to machine learning in design involve large datasets. An alternative approach is exemplified by London-based US computer scientist and musician Rebecca Fiebrink, who develops tools that employ machine learning methods for artistic performance and creative design. Her free and open-source software Wekinator allows users to train machine learning algorithms to respond to different types of input such as facial gestures and bodily motions (Fiebrink et al., 2009). Wekinator users can input a series of gestures into the system via a webcam and associate these to, for example, sound responses. In this way, users craft a small dataset of gestures that the system can use to classify a much wider range of hand gestures during a performance. The result is a highly versatile gestural instrument. Fiebrink's idea of "data as a user interface" nicely illustrates an aesthetic and philosophical commitment to the potential of open-ended and embodied interactions, rather than those of symbolic manipulation, in creative practice (Fiebrink, 2011, 2015). Here, the quality and craft of the dataset are more important than its size.

Both the user-centered work exemplified by Rebecca Fiebrink's work just discussed and the data-focused explorations exemplified by the projects outlined before share with their Cold-War era predecessors an interest in the configuration of stylistically consistent aesthetic systems. Be it through rules, probabilistic descriptions, stochastic processes, neural networks, or grammars, they rely on the codification of aesthetic materials to analyze, describe, generate, or perform. Despite their different technical underpinnings, they also share a long-standing fascination with the potential of computational methods to work inductively: to derive aesthetic results from the analysis of examples.

From this brief overview of machine learning in design, I would like to propose two conceptual moves to understand these technologies' potentials in the design domain. One: understanding the construction of the data, the design of the rules, and the curation of the examples, as *acts of design*. Two: to consider not just outcomes but how these systems *reconfigure relationships* between designers, authors, users, and audiences.

With these, we might explore directions forward that challenge naïf fantasies of design automation, and simplistic approaches to style transfer, and open up analytical and generative potentials for incorporating machine learning methods in design.

The following section discusses three research projects developed at the Computational Design Laboratory at Carnegie Mellon University that help illustrate the conceptual moves stated above and outline some emerging potentials and limitations of machine learning in the design domains.

Some new directions

Granular control over algorithmic actions

The first project, developed by computational designer and artist Erik Ulberg, explores new ways of interacting with convolutional neural networks that afford users fine-grain control over the algorithm's behavior. Inspired by the notion of "craft," Erik sought to create an algorithm that enabled the direct, iterative connection artists have with materials when producing work. He developed two computational tools, allowing users to edit and visualize, at different levels of abstraction, a neural network to make line drawings. Together, the tools "provided a crude form of perception for a generative line drawing system to allow it to dynamically respond to preexisting images or emergent structures" (Ulberg, 2020). The first tool, the "Kernel Tuner," allows users to control the weights of a neural network's first layer of convolution, where basic features are extracted from drawings. By adjusting the kernels, users could calibrate the tool to respond to a drawing's specific features—in this case, a line's end. Testing how the Kernel Tuner responded differently to different kinds of drawings, Erik observed that, rather than a general-purpose drawing system, the tool was highly specific to a certain kind of drawing. The process of calibrating the tool seemed to reveal aspects of the network's internal operation. Noting that often many kernels activated at any given pixel, he made the following observation about a network's way of dealing with visual ambiguity:

> …the internal abstractions in a network are better thought of in terms of adjectives on continuous scales rather than one-hot vectors of nouns. Neural networks do not produce clean, easy-to-understand signals. A pixel is not just a "corner." It is "corner"-like, but also "vertical line"-like and "horizontal line"-like. Adjusting the parameters manually facilitates human-led jumps through the search space, but these results suggest we should incorporate computational fine tuning to overcome the complexity of balancing competing activations.
>
> *(Ulberg, 2020)*

The second tool, the "Network Builder," works at a higher level of abstraction. Its visual interface allows users to engage with more complex visual concepts such as "house" or "bottle," correcting the weights to privilege certain activations. Working in conjunction with the Kernel Tuner, the Network Builder can produce intriguing compositions based on these visual concepts (Figure 2.6). The tools did not fully accomplish Erik's goal to facilitate an engagement with neural networks, resembling that of an artist with their material. However, they did offer a new type of algorithmic scaffolding for visual experimentation, and intriguing visual results. In addition, the visualization offered insight into the workings of the algorithm itself—for example, about how CNNs handle visual ambiguity. Erik's project foreshadows future developments into computational methods that experiment with the very architecture of machine learning algorithms, and with their user interfaces, for expressive purposes.

Architectural distant readings

The second project asks how machine learning methods might enable the analysis of large collections of architectural data. Researchers in the digital humanities have developed the concept of "distant reading" to describe analyses of large datasets enabled by computational

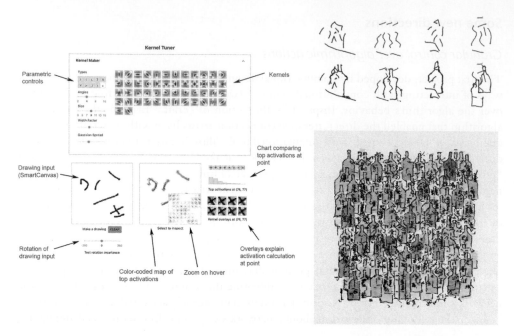

Figure 2.6 Tools to visualize and manually alter the behavior of a neural network in real time allows for a new kind of image manipulation (Image credit: Ulberg, 2020).

methods. These researchers contrast this approach with that of "close reading," which typically focuses on a single literary, visual, or technical work. For example, instead of focusing on one work by a single author, such as a novel or a memoir, or even the entire works of a single author, researchers using this concept have explored entire genres or periods of literary production. Relying on computational techniques such as text mining and network analysis, distant reading practices seek to identify continuities or variations across vast collections that would be difficult to perceive with the conventional toolkit of the literary scholar (Underwood, 2017). With similar ideas in mind, architect and computational designer Cecilia Ferrando and collaborators conducted an experiment on "architectural distant reading" wherein architectural characteristics such as visual and spatial connectivity can be read across a large body of buildings, potentially identifying typological and configurational variations and similarities (Ferrando et al., 2019). To test this idea, the team laboriously composed a small dataset of religious buildings, which they represented as graphs—with nodes as individual spaces and links as indicators of spatial connectivity. They implemented a graph-based kernel to quantify the similarity between graphs based on the length of random walks and clustered the buildings in the dataset by the similarity of their spatial structures. This enabled them to find correlations between spatial structure and typological or functional traits. For example, the team observed that buildings cataloged as mosques in the dataset had a relatively horizontal, or shallow, spatial structure compared to monasteries. Their graphs resembled "flowers," with a central space and a number of connected spaces forming on a level of spatial "depth" (Figure 2.7). In contrast, monasteries were more hierarchical, with spaces often chained into sequences. The clustering inspired the team to think of the concept of a "typological gradient," which helps to think about building types not as exclusive categories but rather as overlapping ones.

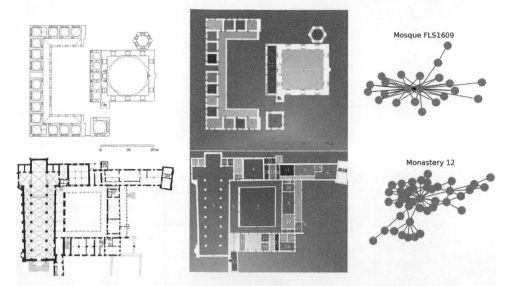

Figure 2.7 An experiment in "architectural distant reading." A graph-based spatial analysis helps analyze "typological gradients" in collections of architectural data (Image credit: Ferrando et al., 2019).

Cecilia and team's findings suggest that spatial structure in conjunction with machine learning methods can be used as an effective typological classifier—they were able to classify the buildings in the dataset with 93% accuracy. But, more importantly, they sketch out a way for machine learning methods to support architectural analysis and design—not as replacements of but as resources for architects and researchers.

New urban cartographies

The third project offered here for discussion is Jinmo Rhee's study of Pittsburgh's urban fabric using machine learning algorithms (Rhee et al., 2019). Despite being a relatively small city, Pittsburgh's fabric is notably heterogeneous, with many neighborhoods, each with a distinctive urban character. Noting how research into computational aids to design has historically fallen short of acknowledging the importance of urban contexts, Jinmo developed a computational method to help understand the city's rich patchwork of urban fabrics. The way architectural and urban data is conventionally represented digitally in urban data—without any link between urban context and architectural unit—makes this type of analysis difficult. To address this limitation, Rhee designed a data structure combining information about architectural units, such as their height, function, dimensions, occupancy, and their immediate urban contexts (Rhee, 2018). Working with GIS data provided by the city's and county's governments, Rhee generated a new dataset of images of each one of Pittsburgh's 48,913 buildings, surrounded by its immediate urban context. Using t-distributed stochastic neighbor embedding, a dimensionality reduction technique, he was able to cluster buildings based not only on their individual characteristics but also on their contexts. Mapped back into space, this clustering produces a new type of morphological plan that redistricts the city based on subtle distinctions in its urban fabric (see Figure 2.8).

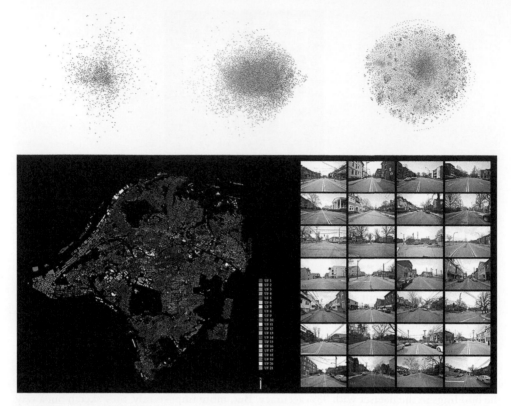

Figure 2.8   New data structures comprising building and urban data allow for fine-grain morphological analyses using machine learning techniques (Image credit: Rhee et al., 2019).

Jinmo supplemented his study with field visits to what appeared to be boundary conditions in the dataset, and with visits to the city archives, enriching his analysis with qualitative observations. These on the one hand helped confirm that the boundaries identified by his method corresponded with observable urban phenomena and on the other helped enrich his study with a deeper understanding of the historical origins of Pittsburgh's morphological diversity. The study, which Jinmo is currently expanding as part of his PhD, opens up both analytical and generative opportunities. On the one hand, the enriched urban dataset affords the detailed study of a city's morphology, which opens up nuances and suggests the possibility of comparative analyses of urban form. On the other, these techniques may be developed into a design toolkit allowing designers to, for example, assess architectural or urban design hypotheses in terms of their fit with existing, or desired, contexts.

Discussion

From rule-based music and synthetic Palladian villas to distant readings of architectural collections, handcrafted neural networks, and data-rich urban analyses, this chapter has delineated an experimental tradition in computational art and design based on inductive processes. Via rules, statistical controls, or machine learning algorithms, this tradition has focused on shaping spaces of design possibility. But I have also tried to show that the units of these computational transactions (encoded melodies, shapes, "data") have a materiality and a plasticity of their own, that they are irreducibly contingent upon human labor and creativity, and that, it is precisely there, on those materialities, labors, and creative acts, that the critical and aesthetic potentials of machine learning in design are realized. And yet, these labors are commonly hidden by rhetoric centered on the supposed autonomy of computational systems. By discussing a series of recent experiments, I have tried to show how the poetics of machine learning is also the poetics of data—how we as researchers, willingly or unwillingly, design and construct them. In other words, practices of data structuring, collection, and manipulation are acts of design at the root of the new aesthetics emerging around AI and machine learning methods.

Accordingly, the projects discussed suggest the emergence of new authorial roles related to how data is collected, curated, processed, and visualized. The explicit and implicit labors of designing and constructing a dataset are not only the defining component of the process. They also appear as the key arena for both critical and creative inquiry.

To finalize, drawing from the examples provided, I would like to offer for discussion three specific arenas where these practices open up opportunities for creative and critical engagements with AI and machine learning in design.

Codification and "translation" as creative practices

As recent studies of science and technology remind us, rather than objective and neutral, data are laboriously designed and constructed. They are enmeshed with and at the same time shape their social and material settings. It is thus important to recognize codification—the construction of these data—as a creative practice worthy of critical consideration. In encoding Palestrina's compositional principles into computer subroutines, for example, Hiller and collaborators constructed a specific kind of dataset on which to train their stochastic system. In encoding 37 musical pieces as numerical strings, Brooks and collaborators not merely translated but also took a position about the nature of music as media, making it computable as a space of probabilistic inference. In encoding Palladian architecture in a finite set of visual rules, Stiny and Gips adopted (or reinforced) a stance about orthographic architectural representations' capacities to codify what is important about architecture. These decisions should not be seen as innocent but as key *design* decisions crucially structuring design spaces. Of course, no translation is transparent nor leaves original meanings untouched. For example, in Cecilia Ferrando's "architectural distant readings," the decision to codify buildings as graphs shaped the kind of questions she and her coauthors were able to ask of the dataset—privileging notions of spatial structure and hierarchy (and overlooking other, arguably essential, factors of architectural quality). In Jinmo Rhee's study of Pittsburgh, the analytical and generative potential of the machine learning framework is realized in the design of a new data structure specifically designed to codify aspects of a building's urban context. As these examples show, critically engaging with codification practices can unlock opportunities for creative engagement in a design culture increasingly defined by data.

Disciplinary and methodological hybridity

Computational methods have always worked in conjunction with other knowledge domains and draw from a broad range of conceptual and methodological toolkits. Computational design practices are not an exception. In Hiller's experiments in musical composition, for example, molecular structures served as conceptual scaffoldings for melodic ones. In Stiny and Gips' work, a centuries-old tradition of orthographic architectural representations was used to produce a generative description of an entire body of architectural work. This conceptual openness imposes critical demands on computational design practices, because they are never safely contained within a disciplinary or methodological bucket. Failing to recognize these demands will likely result in yet another simplistic attempt to style transfer, yet another naïf fantasy to automate design, or yet another misguided effort to quantify architectural quality. The rigor with which the different domains are explored and articulated will determine the quality of both the creative outputs and critical insights offered.

There is no formula for creatively putting different forms of expertise in motion "in the wild" nor for accessing methodological or disciplinary hinterlands effectively through computational methods. However, the chapter offers some hints: Jinmo's attention to historical archives and to evidence collected "on the field" productively puts architectural and urban sensibilities in conversation with computational expertise. Erik's artistic sensibility and practice not only motivated his inquiry but also shaped the two computational tools he developed, as well as their outputs. Cecilia's architectural training and scholarly understanding of spatial analysis methods, along with her deep understanding of machine learning, shaped the choices she made about codification as well as the questions she asked of the dataset.

Slowdowns and interruptions at the interface

The design of interfaces for users to interact with data in machine learning contexts offers opportunities for creativity and innovation. Interfaces developed with particular users or user groups in mind can help support new kinds of creative exploration. In Rebecca Fiebrink's "Wekinator," for example, we see an early expression of interfaces allowing musicians, visual artists, and other creative practitioners to easily create and manipulate training datasets. Using their bodies to iteratively sculpt the training data, users shape these data and create frameworks of inference that suit their expressive goals—a computational design space. Similarly, Erik Ulberg's "Kernel Tuner" and "Network Builder" engineer a type of interaction that affords artists low-level, granular control over the algorithmic machinery of a convolutional neural network. Importantly, the interface actually *slows down* a computational process that is typically in the background and creates opportunities for interruptions and adjustments, which enable artistic experimentation. Of interest here is that the focus is not placed on the design of new, faster algorithms, but on the design of an interaction that facilitates new kinds of engagement with a computational process—making it less rigid, and less predictable.

Acknowledgments

I am thankful to the graduate students in the Computational Design Laboratory at the School of Architecture at Carnegie Mellon University with whom we discussed many of the ideas in this paper and in particular to Jinmo Rhee, Erik Ulberg, Cecilia Ferrando, and Ardavan Bidgoli. I am also thankful to Rebecca Fiebrink for insightful discussions about her work.

Note

* An earlier version of this article was published in German in: *Machine Learning: Medien, Infrastrukturen und Technologien der Künstlichen Intelligenz*, edited by Christoph Engemann and Andreas Sudmann. Bielefeld: Transcript, 2017.

References

Bense, M. (1971). The projects of generative aesthetics. In *Cybernetics, Art and Ideas* (ed. Jasia Reihardt) (pp. 57–60). Studio Vista. http://www.computerkunst.org/Bense_Manifest.pdf

Bewley, J. (2004). *Lejaren A. Hiller: Computer Music Pioneer.* http://library.buffalo.edu/libraries/units/music/exhibits/hillerexhibitsummary.pdf

Birkhoff, G. D. (1933). *Aesthetic Measure.* Harvard University Press.

Boyd, D., & Crawford, K. (2012). Critical Questions for Big Data. *Information, Communication & Society, 15*(5), 662–679. https://doi.org/10.1080/1369118X.2012.678878

Brooks, F. P., Hopkins, A. L., Neumann, P. G., & Wright, W. V. (1957). An Experiment in Musical Composition. *IRE Transactions on Electronic Computers, EC-6*(3), 175–182. https://doi.org/10.1109/TEC.1957.5222016

Caplan, L. (2020). The Social Conscience of Generative Art. *Art in America, January 2020, 108*, 50–57.

Cardoso Llach, D. (2015). *Builders of the Vision: Software and the Imagination of Design.* Routledge.

Chomsky, N. (2015). *Syntactic Structures.* Martino Fine Books.

Computational Design Laboratory. (2016). *Code Lab.* http://code.arc.cmu.edu/

Crawford, K., & Paglen, T. (2019, September 19). *Excavating AI: The Politics of Images in Machine Learning Training Sets.* https://www.excavating.ai

D'Ignazio, C., & Klein, L. F. (2020). *Data Feminism.* The MIT Press.

Domingos, P. (2015). *The Master Algorithm: How the Quest for the Ultimate Learning Machine Will Remake Our World.* Basic Books.

Drucker, J. (2011). Humanities Approaches to Graphical Display. *Digital Humanities Quarterly, 5*(1). http://www.digitalhumanities.org/dhq/vol/5/1/000091/000091.html

Ferrando, C., Cardoso Llach, D., Dalmasso, N., & Mai, J. (2019). Architectural Distant Reading: Using Machine Learning to Analyze Architectural Traditions. *CAAD Futures 2019: Hello, Culture.* CAAD Futures 2019, Daejeon, Korea.

Fiebrink, R. (2011). *Real-time Human Interaction with Supervised Learning Algorithms for Music Composition and Performance.* Princeton University.

Fiebrink, R. (2015, July 9). Data as Design Tool. How Understanding Data as a User Interface Can Make End-User Design More Accessible, Efficient, Effective, and Embodied, While Challenging Machine Learning Conventions. *International Conference on Auditory Display (ICAD) 2015.* http://iem.kug.ac.at/icad15/icad15.html

Fiebrink, R., Trueman, D., & Cook, P. R. (2009). *A Meta-Instrument for Interactive, On-the-Fly Machine Learning—Semantic Scholar.* NIME - New Interfaces for Musical Expression, Carnegie Mellon University. /paper/A-Meta-Instrument-for-Interactive-On-the-Fly-Fiebrink-Trueman/0652e6120d-72dc0162a17b5b0e49e9f5e12bc668

Gatys, L. A., Ecker, A. S., & Bethge, M. (2015). A Neural Algorithm of Artistic Style. *ArXiv:1508.06576 [Cs, q-Bio].* http://arxiv.org/abs/1508.06576

Karpathy, A. (2015a). *Char-rnn.* GitHub. https://github.com/karpathy/char-rnn

Karpathy, A. (2015b, May 21). *The Unreasonable Effectiveness of Recurrent Neural Networks.* http://karpathy.github.io/2015/05/21/rnn-effectiveness/

Knight, T. W. (1994). *Transformations in Design: A Formal Approach to Stylistic Change and Innovation in the Visual Arts.* Cambridge University Press.

Kogan, G. (2015). *Style Transfer.* Genekogan.com. http://www.genekogan.com/works/style-transfer.html

Le Cun, Y. (2014, June 2). Convolutional Network Demo from 1993. https://www.youtube.com/watch?v=FwFduRA_L6Q

LeCun, Y., Bottou, L., Bengio, Y., & Haffner, P. (1998). Gradient-based Learning Applied to Document Recognition. *Proceedings of the IEEE, 86*(11), 2278–2324. https://doi.org/10.1109/5.726791

Levin, G., Newbury, D., & McDonald, K. (2016, May 24). *Terrapattern_alpha*. Terrapattern.Com. http://www.terrapattern.com/

Loukissas, Y. A. (2019). *All Data Are Local: Thinking Critically in a Data-Driven Society*. The MIT Press.

McDonald, K. (2016, October 7). *A Return to Machine Learning*. Medium. https://medium.com/@kcimc/a-return-to-machine-learning-2de3728558eb

Mordvinstev, A. (2015, July 13). *Inceptionism: Going Deeper into Neural Networks*. Research Blog. https://research.googleblog.com/2015/06/inceptionism-going-deeper-into-neural.html

Mordvinstev, A., Tyka, M., & Olah, C. (n.d.). *Deep Dream*. GitHub. Retrieved January 5, 2017, from https://github.com/google/deepdream

Paglen, T. (2016, December 8). *Invisible Images (Your Pictures Are Looking at You)*. The New Inquiry. http://thenewinquiry.com/essays/invisible-images-your-pictures-are-looking-at-you/

Park, J. H. (2015). *Synthetic Tutor: Profiling Students and Mass-Customizing Learning Processes Dynamically in Design Scripting Education* [Thesis, Massachusetts Institute of Technology]. http://dspace.mit.edu/handle/1721.1/101544

Rhee, J. (2018). *Diagrammatic Image Dataset Pittsburgh (DID-PGH)*. Jinmo Rhee. http://www.jinmorhee.net/jinmorhee_2-multiimage/didpgh.html

Rhee, J., Cardoso Llach, D., & Krishnamurti, R. (2019). Context-rich Urban Analysis Using Machine Learning—A case study in Pittsburgh, PA. *Architecture in the Age of the 4th Industrial Revolution - Proceedings of the 37th ECAADe and 23rd SIGraDi Conference, 3*, 343–352. http://papers.cumincad.org/data/works/att/ecaadesigradi2019_550.pdf

Stiny, G., and Gips. J. (1972). "Shape Grammars and the Generative Specification of Painting and Sculpture." In *IFIP Congress, Information Processing* 71, 1460–65.

Stiny, G., & Mitchell, W. J. (1978). The Palladian Grammar. *Environment and Planning B, 5*, 5–18.

Ulberg, E. (2020). *Crafting the Weights of a Convolutional Neural Network to Make a Drawing* [MS]. Carnegie Mellon University.

Underwood, T. (2017). A Genealogy of Distant Reading. *Digital Humanities Quarterly, 11*(2). http://www.digitalhumanities.org/dhq/vol/11/2/000317/000317.html

Zaripov, R. Kh., & Russell, J. G. K. (1969). Cybernetics and Music. *Perspectives of New Music, 7*(2), 115–154. https://doi.org/10.2307/832298

3

Mapping generative models for architectural design

Pedro Veloso and Ramesh Krishnamurti

Mapping generative models for architectural design

Natural sciences are concerned with how things are; design, on the other hand, is concerned with how things ought to be (Simon, 1996, p. 114). Likewise, their respective models resonate this distinction between analysis and synthesis. Models in natural sciences are instruments to investigate hypothetical or existing phenomena and are generally based on symbolic and mathematical concepts. In contrast, architectural designers traditionally use a vast range of visual media, such as in sketches or physical prototypes (which can be considered as models as well) to express relevant characteristics of an as-yet-unknown spatial construct.

Architects modify and refine models that partially represent a spatial construct that is under construction with the models themselves (see Figure 3.1: A). Working as a material and stimuli for design interaction, models in architecture support what design theorists consider a specific form of creative and cyclic reasoning (Anderson, 1966; Schön, 1983; Corona-Martínez, 2003; Lawson, 2005; Gänshirt, 2007). Particularly in the early stages of design, interaction with the partial representations is important for acquiring knowledge,

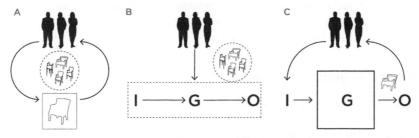

Figure 3.1   A: Design ideation: the direct interaction of designers with visual media to build an imaginary design world. B: formulation of a generative model: the definition of input (I) and generator (G) implies the existence of design space to navigate and look for output design alternatives (O). C: execution of a generative model: designers control an input, the generator synthesizes a design alternative as an output, which is observed by the designers.

creating a frame of reference, and reformulating the problem and solution in parallel (Cross, 2006). In this process, "(…) the designer constructs the design world within which he/she sets the dimensions of his/her problem space and invents the moves by which he/she attempts to find solutions" (Schön, 1992, p. 11).

Notwithstanding being a well-established practice, the direct and intuitive engagement with design media is not the only alternative for design conception. Instead of using static models for visual and tactile feedback, designers can employ models that embed some form of decision-making, such as instructions or behaviors, to generate design alternatives, which is the essence of generative models.[1] Our basic representation of a generative model[2] has two stages—formulation and execution—and three main components: input (I), generator (G), and output (O).

In the formulation stage (Figure 3.1: B), the designer develops the representations for the input, for the output, and the algorithm to be encoded in the generator. This algorithm specifies how to synthesize the output design alternatives, conditioned on the input information. In contrast to conventional design ideation, where designers imagine design worlds by interacting with design media, generative models induce the space of possible designs (design space) and the ways that the designer can navigate between solutions.

In the execution stage (Figure 3.1: C), designers interact with the generator by changing the input information and observing design alternatives as feedback in the output of the model. They can either exploit a subspace of solutions that satisfy certain goals or explore unexpected alternatives. Potentially, this stage can lead to a reformulation of the model.

Notice that this representation is not restricted to the use of computational models. It can (retrospectively) include existing methods, such as form-finding models, like pneumatic, soap bubbles, soap-film, sand, and suspended chain models (Otto, 2009; Vrachliotis et al., 2017), or the procedures to generate building elements and configurations from architectural treatises (Lucan, 2012).[3] Nevertheless, the abstraction and generality of numerical and symbolic computation enable the control over all the elements and stages of a generative model and can subsume most existing generative models. With computers, it is not only possible to explicitly model geometry and building information—as in CAD and BIM software—but also to simulate form-finding models, to automate the generation of building types, and to create custom generative models.

Generative models are constructs situated between design and computational logic. Their agency can be inspired by different sources, such as human cognition, expert knowledge, brain architecture, social organisms, natural processes, and dynamics. They are a powerful and compelling alternative for design that benefits both from the rigor of scientific modeling and the open-endedness of the design artifacts.

A taxonomy for generative models

Despite the resurgent interest in generative modeling for architecture, there is a lack of consistency and rigor in the treatment of underlying ideas and terms (Caetano, Santos, & Leitão, 2020). The knowledge on generative models is fragmentary, and the techniques to develop custom generative models are not systematized; so their incorporation in design education is still challenging.

Early computational generative models focused on the synthesis of architectural layout and relied on techniques from operations research (optimization) and symbolic artificial intelligence (heuristic search) (Eastman, 1975; Mitchell, 1977; Bijl, 1990; Flemming &

Woodbury, 1995; Simon, 1996). Over time, optimization became a dominant technique for generative models with the incorporation of black-box methods, such as genetic algorithms. Additionally, rule-based and agent-based models, such as fractals and L-systems, cellular automata and swarm algorithms, or simulation techniques, such as physics simulation, further extended this repertoire (Fischer & Herr, 2001; Kalay, 2004; Kolarevic, 2005; Oxman, 2006; Grobman, Yezioro, & Capeluto, 2009; Vishal & Gu, 2012). Ideas from machine learning are also being incorporated in generative models to infer the generator automatically from data or experience (Kalay, 2004; Bidgoli & Veloso, 2018; Veloso & Krishnamurti, 2019).

Generative models are occasionally assimilated into design studios and workshops via predefined computational workflows and plug-ins as a platform to explore a certain design agenda. They have been integrated into changing trends and design narratives related to aesthetics, mathematics, biology, or to aspects of production, such as tectonics, performance, or fabrication (Mitchell, Liggett, & Kvan, 1987; Mitchell, 1990; Coates & Thum, 1995; Frazer, 1995; Terzidis, 2006; Coates, 2010; Hensel, Menges, & Weinstock, 2010; Oxman & Oxman, 2014; Henrique et al., 2019).

We have created a taxonomy to contribute to the systematization of existing generative models and development of new ones (Figure 3.2).[4] We introduced this taxonomy in computational design courses at Carnegie Mellon University, and it resulted in insightful feedback and interesting projects—some of these projects are displayed in this chapter as examples. It is based on components or building blocks of generative models, which are organized in three levels according to their function: expression, synthesis, or learning. Each generative model is represented in the taxonomy as a combination of the building blocks. The vertical and diagonal connections between building blocks in different levels represent the combination of components for models with multiple functions. The horizontal connections represent the hybridization of components for the same function. The thickness of the lines indicates affinity. Thus, agent-based models have a relatively stronger affinity with simulation as compared to rule-based models with composition and, likewise, even more so than parametric models with optimization.

The blocks in the first row are the three common expressions of a generative model: parametric, rule-based, and agent-based. These blocks are essential because they define specific formulations for the models that result in different types of design spaces and forms of design navigation. The second row contains computational methods for automatic design synthesis, such as optimization,[5] composition, and simulation. These blocks support the execution stage, where the designers can explore design alternatives by interacting with the design input and outputs. Finally, the third row contains the blocks of generative learning and behavioral learning, which are computational strategies to automate the formulation of the model using data or experience.

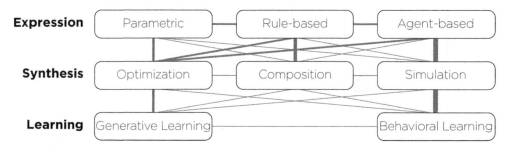

Figure 3.2 Taxonomy for building blocks of generative models.

Pedro Veloso and Ramesh Krishnamurti

Expressions of generative models

Parametric model

One of the more popular ways of expressing design synthesis is through parametric modeling, which has precedents in the history of rationalist architecture and computational modeling (Davis, 2013a). Roughly, a parametric model can be defined as an explicit representation of the design logic that can be controlled by independent variables (or input). Mathematically, these variables are named parameters and are associated with equations that map them to a certain quantity in the output (Davis, 2013b, pp. 21–22). For example, the explicit representation of the coordinates of a hyperbolic paraboloid parameterized on the straight lines maps the input parameters (u, v, a) to the coordinates of the surface (u, v, uva) (Figure 3.3). The parameter a is of special interest because it can be used to change the height of the hyperbolic paraboloid.

In design, the notion of a parametric function is more general than a mathematical function, because it can also comprehend any type of modeling operation available in design software. Thus, parametric modeling is employed as a method to explore and visualize variations of architectural solutions, based on an algorithm that receives an input, executes a finite sequence of well-defined, geometric, symbolic, or even numerical operations, and generates the design alternatives as output. In other words, the generator is typically a fixed structure where the changes in the parameters propagate through all the dependencies, updating the representation.

In the early programming courses for design (Mitchell, Liggett, & Kvan, 1987; Coates & Thum, 1995), this explicit parametric function was developed procedurally to generate a certain shape. Furthermore, the designer could change some of the parameters of this program, re-execute it, and watch the change propagate through the function to update the shape. Today, most current parametric editors for design are propagation-based, in which the parametric function is explicitly modeled as an acyclic graph with dependencies, modeling operations, and entities (Woodbury, 2010, p. 12; Janssen & Stouffs, 2015, pp. 158–162). Any change in the input information or some component of this graph will trigger the re-execution of the function, updating the output.

Parametric modeling enables fast change in a predefined range of variation, which relies on the domain of the parameters and the parametric function. If the parameters are all numerical or each parameter can be depicted on a separate axis, then the design space can be represented by a multidimensional parameter space. The designer can explore a combination of parameters, which are mapped to a geometric solution by the parametric function (if such

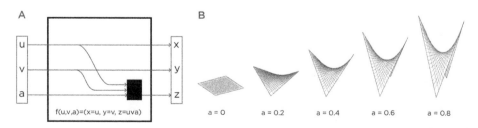

Figure 3.3 A: function to generate the coordinates of a hyperbolic paraboloid. B: representation of the surfaces in a specific domain of u and v, based on the variation of the parameter a.

a solution is possible) (Figure 3.4). In the cases where the input is geometrical, the variations can also be achieved by conventional modeling operations that affect the input.

Different parametric models can capture different design intentions (Figure 3.5). Owing to a commitment to a parametric structure, the design of a good model requires significant frontloading. The designer should anticipate and accommodate the intended interdependencies, changes, and future explorations. Otherwise, design decisions and changes in the design space will require reconstructing a part or the whole of the parametric function (Davis, 2013b, pp. 37–47).

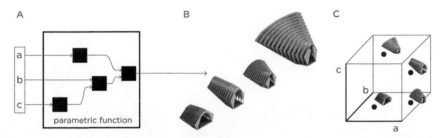

Figure 3.4   A: diagram of a generative model based on the parameters a, b, and c and on an internal network of operations. B: variations of the geometry. C: diagram of parameter space of the model, associating the coordinates of the parameters with the resulting designs. The model depicted in B and C was developed by Adie Alnobani (Parametric Modeling, CMU, Spring 2016).

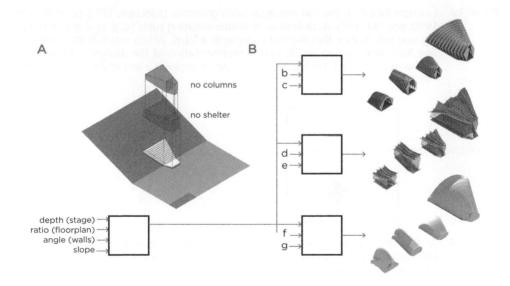

Figure 3.5   Exercise for parametric modeling (CMU, Spring 2016): outdoor theater. A: base parametric model, with requirements for the theater (seats, volume with no columns, and volume to shelter). B: three different parametric models to create a structure for the base model (authors from top to bottom: Adie Alnobani, Atefeh Goloujeh, and Cecilia Ferrando). These models respond to the changes of the parameters of the base model and their own. The diagrams of the parametric functions and the input values are schematic.

Rule-based model

Rule-based modeling encapsulates a kit-of-parts approach. The parts of the kit are blocks, which can be selected and, with custom transformations, applied to a design representation to build alternatives. These blocks can be represented as a set of instructions or be formalized into productions or if-then rules (see rules x, y, z, and w, in Figure 3.6: A and in Figure 3.7: A: item 1).

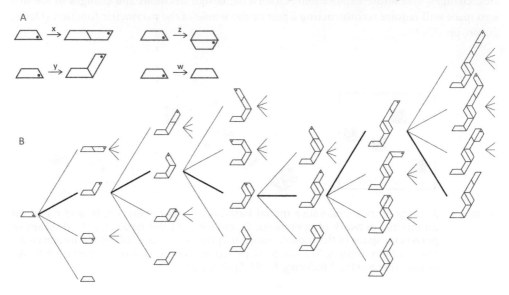

Figure 3.6   Example based on the half-hexagon table grammar (Mitchell, 1977, pp. 436–439; 1990, pp. 143–147). A: definition of nonterminating rules (x, y, z) and a terminating rule (w). Notice that the dot represents a label, which restricts the precondition for future derivations. B: partial representation of the design space induced by the rule set. A thicker line represents an example of a sequence of derivations.

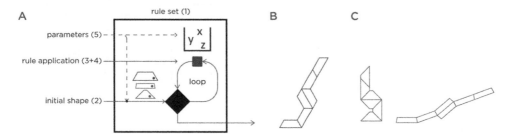

Figure 3.7   A: diagram of a rule-based generative model using a variation of the half-hexagon table grammar. B: example of resulting design; C: two variations using parameters for angle and width.

In the case of if-then rules, the design transformation maps two elements:

The if or left-hand side (lhs) represents the preconditions for the application of the rule. The then or the right-hand side (rhs) depicts the result of the transformation.

Rules are either terminating or nonterminating. Nonterminating rules contain elements that represent preconditions, which enable further derivation of the design. Terminating rules do not have preconditions on the right side, that is, they prevent further changes in the representation. During the execution of a rule-based model (Figure 3.7: A), an initial design representation (usually, the input of our generative model) will be incrementally changed by the rules available in the rule set.

Designing with rule-based models is equivalent to selecting the preconditions and rules incrementally—that is to say, the decision process is represented by sequences of derivations. The designer or the generator interprets the current design state to detect existing preconditions (see Figure 3.7: A: item 3). Detecting the preconditions is simple in the case where it is an atomic representation, such as a character, a string, or a line. Moreover, geometric preconditions can be subject to geometric transformations, such as rotation or scaling. However, when the representation is ambiguous, forms and preconditions that are unanticipated during the development of the rule set can emerge with the derivations. In these cases, interpreting preconditions in the representation can be hard. After discovering preconditions, it is necessary to pick a rule compatible with one of the available preconditions (see Figure 3.7: A: item 4). If there is only one rule application available for every state of the representation, the model is deterministic, and it will generate a single trajectory of changes, as in standard fractals or simple L-systems. However, if multiple preconditions and/or multiple rules can be selected, the design space is a network of possible design alternatives formed by the distinct paths of transformations, starting from an initial representation (Figure 3.6: B).

Models with if-then rules have been widely adopted and formalized in different fields, such as logic (Bratko, 2011), shape grammars (Stiny, 2006), L-systems (Prusinkiewicz & Lindenmayer, 2004), and fractals (Mandelbrot, 1983). Overall, rule-based modeling covers a vast variety of application areas and as such results in different nomenclature and specificities. Table 3.1 characterizes three different formalisms.

Table 3.1 Different formalisms based on rules

	L-Systems	*Shape Grammars*	*Fractals*
Representation	String with constants and variables from a fixed alphabet	Shapes composed of maximal lines	Atomic geometric entities (lines, polygons, etc.)
Original area of application	Developmental biology	Spatial design and visual arts	Mathematics of self-similarity
Rule set	Set of production rules based on a fixed alphabet	Set of rules in a grammar	Typically, one rule defines a fractal
Left-hand side (lhs)	Variable from the alphabet	Shape	Initiator geometry
Right-hand side (rhs)	String with variables and/or constants	Shape	Generator geometry (a set of transformed initiators)
Interpreter	Detect substrings	Detect subshapes	Detect initiators
Mode of application	Parallel	Serial	Parallel
Types of operations	String rewriting	Shape substitution	Shape substitution
Post-processing	A mechanism converts the string into geometry.	–	–

Inspired by Gips and Stiny (1980).

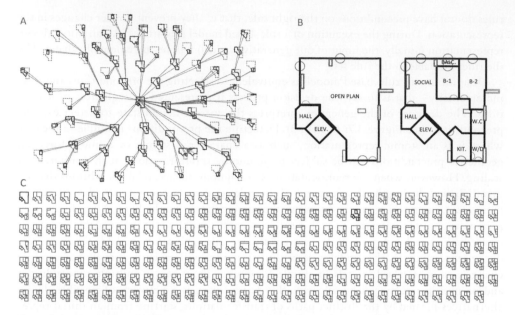

Figure 3.8 Example of grammar for the customization of an apartment layout (Veloso, Celani, & Scheeren, 2018). A: rule set organized in a graph. B: two examples of floor plans that can be generated by the rules. C: all the floor plans that can be generated.

Among these, shape grammars are historically the main formalism for rule-based architectural design (March, 2011). Shapes are based on sets of maximal lines (Krishnamurti, 1980; Stiny, 1980) with rewriting rules that enable the substitution of shapes and, potentially, the emergence of unanticipated shapes (Knight & Stiny, 2001, pp. 364–372). Starting from an initial shape and following the rules defined by a certain grammar, it is possible to explore designs with a certain characteristic (a design language). The grammar produces shapes, which can resemble floor plans, sections, or even 3D models.

For example, in grammar for apartment layout customization (see Figure 3.8), the generation might start with a predefined footprint followed by operations to divide it into sectors. Then, each sector can be divided into rooms. The navigation in the space of possible layouts can be executed by a human or algorithm that selects the precedent floor-plan shapes and rules.

Parameter- and rule-based models capture complementary aspects of design logic. In parametric modeling, the parameters typically define and bound the design space, while in rule-based models, it is a network that, with proper rules and preconditions, can be indefinitely expanded. Despite these differences, they can be combined in hybrid models. A parametric function can represent a finite trajectory of rule derivations explicitly, with the preconditions and rule selection controlled by the input. On the other hand, rule-based models can be extended with a parametric layer, such as in parametric shape grammars (see Figure 3.7: A: item 5, and C) or in parametric L–Systems.

Agent-based model

The design decisions and transformations can potentially be decentralized and encapsulated by a collection of discrete entities. In many domains, the motivation to decentralize the computation in these entities is to model the behavior of real-world phenomena, such as fluid flows, pattern formation, reaction–diffusion of chemicals, physics, or even urban dynamics. In simple cases, these entities are objects that react to external signals, such as in particle simulations. When these discrete entities of the simulation have a degree of autonomy and can engage in interactions, they are called agents.

The domain of fields studying agent-based computing is vast, and this can lead to confusion with regard to semantics (Niazi & Hussain, 2011, p. 2). For example, in AI, multiagent systems are goal oriented, and the term "agent" is used to describe autonomous computer programs that are situated in an environment and are capable of autonomous action to solve a certain task rationally (Russel & Norvig, 2010). In agent-based modeling (ABM), the agent is a unit of representation in the computational modeling of social dynamics related to natural or artificial phenomena (Wilensky & Rand, 2015). These models are used to predict certain configurations or behaviors based on the interaction of the agents in a shared environment.

Agent-based modeling relies on the interaction between the different components, such as agent–self, environment–self, agent–agent, environment–environment, and agent–environment interaction (Wilensky & Rand, 2015, pp. 257–262). All these interactions typically depend on the configuration of agents and environment in a certain spatial representation, such as cellular grids, topological networks, or coordinate systems. Particularly, the local interactions of the agents are restricted by a notion of neighborhood, which is paramount to agent-based computing.

An agent observes its internal state, other agents, and the information from the environment. When the agent is represented in a grid, its neighborhood can be defined in various ways, for example, Moore neighborhood, von Neumann neighborhood (Figure 3.9: A and B), or by an arbitrary collection of cells. Agents in Euclidean space can receive the information constrained by a certain radius (Figure 3.10: A) by signals from radial pulses or any other form of perception. The internal program of an agent or its policy defines what action to take conditioned on the information received by the agent over time. This policy can be a simple reactive strategy (e.g., follow the gradient of pheromone or move toward the closest neighbor), a set of if-then rules that looks for preconditions in the input to select the action, a set of cumulative behaviors (Figure 3.10: B), or a more sophisticated function that chooses an action, based on an estimate of the future performance (see example in Figure 3.20).

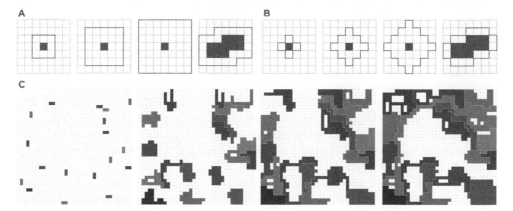

Figure 3.9 A: Moore neighborhood with different radii for a single-cell agent and a multicellular agent. B: von Neumann neighborhood with different radii for a single-cell agent and a multicellular agent. C: simulation with multiple agents that use two cells for expansion (model by Pragya Gupta, Design and Computation 2, Fall 2018).

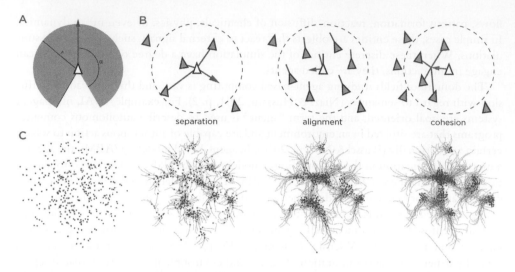

Figure 3.10 Boids: a model that simulates the flocking behavior of a bird. A: neighborhood based on radius and visibility angle. B: three basic behaviors (separation, alignment, and cohesion) which add forces to the agent conditioned on the state of the neighbors. A and B are based on diagrams by (Reynolds, 1999). C: Boids interacting in a simulation.

In terms of actions, in a grid, an agent might be able to switch the states of its current cell, such as in cellular automata. In other cases, it might be able to move to another cell, such as in ant algorithms, or even expand or retract to change its shape if its representation allows multiple cells (Figure 3.9: C). In the Euclidean space, an agent can move using acceleration (Figure 3.10: C) or change aspects of its shape, such as the position of vertices of polygons. The behavior of agents in a shared environment results in interaction and changes in the design representation.

In Table 3.2 we show models that are applicable to agent-based form exploration, and architectural and urban design.

For deterministic agents and environment, the design space is a single trajectory of states, parameterized by the initial configuration of the agents, as in standard cellular automata. On the other hand, if the agents can take multiple actions for the same circumstance, the space of design alternatives is a large network based on the joint states (nodes) and actions (edges) of the agents in the environment. Each of the possible paths of this network displays a certain evolution of patterns over time.

The design navigation relies on a sequence of interactions that change the representation. Overall, the designer can explore the different patterns by configuring the program of the agents, the characteristics of the environment, or the initial state (Figure 3.11: A). In the simulation, the model will update the states of the agents and the environment over multiple time steps (Figure 3.11: B).

Agent-based models can emulate properties of natural phenomena, such as self-organization, robustness, scalability, and flexibility. Particularly, it supports the coherent arise of patterns at the macrolevel from the interactions between the parts at the microlevel—which is generally referred to as emergence (Simon, 1996, pp. 169–172; Holland, 1998, pp. 115–124; De Wolf & Holvoet, 2005). The compelling aspect of emergence for design is that the emerging patterns are not represented explicitly in the initial configuration of the agents

Table 3.2 Examples of agent-based models

	Discrete models		Swarm models		Growth models	
Example	Cellular Automata (Wolfram, 2002)	Reaction-diffusion (Turing, 1952; Pearson, 1993)	Ant foraging (Bonebau, Dorigo, & Theraulaz, 1999)	Boids (Reynolds, 1987, 1999)	Diffusion-limited aggregation (Witten Jr & Sander, 1981)	Differential Growth
Standard Environment	Grid	Grid	Grid or graph with pheromone markers, food, and nest	Euclidean	Euclidean	Euclidean
Agent	Cell with binary states	Cell with a concentration of two chemicals	Ant that occupies a cell	An agent with a position, velocity, and acceleration	Particles that move; aggregated particles	A network of connected discs
Standard neighborhood	Moore	Moore	Adjacent cells/ nodes	Agents within distance and visual field	–	Connected discs
Action	Update state based on neighborhood	Update state based on the reaction of chemicals	Move to the adjacent cell based on pheromone; deposit pheromone	Behaviors update trajectory	Random movement; attach particles close to aggregation	Disc repulsion; extended link creates a new agent
Result	Dynamic patterns	Dynamic patterns with chemicals	Pheromone network between food and nest	Flocking patterns	Brownian trees	Self-folding curve or mesh

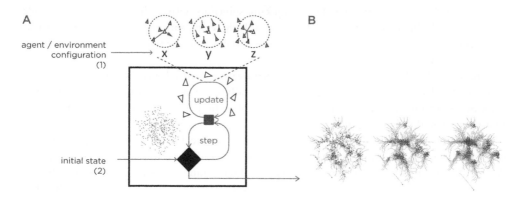

A

agent / environment configuration (1)

X Y Z

update

step

initial state (2)

B

Figure 3.11   A: diagram of the agent-based model. The bottom loop represents the time steps and the top loop represents the updates of the agents for an one-time step. B: three distinct steps of the simulation.

and environment. The large design space of agent-based models can contain unexpected collective behaviors or formations that are revealed during the execution of the generative model, because the actions of the agents are conditioned by their surroundings. Emergence comes at the cost of lack of control, which is a trade-off that should be considered during the development of the model.

Synthesis

Once the expression of the model has been formalized, it is possible to explore design alternatives with some form of user control. The design representation can be modified, the parameter values of parametric models can be tweaked, and rule-based models can be computed by selecting shapes and rules. However, generative models typically incorporate a strategy to navigate in the design space and automatically synthesize design alternatives.

Optimization

Synthesis by optimization involves searching for the best solutions in a certain design space, with regard to some quantifiable criteria of performance. It is often associated with a parametric model, which expresses the design outcome as a function of specific input parameters. It adds two components to the generative model: a fitness function and an optimization algorithm.

The fitness function typically evaluates the performance of a design mathematically. It receives the design output from our generator and returns its performance values, subject to constraints. The fitness function can be as simple as a function that measures the surface area of a solution or as complex as a structural or energy simulation. Constraints can be values, combinations of, or relations between parameters that either are unacceptable or result in an unacceptable solution. These constrained solutions can be either avoided or eliminated from the model in the generation process or be represented in the fitness function as penalization.

By outputting a fitness value, this function creates a new space for the generative model: the fitness space. In this context, exploring design alternatives involves understanding the relation between the space of possible choices (usually, the parameter space of the model) and the space of the performance. If the fitness function is based on a single objective or performance value, each design alternative tested can be ranked on a one-dimensional space, which makes selection easy—i.e., by just picking solutions with higher value—for example, in Figure 3.12, the ones closer to the darker area. If there are multiple performance criteria to be represented in a fitness function, it is necessary to define some strategy to address tradeoffs and rank solutions.[6]

The second additional component is an optimization method that can automatically navigate in the decision space of our generator (usually the parameters) to incrementally find solutions with better fitness values—i.e., by finding the parameters, subject to constraints, that maximize this fitness function.

Generative models originally inherited optimization techniques used in operations research for decision-making in military operations and industrial organization (Churchman, Ackoff, & Arnoff, 1957, p. 3). These mathematical techniques for decision-making relied on specific analytical forms of the problem description[7] (Mitchell, 1977, pp. 468–472; Radford & Gero, 1988). Nevertheless, the elements of generative models, such as the parameters, generator, the constraints, or even the fitness function, extrapolate the forms required by mathematical optimization. They require techniques with less mathematical restrictions and

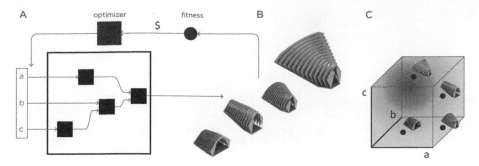

Figure 3.12   A: parametric model with a fitness function and an optimizer controlling its parameters. B: variations of the design. C: fitness landscape: diagram representing the fitness value of every solution in the parameter space (darker means higher value). B–C: a model developed by Adie Alnobani.

that enable designers to explore partial solutions or to learn about the correlation between decisions and performance.

Over the past decades, with the development of novel black-box methods—namely, algorithms that do not require knowledge of the fitness function—optimization became predominant in generative modeling. There are three categories of black-box algorithms: metaheuristics, direct search, and model-based (Wortmann, 2018, pp. 100–114). Recently, genetic algorithms, simulated annealing, particle swarm optimization,[8] and many other black-box techniques have been incorporated into parametric modeling as plug-ins (Rutten, 2013; Wortmann, 2017). These techniques contain different strategies to navigate in the parameter space of the model based on the fitness signal of the objective function. Particularly, metaheuristics use higher-level strategies.

Optimization of parameters

Optimization is a very general method and allows design synthesis for different formulations of generative models. Typically, optimization is applied to the parametric model to choose the parameters that increment the fitness values of the resulting design alternatives. However, it allows for many other applications.

Optimization of parameters can also be applied to rule-based and agent-based models. In the former, the parameters can represent a way to select the initial state (see Figure 3.13), precedents, rules, and the number of time steps. The fitness function can evaluate the characteristics of the designs achieved by these parameters. In the latter, the parameters of the agents or the environment can be considered the parameters of the model. The fitness function will evaluate the performance of the agent or the overall model after one or more simulations.

Optimization of programs

In the previous optimization examples, the topological structure of the parametric model or the logic of the algorithm is predefined, so the optimization can focus on the parameter space. However, it is possible to use a metaoptimization to induce generative programs. The challenge is that the algorithms should be able to operate on data structures more complex than a list of parameters, such as trees or directed graphs with variables and operations. Conventionally, the algorithm used for this task is genetic programming (Koza, 1992), an

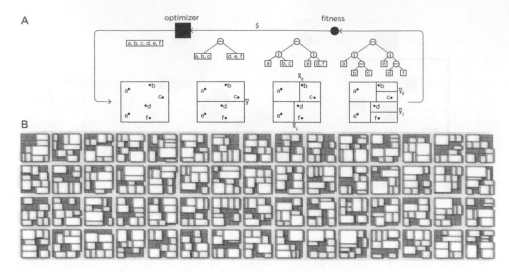

Figure 3.13 A: optimization of floor plans with genetic algorithms and KD-Tree, inspired by Knecht & König (2010). Parameters are the coordinates for the points used as input for a KD-Tree partition. B: examples of resulting designs.

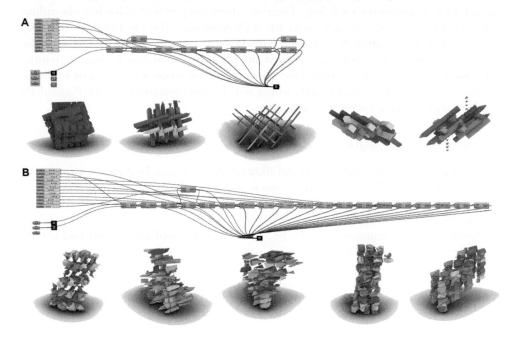

Figure 3.14 Use of genetic programming (plug-in Embryo) to generate parametric definitions for sculptures (Michael Stesney, Generative Models for Design, CMU, Fall 2019). A–B: two parametric graphs with custom operations and variations of the resulting sculpture below.

extension of genetic algorithms that deals with hierarchical computer programs of dynamically varying sizes and shapes. It uses variations of the same genetic operators as the genetic algorithm, namely, selection, crossover, and mutation, to evolve a program (Figure 3.14). This approach can also be employed for generating programs such as parametric functions

(Harding, 2016) or internal programs of agents. In the former case, the algorithm generates parametric functions and uses a fitness function to evaluate the performance of their output. In the latter case, the optimization creates the program of an agent and evaluates its performance in a simulation. Overall, inferring the program to achieve a certain goal is a task that is close to the two categories of learning in taxonomy.

Composition

In the decision-theoretic paradigm of symbolic AI, design synthesis can be modeled as a sequential decision process based on the search of "satisficing" solutions rather than optimizing performance (Simon, 1975; 1996, pp. 114–122). In this case, the generative process starts with an initial representation of the design. The designer uses some form of heuristics to select incremental transformations, which can be interpreted as a sequential composition.[9] While the interaction of the designer with any type of model can be interpreted as a sequential decision process, this type of synthesis is built-in in rule-based models, where the design space is defined by an implicit network with design alternatives.

Sampling

To explore the design space of a rule-based model without being committed to specific goals, it is possible to sample solutions using a stochastic or deterministic strategy to select preconditions and rules. This can result in solutions with certain qualities. For example, we created an atomic shape grammar called Q-growth as an educational experiment to explore both the precondition and rule selection that lead to certain types of formal configurations (Figure 3.15). It contains three rules that can be applied to any convex quadrilateral—x: expansion, y: parametric division, and z: elimination. All the quadrilaterals in the representation are preconditions. They can be ordered for the next derivations based on a fixed

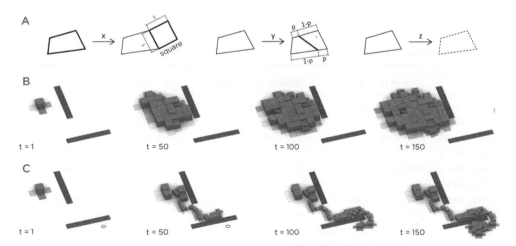

Figure 3.15 A: rules of qGrowth grammar. B-C: generating forms with stochastic selection of rules (rule x: 60%, rule y: 30%, rule z: 10%) and parameter p (0.2: 50%, 0.8: 50%). B: precondition selection with a queue (quadrilaterals added first to the frontier are selected first). C: precondition selection with a priority queue (quadrilaterals closer to the circle are selected first).

logic, such as a queue (first in, first out), a stack (last in, first out), or a priority queue (order according to a property). The rules and parameters for the derivation are sampled from a probability distribution defined by the designer. A collision test is used to prevent new quadrilaterals to collide with preexisting elements in the environment (other quadrilaterals and obstacles).

Search

For a more systematic composition, the following are necessary: (1) a goal function to evaluate the qualities of the design alternatives in the design space and (2) a systematic search strategy to build solutions. In contrast to the fitness function used for optimization, which returns a numerical value indicating performance, the goal function typically indicates if a design is satisficing or not, based on experience, preferences, or any other criteria. A search algorithm starts at the root of a search tree and explores multiple paths incrementally until it eventually synthesizes "satisficing" designs based on designer aspirations and criteria (Simon, 1975, pp. 297–301; 1996, pp. 119–121). The search can rely on personal criteria or strategies from AI (Russel & Norvig, 2010, pp. 64–119), such as the ones described in Table 3.3.

One of the classical examples for applications of search in design is in layout automation. For example, Autoilet (Figure 3.16) combines a parametric and rule-based model with a search to automate the design of single-user toilet rooms according to the standards of the Americans with Disabilities Act (ADA). The inputs for the algorithm are the dimensions of the room, whether the room is L-shaped or not, the dimensions of the corner, and the position of the door. For each element of the toilet, there is a geometric entity as well as clearance. The goal function requires that the geometry and clearance of each element should be within the boundary of the room and there should be no conflicts between objects and clearances. A depth first search (DFS) is used to sequentially place all the equipment elements and return satisficing solutions.

Table 3.3 Examples of search algorithms

	Type of knowledge	Order of exploration	Data structure
Breadth-first search (BFS)	Order of branches	Level-by-level	Frontier: Queue (first in, first out)
Uniform-cost search (UCS)	Path cost	Best path cost first	Frontier: Priority queue (highest priority first out)
Depth-first search (DFS)	Order of branches	The deepest nodes first	Frontier: Stack (last in, first out)
Greedy best-first search	Estimate of value of next nodes	Best estimate to reach goal first	Frontier: Priority queue (highest priority first out)
A*	Path cost and estimate of value of next nodes	Best path cost and estimate to reach goal first	Frontier: Priority queue (highest priority first out)
Monte Carlo Tree Search (MCTS)	Estimate of node values based on sampling and backpropagation	Policy that balances exploration and exploitation of current estimates. Random search for unexplored nodes	Estimates are stored at the nodes of the tree

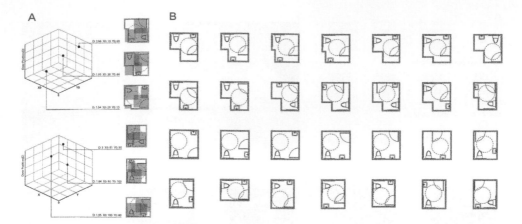

Figure 3.16 Autoilet (Jichen Wang and Joon Young Choi, Generative Models for Design, Fall 2019). A: parameter space of the input (boundary, corner, and door placement) for rectangular and L-shaped footprints. B: examples of solutions using depth first search (DFS) for placement of toilet, sink, and Americans with Disabilities Act (ADA) circle.

Conventional search techniques can be of limited use for large design spaces. However, it is possible to eliminate large portions of the search tree at once by identifying combinations that violate certain constraints, such as collisions, area, etc. Besides, modern techniques, such as Monte Carlo Tree Search, can be combined with neural networks to address extremely large state spaces, such as in the game of Go (Silver, Hubert, et al., 2017; Silver, Schrittwieser, et al., 2017). This can lead to the development of search-based models to address more complex design problems.

Traversal

In some cases, the designer enumerates all the possible solutions under a certain criterion— such as all possible rectangular and nondimensional floor plans up to a certain number of rooms (Steadman, 1973, 1983; Krishnamurti & Roe, 1978). While this type of enumeration can be done by sampling multiple solutions and organizing the unique results in a set, it is more efficient to use a search algorithm to explore the solutions systematically. However, instead of stopping the search when a certain goal function is satisfied, the algorithm should keep exploring and accumulating all the satisficing solutions until the search tree is exhausted or a certain stopping condition is triggered.

Simulation

In the case of agent-based models, the mechanism for decision-making is already embedded in the program of the agents. The algorithm to form solutions relies on executing the interaction of the agents in the environment over time—that is, a simulation. To explore different alternatives in a simulation, the designer must push the simulation toward certain directions by customizing the environment and the agents. This customization can involve tasks such as, parameter tuning (see Figure 3.17), the design of new behaviors, or simply adding randomness. See the Section "Agent-based model" for more details.

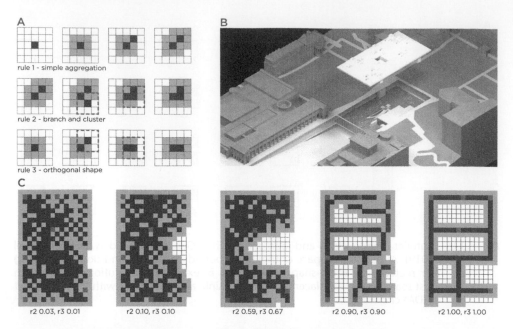

Figure 3.17 Agents generating an underground gallery on campus (Jinmo Rhee, Generative Models for Design, CMU, Fall 2019). A: stochastic program with three rules. B: design of campus gallery based on agents with r2 = 0.59 and r3 = 0.67 at time step 200. C: the resulting spatial configuration for the same initial environment with different parameter: r2 and r3 increase the probability of choosing rule 2 and rule 3 respectively.

Learning

The previous categories rely on the designer explicitly encoding the generative knowledge with different formulations (parameter-based, rule-based, or agent-based) and strategies for synthesis (optimization, composition, or simulation). However, the generative rationale to formulate a model might not be available—e.g., when designers rely on their cumulative experience to interact with the design media and respond to immediate problems based on unconscious mental processes, with no need for an explicit rationale. One alternative to incorporate implicit design knowledge is to use design data or experience to infer the generative logic of a model. This possibility is explored in machine learning (ML), a multidisciplinary field concerned with the question of "how to construct computer programs that automatically improve with experience" (Mitchell, 1997, p. xv). In the past decade, ML gained momentum with the development of techniques based mainly on deep neural networks—which originated the field known as deep learning (Goodfellow, Yoshua, & Aaron, 2016).

A neural network is a parametric model vaguely inspired by the human brain and by its capacity to change its own pattern according to different experiences from the world. In contrast to parametric models from architecture, which largely rely on a graph with geometric operations, neural networks are usually formulated as a network of simple differentiable mathematical operations and functions. A typical neural network is organized as a feed-forward sequence of fully connected layers. Each of these layers represents a matrix-vector multiplication followed by a nonlinear activation function. More specifically, the layers are composed of a series of small units called neurons, connected to the units of the next layer. Each unit linearly combines the previous layer's output values and the local parameters (weights and bias). Then, it passes the result through a nonlinear activation function, which expresses how "activated" the node is. Neural networks can use other patterns of connection and types of operations to address geometric or spatial information. For example, convolutional neural networks (CNNs) use special operators called convolutions for tasks involving images or any grid-based data. Other network architectures and operations can address sequential data, graphs, point clouds, and meshes.

Neural networks can adapt and approximate functions. For example, in supervised learning tasks, such as regression or classification, a labeled dataset with pairs of input and output elements works as an instructor to tell the model what function to approximate (Goodfellow, Yoshua, & Aaron, 2016, p. 105). In the context of design, the input (independent variables) can represent a context or the requirements for a project and the output is some aspect of the design to be predicted or classified. In this supervised setting, the training feeds the neural network with input—output pairs from the known data. It uses an error function that measures the difference between the known output (target) and the output predicted by the neural network, given the input. Then, an optimization algorithm changes the internal parameters of the neural network to minimize this error and, consequently, approximate the target function. Part of the known data is removed from the training and used to test if the function can generalize to new and unseen input data.

An adaptive model such as a neural network enables designers to build components of a generative model without explicitly describing its logic, which is an important step to bridge computation and intuitive design. With the recent advancements of ML, these components can be as varied as a fitness function, a parametric model, the program of agents, or a search mechanism. This brings learning algorithms to the formulation stage (Figure 3.18: A). The logic of the component can be inferred from different sources, such as a dataset curated by the designer or simulations. Then, in the execution stage, the component will support the generation of design alternatives and can even be refined with further training (Figure 3.18: B).

Generative learning

There are many techniques in using a neural network as part of the generator. This is an open area of research in design, so we will briefly mention the most notable examples, such as deep dream, neural style transfer, autoencoder, and GANs.

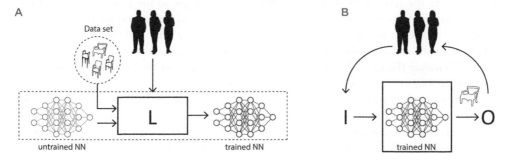

Figure 3.18 A: the formulation of generative model using a data set (D), a neural network (NN), and a learning algorithm (L). B: execution of a generative model: designers control an input (I); the trained neural network works as part or as the whole generator (G) and synthesizes a design alternative as an output (O).

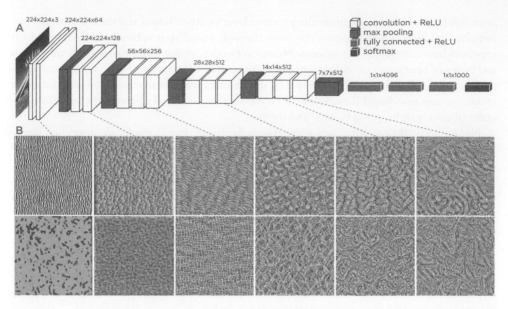

Figure 3.19 A: architecture of VGG-16; B: every column contains synthetic images for the visualization of two features of different layers of the network (indicated by the dotted line). Based on a repository (Ozbulak, 2017).

Let us start with a simple model: VGG16 (Simonyan & Zisserman, 2015) (Figure 3.19: A), a CNN trained for classifying an input image in 1,000 classes of objects, such as teapots, Siberian huskies, and churches. After successful training, the network classifies the input image by using a series of layers, which result in increasingly complex internal representations. These representations are called feature maps, and they are the knowledge used by the model to classify the input. In the first layers, these feature maps might capture abstract patterns such as the occurrence of horizontal lines. Closer to the end, they can capture more sophisticated shapes of the objects to be classified.

Deep dream (Mordvintsev, Olah, & Tyka, 2015) was originally invented to investigate what the neural network "sees" when it receives a given input image. This is a hybrid model, as it uses optimization for synthesis. It incrementally changes the pixels of an input image to maximize the activations of one or multiple feature maps, so the patterns of the selected feature maps start to emerge like a hallucination. While this process typically starts with an image with random noise, a real photo and drawing can be used and transformed. For example, we used this algorithm to change an image of the Cathedral of Brasilia, designed by Oscar Niemeyer (Figure 3.20: A). We selected a feature map in the last convolutional layers to generate a more complex pattern of hallucination.

In the case of neural style transfer (Gatys, Ecker, & Bethge, 2016), optimization is associated with the trained neural network to create an image that has abstract qualities of a style image and the concrete qualities of a content image. In this case, different feature maps are used as a mechanism to measure the similarity between the synthesized image with the original content image and the style of the original style image. Optimization is used to change the pixels and minimize these differences, which results in a stylized image (Figure 3.20: B, C, and D).

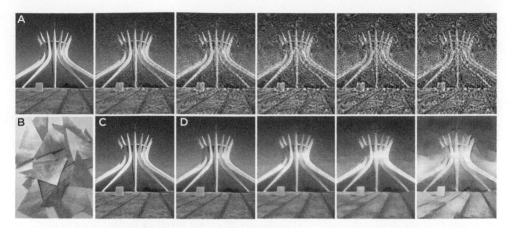

Figure 3.20 A: applying deep dream to an image of the Cathedral of Brasilia (photo by the first author), based on feature 286 of the last convolutional layer (activated by the top right image on Figure 19: B). Based on a repository (Ozbulak, 2017). B–D: custom style transfer based on the code from Jacq n.d.. B: Style image produced by Kate McLean. C: content image. D: content image incorporating style.

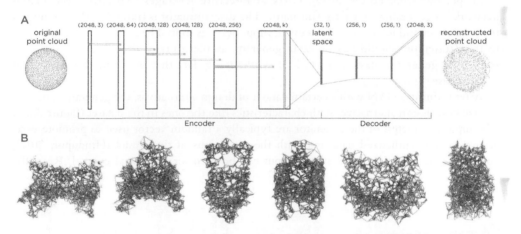

Figure 3.21 Deepcloud. A: architecture of autoencoder trained on a dataset of point clouds of chairs. B: monstrous chair series generated by exploring the parameters of the latent space as input.

While these examples are interesting, they are still only hybrid optimization models that rely on the knowledge embedded in a model trained for classification. On the other hand, generative models from machine learning[10] can explicitly or implicitly learn the distribution of a certain dataset, which enables sampling novel things from it (Bishop, 2006, p. 43; Foster, 2019). Generative modeling is one of the current frontiers in ML and has been responsible for many of the advances in art, image, and video synthesis. There are several generative models in ML, including but not limited to autoencoder and generative adversarial networks (GANs).

An autoencoder (AE) is a model composed of two parts: an encoder and a decoder (Foster, 2019) (see Figure 3.21). The encoder learns how to compress the samples of a data distribution into points in a lower-dimensional representation (latent space) or into a normal distribution around this point[11] in the case of a variational autoencoder (Goodfellow, Yoshua, & Aaron, 2016, pp. 696–699; Foster, 2019). The decoder learns how to reconstruct the original input based on the observed values in this compressed representation. They are trained simultaneously to compress and reconstruct each of the samples in a dataset with a consistent representation, such as images or point clouds. After training, the decoder can be decoupled and used to synthesize new output data, using the compressed vector as the input parameters.

In the context of generative models, autoencoders can be trained to reconstruct a set of design examples with certain characteristics. For example, in DeepCloud (Bidgoli & Veloso, 2018) (Figure 3.21), an AE reconstructs point clouds from datasets of chairs, cars, hats, and tables. After training, DeepCloud captures structural aspects of the dataset in the space of the compressed vector. Therefore, the user can manipulate the parameters of the decoder to reconstruct the design examples in the dataset or create novel or hybrid designs based on different parameter values.

In contrast to autoencoders, which learn a lower-dimensional representation, GANs are generative models created with the primary purpose of synthesizing new data that look like sampled from a dataset (Goodfellow et al., 2014; Goodfellow, Yoshua, & Aaron, 2016, pp. 699–703; Foster, 2019). GAN architecture leverages two adversarial neural networks, a generator, and a discriminator. The discriminator is trained with the samples from a dataset and learns to test if a given input belongs to it. The generator has no access to the dataset and should learn how to generate samples to trick the discriminator. As a result, the generator masters the task of synthesizing data that fit in the distribution of the database.

After training a GAN with a certain dataset of design alternatives, the generator can synthesize new design alternatives with characteristics like the ones in the dataset (Figure 3.22). The input parameters of the generator are typically a random vector used to promote variations on the synthesized data, but with the extensions of the model (Hindupur, 2017), conditional information or even user input can be used for additional control. Recently,

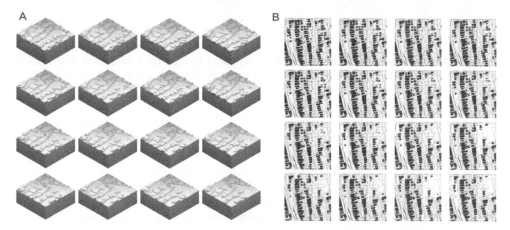

Figure 3.22 Urban structure synthesizer (Jinmo Rhee, Generative Models for Design, CMU, Fall 2019): 3D models (A) and 2D diagrams (B) with incremental variations of an urban fabric. The diagrams were generated with a model (WGAN-GP) trained on a dataset of images from Pittsburgh, USA.

GANs have been widely applied to architectural design to analyze and generate building representations, such as floor-plan layouts (Huang & Zheng, 2018; Zheng, 2018; Chaillou, 2019; Newton, 2019; Nauata et al., 2020).

Behavioral learning

Behavioral learning emphasizes decision-making of agents that interact with an environment over time to achieve a certain goal. This is particularly compelling for research on agent-based generative models, which currently relies on the predefined behavior of existing models, such as swarm algorithms (flocking and pheromone navigation), cellular automata, reaction-diffusion, and custom physics simulation.

One of the main sources for this category is the field of reinforcement learning (RL), which addresses agents that learn by interacting with the environment and discovering behaviors that can maximize their performance with the respect to certain goals defined by the designer. In RL, problems are expressed in the formal framework of the Markov decision process. There is a set of states (S), which represents different configurations for the agent and the environment in any context, such as games, driving, or even configuring layouts. The agent observes the current state (s) and it takes one of the available actions (a). The environment sends information about the new state (s') and evaluative feedback in the form of a reward (r), which reinforces certain behaviors positively or negatively.[12]

The design of the function that returns the scalar reward signal for the agent transitions is critical for RL. This reward function can be explicitly defined by the designer or potentially learned from desired behavior. An ill-formulated reward function can lead to unexpected and undesirable behavior. Also, a function that returns only sparse reward signals can make learning extremely hard.

Given a proper reward function, the goal of the agent is to learn a policy, a function that, given any state, selects an action. Neural networks can be used to learn a policy that maximizes the long-term cumulative rewards and/or a function that estimates the future cumulative rewards, given any state and action. While datasets with existing trajectories can be used for training, it typically relies on experiences generated in simulations of the agent interacting with the environment. This approach characterizes the field of deep reinforcement learning (DLR) (Sutton & Barto, 2018), which gained notoriety with the recent success in learning how to master playing videogames (Mnih et al., 2013; Vinyals et al., 2019) and board games such as go, chess, and shogi (Silver, Hubert, et al., 2017; Silver, Schrittwieser, et al., 2017). Multi-agent deep reinforcement learning (MADRL) (Nguyen, Nguyen, & Nahavandi, 2018) extends DRL with algorithms to address multiple agents.

To explore the potential of RL for training custom agent-based models for architectural design, we have developed a proof of concept in which agents are trained to generate a floor-plan diagram (see Figure 3.23). Each agent is a set of grid cells that share edges. It uses basic expansion and retraction actions to compose more complex behaviors such as moving, re-shaping, or even jumping. Its goal is to reach a specific area, be adjacent to other agents, and satisfy certain shape constraints. The agents interact in a grid environment with obstacles to satisfy these goals. After the agents are trained and they know what actions to take to pursue their goals, a designer can interact with them in a simulation. The designer can not only customize the objective parameters (e.g., increase the area of an agent) but also reconfigure the cells of the agents and the environment. The trained agents will react and incrementally form a spatial configuration compatible with the current goals.

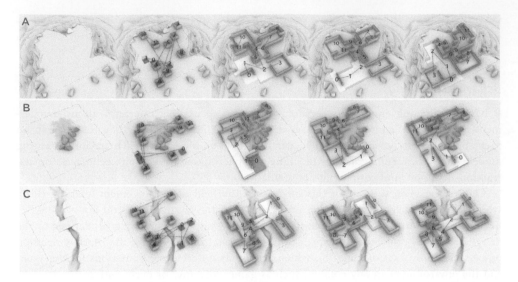

Figure 3.23 Twelve spatial agents generating a two-bedroom house (0: patio, 1: living room, 2: dining room, 3: kitchen, 4: corridor, 5: half-bath, 6: corridor, 7: bedroom, 8: bath, 9: closet, 10: bedroom, 11: bath) in different environments. A: a terrain on the top of a hill with irregular boundaries. B: terrain with central obstacles. C: a terrain with a stream and a bridge.

Final considerations

The proposed taxonomy is not only a gateway to generative models in design education but also a register of an ongoing redefinition of creative practices with different computational paradigms. The maturity of generative methods in design culture provides fertile territory for many of the recurrent visions of artificial intelligence and design, such as the symbiosis of human designers and architectural machines (Licklider, 1960; Negroponte, 1970). With some form of creative agency, generative models can support a productive human–machine partnership to enable design workflows that are not possible by either of the "designers" alone. However, to become part of a practice and address real-world problems, a symbiotic design would depend not only on advancements in artificial intelligence but also on the development of a fluid interplay between humans and machines.

The taxonomy focuses on the generative logic of computational models, which has a direct influence on the knowledge of the generator and the granularity of the possible design interaction. However, with proper interactive strategies and mechanisms, generative models can support more natural forms of interaction with design alternatives. External factors, such as user experience and human–computer interaction, are essential to explore the possible modes of interactions, such as hand-mediated, multimodal, experimental, and virtual reality- and augmented reality-based systems (Erdolu, 2019).

Besides, fluid construction of generative models is an important step toward the symbiotic exploration of design worlds by humans and machines. Creative design exploration cannot be restricted to a linear process or a single generative model. Designers address complex design situations by changing, on the fly, both the formulation of the design solution and the problem. Open-ended design exploration requires a flexible reformulation of models to explore varied design spaces. While some of the models presented are more flexible for restructuration, the formulation and reformulation of generative models typically require explicit knowledge about the generative logic and expertise on different programming languages, modeling software, and plug-ins. Soon, it might be possible to infer and tune varied models from databases or directly from the designers' preferences or behaviors, dissolving the boundary between formulation and execution.

Many of the challenges for symbiotic architectural design are still uncharted. Nevertheless, the current landscape of generative design already provides elements to review essential components of practice and education, such as the notions of authorship, collaboration, originality, and the sources of architectural configuration.

Acknowledgments

We would like to express our gratitude to Adie Alnobani, Atefeh Mahdevi Goloujeh, Cecilia Ferrando, Jichen Wang, Pragya Gupta, Michael Stesney, Kate McLean, and Jinmo Rhee for authorizing the use of their projects in the examples and diagrams in this chapter. Also, we would like to thank Jinmo Rhee, Javier Argota Sánchez-Vaquerizo, and Kate McLean for their comprehensive review of the draft, and Professor Thomas Wortmann for his insightful comments and suggestions on the Section "Optimization". Finally, this work would not have been possible without the PhD scholarship granted to the first author by the Brazilian National Council for Scientific and Technological Development (CNPq).

Notes

1 There are many terms used in the literature, such as generative system, generative model(ing), and generative design. In fields such as systems engineering and cybernetics (Ashby, 1956), system is used to comprehend the studied phenomenon as a cohesive organization composed of interacting parts that together produce results not obtainable by the parts in isolation. The term model refers to the representation of a system. We opted for the term generative model for three reasons: (1) it describes representations of concrete generative systems; (2) it can be considered an instance of models used for design conception; (3) it also unifies the nomenclature of the diverse areas addressed in the chapter, such as mathematical models, geometric modeling, parametric modeling, agent-based models, rule-based models, and adaptive models in machine learning. We use the term generative design when we refer to an architectural practice or method that uses generative models.

2 While our representation is unique and represents our approach to the topic, it certainly has precedents in the literature, such as Fischer and Herr (2001), Cagan et al. (2005, p. 172), Gänshirt (2007, pp. 78–79), Bohnacker et al., (2012, p. 461), Veloso and Krishnamurti (2019).

3 In the case of form-finding models, the formulation requires constraining existing natural phenomena to make their behavior work as an algorithm for form exploration. In the case of a written procedure to generate a building element, the execution stage depends on the designer.

4 While the taxonomy shown here is not exhaustive, it is broad enough to subsume earlier classifications that were based, perhaps, on finer considerations, for example, AI techniques such as knowledge representation, case-based reasoning, and expert systems. Some of the techniques might be a special case of the existing blocks or might fit in between the blocks.

5 These building blocks are related to a specific aspect of generative modeling, so it is important to distinguish them from the algorithms that they comprehend. For example, the Category "Optimization" is mostly based on optimization algorithms for design synthesis. However, optimization algorithms are very general and can be applied for other ends, such as training neural networks (see Section "Learning").

6 For example, it is possible to rank sets of solutions based on their hypervolume in the objective space, to combine the different objectives in a singular fitness dimension, or to look for the non-dominated elements in the set of solutions. Dominance is characterized between two solutions.

A solution "a" dominates a solution "b" if it is no worse than "b" in all objectives and it is better than "b" in at least one objective. A solution is nondominated if no other solution in the set dominates it.

7 For example, calculus requires access to a continuous and differentiable function, and classic optimization techniques usually restrict the problem formulation to a specific analytical form, such as a convex space (Radford & Gero, 1988, pp. 48, 90; Boyd & Vandenberghe, 2004, pp. 1–2).

8 These examples are metaheuristics that use higher-level strategies inspired by nature to explore good solutions to an optimization problem (Brownlee, 2012). Genetic algorithm is inspired by evolutionary biology and uses natural selection operators (crossover and mutation). Simulated annealing is inspired by the process of annealing in metallurgy and uses a decreasing temperature to reduce the exploration of random solutions over time. Particle swarm optimization is inspired by the swarm behavior, such as flocking, and uses multiple particles to move, based on shared information of the positions of the best-known solutions.

9 The term composition is related both to function composition and architectural composition. In mathematics, this is an operation that sequentially applies two or more functions (e.g., $g(f(x))$). In architecture, it is related to the process of creating an architectural configuration.

10 While there is an overlapping, it is important to distinguish the idea of generative models for design (the topic of this chapter) from generative models in machine learning.

11 Usually it is assumed that there is no correlation between the dimensions, so the encoder can output the vectors with the mean and the variance (or the logarithm of the variance).

12 This workflow relies on the Markov property, so the probability of moving to a state s and receiving a reward r is only dependent on the information stored in s and the action a selected.

References

Anderson, S. (1966). *Problem-Solving and Problem-Worrying.* Retrieved from http://web.mit.edu/soa/www/downloads/1963-69/TH_AALond-Lect_66.pdf

Ashby, W. R. (1956). *An Introduction to Cybernetics.* London: Chapman & Hall.

Bidgoli, A., & Veloso, P. (2018). DeepCloud: The application of a data-driven, generative model in design. In P. Anzalone, M. Del Signore, & A. J. Wit (Eds.), *Recalibration: On Imprecision and Infidelity. Proceedings of the 38th ACADIA Conference* (pp. 176–185). Mexico City: Universidad Iberoamericana. Retrieved from http://papers.cumincad.org/cgi-bin/works/paper/acadia18_176

Bijl, A. (1990). *Computer Discipline and Design Practice: Shaping Our Future.* Edinburgh: Edinburgh University Press.

Bishop, C. M. (2006). *Pattern Recognition and Machine Learning.* New York: Springer-Verlag.

Bohnacker, H., Gross, B., Laub, J., & Lazzeroni, C. (2012). *Generative Design: Visualize, Program, and Create with Processing.* New York: Princeton Architectural Press.

Bonebau, E., Dorigo, M., & Theraulaz, G. (1999). *Swarm Intelligence: From Natural to Artificial Systems.* New York: Oxford University Press.

Boyd, S., & Vandenberghe, L. (2004). *Convex Optimization.* Cambridge: Cambridge University Press.

Bratko, I. (2011). *Prolog Programming for Artificial Intelligence* (4th ed.). Harlow: Pearson Education.

Brownlee, J. (2012). *Clever Algorithms: Nature-Inspired Programming Recipes.* Self-published. Retrieved from https://github.com/clever-algorithms/CleverAlgorithms

Caetano, I., Santos, L., & Leitão, A. (2020). Computational design in architecture: Defining parametric, generative, and algorithmic design. *Frontiers of Architectural Research,* 9(2), 287–300. https://doi.org/10.1016/j.foar.2019.12.008

Cagan, J., Campbell, J. I., Finger, S., & Tomiyama, T. (2005). A framework for computational design synthesis: Model and applications. *Journal of Computing and Information Science in Engineering,* 5(9), 171–181. https://doi.org/10.1115/1.2013289

Chaillou, S. (2019). *AI + Architecture: Towards a New Approach* (Master's thesis, Harvard). Harvard, Cambridge. Retrieved from https://view.publitas.com/harvard-university/ai-architecture-thesis-harvard-gsd-stanislas-chaillou

Churchman, C. W., Ackoff, R. L., & Arnoff, E. L. (1957). *Introduction to Operations Research.* New York: Wiley.

Coates, P. (2010). *Programming Architecture.* London: Routledge.

Coates, P., & Thum, R. (1995). *Generative Modelling*. London: University of East London. Retrieved from http://roar.uel.ac.uk/948/

Corona-Martínez, A. (2003). *The Architectural Project* (M. Quantrill, Ed.; A. Corona-Martínez & M. Quantrill, Trans.). College Station: Texas A&M University Press.

Cross, N. (2006). *Designerly Ways of Knowing*. London: Springer.

Davis, D. (2013a). *A History of Parametric*. Retrieved January 22, 2020, from Daniel Davis website: https://www.danieldavis.com/a-history-of-parametric/

Davis, D. (2013b). *Modelled on Software Engineering: Flexible Parametric Models in the Practice of Architecture* (Doctoral dissertation, RMIT). RMIT, Melbourne. Retrieved from https://researchrepository. rmit.edu.au/

De Wolf, T., & Holvoet, T. (2005). Emergence versus self-organisation: Different concepts but promising when combined. In S. A. Brueckner, G. Di Marzo Serugendo, A. Karageorgos, & R. Nagpal (Eds.), *Engineering Self-Organising Systems: Methodologies and Applications*. Berlin: Springer. https:// doi.org/10.1007/11494676_1

Eastman, C. M. (1975). *Spatial Synthesis in Computer-Aided Building Design*. New York: Elsevier Science Inc.

Erdolu, E. (2019). Lines, triangles, and nets: A framework for designing input technologies and interaction techniques for computer-aided design. *International Journal of Architectural Computing*, 17(4), 357–381. https://doi.org/10.1177/1478077119887360

Fischer, T., & Herr, C. M. (2001). Teaching Generative Design. In *Proceedings of the 4th Conference on Generative Art*. Milan: Politechnico di Milano University.

Flemming, U., & Woodbury, R. (1995). Software environment to support early phases in building design (SEED): Overview. *Journal of Architectural Engineering*, 1(4), 147–152. https://doi.org/10.1061/ (ASCE)1076-0431(1995)1:4(147)

Foster, D. (2019). *Generative Deep Learning: Teaching Machines to Paint, Write, Compose and Play*. Sebastopol: O'Reilly Media.

Frazer, J. (1995). *An Evolutionary Architecture*. London: Architectural Association.

Gänshirt, C. (2007). *Tools for Ideas: Introduction to Architectural Design*. Basel: Birkhäuser. https://doi. org/10.1515/9783034609241

Gatys, L. A., Ecker, A. S., & Bethge, M. (2016). *Image Style Transfer Using Convolutional Neural Networks*. 2016 IEEE Conference on Computer Vision and Pattern Recognition (CVPR), 2414–2423. Las Vegas, NV: IEEE. https://doi.org/10.1109/CVPR.2016.265

Gips, J., & Stiny, G. (1980). Production systems and grammars: A uniform characterization. *Environment and Planning B: Planning and Design*, 7, 399–408. https://doi.org/10.1068/b070399

Goodfellow, I., Pouget-Abadie, J., Mirza, M., Xu, B., Warde-Farley, D., Ozair, S., Courville, A., & Bengio, Y. (2014). Generative adversarial nets. In Z. Ghahramani, M. Welling, C. Cortes, N. Lawrence and K.Q. Weinberger (Eds.), *Proceedings of NIPS: Advances in Neural Information Processing Systems*, 2672–2680. Montreal, Canada.

Goodfellow, I., Yoshua, B., & Aaron, C. (2016). *Deep Learning*. Cambridge, MA: The MIT Press. Retrieved from http://www.deeplearningbook.org

Grobman, Y. J., Yezioro, A., & Capeluto, I. G. (2009). Computer-based form generation in architectural design: A critical review. *International Journal of Architectural Computing*, 7(4), 535–553. https:// doi.org/10.1260/1478-0771.7.4.535

Harding, J. (2016). Evolving parametric models using genetic programming with artificial selection. In H. Aulikki, T. Österlund, & P. Markkanen (Eds.), *Complexity & Simplicity: Proceedings of the 34th eCAADe Conference* (Vol. 1, pp. 423–432). Oulu: eCAADe.

Henriques, G. C., Bueno, E., Lenz, D., & Sardenberg, V. (2019). Generative systems: Interwining physical, digital and biological processes, a case study. In J. P. Sousa, G. C. Henriques, & J. P. Xavier (Eds.), *Architecture in the Age of the 4th Industrial Revolution: Proceedings of the 37th eCAADe and 23rd SIGraDi Conference* (Vol. 1, pp. 25–34). Porto: eCAADe-SIGraDi-FAUP.

Hensel, M., Menges, A., & Weinstock, M. (2010). *Emergent Technologies and Design*. New York: Routledge.

Hindupur, A. (2017). *The GAN Zoo* [GitHub]. Retrieved January 28, 2020, from The GAN Zoo website: https://github.com/hindupuravinash/the-gan-zoo

Holland, J. H. (1998). *Emergence: From Chaos to Order*. New York: Basic Books.

Huang, W., & Zheng, H. (2018). Architectural drawings recognition and generation through machine learning. In P. Anzalone, M. Del Signore, & A. J. Wit (Eds.), *Recalibration on Imprecision and Infidelity: Proceedings of the 38th Annual ACADIA Conference* (pp. 156–165). Mexico City: ACADIA.

Jacq, A. (n.d.). *Neural Transfer Using PyTorch* [Tutorials]. Retrieved June 26, 2020, from PyTorch website: https://pytorch.org/tutorials/advanced/neural_style_tutorial.html

Janssen, P., & Stouffs, R. (2015). Types of parametric modelling. In Y. Ikeda, C. M. Herr, D. Holzer, S. Kaijima, M. J. Kim, & M. A. Schnabel (Eds.), *Emerging Experience in Past, Present and Future of Digital Architecture: Proceedings of the 20th CAADRIA Conference* (pp. 157–166). Hong Kong: CAADRIA.

Kalay, Y. E. (2004). *Architecture's New Media: Principles, Theories, and Methods of Computer-Aided Design.* Cambridge, MA: The MIT Press.

Knecht, K., & König, R. (2010). Generating Floor Plan Layouts with K-d Trees and Evolutionary Algorithms. In C. Soddu (Ed.), *Proceedings of the 13th Generative Art Conference* (pp. 238–253). Milan: Politechnico di Milano University. Retrieved from http://www.generativeart.com/

Knight, T., & Stiny, G. (2001). Classical and non-classical computation. *Arq: Architectural Research Quarterly*, 5(4), 355–372. https://doi.org/10.1017/S1359135502001410

Kolarevic, B. (2005). Digital morphogenesis. In B. Kolarevic (Ed.), *Architecture in the Digital Age: Design and Manufacturing* (pp. 12–28). London: Taylor & Francis.

Koza, J. R. (1992). *Genetic Programming: On the Programming of Computers by Means of Natural Selection.* Cambridge, MA: The MIT Press.

Krishnamurti, R. (1980). The arithmetic of shapes. *Environment and Planning B: Planning and Design*, 7(4), 463–484. https://doi.org/10.1068/b070463

Krishnamurti, R., & Roe, P. H. O. (1978). Algorithmic aspects of plan generation and enumeration. *Environment and Planning B: Planning and Design*, 5(2), 157–177. https://doi.org/10.1068/b050157

Lawson, B. (2005). *How Designers Think: The Design Process Demystified* (4th ed.). Amsterdam: Elsevier.

Licklider, J. C. R. (1960). Man-computer symbiosis. *IRE Transactions on Human Factors in Electronics*, HFE-1(1), 4–11. https://doi.org/10.1109/THFE2.1960.4503259

Lucan, J. (2012). *Composition, Non-Composition: Architecture and Theory in the Nineteenth and Twentieth Centuries.* Lausanne: EPFL Press.

Mandelbrot, B. B. (1983). *The Fractal Geometry of Nature.* New York: W. H. Freeman and Company.

March, L. (2011). Forty years of shape and shape grammars, 1971–2011. *Nexus Network Journal*, 13(1), 5–13. https://doi.org/10.1007/s00004-011-0054-8

Mitchell, T. (1997). *Machine Learning.* Boston: McGraw-Hill.

Mitchell, W. (1977). *Computer-Aided Architectural Design.* New York: Mason Charter.

Mitchell, W. (1990). *The Logic of Architecture: Design, Computation, and Cognition.* Cambridge, MA: The MIT Press.

Mitchell, W., Liggett, R., & Kvan, T. (1987). *The Art of Computer Graphics Programming: A Structured Introduction for Architects and Designers.* New York: Van Nostrand Reinhold Company.

Mnih, V., Kavukcuoglu, K., Silver, D., Graves, A., Antonoglou, I., Wierstra, D., & Riedmiller, M. (2013). *Playing Atari with Deep Reinforcement Learning.* ArXiv Preprint ArXiv:1312.5602. Retrieved from https://arxiv.org/abs/1312.5602

Mordvintsev, A., Olah, C., & Tyka, M. (2015, June). *Inceptionism: Going Deeper into Neural Networks.* Retrieved June 16, 2020, from Google AI Blog website: http://ai.googleblog.com/2015/06/inceptionism-going-deeper-into-neural.html

Nauata, N., Chang, K.-H., Cheng, C.-Y., Mori, G., & Furukawa, Y. (2020). *House-GAN: Relational Generative Adversarial Networks for Graph-constrained House Layout Generation.* ArXiv:2003.06988 [Cs]. Retrieved from http://arxiv.org/abs/2003.06988

Negroponte, N. (1970). *The Architecture Machine: Toward a More Human Environment* (1st ed.). Cambridge, MA: The MIT Press.

Newton, D. (2019). Generative deep learning in architectural design. *Technology|Architecture + Design*, 3(2), 176–189. https://doi.org/10.1080/24751448.2019.1640536

Nguyen, T. T., Nguyen, N. D., & Nahavandi, S. (2018). *Deep Reinforcement Learning for Multi-Agent Systems: A Review of Challenges, Solutions and Applications.* ArXiv:1812.11794 [Cs, Stat]. Retrieved from http://arxiv.org/abs/1812.11794

Niazi, M., & Hussain, A. (2011). Agent-based computing from multi-agent systems to agent-based models: A visual survey. *Scientometrics*, 89(2), 479–499. https://doi.org/10.1007/s11192-011-0468-9

Otto, F. (2009). *Occupying and Connecting.* Stuttgart: Edition Axel Menges.

Oxman, R. (2006). Theory and design in the first digital age. *Design Studies*, 27(3), 229–265. https://doi.org/10.1016/j.destud.2005.11.002

Oxman, R., & Oxman, R. (2014). From composition to generation. In *Theories of the Digital in Architecture* (pp. 55–61). New York: Routledge.

Ozbulak, U. (2017). *Pytorch CNN Visualizations* [GitHub]. Retrieved June 20, 2020, from https://github.com/utkuozbulak/pytorch-cnn-visualizations

Pearson, J. E. (1993). Complex patterns in a simple system. *Science*, 261(5118), 189. https://doi.org/10.1126/science.261.5118.189

Prusinkiewicz, P., & Lindenmayer, A. (2004). *The Algorithmic Beauty of Plants*. New York: Springer-Verlag. Retrieved from http://algorithmicbotany.org/papers/abop/abop.pdf

Radford, A. D., & Gero, J. S. (1988). *Design by Optimization in Architecture, Building, and Construction*. New York: Van Nostrand Reinhold Company.

Reynolds, C. (1987). Flocks, herds and schools: A distributed behavioral model. *ACM SIGGRAPH Computer Graphics*, 21, 25–34. ACM. https://doi.org/10.1145/37402.37406

Reynolds, C. (1999). *Steering Behaviors for Autonomous Characters*, 763–782. San Jose. Retrieved from http://www.red3d.com/cwr/steer/gdc99/

Russel, Stuart J., & Norvig, P. (2010). *Artificial Intelligence: A Modern Approach* (3rd ed.). Upper Saddle River, NJ: Prentice Hall.

Rutten, D. (2013). Galapagos: On the logic and limitations of generic solvers. *Architectural Design*, 83(2), 132–135. https://doi.org/10.1002/ad.1568

Schön, D. (1983). *The Reflective Practitioner: How Professionals Think In Action*. New York: Basic Books.

Schön, D. (1992). Designing as reflective conversation with the materials of a design situation. *Knowledge-Based Systems*, 5(1), 3–14. https://doi.org/10.1016/0950-7051(92)90020-G

Silver, D., Hubert, T., Schrittwieser, J., Antonoglou, I., Lai, M., Guez, A., … Hassabis, D. (2017). *Mastering Chess and Shogi by Self-Play with a General Reinforcement Learning Algorithm*. ArXiv:1712.01815 [Cs]. Retrieved from http://arxiv.org/abs/1712.01815

Silver, D., Schrittwieser, J., Simonyan, K., Antonoglou, I., Huang, A., Guez, A., Lanctot, M., Sifre, L., Kumaran, D., Graepel, T., Lillicrap, T., Simonyan, K., & Hassabis, D. (2017). Mastering the game of Go without human knowledge. *Nature*, 550(7676), 354–359. https://doi.org/10.1038/nature24270

Simon, H. A. (1975). Style in design. In C. M. Eastman (Ed.), *Spatial Synthesis in Computer-Aided Building Design* (pp. 287–309). New York: Elsevier Science Inc.

Simon, H. A. (1996). *The Sciences of the Artificial* (3rd ed.). Cambridge, MA: The MIT Press.

Simonyan, K., & Zisserman, A. (2015). *Very Deep Convolutional Networks for Large-Scale Image Recognition*. ArXiv:1409.1556 [Cs]. Retrieved from http://arxiv.org/abs/1409.1556

Steadman, P. (1973). Graph theoretic representation of architectural arrangement. *Architectural Research and Teaching*, 2(3), 161–172.

Steadman, P. (1983). *Architectural Morphology: An Introduction to the Geometry of Building Plans*. London: Pion.

Stiny, G. (1980). Introduction to shape and shape grammars. *Environment and Planning B: Urban Analytics and City Science*, 7(3), 343–351. https://doi.org/10.1068/b070343

Stiny, G. (2006). *Shape: Talking about Seeing and Doing*. Cambridge, MA: The MIT Press.

Sutton, R. S., & Barto, A. G. (2018). *Reinforcement Learning: An Introduction* (2nd ed.). Cambridge, MA: The MIT Press. Retrieved from http://incompleteideas.net/book/the-book.html

Terzidis, K. (2006). *Algorithmic Architecture*. Oxford: The Architectural Press.

Turing, A. M. (1952). The chemical basis of morphogenesis. *Philosophical Transactions of the Royal Society of London*, 237(641), 37–72.

Veloso, P., Celani, G., & Scheeren, R. (2018). From the generation of layouts to the production of construction documents: An application in the customization of apartment plans. *Automation in Construction*, 96(9), 224–235. https://doi.org/10.1016/j.autcon.2018.09.013

Veloso, P., & Krishnamurti, R. (2019). *From Black Box to Generative System. BLACK BOX: Articulating Architecture's Core in the Post-Digital Era*. Presented at the 107th ACSA Annual Meeting, Pittsburgh, PA.

Vinyals, O., Babuschkin, I., Czarnecki, W. M., Mathieu, M., Dudzik, A., Chung, J., … Silver, D. (2019). Grandmaster level in StarCraft II using multi-agent reinforcement learning. *Nature*, 575(7782), 350–354. https://doi.org/10.1038/s41586-019-1724-z

Vishal, S., & Gu, N. (2012). Towards an integrated generative design framework. *Design Studies*, 33(2), 185–207. https://doi.org/10.1016/j.destud.2011.06.001

Vrachliotis, G., Kleinsmanns, J., Kunz, M., & Kurz, P. (Eds.). (2017). *Frei Otto: Thinking by Modeling*. Leipzig: Spector Books.

Wilensky, U., & Rand, W. (2015). *An Introduction to Agent-based Modeling: Modeling Natural, Societal and Engineered Complex Systems with Netlogo*. Cambridge, MA: The MIT Press.

Witten Jr, T. A., & Sander, L. M. (1981). Diffusion-limited aggregation, a kinetic critical phenomenon. *Physical Review Letters*, 47(19), 1400. https://doi.org/10.1103/PhysRevLett.47.1400

Wolfram, S. (2002). *A New Kind of Science*. Champaign: Wolfram Media.

Woodbury, R. (2010). *Elements of Parametric Design*. New York: Routledge.

Wortmann, T. (2017). Model-based optimization for architectural design: Optimizing daylight and glare in grasshopper. *Technology|Architecture + Design*, 1(2), 176–185. https://doi.org/10.1080/2475 1448.2017.1354615

Wortmann, T. (2018). *Efficient, Visual, and Interactive Architectural Design Optimization with Model-based Methods* (PhD Dissertation). Singapore University of Technology and Design, Singapore.

Zheng, H. (2018). Drawing with Bots: Human-computer collaborative drawing experiments. In T. Fukuda, W. Huang, P. Janssen, K. Crolla, & S. Alhadidi (Eds.), *Learning, Adapting and Prototyping: Proceedings of the 23rd Annual CAADRIA Conference* (pp. 127–132). Beijing: CAADRIA.

4

The network of interactions for an artificial architectural intelligence

Can Uzun

> The buildings and communities of the near future will be planned with the aid of some development of these theories (new technologies). Whether or not they are planned by architects may pretty well depend on the way architects today prepare to use such tools.
>
> *(Eames, 1954)*

Joao Rocha (2004) recalled that architectural theory is an intellectual bridge between architecture and other disciplines. In this context, architecture has established various relationships with different disciplines. One of these relationships is computational thinking. Joao Rocha's thesis describes the intellectual mediation between computational systems and architectural theory. This relationship, which emerged between architecture and computational systems, between 1960 and 1980, led to the development of computational theory in architecture. Rocha explained the first steps of the theory of computation in architecture with a network visualization on the first page of his thesis. In this network, individuals, and institutions that enable the development of the basic ideas of computation theory in architecture, can be seen. Despite the simplicity and understandability of the network, Rocha's thesis explains the comprehensive intellectual interactions of computational architecture theory.

We can see from the literature that the computational theory of architecture interacted intensely with artificial intelligence and cybernetics in the 1960–1980 period. As a result of this interaction, a lot of research has been done, from self-referential building ideas to autonomous design actions. When the interactions in the literature are examined in detail, we can understand that all intellectual interactions give rise to quite a large social network. This text presents a larger and more complex network of intellectual interactions through a large literature that may be related to artificial architectural intelligence (AAI). In other words, this text presents the brain of the idea of AAI, consisting of intellectual interactions that started in the 1950s and still continue today.

A complex social network (or the brain) of the AAI

> In 1968 one could read all existing literature in English on the subject of "artificial intelligence" within one month. It now takes about six months. The field is still small and ill defined (as even the name suggests), and can be roughly characterized by two contrasting approaches to achieving a machine intelligence.
>
> *(Negroponte, 1975)*

Forty-five years have passed since this statement of Negroponte. Within 50 years, countless researches have been done and lots of research on AI continues. Today in the year 2020, the artificial intelligence field is far broader than it was in 1968. Even reading the headings of each literature within the field may take months. In the 1960s, AI had two approaches—as connectionist and symbolist. But today, AI has lots of subfields with different approaches. These approaches are evolutionaries, Bayesians, symbolists, anologizers, and connectionists (Domingos, 2015). All these fields also have subfields. Each of these subfields includes hundreds of algorithms. We can count at least 500 generative adversarial network (GAN) algorithms, which are the subfield of the connectionist AI's generative algorithms. It is hard to have a good knowledge of the whole AI field. But it is even hard to see all the relations and interactions among the literature of the AI field. All these huge amounts of information in the AI field create a network. We can understand the important interactions and actors of the network by analyzing it.

The field of artificial intelligence has become so widespread that it can even interact with the discipline of architecture. But this interaction is not that new. Till now a number of researches have been done in between the fields of AI and architecture. For this text, the most important and the most related articles, the actors (author(s) of the publications) in the field of "AI and architecture" and interactions between them are listed. The article count that is analyzed in this text is 177, and the actors' count is 109. So the node count in this network is 286. The interaction count between articles and actors is 673. These numbers are given to show the complexity of the field even if it is too specific a field as "AI and architecture." Comprehensively understanding this field's advent and evolving branches can be possible by analyzing all the interactions in detail.

Social network analysis is the key method to analyze these interactions between AI and architecture. Hummon and Doreian (1990) stated in their study "Computational methods for social network analysis" that search algorithms used in computer science can be used in the analysis of social networks. And they have developed a network visualization software in which the relationships of the data are visualized. Since then, utilizing network visualization showed lots of interesting details hidden in the networks.

Interaction between the fields of AI and architecture creates an intellectual social network with the articles, books, theories, and the author(s) of all these publications. Using visualization of this social network will help to understand the important intersections and connection of the network. I created the social network of "AI and architecture" with the network visualization software called Cytoscape (Demchak, 2002). This software is commonly used in molecule interactions; however, we can use this software for social interaction analysis too. Besides visualization, Cytoscape gives lots of statistical information from the social network by visualizing it.

The data collection process related to the field "AI & architecture" covered the period from the cybernetics era to today. I collected all the data according to the rule that either the data must be directly or indirectly related to the "AI and architecture" field. The publications

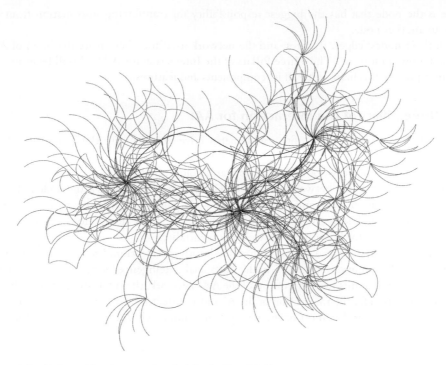

Figure 4.1   AI & architecture network / the brain of AAI.

that are directly and indirectly related are decided by looking at the publications' references and scope of the research. Direct relation is defined as the publications that fit exactly within the discipline in between AI and architecture, while indirect relations are defined through the referencing system. For example, if there is one publication directly related to the AI field and if this publication is cited by an architectural publication, then it becomes indirectly related to the AI and architecture field. Each citation and reference connects all the publications and the actors. In this way, the social network is obtained. This process includes a highly intense and detailed searching process. After completing all the data collection processes, "AI & architecture" relations data were stored in an excel sheet. In Cytoscape software, this excel sheet is converted into a visualized social network to be analyzed later. Figure 4.1 shows the first result of the social network of AI & architecture. At first glance, we can have an idea about how complex it is to evaluate these relations. In Figure 4.1 all the curves are the connections between the actors and the publications. These curves are called edges in social networks. The actors, the publications, the fields, and the topics become nodes in a social network. And edges are the connections between all these nodes.

To evaluate all the networks with their nodes and edges, I utilized Cytoscape analyzing tools. All the networks have common features such as degree, closeness centrality, and be-tweenness centrality. Cytoscape provides all these features too.

In this text, I use degree and betweenness centrality values. A degree is the value for the number of connections per node. The betweenness centrality value relates to how much a node is used to transfer information within the network. In other words, it is about the node acting as a bridge in the transfer of information. The node with a high betweenness centrality value is the node that has the biggest responsibility for transferring information from one node to another node.

All these nodes, edges, features, and the network itself together create the brain of AAI. In the following section "The Three Pillars of the Interaction for AAI," I will be evaluating and interpreting this brain with all its components and features.

The three pillars of the interaction for AAI

In this chapter, I will present quite a wide perspective for AAI with the help of social network visualization of the AAI system. Figure 4.2 shows all the betweenness centrality values hierarchically for the network of AAI. The warm colors and the radius of the circles are directly proportional to the betweenness values. Here, each of the circles is the node indicating each actor, publication, field, and topic in the network. And, all the edges have a betweenness value with their thicknesses, which shows the importance of the interactions. Edge thickness value correlates positively with the betweenness centrality.

At first glance at the social network, three nodes attract attention. From right to left, these are respectively "autonomous plan" node, "artificial intelligence node," and "cybernetics node." According to this first impression of the AAI network, the interesting thing is that the biggest motivation for the interaction of the AI and architecture has been to obtain an autonomous plan generator. So, most of the interactions among cybernetics, AI, and architecture

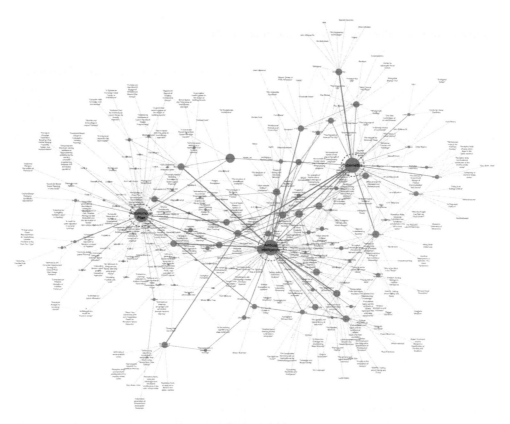

Figure 4.2 Betweenness centrality visualization of the AAI.

occurred due to the autonomous plan generation field. In this chapter, I will focus on these three nodes and explain the actors' interaction in a detailed way.

In this chapter, I will be explaining the different clusters with their different tendencies for obtaining an AAI. According to the social network visualization, there are three main tendencies; I called them the three pillars of the interaction. Those are cybernetics, artificial intelligence, and autonomous plan nodes. For the cybernetics pillar, the interaction among Gordon Pask, Cedric Price, Joan Littlewood, Norbert Wiener, the interaction among György Kepes, Norbert Wiener, Kevin Lynch, J.C.R. Licklider, and the interaction among Charles Eames, Ray Eames, Claude Shannon, and IBM will be explained. For the artificial intelligence node, interactions among Cedric Price, Christopher Alexander, Gordon Pask, Nicholas Negroponte, Lionel March, George Stiny, and James Gips will be important. For the autonomous plan generation node, I will present the various ideas among various architects and computer scientists. While all these interactions give a comprehensive idea for chronological developments in the field of AAI, we can see the clusters that are separated in terms of the methodology that is used for an AAI.

Architectural cybernetics

The cybernetic theory can also claim some explanatory power insofar as it is possible to mimic certain aspects of architectural design by artificial intelligence computer programs (provided, incidentally, that the program is able to learn about and from architects and by experimenting in the language of architects, i.e, by exploring plans, material specifications, condensed versions of clients' comments, etc). Such programs are clearly of value in their own right. They are potential aids to design; acting as intelligent extensions of the tool-like programs mentioned at the outset. Further, they offer a means for integrating the constructional system (the 'machinery of production') with the ongoing design process since it is quite easy to embody the constraints of current technology in a special part of the simulation.

(Pask, 1969)

Gordon Pask is a cybernetician scientist who has an important role in the social network within AAI. Gordon Pask had direct contact with Norbert Wiener for his cybernetics studies. This contact between Norbert Wiener and Gordon Pask allowed the formation of a new theory in architecture. Pask (1969), in his publication, "The Architectural Relevance of Cybernetics," explains that architecture and cybernetics are very closely related. He argued that cybernetics is compatible with architecture in terms of architects being system designers. In this regard, he said that cybernetics is an important subtheory in architecture. This clear and strong relationship between Pask and cybernetics and architecture emerges as an important part of the social network of AAI. Gordon Pask interacted with important actors not only during the cybernetic period but also in the field of artificial intelligence. In the quotation from Gordon Pask above, he proposed that artificial intelligence can be taught with the architectural language; moreover, even AI can explore plan schemes autonomously. This idea of Pask corresponds to the recent research on autonomous plan generation with today's artificial intelligence algorithms.

The interaction of Gordon Pask had an important interaction with architect Cedric Price who has a valuable foresight on the future of architecture. Figure 4.4 shows the location of Cedric Price in the network and the close neighbors of Price. There are many interactions of Cedric Price, and one of them is Joan Littlewood. Cedric Price and Joan Littlewood

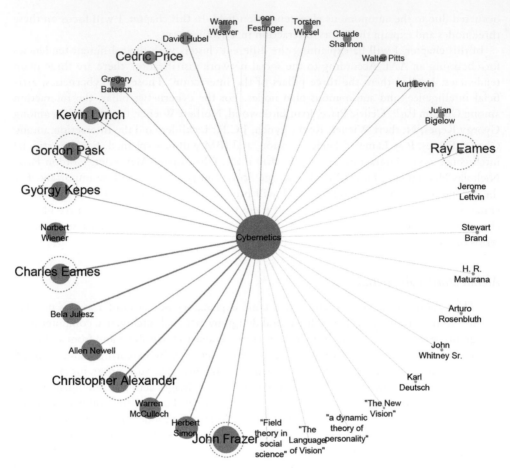

Figure 4.3 Cybernetics connections with architecture.

proposed the Fun Palace project before Price developed the project Generator in 1962. The most important point of this project is that Price and Littlewood created the Fun Palace with analog feedbacks that form the basis of cybernetics theory. The space (Fun Palace) had been turned into a responsive place with analog feedback. Gordon Pask contributed to the Fun Palace project too. Gordon Pask proposed a responsive theater that reacted by changing its light and sound according to the effects of the theater audience. Pask called this theater cybernetic theater. With its responsiveness, that space had become, for the first time, a self-referential space in the 1960s.

Another project that led Cedric Price to be in the social network is the Generator project. For the Generator project, Cedric Price worked with John Frazer, who later became the author of the book *An Evolutionary Architecture*. The Generator project was a project directly related to cybernetics as it combines space syntax, automata, and cybernetics into one project (Pertigkiozoglou, 2017a). In the Generator project, for the first time, a building was called an intelligent building in 1980. Fun Palace was only a fictional verbal proposal. But the Generator project gained a physical reality as an intelligent building (Hernandez, 2015). An intelligent structure (Generator) organizes itself with a real feedback mechanism that responds to user needs and recreates the spatial organization according to the changing needs of the users.

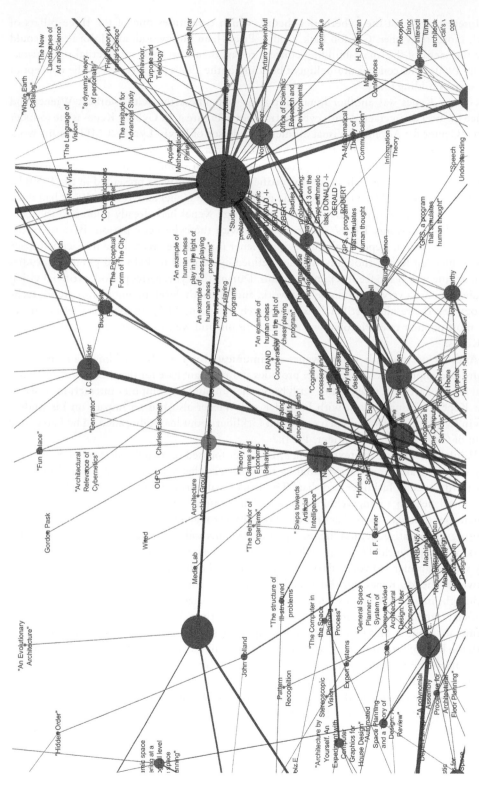

Figure 4.4 Location of Gordon Pask and Cedric Price in the network (locations are according to betweenness centrality value).

Interacting about the cybernetics theory, which constitutes one of the three pillars of AAI, Norbert Wiener, Gordon Pask, Cedric Price, Joan Littlewood, and John Frazer could sow the seeds of the smart-building concept today, thanks to their intellectual interactions in the 1960s. The concept of intelligent building of the 1960s is converted to the concept of the smart building today.

György Kepes was another important actor who interacted with Norbert Wiener and hence he directly interacted with cybernetic theory (Figure 4.3). György Kepes is the founder of the Center for Advanced Visual Studies and advisor of Kevin Lynch at MIT. In his work on vision, Kepes argued that the vision had to have a formal explanation. It is interesting to note that although Kepes' attempt to formally explain vision was not related to artificial vision in technical terms, theoretically, artificial vision ideas were presented in the 1950s by an art professor at MIT in the cybernetic period. Before Hubel and Wiesel (1962) had done their famous experiments on vision in cats, György Kepes had already published the *Language of Vision*. György Kepes' studies coincide with the cybernetic period. Because of the cybernetics period, Kepes' dialogues with Wiener might have created the intellectual space that influenced Kepes' thoughts. Wiener defined cybernetics in 1948 and published studies on machine vision and feedback mechanisms. During the cybernetics period, artificial vision studies became a very common field of work, and Wiener's development of antiaircraft technology was the result of artificial vision research (Halpern, 2015). In the cybernetics period, the most popular research topic was artificial vision, and we can see the effects on the ideas of Kepes.

Another person with whom Kepes communicated is J. C. R. Licklider, an important figure in computer science. Licklider provides an important base for the theoretical and practical fields of artificial intelligence with his studies on human–computer interaction. It seems that Kepes' communication with Licklider and Wiener also had an impact on his student Kevin Lynch (Figure 4.5). Lynch contacted Licklider about his study called "The Perceptual form of City" (Lynch & Licklider, 1954).

While interpreting the text of Lynch, Licklider focused on Lynch's desire to describe the city with its grammar and its vocabulary but criticized that it was necessary to add meaning as a third concept. Licklider said that "The Perceptual Form of City" text went from a psychological field to a nonpsychological field. The reason behind Licklider's criticism is that Lynch tries to make a formal definition of the city through grammar and vocabulary. Instead of using a qualitative method, he uses quantitative methods to analyze the city. The seminal work of Kevin Lynch, *The Image of the City* (1960)—the result of his efforts to understand the city with grammar and vocabulary—presents a formal definition of the city. The interaction between Wiener, Kepes, Licklider, and Lynch could demonstrate the city's logic formally. Although, in a technical sense, it is not correct to associate Lynch's work directly with the artificial intelligence field, in the 1950s, for the first time, Lynch described the city with its grammatical rules. This first attempt is an important step in reading the city formally. Today, with the help of formal reading of the city, we can build smart cities. Instead of grammar and vocabulary, the technology uses segments of the city (pedestrians, pavement, vehicle roads, traffic signs, buildings, etc.) to build itself autonomously. Intelligent vehicles can read all the segments of the city and find their way autonomously. While the interactions among Norbert Wiener, Gordon Pask, Cedric Price, Joan Littlewood, and John Frazer laid the foundations for the smart-building concept, the interactions among György Kepes, Norbert Wiener, Kevin Lynch, and J. C. E. Licklider can be a starting point for today's smart-cities concept.

Charles Eames and Ray Eames are the other actors that interact with the cybernetics concept in the social network. In the cybernetics period, Charles and Ray Eames produced tens

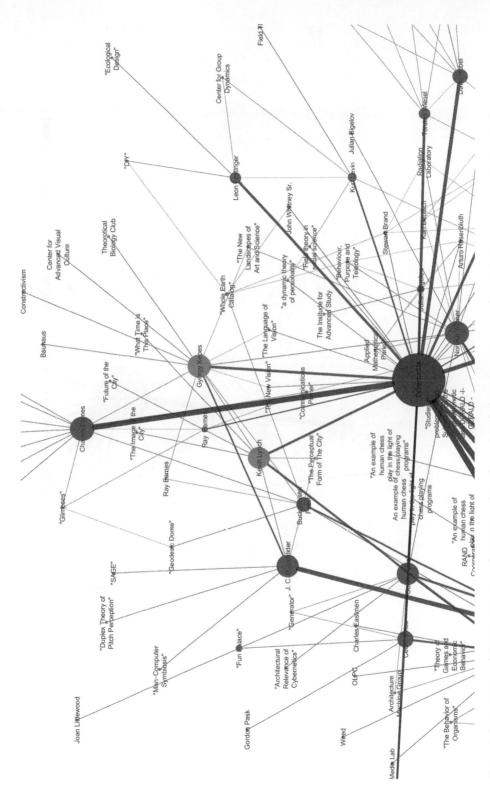

Figure 4.5 Location of György Kepes and Kevin Lynch in the network (locations are according to betweenness centrality value).

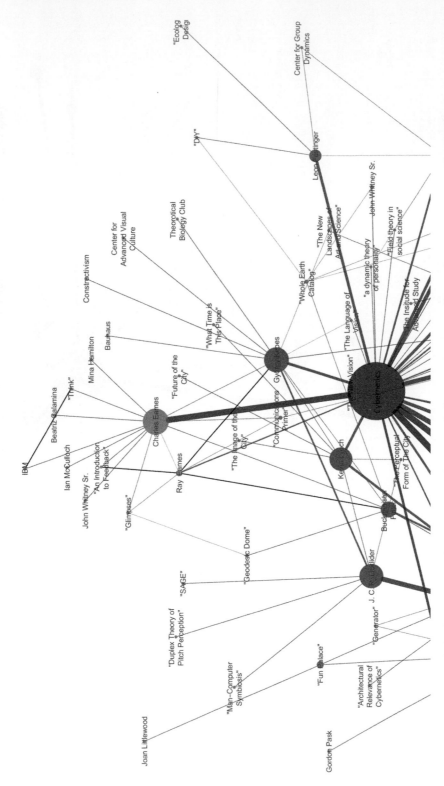

Figure 4.6 Location of Charles Eames and Ray Eames in the network (locations are according to betweenness centrality value).

of videos that were related to the topic AAI. Each video they produced was directly linked to algorithmic logic and the cybernetic thinking system. "A Communication Primer" is one of these videos. "A Communication Primer is directly related to the book, *A Mathematical Theory of Communication*, by Claude Shannon, a leading information theorist of the period. The effect of *A Mathematical Theory of Communication* on science and technology is undeniable. "A Communication Primer" simply presented the logic of *A Mathematical Theory of Communication* and aimed to make architects aware of recent technological advances. In the 1960s, Eames also produced two videos for IBM called "An Introduction to Feedback" and "Think." "An Introduction to Feedback" is directly related to cybernetics, and it presents the system of feedback mechanism. On the other hand, in "Think," Eames explained IBM's problem-solving process and how the organization and analysis process of the information took place. "Think" was also an important attempt in the way it was presented. In the problem-solving method of the machines, machines solved the problems by dividing the problem into subparts. Likewise, in the demonstration held in IBM Pavilion, "Think" was shown from a screen that included many subscreens (Schuldenfrei, 2014). Another important video production of Eames is "Glimpses." In "Glimpses," Eames explained life in the USA with a video that consisted of more than 2,200 images. Although "Glimpses" is not directly related to cybernetics or artificial intelligence, videos produced with more than 2,200 images can be an important reference for big data. These images form an American pattern. The learning path of today's artificial intelligence algorithm is to find the embedded pattern in the big data and establish relationships. So, maybe for the first time, an image dataset that represents the idea of a country was produced in a video called "Glimpses."

Catalysts of artificial intelligence in architecture

> As time goes on the designer gets more and more control over the process of design. But as he does so, his efforts to deal with the increasing cognitive burden actually make it harder and harder for the real causal structure of the problem to express itself in this process. What can we do to overcome this difficulty? On the face of it, it is hard to see how any systematic theory can ease it much.
>
> *(Alexander, 1964)*

In this section, I will introduce concepts such as algorithmic aesthetics, artificial intelligence and aesthetics, architectural machines, and design machines. These concepts were not the futuristic thoughts in the architectural discipline in the 1970s, but the titles of publications developed an autonomous architectural thought which have many interactions with artificial intelligence references. The network in this study shows the pioneers of artificial architectural intelligence as follows: Nicholas Negroponte, Christopher Alexander, George Stiny James Gips, Lionel March, Cedric Price, and Gordon Pask (Figure 4.7). I call all these genius people catalysts of artificial intelligence in architecture. In this chapter, I will focus on the works of Christopher Alexander, George Stiny, James Gips, and Negroponte.

This network shows node points placed according to the betweenness centrality values. There is no randomness in this network. Therefore, we can understand better the interaction of any node with its close neighbors and its importance in the social network. I first start this chapter with Christopher Alexander. We can see the position of Alexander in the network in Figure 4.8. Hence we can understand the importance of Alexander with his position in the network.

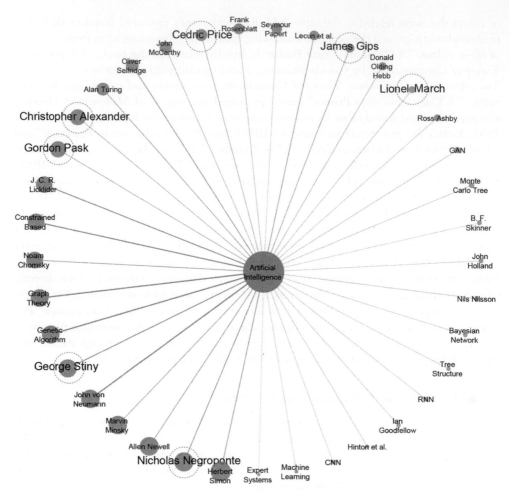

Figure 4.7 Artificial intelligence connections with architecture.

The works of Alexander in the design discipline and artificial intelligence intersection is to explain the system of the design process with its patterns. Alexander's *Notes on the Synthesis of the Form* (1964) is a book to understand the recurring systematic in the design process. While Alexander explained this systematically, he directly referred to the references of Noam Chomsky, Ross Ashby, Norbert Wiener, Allen Newell, John von Neumann, B. F. Skinner, and Marvin Minsky. The explanation of the design action in architectural discipline with these references in the artificial intelligence field has also influenced and developed the ideas of artificial intelligence in architecture.

Alexander emphasized the need to look for systematic solutions to the design problem, as the architecture increases the cognitive load while he/she designs. He supported the idea of the necessity of having an efficient architectural project process by reducing the cognitive load in design rather than an autonomous design action.

In his book *Notes on the Synthesis of the Form* (1964), Alexander emphasized the need for symbolic representation of solutions and the constraints within the problem. Negroponte (1975) says that Alexander's trying to analyze the design by dividing it into subproblems is directly associated with Minsky's symbolic AI definition. Symbolically, Alexander explained

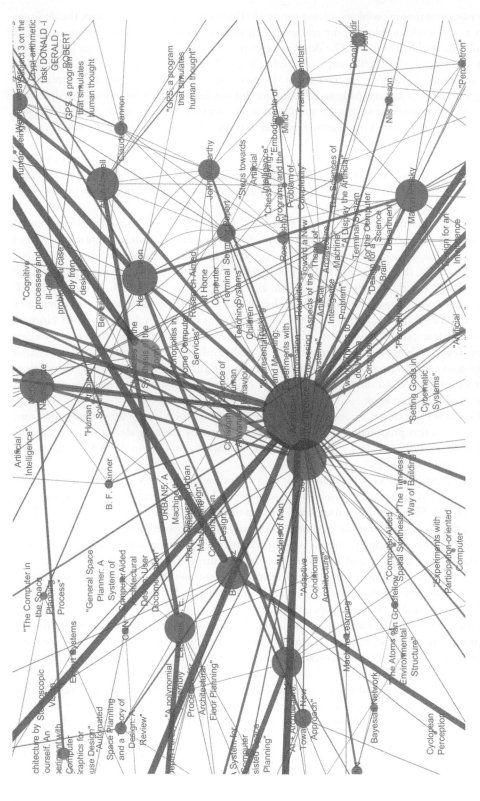

Figure 4.8 Location of Christopher Alexander and his book *Notes on the Synthesis of the Form* in the network (locations are according to between-ness centrality value).

the systematic design problem-solving process in three steps. In the primary step, the designer faces a real-world problem in the real world. In the second step, the designers' awareness of the design problem is high. The designer tries to find a solution to the design problem by communicating with his/her experiences. In the third stage, the design problem is converted into an abstract symbolic representation. In this stage, Alexander proposed to explain the design problem with sets. Although Alexander did not describe an autonomous architecture, he proposed a symbolic system for autonomous architecture. In *Notes on the Synthesis of Form* (1964), Alexander stated the learning definition of BF Skinner is valid for the designer too. Skinnerian learning has been the basis of today's reinforcement learning method. As in reinforcement learning, Skinnerian learning theory describes the learning process with success or failures from one's repetitive experiences. According to Alexander (1964), the designer develops his workmanship, which he started as a novice, by practicing and learning from his/her mistakes.

In addition to the systematic design processes, Alexander also mentioned a self-referential building by interacting with its environment. In this respect, Alexander mentions a system similar to that of Cedric Price's Generator project. However, Alexander (1964) talks about a house design that responds to social changes. A building could communicate with the social changes with a feedback mechanism, allowing the structure to be redefined by itself. Alexander (1964) described the building that interacts and responds to its environment as a good fit. Alexander made this definition directly using the feedback definition of Norbert Wiener in the cybernetics theory. The idea of the systematic nature of Alexander's design action revealed both the autonomous design action and the self-referential building system discussions in *Notes on the Synthesis of Form*. All this information about Alexander shows that, with its references and interactions, the book *Notes on the Synthesis of Form* is an important node in the AAI network.

Two other important actors emerged in AAI in the 1970s: George Stiny and Jame Gips. These two actors proposed the theory of shape grammar by creating algorithms with shapes instead of symbols. Figure 4.9 shows the location of Stiny and Gips in the AAI network and their close surroundings.

In 1972, Stiny and Gips, in their text, "Shape Grammars and the Generative Specification of Painting and Sculpture," presented an artwork production algorithm with the shape rules they defined. Shape grammar uses shapes instead of symbols while creating algorithms. With shape grammar theory, for the first time, Stiny and Gips proposed a calculation with shapes instead of symbols. Shape grammar is an important theory in explaining the systematics of the algorithm for seeing and evaluating the shapes. Shape grammar explains the syntax of shapes, as in the language grammar, but using a different method. Instead of using symbols, Stiny and Gips offered the part-whole relations in the shapes. So, the syntax of the shapes will not be the exact definition of shape grammar.

Language and grammar studies have been frequently emphasized in language processing studies in the field of artificial intelligence. It has been an important aim, especially for artificial intelligence, to perceive the language we use to communicate with a human. Therefore, grammatical rules and meaning or syntax and semantics are necessary for the language to be understood and spoken autonomously. Stiny and Gips were influenced by the grammar studies of the language theorist Noam Chomsky. The work of Chomsky has been particularly criticized by Minsky. Minsky argued that language can be understood not only with grammatical rules but also with semantics (Stiny, 2006). Chomsky, on the other hand, explained that we can understand a sentence that we have never heard of, with our sincerity towards the grammatical rules of the language. Birkhoff's (1933) book, *Aesthetic Measure*, and

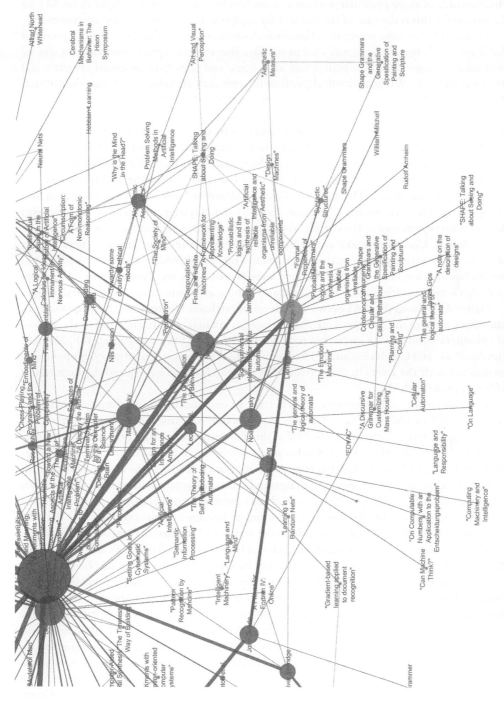

Figure 4.9 Location of George Stiny and James Gips in the network (locations are according to betweenness centrality value).

the discussion of Minsky and Chomsky formed the basis for the shape grammar theory. Even though there are lots of philosophical backgrounds of shape grammar theory, the biggest application area of shape grammar is its use as a method for plan production algorithms. Maybe the reason for this is the ease of the method for applying the plan production algorithms.

Stiny and James Gips wrote the *Algorithmic Aesthetics* in 1978. The formal descriptions of the shapes with the grammar rules led to the idea that the concept of aesthetics can also be explained via algorithms. To realize this idea, Stiny and Gips have proposed criticism and design algorithms. While criticism algorithms interpret any art value, the design algorithm is the algorithm that produces art with value (Stiny & Gips, 1978). Both algorithms have a receptor and an effector algorithm to work. The criticism algorithm analyzes the information from the receptor with the aesthetic system and reports the evaluation result with the effector. The design algorithm produces a design product output from the effector by synthesizing the information from the receptor with an aesthetic system (Stiny & Gips, 1978). All this system provides is a basic algorithm for AAI. This work was the basis of the "Design Machines" (1981) of Stiny and March. The design machine proposed by Stiny and March consists of four components. These are receptor, effector, architectural language, and theory. The receptor defines what is perceived in the outside world, and the effector outputs the product according to the design. Communication on the theory between the receptor and the effector takes place in the language of architecture. This creates the entire model of a design machine. In the studies of Stiny, Gips, and March, there were proposals on the algorithms of the concept of design action, which is more inclusive than defining an autonomous architectural system.

Figure 4.10 shows the AAI network location of Nicholas Negroponte. Negroponte is an important node in the AAI network that is closer to artificial intelligence and in the middle of cybernetics and AI. He interacted with Marvin Minsky, Seymour Papert, B.F. Skinner, Gordon Pask, and Charles Eastman. The indirect and direct interactions that Negroponte has established with the actors in the network and its neighbors have increased the importance of Negroponte in AAI.

This interaction of Negroponte was effective in establishing the Architecture Machine Group at MIT in 1967 with Leon Groisser. Architecture Machine Group has continued numerous intellectual interactions until 1985 at the intersection of computer graphics, software, and architectural discipline. In 1985, it became a new research environment as the MIT Media Lab. Today, MIT Media Lab has played an important role in the production of new technology with the interaction between design and science disciplines in many different fields from neuroscience to robotics for years. With this great influence of this journey that started with the Architecture Machine Group, Negroponte became an important node in the AAI network, and he plays an important role in the transfer of intellectual knowledge. Vardouli (2012) stated that Licklider's work on human–machine symbiosis had a great influence on the Architecture Machine Group. Besides, Gordon Pask and Yona Friedman had been influential names in Negroponte's proposal for an architectural machine. In the cybernetics topic, I explained in detail the responsive theater of Gordon Pask at Fun Palace and said that Gordon Pask thought that architecture is a parallel discipline with cybernetics. And Pask had many visits to the Architecture Machine Group at MIT (Pertigkiozoglou, 2017b). These visits provided important interactions with Negroponte. One of the other important interactions with Negroponte was Yona Friedman. Yona Friedman (1975) proposed Flatwriter, a system that produces autonomous plans in *Toward a Scientific Architecture* (Vardouli, 2019). So, with these interactions and intersections of the areas of interest, the Architecture Machine Group has created a large intellectual space for the development of many new technologies in the relationship between architects and machines.

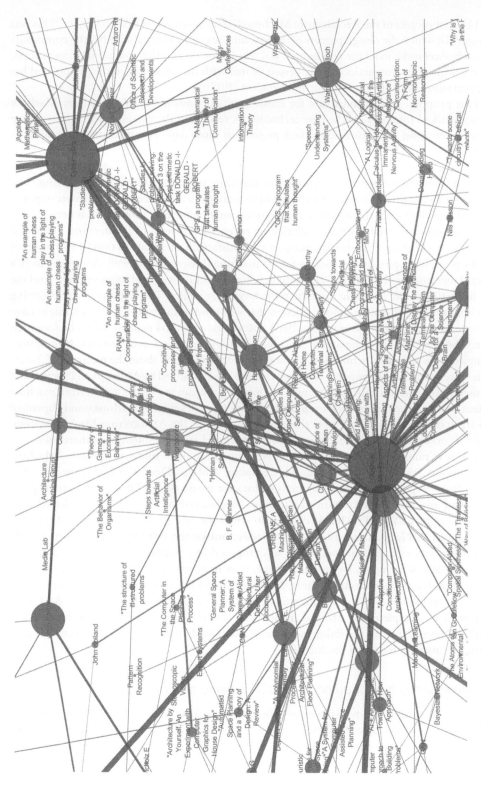

Figure 4.10 Location of Nicholas Negroponte in the network (locations are according to betweenness centrality value).

The first project of the Architecture Machine Group was the URBAN 5 project. This was a project in which the design process of the machine was investigated whether the communication between the machine and human was feasible or not. In the communication process, the machine gives instructions to the person, learns with the answer from the person, and has a conversation with the person (Pertigkiozoglou, 2017b).

This proposal seemed futuristic for those days, but instead, the Architecture Machine Group worked intensely on the new technologies related to the design field. So there were lots of interesting and futuristic research projects in those days. Another important, and interesting, work of Negroponte is "Toward a Theory of Architecture Machines." In this text, Negroponte (1969) explained that the architecture machine could be made possible by performing four actions: heuristic learning, rote learning, reward selection, and forgetting. The heuristic mechanism is necessary for the machine to follow a method appropriate to its response to similar problems for the first time it encounters an architectural problem. It is necessary to make memorization and to develop solutions to repetitive problems in architecture. The award selection works with a Skinnerian perspective. Satisfaction or dissatisfaction of the designer works as a reward penalty mechanism for the machine (Negroponte, 1969). According to this reward mechanism, the machine can learn in which direction it should improve itself. And the last feature of the architecture machine is the forgetting ability. The importance of forgetting is related to the fact that an action in design that was valid in the past as a solution might have become outdated today (Negroponte, 1969). Information that has expired should be forgotten to not be used by the architectural machine. And with all these four features, Negroponte completed his architecture machine. There is an interesting detail about the receptors of the architecture machine. Negroponte proposed that the eye developed by Minsky and Papert could be used as the sensor of the architecture machine. As we can see in the architecture machine system, most of the theories and even the hardware (eyes developed by Minsky and Papert) of the artificial intelligence field were thought to be used for the Architecture Machine system. And this makes the interaction between architecture and artificial intelligence more solid.

The text published by Weinzapfel and Negroponte in 1976 under the project "Machine Recognition and Inference Making in Computer Aids to Design" in "Architecture-by-yourself: an experiment with computer graphics for house design" had an important place in human–machine interaction in architecture. "Architect-by-yourself" was developed with the philosophy of Yona Friedman (1975), who wrote the text of *Toward a Scientific Architecture* (Weinzapfel & Negroponte, 1976). In this study, unlike the software that supports mostly drafting processes today, an application was proposed to a nonarchitect as an aid in design. This proposal, which goes far beyond its time, is an important resource for teaching the machine with design constraints. In short, Negroponte had lots of interactions that gave rise to dozens of technologies in the architecture field. And he is one of the leaders in the AAI field.

I want to complete the artificial intelligence catalysts section in architecture with the work of Negroponte. In the following section, I will explain the third pillar of the AAI network, the autonomous plan productions.

Architecture machine or autonomous plan schema generator

> … purpose of this paper is to more fully introduce this problem domain to the artificial intelligence literature. Not only is it an interesting problem class now only the province of humans, but it has wide applications. Throughout the presentation, both the commonalities and disparities of this task domain with other AI tasks are explicated.
>
> *(Eastman, 1973)*

In the previous sections, I explained many methods in which architecture interacts with the field of artificial intelligence and cybernetics. However, until this section, most studies have suggested understanding architecture and proposing an algorithm of architecture or design. Design machines and architectural machines are quite large architectural problems. On the other hand, plan solution in architectural discipline is a more defined problem than the architecture problem is. All the literature I explained earlier argued that the problem of architecture is too complex to solve. Although the plan layout problem is specific, the problem definition has not been clear yet. However, when we look at the autonomous plan production studies in the literature, we can observe that research on autonomous plan layout generation has a big part in the artificial intelligence field. According to the network analysis, an autonomous plan generator took the third important part of AAI.

I started this chapter with a quotation from Eastman's "Automated Space Planning," which I think is important. Eastman said in the quote very clearly that he aimed to explain autonomous plan production to the AI field and indicated that autonomous space planning is in the artificial intelligence problem domain. Eastman published "Automated space Planning" in the "Artificial Intelligence" journal. This is another proof that "Autonomous Space Planning" is directly related to the AI field. In the network, we can infer that Eastman has an important role in transferring the information between artificial intelligence and autonomous plan generation studies. Furthermore, we can say that the intellectual interactions among the AAI network increased more with the studies of Eastman. Figure 4.11 shows Eastman's interactions and his close neighbors in the network through the betweenness centrality value.

Lobos and Donath (2010) stated there are many attempts to achieve an efficient system for the space layout planning (SLP) technique. Researchers used various methods for SLP such as generative systems, constrained-based systems, shape grammars, and expert systems. Lobos and Donath (2010) indicate that, as the architectural space layout problem is ill-defined (Yoon, 1992), and over-constrained (Arvin & House, 1999), although there are many attempts, these techniques cannot produce suitable tools for the use of architects.

Although the plan production problem has not been fully defined yet, producing efficient autonomous plan layout samples with recent algorithms is possible today. According to Eastman (1973), the goal in autonomous spatial planning researches is not to completely remove the architect from the design process. But the aim is to automate the repeating process in the architectural design discipline. This interpretation was an important explanation for the borders of autonomous architecture research. As Eastman said, the aim of AI algorithms is already to automate the repetitive process.

Two of the most repetitive processes in architecture are deciding the plan scheme organization and drafting the plan schemes. Because of this, there are many attempts to automate this repetitive process. I did not add all these attempts to the network, but I added the ones which have an interaction with the AI field. But, still, the number of researches is so big that Shaviv (1986) stated: "It seems that any architect who entered the area of CAAD felt that it was his responsibility to find a solution to this prime architectural problem." With the prime architectural problem, Shaviv indicated the autonomous plan layout generation.

When I scanned the literature chronologically, the first study in the field of autonomous plan production I encountered was Buffa's "Sequence analysis for functional layouts" in 1955. However, in 1957, Koopmans said that the first studies on plan production problems date back to about 25 years. It means, in the 1930s, the studies on autonomous plan layout generation started. Shaviv (1986) argued that, between 1957 and 1970, more than 30 applications were developed on autonomous plan design. This information shows that autonomous plan production studies have a history of approximately 90 years. Numerous methods have been

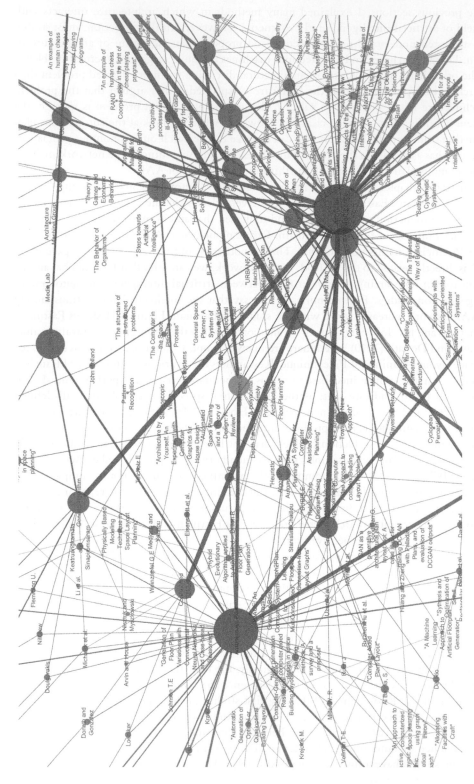

Figure 4.11 Location of Charles Eastman in the network (locations are according to betweenness centrality value).

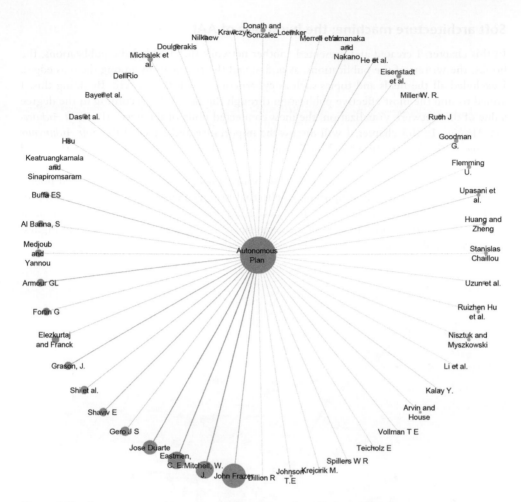

Figure 4.12 Autonomous plan node and its connections in the network.

used in this field that has a history of 90 years. These methods include shape grammar, graph theory, genetic algorithm, expert systems, tree structures, constrained based models, many hybrid machine learning methods, Bayesian networks, RNN, CNN, and most recently, GAN algorithms.

The autonomous plan production field has become an even more charming field with the new algorithms of artificial intelligence. Most of the studies in the autonomous plan production field used the graph theory method (Hu et al., 2020; Medjdoub and Yannou, 2001; Fortin, 1978; Ruch, 1978; Al Banna & Spillers, 1972; Grason, 1971; Miller, 1970). But recently, the autonomous plan studies, particularly with the artificial neural networks, have been increasing rapidly (Uzun et al, 2020; Chaillou, 2019; Eisenstadt et al., 2019; Huang & Zheng, 2018; Bayer et al., 2017).

One chapter will not be enough to completely describe the autonomous plan layout research area, which I presume, has a history of about 90 years. So, this chapter could be just a summary to highlight the reasons for the importance of autonomous plan production in the AAI field.

Soft architecture machine: the backbone of AAI

In this chapter, I created and presented another network that I added the publications, the books, the writers of the publications, as nodes, and the interactions among them as edges. I excluded all the fields and topics such as cybernetics, graph theory, etc. By doing this, I aimed to find the most effective publication through the network. According to the degree value of this network visualization, the most connected node of the network is *Soft Architecture Machine*. In this chapter, I will discuss the importance and effect of the *Soft Architecture Machine*, so the Architecture Machine Group. And, I will explain the secondary, tertiary, and quaternary important publications as well.

When we look at Figure 4.13, we can see some thick red connections between nodes. These thicknesses show the important intellectual bridges that convey the information of AAI to all nodes in the network. So, they have a big role in the network. When we look at the thick red connections, the core of the network is *Soft Architecture Machine* with its highest degree value, 35 interactions among the network nodes.

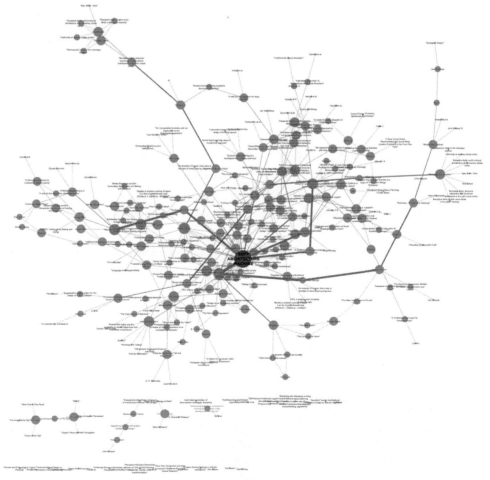

Figure 4.13 Citation and references among publications.

Negroponte, with his pioneering role in the Architecture Machine Group, led the development of the intellectual field between architecture and artificial intelligence. Negroponte's "Toward a Theory of Architecture Machine," *Soft Architecture Machine*, "Architecture-by–yourself: an experiment with computer graphics for house design," *URBAN5: A Machine that Discusses Urban Design* publications are exactly the works that correspond to the AAI.

In his book, Negroponte (1975) stated that he summarized the computer program status not technically, but philosophically. Because of this reason, in *Soft Architecture Machine*, there are lots of references to the important publications of AI leaders. Some of those are Warren McCulloch, John McCarthy, Marvin Minsky, Herbert Simon, Allen Newell, John von Neumann, Alan Turing, Oliver Selfridge, Seymour Papert, Noam Chomsky, and Ross Asby. Besides all these important actors, there are important references to some of the architects such as Buckminister Fuller, Christopher Alexander, Charles Eastman, William Mitchell, and more. Negroponte summarized all the related works between the field of artificial intelligence and architecture. So, this book became a seminal book.

The most important interactions that the book establishes are represented with the branches in the network. In Figure 4.13, we can see these three most important branches in the network with the red and thick connections between nodes. The first important branch includes *Algorithmic Aesthetics* (Stiny & Gips, 1978), *The Sciences of the Artificial* (Simon, 1969), and *Soft Architecture Machine* (Negroponte, 1975). The second branch includes *The Human Use of Human Beings* (Wiener, 1950), and *Notes on the Synthesis of Form* (Alexander, 1964). The third one includes *Heuristic Algorithms for Automated Space Planning* (Eastman, 1971b), "GSP: A System for Computer Assisted Space Planning" (Eastman, 1971a) publications. The main highway for information transmission among the network is these connections. All these branches are the connections among the cybernetics theory, shape grammar theory, and autonomous plan generation field. And, *Soft Architecture Machine* connects all these branches. For this reason, I named this section "Soft Architecture Machine: the Backbone of AAI."

The most important factor in the creation of this book is the Architecture Machine Group that Negroponte founded with Groisser. The strong interactions of this group with computer science have increased the intellectual power of Negroponte. It is clear that Negroponte has a large inclusive role in AAI, and therefore, the book *Soft Architecture Machine* is important for AAI.

I created the chord diagram of the interaction of each publication with references via each other in the R coding language to find important publications other than *Soft Architecture Machine* . I create a visualization of references. Figure 4.14 shows the list of publications within the AAI network and the reference relationship they have among them. If we check the publications' connections carefully, the most important ten nodes are : *Soft Architecture Machine, Notes on the Synthesis of Form, Algorithmic Aesthetics,* "Toward a Theory of Architecture Machines," "New generation of computer-aided design in space planning methods: A survey and a proposal," *SHAPE: Talking about Seeing and Doing, Perceptron, IMAGE: An Interactive Graphics based Computer System for Multi-constrained Spatial Synthesis, Heuristic Algorithms for Automated Space Planning,* and "Hybrid Evolutionary Algorithm applied to Automated Floor Plan Generation."

All these studies established this great intellectual AAI network with the references among them. Each of the studies has a unique quality that develops this intellectual AAI network. We can see that a great accumulation of knowledge has been hidden within this network for years. The AAI network looks like this in 2020. How it will be represented in the future will be determined by ongoing studies.

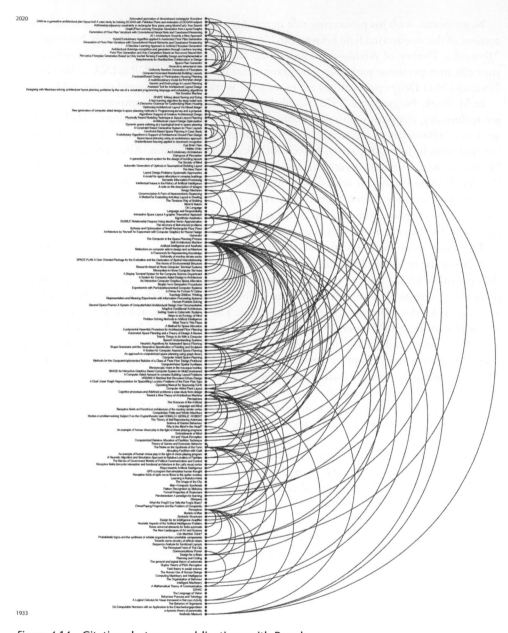

Figure 4.14 Citations between publications with R code.

What is next for AAI?

In this section, I will explain the chronological development of autonomous plan production methods in the AAI network. Figure 4.15 shows the publications made in the corresponding concepts in chronological order. In the 1940s, the concept of cybernetics first emerged, and we can see that studies in the field of artificial intelligence started in the 1940s. Similarly, the beginning of the studies on artificial neural networks coincides with the 1940s.

Figure 4.15 Chronological chart for the advances in the field of AAI (column y indicates the advances of the methods of AAI chronologically, column x indicates the dates).

Koopmans et al. (1957) stated that autonomous plan research started in the 1930s, but since I was able to reach only Buffa's (1955) text as the first source, autonomous plan production studies are seen as starting in the 1950s on the graph. When we look at the methods of autonomous architectural plan production on the graph, many methods started in the early 1950s. The most used method, graph theory, which started to be used in the 1960s, in the production of autonomous plan schemes, continues today. This is because space syntax can be explained easily with graph theory. However, as architects, we should ask ourselves the question whether space syntax is the only important concept in plan production. I would like to remind you that Minsky criticized Chomsky over syntax.

We can read from the below chart that the second most-used method is the constrained based method. Constrained-based studies started in the 1970s and the number of researches related to constrained-based studies increased between 2000 and 2010. Another important theory on plan scheme generation is shape grammars. Shape grammar theory has been used in numerous studies related to the autonomous plan layout generation after the 1970s. On the below graph, we cannot see so much density on shape grammar theory. I selected all the nodes in the social network in this study. Accordingly, the nodes have direct or indirect interactions with artificial intelligence or cybernetics. For this reason, I do not include all the publications on shape grammars. Instead, I selected the ones most related with the topic of AAI. The other method for the autonomous plan scheme generation is the expert system. We can see some examples of expert systems in the 2000s and Bayesian algorithms towards the 2010s. Starting since the 1970s, generative algorithms have been used for autonomous plan generation.

As you go to the right on the graph, we can notice an increase in the direction of y-axis. The reason for the increase is artificial neural networks, which are the most recent developments in the artificial intelligence field. Today most of the artificial intelligence algorithms develop over artificial neural networks. The most powerful feature of today's artificial neural networks (CNN, RNN, GAN, etc.) is its data processing power. Although the data inherent in the image information occupies a large area due to the color values and location values, the neural networks are highly developed in processing image data due to their processing power. The neural networks have enabled the architectural plan schemes, as a visual data type, to be processed easily. For this reason, we can see an increase in the graph. Autonomous plan production studies have been carried out using various artificial neural network algorithms. On the other hand, when we compare the studies in the past with today's studies on autonomous plan scheme generation, we can obtain quite high autonomous generated plan scheme qualities with the power of artificial neural networks.

The near future shows that we will use the neural networks for the production of autonomous plans. However, we know that the relationship between architecture and artificial intelligence is established not only with the plan scheme generation. So the question is what the next is. We can predict which algorithms will have the highest potential for autonomous plan generation. However, the question of what will be the new aim in the relationship between architecture and artificial intelligence is the most important.

Perhaps, past studies may offer a clue. Whatever is thought in the past, the same things are considered today. Only the methods are more advanced. Now, the methods that were used for an automated design in the past are outdated; but assertions, proposals, and thoughts are still up-to-date. So, the answer to what the next is will be together the past and today. Shortly, this AAI network will develop even faster. The current state of the AAI's network indicates that development will be most probably on the autonomous plan scheme generation field and artificial neural networks field.

When I look at the network, I can say that the Future is older than we thought. While looking at the recent studies we should also look at the studies in the past. When we check the projects in the architecture machine group, today most of those technologies are in our hands for our daily life uses. This is a big hint for the future. Looking at not only the recent works but also the previous studies will broaden our imaginations. So, we should always have a holistic viewpoint on history from past to future. Today's research will be tomorrow's daily life tools. So the network in this study shows a holistic viewpoint to the field of AAI which can give lots of hints for the future of AAI.

Bibliography

Al Banna, S., & Spillers, W. R. (Eds.) (1972). SOMI – An interactive graphics space allocation system, technical report, Departments of Civil Engineering and Graphics, Columbia University, May.

Alexander, C. (1964). *Notes on the synthesis of form* (Vol. 5). Cambridge, MA: Harvard University Press.

Alexander, C. (1979). *The timeless way of building* (Vol. 1). New York: Oxford University Press.

Alexander, C. (1984). "The Atoms of Environmental Structure." In *Developments in Design Methodology*, edited by Nigel Cross. New York: John Wiley and Sons, 1984.

Armour, G. C., & Buffa, E. S. (1963). A heuristic algorithm and simulation approach to relative location of facilities. *Management Science, 9*(2), 294–309.

Arvin, S. A., & House, D. H. (1999). Modeling architectural design objectives in physically based space planning. *Automation in Construction, 11*(2), 213–225.

Ashby, W. R. (1952). *Design for a brain*. Chapman and Hall.

Ashby, W. R. (1956). Design for an intelligence-amplifier. *Automata Studies, 400*, 215–233.

Banna, S. A., & Spillers, W. R. (1972). An interactive computer graphics space allocation system. In *Proceedings of the 9th Design Automation Workshop* (pp. 229–237). New York, NY, USA.

Bateson, G. (1979). *Mind and nature: A necessary unity* (Vol. 255). New York: Bantam Books.

Bateson, G. (2000). *Steps to an ecology of mind: Collected essays in anthropology, psychiatry, evolution, and epistemology*. Chicago, IL: University of Chicago Press.

Bayer, J., Bukhari, S. S., & Dengel, A. (2017). Floor plan generation and auto completion based on recurrent neural networks. In *2017 14th IAPR International Conference on Document Analysis and Recognition (ICDAR)* (Vol. 2, pp. 49–50). Piscataway, NJ: IEEE.

Birkhoff, G. D. (1933). *Aesthetic measure*. Cambridge, MA: Harvard University Press.

Brand, S. (Ed.). (1981). *Whole earth catalog: Access to tools*. New York: Point, Random House.

Buckminster Fuller, R. (1969). *Operating manual for spaceship earth*. New York: EP Dutton & Co. Available at http://www.bfi.org/node/422 (accessed 8 September 2009).

Buffa, E. S. (1955). Sequence analysis for functional layouts. *Journal of Industrial Engineering, 6*(2), 12–13.

Buffa, E. S. (1964). Allocating facilities with CRAFT. *Harvard Business Review, 42*(2), 136–159.

Chaillou, S. (2019). *AI+ architecture: Towards a new approach*. Cambridge, MA: Harvard University.

Chang, C. L., & Lee, R. C. T. (1972). *Problem-solving methods in artificial intelligence*. Nils J. Nilsson.

Chomsky, N. (1957). *Syntactic structures*. Berlin: de Gruyter Mouton.

Chomsky, N. (1959). On certain formal properties of grammars. *Information and Control, 2*(2), 137–167.

Chomsky, N. (2006). *Language and mind*. Cambridge: Cambridge University Press.

Das, S., Day, C., Hauck, J., Haymaker, J., & Davis, D. (2016). Space plan generator: Rapid generationn & evaluation of floor plan design options to inform decision making. *Proceedings of the 36th Annual Conference of the Association for Computer Aided Design in Architecture (ACADIA)* (pp. 106–115). Ann Arbor, MI.

Del Rio-Cidoncha, G., Martínez-Palacios, J., & Iglesias, J. E. (2007). A multidisciplinary model for floorplan design. *International Journal of Production Research, 45*(15), 3457–3476.

Demchak, B. (2002). *Cytoscape product roadmap*. Retrieved September 9, 2020, from https://cytoscape.org/roadmap.html

Deutsch, Karl W. (1963). *The nerves of government: Models of political communication and control*. Glencoe, IL: The Free Press of Glencoe, Collier-MacMillan.

Domingos, P. (2015). *The master algorithm: How the quest for the ultimate learning machine will remake our world*. New York: Basic Books.

Donath, D., & Böhme, L. F. G. (2008). Constraint-based design in participatory housing planning. *International Journal of Architectural Computing, 6*(1), 97–117.

Doulgerakis, A. (2007). *Genetic and embryology in layout planning.* Master of Science in Adaptive Architecture and Computation, University of London, 2.

Duarte, J. P. (2005). A discursive grammar for customizing mass housing: the case of Siza's houses at Malagueira. *Automation in Construction, 14*(2), 265–275.

Eames, C. (1954). "Letter to Ian McCallum, Esq. of the Architectural Review (London)," The Work of Charles and Ray Eames Collections of the Manuscript Division, Library of Congress, Box 218.

Eastman, C. M. (1969). Cognitive processes and ill-defined problems: A case study from design. In *Proceedings of the International Joint Conference on Artificial Intelligence: IJCAI* (Vol. 69, pp. 669–690). Washington, DC.

Eastman, C. E. (1971b). GSP: A system for computer assisted space planning. In *Proceedings of the 8th Design Automation Workshop* (pp. 208–220), New York.

Eastman, C. M. (1971a). *Heuristic algorithms for automated space planning.* Pittsburgh, PA: Institute of Physical Planning, Carnegie-Mellon University.

Eastman, C. M. (1972a). *Adaptive conditional architecture.* Pittsburgh, PA: Institute of Physical Planning, Carnegie-Mellon University.

Eastman, C. M. (1972b). *Automated space planning and a theory of design: A review.* Pittsburgh, PA: Institute of Physical Planning, Carnegie-Mellon University.

Eastman, C. M. (1972c). *General space planner: A system of computer-aided architectural design; user documentation.* Pittsburgh, PA: Institute of Physical Planning, Carnegie-Mellon University.

Eastman, C. M. (1973). Automated space planning. *Artificial Intelligence, 4*(1), 41–64.

Eastman, C. M. (2016). Requirements for men–machine collaboration in design. In W. Preiser (Ed.), *Environmental design research: Volume one–Selected papers* (pp. 396–413). New York: Routledge.

Eisenstadt, V., Langenhan, C., & Althoff, K. D. (2019). Generation of floor plan variations with convolutional neural networks and case-based reasoning-an approach for transformative adaptation of room configurations within a framework for support of early conceptual design phases. In *Proceedings of the 37th eCAADe and 23rd SIGraDi Conference – Volume 2* (pp. 79–84), University of Porto, Porto, Portugal.

Elezkurtaj, T. & Franck, G. (1999). Genetic algorithms in support of creative architectural design. In *European Computer Aided Architectural Design And Education,* 17 (pp. 645–651), September 15–17, 1999, Liverpool.

Elezkurtaj, T., & Franck, G. (2002). Algorithmic support of creative architectural design. *Umbau, 2,* 16.

Flemming, U. (1986). On the representation and generation of loosely packed arrangements of rectangles. *Environment and Planning B: Planning and Design, 13*(2), 189–205.

Flemming, U., Coyne, R., Glavin, T., & Rychener, M. (1986). A generative expert system for the design of building layouts. In D. Sriram & R. Adey (Eds.), *Applications of artificial intelligence in engineering problems.* Berlin: Springer. https://doi.org/10.1007/978-3-662-21626-2_66

Fortin, G. (1978). BUBBLE: Relationship diagrams using iterative vector approximation. In Proceedings of the *15th Design Automation Conference* (pp. 145–151), June 19–21, Las Vegas, NV.

Frazer, J. (1995). *An evolutionary architecture.* London: Architectural Association.

Friedman, Y. (1975). *Toward a scientific architecture.* Cambridge, MA: MIT Press.

Gero, J. S. (1973). A system for computer-aided design in architecture. In J. Vlietstra and R. F. Wielinga (Eds.), *Principles of Computer-Aided Design* (pp. 309–326). Amsterdam North-Holland Publishing Company.

Gips, J., & Stiny, G. (1975). Artificial intelligence and aesthetics. *IJCAI, 75,* 907–911.

Goldstine, H. H., Von Neumann, J., & Von Neumann, J. (1947). *Planning and coding of problems for an electronic computing instrument.* Princeton, NJ: The Institute for Advanced Study.

Goodfellow, I. (2016). *NIPS 2016 tutorial: Generative adversarial networks.* arXiv preprint arXiv:1701.00160.

Goodman, G. (2019). *A machine learning approach to artificial floorplan generation.* Theses and Dissertations—Computer Science. 89.https://uknowledge.uky.edu/cs_etds/89

Grason, J. (1970a). A dual linear graph representation for space-filling location problems of the floor plan type. In G. T. Moore (Ed.), *Emerging methods in environmental design and planning* (pp. 170–178), Cambridge, MA: MIT Press.

Grason, J. (1970b). *Methods for the Computer-Implemented Solution of a Class of "Floor Plan" Design Problems, unpublished Ph.D* (Doctoral dissertation, dissertation, Pittsburgh: Carnegie-Mellon University).

Grason, J. (1971). An approach to computerized space planning using graph theory. In *Proceedings of the 8th Design automation workshop* (pp. 170–178), New Jersey, USA.

Halpern, O. (2015). *Beautiful data: A history of vision and reason since 1945.* Duke University Press.

He, Y., Liang, J., & Liu, Y. (2017). Pervasive floorplan generation based on only inertial sensing: Feasibility, design, and implementation. *IEEE Journal on Selected Areas in Communications, 35*(5), 1132–1140.

Hebb, D. O. (1949). *The organization of behavior: A neuropsychological theory.* New York: John Wiley & Sons.

Hernandez, J. (2015). From the fun palace to the generator cedric price and the conception of the first intelligent building. *ARQ*, 90, 48–57.

Hinton, G. E., Osindero, S., & Teh, Y. W. (2006). A fast learning algorithm for deep belief nets. *Neural Computation, 18*(7), 1527–1554.

Holland, J. H. (1995). *Hidden order: How adaptation builds complexity.* New York: Perseus Books.

Hsu, Y. C. (2000). Constraint based space planning: A case study. *ACADIA Quarterly*, 19, 3, 2–3.

Hsu, Y. C., & Krawczyk, R. J. (2003). New generation of computer aided design in space planning methods–a survey and a proposal. In *Proceedings of the 8th International Conference on Computer Aided Architectural Design Research in Asia* (pp. 101–116), Bangkok Thailand.

Hu, R., Huang, Z., Tang, Y., van Kaick, O., Zhang, H., & Huang, H. (2020). *Graph2Plan: Learning floorplan generation from layout graphs.* arXiv preprint arXiv:2004.13204.

Huang, W., & Zheng, H. (2018). Architectural drawings recognition and generation through machine learning. In *Proceedings of the 38th Annual Conference of the Association for Computer Aided Design in Architecture* (pp. 18–20), Mexico City, Mexico.

Hubel, D. H. (1995). *Eye, brain, and vision.* New York: Scientific American Library/Scientific American Books.

Hubel, D. H., & Wiesel, T. N. (1960). Receptive fields of optic nerve fibres in the spider monkey. *The Journal of Physiology, 154*(3), 572–580.

Hubel, D. H., & Wiesel, T. N. (1962). Receptive fields, binocular interaction and functional architecture in the cat's visual cortex. *The Journal of Physiology, 160*(1), 106–154.

Hubel, D. H., & Wiesel, T. N. (1968). Receptive fields and functional architecture of monkey striate cortex. *The Journal of Physiology, 195*(1), 215–243.

Hubel, D. H., & Wiesel, T. N. (1970). Stereoscopic vision in macaque monkey: Cells sensitive to binocular depth in area 18 of the macaque monkey cortex. *Nature, 225*(5227), 41–42.

Hubel, D. H., & Wiesel, T. N. (1974). Uniformity of monkey striate cortex: A parallel relationship between field size, scatter, and magnification factor. *Journal of Comparative Neurology, 158*(3), 295–305.

Hummon, N. P., & Doreian, P. (1990). Computational methods for social network analysis. *Social Networks, 12*(4), 273–288.

Jo, J. H., & Gero, J. S. (1998). Space layout planning using an evolutionary approach. *Artificial Intelligence in Engineering, 12*(3), 149–162.

Johnson, T. E. (1970). *IMAGE: An interactive graphics-based computer system for multi-constrained spatial synthesis.* Cambridge, MA: Department of Architecture, Massachusetts Institute of Technology.

Julesz, Bela. (1995). *Dialogues on perception.* Cambridge, MA: MIT Press.

Kalay, Y., & Shaviv, E. (1979). A method for evaluating activities layout in dwelling units. *Building and Environment, 14*(4), 227–234.

Keatruangkamala, K., & Sinapiromsaran, K. (2005). Optimizing architectural layout design via mixed integer programming. In *Proceedings of the 11th International Conference on Computer Aided Architectural Design Futures* (pp. 175–184), Vienna, Austria.

Kepes, G. (1956). *The new landscape in art and science.* Chicago, IL: Paul Theobald & Co.

Kepes, G. (1995). *Language of vision.* Chelmsford, MA: Courier Corporation.

Koopmans, I. C. et al. (1957). Assignment problems and the location of economic activities. *Econometrica, 25*(1), January, 53–76.

Krawczyk, R. J., & Dudnik, E. E. (1973). Space plan: A user oriented package for the evaluation and the generation of spatial inter-relationships. In *Proceedings of the 10th Design Automation Workshop* (pp. 121–138), Portland, Oregon.

Krejcirik, M. (1969). Computer-aided plant layout. *Computer-Aided Design, 2*(1), 7–19.

LeCun, Y., Bottou, L., Bengio, Y., & Haffner, P. (1998). Gradient-based learning applied to document recognition. *Proceedings of the IEEE, 86*(11), 2278–2324.

Lettvin, J. Y., Maturana, H. R., McCulloch, W. S., & Pitts, W. H. (1959). What the frog's eye tells the frog's brain. *Proceedings of the IRE, 47*(11), 1940–1951.

Lewin, K. (1936). A dynamic theory of personality: Selected papers. *The Journal of Nervous and Mental Disease*, 84(5), 612–613.

Lewin, K., & Cartwright, D. (1951). *Field theory in social science.* New York: Harper & Row.

Li, S. P., Frazer, J. H., & Tang, M. X. (2000). A constraint based generative system for floor layouts. In *Proceedings of the Fifth Conference on Computer Aided Architectural Design Research in Asia* (pp. 441–450), Singapore.

Licklider, J. C. (1960). Man-computer symbiosis. *IRE Transactions on Human Factors in Electronics*, *1*, 4–11.

Licklider, J. C. R. (1951). A duplex theory of pitch perception. *The Journal of the Acoustical Society of America*, *23*(1), 147.

Lobos, D., & Donath, D. (2010). The problem of space layout in architecture: A survey and reflections. *Arquiteturarevista*, *6*(2), 136–161.

Lömker, T. M. (2006). Designing with machines: Solving architectural layout planning problems by the use of a constraint programming language and scheduling algorithms. In *Proceedings of the Dresden International Symposium of Architecture 2005* (pp. 225–229), Technische Universitaet Dresden, Germany.

Lynch, K. (1960). *The image of the city* (Vol. 11). Cambridge, MA: MIT Press.

Lynch, K. (1972). *What time is this place?* Cambridge, MA: MIT Press.

Lynch, K., & Licklider, J. C. R. (1954). *The letters between Lynch and Licklider.* Retrieved June 12, 2020, from https://dome.mit.edu/bitstream/handle/1721.3/35616/KL_002005.pdf? sequence=1

Marvin, M., & Seymour, A. P. (1969). *Perceptrons.* Cambridge, MA: MIT Press.

McCarthy, J. (1973a). A display terminal system for the computer science department Stanford University. *Artificial Intelligence Memo* No. 1436.

McCarthy, J. (1973b). Monopolies in home computer services Stanford University. *Artificial Intelligence Memo* No. 1428.

McCarthy, J. (1973c). Research aimed at home computer terminal systems Stanford University. Artificial Intelligence Laboratory Proposal to The National Science Foundation.

McCarthy, J. (1980). Circumscription: A form of non-monotonic reasoning. *Artificial Intelligence*, *13*(1–2), 27–39.

McCulloch, W.S. (1950). Why the mind is in the head? *Dialectica*, 4, 192–205.

McCulloch, W. S. (1956). Towards some circuitry of ethical robots. *Acta Biotheoretica*, 11, 147.

McCullouch, W. S. (1965). *Embodiments of mind.* Cambridge, MA: MIT Press.

McCulloch, W. S., & Pitts, W. (1943). A logical calculus of the ideas immanent in nervous activity. *The Bulletin of Mathematical Biophysics*, *5*(4), 115–133.

Medjdoub, B., & Yannou, B. (2001). Dynamic space ordering at a topological level in space planning. *Artificial Intelligence in Engineering*, *15*(1), 47–60.

Merrell, P., Schkufza, E., & Koltun, V. (2010). Computer-generated residential building layouts. In *ACM SIGGRAPH Asia 2010 Papers* (pp. 1–12), New York, United States.

Michalek, J., Choudhary, R., & Papalambros, P. (2002). Architectural layout design optimization. *Engineering Optimization*, *34*(5), 461–484.

Michell, W. J., Streadman, J. P., & Liggett, R. S. (1977). Synthesis and optimization of small rectangular floor plans. *Environment and Planning B*, *3*, 37–70.

Miller, W. R. (1970). Computer-aided space planning. In *Proceedings of the 7th Design Automation Workshop* (pp. 28–34), New York, United States.

Minsky, M. (1956a). *Heuristic aspects of the artificial intelligence problem.* Washington, DC: Armed Services Technical Information Agency.

Minsky, M. (1956b). Some universal elements for finite automata. *Shannon and McCarthy*, 34, 117–128.

Minsky, M. (1961). Steps toward artificial intelligence. *Proceedings of the IRE*, *49*(1), 8–30.

Minsky, M. (1974). *A framework for representing knowledge.* Cambridge, MA: MIT Press.

Minsky, M. (1982). *Semantic information processing.* Cambridge, MA: MIT Press.

Minsky, M. (1988). *Society of mind.* New York: Simon & Schuster.

Minsky, M. (2007). *The emotion machine: Commonsense thinking, artificial intelligence, and the future of the human mind.* New York: Simon & Schuster.

Minsky, M., & Selfridge, O. G. (1960). *Learning in random nets.* Vol. 46. MIT Lincoln Laboratory.

Minsky, M., & Papert, S. (1972). *Artificial intelligence.* Cambridge, MA: M.I.T. *Artificial Intelligence Memo* No. 252.

Minsky, M. L. (1967). *Computation.* Englewood Cliffs, NJ: Prentice-Hall.

Mitchell, W. (1972). Experiments with participation-oriented computer systems. *Design Participation*, 73–78.

Mitchell, W. J. (1970). *Computer-aided spatial synthesis.* Association.

Mitchell, W. J. (1970). A computer-aided approach to complex building layout problems. In *Proceedings of EDRA2 Conference* (pp. 391–397), October 1970, Pittsburgh, PA.

Mitchell, W. J. (1972). Simple form generation procedures. In *Proceedings of the International Conference on Computers in Architecture* (pp. 144–156), September 1972, University of York, UK.

Mitchell, W. J., & Dillon, R. (1972). A polyomino assembly procedure for architectural floor planning. In W. J. Mitchell (Ed.), *Environmental design: Research and practice*. Los Angeles, CA: University of California.

Negroponte, N. (1969). Toward a theory of architecture machines. *Journal of Architectural Education*, *23*(2), 9–12.

Negroponte, N. & Leon B. Groisser (1970). *URBAN5: A machine that discusses urban design*. Emerging Methods in Environmental Design and Planning, Gary T. Moore (Ed.), Cambridge, Mass: MIT Press.

Negroponte, N. (1975). *Soft architecture machines*. Cambridge, MA: MIT Press.

Newell, A. (1967). *Studies in problem solving; subject 3 on the crypt-arithmetic task*. Donald + Gerald = Robert.

Newell, A. (1971). *Speech-understanding systems: Final report of a study group*. Pittsburgh, PA: Carnegie-Mellon University.

Newell, A. (1982). *Intellectual issues in the history of artificial intelligence* (No. CMU-CS-82–142).

Newell, A., Shaw, J. C., & Simon, H. A. (1958). Chess-playing programs and the problem of complexity. *IBM Journal of Research and Development*, *2*(4), 320–335.

Newell, A., & Simon, H. A. (1961). *GPS, a program that simulates human thought* (No. P-2257). Santa Monica, CA: RAND Corporation.

Newell, A., & Simon, H. A. (1964). *An example of human chess play in the light of chess playing programs*. Pittsburgh, PA: Carnegie Institute of Tech.

Newell, A., & Simon, H. A. (1972). *Human problem solving*. Englewood Cliffs, NJ: Prentice-Hall.

Nilkaew, P. (2006). Assistant tool for architectural layout design by genetic algorithm. *Proceedings of the 11th International Conference on Computer Aided Architectural Design Research in Asia* (pp. 641–643), Kumamoto, Japan.

Nisztuk, M., & Myszkowski, P. B. (2019). Hybrid evolutionary algorithm applied to automated floor plan generation. *International Journal of Architectural Computing*, *17*(3), 260–283.

Papert, S. (1972). Teaching children thinking. *Programmed Learning and Educational Technology*, *9*(5), 245–255.

Papert, S., Solomon, C.,(1971). *Twenty things to do with a computer*. Report No. 1971 248. MIT AI Laboratory.

Pask, G. (1969). The architectural relevance of cybernetics. *Architectural Design*, *39*(9), 494–496.

Pertigkiozoglou, E. (2017a). 1976. Retrieved June 11, 2020, from https://medium.com/designscience/1976-22121bb498c4

Pertigkiozoglou, E. (2017b). 1973. Retrieved June 11, 2020, from https://medium.com/designscience/1973-a1b835e87d1c.

Price, C., & Littlewood, J. (1968). The fun palace. *The Drama Review: TDR*, *12*(3), 127–134.

Rocha, A. J. M. (2004). *Architecture theory, 1960–1980: emergence of a computational perspective* (Doctoral dissertation, Massachusetts Institute of Technology).

Rosenblatt, F. (1958). The perceptron: A probabilistic model for information storage and organization in the brain. *Psychological Review*, *65*(6), 386.

Rosenblueth, Arturo, et al. (1943). Behavior, purpose and teleology. *Philosophy of Science*, *10*(1), 18–24. doi:10.1086/286788.

Ruch, J. (1978). Interactive space layout: A graph theoretical approach. In *15th Design Automation Conference* (pp. 152–157), June 19–21, Las Vegas, NV.

Schuldenfrei, E. (2014). *The films of Charles and ray eames: A universal sense of expectation*. London: Routledge.

Selfridge, O. G. (1959). *Pandemonium: A paradigm of learning*. Mechanization of Thought Processes, NPL Symposium 10.

Selfridge, O. G. (1972). *A primer for FORTRAN IV: on-line*. Cambridge, MA: MIT Press.

Selfridge, O. G., & Neisser, U. (1960). Pattern recognition by machine. *Scientific American*, *203*(2), 60–69.

Shannon, C. E. (1948). A mathematical theory of communication. *Bell System Technical Journal*, *27*(3), 379–423.

Shaviv, E. (1986). Layout design problems: Systematic approaches. In *CAAD Futures Conference Proceedings* (pp. 28–52), Delft, the Netherlands.

Shi, F., Soman, R. K., Han, J., & Whyte, J. K. (2020). Addressing adjacency constraints in rectangular floor plans using Monte-Carlo Tree Search. *Automation in Construction, 115*, 103187.

Siklóssy, L., & Simon, H. A. (Eds.). (1972). *Representation and meaning: Experiments with information processing systems.* Upper Saddle River, NJ: Prentice-Hall.

Simon, H. A. (1957). *Models of man: Social and rational.* Hoboken, NJ: Wiley.

Simon, H. A. (1969). *The sciences of the artificial.* Cambridge, MA: MIT Press.

Simon, H. A. (1977). The structure of ill-structured problems. In H. A. Simon, *Models of Discovery* (pp. 304–325). Boston Studies in the Philosophy of Science, Vol 54. Dordrecht: Springer.

Skinner, B. F. (1938). *The behavior of organisms: An experimental analysis.* New York: Appleton-Century.

Skinner, B. F. (1965). *Science and human behavior.* New York: Simon & Schuster.

Sliavid, E., & Gali, D. (1984). A model for space allocation in complex buildings: A computer grapliic approach. *Build International, 7*, 439–518.

Stiny, G. (1981). A note on the description of designs. *Environment and Planning B: Planning and Design, 8*(3), 257–267.

Stiny, G. (2006). *Shape: Talking about seeing and doing.* Cambridge, MA: MIT Press.

Stiny, G., & March, L. (1981). Design machines. *Environment and Planning B: Planning and Design, 8*(3), 245–255.

Stiny, G., & Gips, J. (1971). Shape grammars and the generative specification of painting and sculpture. *IFIP Congress, 71*, 1460–1465.

Stiny, G., & Gips, J. (1978). *Algorithmic aesthetics: Computer models for criticism and design in the arts.* Berkeley, CA: University of California Press.

Teicholz, E. (1975). The computer in the space planning process. In *Proceedings of the 12th Design Automation Conference on Design Automation* (pp. 331–344), Boston, Massachusetts, USA.

Turing, A. M. (1938). On computable numbers, with an application to the Entscheidungsproblem: A correction. *Proceedings of the London Mathematical Society, 2*(1), 544–546.

Turing, A. M. (1948). Intelligent machinery. (Report No. 67 228). National Physical Laboratory.

Turing, A. M. (1956). Can a machine think. *The World of Mathematics, 4*, 2099–2123.

Turing, A. M. (2004). Computing machinery and intelligence (1950). In B. Jack Copeland (Ed.), *The essential turing: The ideas that gave birth to the computer age* (pp. 433–464). Oxford: Oxford University Press.

Upasani, N., Shekhawat, K., & Sachdeva, G. (2020). Automated generation of dimensioned rectangular floorplans. *Automation in Construction, 113*, 103149.

Uzun, C., Çolakoğlu, M. B., & İnceoğlu, A. (2020). GAN as a generative architectural plan layout tool: A case study for training DCGAN with Palladian Plans, and evaluation of DCGAN outputs. *A|Z ITU Journal of Faculty of Architecture, 17*, 185–198.

Vardouli T (2012). *Design-for-empowerment-for-design: Computational structures for design democratization.* PhD thesis, Massachusetts Institute of Technology, Cambridge, MA.

Vardouli, T. (2019). *Nicholas Negroponte: An interview.* Retrieved June 12, 2020, from https://openarchitectures.com/2011/10/27/an-interview-with-nicholas-negroponte/).

Von Neumann, J. (1951). The general and logical theory of automata. In L. A. Jeffress (Ed.), *Cerebral mechanisms in behavior: The Hixon Symposium* (pp. 1–41). New York: Wiley.

Von Neumann, J. (1956). Probabilistic logics and the synthesis of reliable organisms from unreliable components. *Automata Studies, 34*, 43–98.

Von Neumann, J., & Burks, A. W. (1966). Theory of self-reproducing automata. *IEEE Transactions on Neural Networks, 5*(1), 3–14.

Weinzapfel, G., & Negroponte, N. (1976, July). Architecture-by-yourself: An experiment with computer graphics for house design. In *Proceedings of the 3rd Annual Conference on Computer Graphics and Interactive Techniques* (pp. 74–78), New York, USA.

Wiener, N. (1950). *The human use of human beings: Cybernetics and society* (No. 320). Cambridge, MA: Da Capo Press.

Yamanaka, K., & Nakano, S. I. (2013). *Uniformly random generation of floorplans.* IEICE Trans. Inf. Syst., 99-D, 624–629.

Yoon K. B., (1992). *A constraint model of space planning.* Southampton: Computational Mechanics Publications.

Part 2
AI tools, methods, and techniques

5

Machine learning in architecture

An overview of existing tools

Ilija Vukorep and Anatolii Kotov

While there is a broad spectrum of architectural design and analysis methods, machine learning (ML) tools are filling a narrow niche commonly used by architects with affiliation to software and programming. While some bigger architectural offices are running a computational division, more common are smaller specialized independent teams that are engaged by architects, engineering and construction companies, designers, project developers, and authorities. This means that many ML tools are "pushed by the problem" and that they often serve as an interface to adjacent disciplines. Furthermore, these tools are used inside of project and research teams without being brought to the public.

One of the first architects to use ML for his work in 1992 was Bojan Baletic, currently professor for architecture at the University of Zagreb. His PhD thesis entitled "Information Codes of Mutant Forms" (Baletic, 1992) used a neural network to specify patterns in floor planning to help architects in their future planning. For his research, he used software called NeuroShell, from wardsystems.com, which nowadays is mostly used for financial forecasting.

The biggest group of artificial intelligence (AI) tools in architecture we can find is part of existing software solutions. They come as add-ons to parametric extensions of programs like McNeel Rhino 3D and Autodesk Revit. The next group is ML solutions developed as part of research work. These are characterized by very individual software solutions that deal with the individual research question and can only in very few cases be transferred to other problems. The other group contains self-standing software solutions in various areas of the architectural field, from VR to construction supervision. The last group includes all AI solutions inside CAD/BIM software for architects for solving specific functions.

In this article, we present short reviews and categorize the tools that are publicly available. Publicly available tools are those that can be downloaded and installed, e.g., food4rhino. com, autodesk.com, archicad.com, github.com, gitlab.com, and other sources. Next to a performance benchmark, we evaluate several functional quality categories such as usability, complexity, documentation, and target user group. As this article addresses ML in architecture, we emphasize the architectural point of view in the text. Sometimes, it is not possible to directly compare tools if they are solving different problems. An examination of robotic-AI tools (openAI- Robot Operating System – ROS and others) as well as topology analysis or optimization tools is not part of this paper.

Plug-in tools

In the field of architecture and design, most problems are a very unique combination of complexity and variety. It can be assumed that it is an almost impossible task to create a universal problem-solving instrument that will be applicable for each individual architect and designer. This leads to the case where architects/designers or IT departments in big studios are developing their own tools in-house. Such firms as Grimshaw Architects, Foster+Partners, UN Studio, and Zaha Hadid Architects are famous for their innovations in parametric design and its application. Historically, the use of scripting languages for diverse programs such as Autocad, Autodesk Maya, Rhino, and Microstation paved the path toward more sophisticated tools (beginning with Generative Components from Bentley's Microstation).

However, such a level of tools was not available for most of the architectural society. The development of plug-ins for CAD/CAM programs played a significant role in the democratization of ML tools applications in architecture. One of the best-known programs with such an ecosystem is Rhino by McNeel. It is popular not only for its performant non-uniform rational B-spline (NURBS) workflow (NURBS) is a mathematical model for the representation and generation of curves and surfaces) but also for its plug-in, Grasshopper, which is now an integrated part of the program and has been a great innovation by introducing a visual node programming approach and lowering the entry-level for the usage of complex parametric tools. Subsequently, the Dynamo plug-in in Autodesk Revit and Marionette in Vectorworks were created and conceptually offer some similar functionality.

Optimization solvers

Pioneered in 2010 by the Galapagos component in Grasshopper, a huge class of tools called "optimization solvers" began to be developed. These tools possess a variety of incorporated ML algorithms aimed to find the best solution for the required goal. The following sections will analyze the base concept of each and compare them in terms of performance and user experience.

Concept of optimization

The class of optimization solvers is perhaps one of the most intuitive tools in the whole palette of ML methods and is amazingly powerful. Usually, we start by defining the problem. For example, to create the highest possible building using a set of model parameters, such as the number and height of floors, the goal would be to maximize the height of the building. Therefore, the goal of the optimization solver will be to maximize height by changing the available parameters. By changing the number and height of the floors, the solver can maximize the height because there is a linear relationship between level count, floor and building height.

Such desired goals are called fitness functions and represent the space of potential combinations of parameters of the model with a value for each state. Maximizing or minimizing the output of the fitness function defines the fitness function for the solver. It could be maximizing the volume of buildings while minimizing construction costs or just minimizing the usage of the materials for the facade.

Fitness landscape and fine-tuning

To better understand fitness function, we refer to the fitness landscape to visually represent the search of the algorithm for some maximum or minimum. Although humans cannot

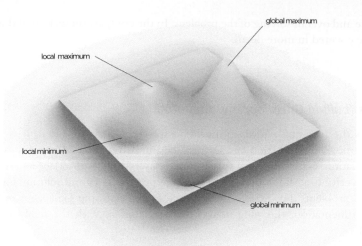

Figure 5.1 Visualization of a three-dimensional fitness landscape.

comprehend fitness landscapes of more than three dimensions, normally they are hypersurfaces in *n*-dimension space, where *n* is the number of goals. The properties of this landscape are crucial to the overall performance of the optimization solver. For instance, when the goal is to minimize the fitness function, it means searching for the global minimum on this hypersurface. If the slope is too high or too sharp, then it can lead to a situation where the algorithm cannot find the global minimum and is stuck in a suboptimal position or local minimum. This applies to many other fields of ML such as neural networks, etc. The problem formulation, definition of the goals, and variable parameters of the model directly form the potential fitness landscape. Some problems tend to create harder fitness landscapes while others are easier by being much smoother.

The countermeasure for getting in local minima is by fine-tuning the hyperparameters of a particular optimization solver, neural network, or other tool. However, we do not cover this aspect here as we are running all tools and solvers with their default values and parameters (Figure 5.1).

Single- or multi-goal problem definition

The usage of most optimization solvers is quite similar. It is required to set one or more target goals to be used as fitness functions. In addition, we can set some additional parameters that the solver can change in the process of optimization. Finally, it is required to set solving options, i.e., maximizing or minimizing for fitness function(s), possible time limitation, population parameters, thresholds for values, etc.

The fitness function can be a complex composition of other functions, and setting only one end goal will be a single-goal optimization or single-objective optimization (SOO) task because the output comprises only one value.

Optimization problems are often more complex and require more than one goal. For instance, we want to maximize the available commercial space of a building while minimizing its construction costs. This is a multi-goal optimization or multi-objective optimization (MOO) task because we have more than one goal.

Not all solvers support multi-goal optimization; thus, the excellent option is to combine goals into a single fitness function. Surprisingly, this can be even more efficient in terms of performance and overall solving of the problem. In the comparison section of this article, this issue will be covered in more detail.

Solvers

Galapagos (built-in Grasshopper v. 1.0.0007)

Galapagos is the first single-goal optimization solver by David Rutten. It is based on the genetic evolution representation and features an annealing solver. In testing, we have used genetic simulation. Galapagos has a very intuitive, user-friendly interface and is a quite complex and powerful tool. It is a built-in in Grasshopper and is a good solution for both simple and complex problems. For many architects and engineers using Galapagos in Grasshopper with its documentation, this plug-in was the first contact with the field of optimization (Figure 5.2).

Octopus (v. 0.4)

Octopus was created by Robert Vierlinger at the University of Applied Arts Vienna and Bollinger+Grohmann engineers. It features SPEA-2 (Zitzler, Laumanns & Thiele, 2001) and HypE algorithms (Bader & Zitzler, 2011) from ETH Zurich. The major difference from Galapagos is the implementation of multiple-goal search. It features a powerful interface for navigation through generations and a possibility to select desired goals, goal parameters, and

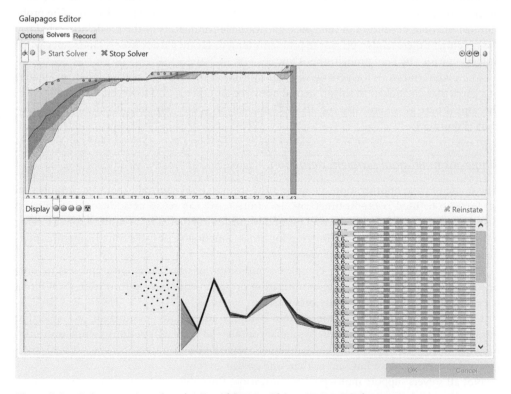

Figure 5.2 Galapagos interface by David Ruten, Rhino 3D/McNeel.

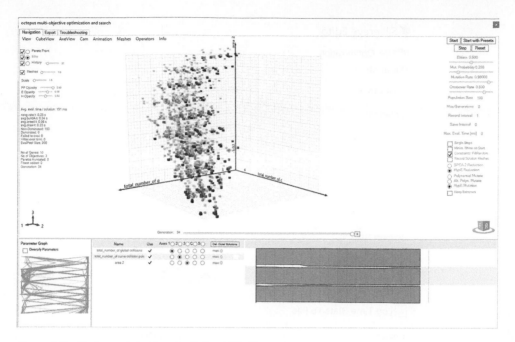

Figure 5.3   Octopus interface by Robert Vierlinger.

exact population members as a primary search sample as well as many other options. Surprisingly, with the latest release in 2016, it still has the best ability to control desired goals, limitations, and thresholds. This means control over which goal is more important for the final solution. With thresholds, it is possible to select target numeric domains or values for goals. The interface of the program offers many options while maintaining an intuitive way of displaying the space of solutions and other settings. The ability to manually select preferred objectives and values was not used in the comparison because it is a form of parameter fine-tuning (Figure 5.3).

SilverEye (v. 1.1.0)

Developed by Judyta M. Cichocka, Agata Migalska, Will N. Browne, and Edgar Rodriguez, SilverEye features single-goal optimization based on the particle swarm optimization (PSO) algorithm (Cichocka, Migalska, Browne & Rodriguez, 2017). User experience is good because the plug-in offers an intuitive minimalistic interface and excellent program stability. However, the interface only displays the current fitness value as a numeric value of graphs or complex 3D charts (Figure 5.4).

Wallacei (v. 2.6)

Wallacei is an optimization solver from the family of evolutionary optimization solvers and features single- and multi-objective optimization. It has an explicit user interface for the comparison of different generations, results, goals, etc. Despite the very advanced interface, it is not possible to affect the optimization process by selecting preferred values of goals like in Octopus. Nevertheless, it offers great opportunities for the analysis of the outcomes and has good program performance (Figure 5.5).

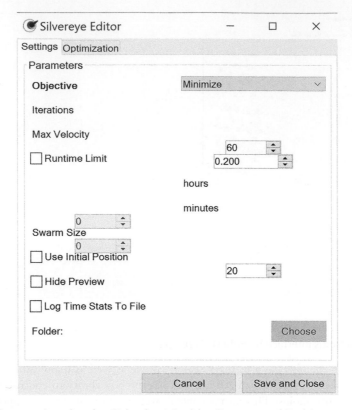

Figure 5.4 Octopus interface by Cichocka, Migalska, Browne, and Rodriguez.

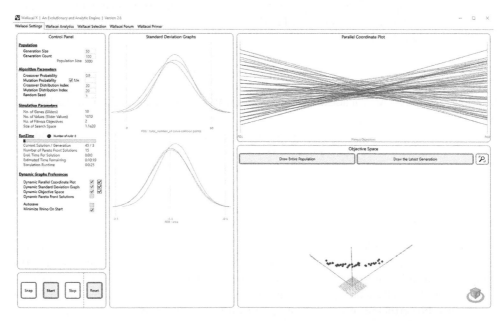

Figure 5.5 Wallacei interface by Mohammed Makki and Milad Showkatbakhsh.

Opossum (v. 2.0)

Opossum, by Thomas Wortmann, features model-based, gradient-free, and global optimization and uses the RBFOpt algorithm (Costa & Nannicini, 2018). There are also other available algorithms like NSGA-II that can be activated (Deb, Pratap, Agarwal & Meyarivan, 2002). The program performance is very stable, and it has a comprehensive list of available algorithms. Some problems of instability occurred during the process of the MOEA/D algorithm (Zhang & Li, 2007); however, this is a very capable tool overall due to the RBFOpt algorithm (Figure 5.6).

Optimus (v. 1.0.2)

Optimus was developed at the Chair of Design Informatics, TU Delft, and is an implementation of the self-adaptive differential evolution with ensemble of mutation strategies (jEDE) (Cubukcuoglu, Ekici, Tasgetiren & Sariyildiz, 2019). While the concept and performance of this solver are quite adequate, it lacks in user-friendliness. It does not use default "gene" components from the Grasshopper, and it is necessary to manually set up all ranges for variable parameters and the parameters themselves as well. Although this part can be automatized with Grasshopper or scripting, it is still not easy to use. Furthermore, Optimus uses the Hoopsnake plug-in to create the loops inside the Grasshopper. This could be a reason for the lack of stable results as the interface of Rhino/Grasshopper tends to freeze. Because Optimus is in fact a set of node components, there is no specified GUI.

Feature overview

Comparison

Because many of the solvers' authors are claiming that their solution is superior, we have created our own test bed in two particular problem subjects: architecture design (Task 1) and structural optimization (Task 2). The idea was to benchmark solvers on some close-to-real-life tasks instead of synthetic math problems. Therefore, this comparison does not cover all potential problem spaces. The fine-tuning of each of the optimization solvers can also dramatically vary the final results.

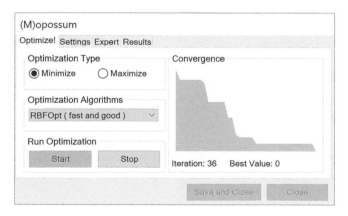

Figure 5.6 Opossum interface by Thomas Wortmann.

Table 5.1 Feature overview

Category/Plug-in	Galapagos	Octopus	Opossum	SilverEye	Wallacei	Optimus
Algorithms	GA	SPEA-2 HypE	MOEA/D NSGA-II NSPSO RBFMOpt CMAES RBFOpt	PSO	NSGA-II	jEDE
GUI	●	●	●	●	●	○
MOO	○	●	●	○	●	○
MOO Control	○	●	○	○	○	○
Visualization	●	●	●	○	●	○
Data Analysis	○	●	○	○	●	○

All optimization solvers were run with their default parameters with no parameter fine-tuning. The multi-goal definition was applied where possible; otherwise, all goals were summed in one single-goal fitness function. In the case of no default parameters, the parameters from the example files provided were taken (hardware configuration: Intel i7 9750H with 32 GB of RAM). Each solver ran three times for 30 minutes, and the best result was left for the comparison. The final chart illustrates the fitness/speed ratio: Lower/Faster is better.

Architecture design problem (Task 1)

The general goal was to maximize the area of circles while managing zero collision with each other and obstacles. Optimization objectives were to maximize the circle area, minimize the number of collisions, and minimize collision points (Figure 5.7).

Structural optimization problem (Task 2)

The general goal was to optimize the structural qualities of the roof-like form. The optimization objectives were to calculate surface area, energy, and mass (Figure 5.8).

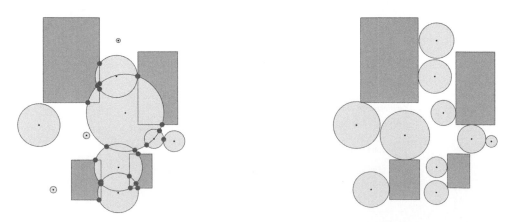

Figure 5.7 Left image with random initialization and right image with a possible solution.

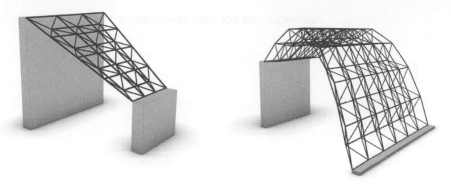

Figure 5.8   Left image with random initialization and right image with a possible solution.

Conclusion

The results of the comparison present an interesting picture of the solvers' performance. Tasks 1 and 2 have different fitness landscapes, and it can be clearly seen on the charts that most solvers fully solved the structural problem (Task 2) although some were not able to find the global optimum for the architectural design problem (Task 1). Figure 5.9 illustrates that even relatively simple tasks hold the potential for dead ends in local minima, and solvers simply cannot find a path toward the best solution. The structural problem (Task 2) shown in Figure 5.10 has a smoother fitness landscape; therefore, many solvers managed to find a global minimum. Most likely, the majority of the solvers can perform better, but that will require a fine-tuning of their parameters, which is outside the scope of this comparison. One specific characteristic of solvers is that they all start from random initial positions. This could potentially affect the results because some solvers can be "luckier" in their initial placement.

The best results were performed by Wallacei and Octopus in single-objective mode while second and third places are shared by Opossum SOO and MOO modes, respectively. Figure 5.11 depicts the overall performance of solvers across both tasks. The numerical data and rankings are shown in Table 5.2. Surprisingly, MOO versions of algorithms behaved worse than SOO versions. This result is quite intriguing because MOO methods are more advanced than SOO and should generally provide better solutions. This is possible via a superior understanding of the fitness landscape and the mutual influence of parameters on each other as well as other optimization techniques. However, this situation can also be fixed by fine-tuning the parameters. Detailed data for the performance and timings can be observed with charts and a table.

Interactive evolution

Biomorpher (v. 0.7.0)

The Biomorpher plug-in was developed by John Harding and Cecilie Brandt-Olsen. It is a very unique plug-in, featuring the interactive evolution of a genetic system. This system offers very similar functionality to the previously mentioned Octopus but with a few more functions. It is possible to selectively target goals whether they should tend to be maximized or minimized. However, the most interesting option is to manually select one of

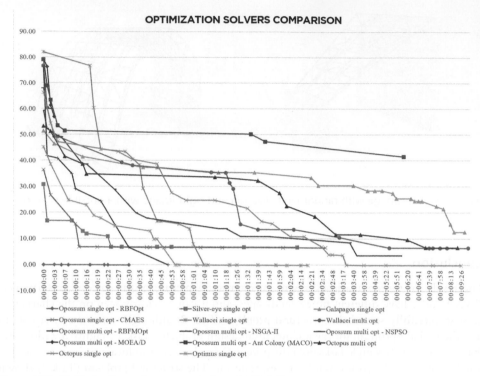

Figure 5.9 Optimization solvers comparison for Task 1.

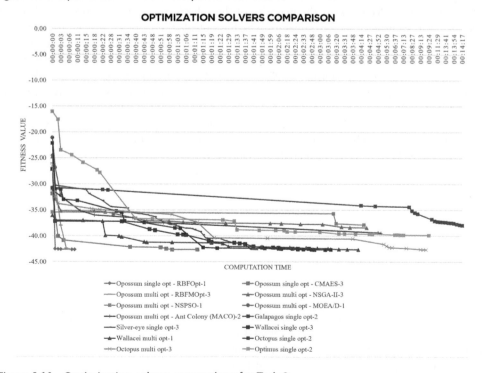

Figure 5.10 Optimization solvers comparison for Task 2.

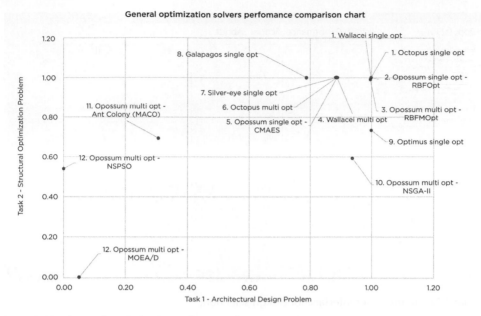

Figure 5.11 General optimization solvers performance comparison.

Table 5.2 Comparison of function output and normalized values

Solver name	Task 1		Task 2		Average performance normalized	Rank
	Fitness	Normalized	Fitness	Normalized		
Galapagos single opt	12.57	0.7886	−42.62	1.0000	0.8943	8
Octopus multi opt	6.66	0.8871	−42.62	1.0000	0.9435	6
Octopus single opt	−0.11	0.9998	−42.62	1.0000	0.9999	1
Opossum multi opt— Ant Colony (MACO)	41.5	0.3067	−39.43	0.6939	0.5003	11
Opossum multi opt—MOEA/D	56.9	0.0501	−32.2	0.0000	0.0251	13
Opossum multi opt—NSGA-II	3.61	0.9379	−38.39	0.5941	0.7660	10
Opossum multi opt—NSPSO	59.91	0.0000	−37.84	0.5413	0.2706	12
Opossum multi opt—RBFMOpt	0	0.9980	−42.53	0.9914	0.9947	3
Opossum single opt—CMAES	6.6	0.8881	−42.62	1.0000	0.9440	5
Opossum single opt—RBFOpt	−0.08	0.9993	−42.62	1.0000	0.9997	2
Optimus single opt	−0.12	1.0000	−39.85	0.7342	0.8671	9
Silvereye single opt	6.8	0.8847	−42.62	1.0000	0.9424	7
Wallacei multi opt	6.49	0.8899	−42.62	1.0000	0.9449	4
Wallacei single opt	−0.11	0.9998	−42.62	1.0000	0.9999	1

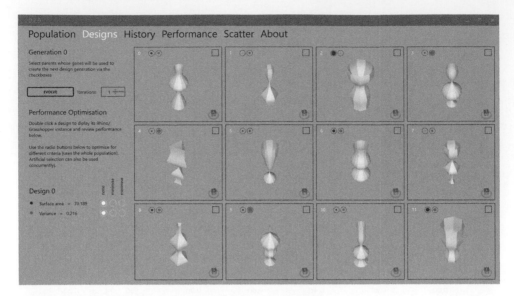

Figure 5.12 Biomorpher interface for design selection.

the "designs" as a target example for the evolution solver, which allows operation without a fitness function. Then, select the best form or best solution and the next generations will be automatically more similar to the selected solutions. Given such interesting and unique qualities, the Biomorpher can be used not only just for optimization purposes but for even more general ones like an artistic search of form and shape.

However, it is important to realize that the installation of this plug-in can cause conflict with the Octopus, causing the Rhino to crash. In this case, the solution is to move the Biomorpher out of the plug-in folder of the Grasshopper and into the other directory (Figure 5.12).

General-purpose machine learning

This type of components and plug-ins features general-purpose algorithms and tools. This includes simulation tools for artificial neural networks (ANNs or NNs), support vector machines (SVMs), tools for nonlinear optimization, clustering, tools for working with graphs and fields, regression problems, etc. It is important to mention that the efficient usage of these methods requires at least a minimum understanding of the math behind those concepts. Otherwise, in most cases, the result may be simply noninterpretable.

Architectural applications of these advanced methods are very different due to the vast generality of the given methods. However, those applications should be mentioned: optimization of geometry elements/geometry elements' interrelations; agent simulation; form-finding; general parameter optimization; etc. For instance, optimization is performed on building form/position with respect to sunlight and form-finding of the facade elements to reduce the number of unique elements. The potential problems are very much the same as the problems explained in the Section "Optimization solvers." Indeed, different fields of ML are sharing a lot of common problems and concepts. One other potential application may be the advanced statistical analysis of the given data, e.g., analysis of the data on the materials, prices, and components to optimize the production costs of a building.

Due to the high variety, complexity, and general approach of these tools, there is no good way to make an objective comparison. The other reason is that they offer different options for the same structures. For instance, the exact available NN activation function may vary. Therefore, a brief overview of the capabilities of these plug-ins is the best option; however, if you want to implement state-of-the-art AI/ML models or do deep ML, then it is better to go for other tools (refer to Section "Research Tools").

Owl (v 2.1.0.0)

Owl was created by Mateusz Zwierzycki and is partially based on the Accord.NET library. The plug-in offers an extensive set of components for the creation, editing, and tuning of neural networks, tools for reinforcement learning, supervised and unsupervised learning, K-means clustering, Markov chain, etc. One of the best things about Owl is that you can create highly customized neural networks inside the Grasshopper interface while maintaining the relative simplicity of the definition.

Lunchbox (v. 2018.11.16)

Created by Nathan Miller, Lunchbox features a simple implementation of neural networks, where you cannot change the fundamental structure of the net; thus, it is always a network with one hidden layer. The other limitation is that the activation function is limited only to sigmoid. There are also components for regression problems, e.g., linear, nonlinear, multivariate, and logistic. Lunchbox also has useful tools for clustering and classification such as Gaussian mixture, K-means, and Naive Bayes. Except for traditional ANN with one hidden layer, Lunchbox also provides the Hidden Markov model and Restricted Boltzmann Machines.

Octopus (v. 0.4)

Along with an already analyzed genetic optimization solver, Octopus features tools for the modeling of ANN and SVM. The interesting point here is the availability of algorithms for ANN optimization: NEAT algorithm and RPROP, as an optimization algorithm, which can be more efficient than standard SGD (Mosca & Magoulas, 2015). Furthermore, it features tools for KD-Tree operations.

Dodo (v. 0.3)

Created by Lorenzo Greco, Dodo features an extensive set of components for ANN, supervised and unsupervised learning, scalar, vector, and tensor field operations, various mathematical operations (e.g., Fourier transform), graph operations, etc. Although other plug-ins like, for instance, Owl are also featuring unsupervised learning, only Dodo has the opportunity to model self-organizing map (SOM) and elastic network. The last one can solve complicated problems such as the traveling salesman problem (Table 5.3).

Table 5.3 Comparison table of features and properties

Category / Plugin	Owl	Dodo	Lunchbox	Octopus
ML Model types	Multilayer NN; Reinforcement Learning	Multilayer NN; SOM; Elastic Network	Multilayer NN; Markov Model; RBM	Multilayer NN; SVM
Activation function(s)	Linear; Relu; Sigmoid Tanh	Sigmoid; Bipolar Sigmoid	Sigmoid	Steepened Sigmoid
Algorithms	BackProp	BackProp	BackProp	NEAT; RPROP
Adv. math tools	○	●	○	○
Graphs	○	●	○	○
Clustering	●	●	●	●

Research tools

In scientific papers that deal with architectural topics, we can observe a very diverse and rather incomparable variety of used tools. Still, we can make some grouping of those most connected to programming languages and embedded systems.

Python

Although Python is the most widely used programming language in scientific circles, the observation of recent papers shows that it is not predominant in the architectural field. Still, its capacities are special when it is connected to common architectural designing parametric tools such as the Grasshopper for Rhino or the Dynamo for Revit, and it can be enormously powerful when it comes to transforming numerical results into geometrical form. As GH for Rhino does not have the capability to use external libraries, mostly the add-ons like GH_CPython or GHPython remote are establishing this connection. Here is an overview of the most used Python-based libraries and frameworks:

- SciPy is a basis for several other ML libraries like scikit-learn and provides many tools for numerical operations, statistics, and linear algebra.
- PyTorch (Facebook), Tensorflow (Google), and Theano are the most used ML frameworks and have different programming approaches, GPU-support, and performance levels depending on the task.
- Jupyter Notebook is a very widely used web application on top of the local Python installation that is showing the code result live, visualizing the output, and sharing and publishing it simply. It is usually installed as part of the Anaconda package that provides consistent library management and software distribution.

Environments

Toolkits with a predefined set of environments are very helpful when we need to quickly test our code/algorithm and do not want to waste time building up sandboxes with some properties. Due to standardized environments and a very easy setup, usage is primarily for testing and benchmarking algorithms, for example:

- OpenAI—Gym (Elon Musk as founder and Microsoft) is a toolkit for reinforcement learning with predefined worlds and is used mostly in research. The programming language is Python; it can run multiple instances simultaneously; and it has a great interface for importing other environments.
- Gridworld is a concept for very simple but quickly and easily adaptable environments and is used for testing reinforcement learning algorithms. It is a matrix with defined space, walls, or any other objects with specific properties. Researchers can build their own gridworld that responds to their own research question. There are a lot of predefined gridworld environments and some are also based on the openAI-Gym framework.
- Unity3D is a game engine that has supported ML development since 2017. The program has highly developed setup possibilities for environments and players, a good incorporated physics-engine, and very practical perception tools. It is used for reinforcement learning projects as well as for the creation of synthetic data. It also has predefined environments and agent packages. The main programming language is C# although using Python is also possible. An environment export to openAI Gym is available.

Instruments for numerical routines

There are several strong mathematical-based software packages that deal with matrix operations and huge numbers and that can perfectly serve for ML purposes. Most specific ML procedures can be done directly without having additional libraries in between. There are several benefits in using libraries for numerical routines, e.g., real understanding of the operations that are lying behind most ML procedures and often speedier results. Examples of packages that have been used in recent papers include the following:

- Matlab is a predominant complete software package with everything needed from heavy calculations to representation, its own programming language, IDE, ML-Toolkits, and ML-Environments. It is widely used at universities in teaching and research as well as in industrial projects.
- Octave is an open-source package similar to Matlab and very much compatible with it. There are some differences in the software syntax that makes it problematic for bigger projects. Because it is free, it is a good program for learning to program numerical routines toward Matlab.

Other tools

Semantic and graph tools as AGraphML connect semantic-building information from various CAD and BIM tools and use them for spatial and topological analysis as well as for design work (Ayzenshtadt et al., 2015).

Built-in tools

In contrast to graphic software packages that have some ML tools as content-based filling, select and sharpen functions, major software packages for architects lack built-in tools with special abilities based on ML. The trend is toward self-standing solutions, e.g., Autodesk invested in seven construction start-ups in 2017 and 2018 (3DR, io, Project Frog, Manu-factOn, Assemble Systems, eSub, Rhumbix), and acquired Assemble Systems and PlanGrid. Autodesk has also signed a definitive agreement to acquire "BuildingConnected," and big software companies are getting more involved in the direct construction field (Smith, 2019). This is not surprising as building design becomes digital; it is only a matter of time before Autocad and Nemetschek will be involved in the direct production of buildings.

Revit refinery

Refinery is a very good example of a tool made for normal users that was developed for Dynamo for Revit where it still plays a role. It implements the best practices of the widely known GA-tools in Grasshopper. It has objective selection and a preview of the genotypes and supports minimization and maximization of the fitness function. It is interesting to observe how this tool will transform in the future development of Revit, especially as an optimizer inside a BIM environment with all the metadata these files contain.

Further development

The past ten years of development of software used by architects represent an incredible leap toward systems that can help designers deal with complex forms and invent new shapes and sustainable constructions with the help of ML tools. The most presented approaches are conceptually using old and good methods of ML but we are missing implementations and new approaches in architecture, engineering and construction (AEC) fields. This can be several things: deep geometrical learning, reverse engineering tools from geometry to parametric models, better human interfaces, AR/VR-aided modeling, profound predictions based on big data analysis of architectural-related data, and much more. We can speculate what kind of company approaches (Autodesk with internal research departments vs. McNeel with its community-driven research) will have bigger success in the future. Because we see the fast pace of technology development, there is no solid way to predict the evolution of AI tools in architecture.

References

Ayzenshtadt, V., Langenhan, C., Bukhari, S. S., Althoff, K. D., Petzold, F., & Dengel, A. (2015, December). Distributed domain model for the case-based retrieval of architectural building designs. In *Proceedings of the 20th UK Workshop on Case-Based Reasoning: UK Workshop on Case-Based Reasoning (UKCBR-2015), located at SGAI International Conference on Artificial Intelligence, December* (pp. 15–17). Cambridge, UK.

Bader, J., & Zitzler, E. (2011). HypE: An algorithm for fast hypervolume-based many-objective optimization. *Evolutionary Computation, 19*(1), 45–76.

Baletic, B. (1992). Information codes of mutant forms. In *Proceedings of the ECAADE 1992 Conference* (pp. 173–186). Barcelona, Spain.

Cichocka, J. M., Migalska, A., Browne, W. N., & Rodriguez, E. (2017, July). SILVEREYE: The implementation of particle swarm optimization algorithm in a design optimization tool. In *International Conference on Computer-Aided Architectural Design Futures* (pp. 151–169). Springer, Singapore.

Costa, A., & Nannicini, G. (2018). RBFOpt: An open-source library for black-box optimization with costly function evaluations. *Mathematical Programming Computation, 10*(4), 597–629.

Cubukcuoglu, C., Ekici, B., Tasgetiren, M. F., & Sariyildiz, S. (2019). OPTIMUS: Self-adaptive differential evolution with ensemble of mutation strategies for grasshopper algorithmic modeling. *Algorithms, 12*(7), 141.

Deb, K., Pratap, A., Agarwal, S., & Meyarivan, T. A. M. T. (2002). A fast and elitist multiobjective genetic algorithm: NSGA-II. *IEEE Transactions on Evolutionary Computation, 6*(2), 182–197.

Mosca, A., & Magoulas, G. D. (2015). Adapting resilient propagation for deep learning. *arXiv preprint arXiv:1509.04612*.

Smith, S. (2019). AECCafe Industry Predictions for 2019– Part 2. *AECCafe*. https://www10.aeccafe.com/blogs/aeccafevoice/2019/01/17/aeccafe-industry-predictions-for-2019-part-2/

Zhang, Q., & Li, H. (2007). MOEA/D: A multiobjective evolutionary algorithm based on decomposition. *IEEE Transactions on Evolutionary Computation, 11*(6), 712–731.

Zitzler, E., Laumanns, M., & Thiele, L. (2001). SPEA2: Improving the strength Pareto evolutionary algorithm. *TIK-report, 103*.

6

Fundamental aspects of pattern recognition in architectural drawing

Tyler Kvochick

To understand how artificial intelligence might be applied to architecture, first we must understand what artificial intelligence is. In *Artificial Intelligence: A Modern Approach*, Russell and Norvig (2019) write that an artificially intelligent computer system would need six capabilities in order to pass a total Turing test:

1 Natural Language Processing: to communicate in [human language]
2 Knowledge Representation: to store what it knows or hears
3 Automated Reasoning: to use stored information to answer questions and draw new conclusions
4 Machine Learning: to adapt to new circumstances and to detect and extrapolate patterns
5 Computer Vision: to perceive objects
6 Robotics: to manipulate objects and move about

The authors, by their own admission, are interested in "…general principles of rational agents and on components for constructing them" (Russell and Norvig, 2009). Therefore, in order to understand how artificial intelligence relates *specifically* to architecture, it is constructive to reinterpret these capabilities as domain-specific proficiencies. If we are to recognize something that approximates artificial intelligence in architecture, we can speculate on what this hypothetical system might be capable of ahead of time. In this context, we will define the domain of architecture to be the analysis and generation of design documents for buildings that are intended for construction. Within this constraint, we might recast Russell and Norvig's capabilities as follows:

1 Natural Language Processing: to relate character strings in design documents to domain-specific concepts or physical entities
2 Knowledge Representation: to understand how construction conditions are represented in design documents
3 Automated Reasoning: to infer what is not represented by what is represented
4 Machine Learning: to map different representations of a category of objects to real or categorical values in the presence of noise

5   Computer Vision: to analyze digital imagery
6   Robotics: to drive computer numerically controlled fabrication, robotic drawing, and robotic buildings

Natural language example

If we had a computational system that possessed the capabilities above, we could reasonably expect to see it step through a causal chain that takes an architectural document as input, and

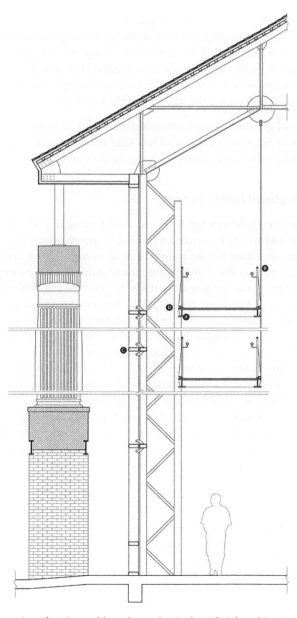

Figure 6.1   A wall section that is read by a hypothetical artificial architectural intelligence.

proposes options for updating that same document as output. For example, take the adjacent architectural detail drawing (Figure 6.1).

> Because this feature (A) is represented with a heavy line weight, I know it must be cut by the imaginary plane of this drawing. Because it is underneath the deck, and because gravity's vector is down in the plane of the drawing, I know that it must structurally support the thing above. Because there is a cable attached to the other side (B), the compression member must not be enough to support this feature. Because I see no other methods of support, the capacity of the compression member plus the capacity of the tensile member must need to be equal to the maximum load on the walkway. There is a large curtain wall (C) covering the entire face of the building to the left of the feature, which means that the walkway will be visible from the outside of the building. Because, at the last meeting with the client, they said they did not like "glass boxes," I think we may need to change the exterior envelope system. The exterior envelope is backed by a vertical truss system (D) that is also what the compression member (A) is supported by. Changing the exterior envelope would require changing this truss system, which will impact the structure of the walkway.

While computational systems may not articulate their logic in human language, this hypothetical system would need to be capable of this kind of inference to come to a similar conclusion about the structural implications of changing the envelope.

Artificial architectural intelligence

This example provides guidelines for how one might recognize an artificial architectural intelligence (AAI). AAI would be capable of taking in specifications of a problem for which to generate a design, searching for the information necessary to form criteria of what makes a good or bad design, parsing that information into domain-specific concepts, applying those concepts to the context of the input specifications to generate a possible solution, evaluating the established criteria, and making updates to the generated solution to more closely satisfy the criteria. This specification of capabilities, though only qualitative, is necessary to put the current work in the context of a more significant goal. The history of artificial intelligence is full of examples of iterative, minor developments that appear to suddenly solve some intractable problem. Chess, free-form image recognition and Go have all been said to be impossible for a computer system to solve for years until, one day, they are solved. The design of buildings, structures, and cities is likely on this same trajectory.

Any application that possesses the capabilities of AAI would be an amazing technical feat, but the implementation will be made of evolutionary updates to contemporary work that rests on relatively simple mathematical bases of information theory, belief updating, and the manipulation of multi-dimensional mathematical objects.

Coding

There are minor differences between the way contemporary machine learning techniques are applied to typical datasets and the way they are applied to the domain of architecture. However, the field of artificial intelligence (of which machine learning is a more strictly defined subfield) is based on the study of *information* in the fundamental, mathematical sense. Anything that can be construed as information is a potential subject for analysis with the tools of machine learning. As with most fields of technology and business, the production, exchange, and consumption of architectural documents happen or can happen digitally. This digitization means that almost every aspect of the practice of architecture can be manipulated by machine learning models.

In the practice of architecture, drawings are legally binding documents between the architect, owner, and contractor (Architects, n.d.a). Drawing sets also form a repository of project information from the general appearance of an architectural work to the exact dimensions and numerical specifications of the materials that should be used to execute it. When all of these things are digitized, either directly from software or indirectly through digital photography, they become information.

To understand how architectural production can be subsumed into machine learning, we must first understand how drawings carry information. In *A Mathematical Theory of Communication*, Claude Shannon describes the mathematical definition of information as follows:

> These semantic aspects of communication are irrelevant to the engineering problem. The significant aspect is that the actual message is one selected from a set of possible messages…. If the number of messages in the set is finite then this number or any monotonic function of this number can be regarded as a measure of the information produced when one message is chosen from the set, all choices being equally likely.
>
> *(Shannon 1948)*

In architectural production, we will assume one drawing constitutes one of Shannon's "messages." We will also conflate drawings and images as the sparse, vector formats that constitute a digital drawing, such as scalable vector graphics (SVG) (Editors, n.d.), are rendered to images for human interpretation. We will assume that the pixels in the drawings with which we are working can hold one byte of information, or 2^8 bits, and that these bits are used to represent values in the range:

$$\left[\frac{0}{255}, \frac{255}{255}\right]$$

Or 256 unique values. This is enough to represent an example of an architectural message: a plan drawing (Figure 6.2).

To return to Shannon's definition of information from the above, how does one measure the amount of information here? To do this, we must determine "the number of messages in the set." The drawing above has spatial dimensions of 1024×1024 pixels. Combined with the bit depth defined above, the number of possible images in the space, and one of the possible measures of information, is 256^{1024^2}. This specific value is not as interesting or useful as a general measure of the information content of architectural drawing. To find this, we could say that, in general, the information content is produced from the following:

1 $|S|$: The number of symbols from which to choose (here, one of the 256 values for pixel brightness).
2 w: The spatial width of the drawing as a number of pixels.
3 h: The spatial height, also in pixels.

So in general, the formula for finding the information content of a drawing would be:

$$I = |S|^{w \times h}$$

Under this definition, all the images below have the same information content. Of course, this is one particular definition of the term *information*, but an important definition to consider.

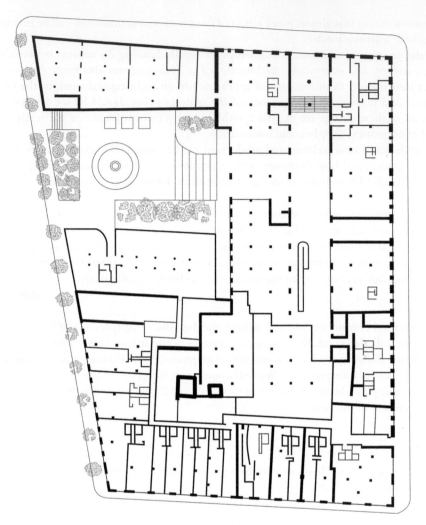

Figure 6.2 Westbeth artist's housing, and Richard Meier architects: examples of architectural symbols.

The goal of engineering a communication channel, from a telegraph wire to a fiber-optic network, is to be able to transmit architectural drawings, phone calls between friends and family, and pictures of cats all with the same fidelity. But, this does not comprise information with a domain-specific meaning.

The question then becomes: If communication theory gives us a way to measure what we might call zeroth-order information (information without meaning), how does one measure something meaningful?

An alphabet of architectural drawing

One of the key assumptions necessary to Shannon's definition of information is the ability to identify the term S, the alphabet of symbols that are transmitted across a wire and assembled into messages which may or may not have meaning in human consumption.

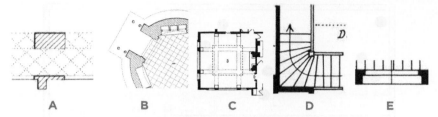

Figure 6.3 Architectural symbols: examples of architectural symbols. A: column; B: door; C: room; D: stair; and E: window.

In general human language, this is fairly easy. All human languages are made of collections of symbols identifiable to the populations that use that language. If these symbols are graphical, it is possible to find examples of encoding them in as few as 3×4 binary pixels (Coyove, n.d.). In architectural design, it is not as easy to identify what exactly constitutes a "symbol." While there are guidelines for typical symbols (Architects, n.d.a), they are not always adhered to. This is not necessarily a bad thing. It is advantageous, even, to have some level of indeterminacy to allow for creativity in the use of all languages, whether that language is Japanese, English or architectural drawing. So how would one establish an architectural alphabet in the presence of this indeterminacy? This turns out to be exactly the *raison d'être* for machine learning.

To measure the information content of a drawing, we assumed that a drawing can be represented as a grid of pixels where each pixel has only one of the 256 brightness values. If we take a drawing as the graphical analog of a sentence (or series of sentences), then we are trying to identify the letters and words. We could recursively define the drawing to be made of many drawings each with a width and height less than or equal to the width and height of the enclosing drawing or $w_s \leq w_D, h_s \leq h_D$.

Each of the images in Figure 6.3 is an example of a potential letter in an alphabet of drawing. Each is a drawing in its own right but expresses a complete, if disjoint, architectural entity such as a door, window or stair. Each exists in a space of similarly represented entities without ever being exactly the same.

At this level of information, it is necessary to go beyond arithmetic or combinatorial measures of information to develop an understanding of semantic meaning. To do this, contemporary machine learning allows us to simply collect examples of architectural symbols which we would like to be able to identify and retrain a state-of-the-art classification network on them. Understanding how this works first requires a basic level of understanding of the general mathematical principles of pattern recognition.

Bayesian reasoning

One of the practices of pattern recognition is to mathematically encode how one establishes an initial probability of the occurrence of some known pattern and then updates that prediction based on the acquisition of new evidence. Arguably the most significant rule of this practice is Bayesian reasoning.

Bayesian reasoning is based on a simple rule devised by Thomas Bayes and was first published in 1763 (Mathematics, n.d.a). The rule can be expressed symbolically as:

$$p(x \mid y) = \frac{p(y \mid x) p(x)}{p(y)}$$

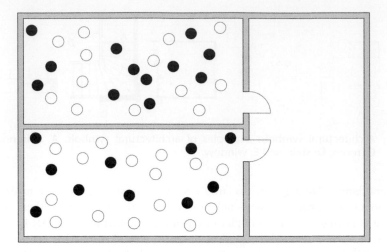

Figure 6.4   Upper and lower rooms of white and black seat.

In a nutshell, this is an algebraic statement that describes how to update the prior probability $p(x)$ that one assigns to some uncertain event x after taking into account some new evidence y which was unknown at the time of assigning $p(x)$. We could translate from the algebraic expression into English as follows:

The probability of seeing x after seeing the new evidence y is proportional to the probability of seeing y if we had already known that x was true, times the initially assigned probability of ever seeing x, divided by the initially assigned probability of ever seeing y.

Since this English translation is, amazingly, even less clear than the algebraic expression, we will use the diagram below to illustrate this relationship. The simplest example that can be used to demonstrate the usefulness of Bayes' rule has two degrees of freedom, both of which can take on two values. In this example, we will use colors: white w and black b; and rooms: upper u and lower l (Figure 6.4).

Imagine rearranging a selection of black and white seats from the upper and lower rooms in the simple plan into the third room (say, for a special event) but with the restriction that the seats must be put back into the room where they started. While rearranging the seats, you are interrupted by a call from the catering company. When you return to setting up the seats, you cannot remember from which room you selected the last seat to mark it for return at the end of the night. How do you decide which room was more likely?

Bayes' rule is meant for exactly this condition, when one is *reasoning under uncertainty*. If you were to pick randomly, there are only raw prior probabilities based on the proportions of the colors of seats in each room, which were conveniently recorded before setting up for the event.

There are 50 total seats.

$$(12+13)+(10+15)=50$$

There are 25 each in either room, so the prior probability of either room is 0.5.

$$p(u)=\frac{25}{50}=p(l)=0.5$$

Twenty-two out of 50 seats are black, so $p(b) = 0.44$, and 28 out of 50 seats are white, so $p(w) = 0.56$.

$$p(b) = \frac{12 + 10}{50} = 0.44$$

$$p(w) = \frac{13 + 15}{50} = 0.56$$

If you had to choose a room at this point, the best bet is to just pick upper or lower randomly because both are equally likely. This situation is the most uncertain that one can be in. However, if you take into account the color of the seat in question (which you observe to be white), you now have a new bit of information. At this point, Bayes' rule becomes useful! If you pick the lower room to focus on, you can now see if the odds have increased or decreased in its favor. Again, this question can be formulated in English as follows:

What is the probability that the seat came from the lower room, given that you know the seat is white? And algebraically as:

$$p(l \mid w) = \frac{p(w \mid l) p(l)}{p(w)} = \frac{\dfrac{15}{25} \cdot \dfrac{25}{50}}{\dfrac{28}{50}} = \frac{0.6 \cdot 0.5}{0.56} = 0.53$$

Since we started with a probability of the lower room at 0.5 and since probabilities must sum to 1, then the odds have risen in favor of the lower room and, correspondingly, have fallen in favor of the upper room. This makes the best chance at returning the seats correctly to mark the unknown seat for the lower room.

The application of Bayesian reasoning in contemporary machine learning follows directly from this simple example. In the case of designing a neural network to identify several classes of architectural symbols such as columns, doors, windows, stairs, and rooms, we would first

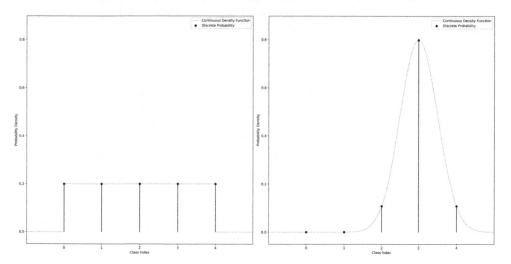

Figure 6.5   The intended effect of training: transition from uniform probability over all classes to maximal probability over the correct class.

design the network to output a prior probability of $\frac{1}{5}$ or a uniform distribution over the five possible classes that an image could be assigned. Upon passing the image to the network, we now have new information, namely the pixel values of the image, and we can update the probability that the image belongs to one of the five classes based on that new information (Figure 6.5).

Tensors

The term tensor comes from William Rowan Hamilton's work on describing three-dimensional rotation mathematically which he accomplished with a concept that he called quaternions. To Hamilton, the tensor was a term that "stretched" the quaternion (Hamilton, n.d.). Throughout the 19th century, several special cases of tensor were used to describe physical phenomena such as stress and deformation (Mathematics, n.d.b). On the more modern usage of the term, Taha Sochi (2017) writes: "A tensor is an array of mathematical objects (usually numbers of functions) which transforms according to certain rules under coordinates change."

There are many good references on tensor algebra and calculus such as the Sochi text. But we can examine some key principles here.

Space

Tensors create a precise mathematical language for describing the physical world. We describe tensors as having a number of "dimensions" in the same way that we say that we live in three-dimensional space. When we express a physical quantity such as force, for instance, we can express it as a three-dimensional quantity. This is a kind of arrow in space with three components relative to a chosen coordinate system.

In a simplified physical system consisting of an apple sitting on a table, there is a vector that is pointing down everywhere that corresponds to acceleration due to gravity. This has three components $[x, y, z]$. It is well known that physical force is the product of mass and acceleration: $F = ma$. Since the apple has mass M, we can multiply $M \cdot [x, y, z]$ and find the force vector on the table due to the apple.

Coding

The number of dimensions that can be represented with tensors can go far beyond what is familiar in the physical world, however. In machine learning, tensors are used to express everything. A simple example is known as one-hot encoding where we have some number of things to encode, such as the letters "a" through "z." Since we know that there are 26 letters, we can code each letter in a word as a 26-dimensional vector where the number of that letter (a: 0, b: 1, …, z: 25) is set to 1.0 and every other dimension is set to 0. This may sound inefficient, but it allows new abilities like being able to express a word as a rank-2 tensor of $n \times 26$ elements, where n is the length of the word (Figure 6.6).

Because tensors can subsume complex, nonscalar data such as alphabets and physical relationships into a data type with a defined algebra and calculus, they are an ideal mathematical object to express nonlinear relationships, such as the relationship between a collection of pixels and the semantic label of "door/not door." The numeric values are able to carry data, while the indices of the tensor and the functions between them define how much each dimension affects the others.

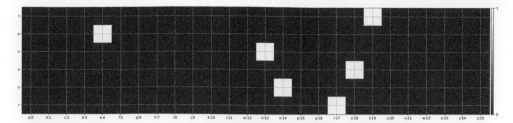

Figure 6.6   The string "tensor" one-hot-encoded and rendered as an image.

Application scenario

Suppose that you work for Opening Day Door Company and that you wanted to create an application that was capable of reading architectural plans to count up how many doors there are so that you can estimate how much an architect's door order will cost them. Although building information models are capable of producing this information directly, standard contracts still assume that two-dimensional drawing sets form the "instruments of service" of a building project and require extra exhibits, otherwise (Architects, n.d.b). Furthermore, all structures that were designed before the advent of three-dimensional modeling are documented in drawing sets and many contemporary practices continue to rely on the production of two-dimensional drawings to deliver their services. Thus, the application of computer vision models to architectural drawings remains an important practical application of contemporary artificial intelligence to the design and construction of buildings.

In order to read these drawings without machine learning, one would have to express qualities that indicate "doorness" in a drawing as some arithmetic or Boolean combination of pixel values. Take the three images of door symbols below (Figure 6.7).

In order to define discrete rules based on these examples, we could start by dividing the drawings into grids and finding common factors of each of our examples within those grids.

In the three examples, A and B have some feature in the middle left grid square, C has feature in the lower middle square, and all three have some feature in the middle right square. So we might derive a filter for "doorness" that takes these into account, and represent our analysis as pixel values like in Figure 6.8.

We could then preprocess input images by downsampling them at a similar ratio to the 3×3 grids here and take a majority vote of the pixels to determine if the grid square should be white or black. We could then perform a Boolean "and" between these filters at every location in an input image and, where the result is "true," we say that we have found a door. We could go a step further and weight the results more strongly on filters A and B since our data show that those filters are more common than C.

But what happens when we encounter a new door with a previously unseen symbol and our filter doesn't react strongly enough? What happens if a section of a plan that is actually representing a window closely matches our filter and the program matches very strongly on an incorrect part of the plan? We will have found failure modes of our application that lead to over- or undercounting of the number of doors in the plan, and our estimate for the architect will be wrong.

The solution of machine learning was created to solve this exact problem: when a program is easier to express by example rather than by enumerating rules. Rather than having to examine examples and try to use them to establish the decision paths of whether a data point fits

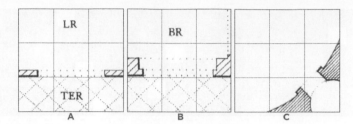

Figure 6.7   Examples of door symbols broken down into simpler grids.

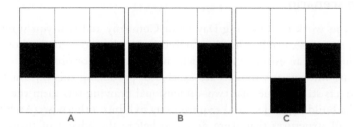

Figure 6.8   Manually filtering images by filling in simple grids with values that approximate the symbols.

into a certain class or not, machine learning is designed to create hundreds or thousands or more decision paths in a program. Then, in the process of training, these paths are reinforced or suppressed based on how well they allow the transformation from input to label.

Training a model

Data

Data are arguably the most important aspect of training a machine learning model. Training a model is effectively a kind of "programming with data." In order to train a drawing-reading machine learning model, we can present it with examples of the architectural symbols which we would like to be able to recognize in drawings, such as the previously seen five classes of door, window, stair, room, and column. We can pair each input image with an extra five bits of information that is used to one-hot-encode the labeled class in a five-dimensional tensor. The training data are typically split into at least two subsets with the largest proportion used for training and the smaller proportion withheld from training to be used for validation to ensure that the model is not just memorizing values that work only for the training data (Figure 6.9).

Hundreds or thousands of examples in each category must be collected in order to appropriately describe the possible values that represent these categories. The process of collecting data is also a notoriously easy way to bias the training of a model if the dataset does not sample uniformly from the real distribution of values or has many more samples of one class than another.

Datasets for common vision tasks such as ImageNet (Deng et al. 2009) or COCO (Lin et al., 2014) are often comprised of tens of thousands or millions of images organized into thousands of categories.

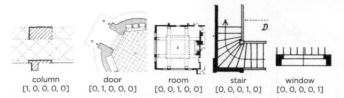

Figure 6.9 An example dataset of architectural features for classification and one-hot-encoded labels.

Preprocessing

Preprocessing prepares the data for the model and may optionally mutate the data in some way in an effort to make the model that is being trained generalize better than seeing the raw data. Typical preparation steps include normalizing the data to a known numeric range or resampling to a size that is appropriate for the model that is being used. The optional mutations can include random flipping, rotation, and cropping as well as affine transformations such as shearing and scaling.

Nascent approaches to preprocessing include the application of model that has been trained to augment data in ways that are more effective than hard-coded random flips and rotations (Zoph et al., 2019).

Model

The model is typically the component that gets the most attention in deep learning. AlexNet, ResNet, Inception, and GPT-2 are all examples of specific model architectures. The model is a series of transformations on the data. Rather than pairing data with explicitly defined functions as is typical in software development, the model is a kind of program that progressively transforms the input data in stages known as layers. A layer is itself just a kind of software module. For vision models, one of the basic building blocks is a convolutional layer. A simple convolutional layer can be specified by a collection of weights (also called filters or kernels), a collection of biases, a stride, and a padding. Each of these is expressed as a tensor. A simplified two-dimensional case could pair an input image with one channel with known weights such as the Sobel operator (Nixon and Aguado, n.d.) in order to perform edge detection. These weights are then convolved, or multiplied and summed at many locations, with the input, and then optionally normalized to produce the output of this layer. This output can then be fed into the next layer in a recursive structure (Figure 6.10).

Contemporary vision models can contain hundreds of layers like this and others for particular types of transformation such as resampling to different sizes, only allowing particular numerical values through, and randomly dropping outputs.

Loss function

To determine the performance of the model, its output is compared to a target value using a loss function. Loss functions need to be paired specifically with models as not all loss functions are defined over the output range of the model. For instance, binary cross-entropy must be paired with a model that can only output in the range $[0, 1]$ as that is equivalent to BCE's domain.

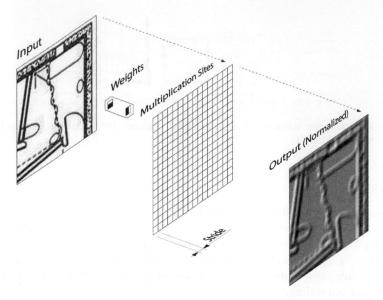

Figure 6.10 Conv_diagram: simplified diagram of a 2D convolution.

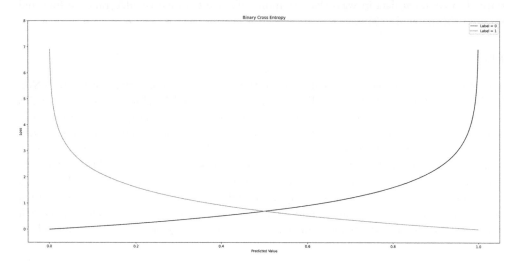

Figure 6.11 Plot of the values of binary cross-entropy with the intended label equal to zero or one.

Binary cross-entropy is defined as follows:

$$bce(y, \hat{y}) = -\left[y\log(\hat{y}) + (1 - y)\log(1 - \hat{y}) \right]$$

Here, y represents the true label, and $\hat{y}$ represents the model's prediction (Figure 6.11).

Binary cross-entropy is useful because it produces very large loss values when the prediction is very far off and very small values when the prediction is close to the intended label. The rate of change of binary cross-entropy also decreases as a model moves from very wrong predictions to better predictions, which creates loss signals that prompt decreasing updates to the model weights. This allows training to proceed quickly in the early stages and more slowly in later stages as the model performances increases.

Back-propagation

Back-propagation is a way of taking the value produced by the loss function and attributing how much of that loss came from each part of the model. The algorithm has a long history and a complex derivation, but it amounts to an iterative application of the chain rule from differential calculus to each layer of a model in order to assign a rate of change, or gradient, of the loss to that stage of the model, with respect to the input data for which that loss was generated.

An excellent overview of the history and technical details of back-propagation can be found in Jurgen Schmidhuber's *Deep Learning in Neural Networks: An Overview* (Schmidhuber, 2015). The article that is commonly credited with popularizing the approach in contemporary machine learning is Rumelhart et al. (1986).

Optimization

Once back-propagation has been used to attribute the rate of change of the output to each tensor that comprises the model, an optimizer can be used to update the weights in the model in a way that will reduce the loss at the next iteration. There are many different optimizers that are used in contemporary machine learning practices, such as ADAM, AdaGRAD, and stochastic gradient descent (SGD). An empirical comparison of many different optimizers can be found in *On Empirical Comparisons of Optimizers for Deep Learning* (Choi et al., 2019). SGD is one of the most commonly applied optimizers. Its name refers to moving the model weights in the direction pointed by the gradient that was found through back-propagation where the data point that produced the loss is selected randomly in order to avoid taking computationally infeasible derivatives of the thousands or millions of training examples.

The loop

All of these components are combined into a system that resembles the diagram below (Figure 6.12).

For each subset of the data (known as a batch) that is pulled from the dataset, the whole system completes one forward and one backward pass of the model. After seeing every batch from the dataset, the model is said to have completed one epoch of the training loop. The number of epochs that is required varies but, if it gets too large, can result in over-training where a model can start to overfit to the data in the dataset and not generalize well to unseen examples or applications that take in new data.

For the small dataset trained on here, we used ~200 examples of each of the five classes trained over 20 epochs in batches of 16 using SGD to optimize DenseNet121 (Huang, Liu, and Weinberger, 2017). The loss graph from training shows the model nearing convergence (loss values very near 0) over the course of training, though the sporadic increases and decreases throughout training suggest that collecting more data or using more augmentation techniques could improve model performance (Figure 6.13).

At each epoch, we validate the model performance on a withheld subset of ~20 examples of each class that are always seen in the same order so that we can compare the loss values between epochs. Again, this shows an improvement over the course of training, though the

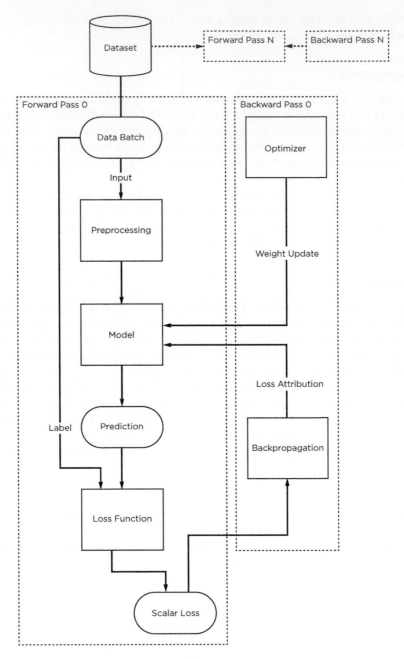

Figure 6.12 Process diagram of a training sequence.

repeating pattern suggests endemic characteristics of the data that could be examined to draw out the features that are and are not being generalized well by this model and dataset. And the single large spike shows an instance of an update to the model from one batch degrading performance at the next batch which was subsequently accounted for (Figure 6.14).

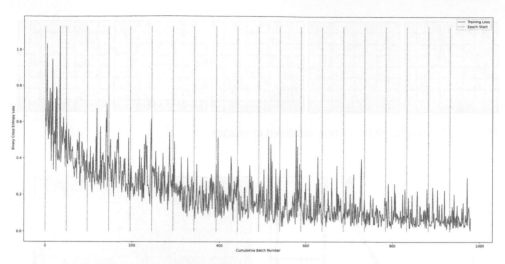

Figure 6.13 A plot of DenseNet121 loss over time in training to recognize architectural symbols.

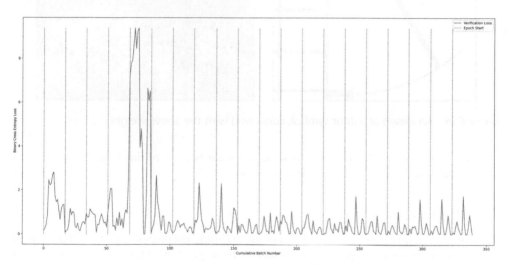

Figure 6.14 A plot of DenseNet121 loss over time in validation on withheld examples of architectural features.

What does a model learn?

Weights

The cumulative effect of training on models can be examined by extracting the weight tensors of layers of the network and rendering them as images. In the examples below, the 64 weights of the first convolutional layer of DenseNet121 are rendered at epochs 0, 2, 4, 8, and 16. The effect of the propagation of early, large losses can be seen the sudden transition from purely random weights at epoch 0, to weights with definite (if difficult to describe) structure,

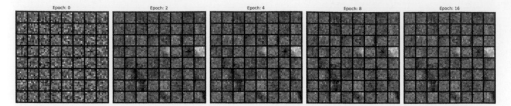

Figure 6.15   Weights of DenseNet, rendered as images.

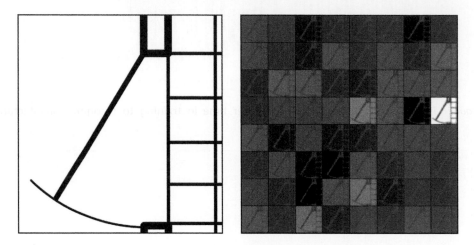

Figure 6.16   An image of a door symbol, convolved with the above weights.

which is then changed slowly in the subsequent epochs because of the decreasing loss signal as the model progressively improves (Figure 6.15).

Output of intermediate layers

If we use the weight tensors that result from this training and convolve them manually with one of the verification images, we can visualize one stage of the internal transformations of the data inside the trained model (Figure 6.16).

Even this small collection of weights shows diversity in the transformations that are learned by the network. In the collection of convolution results, there are many variations of edge detection, inversion, blurring, contrast enhancing, and so on. This representational power is multiplied across the number of layers and weights in each of those layers, throughout the depth of the network. This representational power is what allows deep neural networks to learn semantically meaningful mappings of domain-specific training data. This mapping is subsequently what enables the application of machine learning models to reading architectural drawings for practical and theoretical applications.

Conclusion

We have speculated on what artificial intelligence applied to the domain of architectural design might be capable of. We have also examined the mathematical bases and the practical implementation of these bases in solving a real task that is important to the domain of architecture. Finally, we have examined what this "learning" amounts to in real effects on a neural network. Though this does not apparently approach the six identifying capabilities from which we started, it does make significant progress toward one of them: machine learning as a tool for recognizing domain-specific symbols in the presence of noise. The tools and information to do this are now widely available and are beginning to be applied in commercial products.

How close are we to AAI?

How close are we to the earlier example of a computational system that is capable of reading an architectural drawing, reasoning through its aesthetic and performative characteristics, and proposing changes to that drawing? Closer than it seems. Contemporary deep-learning models that have been applied to the domain of architectural design are capable of generating visually realistic drawings and reasoning through their adjacency implications (Nauata et al., 2020), and even reasoning about spatial conditions between perspective and orthographic projections (Eslami et al., 2018). None of these approaches are based on encoding tomes of architectural knowledge into computer programs, but are instead based on the same mathematical bases we laid out here: information theory, iterative updates to statistical models, and manipulation of higher-order mathematical objects.

The bitter lesson

In *The Bitter Lesson*, Richard Sutton writes:

> …the human-knowledge approach tends to complicate methods in ways that make them less suited to taking advantage of general methods leveraging computation. There were many examples of AI researchers' belated learning of this bitter lesson, and it is instructive to review some of the most prominent.
>
> *(Sutton, n.d.)*

Sutton goes on to describe how, in the strategy games chess and Go, early research in the application of artificial intelligence to these domains focused on building domain-specific models into the programs. That is, domain experts tried to recreate in a program how human experts thought the games should be played. Ultimately, in both cases, more general computational methods with no domain-specific model were far more successful, especially in the case of AlphaZero (Silver et al., 2018), which, in a matter of days, taught itself to be superior to any human player and to past artificially intelligent programs in chess, shogi, and Go.

This begs the question: Will there be a deep understanding of architectural theory, drawing, formal analysis, geometry, construction, and social and cultural values built into this "artificial architectural intelligence" by architects, engineers and builders? Or are there simple computational methods that ultimately will be discovered and have enough processing power put behind them to generalize to any task?

I think it is safe to say that there will be nothing special about the future applications of artificial intelligence to architecture. The human brain, for instance, does not seem to have an intrinsic model of architectural theory, aesthetics, and so on. Any model that is able to approximate the six capabilities described here will still be based on information in the sense of *A Mathematical Theory of Communication*, updating predictions based on new data, and the efficient manipulation of high-dimensional encodings of those data. Those who are engaged in the design and construction of buildings will need to become well-versed in these fundamental aspects if they are interested in participating in the future application of artificial intelligence to the built environment.

References

Architects, The American Institute of. n.d.a. "A201–2017 General Conditions of the Contract for Construction." https://www.aiacontracts.org/contract-documents/25131-general-conditions-of-the-contract-for-construction.

———. n.d.b. "E203–2013 Instructions." https://contractdocshelp.aia.org/Get_Document_Answers/Document_Instruction_Sheets/By_Series/E-Series/E203-2013.htm.

Choi, Dami, Christopher J. Shallue, Zachary Nado, Jaehoon Lee, Chris J. Maddison, and George E. Dahl. 2019. "On Empirical Comparisons of Optimizers for Deep Learning." http://arxiv.org/abs/1910.05446.

Coyove. n.d. "Pixii." https://github.com/coyove/Pixii.

Deng, J., W. Dong, R. Socher, L.-J. Li, K. Li, and L. Fei-Fei. 2009. "ImageNet: A Large-Scale Hierarchical Image Database." In *CVPR09: 2009 IEEE Conference on Computer Vision and Pattern Recognition* (pp. 248–255), Miami, FL.

Editors, W3C. n.d. "Scalable Vector Graphics (Svg) V2." https://svgwg.org/svg2-draft/Overview.html.

Eslami, S. M. Ali, Danilo Jimenez Rezende, Frederic Besse, Fabio Viola, Ari S. Morcos, Marta Garnelo, Avraham Ruderman, et al. 2018. "Neural Scene Representation and Rendering." *Science* 360(6394): 1204–1210. https://doi.org/10.1126/science.aar6170.

Hamilton, William Rowan. n.d. "ON Quaternions, or on a New System of Imaginaries in Algebra." Edited by David R. Wilkins, *The London, Edinburgh and Dublin Philosophical Magazine and Journal of Science*. https://www.maths.tcd.ie/pub/HistMath/People/Hamilton/OnQuat/OnQuat.pdf.

Huang, Gao, Zhuang Liu, and Kilian Q. Weinberger. 2017. "Densely Connected Convolutional Networks." In *2017 IEEE Conference on Computer Vision and Pattern Recognition (CVPR)* (pp. 2261–2269), Honolulu, Hawaii, United States.

Lin, Tsung-Yi, Michael Maire, Serge Belongie, James Hays, Pietro Perona, Deva Ramanan, Piotr Dollár, and C. Lawrence Zitnick. 2014. "Microsoft Coco: Common Objects in Context." Lecture Notes in Computer Science, 740–755. https://doi.org/10.1007/978-3-319-10602-1_48.

Nixon, Mark S., and Alberto S. Aguado. n.d. "Sobel Edge Detection." https://www.sciencedirect.com/topics/engineering/sobel-edge-detection.

Mathematics, Encyclopedia of. n.d.a. "Bayes, Thomas." http://encyclopediaofmath.org/index.php?title=Bayes,_Thomas&oldid=39173.

———. n.d.b. "Tensor Calculus." https://encyclopediaofmath.org/wiki/Tensor_calculus.

Nauata, Nelson, Kai-Hung Chang, Chin-Yi Cheng, Greg Mori, and Yasutaka Furukawa. 2020. "House-Gan: Relational Generative Adversarial Networks for Graph-Constrained House Layout Generation." http://arxiv.org/abs/2003.06988.

Rumelhart, Hinton, David E. 1986. "Learning Representations by Back-Propagating Errors." *Nature*. 323: 533–536. https://doi.org/10.1038/323533a0.

Russell, Stuart, and Peter Norvig. 2009. *Artificial Intelligence: A Modern Approach*. 3rd ed. Upper Saddle River, NJ: Prentice Hall Press.

Schmidhuber, Jürgen. 2015. "Deep Learning in Neural Networks: An Overview." *Neural Networks* 61 (January): 85–117. https://doi.org/10.1016/j.neunet.2014.09.003.

Shannon, Claude E. 1948. "A Mathematical Theory of Communication." *The Bell System Technical Journal* 27 (3): 379–423. http://people.math.harvard.edu/~ctm/home/text/others/shannon/entropy/entropy.pdf.

Silver, David, Thomas Hubert, Julian Schrittwieser, Ioannis Antonoglou, Matthew Lai, Arthur Guez, Marc Lanctot, et al. 2018. "A General Reinforcement Learning Algorithm That Masters Chess, Shogi, and Go Through Self-Play." *Science* 362 (6419): 1140–1144. https://doi.org/10.1126/science.aar6404.

Sochi, Taha. 2017. *Principles of Tensor Calculus.* CreateSpace. https://isbnsearch.org/isbn/ 9781974401390

Sutton, Richard S. n.d. "The Bitter Lesson." http://www.incompleteideas.net/IncIdeas/BitterLesson. html.

Zoph, Barret, Ekin D. Cubuk, Golnaz Ghiasi, Tsung-Yi Lin, Jonathon Shlens, and Quoc V. Le. 2019. "Learning Data Augmentation Strategies for Object Detection." http://arxiv.org/abs/1906.11172.

7

AI as a collaborator in the early stage of the design

Sam Conrad Joyce

Architectural design is a complex, multifaced, effort-consuming process that goes through many phases of development from indeterminate beginnings to concrete actualized construction. Most professional bodies break this design process down to a similar number and scope of stages. As formally defined professionally by the American Institute of Architects these design stages are denoted as programming, schematic, design development, construction documentation, tender bidding, and construction support. This chapter is focused on the early stages of design. The "schematic" or "concept" stage sees the site analyzed, and from a blank sheet an initial form and arrangement are explored and defined so that more in-depth design can move forward in later stages.

The early-stage attempts to find one or more configurations that answer the main needs of the brief, using minimal detail to ensure the process is fast and iterative, responsive to feedback, and in many cases simplistic, ignoring some practical aspects to enable greater design freedom. The process is typical of divergent exploration and synthesizing complex high-level and subjective inputs into possible output solutions for the client and users to comment on, further refining the brief then design. This is the context of the application of artificial intelligence (AI) for these processes in this chapter.

The exploratory nature of this phase presents novel challenges for computation and AI, specifically issues such as responding to context, designing from "scratch," generating a range of creative solutions, realizing the performance objectives, reacting to user input and design feedback. However, perhaps it is the more subjective and style-driven design that lends itself better to neuron-inspired and stochastic types of AI, as opposed to a later stage and often more objective design where solutions are already successfully deployed using analytical-geometry, numerical solvers, and optimization.

This chapter will first define what concept stage design is and how AI can be applied to it. Specifically, it considers the role that interaction and feedback from the designer/user have to help tune or inform AI, to give it something approaching experience, intuition, or design sense that is central to concept stage ideation. Finally, it goes on to review some examples of applied AI in architecture and how they support design in new ways not possible before.

Features of early-stage design

It is important to consider what makes this phase challenging even as a human-driven process, so that the requirements of any complementary AI system may be fully understood. During this concept stage, there are iterated periods of rapid ideation, where many solutions are made, discussed by designers, client, and users, then discarded or refined into improved variations. This often involves exploring competing options or sometimes revising and restarting the whole design process and even rewriting the underlying brief. A deeper analysis of the early-stage ideation process and its application in practice can be found in Ryūji Fujimura (2018). For example, one approach used is called "super linear design," where the process is organized into steps defining first the volume, then the plan, the structure, and finally, the roof, only proceeding to the next step once all before being confirmed. While for most architects the concept design process is not as formalized, most share similar incremental development over time from simple volumetric definitions to gradually more detailed design (Figure 7.1).

During this exploratory process, practical and functional requirements are considered, but the in-depth analysis is eschewed for experienced intuition and rule-of-thumb, to maintain development speed, while integrating and testing many ideas preventing limited search of the design space or fixation on one solution or issue. The challenges in this stage have been well characterized as a "wicked problem" by Rittel and Webber (1973), where the problem and solution are developed in unison; differentiating it from many engineering problems where requirements are well defined, preemptive, objective, and measurable. Design is a process that cycles among defining the purpose, to how it should be performed, to how it should be configured, to how it actually performs, as explained by Gero and Kannengiesser (2004) in their "situated function-structure-behavior" ontology.

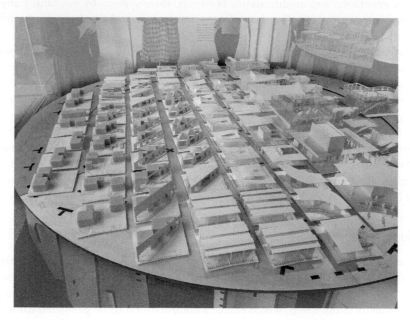

Figure 7.1 Development of a project from site massing to detail design by Ryūji Fujimura Architects.

Finally, it is important to note that this process is willful and reductive because due to the unconstrained combinatorial nature of design, the number of possible solutions is vast. And without some predetermined goals, design-experience, or style preferences to confine the design space, the problem soon succumbs to the "curse of dimensionality," where there are so many degrees of freedom that becomes effectively infinite possible solutions and thus, they cannot all be meaningfully considered in a reasonable time. However, due, in part, to the generative design making this problem more acute, methods are being explored to sample and arrange these spaces (Harding & Brandt-Olsen 2018; Ibrahim & Joyce 2019; Matejka et al. 2018) as well as interpolative meta-model methods to support more perforce directed exploration (Tseranidis, Brown & Mueller 2016; Xuereb & Kaijima 2018).

Background of AI applied to early-stage design

At the early stage of design, it could be argued that AI has a long history but equally has only just started to be earnestly applied. Much of the pioneering examples in architecture were often forward-thinking and deeply considered the potential of machine intelligence but operated at the level of projective discussions; only able to explore rudimentary implementations due to hardware and algorithmic limitations.

Most of the initial developments in design computation were in drawing tools that would ultimately become computer-aided design (CAD). The prototype system "sketch pad" developed by Ivan Sutherland in 1963, incorporated advanced drawing concepts allowing it to emulate and go beyond the capabilities of the drafting table. However, many concepts from this would not be widely adopted until much later with the advent of building information model (BIM) and parametric-modeling software. These platforms empower users by capturing their relational intent between the bundling elements and leveraging computing to enable fast generation and modifications. However, these systems by not taking any initiative to learn or problem solve by themselves do not represent AI and are simply defined as sophisticated tools.

Discourses on AI for building design was explored as early as Nicholas Negroponte's *The Architecture Machine* (1970) and *Soft Architecture Machines* (1975). These works explore ideas of "thinking" machines, applied by people such as Gordon Pask. Cybernetics, a precursor to modern machine learning (ML), researched information processing systems, relying on feedback to tune them. Ideas of artificial Neural networks (NN), could be traced before Minsky to Ross Ashbys book *Design for a Brain* published as early as 1951 (Ashby 1960) discussing simulating neurons and homeostasis, and how it might be used to learn and adapt to dynamic input. As discussed in *Soft Architecture Machines*, these are mostly "isolated" systems, but in a later chapter, "participatory design" is discussed by Yona Friedman. The potential and drawbacks of both should be considered for any modem system, and are discussed below.

Individual AI design

In this case, the AI is considered to be working by itself in isolation, typically referring to systems that are "taught" to make or explore solutions, either inductively using existing data or deductively by applying rules and logic to generate new things. Some early examples are Shape Grammars (Stiny 1980), which enable a complex form to be generated from a simple seed of information, which could be the site and the style, and then applies transformation rules to build-up a full design.

Effectively such systems are designed as single-pass processors and usually would be expected to make the same or similar design every time if provided with the same input. Unless the system itself was redesigned, thus, they cannot easily be updated with new information like additional case-studies, or can allow for feedback. However, being self-contained means that they are readily understandable and generate known or expectable results. They also require little in the way of integration as they do not need to be interfaced into other systems or require major input from users.

Participatory AI

Another class of AI is participatory systems that are especially relevant in the early stage. These allow for the user input during the design process, to learn and adapt to the users input. This is often in the configuration of a feedback cycle of the computer creator and user critic/appraiser. Thus, these systems are effectively active agents in a wider design process. How exactly they do this and what they contribute is the choice of the systems designer.

In considering human–machine collaborative design, influential early projects by John and Jane Frazer are captured in the book *An Evolutionary Architecture* (1995). This work considers the use of early NN in learning and pattern recognition for architecture, most notably the Generator project in 1978 where Cedric Price investigated the use of computers integrated into a collaborative and responsive design process that drove the configuration of a modular building system. He even considered what if computers got "bored," such as when a design remained too static and had them react by producing unsolicited designs to provoke human creativity, and went so far with this idea to propose that a "feeling" building might demolish itself if it got "depressed" from neglect or misuse.

Despite the hyperbole, the early implemented systems were limited by processing and had relatively simple algorithms compared to today. In the Generator project, the design "thinking" incorporated numerical input tables for user needs, linked to a constrained space allocation algorithm that provided simple grid-based layouts. This enabled user adaption by the way of applying algorithms similar to the "Menace" game system by Donald Michie (1963), an essentially early stochastic reinforcement learning. This allowed users, over several interactions, to steer the generation of designs returned by the system toward those with similar steps as those previously preferred by users in the same way that Menace preferred game moves that had been successful in the past.

Applying AI in early-stage design

The use of AI in early-stage design can be applied over a range of activities and processes. The design of a design process is itself a complex one and often integral to the personal or commercial style of practice. For example, the sculptural aesthetic approach of Frank O. Gehry is centered around a holistic expressive physical model-driven form generation method and his taste for feedback. This is contrasted with the functionally driven approach of Richard Rogers where the performance and space needs are defined early on, and technology is then assembled around the space to enable and support it, seemingly without considering the aesthetic of the result but carefully coordinated over limited targeted drawings.

Involving AI into the early-stage design also defines a unique process, so there are important fundamental creative questions about how the design should operate such that each designer implementing such approaches needs to be aware of and have their stance on. Using

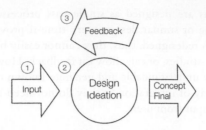

Figure 7.2   A simple process diagram of the concept design process.

AI in concept design also raises questions about the extent of AI agency and creative contribution to the design.

The early-stage design might be simplistically divided into three main sections:

1   Initial processing
2   Design creation
3   Design development from the feedback

As demonstrated by Figure 7.2. This section will consider how AI can contribute to each aspect in order.

Initial processing

The first stage typically involves assessing the design context such as the design brief, site, and surrounding buildings of the project. The site defines constraints as well as the degrees of freedom that the design can utilize, typically the buildable volume but in some cases, it may be more complex. The surrounding buildings might present a local style that wants to be emulated or challenged, as well as represent examples of designs that have been successfully built there before the concerning building-code or environmental performance. During the initial process, reference buildings might be analyzed and reviewed. This can include buildings from the architect's repertoire, to reference for general design solutions or style, and also typologically similar buildings that can give data and insight into the unique needs or trends of that typology. The relevance of context over external examples depends on the project. For example, airports rarely copy buildings close to them, instead compare themselves against other airports. Conversely, private homes will often aim to fit in and adapt to local conditions over following global housing standards or style.

Design creation

After compiling input data, design ideation is next. During this period prototypes are typically made quickly to explore what is possible. The methods to do this can be personal to the designer and in some cases relatively arbitrary, in others more logical. For example, architects like Santiago Calatrava often reference external inspiration like animal shapes for the form of a building. Or designers like David Chipperfield might take the massing of an existing building but simplify and hone this to generate new volumes. Others like UN studio are driven by the analysis of the user flow to different programs in a building and how to heighten this to generate social and cultural spaces. These examples highlight the range of possible approaches; while none are perfect or wrong, they all show that some functional and reactive approach to form-making is required for the design.

Design feedback

Critical during the early concept stage is the feedback process. This is arguably the engine that drives this phase. Generating prototypes has no meaning if they are not appraised and tested against objective and subjective demands, ultimately leading to a final option to be carried through to detail design. Typically, this requires a range of options to be considered as even objective measurements have no meaning unless compared relative to benchmark-baselines, existing buildings, or other design options. By comparing trade-offs between different options, the aspects of design become explicit, and designers and clients are required to externalize and confirm their preferences. During this process, visual and performative assessments are key, but also experiential, formal, and even iconographic aspects can be important.

Even this incomplete expanded diagram of the design process shown in Figure 7.3 demonstrates the many processes that AI may support. The below section will explore the implemented examples of intervention by AI in aspects of - the early-stage design process enabling new systems of design and the human-designer collaboration to be realized.

Application of ML to early-stage design

For these applied examples of concept stage design AI, we will break the projects into the three main components of concept stage design as identified in the process analysis:

Input
The initial site and contextual analysis, existing solution sense-making and processing

Ideation
Generation of new and derived designs for consideration

Feedback
Approaches to learning from feedback and adapting subsequent models

The projects are developed on the premise that AI is most usefully applied to support the designer in specific aspects rather than attempting to replace the architect or the process as a whole. What will follow for each project is an explanation of the design context, what the

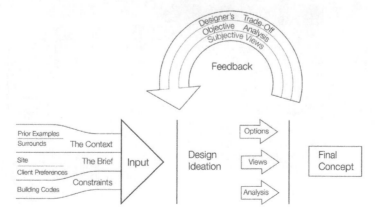

Figure 7.3 Expanded concept stage process diagram.

general design challenge was and how this translates to specific process goals, then explaining how the AI was implemented, both the data and algorithm used, and finally, discussing its suitability, capability, and effectivity.

Design input support using AI

This first section will look at how AI can assist early on before any design is undertaken. By supporting the designer with more topic knowledge, data processing, and contextual understanding, beyond what is possible with the human experience alone.

Mining site images for typology comparison at scale

An initial review of similar projects is important for a designer to develop a sense of what is typical and desirable for their own. This is arguably best gained by having designed similar buildings, but there is also utility in visiting and analyzing similar works. However, often the number of studied examples is limited by designer experience, and a wider data-driven approach can find unknown examples that are useful to focus on concerning a new project. This acquisition of knowledge by observing other design examples can be supported by AI, and has good potential as it has the capacity and speed to process many more case studies than a human alone could consider and also uncover links that humans may not.

For urban design and building site exploration, aerial images have much potential. This section looks at a project involving airport sites. While placed all over the world, their function is internationally regulated, and so many airports share similar features. Using the publicly available locations of airports, it is possible using open satellite APIs to obtain high detail aerial imagery (10 × 10 m per pixel) for any location at regular times. By automating this process, a large corpus of aerial images can be built; in this case, a 10 × 10 km aerial image was produced for over 1,000 of the largest airports by annual passenger numbers. A sample of these data is shown in Figure 7.4.

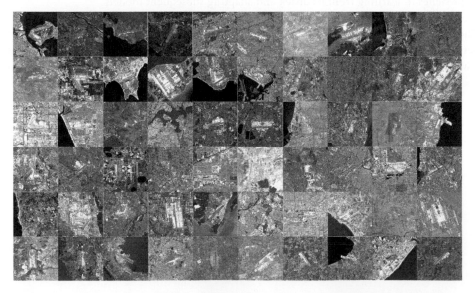

Figure 7.4   A sample of an algorithmically sourced corpus of 1,000 airport aerial images.

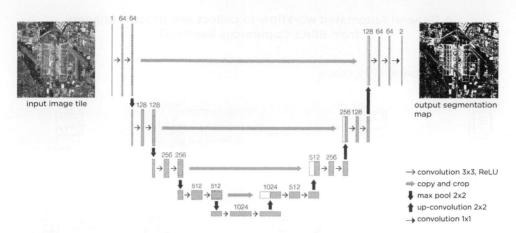

Figure 7.5 Example of plan land use detection using U-Net.

This by itself enables a much larger number of examples to be compared than would be compiled by manual research. Additionally, this can be matched with technical and performance data about the airports so that correlations and links can be made. Images can be organized by the number of terminals, length of runways, distance from city center, and so on, if that information is available from other sources and merged as labels to the data set.

However, with these aerial images, further processing is required to gain meaningful high-level information, such as land use statics. In this case, there was value in knowing areas in these pictures that were unbuilt and might be developed, areas that had a high population and might be affected by expansion, and also the impact on nature either by land reclamation or removing vegetation. Working out the location and area of vegetation, water, and buildings manually on each image is possible, but on a collection of 1,000, this would be impractical. This represents a common problem in – early-stage design, especially those involving compiling similar existing projects to generate more data/analysis but is often limited by the time someone can take before they have to start designing.

In this case, a small subset of 50 images was manually masked indicating if the area was one of the major land uses: water, buildings, vegetation, or empty, which was possible in a reasonable amount of time. With this small corpus of labeled data, it was possible to then use approaches such as U-Net to learn from these features and identify land use areas on the rest of the set (950 images). U-Net is a deep convolutional approach (Ronneberger 2015), which using progressively convoluted kernels of the images, learns features of local groups of pixels in images, at different levels of resolution as shown in Figure 7.5. This allows it to effectively break up one sample image into a bigger number of learning examples, thereby, improving the learning rate from a relatively small number of labeled images. The whole process is shown in Figure 7.6.

It is important to check the output, using typical accuracy measurements (learn with 80% of the data, test with the remaining 20%), as well as manually verifying the sample predictions and, in this case, can be visually estimated quickly by a designer with experience. Vitally edge cases should be also checked such as an atypical terrain; if the learning does not pick these up, more manual labeling can be added to the underrepresented data set. But one should be careful not to overly skew the learning in this way and keep the training set relatively representative of the larger corpus. In extreme cases, segmenting the data into

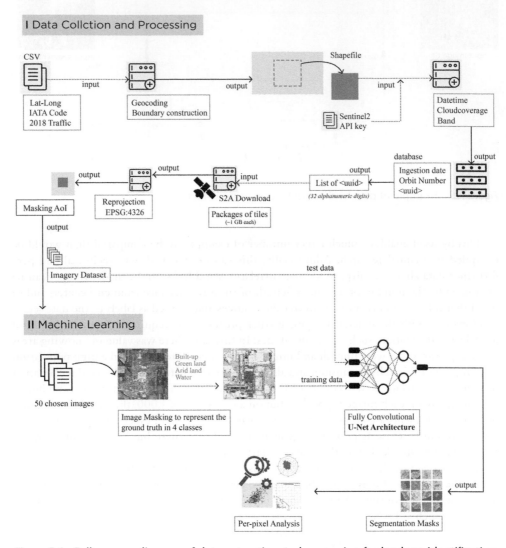

A General Automated workflow to collect and process Imagery from ESA's Copernicus Sentinel2

I Data Collction and Processing

II Machine Learning

Figure 7.6 Full process diagram of data extraction and processing for land use identification.

different groups, and processing them separately may produce better results. For this work, and eventual accuracy was obtained of over 95%, which is more than useful; an example can be shown in Figure 7.7.

From this, data analysis can be undertaken to find valid expansion areas for airports. By post-processing these maps to remove smaller properties, large contagious areas that could be expanded with minimal demolition and disruption can be identified. This could be achieved using a "flood-fill" approach, or the largest fit of rectangles, to show more usable space for structures like runways as shown in Figure 7.8 and processed to compute those locations relative to the center of the airport that are easiest to expand to. When applied at scale, this

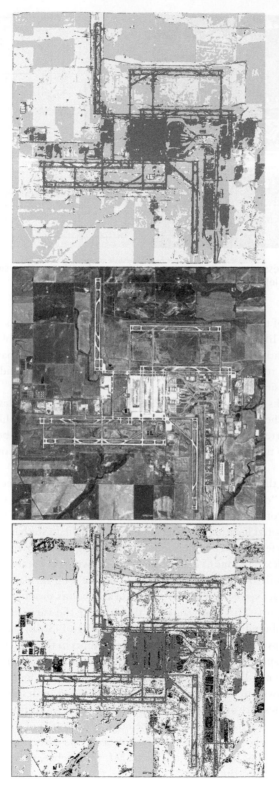

Figure 7.7 A ML-based system able to highlight land use and areas of potential development. The middle is the base aerial image, left is the input mask, and right is the U-Net prediction.

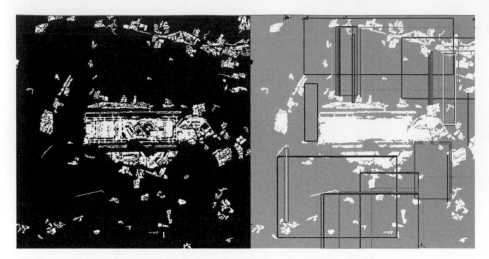

Figure 7.8   A post-processed airport expansion zoning exploration with a simplified built-up area on the left and indicative larger land trances on the right.

gives a global picture of the future expansion capacity of the existing sites, as well as shows locations of cities with likely new terminals and those that will have problems and may require new sites. Alternatively, the method can be used to indicate areas that would gain the most from airport size reduction by computing how much-inhabited land would be freed from engine noise and similar benefits (Figure 7.9).

Beyond targeted tasks to gain specific data from a collection of examples, one might also benefit from ordering them in a more subjective way to explore the data. Unsupervised ML approaches that can correlate similar examples without user-labeling can be useful in effectively allowing users to make unpredicted connections not driven by preconceived designer bias.

In the airport case, this was undertaken to explore airports that shared landscape color similarities. To do this "dimensionality reduction" was used; where, data with a high number of dimensions are converted into a low number of dimensions. These translations try to maintain the relative spatial location or distances between the data so that their relationships are preserved, but with few enough dimensions that they might be shown graphically. Typically, this allows complex relations of data points to be shown as 2D scatter plots that can be seen and understood easily by humans, which is not the case for a similar 10D or 100D plot. In this case, the input data were the ten dominant land area colors producing a 10 by 3(RGB) size vector for each airport. This plot wanted to demonstrate the variation of landscape differences; thus, a t-distributed stochastic neighbor embedding (T-SNE) was used (Maaten & Hinton 2008). This maps the similarity between all data points in the high dimensional space of the dominant landscape tones and then builds a spatial relational map in 2D (Figure 7.10).

This approach might not directly help decision-making but allows for a new way of seeing the data. Here, this shows similar airport sites clustered by being in desert areas, urban centers, and near water. These are arrangements that would be time-consuming to do in person but help in discovering sites that are similar to the target site or area of study. They can be a valuable sense-making tool overviewing the whole data set and integrating the varying and complex relations of the data. But like all unlabeled ML approaches, they require the user to interpret and give meaning to the results.

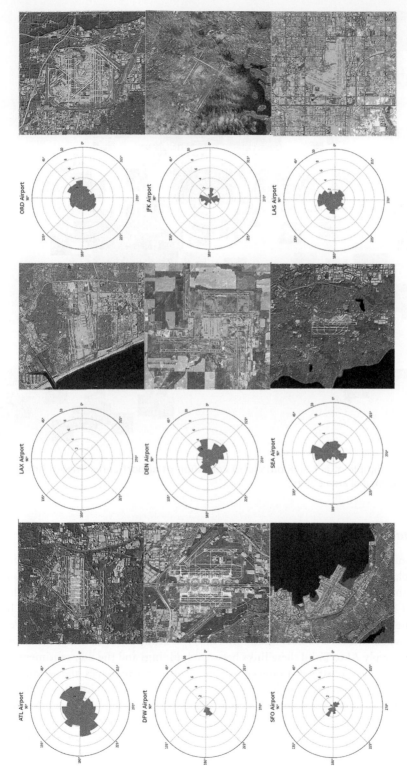

Figure 7.9 Airport expansion possibility by 16 radial zones as shown for a sample of international airports on the right.

141

Figure 7.10   A sample of a T-SNE organized collection of airport aerial images organized by principal area colors.

Urban data and social feedback for site investigation

Alongside directly observable aspects of a building site, a designer needs to understand more nuanced relations between how users interact and "feel" toward their built environment. Typically, this is where experience and observation excel and enable a designer to understand and predict how people will act and respond to a particular space. However, this is limited by a designer's prior interactions, which makes them prone to small sample inductive biases and errors when extended to new locations. Thus, it is attractive to use larger user feedback volumes and apply AI to build these links between buildings and the user sentiment.

This example demonstrates a project where social media messages and urban building configuration were correlated for design insight. In this case, the building plot outlines from Singapore and a corpus of all public Twitter messages sent in Singapore over three years. Each message was tagged to its nearest building plot to derive a collective message corpus per building. This city-wide per building message corpus was then turned into a word vector, specifically used here was the term frequency-inverse document frequency approach removing unimportant "stop words." At the city scale, this is a large amount of data; however,

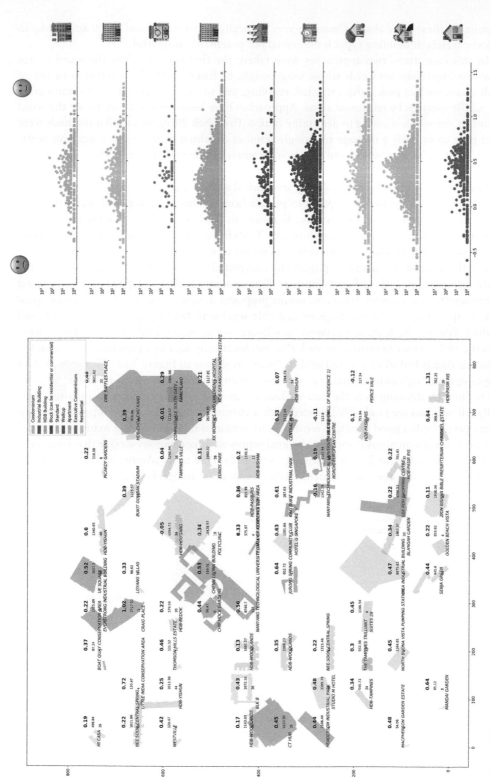

Figure 7.11 An example of building footprints on the left; linked to social media sentiment on the right, typologies sperate plots and the messages shown in the x-axis by positive or negative sentiment and message volume in the y-axis.

organizing these large abstract word vectors (typically between 100 and 1,000 keywords) to observe trends in building types is nontrivial but potentially insightful.

In this case study, two approaches were taken; the first was to reduce the word vector down to important keywords whose usage might be linked with the perception or use of built space, such as park, busy, crowded, relaxing, and so on. The second was to summarize the whole message by sentiment alone. Approaches have been devised to try to use the word vector or the whole message to determine (Pak & Paroubek 2010), and similar methods were used here to simplify a message to a single number of which negative was a negative sentiment, positive being positive, and zero being completely neutral (Figure 7.11).

In this case, there was a large discrepancy in the per building word vectors, where some had many messages and others had very few, linked to different activities in public buildings like museums and malls as compared to private homes. Due to this, global dimensionality reduction approaches to cluster data like K-means are likely to be skewed by the nonuniform variation. In these situations, algorithms like T-SNE would pick up on the larger variation, but this could not be mapped onto new data unless rerun/updated.

For this case, it was useful to project the complex data to a continuous space so that the building messages with similar "sentiments" or content might be mapped and understood in relation to one another. This also means proposed designs could be placed in that space and compared to similar buildings or desirable sentiment buildings, could be located, and studied. For this the Kohonen network or self-organizing map (SOM) is useful. This system uses the full data set to train a network that can locate any data to a preferred neuron in the network that is linked to a spatial grid or "map" as shown in Figure 7.12. This grid enables mapping from high dimensional spaces to low dimension spaces, typically two. The neurons are trained by iterating over the data set linking most similar data points to a neuron. Initially, all neurons are randomly initiated with a vector the same size as the input data. Once a data point finds a good match, it reinforces its vector to the neighboring neurons arranged in a grid. Over numerous iterations, the grid represents a continuous surface that covers the high dimensional input data as uniformly as possible. Due to its adaptive grid behavior, the mapping is not like the usual dimensionality reduction, and makes fuller use of the node

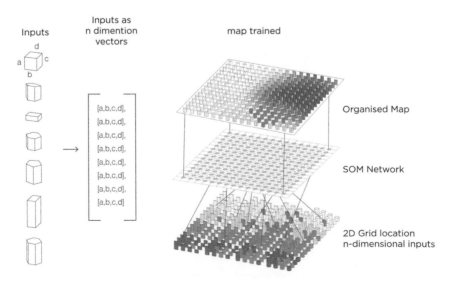

Figure 7.12   Kohonen network processing of a 4D input space and translation to a 2D map.

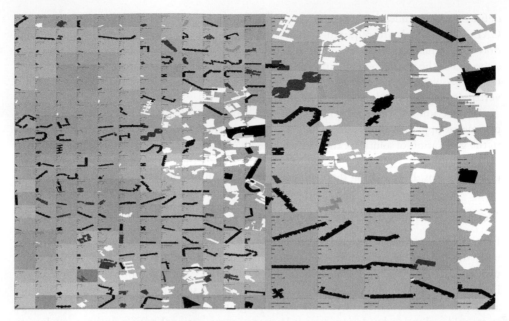

Figure 7.13 Example of building footprints mapped by social media messaging similarly. Left: larger view; right: zoom in showing buildings close to each other on the map linked by similar social sentiment.

space, and can position disjoint regions of the target high-dimension data close together, resulting in a compact rectangular-shaped map of a space rather than typical "ball" shaped data projections of T-SNE and similar.

In this case, the mapping was undertaken considering the two types of data per building: the social and spatial. Training the SOM using just spatial data allows for a map that can take the target design and find those similar indicated by being close in the SOM. Using just social sentiment to train, gives a map based purely on how people message about them. By visualizing this with the footprints, one can find the types of buildings with a similar sentiment but possibly very different physical configurations. Finally, by combining both spatial and social data in one large space, the interaction between the buildings and their user experiences can be visually shown as in Figure 7.13.

These methods allow for sense-making across disparate data types through positional correlations on the map, giving a designer the ability to navigate and digest many examples. It also allows one to compare an existing site or location of a proposed configuration by providing a continuous mapping between the social and design space. However, this mapping is limited to examples that have sufficient data to train with, which is why it is more relevant tourban data with many data points. Furthermore, any correlation between the two aspects could also be skewed by factors that are not captured in the data such as business uses or specific incidents that are not related to the area. Thus, when using social media data, care must be taken to conservatively use this where it is most likely to give meaningful correlations.

Design ideation

The next challenge after analyzing the site is to generate design solutions. Typically, this is not a "single-shot" process but an iterative exploration, driven by performance and taste, defined, and bounded by how it is communicated or represented. In later stages, typically CAD/BIM models are required as they have the details to make cost estimates, provide drawings to planning authorities, build a structural model, and so on. However, in the early-stage phase, the media used to explain and develop designs in a much more open, often favoring expressiveness over accuracy. Early designs may include sketches, renders, flow-diagrams, verbal descriptions, and massing models; all are valid.

This section will present two very different approaches to using AI to generate designs: a parametric approach and an image-based ML approach. They represent opposing paradigms in the generation of solutions; the former, a deductive method, a built-up based on basic first principal rules. As opposed to the latter, an inductive method using inference derived from prior solutions. Both exhibit their unique benefits and limitations.

Meta-parametric building design exploration

Parametric modeling is widely used to build sophisticated geometric models, usually manually through visual programming tools to make associations between geometry objects. It uses assemblies of "components" where the output data of one component are used as the input data of another and uses replication rules applied to structured data to replace for loops and other conventional iterative state-based programming. This relative ease of use has led to its wide adoption by designers as it leverages computational power without needing to write code.

The use of such systems at the early stage has led to criticisms due to its intellectually intensive demand, specifically when making and editing models to change the generative logic, as opposed to just parametrically different, where simply sliders and input variables are changed (Davis 2013). An alternate approach considered here is meta-parametric design (Harding & Shepherd 2017). This method operates on the intrinsic structure of parametric models (PMs) as "directed acyclic graphs," meaning that all data must move in one direction without feedback loops. Thus, a PM can be defined using three things: a rational number vector "M," an integer matrix "F," and an integer tensor "T." The size of M defines the number and value of the input parameters. The size of F defines the number of functional and geometric components in the model arranged in a grid, and the integer value for each defines which type out of a list of components is used for each grid point. The tensor T being the same gird size as M defines, for each component, which previous components it is linked to. From this, the whole PM may be defined as a special type of graph demonstrated in Figure 7.14.

This "genome" definition of a PM enables the computer to manipulate it without human effort. They can be modified or "mutated," and the resultant geometry model is analyzed to see whether it performs, and is used for general exploration and optimization. This allows for the computer to make novel solutions from scratch using a palette of predetermined components. The challenge ensures that the approach can make something meaningful to the design; some objective goal must be given, otherwise, the options generated have no "target" to design for. An evolutionary optimization or simulated annealing approach may be applied to drive the design. This makes a closed-loop system, which must run for several iterations before returning an optimal design or a range of trade-offs (Pareto-optimal front)and only return solutions that achieve functional performance on measurable objective properties.

This type of optimization is not responsive to the interactive iterative nature of the design process. However, an approach called interactive evolutionary optimization supplements objective variables by including the user preference as a scalar or categorical objective measure

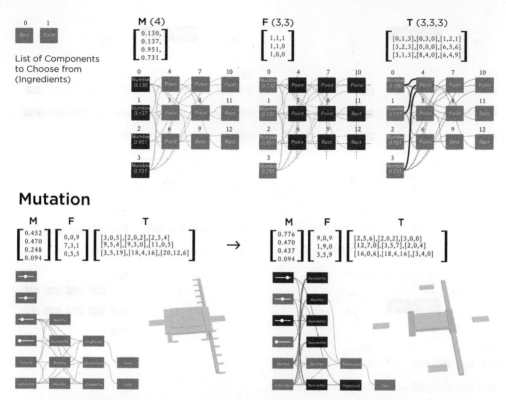

Figure 7.14   Meta-parametric model representation encoded as a component matrix "F," typology tensor "T," and parameter vector "M" above, and showing a model bottom left undergoing a mutation to become the model in the bottom right.

of "fitness" for each design. This feedback applied over several iterations means that preferred designs are reinforced. This approach when applied to simply slider values on a PM has worked well for working out optimum slider values (Mueller & Ochsendorf 2015). The meta-parametric design takes this beyond just the sliders "M" and allows manipulation of the components "F" and typology "T" as well. However, being a much larger design space, using a single preference input may take a user many hundreds of iterations to get the desired outcome, as a preference for parts of the design cannot be indicated.

A more targeted meta–parametric approach allows for users to change specific aspects at the phenotype (design) level. This takes on a "mutation" rather than "mating" operator shown in Figure 7.15, where updated models are not combinations of two models consistent with usual evolutionary approaches, but rather a modification to a singular design. In this way, the extent of change may be controlled. For example, if a specific geometry needs modification, the related components, associations, and parameters are changed and can be more directed than the mass mating changes (Joyce & Ibrahim 2017). General high-level changes can be imposed by adding extra components or variables to an area of the design. This replicates the early-stage design process more closely, where models are iteratively worked on with the user and designer feedback. However, in this case, the design changes are decided by the AI either via stochastic or by Markov-based reinforcement learning, directing the changes to a model based on a training set of prior working models, similar to how autocorrection works.

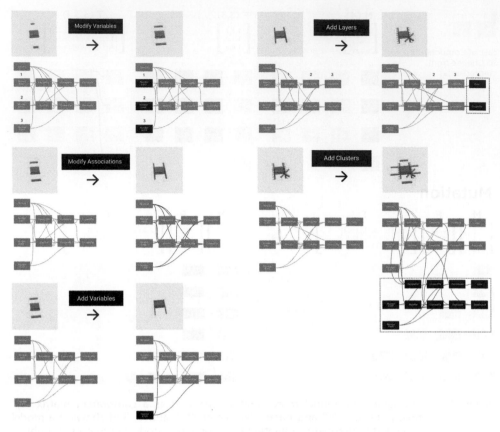

Figure 7.15   Meta-parametric replacement rules applied to transform a parametric representation.

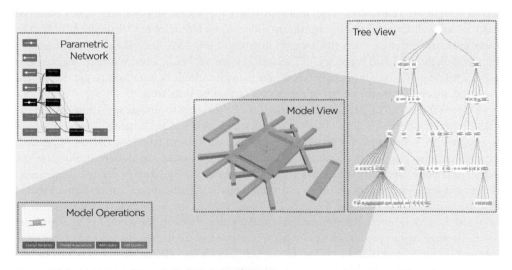

Figure 7.16   User interface of AI driven co-designer.

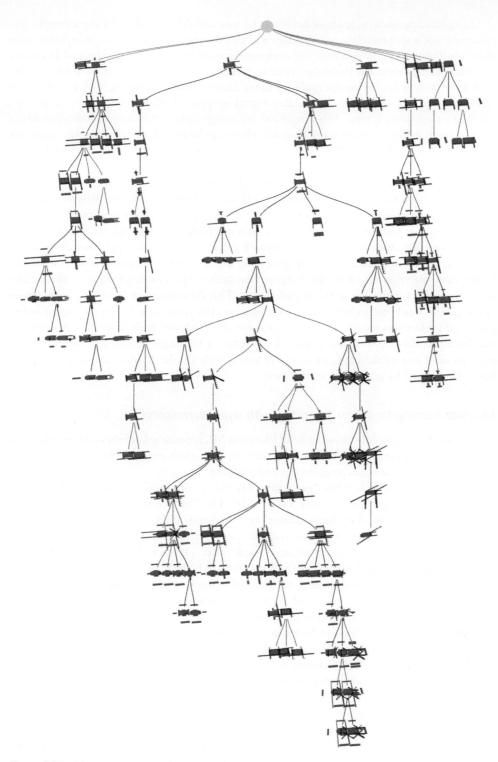

Figure 7.17 Meta-parametric design exploration session tree by a single user.

Using this approach, a dialogue between the user and AI is possible. In one example implementation, a web interface was developed to enable airport terminal design exploration as shown in Figure 7.16. In this case, the components used were specifically defined as airport elements such as terminal buildings, satellite terminals, finger piers, and air-bridges. This allows the system to develop the typology more directly when beginning with a seed design of a basic terminal. Using this, the iterated mutation approach allows the progress to be captured in a phylogenetic tree. This formalizes the design option exploration process enabling users to track, compare, and extend from anywhere on the tree. A meta-parametric approach makes modifying the model "inexpensive"; however, being stochastically generated, it requires a user comparing versions (widening the tree) but also iterating to refine the design (lengthening the tree) before getting it "right" (Figure 7.17).

An interactive meta-parametric approach allows for a type of dialogue between the human and machine, where a range of concrete design options can be developed and made more detailed as the design progresses, by moving from using modification operators to adding more operators. However, this approach requires significant input from designers as shown in an example design session (Figure 7.18) where nearly 200 options were considered. In this case, the requirement by the designer is to steer the process targeting both the performance as well as subjective aesthetic preferences. This AI interaction is focused on one user although this could be undertaken by multiple users but is unlikely to be convergent unless goals and preferences are shared, but this is consistent with any multiclient design situation. Furthermore, this approach has no prior knowledge of the target design, so unless the components used and/or the configurations are tuned with similar Markov models, the design has to be derived by interaction by the user.

Machine learning for design generation with style interpolation

Generative ML is a rapidly growing field; like most ML approaches, it relies on learning from a pool of prior examples but unlike most can produce their own "designs" after training rather than typical tasks of categorizing or identifying.

One popular approach is the "generative adversarial network" (GAN), which pits two NNs against each other as shown in Figure 7.18. The "generator" is a self-contained NN that makes content, and the "discriminator" tries to decide if the content is real (original) or fake (generated). The whole system is trained over a series of epochs. The discriminator is randomly given several real and generated samples that it labels real or fake. If the discriminator predicts correctly, then it is positively reinforced. If the image is a generated one and it is good enough to trick the discriminator into believing it is real, then the generator is reinforced and the discriminator penalized. Repeating this mutually improves both the generator and discriminator, respectively. The generator alone can now make outputs believably like the input training data. This can be applied to many data types but has been most successfully used with photographs (Karras et al. 2020). But it has been effective in generating 2D building plans (Chaillou 2020) as well as 3D chairs (Wang et al. 2017).

Typically, we have found at least more than 1,000 unique training samples are needed to train a GAN depending on the complexity of what is being imitated. The training data need to be similar and comparable, for example, images shot from the same angle. If not, then there is a likelihood that the way the data are represented, such as the shot angle, will be misconstrued with actual data feature variation, and the generated data will show variation in representation instead of design.

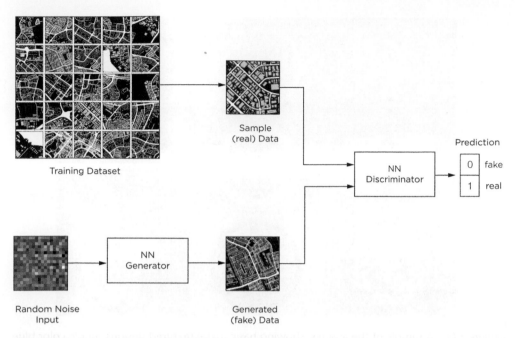

Figure 7.18 **Representation of a GAN.**

Because of the requirement for large amounts of consistent training data, applications of GANs are limited to where data are readily available. In the early stages, generated data are still usable even if they are quite basic, which broadens what is possible, but conversely, the time for finding/making and processing these data are reduced as the duration for design is limited. One remedy for this is to focus on general-purpose uses such as a floor plan generator that can be used over a range of projects, and so time can be invested to fully develop and build useful data sets. Conversely, if the target is more focused, it can help to limit what is required, and it will likely not be useful outside of the specific cases; however, it can be done more rapidly but usually is reliant on opportune data sources.

For this section, we will consider a piece of urban furniture design—the simple manhole cover. In Japan, there are many unique regional manhole designs with abstract patterns, textures, images designed to relate to the use (fire hydrant, electricity, water, etc.) or depicting local mascots, folktales, food delicacies, and famous landmarks/buildings. They represent a huge amount of unique cultural design innovation and so is interesting to explore how a computer might be able to generate and, in the process, learn about what makes a manhole cover design unique.

This example used a community collected set of over 25 thousand manhole cover images with similar framing, as shown in Figure 7.19. They were resized to be the same pixel size, and abnormal images were removed by looking at background colors and verifying reasonable size circle and square shapes with the OpenCV library.

A basic GAN was trained on this data set, which showed progressively better generations of new solutions as the number of epochs increased. We can see from Figure 7.20 that over time, not only the shape of the input data but also the main indicative types are reproduced. What we do notice, however, is that many of the generated designs are the more common metal textured types and rarely try to represent the pictorial designs, and when they do, they look smudged.

Figure 7.19 A sample of the images, showing basic metal textured designs, single color blue water, and yellow fire hydrant designs, as well as more complex patterned city and prefecture based multicolor pictorial designs.

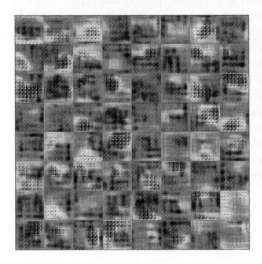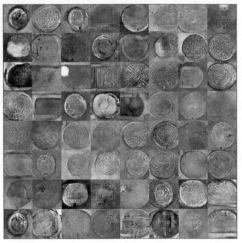

Figure 7.20 Random samples of the latent space from the 20th epoch (left) trained on the whole data set. In the early stages, vague general shapes, colors, and unrealistic repetitive textures may be seen. By epoch 200 (right) examples are mostly well-formed with small-scale texture that is are either periodic and some pseudo-pictorial or radially orientated designs.

To counter this "mundane" output, the training data were curated to only include the more colorful examples. In this case, a K-means clustering on a sample of the pixels of each image was used to find the most dominant six colors as shown in Figure 7.21. These colors were then measured for their average "value" using the Hue Satuaration Ligtness (HSV)

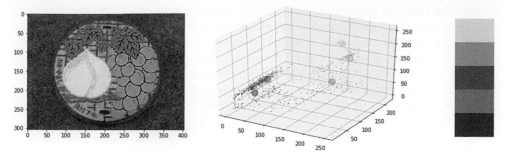

Figure 7.21 Example of the five-main color (right) identification showing centroid positions in RGB space (middle) next to sample pixels from the target image (left).

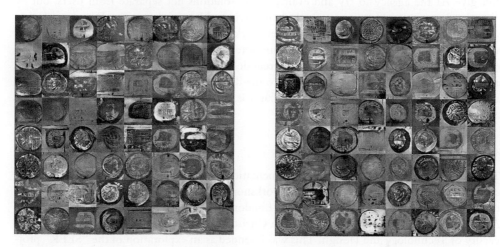

Figure 7.22 Example output from training the GAN on the curated "colorful" Manhole data-set after 3,000 and 4,000 epochs.

color space, where a high value is given to vibrant colors. Images with high average values were retained and the duller images removed.

A GAN trained on this new set showed a markedly different design language as shown in Figure 7.22, and this could then be extended to only using images with certain dominant colors or only from a certain region to further control the output. However, this design direction approach can drastically reduce the training data size, which is undesirable and requires retaining the GAN. An alternative is to capture these properties as "latent variables" that control inputs that influence the taught image generation. These can be specific, such as dominant color, high-level labels such as "logo" or "mascot," but also more abstract, such as style markers "naturistic" or "graphical." By integrating this, one can have considerably more control over the output and even explore the "latent space," which is a continuous space of these inputs, and potentially be able to interpolate between them.

This GAN approach shows interesting results that could be improved with more advanced training. However, at this level, it is limited to being a starter for design as things like text and functional markings are not reliably reproduced by most GANs. More fundamentally, due to the inherent inductive paradigm of the approach, outcomes are rarely surprising, being derived from real examples rather than first principals. They are also bound to use the same data format as the input data, so in this example, both input and output are images, while typically vector graphics would be the most useful way to show a design like this. Unfortunately, most advanced examples of GAN use convolution for capturing different scale data on uniformly distributed (vector/tensor) and locally related data (neighboring pixels), which while good for images are not well adapted to other data structures.

AI and user symbiosis

In the prior section, we explored the capability of AI to help design both logically and from an example. The previous section showed systems to leverage large amounts of data to support the understanding of the site. This last section touches on ideas to bring these together and give AI the agency to try and evaluate new solutions not separate from users, but by directly observing and interacting with them—where AI controls an actual space, and users simply inhabit it; their activity being the feedback in which the AI hones its understanding and tries to improve the design by itself. This potentially circumvents the effort of requiring explicit human input. This opens up a different debate as to the human role, in this case only able to influence the AI through reacting to the designs; furthermore, there is still systemic agency from the AI developer dictating what it is trying to achieve, and the design degrees of freedom available to it.

AI for situational learning and design

This section looks at a prototypical implementation of this concept. An AI system that was developed for the 2018 Smart Geometry workshop along with Kate Jeffery, behavioral neuroscience professor at University College London, Jonathan Irawan and Maurice Brooks, Architects from Hassell Studio, and Verina Christie, a Ph.D. Researcher at Singapore University of Technology and Design. This was intended as an exploration of the "SEEK" project by the architecture machine group from MIT in the 1970s. SEEK looked to make an environment for gerbils (a rodent) that was dynamically modified by a computer. At the time of sensing and actuating, AI technology was in its infancy. This workshop with support from the participants aimed to see what could be done with modern technology albeit in much shorter time frames.

This project worked with ants as "users" in the system, rejecting gerbils due to practical and ethical issues of using mammals in experiments. Ants were advantageous with their size allowing for more individuals, thus, data per session. The project made a habitat as shown in Figure 7.23, which used a solenoid-controlled floor controlled by an Arduino, allowing it to move a grid of 10 by 30 of independent 3 cm squares to any height. The grid was covered, making a reconfigurable landscape for the ants to inhabit. Above this was a camera that was able to capture a live 2D plan video of activity over the whole environment. For each configuration, the ant colony was released and allowed to freely explore. The result is a computer-controlled and observed environment that given the right programming can respond to its small but numerous users.

Beyond the technical complexity of a system driving solenoids to determine the configuration and the video feed to capture the ants' activity, the real challenge is how to meaningfully link these two activities. This is effectively the role of a designer to build designs that have desirable effects on its users. Considering how architects learn to do this, we may

Figure 7.23 The prototype AI driven ant environment, including above the apparatus of the tracking system, spatial organization system with actuators below, and the ant colony in vials on the white surface in a flat configuration in the middle. Some live tracking is shown behind the screen.

propose that at a basic level, they observe their surroundings and understand the impact that the existing built environment has on users, then apply this understanding to realize "good" designs.

The prototype developed for this study attempted something similar by having a system that observed users and then sought to correlate this with the environment to develop predictions. The work did not attempt to directly tackle the issue of making good designs as this value assessment is problematic. In humans, this might be possible, linking a building design to being healthy, happy, or productive; but with ants, it is hard to ascertain their desires.

The implementation involved initially predetermined environment configurations with the system trying to learn and predict the impact of the configurations on the movement of the ants. A tracker was set up on the video feed of the new ant habitat, using OpenCV to show where the individual ants moved as shown in Figure 7.24.

The route data can then be processed and superimposed on the environment, transferring the ant's time spent and speed to a user density and the average speed measure for each of the tiles. This was composited as a three-channel tensor, with the width and height of the tensor relating to the environment's 10 by 30 tile grid. The first channel giving a position of that tile of the environment, and the other two channels recording the behavior or use of the space in the form of the normalized seed and density, respectively (Figure 7.25).

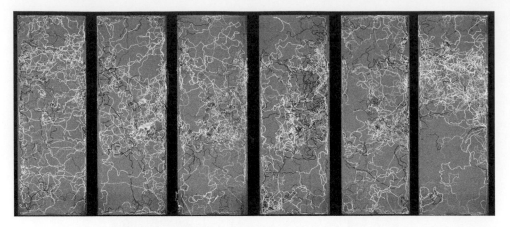

Figure 7.24 Sample of six five-minute samples of ant activity with trails of routes taken by each individual.

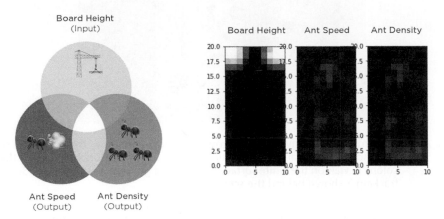

Figure 7.25 The separate channels colored by use and shown on a smaller 20 by 10 example design with two high humps on the top of the environment and ant density and speed in the valley.

A corpus of training data was built consisting of five-minute samples based on the series of input configurations giving the ants some time to respond and settle. Then all the sample data were put through a NN and used to predict what the ant activity would be based on input configuration (Figure 7.26).

This was then taken further to explore the AI itself, developing its own ideas for testing. This was done by training a GAN on the input data, and from this, it was able to generate its own versions of the input data. Although built from limited samples (less than a hundred), simple mound–like environments that were similar to the initial training configurations were shown, while at the same time, predicting the ants' behaviors that were often to stick to the safer edges of the environment as shown in Figure 7.27. It was then possible to feed these back into the configuration, allowing the system to complete a self-designing and apprising loop. Allowed to do this over time, a better understanding of the environment could be possible and even optimized or learned using latent variables linked to the pixels to build designs that enable a demanded activity.

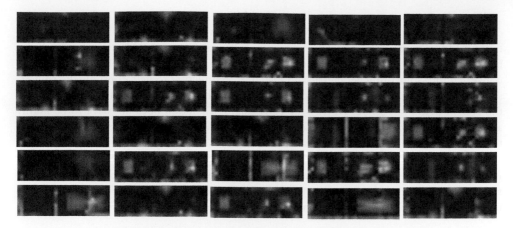

Figure 7.26 Examples of five-minutes input data from the tracking.

Figure 7.27 The separate channels colored by use and shown on a smaller 20 by 10 example design with two high humps on the top of the environment in red and ant density and speed predominantly in the edges.

If this approach was to be applied at a larger human scale and undertaken with daily or even hourly reconfigurations, we could begin to consider a situation in which humans might be intelligently designed for by a system that is simultaneously trying to learn to predict human behavior and also improve the design. This situation could enable micro improvements to be intelligently undertaken all over a city with minimal human input need, opening up new potential for design to be deployed at scale but still be locally sensitive.

Chapter summary

Early-stage concept design is a uniquely free and open part of the building creation. The application of AI here begs the question of how it can be best used to augment this process. To explore more possibilities, the need for data is crucial, whether historical case-studies, design input, or user behavior feedback. AI cannot work in a vacuum as it does not understand the goals of what it is trying to achieve. Fundamentally, this is because the design is for the user and so can only be assessed by them. Creativity is defined by the ability to excite and make new things, so even if there was an objectively novel design in relation to an individual experience, it becomes "old" once seen and cannot be shown again and provide the same level of engagement.

We have shown some examples where AI techniques can be leveraged to know more, to design more, and to interact more. We have also shown different ways that data representation and learning process affect the outcome and capability of the AI Current systems are heavily influenced by their data structures often made of scalar tensors, but these must be converted into something geometric and spatial in architecture to help continue the conversation and exploration. Simultaneously, finding the right resolution and design freedom for the system defines its scope. During the early stages, a solution does not have to be highly accurate, and even in low resolution, a vague solution might beneficially be open to interpretation to find good designs to progress into other stages of the design.

AI itself is still at an early stage of being applied to early-stage design. However, it promises new capabilities in the field and a wealth of untapped potential that needs greater exploration but will likely bring new interfaces leading to the ability for mixed-initiative systems leveraging the best of human and computer capability.

Acknowledgments

The case studies demonstrated here represent the collective effort of the Meta Design Lab over several years, specifically Nazim Ibrahim, Verina Cristie, and Ahmed Meeran, who in many of the above cases lead the principal technical development. Some of the materials in this document were supported by the SUTD-MIT International Design Centre, and the Singapore Ministry of Education.

References

Ashby, W. R. (1960). *Design for a Brain the Origin of Adaptive Behaviour (rev)*. New York: John Wiley & Sons.

Chaillou, S. (2020). *AI+ Architecture: Towards a New Approach* (Doctoral dissertation – Harvard University).

Davis, D. (2013). *Modelled on Software Engineering: Flexible Parametric Models in the Practice of Architecture* (Doctoral dissertation, RMIT University).

Frazer, J. (1995). *An Evolutionary Architecture*. London: AA Press.

Fujimura, R. (2018). *The Form of Knowledge, the Prototype of Architectural Thinking and Its Application*. Tokyo: Toto Publishers.

Gero, J. S., & Kannengiesser, U. (2004). The situated function-behaviour-structure framework. *Design Studies*, 25(4), 373–391.

Harding, J., & Brandt-Olsen, C. (2018). Biomorpher: Interactive evolution for parametric design. *International Journal of Architectural Computing*, 16(2), 144–163.

Harding, J. E., & Shepherd, P. (2017). Meta-parametric design. *Design Studies*, 52, 73–95.

Ibrahim, N., & Joyce, S. C. (2019). User directed meta parametric design for option exploration: In ubiquity and autonomy. In *Proceedings of the 39th Annual Conference of the Association for Computer-Aided Design in Architecture*. University of Texas at Austin.

Joyce, S.C., & Ibrahim, N. (2017). Exploring the Evolution of Meta Parametric Models. Acadia 2017: Disciplines & Disruption. In *Proceedings of the 37th Annual Conference of the Association for Computer Aided Design in Architecture* (pp. 308–317). Cambridge, MA, 2–4 November, 2017.

Karras, T., Laine, S., Aittala, M., Hellsten, J., Lehtinen, J., & Aila, T. (2020). Analyzing and improving the image quality of stylegan. In *Proceedings of the IEEE/CVF Conference on Computer Vision and Pattern Recognition* (pp. 8110–8119). Seattle.

Maaten, L. V. D., & Hinton, G. (2008). Visualizing data using t-SNE. *Journal of Machine Learning Research*, 9(Nov), 2579–2605.

Matejka, J., Glueck, M., Bradner, E., Hashemi, A., Grossman, T., & Fitzmaurice, G. (2018). Dream lens: Exploration and visualization of large-scale generative design datasets. In *Proceedings of the 2018 CHI Conference on Human Factors in Computing Systems* (pp. 1–12). Montreal, Canada.

Michie, D. (1963). Experiments on the mechanization of game-learning Part I: Characterization of the model and its parameters. *The Computer Journal*, *6*(3), 232–236.

Mueller, C. T., & Ochsendorf, J. A. (2015). Combining structural performance and designer preferences in evolutionary design space exploration. *Automation in Construction*, *52*, 70–82.

Negroponte, N. (1970). *The Architecture Machine*. Cambridge, MA: MIT Press.

Negroponte, N. (1975). *Soft Architecture Machines*. Cambridge, MA: MIT Press.

Pak, A., & Paroubek, P. (2010, May). Twitter as a corpus for sentiment analysis and opinion mining. In *Proceedings of the International Conference on Language Resources and Evaluation* (pp. 1320–1326), 17–23 May 2010, Valletta, Malta.

Rittel, H. W., & Webber, M. M. (1973). Dilemmas in a general theory of planning. *Policy Sciences*, *4*(2), 155–169.

Ronneberger, O., Fischer, P., & Brox, T. (2015). U-net: Convolutional networks for biomedical image segmentation. In *International Conference on Medical Image Computing and Computer-assisted Intervention* (pp. 234–241). Springer, Cham.

Stiny, G. (1980). Introduction to shape and shape grammars. *Environment and Planning B: Planning and Design*, *7*(3), 343–351.

Tseranidis, S., Brown, N. C., & Mueller, C. T. (2016). Data-driven approximation algorithms for rapid performance evaluation and optimization of civil structures. *Automation in Construction*, *72*, 279–293.

Wang, W., Huang, Q., You, S., Yang, C., & Neumann, U. (2017). Shape inpainting using 3D generative adversarial network and recurrent convolutional networks. In *Proceedings of the IEEE International Conference on Computer Vision* (pp. 2298–2306), Venice, Italy.

Xuereb Conti, Z., & Kaijima, S. (2018, July). A flexible simulation metamodel for exploring multiple design spaces. In *Proceedings of IASS Annual Symposia* (Vol. 2018, No. 2, pp. 1–8), International Association for Shell and Spatial Structures (IASS).

8

AI in space planning

Danil Nagy

Space planning is the process of arranging programs in space. This can involve laying out rooms within a floor plan or arranging buildings on a site (Figure 8.1). Like any design process, space planning is to some extent a creative exercise that requires a designer's experience, knowledge, and intuition to do well. At the same time, it can be a tedious process, driven less by creativity and more by the need to resolve many competing constraints and requirements within a single layout. Often, the only way to solve a difficult space planning problem is to generate many different options until you find one that works. This can be both a difficult and repetitive process, not well suited to a creative designer.

In many ways, computers are the opposite of human designers. They have no inherent creativity or intuition, or really any way of knowing how to do anything. To accomplish any task, computers must be programmed with specific sets of instructions called *algorithms*. But, once programmed, a computer has no issue with executing the same process over and over and can do so at an amazing speed. This allows computers to process information much faster than any human being and automate many tasks that are challenging for people to do.

It would seem that the often repetitive and tedious nature of space planning make it a perfect candidate for such automation. If we could write an algorithm to follow the same process as a human designer, we could have the computer do all the tedious and repetitive tasks, while allowing the human designer to focus on more creative tasks that require their unique ingenuity and intuition. In fact, many such algorithms and computer programs have been studied and developed over the years, yet none see widespread use in practice today. Given how much progress we have seen in automating industries such as manufacturing, transportation, and finance, why has there been so little development or adoption of tools and technologies for automating design?

This is because space planning, while sometimes routine and repetitive, is still a design process that is individual to each designer and the problem they are trying to solve. Thus, it has been a challenge for the computer software industry to develop automated tools that can fulfill the specific requirements of all designers. In recent years, however, two trends have led to a renewed interest in automated space planning. First, new sophisticated artificial intelligence (AI) approaches have introduced more clever algorithms that can accomplish tasks that were previously thought only possible by humans. Second, the development of easier

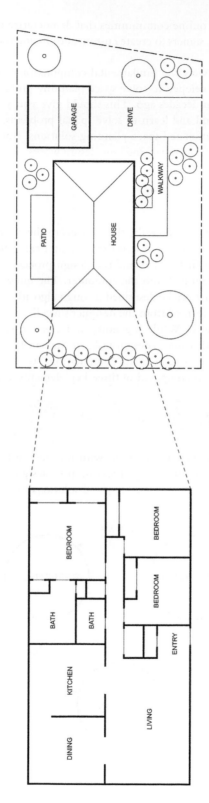

Figure 8.1 Examples of space planning—laying out rooms within a building or a set of buildings on a site.

programming tools and large online communities that democratize the process of computer programming have allowed designers to create custom automation tools to fit their particular needs and design process.

In this chapter, we will review the fundamental computational concepts, strategies, and approaches that have been developed to solve space planning problems since the invention of computers more than seven decades ago. This should give you a good basic intuition for how computers can understand and learn to solve spatial problems, and a solid foundation to start creating your own automated space planning solutions. But before we get into the techniques, let us spend some time unpacking how design works, and what this means for our ability to teach computers how to design.

Automating design

To automate any process, you must describe that process to the computer in the form of an algorithm, or a set of specific instructions that the computer can follow to achieve its goals. To automate design, we must first understand the design process, and then break it into a set of tasks that can be programmed into the computer. The question is, to what extent is design a predictable process that can be described through algorithms, versus a purely artistic expression that emerges fully formed from the designer's head?

In reality it is a mix of both. While ingenuity and creative expression are important, most designers would agree that many design tasks do indeed follow a process, and when that process becomes repetitive, we can create computational tools to automate them for us. In general, the design process is composed of three key elements: creativity, repetition, and learning (Figure 8.2).

Creativity

Creativity is what allows designers to come up with multiple different ideas and concepts to solve a given problem. During the design process, most designers use certain rules, templates, and guidelines that help them generate good solutions to common problems faster.

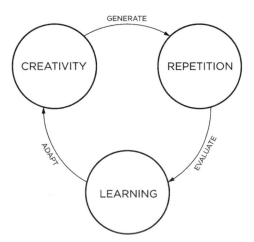

Figure 8.2 A theoretical framework for a design process defined by creativity, repetition, and learning.

These guidelines might be based on the constraints of certain materials, a set of functional requirements, or may be developed consciously as style guides. These style guides ensure that designs stay consistent and make it easier for the designer to create a variety of good solutions in a short period of time.

While we cannot ask a computer to dream up design options on its own, we can create programs that describe the rules and standards of our design process and ask the computer to generate a variety of solutions by following the rules in different ways. To be useful, such a "generator" program also needs to describe the goals of the problem and have a way for the computer to check which solutions are better or worse than others.

In practice, our goals are not always well formalized and may be both quantitative and qualitative. But, if we want to automate the design process, we must be able to describe both the process for creating design options as well as evaluating them in strict computational and quantitative terms. Designing and programming these computational "models" is the most important and most challenging part of automating design.

Repetition

Repetition is critical to any design process since it is very rare for a designer to come up with the best solution to a problem on their first try. Typically, a designer will test many different variations and possible solutions before finally settling on the best one. This iterative process allows the designer to incrementally develop their designs through either improving on existing solutions or starting from scratch and trying something new.

Once we have developed a computational model that can create multiple solutions to a given design problem, we can easily write an algorithm that tests different solutions and tells us which works the best. Computers were built for repetition and using them in the design process allows us to generate and evaluate many more design options than we could "by hand".

However, when a designer is iterating, they are not just creating random solutions. Every time a designer creates a solution they are being guided by their intuition, which is developed over time through practice and seeing what does and does not work. As they iterate, they can also use their analysis of previous designs to guide them to create better designs in later iterations. The designer learns through the design process, and that knowledge can be applied toward solving the current problem as well as other similar problems in the future.

Learning

Creating algorithms that can learn to solve problems autonomously is a core focus of the AI field. Over the years, many AI approaches have been developed including sophisticated algorithms in the related fields of optimization and machine learning (ML). Applied to different domains, these algorithms can help people make complex decisions based on data and even automate entire decision-making processes without requiring any human input.

Using these approaches, we can develop programs that not only generate different design solutions but also learn how to develop better solutions over time. This learning can be done *explicitly* by generating many different solutions from a computational model and figuring out what types of solutions work the best, or *implicitly* by analyzing a large set of good solutions and learning common patterns between them. Explicit solutions use optimization or "search" algorithms to test different solutions to a problem to figure out what types of solutions work best. Implicit approaches use generic computational models such as artificial neural networks (ANNs) which can be made specific through training on a large amount of existing data.

To apply these methods to space planning, we must be able to describe the space planning problem computationally in the form of a model. Over the years, many such models have been developed, but due to the specific nature of design and space planning, no universal model has emerged. Although today there is no single approach to AI in space planning, these precedents provide a set of building blocks that computational designers can use to develop new approaches that satisfy their particular needs and design goals.

Assigning programs to places

One of the earliest approaches to computational space planning deals with the problem of optimally distributing a set of facilities or programs among a set of preselected sites. This is called the quadratic assignment problem (QAP), which was first described by Koopmans and Beckmann in 1957 (Koopmans & Beckmann, 1957).

In the QAP, we define a set of programs and the same number of locations to which the programs can be assigned. The programs can represent any functional unit, for example, rooms of a house, buildings on campus, or office locations throughout the world. Between each pair of programs, we define a "flow" that describes the strength of the connection between them. A flow can represent any important value that depends on the distance between the programs. For example, the number of shipments between two storage facilities or the number of business trips between two offices. Similarly, for each pair of locations, we define a "distance" that describes how far they are apart. This can represent a physical distance or another measure of cost. Given a set of programs and locations, the goal of the QAP is to assign each program to a unique location such that programs with higher flows are placed closer to each other while those with lower flows are placed further apart.

In the QAP, flows and distances are typically stored in matrices or two-dimensional tables of numbers (Figure 8.3). Each cell in the matrix corresponds to the flow or distance between each pair of programs or locations, which are represented by the cell's row and column. The relative success of each solution is called its "cost". This cost can be calculated by first multiplying the flow between each pair of programs by the distance between their assigned locations, which gives you the weighted distance between them. Adding all these values together gives you the total weighted distance between all programs, which describes how good the solution is relative to other possible solutions. Placing programs with high flows

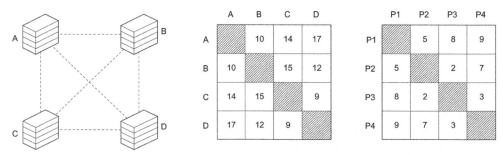

Figure 8.3 A simple QAP with four locations represented by letters A, B, C, and D and four programs represented by numbers P1, P2, P3, and P4.

closer together minimizes this cost, and thus we consider the solution with the lowest cost to be the best solution to the problem.

Heuristics and greedy algorithms

The QAP can be relatively easy to solve by hand when the number of programs and locations is small, but as the number increases, the number of possible solutions starts to grow very quickly. The number of solutions to an assignment problem like the QAP can be calculated by the *factorial* of the number of things being assigned, which grows almost exponentially as the number increases. For example, a QAP with ten programs has 10! = 3,628,800 possible assignments—a large number but relatively easy to work through with a computer. However, just doubling the number of programs creates 20! = 2.4 × 10^18 or *2.4 quintillion* unique solutions. Even with the fastest computer, these types of problems quickly become impractical or impossible to solve directly by trying every solution and returning the best one.

Instead of checking every solution, perhaps we could develop a strategy to solve the QAP directly by working through a series of steps. If we found a strategy that works, we could then program it into a computer as an algorithm so that it can solve the problem for us. Here is one possible algorithm for solving the QAP (Figure 8.4):

1   Start by placing the two programs with the highest flow in the two closest locations
2   Find the program with the largest flow to any program already placed and place it in the unassigned location closest to it
3   Repeat step 2 until all programs are placed

This algorithm can be easily implemented and will create a solution that is very likely to be better than any random assignment. However, because it locks in certain decisions early on, it can prevent the best possible solution from being found. In computer science, these kinds of algorithms are called heuristics. Heuristics can be very effective at solving problems that do not have direct easy solutions, but they are usually specific to the problem they are trying to solve, and do not guarantee that the overall best solution will be found. When an algorithm gets stuck in a solution that is pretty good but not the best possible, we

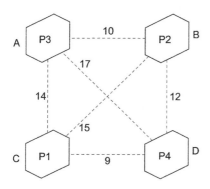

	A (P3)	B (P2)	C (P1)	D (P4)
A (P3)		10*2 =20	14*8 =112	17*3 =51
B (P2)	10*2 =20		15*5 =75	12*7 =84
C (P1)	14*8 =112	15*5 =75		9*9 =81
D (P4)	17*3 =51	12*7 =84	9*9 =81	

Total cost = 846

Figure 8.4 Applying a basic heuristic to solve the QAP.

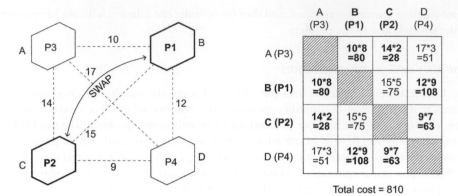

	A (P3)	B (P1)	C (P2)	D (P4)
A (P3)		10*8 =80	14*2 =28	17*3 =51
B (P1)	10*8 =80		15*5 =75	12*9 =108
C (P2)	14*2 =28	15*5 =75		9*7 =63
D (P4)	17*3 =51	12*9 =108	9*7 =63	

Total cost = 810

Figure 8.5 A better greedy heuristic for solving the QAP.

call this a "local optimum", as opposed to the "global optimum" represented by the best solution overall.

Many different heuristics can be developed to solve the same problem, and there is usually a tradeoff between the time it takes to run a heuristic versus the quality of the solution produced. A somewhat better heuristic for the QAP might be:

1   Start with all programs assigned to random locations.
2   For each pair of programs:

    a   Swap their locations and check whether the new locations result in a lower cost.
    b   If the resulting cost is lower, keep the swap and move to the next pair.
    c   If the cost is higher, revert the swap and move to the next pair.

3   Repeat until there is one cycle of pairs during which no lower cost is found.

This type of heuristic is called a "greedy algorithm" because it makes decisions only based on what is good at the moment, without considering what might produce the best results overall. This heuristic would take longer to compute than the previous one, yet it is still deterministic since running the algorithm with the same starting point will always generate the same result (Figure 8.5).

The results produced by the "swap" heuristic are likely to be better than those produced by the first heuristic since many more possibilities are tested before returning the best one. However, since the outcome is highly dependent on the starting condition, this approach is also not guaranteed to produce the overall best result. This is often remedied in practice by running the greedy algorithm many times with different random starting points, and then returning the best result overall.

Planning with grids

A major limitation of the QAP is that it can only be used to assign programs to a predetermined set of spaces. In many cases, however, space planning deals not just with assigning programs to spaces but also designing the physical size and shape of those spaces as well. This is often done by taking a larger area and splitting it up into a set of smaller functional spaces.

For example, we can use walls to divide the floor of a building into rooms, or property lines to divide a site into a set of parcels.

A simple way to model this process computationally is to overlay an even grid onto the area you want to plan and then use the QAP to assign programs to the cells of the grid (Armour & Buffa, 1963). Unlike in the traditional QAP, the number of grid cells (and thus assignment locations) is typically larger than the number of programs, so you must also determine how many cells should be assigned to each program. If the cells in the grid are all the same size, this can be determined by dividing the desired size of each program by the area of one grid cell (Figure 8.6).

Since we are now dealing with spaces sitting next to each other in a floor plan, we are less interested in the exact distance between the spaces and more in the connection between them. For example, if we were planning a house, we would not necessarily care about the exact distance between the center of the bedroom and the bathroom, but we would care if they shared a wall and were connected by a doorway. To represent this relationship between the spaces, we can convert the "distance" matrix of the QAP to an *adjacency matrix*, which uses Boolean values (True/False) to specify those pairs of spaces that are spatially connected (Figure 8.7). We can then define the best solution as the one that maximizes the total flows between programs assigned to adjacent spaces.

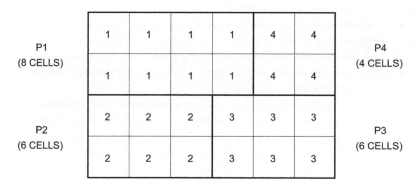

Figure 8.6   A grid-based approach to space planning with four programs.

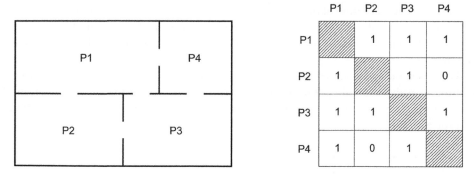

Figure 8.7   Representing adjacencies between spaces using a matrix.

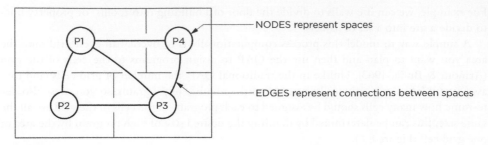

NODES represent spaces

EDGES represent connections between spaces

Figure 8.8 Representing adjacencies between spaces using a graph.

Spaces as graphs

Another way to represent adjacencies between spaces is in the form of a graph. Graphs are data structures (also commonly known as "networks" or "network graphs") that represent things and the connections between them. Every graph is defined by a set of *nodes* that represent elements in a system, and a set of *edges* that connect pairs of nodes to represent a relationship between them. To represent the adjacencies between spaces in a plan, we can create an *adjacency graph* where each space is represented by a node, and spaces that are adjacent to each other are connected with edges. By overlaying this graph onto the plan, we can visualize the connections between its spaces (Figure 8.8).

To describe the strength of the connections, we can assign "weights" to the edges, which produces a "weighted graph". These weights can be derived from any attribute of the system, for example, the distance between locations or the flow between the programs assigned to them. The entire structure of the graph including its nodes and the way they are connected is called the graph's "topology".

Graphs are a very useful data structure and are common in computational design since many design problems deal with understanding relationships between elements in space. Many algorithms have also been developed to calculate useful properties of graphs, for example, the Djikstra algorithm, which can be used to calculate the shortest path between any two nodes in a graph. We will see other applications of graphs later in this chapter.

Subdivision

The grid-based approach gives us some control over the size and shape of our spaces, but it is still limited by the structure of the grid and the shape of its cells. To overcome this constraint, we can create a model that directly controls the way space is divided, in effect creating a custom grid made of cells of different sizes, which more closely fit the needs of their assigned programs.

We can create such a model by starting with the boundary of the space we want to plan and progressively subdividing it into a set of smaller spaces, similar to how a designer might plan a set of rooms by drawing one wall at a time (Figure 8.9). An algorithmic definition of this process might be:

1   Set the boundary as the starting shape.
2   Split the shape to create two new spaces.
3   Select one of the existing spaces and repeat step 2.
4   Repeat steps 2–3 until the desired number of spaces has been generated.

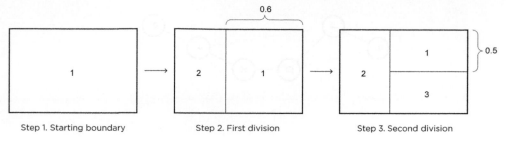

Figure 8.9   Planning a space using subdivision.

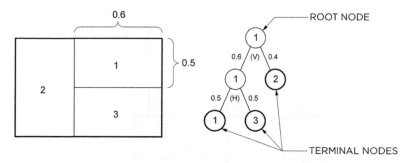

Figure 8.10   Representing the subdivision process with a decision tree.

To control how space is divided, we can use a set of parameters to specify how the spaces are split in step 2 and which space is chosen for further splitting in step 3. By varying these parameters, we can create a variety of different layouts to match our needs.

Decision trees

Because of its iterative nature, we can think of subdivision as a decision-making process driven by a series of decisions where each decision influences the ones that come next. We can represent this decision process in the form of a *decision tree*, utilizing the same graph structure introduced in the last section.

The decision tree starts with a single "root" node representing the starting boundary shape. Every time space is divided, two new nodes are created to represent the two new spaces, each of which is connected by an edge to the original node. The final set of spaces produced from the subdivision are represented by the *terminal nodes* of the graph, which are the set of nodes that were not further divided and thus have no edges coming out of them (Figure 8.10).

The topology of the decision tree represents the sequence in which the spaces are divided to form the final layout. We can also add parameters to the nodes and edges of the tree to store information about how the division is made at each step, for example, the direction in which space was divided or the desired ratio between the areas of the two new spaces produced.

Aggregation

Although the subdivision method provides more flexibility over the size and shape of spaces we can produce, like the grid-based method, it has the limitation of only working within a

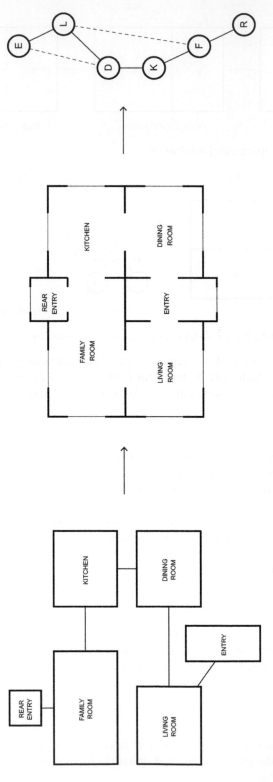

Figure 8.11 Generating a floor plan through aggregation.

predetermined boundary. This works well for cases where this boundary is fixed and known, for example, when laying out rooms or furniture within an existing building or laying out buildings on a fixed site. However, it can be limiting when the boundary is not necessarily fixed or known beforehand, for example, when designing a new building.

To overcome this limitation, we can reverse the process of subdivision and instead start with a collection of smaller components that we wish to assemble into our design. These components may represent individual rooms, pieces of furniture, or components of an entire building. To create a new design, we can "aggregate" the components together by starting from an initial "seed" component and adding to it other components based on some pre-defined *rules*.

For example, if we wanted to generate the floorplan of a house, we could start with the entry foyer, and then add to it spaces based on a certain predetermined sequence. Let us say our sequence is:

entry → living room → dining room → kitchen → family room → rear entry

To generate different designs, we can vary how the rules are applied. For example, we can change the order of rooms in the house generator to create houses with different programmatic layouts (Figure 8.11).

Like subdivision, aggregation is an iterative process and, thus, can also be represented by a decision tree. In this case, the "root" node represents the starting "seed" component (for example, the entry foyer). To this seed component, we can add one or more other components, which are represented by new nodes in the graph connected by edges to the root node. The nodes of the graph can also store information about the rules that dictate which components can be added next.

Fractal geometries and grammars

Subdivision and aggregation are related to each other in that they both define space by starting with an initial condition and then further develop it by following a series of steps or rules. With subdivision, we start with a large space and derive smaller spaces by progressively "cutting" it. With aggregation, we start with smaller components and "grow" them into a larger whole. Both approaches are examples of fractal geometry as first described by Benoit Mandelbrot (Mandelbrot, 1977). Fractal geometries are common in nature and are characterized by self-similar features generated from a sequential process like growth or fracturing (Figure 8.12).

One of the most popular applications of fractal geometries for solving design problems is a concept called "shape grammars", first developed by George Stiny in 1972 (Stiny & Gips, 1971). Just as a language grammar defines the rules for how words come together to form meaning, shape grammars define the components (words) and rules (grammars) for how small components can come together into a larger whole. Shape grammars can be extremely useful for encoding the logic of sequential design processes so that they can be understood by a computer.

Optimizing with "meta" heuristics

With more complex approaches such as subdivision and aggregation, it can start to be difficult to create good heuristics to solve them. Since heuristics are specific to the problem they are

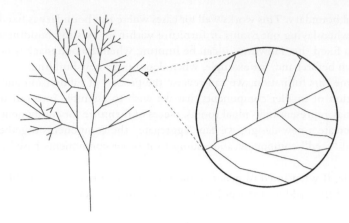

Figure 8.12   Fractal geometry of a tree.

Given a set of parameters: $x = (x_1, x_2, ..., x_n)$

Minimize a set of objective functions: $f_i(x)$

Subject to a set of constraints: $h_j(x) = 0$

$g_k(x) \leq 0$

Figure 8.13   **General definition of an optimization problem based on parameters, objectives, and constraints.**

designed to solve, an algorithm that works well for something like the QAP will not necessarily work for figuring out how to divide a space to get the best set of rooms, or how to aggregate a set of spaces to form a complete plan.

In this case, we can rely on another class of optimization algorithms called "metaheuristics" (Yang, 2010). Like any heuristic, these algorithms can generate solutions to a problem by following a predetermined series of steps. With metaheuristics, however, these steps are not specific to the problem being solved and can be applied to solve any problem as long as it can be represented the right way.

To work with metaheuristics, a design problem must be represented with a computational model that defines a set of parameters for creating various design solutions, and a set of numerical outputs that describe the quality of each solution produced (Figure 8.13). The inputs and outputs of this model create a "design space" that describes all the possible solutions to the problem and the relative performance of each solution. The goal of the metaheuristic algorithm is to explore this design space to find the best possible solution.

The beauty of metaheuristics is that they do not care about the nature of the design problem, how the parameters control the model, or how the outputs are computed. This means that we can easily apply the same algorithm to many different types of problems, without having to create specific heuristics each time.

Most metaheuristic algorithms support two types of outputs that help the algorithm determine the quality of solutions produced. The first is an *objective*, which is a numerical value that should be either minimized or maximized to produce the best solution. Objectives do not define specific targets for what the values should be; they just tell the algorithm to make the values as small or as large as possible. A good example of an objective is the cost calculated in the QAP.

The second type of output is a *constraint*, which defines specific conditions that the solution needs to meet to be deemed valid. For example, in the QAP, we could define constraints based on the maximum distances between certain programs. Unlike objectives, constraints do not define the relative performance between solutions. Any solution that does not meet a constraint is considered "nonfeasible", while all solutions that meet all constraints are considered equally valid.

Objectives and constraints give metaheuristics a way to understand the goals of a problem even without knowing what problem we are trying to solve or how the model actually works. Given a set of parameters to control the model, these algorithms can follow a process to incrementally determine those parameter settings that result in the best objective values that meet all constraints (Figure 8.14).

Another important aspect of metaheuristics is that they often involve some amount of randomness in how they make decisions. Algorithms that incorporate randomness are called *stochastic algorithms*. This randomness allows metaheuristics to explore complex design spaces and avoid getting stuck in local optima, making it more likely that they can find the best overall solution to the problem. The stochastic nature of metaheuristics also means that the algorithms are not deterministic, meaning each time you run a metaheuristic, it can produce different results.

As with any heuristic, there is no absolute guarantee that the best solution will be found within any given amount of time. However, because of their nondeterministic nature, these algorithms can be run continuously and keep exploring the design space and finding better

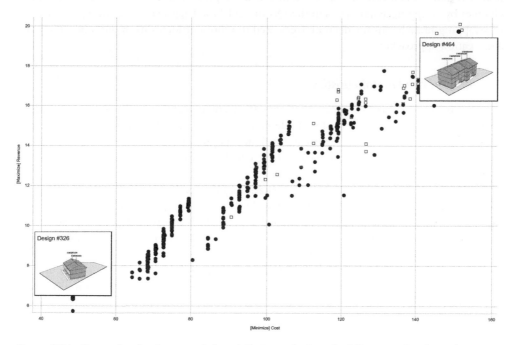

Figure 8.14 Example of using a metaheuristic to optimize a building massing based on a set of objectives and constraints. Each dot in the plot represents a design option explored by the algorithm. The x and y values of the plot represent the two objectives (costs that should be minimized and revenue that should be maximized). Squares represent nonfeasible designs, which broke at least one constraint defined by the site's zoning.

and better solutions if they exist. The tradeoff of this exploration is that metaheuristics usually take more time to achieve good solutions than simpler heuristics or greedy algorithms. Thus, they should not be your first approach and should be reserved only for cases when a simpler heuristic does not exist to solve the problem.

Although many different metaheuristics have been developed over the years, they generally fall into two categories: *trajectory-based* and *population-based*.

Trajectory-based metaheuristics

Trajectory-based algorithms start with a single solution as a starting point and iteratively modify it in a way that leads to better and better solutions over time. This is similar to the "swap" heuristic described earlier, except now the decisions taken at each step are not always predictable. One of the oldest trajectory-based metaheuristics is the simulated annealing (SA) algorithm (Kirkpatrick, Gelatt & Vecchi, 1983), which was inspired by the way molecules in metal alloys organize into regular patterns while the alloy is cooled during a process called annealing.

Like the greedy algorithm we saw earlier, the SA makes progressive changes to a starting condition and accepts each change if it results in a better outcome. However, with SA, there is also some likelihood that a worse result will be accepted. The probability of accepting a worse outcome usually starts high and is reduced while the algorithm is run to encourage wide exploration in the beginning and more and more refinement in later stages (Figure 8.15).

The way in which the design is changed at each stage of the process depends on how the model is defined and how its input parameters are represented. For example, we can make changes by swapping assignments in the QA or grid-based approaches or adding, removing, or swapping branches in the decision trees used to represent solutions in the subdivision and aggregation approaches.

Population-based metaheuristics

Population-based algorithms are another type of metaheuristic which do not work on a single design but instead work on sets of multiple designs simultaneously to progressively improve their performance. One of the earliest and still most popular population-based metaheuristics is the genetic algorithm (GA) (Holland, 1975), which is inspired by the evolutionary process in nature.

The GA starts by creating an initial population of designs as a starting point. It then creates the next generation of designs by selecting high-performing solutions in the first generation and recombining them in a process called *crossover*. This ensures that some characteristics of the good "parent" designs make it into the next generation of "child" designs, with the hope that some of the children will be even better performing than the parents.

There is also a small chance that some of the parameters of the child designs will be randomly changed in a process called a *mutation*. As in evolution, this mutation introduces variation into the process, ensuring that the algorithm can explore the whole design space and avoid getting stuck in local optima (Figure 8.16).

Packing

The aggregation approach allows us to directly determine the size and shape of our spaces, but the way in which they combine must follow a set of predetermined rules. Although this gives us control over how the spaces are aggregated, it can limit the possibilities that the

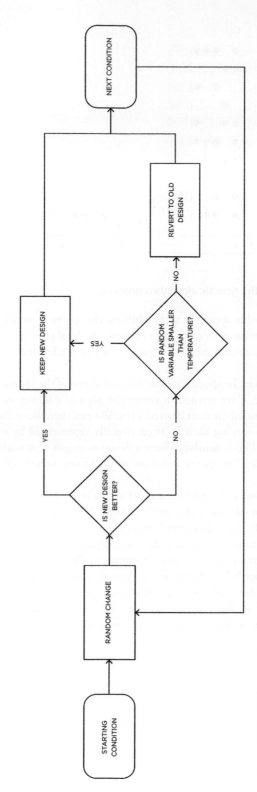

Figure 8.15 Diagram of the simulated annealing process.

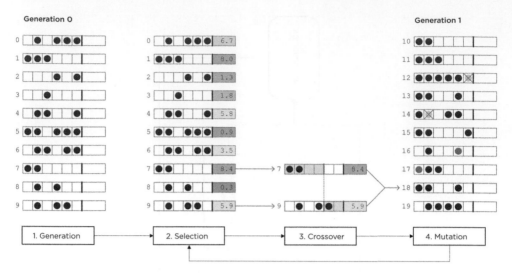

Figure 8.16 Diagram of the genetic algorithm process.

model can produce. Another approach to combining the spaces is to generate them all first, and then let them move relative to each other to form the final plan layout. This is known as a "packing" approach because its goal is to "pack" a set of predefined spaces most efficiently into a layout.

In this approach, we start by specifying the size and shape of the spaces we want to include in the plan. For example, if we wanted to create the plan of a house, we could start with a rectangle for each room based on their desired sizes. We can then move them around in space relative to each other by varying their location (usually represented by x and y coordinates) as well as their rotation. This is similar to how a designer might start with a program brief to generate a "bubble diagram" of spaces, and then arrange them together to form a conceptual plan layout (Figure 8.17).

To generate good layouts, the packing model needs to be programmed with the conditions that constitute favorable and unfavorable results. Typically, a good layout is defined as one that maximizes the desired adjacencies between spaces while avoiding collisions and overlaps between them. To minimize overlaps, we can calculate the intersections among all space boundaries, and set this as an objective to be minimized during optimization. If we want to pack the spaces within a predefined boundary, we can also calculate the portion of all programs that fall outside the boundary and minimize this area as well. Unlike the previous approaches, the packing method gives us the flexibility to either follow a predetermined boundary or not, depending on the space planning problem we are trying to solve (Figure 8.18).

Agent-based systems

Like any optimization problem, we can solve packing problems using metaheuristic algorithms by setting the location and rotation parameters of each program as inputs and the adjacencies and overlaps between programs as objectives and constraints. The downside of this approach, however, is that it creates a huge design space where a vast majority of the potential designs will have overlaps and thus produce invalid designs. This kind of model can be difficult and time-consuming to optimize with a standard metaheuristic that does not consider the particularities of the packing approach.

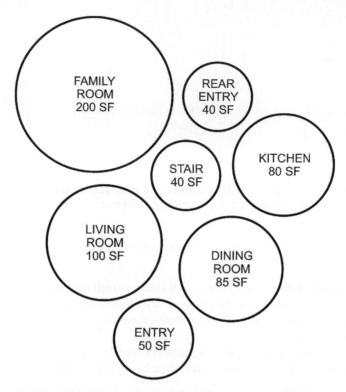

Figure 8.17 Bubble diagram used during the early stages of space planning.

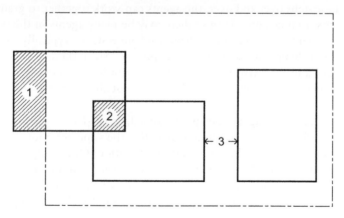

Figure 8.18 Basic rules for a packing problem: (1) minimize program area outside of the boundary, (2) minimize overlapping program area, (3) maximize proximity between programs.

A better approach to solving the packing problem is to develop a custom heuristic that treats each of the spaces that comprise the layout as individual "agents" that are programmed with certain *behaviors* that they follow individually to achieve the best spatial layout. This is called an "agent-based" approach because all the logic is implemented locally in the agents who interact with each other to achieve the overall result. Here is one set of rules that can be programmed into space "agents" to allow them to find the optimal packing (Figure 8.19):

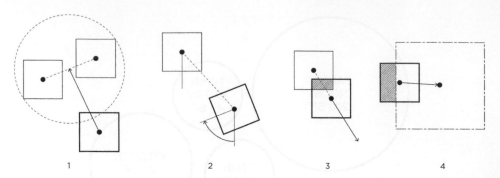

Figure 8.19 A set of rules for packing agents: (1) neighbor affinity, (2) angle matching, (3) neighbor avoidance, (4) boundary avoidance.

1 Start by placing all space agents at random locations in the plan
2 For each agent:

    a Move toward the average center of all agents a small amount
    b Rotate a small amount to match the rotation of the nearest agent
    c If an intersection is found with another agent, move in the opposite direction a small amount
    d If you are trying to fit within a predetermined boundary and you are outside the boundary, move toward the center of the boundary a small amount

3 Repeat these steps for each agent iteratively until a stopping condition is met

By repeating these steps over and over, the agents can work together to gradually achieve better and better spatial layouts. Because there may be many agents in the system and the behavior of each agent influences the behavior of the rest, we typically want the agents to make only small changes at each step of the process. Since there is no way of predicting how long such a process will take, we typically run it continuously until some stopping criteria are met, for example, when the motion of all agents falls below some small threshold.

Depending on how the agents are programmed, agent-based systems can be either deterministic or stochastic. If the agents always follow the same behaviors, they will always produce the same results given the same starting condition. Optionally, we can introduce some degree of randomness or "jitter" to the behaviors to generate variation in the final outcome. Even when the behaviors are deterministic, however, the result can still be difficult to predict, since it comes from the interaction of many agents played out over time.

Intelligent agents

Agent-based systems can be very good at solving problems that can be represented by the interaction of many independent agents following a set of simple rules. However, figuring out what the rules should be is not necessarily obvious and can pose a real challenge for more complex problems. Furthermore, such systems work best when the behavior of each agent is relatively simple since complex rules can overconstrain the system and impose unnecessary and unpredictable limitations on the outcome.

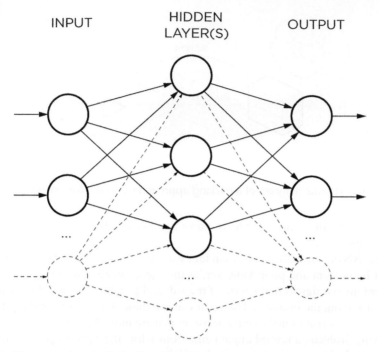

INPUT   HIDDEN LAYER(S)   OUTPUT

Figure 8.20 Diagram of a simple artificial neural network.

In cases where the agent's rules are not clear, we can replace the preprogrammed set of rules with an adaptable model which can learn those behaviors that work best based on the goals of the problem. To create such a model, we can look to ML, a field of AI focused on computational models that are not programmed directly but are trained based on data. With this approach, we start with a generic model containing many parameters and make it specific through a "training" process where we show it data coming from a system and adjust the parameters gradually to make the model fit the data.

The most popular ML model today is the ANN, which is based on the structure of our own brains. An ANN is composed of several layers of individual "neurons" which are connected to other neurons in adjacent layers of the network (Figure 8.20). When data are input into the first "input" layer of the network, it is passed through the neurons based on the parameters stored in each neuron until it reaches the final "output" layer. Typically, the network is initialized with random values for the parameters, so the connection between the inputs and outputs will not be meaningful. To create a specific relationship between the inputs and outputs we can "train" the network by showing it sample data containing inputs and outputs, and progressively adjusting all the parameters in the network until the outputs produced by the network match those seen in the data.

To extend our agent-based approach, we can replace the simple rules programmed into each agent with an ANN that serves as the "brain" of the agent and helps it decide which actions to take at each step of the process. The inputs of the ANN are the conditions or *state* of the agent's environment at each step. For example, the state can be the position of other agents in the system or the distance of the agent to the boundary within which you are trying to pack the programs. The output of the ANN is the *action* that the agent takes based on that

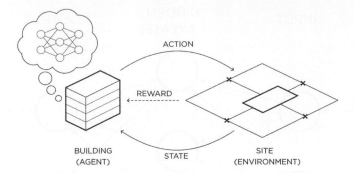

Figure 8.21 Conceptual diagram of a packing approach using reinforcement learning.

state. For example, the action may be to move in a certain direction or to rotate a certain amount (Figure 8.21).

Since the ANN is initialized with random parameters, the decisions made by the agent will at first be random and poor. However, as the agent interacts with its environment, the environment gives it signals in the form of rewards and penalties that tell the agent how well it is doing at solving the problem. The agent can use these signals to train the parameters of its ANN so that it learns to make better decisions that are more likely to maximize its reward. In the packing problem, a reward might come from achieving a proper packing of programs with the desired adjacencies, while a penalty might come from having too many overlaps or placing programs outside of the boundary.

In the ML discipline, this approach is called reinforcement learning (RL). This is a popular method for teaching AI systems to make proper decisions to accomplish specific goals within a well-defined system of rules. One common application is teaching computers to play games such as Chess or Go (Silver, et al., 2016), where the decision is the piece to play in each round, and the reward signal is whether or not you win the game. Similar systems have also been used for self-driving cars, where the decision is how to apply gas, brakes, and steering at every moment of driving, and the reward is whether the car operates safely.

Of the various approaches presented in this chapter, RL is both more modern and more complex to implement. Since it is a relatively new concept, it has not yet been widely applied to solving problems in space planning or design problems in general. However, given its flexibility and ability to learn to solve problems without being directly programmed, this method is very promising, and we are likely to see more applications in the near future.

Conclusion

This chapter has presented a variety of computational approaches, techniques, and tools that have been developed to solve space planning problems since the invention of computers nearly 70 years ago. Despite this long history of development, most of these techniques have only been tested in research, and none have entered common use by designers in their day-to-day practice. Given the impact that computers and automation have made in other industries, you may wonder why these techniques have not made a greater impact on the actual practice of design and space planning.

One reason is that unlike many of the industries that have benefitted from automation, space planning is still largely a creative process. Although many parts of the process are repetitive, the approach taken is often specific to the problem being solved and the particular style and interests of the designer solving it. Another reason is that computer programming has traditionally been a complex and difficult process, involving a high level of training and expertise. Because of this, the computational methods that have been developed have mostly come from professional programmers or academic researchers, not the designers who would use these tools to solve actual design problems.

For this reason, most approaches have focused on creating universal one–size–fits–all solutions that fail to address the actual needs of designers, their unique approaches, and the particularities of the problems they are trying to solve. As a result, the industry has fallen behind in technological advancement, with most designers still following the same manual process they have for decades.

In recent years, however, there has been renewed interest in applying AI to space planning and other design problems. Part of this renewed interest has to do with the emergence of new sophisticated algorithms and approaches like RL that enable computers to solve complex problems without having to be directly programmed by a human. A much bigger reason, however, is the democratization of computer programming through easy-to-use computational design tools like Rhino Grasshopper (grasshopper3d.com) and high-level programming languages like Python (python.org). These tools can be learned by any designer and used to develop custom tools that fit the particular needs of each design project.

By automating routine and repetitive tasks, AI can speed up design processes and unlock new potentials for the human designer. However, the unique and creative nature of design tasks make it unlikely that any universal automation tools will be developed that meet the needs of every designer and every design problem. Instead, designers should learn the concepts behind the computational strategies that have been developed over the years and use them to create their own automation tools that address their specific needs and interests.

References

Armour, G. C., & Buffa, E. S. (1963). A heuristic algorithm and simulation approach to relative location of facilities. *Management Science, 9*(2), 294–309.

Holland, J. (1992). *Adaptation in Natural and Artificial Systems: An Introductory Analysis with Applications to Biology, Control, and Artificial Intelligence.* Cambridge, MA: MIT Press.

Kirkpatrick, S., Gelatt, C. D., & Vecchi, M. P. (1983). Optimization by simulated annealing. *Science, 220*(4598), 671–680.

Koopmans, T. C., & Beckmann, M. (1957). Assignment problems and the location of economic activities. *Econometrica: Journal of the Econometric Society, 25*(1), 53–76.

Mandelbrot, B. B. (1977). The fractal geometry of nature. HB Fenn and Company. *Contents.* Jan, 1.

Silver, D., Huang, A., Maddison, C. J., Guez, A., Sifre, L., Van Den Driessche, G., … & Dieleman, S. (2016). Mastering the game of Go with deep neural networks and tree search. *Nature, 529*(7587), 484–489.

Stiny, G., & Gips, J. (1971, August). Shape grammars and the generative specification of painting and sculpture. In *IFIP Congress (2)* (Vol. 2, No. 3, pp. 125–135).

Yang, X. S. (2010). *Nature-Inspired Metaheuristic Algorithms.* Frome: Luniver Press.

9

Generating new architectural designs using topological AI

Prithwish Basu, Imdat As, and Elizabeth Munch

Automating design is the holy grail of both architecture and AI. The advent of new scalable AI/ML methods and the availability of architectural design data for training is beginning to pave the way for researchers toward reaching this goal. In this chapter, we describe several ways of representing architectural design data that are amenable to further AI/ML processing and also describe AI/ML techniques that can be the steppingstones for automating design eventually.

A key step to automatization of the creative design process is to discover the building blocks of good functional designs. If basic building blocks and design rules of assembly are known *a priori* and finite, new designs can be composed using *shape grammars*—here, design rules dictate which new *shapes* (or designs) can be formed by their repeated application on basic building blocks (Stiny & Gips, 1972). These design rules may be structured or naive (Ruiz-Montiel et al., 2013). In our work, we do not assume knowledge of either the rules of how components are composed into a design or the fundamental building blocks of a design. Instead, our key hypothesis is that both salient and latent design rules can be *discovered* by learning from their repeated occurrence in the design data. This is a challenging problem that we aim to solve by leveraging existing design data and exploiting the synergy between architecture topology-based modeling and AI/ML methods. In particular, our goal is to develop a modern architectural design theory by leveraging hand-in-hand both topology for high-level design considerations and geometry for low-level design considerations. One can potentially incorporate into this framework standard geometric attributes such as dimensions, derived geometric attributes such as maps of heat and air distribution, and key nongeometric attributes in the design such as aesthetics, ambiance, and spirituality into the model—to create a truly holistic design space.

Applied topology can aid design

Topology differs from geometry in that it abstracts away the notion of physical distance while retaining the notions of nearness and continuity. This opens up the potential to explore complex designs at a much higher level of abstraction than allowed by geometry. In fact, a multitude of designs with different geometries could be represented by the same topological space. Examples of topological structures include graphs with nodes and edges (without length) and higher-dimensional analogs of graphs, namely, simplicial complexes with nodes, edges, and higher-dimensional faces. However, these are inadequate to model design data as their mathematical constructions are too rigidly constrained. Recently, there have been proposals to model architectural spaces using concepts from nonmanifold topology (Jabi et al., 2017). Lines, surfaces, and voids can be modeled using *cells*, and a collection of cells is referred to as a *cell complex* or a *cluster*. This resulted in the topologic toolkit, which allows simple binary operations on these structures, e.g., add/delete (Aish et al., 2018). For exploring more complex design problems though, a richer topological space may be necessary. We explore the Closure-finite weak topology *(CW)-complex* (Hatcher, 2002), which is a fundamentally better model for designs since it not only has a sound mathematical foundation but also is computationally tractable.

Topology is also useful for analyzing data. A rich set of *topological data analysis* (TDA) tools is available for characterizing the "essential shape" of complex data. For example, topology-based nonlinear dimensionality reduction tools such as *mapper* (Singh, Mémoli, & Carlsson, 2007) can take a large *point cloud* (set of points lying in a high-dimensional vector space) annotated with real vector-valued attributes and extract the essential topological structure buried in the annotated point cloud, e.g., how many connected components are there? how many holes exist? and so on. This is fundamentally different from other nonlinear dimensionality reduction techniques such as Isomap (Tenenbaum, De Silva, & Langford, 2000) and multidimensional scaling (Cox & Cox, 2008)—these techniques just reduce the dimensionality of the space but do not unearth the *shape* of the point cloud. Our position is that expressing a complex design space as a multidimensional point cloud can allow TDA tools to help simplify this space and unearth interesting nontrivial topological structures, leading to the discovery of design rules as well as untapped potential designs.

Another example is *persistent homology*, which is an algebraic method for measuring topological features of space at different spatial resolutions (Edelsbrunner & Harer, 2010). More persistent features are detected over a wide range of spatial scales and are deemed more likely to represent true features of the underlying space rather than artifacts of sampling, noise, or a particular choice of parameters. The use of persistent homology on the design space, which can have both spatial and temporal scales (for designs whose topology may change over time, e.g., retractable stadium roofs), can help one characterize the sensitivity of the design space to the scale parameter.

AI-based feature learning in topological spaces

Traditionally, the success of deep learning-based AI methods has been demonstrated on unstructured images and text data, for *classification* (Krizhevsky, Sutskever, & Hinton, 2012), *prediction* (Devlin, Chang, Lee, & Toutanova, 2018), or even *generation* (Goodfellow et al., 2014). On the other end of the spectrum, we have structured data (e.g., tables in a spreadsheet) with manually designed features (column names); traditional ML tools, as well as deep learning tools, have been successfully applied to such cases. However, for more complex structured data such as graphs, manually designing features is generally inadequate since the arbitrary structure of neighborhoods around each node often makes features on the nodes and edges latent, and hence they need to be learned. Recently, a number of approaches for learning latent feature vectors (representations) of components of graphs have been proposed for homogeneous graphs (e.g., node2vec (Grover & Leskovec, 2016), graph2vec (Narayanan et al., 2017), etc.) and for heterogeneous graphs (e.g., HetGNN

(Zhang, Song, Huang, Swami, & Chawla, 2019)) using *graph convolutional neural networks (NNs)*. These methods embed nodes or groups of nodes in a graph onto a high-dimensional vector space, which facilitates downstream ML tasks such as clustering, link prediction, classification, etc., which are easier to perform on vector data than graphs directly. No such methods exist for learning representations of complex topological spaces such as CW-complexes; hence, our goal is to explore the development of such methods. Broadly speaking, there exist several straightforward applications of AI/ML to design (Nagy et al., 2017), but the use of AI methods to learn the features of existing designs and generate new designs is novel and much more challenging. In this article, we build upon an initial exploration of this topic (As, Pal, & Basu, 2018), which assumed a simplistic representation of designs, i.e., graphs of rooms connected by doors, to propose a more general and universally applicable AI approach based on topology data.

The insertion of topology-based thinking into architectural design alongside the novel application of AI/ML on topological spaces is unprecedented and needs innovative research.

Automatic generation and validation of new designs

We propose two approaches to compose new designs to reflect user-required functions. The first method is the algorithmic composition of building-block CW-complexes, which starts by combining relevant complexes, two at a time, along with the maximum subcomplex common to both (as in Figure 9.1); this is interspersed with lookups into the design "vector" space to fill the gaps or to suggest alternative compositions. Our hypothesis is that since the topological representation learning approach captures containment relationships, vector operations can be a very effective tool for composing smaller elements of design into a fuller design.

The second method leverages generative adversarial networks (GANs) (Goodfellow et al., 2014), which pit two NNs (generator and discriminator) against each other to learn a generative probabilistic model from given data samples. While GANs trained on images have been used to generate new designs (see Chapter 13 by Stanislas Challiou), they can also be used on topological structures for generating user-compliant novel designs directly from design data, thus skipping building-block discovery. The feasibility of algorithm-generated candidate designs can be tested by simulation and crowdsourcing.

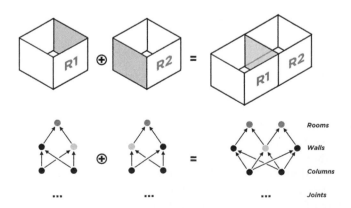

Figure 9.1 Composing building-block designs using posets.

Methodology

Our topological-AI based framework comprises of the following key steps (see Figure 9.2):

1   Translate readily available three-dimensional building information modeling (BIM) models from a vast database of architectural projects on Arcbazar; they are translated into topological datasets to succinctly represent the designs.

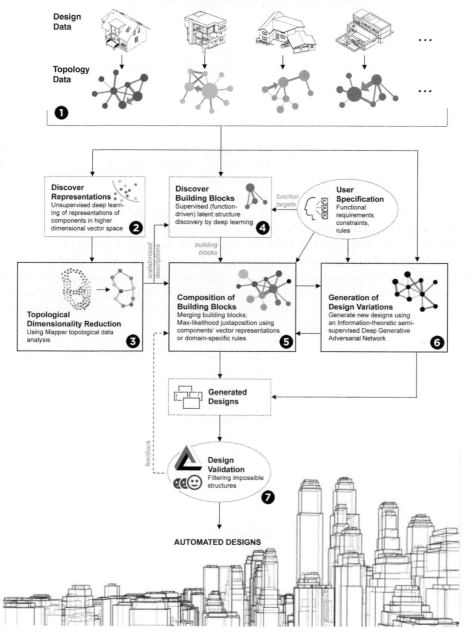

Figure 9.2   Methodology for generating novel architectural designs using topological AI.

2   Use unsupervised deep learning methods to project these complexes in higher-dimensional vector spaces.

3   Apply topology-based dimensionality reduction techniques to simplify the design space. This will aid our ML system to compute essential topological invariants and signatures.

4   The ultimate goal is to learn design rules and essential building blocks in each design sample. To this end, graph convolutional NNs are trained in topological data structures.

5   Compose discovered building blocks into new designs via a composition algebra that is aided by vector embeddings or domain-specific architectural rules.

6   Use GANs to generate entirely new and unprecedented design topologies, not just an intelligent mixture of building blocks as in step 5.

7   Validate the viability of certain generated designs through crowdsourcing and manual scoring processes. In this way, we will be able to dismiss impossible designs and identify valid solutions.

Using topology to represent architectural designs

Traditionally, architects use orthographic drawings (plan, section, and elevation) to represent/encode architectural designs: (a) The plan is a diagram depicting the disposition of a given building program, e.g., bathrooms, kitchens, etc., onto a two-dimensional picture plane. In this type of projection, the building is cut through a horizontal cutting plane and looked upon from the top to get a flat, map-like view of the floor plate; (b) the section drawing cuts the building similarly with a vertical cutting plane; and (c) an elevation is an exterior flat view of the building from one side. These drawings are drafted onto a single sheet together with the help of a T-square—lines from the plan are extended to construct the section and elevation views. There are also other combinatorial orthographic projections, such as isometric and axonometric projections, where plans, sections, and elevations are combined into a single three-dimensional view, keeping the elements to scale, and showing the relationship between several sides of the same object, so that the complexities of a shape can be better understood. Representing an object or a building in its entirety requires this triumvirate of the plan, section, and elevation. They constitute the proxy of a complete artifact and rely on an abstract graphic language (based on projective geometry) and is linked by syntactic connections (As & Schodek, 2008).

In the last couple of decades, architects started using more information-rich BIM tools to encode architectural designs. BIM is an object-oriented format, in which each design element (e.g., room, wall, door, rivet, etc.) is an object, and the relationship between objects is encoded appropriately as well. BIM encodes a "complete" description of a design to the last bolt and is often used by GUI tools such as Revit and ArchiCAD by architects for manipulation/modification of designs. In addition to geometry, these tools can also simulate building performance and behaviors, such as airflows, thermodynamic conditions, and other site-specific information, which opened up a new spectrum of measurable factors that can be accurately and systematically woven into design deliberations. However, BIM is too voluminous and cumbersome to be directly useful for the effective learning of latent design patterns by the use of state-of-the-art AI/ML tools. Moreover, while the geometry of a design is important (and accurately captured in BIM), often the inter-relationships between the design objects are inherently topological and are key for understanding its essence. Topology cares about modeling the essential shape of a potentially complex spatial object after subjecting it to continuous deformation, i.e., using *stretching* or *compressing* but without *tearing* or *gluing*. For example, a motel with a linear row of ten rectangular rooms is topologically isomorphic to another motel with an L-shaped or U-shaped arrangement of ten much larger rooms with complex shapes, but it is not isomorphic to ten rooms arranged in a circular pattern.

Representation using graphs

Topology is a vast field in mathematics, with many variants. The variants of topology that are algebraic and combinatorial in nature are more amenable to computational processing than the others. The simplest topological structures are graphs that are combinatorial objects that can be easily processed by computational/algorithmic methods. As a case in point, recent work by As et al. (2018) explored the use of graph theory to model the essential relationships within designs—design samples were represented as attributed graphs (see Figure 9.3) that were then processed using graph convolutional NNs to learn significant design building blocks (as subgraphs of the graphs corresponding to design samples).

Representation using higher-order topological structures

A graph-based representation captures the bare essence of a building's topology, but it abstracts away higher-order topological details that could be exposed to AI. For example, two rooms connected by a door can be modeled by a graph with two nodes (one for each room) and one edge (door) connecting the rooms, and the characteristics of rooms, e.g., floor area, volume, etc., which can be modeled as node attributes. What this representation does not capture is the fact that each room is built out of vertical and horizontal "walls" (e.g., floor and ceiling), which may have vastly different properties such as thickness, material, insulation properties, and so on.

Certain relationships may be k-ary ($k \geq 2$), e.g., walls shared by multiple rooms, and these cannot be succinctly modeled using graphs. Hence, there is a need for a complete yet succinct mathematical representation, which can simultaneously model both low-level concepts such as joints, beams, and walls, as well as high-level concepts such as rooms.

Hypergraphs and their more restrictive yet algebraically nicer cousins, simplicial complexes, can be used to model k-ary relationships, but they are inadequate for the following reasons. A simplicial complex that can be represented by a set of subsets of nodes is closed under the subset operation; this property is often too restrictive for modeling architectural designs. A hypergraph on the other hand does not have this restriction, but it cannot capture essential hierarchical containment relationships that often exist between the elements of architectural design, e.g., a room contains multiple walls that enclose empty space.

Representation using nonmanifold topology

Jabi et al. (2017) propose the use of nonmanifold topology (Aish et al., 2018) to model the structures that occur commonly in architectural design. They define nonmanifold geometric models as combinations of vertices, edges, surfaces, and volumes. For example, Figure 9.4 illustrates how a building can be modeled by a cluster of "cell complexes," where each "cell" models a room; each "cell" consists of "shells," which are themselves composed of a union of "faces" (walls), which are made of "wires," each of which is a collection of "edges" (horizontal or vertical beams), which intersect at "vertices."

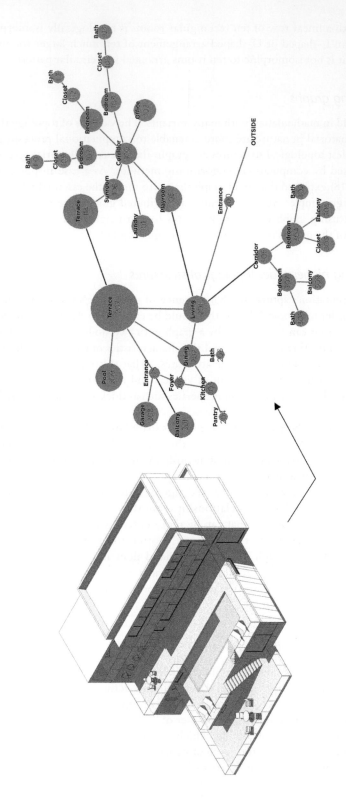

Figure 9.3 Attributed graph model for architectural design: (left) Axonometric view of the house; (right) Graph representation of the house. Nodes (yellow circles) denote rooms, and edges denote connections between rooms. Nodes have attributes such as type, area (indicated by the size of the circle), and volume; and edges have attributes such as type: vertical, open connection, and door. Numbers inside nodes are IDs and denote the floor levels.

Figure 9.4   Nonmanifold topology illustrated (from Aish et al. (2018)).

While traditional solid geometry boundary representations struggle when a surface divides the interior of a polyhedron, an edge is shared by more than two surfaces or ones that combine an isolated vertex, edge, surface, and a solid in one representation; nonmanifold topological representations allow any combination of these elements within a single entity (Jabi et al., 2017). These concepts have been embodied inside the topologic software packages (topologic. app/software).

Representation using annotated CW-complexes

Another topological abstraction that allows richer representation of design samples (for AI-based processing) than Jabi et al.'s (2017) cell complexes is the CW-complex (*Closure-finite weak topology*). This class of topological spaces is broader and has better categorical properties than simplicial complexes but still retains a combinatorial nature that allows for computation (often with a much smaller complex).

Like the case of graphs and simplicial complexes, a CW-complex is a collection of building blocks arranged together in a way that satisfies certain rules. In this case, the building blocks are called *cells* and are defined by a *dimension* having to do with what dimension of space they look like locally. So, 0-cells are vertices, 1-cells are (potentially curvy) lines, 2-cells look like (potentially curvy) disks, and so on. These building blocks are glued together along their boundaries via information in a so-called *attaching map*.

Consider Figure 9.5, architectural design data are simplified down to the basic structures and represented by a collection of vertices, edges, and squares. This can be simplified into its representation by CW-complex given by a sphere with an additional face in through the equator; combinatorially, this can be built with two vertices, two edges, and three faces (the two hemispheres of the sphere along with the middle slice). The attaching maps for each face wrap the boundary of a disk around the equator. The Hasse diagram of the face relation information (i.e., the attaching information for gluing together the pieces into a whole) is given at the far right of Figure 9.5. It is this final construction we will use to create the CW-complex data structure. We note for the expert reader that throughout this chapter all CW-complexes are *regular*, meaning that these attaching maps constitute homeomorphisms. This regularity assumption makes for a well-behaved class of spaces that are more amenable to storage in our data structures.

In addition to boundary maps between cells, each cell in a CW-complex can also be annotated with both geometric and nongeometric information. Examples of geometric information include the length of a beam (1-cell), area of a wall (2-cell), and volume of a room (3-cell). Similarly, examples of nongeometric information include thermal insulation properties of a wall, ambiance, and aesthetics of a room, and so on. These can be expressed as data (vectors) attached to cells in the CW-complex.

It is prudent at this point to provide an aside on some terminology for the different ways that topological spaces are considered "the same." The most restrictive is to say that they are the same if they are *homeomorphic*. Mathematically, this means we can write down a map

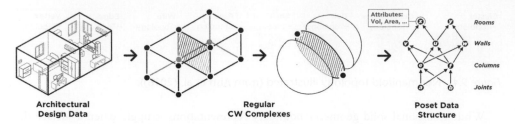

Figure 9.5 Representing architectural designs using topological spaces (CW-complexes) and their computation-friendly representation.

from one space to the other which is invertible. Using a map in the more commonly used layperson's context, a map of Europe and Europe itself are homeomorphic as every place one could stand in Europe is represented by a coordinate on the map and vice versa. In our CW-complexes, we are interested in homeomorphisms as the same structure could have multiple representations as CW-complexes with vastly different numbers of cells, such as the example of Figure 9.5. For this reason, we will often be interested in minimal representations of the space. The work of Nanda (2020) can be utilized to provide an algorithm for constructing minimal representations of a space—where representation here means that the constructed space is homeomorphic to the original—even if it has fewer building blocks. Nonminimal representation is sometimes necessary for composition (see Section "Composing building blocks to generate user–specific designs").

A slightly less restrictive notion of sameness is that of two spaces having the same *homotopy type,* equivalently that they are *homotopic.* In this definition, two spaces are the same if one can be continuously deformed into the other without tearing or gluing. As an example, the letters X and Y have the same homotopy type as they can both be deformed into a single point (this is also called *contractible*), but they are not homeomorphic.

Extraction of CW-complexes from design data

Given a design sample encoded in 3D BIM format, which is the format of choice among architects these days, we need to extract the CW-complex from it. Each component in a given design sample is an object in BIM, with attributes that connect it to other objects; for example, a "door" object has two attributes "fromRoom = x" and "toRoom = y." Parsing a BIM file would lead to the creation of various cells corresponding to joints, columns/beams, floors, walls, doors, rooms, etc., as well as the attachment maps using attribute information and thus would lead to the generation of a naive regular CW-complex with relative ease. Stratification algorithms (Nanda, 2020) can then be applied to generate a simpler CW-complex, which would be useful for further analysis and the application of AI/ML methods.

Machine learning on topological spaces

Conceptual design is the first and arguably the most critical stage of the design and is typically a human-intensive process, where the architect envisions how to compose various structural components to achieve a desired function or goal. An architect often follows the prevalent rules of design and, hence, may miss radically new ideas by failing to explore the multitude of design possibilities, some of which could result in vast improvements in the quality of the design, and some could be highly adaptable to changing goals. Generative designs by the application of known design rules are well-studied, e.g., shape grammars (Stiny & Gips, 1972). However, applying a known fixed set of design rules is unlikely to achieve the level of design diversity that we want. To alleviate this problem, we leverage design data that are increasingly becoming available, e.g., from companies such as Arcbazar. Spurred by its preliminary successes based on graph-based deep learning on available design data (As, Pal, & Basu, 2018), we further explore advanced methods for discovering salient design rules and building blocks that are responsible for achieving certain design functionalities, but which are not explicitly stated in any design manual. Specifically, we propose novel AI/ML methods that are applicable to more general topological spaces, e.g., CW-complexes. Concepts from TDA can be used to *skeletonize* or succinctly summarize the latent space of design relationships that exist in the available data. We also explore two types of methods to generate new designs: (a) systematically composing the discovered building blocks using a combination of tools from graph theory, topology, and representation learning; and (b) generating radical design variations using GANs; all this while taking into account the functional needs specified by a user and various constraints imposed by the built environment.

Discovering representations of CW-complexes and subcomplexes

As the higher-order topological structures can be thought of as different ways to generalize graphs, we take inspiration from the existing work on passing networks to ML algorithms to create ways to represent CW-complexes, whether or not they arise from our architecture design data.

We focus on two kinds of embedding methods for graphs, also known as *graph representation learning*. The first method provides a vector for each input graph, either via handcrafted features or learned features. As opposed to graph comparison methods that return a number to encode the similarity of two input graphs, this collection of methods returns a vector for a given graph to be used for its representation. We refer to this as "graph embedding." The second method, referred to as "node embedding," constructs a vector for each node rather than for the entire graph.

Both graph embedding methods such as graph2vec (Narayanan et al., 2017) and node-embedding methods such as node2vec (Grover & Leskovec, 2016) derive ideas from text document vectorization methods such as word2vec (Mikolov et al., 2013) and doc2vec (Le & Mikolov, 2014), and apply them to graph structures. Essentially, word2vec is a tool from natural language processing, which arises from the idea that words in similar contexts have similar meanings. Each word in a dictionary is represented as a one-hot vector; then, a new word of interest is represented by a weighted combination of words that tend to appear near it. Similarly, node2vec and graph2vec utilize the idea that vertices with similar local neighborhoods should have similar meanings. In graph2vec, local neighborhoods are rooted subgraphs where the root is the node used to create it; whereas, in node2vec, the local neighborhood of a node is generated by sampling fixed-length random walks starting from it. More recently, node-embedding methods have been extended to work on graphs with arbitrary types of node and edge attributes, e.g., HetGNN (Zhang et al., 2019), which apply graph convolutional NNs to learn latent feature vectors for each node using both its neighborhood structure and attribute similarities with neighbors. Recent unpublished work by Basu shows that node embedding is possible on higher-order structures such as hypergraphs, where edges can have two or more nodes. This is achieved by defining suitable random walks on hypergraphs and treating hyperedges as sentences before applying doc2vec.

We take this viewpoint to construct vector representations of CW-complexes. The poset representation of the CW-complex can be directly utilized since this can be viewed as a directed graph and then hand this information to graph2vec for featurization. If two CW-complexes have a significant common substructure (e.g., a subcomplex of several common cells attached in a certain way), it will be reflected as similar local neighborhoods in their corresponding posets. Then the resultant vector representations are likely to be close, as desired. Our hypothesis is that this method can classify architectural designs into various types, e.g., residential, mixed-use, commercial, institutional, etc., since each such type of design would have distinctive topological signatures captured by CW-complexes.

We do not expect that the naive application of node2vec or HetGNN to be useful for looking at substructures of the CW-complex as subgraphs of the diagram do not directly correlate to subcomplexes of the original CW-complex without heavy restrictions on the types of subgraphs required. Thus, for the subcomplex learning task analogous to the node-embedding task for graphs, graph2vec can be used on the subgraphs generated by the subcomplexes of interest. We conjecture that although naive node embedding on the CW-complex poset representation may not yield insights, applying hypergraph node-embedding methods might. Specifically, the neighborhood of each node in a poset can be thought of as a directed hyperedge. We hypothesize that since a poset captures "x-contains-$\{u, v, w\}$" type relationships well, performing vector arithmetic on the vectors corresponding to the lower-dimensional cells $\{u, v, w\}$ can yield a vector for the higher-dimensional cell x. This, if true, can yield a systematic method to compose new designs or perform substitutions.

Summarizing topological representations by dimensionality reduction

Once we have turned our CW-complexes into vectors, we have many options for what to do with this information to explore and otherwise utilize the information. These options open up many new questions for understanding the mathematical behavior of the novel embedding technique described earlier, which will yield new insights into how best to use it for analyzing designs. First, embedding the CW-complex means that we now have a collection of data points in Euclidean space. This, in turn, means we have an obvious notion of a comparison measure between the CW-complexes via the distance of their point representations in space. Clustering can be utilized on these point clouds, which we call *design space*, to determine whether aspects of design and architecture are respected by the embedding. However, we believe it to be more likely that the point clouds generated will function more like a continuum than by distinctly separated clusters. For this reason, the design space can be explored using lower-dimensional embeddings. Standard dimensionality reduction techniques such as Isomap (Tenenbaum, De Silva, & Langford, 2000) or multidimensional scaling (Cox & Cox, 2000) allow an immediate starting place for exploration of the data.

The mapper technique can be used for turning the design space point cloud into a graph (Figure 9.6). The idea behind mapper (Singh, Mémoli, & Carlsson, 2007) is that the point cloud is viewed through the lens of a filter function defined on the points; this is simply a number associated with each data point, which could come either from data specific sources (like a rating of a building's usability) or be automatically computed, e.g., based on the local structure of the point cloud itself. In the example of Figure 9.6, the function is given by height, and we cluster the subclouds consisting of points within one of three cover intervals. Each connected component of the subcloud creates a vertex, and the overlapping nature of

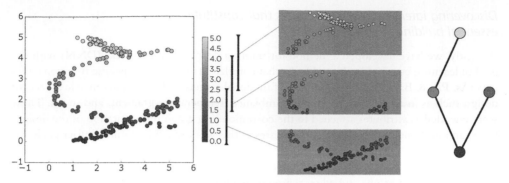

Figure 9.6 An example of a mapper graph (right) constructed from an input point cloud (left) with filter function defined by vertical coordinate.

these subclouds allows for the inclusion of edges where appropriate. The resulting mapper graph can be used to provide a summary of the structure of the point cloud; in this case, we can see the linearity of the global structure reflected in the resulting graph. More refinement of the parameters could also show the smaller linear features of this particular example.

In the context of design space exploration, consider the following scenario for mapper graph utilization. A collection of buildings is represented as a collection of CW-complexes. Each complex is vectorized to provide a point in Euclidean space, and then a mapper is applied to provide a graph for exploration of design space. Each node in this new graph represents a cluster of points in design space with similar characteristics, and adjacent nodes represent other clusters of points with nearby but not identical characteristics. After the construction of the mapper graph, we can highlight nodes by some other target functional score such as usability of the buildings in that cluster (the filter function). If patterns emerge, we can then determine what aspects of the embedding relate to these traits, and in turn, determine what structures in the building themselves contribute to this.

Another potential path for the exploration of design space is that of *persistent homology*. Persistence is an algebraic construction that measures the overall structure of a space, with a propensity for measuring loops and voids. For example, the point cloud of the left-most figure in Figure 9.6 looks like it came from two circles put together. This is easy to determine visually, but the computer's representation sees only a collection of individual points. We can measure the structure of the point cloud by looking at the union of disks of a certain diameter centered at each point in the picture, making it easier to see that there are two circular structures that appear around diameter 0.5, and are filled in by the time the diameter is 2. We represent these structures as points in a persistence diagram, shown on the far right, by recording the diameter for appearance (birth) and disappearance (death) of the circular structures as two points far from the diagonal. The additional points in the persistence diagram represent small circular features that were born shortly before they died. In this way, the persistence diagram encodes information about large regions of design space that are avoided by the point cloud. This can be used to extrapolate information about what sorts of designs are not provided by given buildings; perhaps, these regions are avoided for reasons of practicality, but maybe they present regions of design space that we would want to include as future building blocks to expand the library of available designs.

Discovering latent topological features that constitute essential building blocks of design

Recently, we have developed a method for training deep neural networks (DNN) with the goal of learning essential building blocks that correlate strongly with specific functional targets (As, Pal, & Basu, 2018). Examples of functional targets include nongeometric aspects of design such as *livability* score, aesthetics, ambiance, temperature gradient, and so on. These were encoded as attributes attached to the corresponding graph representation of the design. One can build upon the preliminary successes of this work to achieve much loftier goals. To train DNNs, we derived the data from (BIM corresponding to several annotated conceptual designs available to us from the Arcbazar platform. Designs were represented as simple graphs (nodes represented rooms and edges represented adjacency of rooms). We used a supervised *graph convolutional NN* adapted from a DNN, developed for a molecular fingerprinting application (Duvenaud et al., 2015) to discover latent subgraph patterns that correlate strongly with function targets. In other words, after training on multiple design samples with functional attribute information, it learned subsets of structures and behavioral attributes occurring within designs that are likely to be highly correlated with target functional features (e.g., good aesthetics per user). This process can be adapted to work on CW-complexes/posets. The learning occurs by following the steps summarized below (Figure 9.7).

Data representation

The design data are fed into the DNN one by one with each training sample being represented by a CW-complex as described earlier. Since the CW-complex is stored as a poset, the nodes of the posets are marked with structural or behavioral attributes represented as concatenated vectors of values. These form the input to the DNN at the input layer—with each node vector being input into the neuron responsible for the corresponding node. The DNN's goal is to learn a latent feature vector representation $F = \{F_1, F_2, \ldots, F_S\}$ for each poset, where each F_i is a latent feature, which is then correlated with the design function using a fully connected linear regression layer (as the last layer).

DNN training by graph convolution

During each iteration, each neuron in a certain layer of the DNN corresponding to a poset node holds the average "attribute contributions" from its neighboring nodes and updates its attribute vector of length M. Specifically, neurons in each layer $L \in \{1, 2, \ldots, R\}$ hold the averaged contribution of node attribute values from up to L-hops away in the poset after being multiplied by the hidden layer weights, which are computed separately for each degree-d node at layer L. Thus, the DNN remembers the activation score for each full subposet of radius L centered at a node of degree d. The training method scales well since in the worst

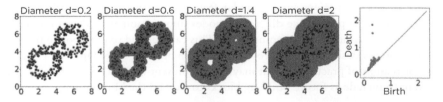

Figure 9.7 Persistence diagrams to unearth robust topological features in the design space.

case, the number of subgraphs examined will be R times the total number of nodes in all the input sample posets, which is linear and not exponential. Now each neuron at layer L additively contributes to the final representation vector F after getting multiplied by the hidden output weights.

Learning building-block subposets from activation

During training, we concurrently perform bookkeeping to learn which subposets tend to produce high activations in each layer and good regression performance. Then F gets regressed with the target function value for the input poset. Elements of F with high positive regression coefficients can be thought of as important factors for determining the target design function. For such factors, we trace back the neurons with high activation scores for each layer L. Finally, we can retrieve the radius L subposets corresponding to these neurons saved

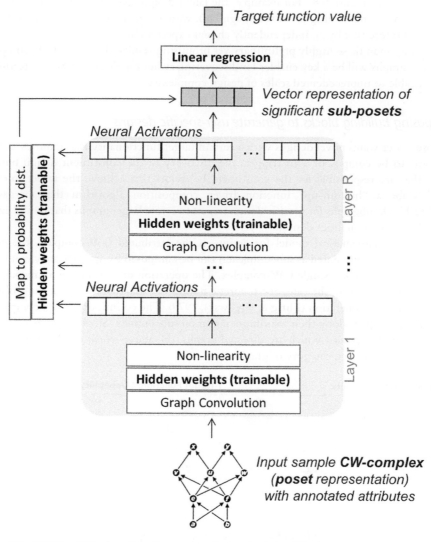

Figure 9.8 DNN architecture for discovering design building blocks.

during the bookkeeping process. The more the number of layers R in the DNN, the greater the propagation of the influence of each node's attributes. The choice of R thus depends on the radius of the poset as well as the sizes of subposets that we desire as building blocks. If R is too small, then only shallow latent subposets would be learned, whereas if R is too large, an entire poset may be returned as a building block.

The DNN training process solves a highly nonlinear optimization problem using stochastic gradient descent to determine the optimal hidden weight matrices. The goal of this optimization algorithm is to minimize the "loss function" that measures the error between the predicted functional target and the actual (user-provided) functional target in each design sample.

In preliminary experiments on a limited number of design samples represented very coarsely as *graphs* of rooms (nodes) and various types of connections (edges), the DNN was able to find interesting building blocks specific to two different target functions (e.g., *livability* and *sleepability* in Figure 9.8). For example, the latent design rule of connecting a large terrace to a dining and a living room (in design H8), which contributed to high livability, was considered interesting by an independently chosen expert architect.

Building upon these highly preliminary yet promising results, the use of CW-complexes instead of graphs will be a key enabler for discovering richer topological design patterns that are applicable to unprecedented scales of design complexity.

Composing building blocks to generate user-specific designs

Suppose a user wants novel designs with a certain target functionality that requires multiple behaviors to be composed. This triggers the discovery of the constituent design building blocks that are responsible for the constituent behaviors that achieve the target function. We describe a "bottom-up" function-driven composition algorithm that merges the building-block subgraphs for specific design targets to create larger graphs that should exhibit the multiple functionalities desired.

Since our mathematical model for designs is the attributed CW-complex, the design building blocks (represented as subcomplexes) can be composed by appropriately combining the subcomplexes into a single CW-complex. The operation of merging two subcomplexes can be formalized using the category-theoretic notion of *colimit* derived from the *pushout* or the *fibered coproduct* operation (Ehrig & Kreowski, 1979). The colimit of two subcomplexes is the merged complex along their maximum common subcomplex. Since the CW-complexes are represented as posets, which are directed graphs, the above *colimit* can be defined in an appropriately associated category of graphs.

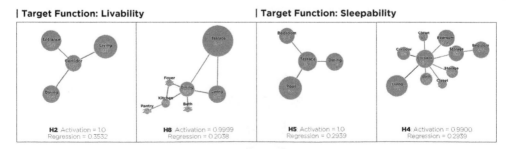

Figure 9.9 Discovering building blocks in the preliminary experiment.

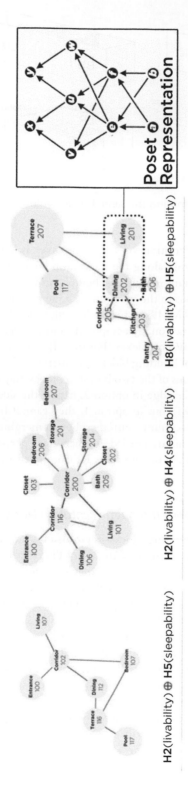

H2(livability) ⊕ H5(sleepability) H2(livability) ⊕ H4(sleepability) H8(livability) ⊕ H5(sleepability)

Figure 9.10 Notional composition of building-block subgraphs. Note that for H2 ⊕ H5, the merger happened along with a common node "Dining" and an additional (bedroom, corridor) edge was created since that edge has a high likelihood of occurrence as per the vector embedding method. This is the outcome of link prediction.

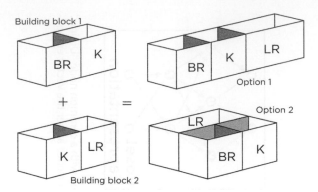

Figure 9.11 Different ways of composing the same building-block designs.

This framework for the composition of CW-complexes is algorithmically realizable in an approximate sense by merging along the maximum common subposet of two CW-complexes. Although the maximum common subgraph problem is NP-hard and hard to approximate, approximate solutions to the maximum clique problem can be a starting point to solve this problem (Barrow & RM, 1976). Figure 9.10 illustrates how some building-block subgraphs (see Figure 9.9) can be notionally composed to form larger designs. Such compositions can be performed with CW-complexes (Figure 9.1) as well. There may be multiple ways of composing the same set of building blocks and merging the posets of the most simplified CW-complex representations of the two building blocks may not work. For example, in Figure 9.11, the K room is at the edge in option 2; hence, the side walls can be collapsed to a hemisphere (like in Figure 9.1), but in option 1, they cannot be. However, if less collapsed posets are retained, then maximum common subposet merging is still possible. Hence, multiscale poset merging algorithms are needed—unnecessary portions of the posets can be collapsed (e.g., LR) whereas critical portions (e.g., K) can be left in an uncollapsed state to enable merging.

Additional composition operations using representation learning

Although merging of essential building blocks is promising, it may not yield a complete conceptual design for the product desired by the user. This is because the user's functions may require the inclusion of auxiliary structures that were not returned explicitly during the building-block discovery step. However, such auxiliary structures can be determined from the embedded space (point cloud) of design samples obtained by applying *representation learning* schemes described earlier. See Figure 9.12 (left) for the case when the design samples are graphs (As, Pal, & Basu, 2018). Given the embedding, one can apply topological skeletonization (e.g., by the mapper algorithm described earlier) to create a *1-skeleton graph* that approximately represents the design rules used by various architects (see Figure 9.12 (right)). This style of composition can be extended to CW-complexes. Once the set of auxiliary nodes is determined, certain nodes of the constituent building-block subcomplexes may be connected by edges derived from the mapper skeleton graph.

We have used attributes/data attached to cells of CW-complexes to learn the building blocks of design that can be composed later. However, the attributes of disparate structures we are trying to compose may be incompatible, e.g., nonmatching geometric dimensions,

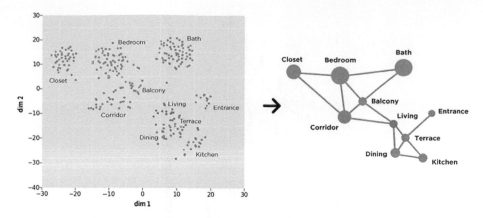

Figure 9.12 Vector representations of various types of rooms in design samples represented as graphs (nodes=rooms).

or incompatible materials, and so on. One can turn to the *theory of sheaves on cell complexes* (Curry, 2013) as a possible method for resolving this issue, as the sheaf requirements impose compatibility of the data attached to cells and thus limit the field of available representations to those that can be composed together.

Generation of radical design variations using GAN on graphs

The composition methods described earlier are likely to yield a novel composition of the discovered building blocks. However, since each building block is left intact during the composition process and there is a large number of degrees of freedom, the exploration of the design space may be limited. Therefore, to generate radical variations in designs, we leverage a generative DNN method named information-theoretic generative adversarial networks (InfoGAN).

GAN has been popular recently for the generation of realistic data samples (e.g., images) after sampling a trove of data. This is achieved by the unsupervised training of two DNNs (generator G and discriminator D) that are playing a minimax game in which G's goal is to convert some input noise into a synthetic data sample to fool D, and D's goal is to always discriminate fake data from real data. Instead of training independently, G and D are trained in tandem. D trains its weights on the real data set and computes the probability p_{fake} that the data generated by G is fake, and G receives feedback from D (the value of p_{fake} for the generated sample) and trains its weights. If the training concludes properly, then a Nash equilibrium of the game is reached, and G always generates data samples for which D computes $p_{fake} = 1/2$. One can compare this to a professor–student relationship in a design studio: The student presents design work to the professor and the professor examines, critiques the design, and points out the shortcomings. The student then iterates on the design and presents it to the professor again. This loop of iterations continues until the professor passes the design as satisfactory. Ideally, at a certain maturity level, the student is then able to generate satisfactory designs without the help of the professor.

Since most work on GANs has been on generating images, the architectures for both D and G are convolutional. Hence, this cannot be applied as such to topology-based generation methods, and the GAN architecture needs to be extended to structured data, in particular

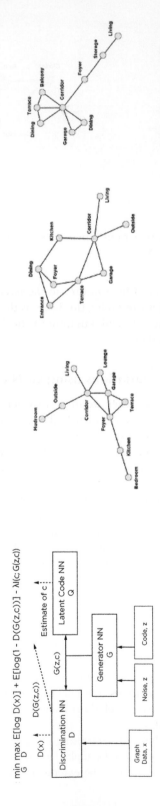

Figure 9.13 Information-theoretic generative adversarial network (InfoGAN), (left) architecture involving simultaneous training of three DNNs, (right) sample graph outputs generated.

graphs or CW-complexes. One shortcoming of GANs is that they do not provide many tools to control the generation process itself and often have low interpretability. Therefore, we leverage a version of GAN, called InfoGANs (Chen et al., 2016) to generate design variations.

InfoGANs work like regular GANs, but they also learn *latent codes*, which can be controlled by the user. In addition to training the discriminator (D) and generator (G) NNs, InfoGAN simultaneously trains a third NN (Q) to minimize the mutual information $I(c, G(z,c))$ between the latent codes c and G's output $G(z,c)$, where z is the input noise that causes variation in sample generation (for example, as in Figure 9.11).

The training problem is set up as a jointly optimized information-regularized minimax game with the objective function specified in the figure. At the maximum value of $I(c, G(z,c))$, we have conditional entropy $H(c \mid G(z,c)) = 0$, which in turn means that the generated sample is closely controlled by the latent code. This results in the disentanglement of the features in the data, which can be effectively controlled by G. For example, if a latent code is found to control whether certain subcomplexes appear in design samples, then one can restrict G to generate new design complexes that contain such subcomplexes. Since the code vector can be multidimensional, different dimensions may be used to control different latent factors.

Our preliminary attempt to generate new design samples (as simple graphs) is shown in Figure 9.13. In these experiments, we only considered rooms, room types, and no other attributes. We observed that InfoGAN can generate interesting and unusual subgraphs that were typically not encountered in the training data set. Our desire is to extend this to generate much richer topologies encoded as CW-complexes.

InfoGAN is known to learn deep representations of "components," thus allowing vector arithmetic in latent code space to add and subtract components in the design space. Thus, it should be possible to use this mechanism to effectively generate design variations that contain certain structures but not others. Also, if latent codes can be coupled with target functions, users have finer grain control over the generative design process.

Generating time-varying architectural designs

There are many examples where the design of a building changes over time to facilitate different use cases, such as retractable stadium roofs, seminar rooms with movable walls to allow for larger or smaller audiences, and automatic shades for temperature-controlled offices. Persistent homology can be used to provide methods for representing and comparing temporally varying designs. Persistent homology can be constructed to investigate input structures beyond simply understanding point clouds. All that is truly required is a 1-parameter varying topological space; sometimes, this is described as a space varying in *time*, although as in the example above, this need not be time itself. Persistent homology can also be used to represent the changing structure of the architectural design, at which point we can incorporate the existing methodology on featurization of persistence diagrams (e.g. Perea, Munch, & Khasawneh, 2019) to immediately interface our work with ML and deep learning methods.

Generating 3D models from generated designs

The final step in the composition process consists of converting a composed design represented as a CW-complex into a *massing model*. To perform this *topology optimization* step, we a physics-based energy minimization method can be used to generate to generate a nice layout of nodes while minimizing constraint violations. Portions of the CW-complex poset that have a tree structure can be laid out independent of the other portions of the poset, since the nodes inside such portions have no relations with the nodes outside. Performing a *tree decomposition* of the poset can break the poset into "communities" of nodes to isolate the nontree like portions from the tree-like portions, and hence yield significant computational speedup. Each community of nodes can be represented as a graph and then laid out in the 3D space using fast graph Laplacian solvers (Vishnoi, 2012).

Conclusions

In this chapter, we described how concepts from topology such as graphs and CW-complexes can be used to succinctly represent architectural design data. Such representations are friendly to AI/ML algorithms, which attempt to discover salient design rules and building blocks that occur in well-rated designs. We also articulated how GANs adapted to graphs or topological spaces can be used to generate the blueprints of novel designs. This is in contrast to image/pixel-based generative algorithms. On one hand, the latter can tap into the vast amount of research in the AI/ML community on similar topics, but on the other hand, these algorithms have limitations, since a pixel in an image is not a semantic unit unlike a node in a graph/topological representation of designs. While we demonstrated our results on graph-based data, in our future work, we plan to extend them to more general topological AI/ML techniques as well—along the lines proposed in this chapter.

Acknowledgments

Any opinions, findings, and conclusions or recommendations expressed in this material are those of the author(s) and do not necessarily reflect the views of Raytheon BBN. This document does not contain technology or technical data controlled under either the U.S. International Traffic in Arms Regulations or the U.S. Export Administration Regulations.

References

Aish, R., Jabi, W., Lannon, S., Wardhana, N., & Chatzivasileiadi, A. (2018). Topologic: Tools to explore architectural topology. AAG 2018: Advances in Architectural Geometry 2018, Gothenburg, Sweden, pp. 316–341.

As, I., & Schodek, D. (2008). *Dynamic digital representations in architecture: Visions in motion.* London: Taylor & Francis, Inc.

As, I., Pal, S., & Basu, P. (2018). Artificial intelligence in architecture: Generating conceptual design via deep learning. *International Journal of Architectural Computing, 16*(4), 306–327.

Barrow, H. G., & RM, B. (1976). Subgraph isomorphism, matching relational structures and maximal cliques. *Information Processing Letters 4* (4): 83–84.

Chen, X., Duan, Y., Houthooft, R., Schulman, J., Sutskever, I., & Abbeel, P. (2016). Infogan: Interpretable representation learning by information maximizing generative adversarial nets. In *NIPS'16: Proceedings of the 30th International Conference on Neural Information Processing Systems* (pp. 2180–2188), December 2016, Barcelona, Spain.

Cox, M. A., & Cox, T. F. (2000). *Multidimensional scaling.* New York: Chapman and Hall/CRC.

Cox, M. A., & Cox, T. F. (2008). Multidimensional scaling. In *Handbook of Data Visualization* (pp. 315–347). Berlin, Heidelberg: Springer.

Curry, J. (2013). Sheaves, cosheaves and applications. *arXiv preprint arXiv:1303.3255.*

Devlin, J., Chang, M. W., Lee, K., & Toutanova, K. (2018). Bert: Pre-training of deep bidirectional transformers for language understanding. *arXiv preprint arXiv:1810.04805.*

Duvenaud, D. K., Maclaurin, D., Iparraguirre, J., Bombarell, R., Hirzel, T., Aspuru-Guzik, A., & Adams, R. P. (2015). Convolutional networks on graphs for learning molecular fingerprints. In *NIPS'15: Proceedings of the 28th International Conference on Neural Information Processing Systems* (Vol. 2, pp. 2224–2232), December 2015, Montreal, Canada.

Edelsbrunner, H., & Harer, J. (2010). *Computational topology: An introduction*. Providence, RI: American Mathematical Society.

Ehrig, H., & Kreowski, H. J. (1979). Pushout-Properties: An analysis of gluing constructions for graphs. *Mathematische Nachrichten, 91*(1), 135–149.

Goodfellow, I., Pouget-Abadie, J., Mirza, M., Xu, B., Warde-Farley, D., Ozair, S., ... & Bengio, Y. (2014). Generative adversarial nets. In *NIPS'14: Proceedings of the 27th International Conference on Neural Information Processing Systems* (Vol. 2, pp. 2672–2680), December 2014, Montreal, Canada.

Grover, A., & Leskovec, J. (2016, August). node2vec: Scalable feature learning for networks. In *Proceedings of the 22nd ACM SIGKDD International Conference on Knowledge Discovery and Data Mining* (pp. 855–864), San Francisco, California, USA.

Hatcher, A. (2002). *Algebraic topology*. Cambridge: Cambridge University Press.

Jabi, W., Soe, S., Theobald, P., Aish, R., & Lannon, S. (2017). Enhancing parametric design through non-manifold topology. *Design Studies, 52*, 96–114.

Krizhevsky, A., Sutskever, I., & Hinton, G.. E. (2012). ImageNet classification with deep convolutional neural networks. In *Neural Information Processing Systems* (Vol. 25, No. 10.1145, p. 3065386).

Le, Q., & Mikolov, T. (2014, January). Distributed representations of sentences and documents. In *International Conference on Machine Learning* (pp. 1188–1196), Beijing, China.

Mikolov, T., Sutskever, I., Chen, K., Corrado, G. S., & Dean, J. (2013, December). Distributed representations of words and phrases and their compositionality. In *NIPS'13: Proceedings of the 26th International Conference on Neural Information Processing Systems* (Vol. 2, pp. 3111–3119), Lake Tahoe, Nevada.

Nagy, D., Lau, D., Locke, J., Stoddart, J., Villaggi, L., Wang, R., ... & Benjamin, D. (2017, May). Project discover: An application of generative design for architectural space planning. In *Proceedings of the Symposium on Simulation for Architecture and Urban Design* (pp. 1–8), Toronto, Canada.

Nanda, V. (2020). Local cohomology and stratification. *Foundations of Computational Mathematics 20*, 195–222.

Narayanan, A., Chandramohan, M., Venkatesan, R., Chen, L., Liu, Y., & Jaiswal, S. (2017). graph-2vec: Learning distributed representations of graphs. *arXiv preprint arXiv:1707.05005*.

Perea, J. A., Munch, E., & Khasawneh, F. A. (2019). Approximating continuous functions on persistence diagrams using template functions. *arXiv preprint arXiv:1902.07190*.

Ruiz-Montiel, M., Boned, J., Gavilanes, J., Jiménez, E., Mandow, L., & PéRez-De-La-Cruz, J. L. (2013). Design with shape grammars and reinforcement learning. *Advanced Engineering Informatics, 27*(2), 230–245.

Singh, G., Mémoli, F., & Carlsson, G. E. (2007). Topological methods for the analysis of high dimensional data sets and 3d object recognition. In *Eurographics Symposium on Point-Based Graphics* (pp. 91–100), Prague, Czech Republic.

Stiny, G., & Gips, J. (1972). Shape grammars and the generative specification of painting and sculpture. In C. V. Freiman (Ed.), *Information Processing 71: Proceedings of IFIP Congress 1971* (pp. 1460–1465). Amsterdam: North-Holland Publishing Company.

Tenenbaum, J. B., De Silva, V., & Langford, J. C. (2000). A global geometric framework for nonlinear dimensionality reduction. *Science, 290*(5500), 2319–2323.

Vishnoi, N. K. (2012). Laplacian solvers and their algorithmic applications. *Theoretical Computer Science, 8*(1–2), 1–141.

Zhang, C., Song, D., Huang, C., Swami, A., & Chawla, N. V. (2019, July). Heterogeneous graph neural network. In *Proceedings of the 25th ACM SIGKDD International Conference on Knowledge Discovery & Data Mining* (pp. 793–803), Anchorage, AK, USA.

Part 3
AI in architectural research

10

Artificial intelligence in architectural heritage research

Simulating networks of caravanserais through machine learning

Guzden Varinlioglu and Özgün Balaban

Roads play a key role in world history. The roads and networks that once connected civilizations have the potential to reveal much about the culture of the age. A prominent example was the Silk Roads, a term first coined by Ferdinand von Richthofen for an interconnected web of routes linking ancient societies of East, South, Central, and Western Asia with the Mediterranean (Chin 2013). These were no single roads, but a diversity of paths, tracks, and roads, changing over time due to shifting topography, regional conflicts, markets, and political power. Silk Roads also create an enormous network of way stations, such as caravanserais, khans, and funduqs (Williams 2015, 22). Caravanserais, arranged along the trade routes a day's journey apart, are enormous accommodation facilities providing shelter, food, and drink for a caravan's full complement of people, animals, and cargo, also meeting the needs of maintenance, treatment, and care. Over several decades, new discoveries have provided architectural evidence for these roads, namely, the traces of way stations. Although there has been a very significant amount of research on the Silk Roads, this consists of individual projects shedding light on specific sections, rather than on the overall network of buildings. Previous research on the caravanserais on the ancient Silk Roads has not attempted to create a global vision of the historical phenomena by mapping precise spatial coordinates, nor have computational tools been used to define and explore the movement in between these waystations.

The accumulation of data in cultural heritage studies has involved a widening range of computerized and computational tools. The uses of these digital tools, however, tend to be limited to management, visualization, and dissemination. The central challenge of this paper is to exploit computational tools to quantify, qualify, represent, and experiment with these ancient networks. Can we reconstruct social networks of the past using computational tools? Can supervised learning (SL) help to automate heritage site prediction? Can we use game engines and deep learning to simulate the movements of caravans and thus locate the paths and caravanserais in this trade network?

This work presents the use of artificial intelligence (AI) in the field of architectural heritage with a case study. As the case study is based on the geographical information

207

system (GIS), we collected and compiled data from the ancient Silk Roads caravanserais of Anatolia during the Seljuk period. AI initially helps researchers predict the geographical coordinates of caravanserais from the satellite imagery through SL. This machine learning (ML) algorithm allows the gathering of caravanserai location data that would not otherwise be available to researchers. The GIS data combined with the terrain data are transferred to the Unity game engine, in which an agent simulates and learns to find the optimal routes in between the caravanserais. This experimental approach employs a simulation environment with the use of deep reinforcement learning (DRL) to estimate the locations of the long-lost urban networks of Anatolia. This research thus integrates digital aspects into architectural heritage studies, using AI as a tool to simulate urban networks of the Anatolian caravanserais.

Digital tools in heritage studies

Howard (2003, 13), in his notes on the importance of heritage, states that "to act as a clear reminder that heritage is about people, write a list of the things which you regard as your most precious heritage—the things which you are keen to pass on to your legatees." He further states that "these things may be as universal as clean air, or as personal as your stamp collection, as concrete as a house or as abstract as a philosophy. What matters so much you take active steps to conserve it" (Howard 2003, 13). Heritage studies have emerged from and remained within, academic disciplines such as art and architectural history, tourism, leisure studies, archaeology, geography, and history. To some, it is not clear why heritage studies are so essential, existing between so many disciplines, although those involved clearly understand its importance. In recent years, heritage gained its place in AI studies, becoming seen as a dataset from humankind that can be copied and learned from by AI algorithms. "We are our distinct and unique cultures, histories, and languages"—a popular blogger recently asserted in an argument for the preservation of cultural heritage via more accurate AI algorithms, with the aim of creating predictions of the future (Ibaraki 2019). As guardians of our unique cultural heritage, which forms the basis of our identities, rather than seeing this as a threat, we should consider the digitized world as having great potential for uncovering the puzzles of the past.

Research in humanities is going through a digital revolution, reflecting the revolution in the life sciences in the last century. Digital humanities, i.e., the integration of digital tools and computational technologies into traditional approaches in humanities, is now considered an academic field in its own right (Berry 2011; Burdick et al. 2012; Hayles 2012). The first wave of digital humanities, "computing in humanities," was seen as technical support for the work of humanities scholars, i.e., large-scale digitization projects of the printed materials. A significant example is the EU funded "Time Machine project," a research project involving the large-scale digitization of European history and culture to create big data from the past (TMP 2019). The project includes an enormous volume of the historical, geographical, museum, and library archival material converted to digital, which is stored and curated, and interacted with, to create the European memory in the digital. The second wave was generative in character, producing, curating, and interacting with that which is "born digital," i.e., the curation of digital collections (Presner 2010). For example, Google Arts and Culture, formerly Google Art Project, is a digital online platform with high-resolution images and videos of artworks and cultural artifacts from partner cultural organizations throughout the world. In this digital system, users can create artwork collections and virtual gallery tours and can also focus on the artwork of their choice, i.e., they curate their own art collections

(Google A&C 2011). The third wave, the current period, concentrates on the underlying computationality of the past for the prediction of the future.

Studies on digital heritage—an integral component in the field of digital humanities—provide a common ground for research across disciplines on the theoretical appraisal of digital media applications by cultural heritage institutions (Cameron & Kenderine 2007). There has been a focus on museums, and the transformation of traditional heritage institutions by digital technologies, and in turn, the transformation of the digital technologies by these institutions. Referring to several practical applications ranging from the research, preservation, management, interpretation, and representation of cultural heritage by professionals, academics, and students, Cameron and Kenderine focus on both theoretical and practical aspects. Similarly, Kalay et al. (2007) contribute to the theorization of virtual or digital heritage, referred to as "new heritage," broadening the definition to address the complexity of cultural heritage and related social, political, and economic issues. Addison (2000) defines digital heritage as an "emergent" discipline made up of three key processes of 3D, namely documentation (from site surveys to epigraphy), representation (from historic reconstruction to visualization), and dissemination (from immersive networked worlds to "in situ" augmented reality). Building on Addison's definition, significant heritage projects are examined as examples of documentation, representation, and dissemination, bearing in mind the permeable character of these categories. The development of AI expands Addison's definition, offering greater opportunities for automating specific tasks and uncovering paradigms by running simulations. A quick review of the existing literature will help the reader to understand the extent of digital tools in architectural heritage studies.

Documentation and analysis of the heritage data

"Archaeologists are the Cowboys of Science" is a reference to the popular Indiana Jones stereotype, an independent outdoor type, who is also patient in research and excavation (Connor 2007, 1). In practice, the forensic methods of archaeology emphasize great precision and accuracy in the collection of archaeological data. A good example is The Earth Archive project (2019), in which archaeologist C. T. Fisher documented extensive sections of the earth with Light Detection and Ranging (LIDAR), a remote sensing method used to examine the surface of Earth. He uses the airborne mapping LiDAR (a.k.a. airborne laser scanning) for rapid archaeological assessments in poorly documented regions (Fisher et al. 2017) and also assumes that such documentation will create a digital record that will survive the coming natural and cultural destruction.

Archaeology often provides less than ideal conditions for documentation. Crowdsourcing lost heritage due to the destruction of cultural heritage has been achieved since 2001. Often photogrammetry, the art and science of deriving accurate fully textured 3D models from photographs, is used in archaeological documentation. Through photogrammetric techniques and algorithms, Grün et al. (2004) worked on reconstructions of the tallest representation of standing Buddhas destroyed by the Taliban, based on several datasets, none of which have been structured for research archaeology. The material collected from tourists was challenging for an accurate reconstruction as the photographs were of poor quality but nevertheless resulted in fairly accurate reconstructions. Similar destruction of heritage sites happened at the end of February 2015, when a video documenting the destruction of cultural heritage at the Mosul museum in Iraq inspired the digital archaeologists C. Coughenour and M. Vincent to initiate a crowd-sourced photogrammetric reconstruction project for the digital visualization of the lost heritage. The Project Mosul seeks to digitally reconstruct the lost heritage, whether through war, conflict, natural disaster, or other means, and preserve its memory through digital preservation schemes (Vincent et al. 2015). The project is a framework for managing the crowd-sourced reconstructions of the lost heritage: Volunteers can upload images onto the website, often photographs from their own tours of specific sites, and then collaboratively group the photos showing the same feature. Alternatively, the challenge might be simply to use unstructured data: N. Snavelyn developed a system that can reconstruct 3D geometry from large, unorganized collections of photographs from Internet photo-sharing sites (Agarwal et al. 2011). In his work, he uses existing photogrammetric data, which were not intended for this specific task. These examples highlight the importance of photogrammetry in archaeological research using collections of images made for various purposes, and similarly, the use of satellite images.

The use of a photogrammetric image in archaeology is even more highly developed in space archaeology, also called archaeology from space. This refers to the usage of any form of air or space-based data to uncover ancient features or sites (Parcak 2009). The space archaeologist Parcak (2019, 4) uses all forms of satellite remote sensing to locate ancient sites, and also to monitor the ongoing destruction. In 2010, Sarah Parcak combined two satellite images of an ancient site, one low resolution and multispectral and the other higher resolution but black and white. Using a variety of types of satellite imagery, she monitors the rate of archaeological site destruction in the Middle East (Parcak 2007). Exploiting crowdsourcing, the power of the public, to analyze the satellite images, GlobalXplorer (2019) is an online platform that enables anyone with a computer and an Internet connection to identify archaeological sites in satellite imagery. Using these techniques, during the pandemic quarantine of spring 2020, Dr. Christopher Smart, the "armchair archaeologist" from the University of Exeter, uncovered dozens of previously hidden archaeological sites (Morrison 2020). As archaeological excavations have been suspended, researchers are turning to LIDAR images and aerial survey data and leading to the discovery of several artifacts. These studies have increased the involvement of the public in archaeology, but also highlighted the time-consuming aspects of this discovery process.

Representation and dissemination of heritage information

Recent developments in emerging technologies have led to the discovery of aspects of heritage, in which digital tools provide new perspectives on archaeological excavations, by improving the collection, analysis, and visualization of data (Forte et al. 2012). Similarly, after a structural fire in 2019 at Notre-Dame de Paris cathedral, the building's reconstruction/restoration will be facilitated by a digital version of the building featured in Unity's 2014 game Assassin's Creed (Gombault 2020, 92). After the fire, Ubisoft, the game creator, collaborated with UNESCO to create a virtual visit to Notre Dame de Paris as it was before the fire. However, the digital models, the game-makers were seeking to create were coherent visuals rather than a precise and accurate reconstruction. Other projects included work by Prof. Nagakura, an expert on the computational representation of architectural space and knowledge, and his team at MIT Faculty of Architecture, who focus on digital heritage visualization through photogrammetric modeling processes and interactive representations in cases in Italy (Nagakura et al. 2015) and in Turkey (Güleç et al. 2016). In photogrammetric reconstruction, developments in scanning technology are improving the accuracy of these digital models; however, in addition to archaeological data, each reconstruction inevitably involves interpretations due to the demand for digital model making. Examples of investigations that virtually reconstruct historical phenomena include Project RomeLab (2013), a leading illustration of a visualization of the evolution of complex architecture; Digital Magnesia, aiming at creating a digital model of Menderes Magnesia (Saldana & Johanson 2013); and other studies focusing on parametric modeling and the analysis of underwater heritage (Varinlioglu et al. 2014). Taking a similar approach, the Digital Teos Project is an interdisciplinary research project investigating and digitally animating the architectural heritage of *Teos*, an important city in *Ionia*. The project included digital fabrication of the reconstructed historical buildings, a revisit through virtual reality (VR) (Varinlioglu & Kasali 2018; Varinlioglu 2020) and augmented reality (AR) devices (Varinlioglu & Halici 2019), as well as a smartphone game application (Varinlioglu et al. 2018).

These prominent examples, focusing on the preservation, visualization, and dissemination of heritage, emerged during the two earlier waves of the digital humanities. However, whether digitized or born-digital, all these tools exploited computational powers to augment the interaction with the cultural heritage. In 1999, the prominent J. Barceló founded the AI / cultural heritage working group to explore the combination of AI and cultural heritage sites (Barceló 2010). In the first theoretical and practical study on the application of AI to archeology, Barceló (2008) argues that computers are able to perform the stages of analysis and interpretation of cultural heritage, acting as automated archaeologists. According to Barceló (2007), heritage refers not to the study of artifacts as mute witnesses of the past, but rather, to the analysis of social actions performed in the past. Archaeologists study data to understand the dynamic nature of society with the goal of discovering the invisible in what is actually visible. Barceló and Del Castillo's (2016) approach to computer simulation seems relevant to this process, in that this presents theories and methods of computer simulation that specifically contribute to the understanding of the past.

Artificial intelligence for digital heritage projects

AI is increasingly influencing choices, behavior, and imagination. AI algorithms suggest music, movies, photographs, recommend friends on social media, and correct our photographs, in short, directing our decisions. The technology companies currently have a great interest in contributing to heritage studies through their AI systems. The projects of Intel combine the drone image collection program with image acquisition and AI to enable projects that contribute to the recording of and having greater control over both natural heritage and cultural heritage (Intel 2018). In the Great Wall Project, AI algorithms have been used to calculate the amount of building material required in the restoration process by detecting the structural defects in the Jiankou Wall. Photogrammetry allows 3D modeling and image processing means that images can be restored more accurately and efficiently. In underwater applications, video images of whales from drones enable whale images to be identified immediately by scanning databases. ML algorithms assess the health status of the whale based on its weight and form. A similar AI and heritage study by Microsoft is AI for Earth, Health, Accessibility, Humanitarian Action, and Cultural Heritage. It envisages projects conducted in partnership with museums, universities, and governments to help protect threatened spoken languages, places of residence, and other heritage works (Microsoft 2019).

Inferences can be made with ML methods based on archaeological data sets. An example in 2D archaeology is Assael et al. (2019), who used AI in the study of ancient Greek inscriptions, regarded as a transcript of history. He tested a system designed to predict the missing fonts (alphabet) in inscriptions based on a deep neural network algorithm called

Pythia. Pythia makes 20 different suggestions that can fill the gap for missing words in inscriptions, with the idea that the best suggestion can be selected via subjective decision and subject knowledge. It compares the predictive ability between a human epigraph and a digital epigraph with reference to the Turing test. Similarly, Sizikova and Funkhouser (2017) propose a method for global reconstruction of 2D wall paintings (frescos) from fragments using a genetic algorithm, which allows a larger and more consistent reconstruction than a local assembly. These efforts at puzzle-solving, reassembling fragmented artifacts and reconstructing missing documents address archaeology's fundamental unresolved issues.

Remote sensing technologies are part of space archeology, and a prominent area of study is the monitoring of the looted archaeological sites using satellite imagery. To prevent the need for time-consuming direct interpretation of images, Bowen et al. (2017) produced an automated image processing mechanism for the analysis of very-high-resolution of satellite images to identify damage to cultural heritage sites. Especially in Middle Eastern sites, which are difficult to access, this mechanism reduces costs and increases time efficiency. A similar study allows automated detection of architectural elements using satellite images. Soroush et al. (2020) used image recognition through deep learning and tested deep convolutional neural networks (CNNs) for qanat detection in the Kurdistan Region of Iraq. They focused on the circular qanat shafts because these potentially valuable targets for pattern recognition cannot be easily captured without automated techniques.

The use of GIS in archaeological studies from the early 1990s provided a step toward an approach to the analysis of human societies and their environment on a full macroscale, with features including the representation of data in layers, the integration of statistical and spatial programs, and most importantly, the ability to work on 3D terrains. In addition, GIS allows agent-based simulation, an approach to modeling systems comprising individual, autonomous, interacting agents (Heppenstall et al. 2012; Macal 2014). Notable examples include the application of network algorithms to connect architectural arrangements, and, on the urban scale, agent-based simulation for investigating urban development processes (Lee & Lee 2018). Similarly, in archaeology, agent-based modeling (ABM) represents a methodology with the potential to revolutionize advances in the overall archaeological research paradigm. Cegielski and Rogers (2016) review the use of ABM and computer simulations, pointing to the great potential of transdisciplinary approaches in archaeological interpretations and analysis.

Within this theoretical framework, using the potentials of computational technologies and, specifically, AI, the project aims to uncover the Anatolian networks of the Seljuk period. The Anatolian road networks, an extension of the Silk Roads, have never before been fully geolocated or simulated in a global setup. For this purpose, the way stations, in our case, caravanserais, are taken as a case study. Assisted by ML, we will be able not only to create a more complete aggregation of locations of caravanserais in Anatolia but also to run simulations to understand trade movements in this network.

Scope

The interaction between individuals and societies has always brought movement, which, rather than occurring randomly in the landscape, is focused on specific ever-changing paths that allow faster and easier connections, or sometimes, preferring longer routes to ensure connections between the heartlands of ancient empires. Roads and routes are mostly, but not limited to, trade networks and are fundamental to the transportation of materials and information between locations. The Silk Roads were a network of routes connecting the ancient societies of East, Central and Western Asia, and the Mediterranean. This network represents one of the world's preeminent long-distance communication networks, covering the Anatolian landscape through caravan routes. The International Council on Monuments and Sites (ICOMOS) thematic study on the Silk Road includes the east–west extent as far as Antioch–modern-day Antakya (UNESCO 2013; Williams 2014). Another relevant study on these trade and urban supply routes is the project of old-world trade routes (OWTRAD), a data transcription system providing a public-access to an electronic archive of geo- and chrono-reference data on Eurasian and African land, river, and maritime trade routes (Ciolek 1999). The system records details of their course, users, chronology, movement speeds, and other variables (Ciolek 2000).

As one of the hubs of the roads, Anatolia, (*Anadolu* in Turkish), also called *Asia Minor*, is the meeting point of three continents, Asia and Europe through the land and in the case of Africa, over water. Anatolia contains some of the world's richest remains of routes, roads, and tracks over the centuries. The history and culture of ancient Anatolia extend from prehistoric times, through Hellenistic, Roman, Byzantine and Seljuk, Ottoman periods, to modern-day Turkey. Research provides architectural evidence of roads from different eras (Bektaş 1999; Yıldırım & Oban 2011), including Roman roads (French 1981), Byzantine roads (Preiser-Kapeller 2015), Silk and Spice Roads (Frankopan 2015), and the Royal Road, an ancient highway reorganized and rebuilt during Persian Empire in the 5th century BCE (Graf 1994), as well as a distribution map on Mediterranean maritime archaeology and ancient trade routes (Robinson & Wilson 2011). However, the research carried out so far indicates how much more work is still needed, especially in examining connections between Anatolia and the Eastern networks. Thus, this study is concentrated on uncovering the networks of Anatolia during the Seljuk period through the examination of way stations, especially focusing on caravanserais.

A caravanserai, literally, caravan palace, or *han* in Turkish, is a roadside inn where travelers could rest and recover from their journeys. These are, ideally, positioned within a day's journey apart, on an average of every 30–40 kilometers. According to the OWTRAD, there are 154 Seljuk caravanserais on the route from Denizli to Doğubeyazıt, Turkey. Several independent studies on the urban networks of Anatolia include a well-known and detailed study by Branning (2019) on the Turkish khans, an edited book on architecture and landscape (Redford 2017), and studies on Anatolian caravanserais (Erdmann & Erdmann 1961; Özergin 1965; İlter 1969; Yavuz 1997; Önge 2007; Özcan 2010), as well as dissertations. The compilation of all these published resources provided evidence for overall 334 caravanserais (Figure 10.1). The focus of the current study will be the caravanserais of Western Anatolia during the Anatolian Seljuk State. The initial efforts of digital heritage projects on the caravanserais of the Anatolian Seljuks include three theses involving the integration of the research on khans into the GIS study (Ertepınar-Kaymakçı 2005; Telci 2011; Jahanabad 2015). Other relevant studies on these trade centers include an examination of urban networks and spatial hierarchies in Anatolia during the Seljuk period (Özcan 2010) and the architectural evidence for the roads (Bektaş 1999). However, lacking in the previous research on the ancient Silk Roads caravanserais during the Anatolian Seljuk period is a global vision for mapping the historical phenomena with precise spatiotemporal coordinates. The substantial research on the period consists of individual projects on specific aspects, but this has shed only limited light on the overall network of buildings. The current research indicates how much more work is still needed, especially in examining connections between Anatolia and the Eastern networks.

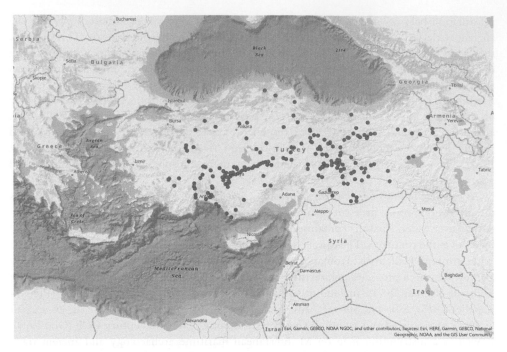

Figure 10.1 The GIS-based database of the caravanserais of Anatolian Seljuks.

Methodology

This work presents the use of AI in a comprehensive analysis of the Anatolian Seljuk trade networks. In the first part of the study, the project team carried out an extensive survey to determine the inventory of caravanserais within the Anatolian region. This manual process involves compiling the data from published materials such as books, theses, papers, and online databases, as stated in the scope. Most caravanserais discussed in the literature lack accurate location data and instead rely on rather vague verbal descriptions that often refer to its position relative to historical settlements or landmarks. However, the process of collating the data is complicated by conflicting information about the location. These descriptions of the location often involve long-forgotten landmarks and village names. Furthermore, since the literature involves many sources, it is very difficult to reconcile different writers' conflicting descriptions of the locations. To enable the collaboration between team members, we digitized these data and manually compiled various written resources in a collaborative database system. A comparative study was carried out to eliminate the ambiguities about the overall numbers and location of the caravanserais. The team used Google Earth satellite images to determine whether the recorded caravanserais were in fact visible in the images. There are two main reasons for not being able to locate these caravanserais manually. Firstly, although they exist in geography, they are not sufficiently clearly referenced for the team to locate them, either because of changes in the location name or the position of the roads. To complement this manual labor of locating the caravanserais that are known to exist in the geography because they are visible on the satellite images but were not found by the team, we employed SL. SL determines areas on the map that are the potential locations of the missing caravanserais, for inspection by the team, thus allowing a more complete survey of caravanserais.

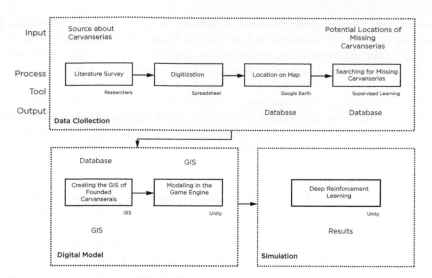

Figure 10.2 Workflow of the methodology.

The second reason for information missing on the caravanserais is that they were ruined or destroyed. To estimate these locations and to further understand the movements of caravans across the trade network, we devised a DRL approach. In the DRL, we created a representation of the topography of Anatolia in a simulation environment in the Unity game engine. In the simulation, an agent travels from its source and tries to reach its destination. In each run, the agent is scored according to its efficiency in locating the destination. The efficiency of the route is evaluated using criteria that reflect the priorities of the caravans of the period, including distance, elevation gain, closeness to major cities, and the need to access water. By tracing these routes, estimating the points at which journeys would need to be broken for rest, and taking the topography into account, the DRL shows potential sites of missing caravanserais.

These two examples show how AI can help to uncover more information in heritage studies and build a more complete analysis. Although these methods are not yet fully automated, they both decrease the labor needed and bring insight into the conditions of the past (Figure 10.2).

Supervised learning

Object detection (OD) is an important toolset for heritage studies (Yarlagadda et al. 2013). Locating a feature in an image is easy for humans, but rather difficult for computers. However, once the computer learns to determine certain features from an image, it can perform the task repeatedly. SL, a branch of ML can be applied for OD (Zhao et al. 2019). In SL, a function is created that maps an input onto an output in a pairwise manner. For our example, the function maps various sets of caravanserai images with the labeled caravanserai, and when it can find a similar feature on a satellite image the algorithm can tag the feature as a caravanserai. Although it is challenging to set up an ML algorithm for the recognition of features from images, tools that connect to GIS to simplify the workflow are available (ArcGIS 2020). In this example, we used ArcGIS and ArcGIS Application Programming Interface (API) for Python, which connects to the Python code responsible for the ML process. As discussed earlier, digitizing the locations of heritage buildings is a meticulous task. In the manual inspection of the caravanserais from Google Earth, our team was able to locate some but not all of the caravanserais for which historical evidence is available, and therefore, we decided to implement SL to automate the search for the remaining caravanserais using satellite image data.

The biggest challenge for developing a successful SL is to create a dataset from caravanserai images to train the algorithm (Fiorucci et al. 2020). SL algorithms need to be trained with a large number of images to produce good results, in general, the more images, the more accurate your model. When creating the dataset, we used ArcGIS to label caravanserai locations. As a base map, we used ArcGIS Map Service 30cm Imagery, and for creating a dataset for the training, we used ArcGIS API for Python. We created a polygon vector layer that marks the caravanserai locations, and these locations can be confirmed through Google Earth and downloaded as 256 × 256-pixel images from satellite imagery from the Esri world imagery layer.

For the training, we used a single-shot multibox detector (SSD), which is an optimized fast algorithm for OD (Liu et al. 2016). The SSD model is built over Resnet-34, which is an image classification model. We used Adam optimizer that uses a one-cycle learning rate schedule for training and employed discriminative learning rates while fine-tuning the model. All of the stated techniques are provided by the fast.ai library. After the training phase, we marked potential areas for caravanserai sites, based on the trade routes operational in the period under study. The search focused only on these areas to increase performance. The marked area was divided into images, the same size as the training dataset, i.e., 256 × 256. This is automatically created from satellite images from ArcGIS. To avoid overfitting in the center, the caravanserais are placed asymmetrically at the corners of the images. After the inference, the (AI marks the tiles with a high probability of containing a caravanserai. To prevent false positives, we inspect the tiles before entering any caravanserai into the database. If the visual inspection is not conclusive, the location is recorded for a subsequent physical examination.

SL was used as a support system in the manual search to locate the caravanserais. In the survey phase, most of the work was performed manually by the research team, but this work was supported by SL leading to the uncovering of some caravanserais missed in the manual search.

Deep reinforcement learning

Reinforcement learning is a branch of ML where agents are trained using rewards for successful behaviors (Kaelbling et al., 1996). Each agent action is positively or negatively rewarded; For each action that brings the agent closer to its goal, it is given a positive reward, and for each action that moves the agent further from its goal, it is penalized. After each action, the state of the environment changes, and another action is taken. This procedure is repeated at each turn. One turn ends when the goal is reached or a termination case occurs, such as the agent crossing the boundary of the simulation or taking more than the maximum allowed actions. After the turn ends, the rewards are calculated for that turn, and the algorithm tries to increase its rewards each turn until an optimized solution is reached. For our example, the agent operates on the topography of Anatolia. The actions that it can take relate to its movement in one of the eight directions: forward, backward, left, right, and the diagonals. The agen's goal is to find the most convenient path from the initial caravanserai to the destination caravanserai (Figure 10.3).

Figure 10.3 Agent leaving traces of movement on the most convenient path from the initial caravanserai to the destination caravanserai.

Development of simulation

The development of the simulation started with the generation of Anatolian topography within Unity. The location of caravanserais comes from the database (Figure 10.1). Esri world elevation services include elevation data covering the world. Both elevation data and caravanserai data are imported into ArcGIS. The area for each simulation is discretized to 100-meter grid cells. Each of these grid cells store data regarding the elevation, presence of any caravanserai, and topographic features such as rivers and bridges. The data are stored in a JSON file and is loaded in the Unity game engine to generate the topography (Figure 10.4).

In the Unity game engine, after receiving the JSON file, the 3D topography of Anatolia is constructed. Tiles are constructed according to the topography data from ArcGIS. In this virtual environment, we place the caravanserais. Once the terrain is generated in the Unity game engine, ML–Agents API is integrated along with its Python end. For the Python libraries, a Python virtual environment is created. After this integration, the development can begin.

For the simulation, we use the Unity ML–Agents package, which integrates into the Unity environment (Figure 10.5). Unity ML–Agents has three parts: brain, academy, and agents (Juliani et al. 2020). First, the brain makes decisions. There are three types of brains that can be implemented: player, heuristic, and ML. In player mode, there is no ML involved;

Figure 10.4 Discrete generation of the topography in ArcGIS.

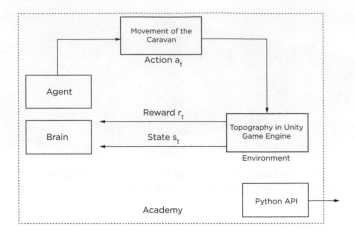

Figure 10.5   Simulation in Unity ML-Agents.

this is a debugging mode and the agent is controlled by the player. The heuristic mode works when Unity cannot connect to the external Python API. It provides simple statistical decision-making rather than ML. This provides an overview of the behavior of the agent. The last option is the connection to Python API, which runs ML. Second, the academy coordinates the learning process. The brain selects the action, and the academy returns the new state and the resulting rewards to the agent. Then the brain selects another action. If needed, the academy can also control multiple agents in the same environment. Lastly, the agent acts with the help of the brain. It records observations and follows the actions determined by the brain. Our aim was to simulate the movements of a caravan in trade routes in the Anatolian topography. Each simulation starts with the selection of the geography and the caravanserais.

Rewards

For a successful agent simulation, the agent's behavior should be reinforced with positive and negative rewards. Careful consideration should be given because the rewarding mechanism determines the agent's actions. For our project, the main behavior required of agents was to find the destination caravanserai; therefore, the highest score, ten points, was given when the agent reached the caravanserai. We also favored the shortest path from one caravanserai to the other; therefore, each move was awarded negative 0.1 points. The river crossings were parametrically coded. Depending on geography, we increased the negative reward for crossing the river, making it an undesirable behavior. Also, this behavior could be reinforced by adding positive rewards for using bridges. Lastly, to prevent the agent from climbing, we gave a negative reward for each move gaining elevation, but the amount varied according to the geography. This rewarding mechanism ensured that the simulation was sufficiently flexible to allow the addition of other features, such as roads and assigning rewards to the agents that follow these and punishing those that ignored them.

Results

In the first part of the research, SL is used to help researchers uncover the missing caravanserais in the survey phase. In the initial search phase, the team was able to find 631 references to caravanserais in different sources. These were collated to a spreadsheet, and all these references were checked several times to eliminate duplicates and combined multiple references to a single caravanserai. Following this step, the number of caravanserais totaled 88. These were the best-known and best-documented caravanserais in the literature. These caravanserais were located using online map services, such as Google Earth.

After the initial search, the team tried to locate the remaining less-known caravanserais using online map services. After a thorough search by the team lasting several weeks, the comprehensive list of caravanserais reached 225 entries. At this point, the manual search could not discover any further caravanserais although the literature suggests there were approximately 300 caravanserais in the region in that era. Also, a visual inspection revealed some areas lacked any caravanserais, and this indicated missing sites, as such an absence would have made it impossible for the caravans to safely travel around the region.

At this point in the research, we used the support system that we developed using SL to locate the remaining caravanserais. To determine the potential success of the system, we created a sample set of 120 caravanserais, from which 100 were selected for the training set and 20 for the testing set. We selected the caravanserais in better conditions, as older ones are often in ruins and difficult to distinguish.

For this study, a true positive case represents the algorithm finding a caravanserai at the site of an actual caravanserai; false-positive case, finding a caravanserai where there is none; the true negative is the algorithm not finding a caravanserai where there is none; lastly, false negative is the algorithm missing a caravanserai. For this study, false-positive cases were not a major concern as the results were checked by the team; in contrast, reducing the number of false negatives was important in locating the missing caravanserais.

After the training of the SL algorithm, we applied the support system to the testing set. From 20 caravanserais, the algorithm managed to find all but two with varying degrees of accuracy. The outcome of the algorithm gives a certainty probability ranging from 0 to 1; the bigger the probability, the more likely the presence of a caravanserai. For the threshold of the algorithm, we selected 0.1 meaning even if the algorithm indicates a 10% chance of a caravanserai in the location, we regard it as a positive case. This threshold selection resulted in the occurrence of many false positives. When we applied the support system to the areas thought to include caravanserai, we received hundreds of false cases in different runs, each of which was inspected and rejected by a researcher. Although this might seem time-consuming, it was still a major improvement over the manual search, which requires inspection of a much larger area. After different tests, the team managed to find nine missing caravanserais. Also, in some cases, the team was uncertain whether the building found by the system was in fact a caravanserai. At this point in the research, as no field study has been performed, the data rely on online map data, and a more comprehensive study involving field inspection is needed.

In the second part of the study, using DRL, we were able to create a simulation environment within the Unity game engine. Each simulation was conducted in a different location and exploited the local terrain with a starting point, destination, and water crossings. In these simulations, from the starting point, the agent traverses the terrain to reach the destination. We ran the simulations in six different scenarios, and in each, the agent managed to arrive at the destination. These routes were considered optimal in terms of the simulation environment. However, in the real world, these routes have some minor differences, due to other factors not factored in, such as the need for safety. These simulations can also be used to estimate the locations of caravanserais that were not identified in the initial survey but presumed to have existed because the nearest known caravanserais are too distant to be reached in one day. Unfortunately, because of the limited available computer power, the experiments were limited to small, clearly-defined areas. It was not possible to run the simulations across the whole of Anatolia, but the size of areas could feasibly be increased using a workstation with a more substantial graphical processing unit.

Conclusion

In cultural heritage studies, computerized tools have become an integral part of data dissemination and visualization. Moreover, the development of AI offers previously unavailable opportunities to automate specific tasks and uncover paradigms through simulations. In this work, we exploited the potential of AI to uncover trade networks of the Anatolian Seljuk period and thus, shed light on the culture of the past. In this process, first, we made an inventory of caravanserais, which are hubs in the trade networks where traveling traders can rest each evening. During the aggregation process, we used the literature to record known caravanserais. However, often the written literature does not provide location data of the caravanserais; thus, the exact locations need to be found manually on an online map, Google Earth. Unfortunately, using this method, we failed to locate more than half of the caravanserais. To locate the still-existing caravanserais that we were unable to locate manually, we trained a CNN using the dataset of images from the caravanserais that we were able to locate. Using inference, we were able to find some of the previously missing caravanserais. After the inclusion of these missing caravanserais, we first set up the network of caravanserais in a GIS, storing various data in a postGIS database. Next, we created a 3D simulation environment using the data in the database contained in the Unity game engine. In this environment, using DRL an agent explores the environment and attempts to move from one caravanserai to another. The simulation environment includes topographical features, and the reward function punishes the agent when it tries to cross rivers or climb uphill but rewards the agent in reaching its destination caravanserai. Moreover, the agent has a limited time to reach its destination, which reflects the real world at the time; caravans needed to reach a caravanserai before the sunset. The outcome of the simulations revealed not only the optimal locations for caravanserais but also the potential sites of as yet undiscovered caravanserais.

Acknowledgment

This project presents the initial findings of Varinlioglu's project entitled "Stigmergy as a Tool for Uncovering Anatolian Urban Networks of the Past" funded by The Fulbright Visiting Scholar Program 2020. This paper is partly presented at the Ph.D. course at Istanbul Technical University (ITU) in the Graduate Program of Architectural Design Computing, MBL 617E Special Topics in Architectural Design Computing, Theory and Methods in Digital Heritage. We would like to thank our graduate students Nur Erdemci, Taner Cafer Üsküplü, Ayşenaz Sönmez, Begüm Moralıoğlu, Hanife Sümeyye Taşdelen, Mustafa Cem Güneş, Varlık Yücel, Feyza Nur Koçer Özgün, Nursena Coşkun Müştekin, and Gülce Kırdar.

References

Addison, A. C. (2000). Emerging Trends in Virtual Heritage. *IEEE Multimedia*, 7(2), 22–25. https://doi.org/10.1109/93.848421

Agarwal, S., Furukawa, Y., Snavely, N., Simon, I., Curless, B., Seitz, S. M., & Szeliski, R. (2011). Building Rome in a Day. *Communications of the ACM*, *54*(10), 105–112. https://doi.org/10.1109/ICCV.2009.5459148

ArcGIS (2020). Retrieved from https://developers.arcgis.com/python/sample-notebooks/detecting-swimming-pools-using-satellite-image-and-deep-learning/.

Assael, Y., Sommerschield, T., & Prag, J. (2019). *Restoring Ancient Text Using Deep Learning: A Case Study on Greek Epigraphy*. Empirical Methods in Natural Language Processing (EMNLP).

Barceló, J. A. (2007). Automatic Archaeology: Bridging the Gap between Virtual Reality, Artificial Intelligence, and Archaeology. In F. Cameron & S. Kenderdine (Eds.), *Theorizing Digital Cultural Heritage: A Critical Discourse* (pp. 437–456). Cambridge, MA: MIT Press. https://doi.org/10.7551/mitpress/9780262033534.003.0023

Barceló, J. A. (2008). *Computational Intelligence in Archaeology*. Information Science Reference.

Barceló, J. A. (2010). Computational Intelligence in Archaeology: State of the art. In *Proceedings of the 37th International Conference on Computer Applications and Qualitative Methods in Archaeology (CAA'10)* (pp. 11–21), Williamsburg, Brooklyn, United States.

Barceló, J. A., & Del Castillo, F. (2016). *Simulating Prehistoric and Ancient Worlds*. New York: Springer International Publishing. https://doi.org/10.1007/978-3-319-31481-5

Bektaş, C. (1999). *A Proposal Regarding the Seljuk Caravanserais Their Protection and Use*. Istanbul: Yapı-Endüstri Merkezi Yayınları.

Berry, D. (2011). The Computational Turn: Thinking about the Digital Humanities. *Culture Machine, 12*, 1–22. https://doi.org/10.2337/DB11-0751

Bowen, E. F., Tofel, B. B., Parcak, S., & Granger, R. (2017). Algorithmic Identification of Looted Archaeological Sites from Space. *Frontiers in ICT, 4*, 4. https://doi.org/10.3389/fict.2017.00004

Branning, K. (2019). The Seljuk Han of Anatolia. Retrieved from http://www.turkishhan.org.

Burdick, A., Drucker, J., Lunenfeld, P., Presner, T. S., & Schnapp, J. T. (2012). *Digital_Humanities*. Cambridge, MA: MIT Press.

Cameron, F., & Kenderdine, S. (2007). *Theorizing Digital Cultural Heritage: A Critical Discourse*. Cambridge, MA: MIT Press. https://doi.org/10.7551/mitpress/9780262033534.001.0001

Cegielski, W. H., & Rogers, J. D. (2016). Rethinking the Role of Agent-based Modeling in Archaeology. *Journal of Anthropological Archaeology, 41*, 283–298. https://doi.org/10.1016/j.jaa.2016.01.009

Chin, T. (2013). The Invention of the Silk Road, 1877. *Critical Inquiry*, 40(1), 194–219. https://doi.org/10.1086/673232

Ciolek, T. M. (1999). Georeferenced Historical Transport/Travel/Communication Routes and Nodes – Dromographic Digital Data Archives (ODDDA): Old World Trade Routes (OWTRAD) Project. Retrieved from www.ciolek.com.

Ciolek, T. M. (2000). Digitising Data on Eurasian Trade Routes: An Experimental Notation System. pp. 1–28 of section 5–122, in: PNC Secretariat (ed.). 2000. *Proceedings of the 2000 EBTI, ECAI, SEER & PNC Joint Meeting 13–17 January 2000*, University of California at Berkeley, Berkeley, CA. Taipei: Academia Sinica.

Connor, M. A. (2007). *Forensic Methods: Excavation for the Archaeologist and Investigator*. Lanham, MD: Rowman Altamira.

Erdmann, K., & Erdmann, H. (1961). Das anatolische Karavansaray des 13. *Jahrhunderts, I*, Berlin.

Ertepınar-Kaymakçı, P. (2005). *Geoarchaeological Investigation of Central Anatolian Caravanserais Using GIS* (Master Thesis, Ortadoğu Teknik Üniversitesi Fen Bilimleri Enstitüsü, Ankara).

Fiorucci, M., Khoroshiltseva, M., Pontil, M., Traviglia, A., Del Bue, A., & James, S. (2020). Machine Learning for Cultural Heritage: A Survey. *Pattern Recognition Letters, 133*, 102–108. https://doi.org/10.1016/j.patrec.2020.02.017

Fisher, C. T., Cohen, A. S., Fernández-Diaz, J. C., & Leisz, S. J. (2017). The Application of Airborne Mapping LiDAR for the Documentation of Ancient Cities and Regions in Tropical Regions. *Quaternary International, 448*, 129–138. https://doi.org/10.1016/j.quaint.2016.08.050

Forte, M., Dell'Unto, N., Issavi, J., Onsurez, L., & Lercari, N. (2012). 3D Archaeology at Çatalhöyük. *International Journal of Heritage in the Digital Era, 1*(3), 351–378. https://doi.org/10.1260/2047-4970.1.3.351

Frankopan, P. (2015). *The Silk Roads: A New History of the World*. London: Bloomsbury Publishing.

French, D. (1981). *Roman Roads and Milestones of Asia Minor: The Pilgrim's Roads*. London: British Institute of Archaeology at Ankara Press.

GlobalXplorer (2019), Retrieved from https://www.globalxplorer.org.

Gombault, A. (2020). Notre-Dame Is Burning: Learning From the Crisis of a Superstar Religious Monument. *International Journal of Arts Management, 22*(2), 83–94.

Google Arts and Culture (2011). Retrieved from https://artsandculture.google.com.

Graf, D. F. (1994). "The Persian Royal Road System". Continuity & Change: Proceedings of the Last Achaemenid History Workshop 1990. *Achaemenid History, 8*, 167–189.

Grün, A., Remondino, F., & Zhang, L. (2004). Photogrammetric Reconstruction of the Great Buddha of Bamiyan, Afghanistan. *The Photogrammetric Record, 19*(107), 177–199. https://doi.org/10.1111/j.0031-868X.2004.00278.x

Güleç Özer, D., Nagakura, T., & Vlavianos, N. (2016). Augmented Reality of Historic Environments: Representation of Parion Theater, Biga, Turkey. *A| Z ITU Journal of the Faculty of Architecture, 13*(2), 185–193. https://doi.org/10.5505/itujfa.2016.66376

Hayles, N. K. (2012). How We Think: Transforming Power and Digital Technologies. In D. M. Berry (Ed.), *Understanding Digital Humanities* (pp. 42–66). Basingstoke: Palgrave Macmillan. https://doi.org/10.1057/9780230371934_1

Heppenstall, A. J., Crooks, A. T., See, L. M., & Batty, M. (2012). *Agent-based Models of Geographical Systems*. Berlin: Springer Science & Business Media. https://doi.org/10.1007/978-90-481-8927-4

Howard, P. (2003). *Heritage: Management, Interpretation, Identity*. A&C Black. https://doi.org/10.1002/jtr.508

Ibaraki, S. (2019). Artificial Intelligence for Good: Preserving our Cultural Heritage. *Forbes*, 28 March, 2019. Retrieved from https://www.forbes.com.

İlter, İ. (1969). *Tarihi Türk Hanları*. Istanbul: Karayolları Genel Müdürlüğü Yayınları.

Intel (2018). Retrieved from https://www.intel.com.tr/content/www/tr/tr/analytics/artificial-intelligence/overview.html.

Jahanabad, H. H. (2015). *Anadolu'da Ticaretin Ulaşım Rotalarının Değişimi Üzerindeki Etkisi: Tarihi-mekansal bir analiz* (Master thesis, İstanbul Teknik Üniversitesi Fen Bilimleri Enstitüsü, İstanbul).

Juliani, A., Berges, V., Teng, E., Cohen, A., Harper, J., Elion, C., Goy, C., Gao, Y., Henry, H., Mattar, M., & Lange, D. (2020). *Unity: A General Platform for Intelligent Agents*. arXiv:1809.02627v2.

Kaelbling, L.P., Littman, M.L., & Moore, A.W. (1996). *Reinforcement Learning: A Survey. Journal of Artificial Intelligence Research, 4*, 237–285. https://doi.org/10.1613/jair.301

Kalay, Y., Kvan, T., & Affleck, J. (2007). *New Heritage: New Media and Cultural Heritage*. London: Routledge.

Lee, J., & Lee, H. S. (2018). The Visible and Invisible Network of a Self-Organizing Town: Agent-based Simulation for Investigating Urban Development Process. In *23rd International Conference on Computer-Aided Architectural Design Research in Asia: Learning, Prototyping and Adapting, CAADRIA 2018* (pp. 411–420), Beijing, China.

Liu, W., Anguelov, D., Erhan, D., Szegedy, C., Reed, S., & Fu, C. (2016). *SSD: Single Shot MultiBox Detector*. arXiv:1512.02325v5

Macal, C. (2014). Introductory Tutorial: Agent-based Modeling and Simulation. In *Proceedings of the Winter Simulation Conference 2014* (pp. 6–20), Savannah Georgia.

Microsoft (2019). AI for Cultural Heritage. Retrieved from https://www.microsoft.com/en-us/ai/ai-for-cultural-heritage.

Morrison, R. (2020). Armchair Archaeology: Dozens of Prehistoric, Roman and Medieval Sites Are Spotted in Aerial Images of South West England by People Working at Home During Coronavirus Lockdown. *Mail Online*, May 13, 2020. Retrieved from https://www.dailymail.co.uk/sciencetech/article-8311455/Dozens-prehistoric-Roman-medieval-sites-discovered-lockdown-archaeologists.html.

Nagakura, T., Tsai, D., & Pinochet, D. (2015). Digital Heritage Visualizations of the Impossible. In *Proceedings of the 20th International Conference on Cultural Heritage and New Technologies* (pp. 1–19), Vienna, Austria.

Önge, M. (2007). Caravanserais as Symbols of Power in Seljuk Anatolia. *Politica, 306*(21), 49–69.

Özcan, K. (2010). The Anatolian Seljuk City an Analysis on Early Turkish Urban Models in Anatolia. *Central Asiatic Journal, 54*(2), 273–290.

Özergin, M. (1965). Anadolu'da Selçuklu Kervansarayları. *Tarih Dergisi, 15*(20), 141–170.

Parcak, S. (2007) Satellite Remote Sensing Methods for Monitoring Archaeological Tells in the Middle East. *Journal of Field Archaeology, 32*(1), 65–81. http://www.jstor.org/stable/40026043

Parcak, S. (2009). *Satellite Remote Sensing for Archaeology*. London: Routledge.

Parcak, S. (2019). *Archaeology from Space: How the Future Shapes Our Past*. New York: Henry Holt & Co.

Preiser-Kapeller, J. (2015). Calculating the Middle Ages? The Project: Complexities and Networks in the Medieval Mediterranean and Near East. *Medieval Worlds, 2*, 100–127. https://doi.org/10.1553/medievalworlds_no2_2015s100

Presner, T. (2010). *Digital Humanities 2.0: A Report on Knowledge.* Retrieved from http://citeseerx.ist. psu.edu/viewdoc/download?doi=10.1.1.469.1435&rep=rep1&type=pdf.

Redford, S. (2017). Foreword. In P. Blessing & R. Goshgarian (Eds.), *Architecture and Landscape in Medieval Anatolia, 1100–1500* (pp. 12–13). Edinburgh: Edinburgh University Press.

Robinson, D., & Wilson, A. (2011). *Maritime Archaeology and Ancient Trade in the Mediterranean.* Oxford: Oxford Centre for Maritime Archaeology. https://doi.org/10.1111/1095-9270.12008_6

Romelab (2013). Retrieved from http://hvwc.etc.ucla.edu.

Saldana, M., & Johanson, C. (2013). Procedural Modeling for Rapid-Prototyping of Multiple Building Phases. *The International Archives of the Photogrammetry, Remote Sensing and Spatial Information Sciences,* XL-5/W1, 205–210. https://doi.org/10.5194/isprsarchives-XL-5-W1-205-2013

Sizikova, E., & Funkhouser, T. (2017). Wall Painting Reconstruction Using a Genetic Algorithm. *Journal on Computing and Cultural Heritage,* 11(1), 1–17. https://doi.org/10.1145/3084547

Soroush, M., Mehrtash, A., Khazraee, E., & Ur, J. A. (2020). Deep Learning in Archaeological Remote Sensing: Automated Qanat Detection in the Kurdistan Region of Iraq. *Remote Sensing, 12*(3), 500. https://doi.org/10.3390/rs12030500

Telci, A. (2011). *Türkiye'deki Ticaret Yolları Üzerinde Bulunan Han ve Kervansarayların Fotogrametrik Belgelenmesi ve Coğrafi Bilgi Sistemine Entegre Edilmesi* (Master thesis, Selçuk Üniversitesi Fen Bilimleri Enstitüsü, Konya).

The Earth Archive Project (2019). Retrieved from https://www.theearcharchive.com.

The Time Machine Project (2019). Retrieved from https://www.timemachine.eu.

UNESCO (2013–2022). Retrieved from https://en.unesco.org/silkroad/content/caravanserais-cross-roads-commerce-and-culture-along-silk-roads.

Varinlioglu, G. (2020). Teos Üzerinden Dijital Mirasta Sanal Gerçeklik Uygulamalarını Anlamak. *Megaron,* 15(1). https://doi.org/10.14744/MEGARON.2019.85619.

Varinlioglu, G., Alankus, G., Aslankan, A., & Mura, G. (2018). Raising Awareness for Digital Heritage through Serious Game. *METU Journal of the Faculty of Architecture,* 36(1), 23–40.

Varinlioglu, G., Balaban, O., Ipek, Y., & Alacam, A. (2014). Parametric Modeling of Archaeological Heritage in the Age of Digital Reconstruction. *SIGRADI 2014,* 614–617. https://doi.org/10.5151/despro-sigradi2014-0127

Varinlioglu, G., & Halici, S. M. (2019). Envisioning Ambiances of the Past. *EAEA 2019, 64.*

Varinlioglu, G., & Kasali, A. (2018). Virtual Reality for a Better Past. In A. Kepczynska-Walczakand S. Bialkowski (Eds.), *Computing for a Better Tomorrow – Proceedings of the 36th eCAADe Conference – Volume 2* (pp. 243–250), Lodz University of Technology, Lodz, Poland.

Vincent, M. L., Gutierrez, M. F., Coughenour, C., Manuel, V., Bendicho, L. M., Remondino, F., & Fritsch, D. (2015, September). Crowd-sourcing the 3D Digital Reconstructions of Lost Cultural Heritage. In *2015 Digital Heritage* (Vol. 1, pp. 171–172). Piscataway, NJ: IEEE. https://doi.org/10.1111/j.0031-868X.2004.00278.x

Yarlagadda, P., Monroy, A., Carque, B., & Ommer, B. (2013). *Towards a Computer-based Understanding of Medieval Images.* Scientific Computing & Cultural Heritage. Berlin: Springer. 89–97. https://doi.org/10.1007/978-3-642-28021-4_10

Yavuz, A. T. (1997). The Concepts that Shape Anatolian Seljuq Caravanserais. In G. Necipoglu (Ed.), *Muqarnas XIV: An Annual on the Visual Culture of the Islamic World* (pp. 80–95). Leiden: E. J. Brill.

Yıldırım, R., & Oban, R. (2011). The Importance of Heritage Roads on the Development of Western Anatolia and Izmir. *Procedia Social and Behavioral Sciences, 19,* 90–97. https://doi.org/10.1016/j.sbspro.2011.05.111

Williams, T. (2014). *The Silk Roads: An ICOMOS Thematic Study.* Paris: International Council of Monuments and Sites (ICOMOS).

Williams, T. (2015). Mapping the Silk Roads. In M. N. Walter and J. P. Ito-Adler (Eds.), *The Silk Road: Interwoven History, Vol. 1, Long-distance Trade, Culture, and Society* (pp. 1–42). Cambridge: Cambridge Institutes Press.

Zhao, Z. Zheng, P., Xu, S., & Wu, X. (2019). Object Detection with Deep Learning: A Review. *IEEE Transactions on Neural Networks and Learning Systems, 30*(11), 3212–3232. https://doi.org/10.1109/TNNLS.2018.2876865

11

A deep-learning approach to real-time solar radiation prediction

Theodoros Galanos and Angelos Chronis

The undoubtedly significant contribution of buildings' performance to the devastating effects of climate change has in the past decades driven research and development efforts in the architecture, engineering, and construction industry (Chokhachian et al. 2017). To enable the shift toward more performance-aware design, environmental simulation tools have become more readily available through the constant development of new interfaces that incorporate state-of-the-art simulation engines in mainstream CAD frameworks. Architects and urban designers have at their disposal today, as part of their design workflows, a wide range of analytical tools that allow them to assess the environmental performance of their designs, to make informed and sustainable design decisions. Further to the incorporation of simulation tools, the recent developments in optimization and generative design methods are fundamentally changing the computational design workflow and enable the exploration of vast design spaces, unconceivable by manual processes.

The established, performance-driven design workflow is still suffering, though, from two significant bottlenecks that prevent it from achieving its full potential. On the one hand, despite the significant developments in the integration of simulation engines, their computational demands are still preventing them from reaching the needs of designers, especially in early stages. The time frames typically set during early design stages demand near-real-time feedback on performance metrics for them to be useful to stakeholders in collaborative design efforts. Moreover, the ability to explore vast solution spaces for design optimization problems with computational tools is currently feasible with very fast-to-quantify performance metrics, which does not allow us to delve into important and more complex performance aspects of our designs. On the other hand, the lack of domain-specific knowledge in architects and urban designers also prevents them from fully achieving a performance-driven design potential. The available simulation tools are either not easily accessible or require expertise on computational tools that is not part of the designers' education. Therefore, the performance optimization processes are mostly reserved by computational experts and researchers that are not usually part of the architectural or urban design process during early stages of design.

With InFraReD, we aim to assess the potential of machine learning (ML) and specifically deep-learning (DL) frameworks in addressing these current challenges of environmental building performance simulation. The framework is focusing on the potential of

ML in augmenting the computational power of environmental simulations, thereby greatly reducing the performance feedback time frame. By integrating models in mainstream CAD frameworks and making vast solution spaces accessible to the designer, the democratization of building performance simulation tools is enabled. Our findings on a first step toward the development of an intelligent framework for resilient design and specifically the development of a DL model to predict solar radiation (SR) in the urban scale have been quite promising. These initial findings are reporting on the methodology, results, and limitations of our current approach but also serve as a step toward a further development of a decision support framework that can greatly benefit resilient designs at early stages in the future.

Background

The use of ML for the prediction of simulation is not novel. ML methods for forecasting SR are, for example, well established for the optimization of the operation of photovoltaic systems, and many different models have been systematically reviewed and researched (Voyant et al. 2017; Wu et al. 2018). Nevertheless, SR prediction through DL remains relatively unexplored in the AEC industry. Specific research on ML-enabled simulation prediction methods has undoubtedly been conducted for buildings, for example, the prediction of hourly energy usage in buildings from yearly simulations (Gokhan et al. 2019) or the prediction of occupants' thermal comfort in buildings, using an intelligent methodology and field data (Wang et al. 2018).

More relevant to our study, the work of Zhang et al. (2018) has shown the significant benefits of using a ML approach to greatly augment the computational design workflow not only by minimizing the simulation time by orders of magnitude, but also by enabling optimized design recommendation based on the solution space generated. The study is also relevant in relation to the framework's interface that allows designers to engage with the model and its performance in an interactive and collaborative manner. However, at present their approach is restricted by a geometric definition that only allows for the use of simple cubes, as well as by the interface itself which is tied to specific hardware. Our work aims to develop a framework that is open for arbitrary geometric input, as well as for the integration within different CAD frameworks. Moreover, we aim to develop a modular and open simulation prediction framework that is independent of the design framework in which it will be used and thus supports the democratization of building performance simulation tools.

Methods

The main objective of our research is to assess the potential of DL in computational environmental design (CED) workflows at the urban scale. A novel workflow is developed, which allows for real-timeSR prediction of arbitrary urban geometries as input. The proposed approach attempts to bring together two until-now-disparate domains of practice, DL and CED, to close the gap between performance feedback and design in the early stages of urban design projects. The selection of SR as a performance indicator was driven by the low computational demands involved in SR simulations and by the established and validated state-of-the-art simulation engines available. This allows us to generate large datasets, in a logical time frame, without questioning the accuracy and efficiency of the SR simulation results.

A different, but equally important, advantage of using SR as a proxy to investigate these new, DL-infused, CED workflows is that it represents a first step toward other, more complex and typically much more valuable, performance evaluations such as thermal comfort and renewable energy potential. Another goal of this study is to be the first step toward a framework that allows such performance evaluations. The software stack involved in our study can be split into two functional parts: (i) computational design tools and (ii) DL models and libraries. The first part took place exclusively within the Rhinoceros and Grasshopper (GH) environment. Ladybug Tools (2019) were used to simulate SR for each geometrical input, using the ray-tracing capabilities of Radiance (Roudsari 2013).

In order to take advantage of the powerful parametric capabilities of GH, we developed custom scripts to allow for an automated generation of 3D urban masses from geographic information system (GIS) data, namely shapefiles containing building information. Custom Python components were developed and used to extract building curves and heights, in order to build the 3D massing models that would be later used in the SR simulations. Each SR result map was saved in the form of an image for later post-processing and use (Figure 11.1). We tried as much as we could to host all the different models, code, libraries and software required, within a single design framework which also gave us the opportunity to evaluate the ability to deploy DL models within GH and operationalize such a model within a coherent design decision support framework.

In order to generate data, case studies were conducted in two countries, the United States (USA) and Austria. For all locations, open-source GIS data for urban massing were used. Several cities across the USA were included in the studies in order to assess the impact of different climatic conditions, specifically sun angles, and urban configurations. The extent of geographical coverage for each study, along with the number of data points (i.e., images of SR maps) generated, varied from location to location. In total, we conducted 20,618 SR simulations within the USA, at a grid scale of 250 m × 250 m, covering a total of 1,288.63 sq. km of urban area. Additionally, we conducted 5242 SR simulations for Vienna, at a grid scale of 100 m × 100 m, covering a total of 52.42 sq. km of urban area.

The case studies developed also differed in terms of building layouts and urban massing complexity. While the building footprints for the US cities were relatively simple, the GIS data for Vienna presented a much higher urban massing complexity (Figure 11.2) that represented an interesting challenge for the DL models.

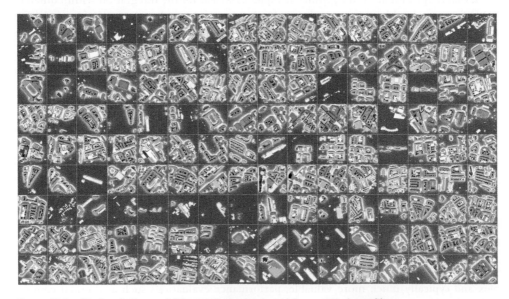

Figure 11.1 SR simulations of 3D massing generated from GIS shapefiles.

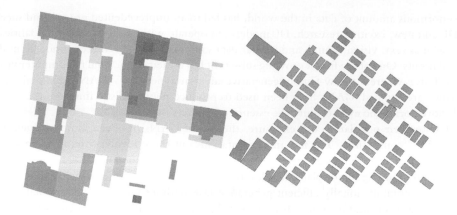

Figure 11.2 Example heightmaps from Boston, Massachusetts (left), and Vienna, Austria (right), showing the difference in urban massing complexity involved in each study.

Machine learning

There are many different definitions and demarcations of the artificial intelligence (AI) domain. In simple terms, AI tries to use computers to solve complex problems. It is focused on automating decisions for tasks that, when done by humans, would typically require intelligence. There are two different modes of AI: the so-called "strong AI," which aims at developing computer programs that can think at a level that meets or surpasses humans and are able to engage in abstract reasoning and thinking; and "weak AI" or "pattern-based AI," which aims at solving problems by detecting patterns in data. While we find ourselves today very far from a successful implementation of the first mode of AI, we have managed to develop many products that we use frequently in our everyday lives based on pattern-based AI.

Another important classification within AI relates to the type of learning that actually takes place. There are three types of learning which divide ML into three main areas of research and practice:

Supervised learning, in which we train a model in order to find the function that best defines, or approximates, the data. The human experts here act as teachers, feeding the computer with data and "showing it" the correct answers.

Unsupervised learning, in which we train a model without labeled data. There is no teacher at all; in fact, typically the model is able to "teach us" something about the data. This mode of learning is particularly useful when we do not know exactly what we are looking for in the data or there are no data available at all (both very common circumstances in real life).

Reinforcement learning, in which we use observations gathered from interaction of agents with their environment, taking actions that typically maximize reward or minimize risk. This mode of learning is iterative, exploring all, or a subset, of possible states of a problem.

Yet another distinction in ML relates to the architecture of models in use. DL typically involves so-called deep neural networks with millions of operations or weights. The rapid diffusion of powerful specialized hardware graphical processing units (GPUs), along with the enormous amount of data in the world, has led to an unprecedented growth and success of DL and new, exciting research. DL models can operate with many different modalities of data such as text, vision, sound, and tabular data sources and can even accommodate multi-modal inputs. One of the fastest growing subsets of DL is their application to computer vision tasks. This is where the now-famous generative adversarial networks (GANs), and their many variants, are situated. GANs have been used to produce photorealistic images, fake videos, and short stories and even capture the essence of painters' styles.

Despite their popularity and exposure, the use of GANs has been almost nonexistent in the AEC community. The few implementations out there revolve around some sort of generative application, whereby the GAN model is charged with generating new, hopefully realistic, designs (e.g., floor plans, facades, renderings). However, all these implementations focus on a computationally efficient generative task without taking the additional step of normative assessment. Our research aims to bridge this gap by using these generative models not to simply generate new designs of some kind but to predict and quantify performance in real time of both existing and generated inputs. This work has the potential to revolutionize the way we approach performance assessment and design allowing us to rapidly assess designs under a variety of performance metrics while providing easy access to typically complex and time-consuming studies.

Results

One model was trained for each location included in the studies, for a total of eight locations, seven in the USA and one in Europe (Vienna). This allowed us to compare the capacity of the model across different geographical locations, climatic conditions related to SR, and massing complexity and diversity. The accuracy of model predictions, in terms of both quantitative and qualitative evaluations, is surprisingly good. The trained models generate extremely accurate predictions of SR, on previously unseen massing configurations, which indicates that they have learned the relationship between urban context, climatic conditions, and SR (Figure 11.3).

The models also seem to perform accurately independently of the scale of the input, within certain limits of course. We tested scale invariance by predicting on a different scale than the one the models were trained without seeing a serious drop in accuracy of predictions (Figure 11.4).

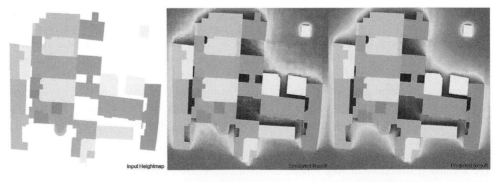

Figure 11.3 An input-simulation-prediction triplet produced by the Vienna model showing the exceptional accuracy of prediction even in complex input geometries.

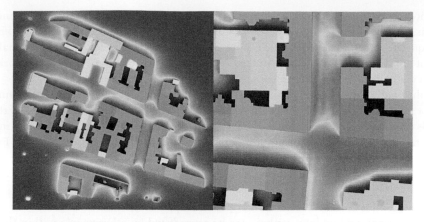

Figure 11.4 An example of scale invariance in model predictions. Left: prediction at 100 m × 100 m grid. Right: prediction at 250 m × 250 m grid.

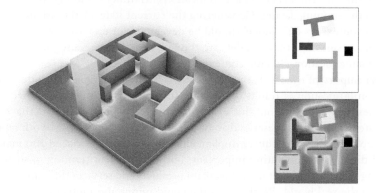

Figure 11.5 The AI-enabled design interface available to the user. Predictions within the design software happen in real time.

Furthermore, in order to assess the workflow's potential within a design decision support framework, GH scripts with custom Python components were developed, which allowed the deployment of the models and the generation of real-time predictions for any urban massing created by the user within GH (Figure 11.5). This gave us the opportunity to both test the model's performance in random user-generated inputs and create an initial test bed that will allow us to assess how real-time performance prediction might alter the user's perspective and choices during early-stage design.

Discussion

While results of the proposed workflow are extremely promising, the work was not without limitations. These can be generally distinguished into two main categories: limitations concerning the design tools used and limitations concerning the applicability and reproducibility of the study itself.

The landscape of design software and tools in the AEC world, both in academia and in practice, is dominated by two widely distributed design environments: Rhinoceros/

Grasshopper and Revit/Dynamo. Both environments have very similar capabilities and limitations. However, none of them is currently AI-capable. In both cases, external libraries are required, and in reality are much more computationally efficient, in order to make the current approach possible, which hinders our capability to develop end-to-end workflows within a unitary design environment.

Additionally, both design environments lack the capacity to handle the large amounts of data and processing involved in this approach, especially during the training of the DL models themselves. Furthermore, while these tools are sufficiently good at handling numerical data, the use, generation, and processing of visual data are far from optimal. Finally, most of the computations involved in this approach happen on the GPU, which creates a small but at times important competition for resources between the design software and DL models.

A crucial dimension of any research or practical application is how easily it can be applied in different contexts and how easily it can be reproduced by other people within the field. The task of urban performance evaluation is deeply influenced by the specific context, both urban and climatic. Generalization, the ability of these models to predict performance accurately in different contexts (e.g., across locations), is difficult and highly dependent on the diversity of the training dataset. Considering the current state-of-the-art and computational demands, a context-specific model should be developed for each case, perhaps even for each location. However, once these models are trained, they can be reused for any similar study within the same location/climatic context.

Another important issue is that we currently lack an intuitive interface that allows for the use and communication of results to different stakeholders of an urban project. We require carefully designed visualizations that can handle the large amounts of data that this approach can generate. Our attempt, described above, of developing such a framework represents only the first step toward more intuitive implementation. The data produced also make the use of cloud and distributed computing important, both for efficient training of such models and for enabling their deployment in downstream products and services that can be used to make decisions in the real world. Working on the cloud might also motivate a bigger disconnect from the typical design environments used locally and make us move toward cloud-based 3D modeling and design interfaces.

Conclusion

This project has clearly shown the potential of utilizing DL models for urban performance prediction, specifically SR prediction. However, more case studies are required in order to validate the approach as well as its accuracy across different urban and climatic contexts. We are currently in the process of developing a multi-city dataset that will span most important locations around the globe. This might also allow us to test our ability to generalize across locations by seeing if it is possible to train a context- and location-insensitive model for prediction of SR at the urban level.

We also need to widen our search within the AI domain and test or develop new architectures that can allow us to predict environmental performance at these scales. We are currently in the process of testing different architectures and models available to us, some simpler and some equally complex. Simpler models will allow us to build strong baselines upon which we can benchmark future research. Additionally, we also aim to enhance existing or to develop novel DL architectures guided by our practical experience and intuition concerning urban design and performance.

Additionally, as discussed, this is only the first step toward more complex and far more time-consuming assessments such as wind flow and thermal comfort prediction. Domain-specific downstream tasks that can transform these models from "prediction engines" to a proper decision support framework need to be developed. Different classification and clustering tasks across many existing and new aggregated measures of performance need to be tested and formalized. In this way, we can potentially use these types of models to create frameworks that allow us not only to answer old questions in new or similar ways, but also to come up with new, interesting questions altogether.

After all, the use of ML within the AEC should not only target on efficiency although that is a crucial part of the connection that we are trying to establish. The overarching goal must be to explore new types of evaluations, to pave the way for new types of designs and even decisions and finally to allow us to create new, positive living experiences. Thought and practice on developing novel downstream assessment tasks are essential and will lead us to new ways to quantify qualitative aspects of our designs, which were previously described as intangible (e.g., cluster all neighborhoods in a city according to how "comfortable it is to walk"). Connecting the dots between all these new types of evaluations will then allow us to "traverse" both our designs and our cities, in ways never before possible.

References

Chokhachian, Ata, Santucci, Daniele and Auer, Thomas. (2017). A human-centered approach to enhance urban resilience, implications and application to improve outdoor comfort in dense urban spaces. *Buildings* 7(4): 113.

Gokhan Mert Yagli, Yang, Dazhi and Srinivasan, Dipti. (2019). Automatic hourly solar forecasting using machine learning models. *Renewable and Sustainable Energy Reviews 105*: 487–498.

Ladybug Tools. (2019, May 28). Retrieved from: https://www.ladybug.tools/

Roudsari, Mostapha S. (2013, July). Ladybug: A parametric environmental plugin for grasshopper to help designers create an environmentally-conscious design. *In Proceedings of the 13th International IBPSA conference in Lyon*, France 2013.

US Building Footprint Data. (2019, May 28). Retrieved from: https://github.com/microsoft/USBuildingFootprints

ViennaGIS. (2019, May 28). *The City of Vienna Geographical Information System*. Retrieved from: https://www.wien.gv.at/stadtplan/en/

Voyant, Cyril, Notton, Gilles, Kalogirou, Soteris, Nivet, Marie-Laure, Paoli, Christophe, Motte, Fabrice and Fouilloy, Alexis. (2017). Machine learning methods for solar radiation forecasting: A review. *Renewable Energy 105*: 569–582.

Wang, Liping, Kubichek, Robert and Zhou, Xiaohui. (2018). Adaptive learning based data-driven models for predicting hourly building energy use. *Energy and Buildings 159*: 454–461.

Ward, G. J. (1994, July). The RADIANCE lighting simulation and rendering system. In *Proceedings of the 21st Annual Conference on Computer Graphics and Interactive Techniques – SIGGRAPH 1994*, Orlando, Florida.

Wu, Zhibin, Li, Nianping, Peng, Jinqing, Cui, Haijiao, Liu, Penglong, Li Hongqiang, and Li, Xiwang. (2018). Using an ensemble machine learning methodology-bagging to predict occupants' thermal comfort in buildings. *Energy and Buildings 173*: 117–127.

Zhang Yan Grignard, Aubuchon, Alexander, Lyons, Keven and Larson Kent. (2018, October). Machine learning for real-time urban metrics and design recommendations. In *Proceedings ACADIA 2018: Recalibration. On Imprecision and Infidelity*, Mexico City.

12

Artificial intelligence and machine learning in landscape architecture

Bradley Cantrell, Zihao Zhang, and Xun Liu

The questions of a rapidly changing climate and increased need for confronting social justice in environmental design pose an epistemological crisis in an age of upheaval. The role of new forms of intelligence becomes particularly important for the discipline of landscape architecture as it embraces the curation and choreography of living matter. The relationship between the designer and the living, the medium of landscape architecture, is fraught with a range of anachronisms that are coming to light in contemporary society.

The discipline of landscape architecture

In response to the environmental movement, the discipline of landscape architecture has adopted ecology as a model stemming from the teaching and practice of Ian McHarg. Through nearly 60 years of co-development with ecology, the early concept that the environment is a homeostatic system continually marching toward equilibrium through ecological succession has shifted toward nonlinearity and indeterminism. The contemporary view that has formed positions the environment in a constant process of unfolding with different landscape types emerging and disappearing. Projects such as the Downsview Park competition entry *Emergent Ecologies (2000)* as well as the Freshkills Park design (2003) have become exemplars for a design paradigm that focuses on emergence and open-endedness; landscape architects articulate process-based strategies that influence processes in different systems—ecological, socioeconomic, cultural, technological—imbuing those systems with agency resulting in landscapes that possess a range of open-ended outcomes.

In the 1990s, post-humanism made its way into the intellectual discourse, and the eco-centric and/or biocentric values in landscape architecture were further enriched by the theoretical frameworks of new materialism, actor–network theory, and object-oriented ontology. Jane Bennett's scholarship has pushed landscape architects to develop a sensibility toward the biophysical world via relationality and through the promotion of agency across objects and beings. Bennett states that "bodies enhance their power in or as a heterogeneous assemblage…" and "…the efficacy of effectivity to which that term [agency] has traditionally referred becomes distributed across an ontologically heterogeneous field, rather than being a capacity localized in a human body or in a collective produced (only) by human efforts"

(Bennett, 2010). Vital materialism acknowledges the network status of things, and "there was never a time when human agency was anything other than an interfolding network of humanity and nonhumanity" (Bennett, 2010). Brett Milligan, founding member of the Dredge Research Collaborative, acknowledges Bennett's thinking, expressing that "we need a language for reading the landscape and a corresponding design sensibility with similar capacities for inclusion and complexity" (Brett, 2011). Post-humanist vocabularies have been incorporated into landscape lexicons, and many designers rely on these concepts to describe the design of landscape as a joint effort of many intelligent agents and assemblages. Therefore, the discipline of landscape architecture is cultivating an understanding that the environment is a result of the co-production of a wide range of intelligent agents, and the role of a designer is moved away from the source of authorship to a choreographer or catalyst among different assemblages that all have certain capacity to influence the environmental processes in a meaningful way. In this manner, landscape design uses process-based strategies to bring forth the potential of different intelligences in the environment and co-produce a shared future.

Challenges

Based on this understanding of the discipline, there are challenges when considering artificial intelligence in the field of landscape architecture. The challenge can be articulated in three areas: anthropocentrism, individualism, and means-end reasoning. First, in AI research, machine intelligence is still conceived as modeling and replicating human intelligence using machines, thus reinforcing human-centric values through AI systems. However, different species, entities, systems or assemblages, including machines, relate to their environment very differently. Imposing a human standard to evaluate machine intelligence essentially limits the potential of AI systems beyond anthropomorphic automation, repeating the known at faster rates. In fact, in many areas, we have already seen examples of AI systems that exhibit unexpected outcomes shedding new light on how human perception can be conceived differently. For example, through deep reinforcement learning (DRL) and self-play technique, DeepMind's AlphaGO series have not only beaten the best human GO player, but also come up with strategies that human GO players have never seen before and are unique to the machine. It should be recognized that the game of GO is a strategy board game originated in China more than 2500 years ago. It is assumed that we have exhausted best strategies to win games. However, AlphaGO has developed strategies based on its own understanding of the game. It challenges the GO players to question how little humans have explored the game. In 2019, using the similar self-play method, DeepMind developed another AI system called AlphaStar that has reached grandmaster level (the highest rank one can reach by competing with other players) in a real-time strategy game StarCraft II. The AI community regards this experiment as a breakthrough because real-time strategy games such as StarCraft are infamously known for their "combinatorial action space, a planning horizon that extends over thousands of real-time decisions, and imperfect information" (Vinyals et al., 2019). After watching or playing with AlphaStar, many professional players reported that AlphaStar has devised many new strategies that they can actually learn from, and they believe AlphaStar was an unorthodox player who has provided new ways to understand the game itself. One commentator even reports that watching the AI play the game is like watching a drunken kung fu master performing martial arts, awkward but somehow outrageously effective (Two Minute Papers, 2019). As we can see, if we start to take on a nonanthropocentric view toward understanding machine intelligence, and intelligence in general, we can see heuristic values in AI systems in helping us form multiple understandings of the environment. AI systems could help to provide a wide range of possible environmental strategies that are beyond contemporary best practices, and such novel strategies are desperately needed when humanity is faced with unprecedented climate change that exists at scales beyond human comprehension.

Second, we tend to apply an individualistic lens when thinking of intelligence, i.e., human intelligence, animal intelligence, and machine intelligence, and overlook the distributive quality of intelligence. The concept of hive intelligence or swarm intelligence speaks to the kind of capacity that only exists among an assemblage of entities, such as a colony of ants. This kind of intelligence can be understood as an emergent quality of the interactions between individuals based on simple rules. To some extent, understanding landscape as a co-produced effort recognizes the emergent intelligence among different agents. This type of hybrid intelligence is beyond the dichotomies of machine intelligence or human intelligence. However, current AI research lacks vocabularies and concepts for a nonindividualistic view for intelligence in both theory and practice. AI systems are considered as separated and distinctive models and algorithms that are designed and trained to perform a specialized task, such as image recognition algorithms with convolutional neural networks. This poses the second challenge for landscape architects to consider AI systems as an intrinsic part of a network of assemblages from which emergent behaviors are generated, thus limiting the designers to consider the open-endedness and the becoming and unfolding of the designed landscapes with embedded intelligent machines. In fact, some landscape experiments have already shown the possibility for hybrid intelligence. For example, designer Leif Estrada tested the sensing–processing–actuating framework in the project *Towards Sentience* using the geomorphology table at the Responsive Environments & Artifacts Lab (REAL) at the Harvard Graduate School of Design. The system is a sandbox consisting of a material feeder and a water outlet on the one end, and a series of sensors including ultrasonic distance detector and Microsoft Kinect sensor. The table can be used to simulate riverine hydro-morphology processes such as erosion and deposition. In one of the experiments, the designer proposed an actuating system called "attuner" that consists of a matrix of acrylic dowels connected to servomotors. Every dowel is separately driven by a servomotor, and the bottom portion of the dowel sticks into the sediments. When the servomotors turn, they drive the dowels moving up and down to influence the flow pattern, thus creating different landforms in the downstream of the sandbox. The topography is then live-tracked by the Kinect sensor above the table, forming a digital elevation model of the sandbox so that a series of high grounds and low grounds can be identified. This information then feeds back to the actuating system so that it could either build more land in a high ground by depositing more sand on it or erode the high ground away by directing more water toward it. The designer reported that the cyborg system exhibited a level of live updates and feedback that was beyond human capacity (Cantrell & Mekies, 2018). Even though there were no machine learning techniques involved in this experiment and the actuating was achieved through predefined rules, the results were inspiring. If we take a border definition of machine intelligence, the experiment represents a form of hybrid intelligence emerging from the interactions between machines and biophysical processes such as erosion and sedimentation.

Third, AI research cannot bypass the inherent means-end reasoning that is deeply rooted in Western thinking. In the Western philosophical tradition, one envisages an ideal form (*eidos*) as a model, and then, the model can serve as a goal (*telos*), which is at the same time an end that calls for actions. As French philosopher Francois Jullien puts:

> with our eyes fixed on the model that we have conceived, which we project on the world and on which we base a plan to be executed, we choose to intervene in the world and give a form to reality.
>
> *(Jullien, 2004)*

Based on this line of reasoning, theory can be differentiated from practice, with the former being the basis for the model and the latter being a set of operations that make the model into reality. Most importantly, with the means–end relationship, the idea of effectiveness and measure can be tied into this habitual reasoning. Once a range of possible tools and actions are at hand, we can evaluate them and decide which one is the most effective. Efficacy becomes the concept that ties the means–end relation together. Finally, because we want to project an ideal model on the world and develop means to achieve this end, unexpected circumstances will always rise to undermine any plan of action and control regime, and thus, uncertainty denotes to those events that are outside the predictions allowed by the conceived model. Most AI systems are envisaged as means to an end; the industry of machine learning can be understood as a new wave of model-making for better prediction and control. Within a means–end reasoning, one is constantly challenged to deal with the tension between control and uncertainty. Nevertheless, contemporary landscape design theory and practice have bypassed the equilibrium and deterministic control paradigm and embraced the paradigm of emergence and an open-ended epistemology. This paradigmatic incommensurability poses another challenge to consider AI in the field of landscape architecture. Ideas such as prototyping are gaining their currency for they providean alternative way for designers to approach ML and AI not as a means to construct simulations and predictive models, but as prototypes that inspire a wide range of possibilities (Figure 12.1).

These specific issues urge landscape architects and scholars to think and theorize AI and ML differently. In this vein of research, responsive landscapes framework is foregrounded to emphasize responsive technologies not as a layer on top of, but as a network that is deeply

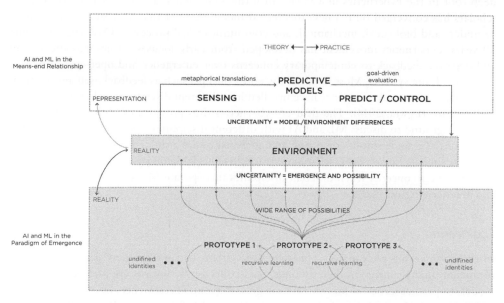

Figure 12.1   Role of AI and ML in different paradigms of environmental practices. Trapped in a means-end relationship, mainstream AI research regards machine learning techniques as effective means in making predictive models for better control strategies (top). In this framework, uncertainty represents the gap between models and the environment, and we are challenged to close the gap by making more accurate models. In contrast, embedded within the paradigm of emergence, machine learning practices become prototyping practices and ML models become prototypes that offer a wide range of possibilities for the future (bottom). Uncertainty becomes the source for emergent behavior and possibilities.

embedded in, the environment (Cantrell & Holzman, 2015). In a thought experiment, scholars have imagined a DRL machine called "wildness creator" that can devise environmental management strategies that are beyond human comprehension and create "wild" places (Cantrell, Martin & Ellis, 2017). Real case studies and unpacking how engineers use machine learning to train models to manage stormwater systems have provided empirical evidence that intelligent machines could be deeply ingrained in the environmental processes. And, more importantly, a post-humanist ethics is needed to overcome anthropocentrism and recognize machine intelligence when theorizing and applying ML and AI in the landscape discipline (Zhang & Bowes, 2019). In light of post-humanism, the concept of "third intelligence" can help to theorize machine intelligence as one of many types of intelligence, such as human intelligence and material intelligence, that coevolve and co-produce the shared environment (Cantrell & Zhang, 2018).

Case studies across disciplines

In the past few years, the environmental management discourse has seen an emerging paradigm of research and practice that revolves around cybernetic models and uses technologies such as sensing networks, artificial intelligence, and machine learning to regulate, control, and manage environmental processes. Design professions have seen similar practices, such as sensing stations for site monitoring, portable sensing kits for participatory planning, and physical responsive models for environmental simulation. These explorations have a deep root in the cybernetics movement since the 1940s when an interdisciplinary team of scholars has converged onto a new theoretical model that is based on system and machine to understand biological, mechanical, and communicational processes. Over the past some 70 years, cybernetics movement has developed from early focuses on homeostatic system and negative feedback to contemporary concerns over emergence and open-ended behaviors of evolving systems. Most importantly, core concepts such as feedback, self-production, self-organization, and emergence have instilled into different disciplines including landscape architecture (Lystra, 2014). The field of cybernetics thus provides us with concepts and a common ground to discuss ML and AI with different disciplines, and cases from across disciplines can be understood, compared, and analyzed under a single framework. We can use concepts such as homeostasis, self-organization, feedback, feedback, and emergence to understand their concerns when different disciplines incorporate ML and AI in their research and practice (Figure 12.2).

Engineering

In the engineering professions, cyber-physical systems become the new frontier for environmental management. In these systems, data collected by sensors are often used to train models to predict scenarios for control strategies. A group of researchers from the University of Michigan is developing real-time watershed control infrastructure. By installing sensors and actuators in a stormwater system, their goal is to develop responsive infrastructures that can be implemented to allow large cities to control flooding and water quality in real time (see urbanlab.umich.edu/project/real-time-watershed-control). Similarly, at the University of Virginia, the School of Engineering has established a research incubator called LinkLab that brings together different engineering professions such as computer engineering, system engineering, and mechanical engineering, to explore cyber-physical systems, from autonomous cars to "smart cities." Many of the models were built with TensorFlow and Keras

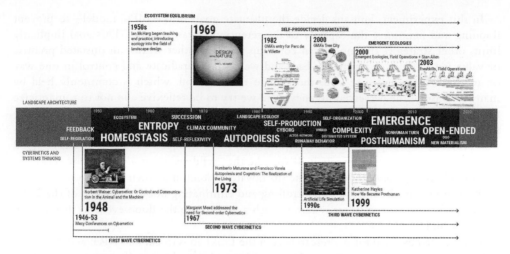

Figure 12.2   Landscape design and systems thinking. The timeline juxtaposes landscape design with the field of systems theory and cybernetics in terms of the development of the concepts in the underlying systems thinking. The discourses have developed from early homeostasis to self-production, and to contemporary concerns for emergence and open-endedness.

(keras.io) and were built on the Rivanna High-Performance Computer (HPC) (arcs.virginia. edu/rivanna), at the University of Virginia, using a graphical processing unit.

For example, a team at the LinkLab uses ML to build correlations between stormwater and transportation systems in a coastal city with the premise that the coupled system can better adapt to environmental disturbances such as sea-level rise and flooding induced by climate change. In order to better use crowdsourced weather data collected by hobbyists and concerned citizens using personal weather stations (PWSs) to facilitate the city's decision-making process, some researchers have developed algorithms to evaluate the trustworthiness of the data collected by these PWSs distributed across the city (Chen, Behl & Goodall, 2018). It can be understood as a reputation system that can automatically score these stations based on their past performances relative to their neighboring stations. The goal is to ensure useful and trustworthy data for creating more reliable models for decision-making. Eventually, the algorithm itself should be able to evolve over time so that it can adapt to increasing numbers of PWSs and re-score stations if their performance was changed.

Another team has adopted model predictive control (MPC) strategy in a simulated stormwater management system. This simulated system has two watersheds converging into one stream. Without any control, downstream will be flooded during rainfall events. Two retention ponds with floodgates were added, one for each watershed before the confluence. Degree of openness and closeness of the floodgates decides how much water the retention ponds can hold. The goal is to close the floodgates before heavy rains so that the ponds can hold more water to prevent flooding in the downstream, or to open the gates to let the water out before the ponds get too full and induce flood in the upstream. The researchers have trained an MPC model that can use weather forecast data to predict the behavior of the stormwater system and device strategies accordingly. In later iterations, the control strategies found by the MPC model can practically eliminate flooding downstream and, at the same time, maintain the water level at the retention pond close to a target level—to maximize the capacity of these ponds (Sadler, Goodall, Behl & Morsy, 2018).

In this experiment, humans decide the ultimate goals of the MPC model—to prevent flooding and maximize the capacity of the retention infrastructures. This goal implicitly limits other strategies the model can come up with. In other words, an unstated premise or value is that flood is ultimately bad, and we need to eradicate and control in one way or another. We sympathize with the goal to reduce flood, which is commonly held by many because of the perceived urgency. And we try to be reflexive and not to romanticize flooding without seeing its damage to people and their lives. As landscape architects, we know the importance of flood events to floodplains and riverine ecosystems. In many design projects, landscape architects tend to design more complex strategies to utilize flood rather than control and eliminate it. If we take the "wildness creator" idea more seriously, can a DRL-based agent understand the stormwater system in its own way thus to come up with its unique goals? Instead of controlling and eliminating flood, can some of the DRL strategies drive the stormwater system in such a way to use the flood event so that we can benefit from the process?

In fact, the next goal for the researchers in the LinkLab is to explore DRL and its potential in environmental management. Here, we have observed a paradigm shift in environmental modeling from physics-based simulation to a state–space modeling approach. In the MPC strategy, the Storm Water Management Model (SWMM) was used to train the agent. SWMM is essentially a physics-based simulation developed by the Environmental Protection Agency (EPA) for stormwater management; it is essentially based on a set of mathematical equations that scientists come up with to describe hydrological systems. Physics-based simulation takes a long time to run, and training the MPC agent requires days of computation on a HPC, whereas, in the DRL approach, what is constructed is essentially a state–space model, which represents a system with a set of input and output as well as state variables. For example, a coastal-city water system can be described through water level on different testing nodes, groundwater level, precipitation, tide level, and other environmental variables. In this representation, no physics is involved. The DRL agent is trying to construct its own representation of the system with these state variables through trial and error. In a way, the DRL method bypasses the physics and mathematical equations that humans come up with to describe a hydrological system. To some extent, the DRL agent "invents" its own rule for the environment. However, in this scenario, the DRL agent is highly mediated by sensing networks. In other words, if there is a flood event in the blind spot of the sensing network, then the DRL will confidently believe that there is no flood in the system at all.

The experiment and research in environmental engineering presents challenges but, more importantly, merits further investigation in the area of DRL-based machine learning techniques and state–space modeling approaches. A paradigm shift can be articulated. The ML techniques are moving away from automation and optimization of existing workflows in environmental management and toward a reconceptualization of different workflows based on human–machine intelligence. Machines play a role that is more than a layer of infrastructure through which humans expand control regimes. Instead, they become an intrinsic part of the socio-technical network for decision-making by providing another pair of eyes, which examines the environment through state–space representation.

Ecology

Rapid advances in technology now offer a number of cost-effective tools to collect ecological and biological data at large spatial landscapes over long survey windows. For example, advances in battery technology have revolutionized wildlife telemetry and mapped out animal movements at continental scales. Visual sensor networks and images collected by satellites, drones, and camera traps have made it easier to track changes at the landscape scale. However, the rise of cheap and powerful sensors has created an increasing amount and type of data, which far exceeds traditional ecological data analysis methods. These new technologies require to couple with faster computing algorithms and automated approaches to process and analyze these data. Machine learning attempts to extract knowledge from messy data, and it is relatively open-minded about the meaning of the data and the relationships between different kinds of data, which are recognized as holding great promise for the advancement of understanding and prediction about ecological phenomena. These modeling techniques are flexible enough to handle complex problems with multiple interacting elements and typically outcompete traditional approaches, making them ideal for modeling ecological systems.

In the last 30 years, it has been widely applied in different subfields in ecology. In 1999, Fielding introduced the machine learning methods to the field through his pioneering book (Fielding, 1999). By integrating computer science, mathematics and statistics, he predicted a future methodological shift in ecological statistics. Currently, machine learning in ecology is mostly used in species distribution modeling and species recognition applications, including audio recognition exercises, species recognition from images, and animal behavior and population dynamics modeling. Some common algorithms include maximum entropy, classification and regression trees, boosted regression trees, random forest, genetic algorithms, Bayesian machine learning, support vector machines, and artificial neural networks (ANNs).

Taking conservation measures as an example, effective wildlife monitoring techniques are a key component of a conservation measure program. However, the standard approach to biodiversity monitoring by human observer is constrained by its costs, survey scale, bias from human observations and disturbance for those sensitive survey sites. Though the cheaper and more powerful hardware may replace human observers, the inherent stochasticity of natural systems—storms, droughts, diseases—adds noise to biological surveys. A greater challenge for large-scale wildlife monitoring projects is the ability to analyze data to quantify events of interest (vocalizations, images of individuals, area covered by vegetation type, etc.) in a cost-effective manner. Better and more cost-effective conservation monitoring methods are needed to improve inference and drive adaptive management of conservation projects. Conservation Metrics, a company that focuses on applying machine learning methods on measurement of conservation outcomes, presents several working case studies, which employ deep learning to empower biologists to analyze petabytes of sensor data from a network of remote microphones and cameras (Klein, McKown & Tershy, 2015). Their software can be used to perform specific tasks such as exploring audio and image data to search for expected species and flag unknown or unexpected events, creating labeled datasets to train and refine models, and manually reviewing and auditing the output of existing models trained to classify events of interest. This system, which is being used to monitor endangered species and ecosystems around the globe, has enabled an order of magnitude improvement in the cost-effectiveness of such projects. The approach can also be expanded to encompass a greater variety of sensor sources, such as drones, to monitor animal populations, and habitat quality, and to actively deter wildlife from hazardous structures. It presents a strategic vision for how data-driven approaches to conservation can drive iterative improvements through better information and outcomes-based funding mechanisms, ultimately enabling increasing returns on biodiversity investments.

Agriculture

Agriculture plays a critical role in the global environment and economy. Due to rampant industrialization and urbanization, the continuous reduction of arable land area and expansion of the population, there are pressures that place urgent demands on smart agriculture to yield rational resource distribution, reduction of production cost, improvements to the environment and an increase in crop quality and yield. With the development of the Internet of things, artificial intelligence and robotics, precision agriculture has arisen as a new field that can use data-driven approaches to increase agricultural productivity while minimizing its environmental impact.

The data are provided by a variety of different sensors from monitoring real-time agricultural environment and status of crop growth. And by using machine learning, more accurate analysis can provide a better understanding of the operational environment (an interaction of dynamic crop, soil, and weather conditions) and the operation itself (machinery data), leading to more accurate and faster decision-making (Liakos, Busato, Moshou, Pearson & Bochtis, 2018). The data-driven strategies in agriculture are quite similar as the applications in ecology. In agriculture, machine learning is widely used in applications such weather data predictions, water and soil management, and crop and livestock management. Most frequently implemented machine learning models include ANNs, SVM, regression, Bayesian models, ensemble learning, and clustering. Yield prediction and disease detection are the most significant topics in precision agriculture and also where machine learning methods are most used.

Yield prediction in precision farming is considered of high importance for the improvement of crop management and fruit marketing planning. Once the yield is site-specifically predicted, the farm inputs such as fertilizers could be applied variably according to the expected crop and soil needs. A variety of approaches, models and algorithms have been presented and used to enable yield prediction in agriculture. Simple linear correlations of yield with soil properties have been proposed based on a limited number of soil samples.

Cartography

As an essential part of landscape design process, the act of mapping is a subjective extraction of landscape structures, features and process into an abstraction expression. This part examines cartography as a discipline, how artificial intelligence is reshaping the traditional methods, with the aim to correlate to the landscape design. The methods of map-making have been closely related to the evolution of technology. Each major evolution in technology, from the first bird perspective observation of the land from balloon to the emergence of technology of photography, satellites images, and private drones, has significantly shifted the way how maps are made. Before machine learning and computer vision technique were used into map-making, computation methods have already been applied through different aspects to enhance the map-making workflow. Taking the example of mapping of vegetation, NDVI (normalized difference vegetation index) is a classical programming approach for mapping greens, by computationally calculation of infrared colored data to enhance the mapping of greens. The later computer vision method is an advanced algorithm with more efficiency and accuracy, while the advent of machine learning algorithm combined with computer vision significantly expands the capacity of automation of mapping. Machine learning algorithms are able to automatically identify, classify and segment the patterns of the satellites images; thus, in the example of mapping vegetations, not only the greens can be mapped out from reds, but the tree canopies can be mapped out of grasslands, by automatically segmenting their different patterns.

Microsoft have used machine learning techniques to map 125,192,184 building footprints in all 50 US states and have published as open-source data to compare with local-sourced data. The automated processes not only significantly release the human labor, but also are much less error-prone, which allow massive data transmission from raster to vector information in such a large-scale project. Besides the mapping of vegetations and buildings, we can imagine that machine learning can be used to identify and automate mapping of any pattern that can be perceived by human eyes. These semantic segmentation methods in the field of computer vision have been extensively employed to map out all the kinds of things from satellite imageries: buildings, roads, swimming pools, wind turbines, oil and gas wells, land use and land cover types, etc. (descarteslabs.com). The sources of data are not limited to satellite images, private drone photography and open-source street images are also widely used as a data resource for mapping elements in the real world. For example, Mapillary, a commercial organization, provides street-level imagery data. They applied semantic segmentation methods to identify the street objects, such as utility poles, streetlights, and mailboxes, and map these elements to serve as data source for cities and private companies. These machine-generated map features are great supplements for traditional survey-based map features.

The machine learning method is also used to analyze the human's perception of the environment, which in traditional ways may not be able to be quantified (Naik, Philipoom, Raskar & Hidalgo, 2014). The social science literature has shown a strong connection between the visual appearance of a city's neighborhoods and the behavior and health of its citizens. However, this research is limited by the lack of methods that can be used to quantify the appearance of streetscapes at high enough spatial resolutions. In the project developed by MIT media lab, "Street Score" is used to describe a scene to understand algorithm that predicts the perceived safety of a streetscape, through training data from an online survey with contributions from more than 7,000 participants. The group first studies the predictive power of commonly used image features using support vector regression. Using Street Score, high-resolution maps of perceived safety for 21 cities were produced for the Northeast and Midwest of the United States at a resolution of 200 images/square mile, through scoring 1 million images from Google Street View images. These datasets are useful for urban planners, economists and social scientists who look to explain the social and economic consequences of urban perception.

In another project, the group used the same strategy but taking time-series street-level imagery, rather than static imagery, to serve as critical data source for mapping the change (Naik, Kominers, Raskar, Glaeser & Hidalgo, 2017). The group used time-series Google Street View to measure changes in the physical appearance of neighborhoods of five US cities. Through critically connecting the output map with economic and demographic data, they correlate the measured changes with neighborhood characteristics to determine which characteristics predict neighborhood improvement, thus providing support for classical urban design theories. By connecting with other geographical data, the value of using computer vision and machine learning algorithms in the field of cartography is not only the replacement of human labor, but the establishment of a critical analysis and an innovative perspective to understand the physical world.

Current uses in landscape architecture

The broad range of scale in landscape discipline separates the application of machine learning across territorial-scale and site-scale formal design. At the territorial scale, the work is most akin to regional planning, a multidisciplinary field overlaying natural sciences such as ecology, geology, and hydrology, and social sciences such as planning and sociology. This correlation enabled a range of applications of artificial intelligence and machine learning explored in these interdisciplinary areas, such as applications of automating land use classification, study of patterns and processes in ecology and river systems, and comprehensive GIS analysis. However, when it comes to the field of design, especially small-scale landscape design projects, there are few public projects. The works include post-occupancy analysis and evaluation, quantification of perception in cultural landscape, and the generative design of topography (Zhang et al., 2018).

Post-occupancy evaluation is a comprehensive examination of the performance of a project after it has been built, to evaluate whether the design goals were met. For landscape design projects, the process of post-occupancy evaluation usually includes rigorous observations and survey of users through a relatively long time range, as well as photographic analysis and behavioral or preference mapping of the place. The use of machine learning would free designers from handling repetitive observation and data-heavy analytical work. Intrigued by the potential of AI for the field of landscape architecture, the XL Research and Innovation Lab at SWA Group, an internationally recognized landscape architecture practice, has experimented with and tested machine learning to better document the spatial distribution of people in small public spaces to identify new patterns of social life (Schlickman, Ying & Zhang, 2019). The measurement methodology is based on the seminal work of William Whyte's book The Social Life of Small Urban Spaces, but with key updates on the survey methods by computer vision and machine learning algorithms. Using ten recently constructed small public sites in New York City as a laboratory, the team collected video footage of each site, and ran the footage through machine learning algorithms to identify people in each space and recorded their movements. What ultimately resulted from the machine learning exercise was a series of pedestrian heat maps, indicating areas of low traffic to areas of high traffic within each site. The new method not only saved time of manually tabulating user behavior data, but also provided much higher resolution of collected data. As a prototype, the methodology shows promise as similar data collection and data processing techniques can be used across a wide array of projects, developing new representation of use patterns, and possibly providing generative potentials for new projects.

Experiments have formed in the application of machine learning research in new forms of pedagogy that test the relationship between the designer and new ways of mapping or seeing the environment. In the summer of 2020, in the workshop "Imaging Landscape: Computer Vision and Landscape Perception" at the DigitalFUTURES 2020 Conference, the group explored the use of computer vision and machine learning in the field of landscape architecture, to develop an effective approach to quantify the subjective perception of landscapes. Previous research on the visual impact of landscape is limited by the lack of methods that can be used to quantify perceptions or analyze large amounts of image data samples. In the workshop, the instructors challenged the conventional perceptual study in the landscape design process. Through data mining and visualization of urban image data, spatial formation, landscape element composition, and landscape perceptions were analyzed from the perspective of machine intelligence rather than the existing empirical measurement methods.

In this one-week workshop, students downloaded 150,000 Google Street View images of the entire Berlin metropolitan area, with a density of 50 meters. Students used semantic segmentation and instance segmentation to quantify the objective environment elements appearing in these street view images and obtained the quantitative measurements of these images such as green vision rate, sky ratio, sidewalk ration, and the number of pedestrians, bicycles, cars, motorcycles, etc. On the basis of these data, 300 pieces of different images were randomly selected as the training set for pairwise comparison, and an online questionnaire system was created to collect students' opinions on style, ecology, sense of security, enclosure, aesthetics, accessibility, etc. The group collected about 2,000 questionnaires and used the Microsoft TrueSkill algorithm to translate the preference model of street view images to a classification model with a score of 0–10. By using machine learning on the classification model, students performed the score prediction of eight personal perception dimensions of the entire Berlin street environment, with a prediction error around only 1.2 score. Through computer vision and machine learning, the participants were able to translate the street view image dataset into high-resolution maps of perception scores of the entire city. Each group of students then developed their own project based on this dataset, to explore social, ecological and economic consequences of urban perception (Figure 12.3).

One of the students' projects was to identify and analyze East Berlin moments in the reunified city through mapping and to systemize their findings through the perception data and ratings. As Berlin was physically divided due to the wall, the government has been working on reunification through integrated developments for decades. The maps of urban functions through points of interest indicate that a reunified, lively central urban area has been formed. Yet traffic network analysis tells that minor divides in the physicality of the urban fabric still exist between the east and west sides behind the veil of a unified Berlin. The students selected Friedrichstrasse Street and Carl-Max-Allee as research objects due to their important roles in the west and east parts. Empirically, sky exposure of Carl-Max-Allee is significantly higher, while ratings for security and accessibility are lower. Through trial and error, they applied different combinations of the data matrix to Berlin's central area, in order to study if specific patterns could help to find leftover fragments of East Berlin. Then, they overlaid the areas with top 10% ratings of tree and sidewalk exposure, and selected where data are clustered as study areas and identify if their characteristics unify the ones in West Berlin. They used the same method to analyze more urban typologies with ratings of

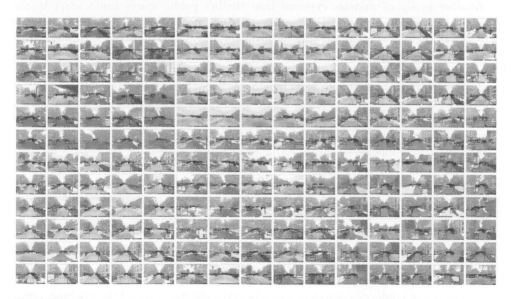

Figure 12.3 Computer vision of streetscape: Semantic segmentation and instance segmentation are used to analyze the landscape elements appearing in street view images. Quantitative measurements are obtained, such as green vision rate, sky ratio, sidewalk ration, and the number of pedestrians, bicycles, cars, motorcycles, etc.

Figure 12.4   Map of perception score of greater Berlin: Through running image segmentation and machine learning on 150,000 Google Street View images, the visual impact of landscape is quantified as eight perception scores on enclosure, aesthetic, accessibility, ecology, etc.

bicycle, building, street, sky and wall to understand if and how such areas keep traces of their past while being physically reunified to a city. Such research method and result will provide valuable reference and guideline to future development of the areas in East Berlin still lacking unified characteristics (Figure 12.4).

Another group of students explored how Berlin's public spaces could adapt to the COVID-19 pandemic with social-distancing measures. To mitigate the demand for outdoor activities in the summer and the need for maintaining safe social distances, they proposed tactical recommendations for Berlin's streets and squares. The proposals were derived from comparative studies with citywide GIS analysis of sidewalk width and points of interests, as well as computer visioning of pre-COVID Google Street Views and post-COVID webcam footages from some of Berlin's popular public spaces. This set of analyses aimed at utilizing technologies to shed light on how urban lifestyle in dense city centers may be sustained under the challenges of a public health crisis.

Another area of interest for the discipline of landscape architecture has been in the generative potential of artificial intelligence and machine learning to produce new methods of topographic analysis and formation. One experimental project uses generative adversarial networks to study topographical features of a set of given sites and trains the machine learning model to automatically design new topography (Bao, 2019). To prepare the large amount of terrain data for the training algorithms, more than 135k samples in a given area were prepared by using 30-m Global Digital Elevation Model (GDEM) data. After enough training sessions, the model can generate new terrain models with similar features as the input terrains, which can be used for further design and research of such terrain patterns. This experiment produces a design heuristic between the designer and the machine, creating comparisons between sites via similar topographic models. As the elevation data of the GDEM 30-m high-altitude resolution are not high enough, the details of the terrain cannot be displayed. But if the model is fed by high-precision data, either natural or designed terrain data, it shows potential to produce design iterations and new ways of exploring various terrain forms. On the other hand, if a similar method is applied for much broader region with different topographical features, the model can also be used for extracting and analyzing features in an unprecedented way.

While not utilizing machine learning, specifically the work of the Harvard Graduate School of Design, REAL is using physical sediment models that are tied to sensing arrays, producing a relationship between real-time sensing and feedback. REAL has conducted research that examines the potential of responsive technologies across a variety of scales focusing on systems at the territorial scale and the manipulation of indeterminate land building using real-time sensing, robotics, and adaptive management techniques. The research and lab have recently found a new home at the University of Virginia School of Architecture where a team of academics, including myself, Brian Davis, Matthew Seibert, Andrea Hansen, Xun Liu, and Zihao Zhang, are developing the platforms and interfaces for a nascent suite of design tools to confront adaptive design protocols. As a prototyping platform, the system has facilitated many research and design projects over the years. The geomorphology table and the ongoing series of experiments shed light on the construction of autonomous systems, devising strategies that are outside of human comprehension (Figure 12.5).

If we take on a more general definition of machine intelligence, then the experiments here present an uncharted territory for exploring artificial intelligence—to explore intelligence as a hybridized and emergent property between technological and biophysical agents. As we have seen, one of the problems in today's machine learning research is that machine intelligence is understood as a localized property within the machine itself, overlooking the

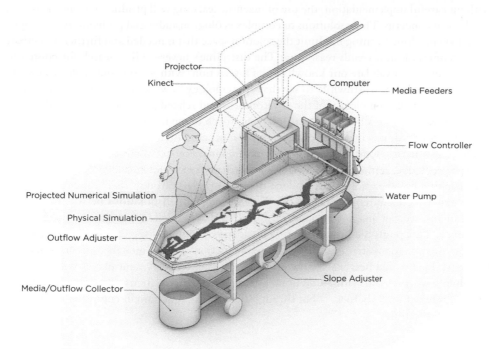

Figure 12.5 Diagram of geomorphology table and instrumentation and sensing systems.

fact that machines have always been deeply embedded in a network of distributed systems. As post-humanist scholars have pointed out, what we understood as agency—be it human or machine—has always been distributed across a field of heterogeneous assemblages. In the process of individuation, "some entities are detached from their background and called 'actors.' They are made to conceal and stand for the web of relations that they cover. They become the place where explanation, moral, causal, and practical stops" (Knappett & Malafouris, 2008).

Adaptation and epistemology

What we understand as machine intelligence is always hybridized by other forms of intelligence within and around a machine, and the "machine" only functions as a carrier of the perceived effectiveness, which is co-produced by many other actors. Within the many cases presented, artificial intelligence and machine learning produce expanded potential but lack ways to address the three concerns of anthropocentrism, individualism, and means–ends reasoning. The research at REAL using the geomorphology table reflects an understanding of intelligence as distributed qualities across the "more than machine whole." In the experiment, the perceived "machine intelligence" is achieved by the processes in not only mechanical systems, but also hydrological and geological systems. Most importantly, the designers off-load their intelligence onto the cyborg, diversifying the "machine intelligence."

What does this then say for the future of machine intelligence within the complex milieu of the environment and the discipline's intent to engage the complexities of ecological and sociocultural systems? Understandably, many methods point to ideological solutions, and without careful implementation, the use of machine learning will produce a strengthening of ideological concerns. These solutions to complex ecological and social problems may be optimized via machine learning but limit the solution space that is needed and further exacerbate the outcomes of means–ends reasoning. The discipline's never-ending search for epistemological frames that validate our knowledge of interactions with society and ecology needs to be reconsidered. Is it worthwhile to say that epistemology as we know it is insufficient? Due to the fact that the complexity of the environment and related problems are beyond human knowledge, requiring a heuristic or adaptive approach to environmental design?

Going forward, it is important to imagine a nascent epistemology of realism, an erasure of ideals that most importantly points to a clear connection between technics, the material, and the predictive. A mode of working in design that asks for biological, geological, climatic, and machine collaborations that produce new knowledge through their interactions. Like many experiments in representation that have developed collaborations between machines and humans, we can imagine an adaptive approach that is aided in real time by machine intelligence. This posits the introduction of an adaptive epistemology that sets goals based on a priori investigations stemming from the construction and maintenance of landscape and territory. This would be scalable, traversing across site, territory, and planet with attempts to connect intervention with prediction. The future of these systems relies on age-old concepts of interaction (cybernetics) but through the extension of human cognition in real time within the machine.

References

Bao, R. (2019). Research on intellectual analysis and application of landscape architecture based on machine learning. *Landscape Architecture Journal, 26*(5), 29–34.

Bennett, J. (2010). *Vibrant matter: A political ecology of things.* Duke University Press.

Brett, M. (2011, September 26). Vibrant matter and relations of things. *Free Association Design*. https://freeassociationdesign.wordpress.com/2011/09/26/vibrant-matter-and-relations-of-things/

Cantrell, B. E., & Holzman, J. (2015). *Responsive landscapes: Strategies for responsive technologies in landscape architecture*. Routledge.

Cantrell, B., Martin, L. J., & Ellis, E. C. (2017). Designing autonomy: Opportunities for new wildness in the Anthropocene. *Trends in Ecology & Evolution, 32*(3), 156–166.

Cantrell, B., & Mekies, A. (Eds.). (2018). *Codify: Parametric and computational design in landscape architecture*. Routledge.

Cantrell, B., & Zhang, Z. (2018). A third intelligence. *Landscape Architecture Frontiers, 6*(2), 42–51.

Chen, A. B., Behl, M., & Goodall, J. L. (2018, November). Trust me, my neighbors say it's raining outside: Ensuring data trustworthiness for crowdsourced weather stations. In *Proceedings of the 5th Conference on Systems for Built Environments* (pp. 25–28). New York, NY, USA. https://doi.org/10.1145/3276774.3276792.

Fielding, A. (Ed.). (1999). *Machine learning methods for ecological applications*. Springer Science & Business Media.

Jullien, F. (2004). *A treatise on efficacy: Between Western and Chinese thinking*. University of Hawaii Press.

Klein, D. J., McKown, M. W., & Tershy, B. R. (2015). Deep learning for large scale biodiversity monitoring. In *Bloomberg Data for Good Exchange Conference*. New York, NY, USA. https://doi.org/10.13140/RG.2.1.1051.7201.

Knappett, C., & Malafouris, L. (Eds.). (2008). *Material agency: Towards a non-anthropocentric approach*. Springer Science & Business Media.

Liakos, K. G., Busato, P., Moshou, D., Pearson, S., & Bochtis, D. (2018). Machine learning in agriculture: A review. *Sensors, 18*(8), 2674.

Lystra, M. (2014). McHarg's entropy, Halprin's chance: Representations of cybernetic change in 1960s landscape architecture. *Studies in the History of Gardens & Designed Landscapes, 34*(1), 71–84.

Naik, N., Kominers, S. D., Raskar, R., Glaeser, E. L., & Hidalgo, C. A. (2017). Computer vision uncovers predictors of physical urban change. *Proceedings of the National Academy of Sciences, 114*(29), 7571–7576. New York, NY, USA. https://doi.org/10.1073/pnas.1619003114

Naik, N., Philipoom, J., Raskar, R., & Hidalgo, C. (2014). Streetscore–predicting the perceived safety of one million streetscapes. In *Proceedings of the IEEE Conference on Computer Vision and Pattern Recognition Workshops* (pp. 779–785). Columbus, OH, USA.

Sadler, J. M., Goodall, J. L., Behl, M., & Morsy, M. M. (2018, September). Leveraging open source software and parallel computing for model predictive control simulation of urban drainage systems using EPA-SWMM5 and Python. In *International Conference on Urban Drainage Modelling* (pp. 988–992). Springer, Cham.

Schlickman, E., Ying, W., & Zhang, A. (2019). Going afield: Experimenting with novel tools and technologies at the periphery of landscape architecture. *Landscape Architecture Frontiers, 7*(2), 84–92.

Two Minute Papers (2019). DeepMind's AlphaStar: A Grandmaster Level StarCraft 2 AI - YouTube. *YouTube*. https://www.youtube.com/watch?v=jtlrWblOyP4

Vinyals, O., Babuschkin, I., Czarnecki, W. M., Mathieu, M., Dudzik, A., Chung, J., … & Oh, J. (2019). Grandmaster level in StarCraft II using multi-agent reinforcement learning. *Nature, 575*(7782), 350–354.

Zhang, C., Huang, Z. Zhang, J., & Ge, J. (2018). Urban tourism destination personality and its cultural landscape representation via machine learning: A case study of Nanjing. *ACTA Geographica Sinica, 72*(10), 1886–1903.

Zhang, Z., & Bowes, B. (2019). The Future of Artificial Intelligence (AI) and Machine Learning (ML) in Landscape Design: A Case Study in Coastal Virginia, USA. *Journal of Digital Landscape Architecture, 4*, 2–9. https://doi.org/doi:10.14627/537663001

Part 4

Case studies of AI in architecture

13

Combining AI and BIM in the design and construction of a Mars habitat

Naveen K. Muthumanickam, José P. Duarte,
Shadi Nazarian, Ali Memari, and Sven G. Bilén

Artificial intelligence (AI) as an academic discipline emerged in the 1950s. Over the years, it has been defined in many different but related ways. One particularly useful definition was put forth by Patrick Winston in his famous textbook *Artificial Intelligence* (Winston, 1992, p. 5), in which he states that "Artificial intelligence is the study of the computations that make it possible to perceive, reason, and act," with the Turing Test used to verify whether a machine is capable of intelligent behavior (Turing, 1948). Since its inception, AI has encompassed different sub-fields and methods including semantic nets, search and optimization, rule-based systems, frames, constraints propagation, backtracking, planning, image and natural language, and learning. In recent years, "learning" has been referred to as "machine learning (ML)" and equated with AI itself, particularly among the general public. The application of AI to design has been present since the beginning, particularly because solving design problems poses interesting and complex challenges that go beyond simple calculations and require a more elaborate kind of intelligence. The application of AI to architecture had important developments in the 1960s with the work of researchers like Ivan Sutherland, who developed the first computer aided design (CAD) system called "Sketchpad" (Sutherland, 1963), and Herbert Simon's influential book *The Sciences of the Artificial* (Simon, 1969). In the decades that followed, several authors used different AI techniques and paradigms to address architectural problems. One meaningful reference for the work described in this chapter was José Duarte's discursive grammar for Álvaro Siza's Malagueira houses (Duarte, 2001). In his work, he used shape grammars (Stiny & Gips, 1972), a rule-based system, to encode Siza's design rules and define the space of design solutions, a series of metrics to compare the evolving solution to the desired one, and best-first search to guide the generation of solutions towards the desired goal. The outcome was customized housing solutions in Siza's style, who was unable to distinguish solutions generated by the system from his own designs, thereby validating the "intelligence" of the system through this modified version of the Turing Test.

The current work also aims to find solutions that best fit predefined conditions and uses a similar conceptual framework, encompassing generation, simulation, and optimization, as described in Duarte (2019). Its implementation has, nevertheless, some noteworthy differences: a parametric design system replaced shape grammars as the basis for the generative system; sophisticated software simulated the performance of candidate solutions from different viewpoints, including structural and environmental; and multicriteria optimization was used to find solutions that fitted different scenarios. ML was used in the optimizer to look at information about previous searches and utilize it to speed up the search process. Another important difference is that a new system incorporated information about the process used to materialize the solutions, which was also considered when searching for appropriate designs. In addition, the new system was developed on a building information model (BIM) platform, which permitted the control of the various software used for the generation, simulation, and search operations and support the progressive development of the design. This platform was used not just to design the habitat, but also the process for making it, including the printing system, its transportation, and set up. The use of such a platform was necessary to solve the complexities involved in the multifaceted design problem, which included the consideration of two completely different locations, Mars and Earth, with very different environmental conditions with significant impact on design performance and the autonomous robotic construction process.

Robotic construction is beginning to make inroads into the architecture, engineering, and construction (AEC) field to assist in complex and repetitive tasks and to support construction in remote and challenging environments. Before deployment to such places, it is imperative to simulate the sequence of robotic movements and the subsequent behavior of material delivery and construction logistics to ensure accurate and safe realization of the building design. Robotic construction techniques such as additive concrete construction, in particular, are highly dependent on material-specific (concrete flowability, setting time, etc.) and robot-specific properties (robotic arm speed, toolpath direction, etc.). Simulating the construction process while also considering these properties early in the design phase is essential as they play a crucial role in determining the constructability of the building shape. The resulting building shape, in turn, impacts other performance factors such as structural integrity, indoor environmental quality, and construction cost. Hence, in addition to simulating the construction sequence, it is also essential to analyze the building design for these additional performance factors. For instance, Figure 13.1 illustrates an industrial robot used to 3D print a simple concrete cylinder by depositing material in a concentric circular toolpath layer by layer. Here, as time progresses from t, it can be noted that the cylinder deposited by the robot behaves nominally until $t+5$ min, after which it starts failing. BIM-based techniques such as a digital twin (close-to-accurate digital representation of the robotic setup) can be used to simulate the construction sequence (i.e., a "4D" simulation). However, additional techniques like structural analysis using finite element modeling (FEM) tools and physical tests are needed to predict such unforeseen failures beforehand and address them in the design stages. More complex geometrical shapes at larger scales, such as that of a building, need to be analyzed and simulated for additional factors such as indoor environmental quality (IEQ) and building cost. Additionally, it is also possible to utilize advanced computer vision sensors to capture real-time data on structural deformation during the concrete 3D-printing process and adjust material- and robot-specific variables accordingly to rectify or correct such deformations. However, this requires sophisticated use of ML algorithms for predictive analytics and robotic process automation for timely implementation of the corrections. The former method, in which rigorous multidisciplinary analyses and simulations are used to ensure realization of the envisioned building design, can be considered analogous to the processes involved in the design of products in other engineering fields such as the automotive and airplane design and manufacturing sectors. On the other hand, the method in which real-time data collection, predictive analytics, and ML are used to prevent structural deformations can be considered analogous to the autonomous systems used in the landing of a reusable space

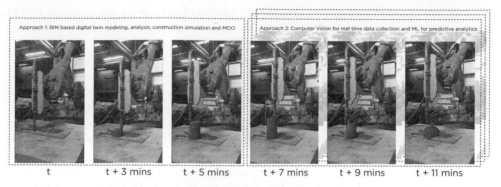

Figure 13.1   Conceptual overview of a failing printing test.

vehicle, in which the system automatically adjusts the various flight parameters to ensure the spent rocket follows a nominal landing trajectory.

This chapter focuses on the former approach, i.e., leveraging BIM as a connected software ecosystem for parametric modeling and generation of large sets of design alternatives, integrated multidisciplinary analysis, optimization, and construction simulation in a robotic construction project (specifically, additive concrete construction). An overview of the process underlying design for additive manufacturing (Df) along with challenges and technological knowledge gaps associated in implementing a similar framework to enable design for additive construction (DfAC) in the AEC field are discussed in the next section. This is followed by a section outlining the features of a novel BIM-based framework, which was developed and used for the design of a 3D-printed Mars habitat satisfying multidisciplinary requirements. Additionally, a brief overview of how computer vision techniques and ML could be leveraged for avoiding structural deformations and failure in robotic construction is also discussed along with potential avenues for future research.

Background

Design for Additive Manufacturing (DfAM)

Additive manufacturing (AM) technologies have grown tremendously in the last two decades, enabling new strategies for rapid prototyping of designs and custom production within the manufacturing sector. The capability of AM technologies to place, bond, or transform raw materials layer-by-layer or voxel-by-voxel (elemental points in 3D space) enable the rapid production of a wide range of physical objects ranging from small artifacts to complex industrial components such as automobile and electronic parts. A wide range of AM processes such as powder bed fusion, material extrusion, and sheet lamination are used in the production of such parts and components (cf., Thompson et al., 2016). With such wide ranging AM processes, it is crucial to note that the quality of the raw material at each voxel depends on multiple factors specific to raw material(s) type, manufacturing equipment (e.g., the build platform precision, nozzle geometry, and light or laser beam wavelength), and process parameters (e.g., the nozzle temperature, light or beam intensity, and traverse speed) (Thompson et al., 2016). These variables affect the performance, quality, and cost of production of the parts and, in turn, impact design decisions. Therefore, it is necessary to analyze the design of the product for various performance factors with respect to these variables. Motivated by these, architecture and engineering design fields have worked to develop appropriate DfAM frameworks under the larger body of work focusing on design for manufacturing and assembly (DfMA).

Typically, DfMA frameworks (generalized process shown in Figure 13.2) enable designers and engineers to design and optimize a product for various performance factors while concurrently considering its manufacturing constraints (imposed by the production system) in order to reduce production time and cost while increasing their performance and quality. Most of the product design processes (Figure 13.2) start with the generation of 2D sketches and 3D models of a few conceptual ideas envisioned by the designers. Subsequently, these models are then iterated at an appropriate level of detail and subject to multidisciplinary analyses specific to the product type and intended use case. Based on such multidisciplinary analyses and inputs from multiple stakeholders, the generated design alternatives are optimized to meet multiple performance factors, including manufacturing constraints of the specified production system(s), while optimal design(s) are selected based on trade studies (trade-off exploration). In order to ensure efficient manufacturing and production of the product, sophisticated toolpath (robotic or 3D-printer nozzle motion) simulations are used.

Considering the more nuanced outline of the process underlying DfAM shown in Figure 13.3, the process begins with the generation of a 3D model, which is then sliced/contoured (typically along the vertical axis) with each layer containing a toolpath (route map) along which the nozzle traverses. This is accomplished using a variety of specialized slicing software as listed in Figure 13.3. Based on the geometry of the part and the type of

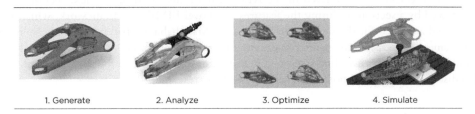

| 1. Generate | 2. Analyze | 3. Optimize | 4. Simulate |

Figure 13.2   Design for manufacturing and assembly (DfMA) framework. Adapted from www.autodesk.com/product/fusion-360.

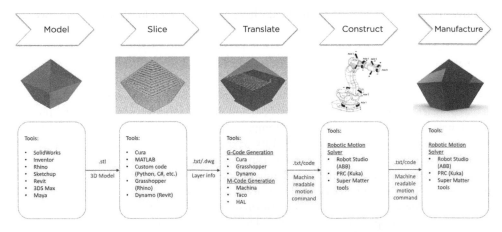

Figure 13.3   Design for additive manufacturing (DfAM) framework.

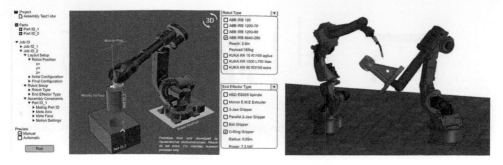

Figure 13.4   (Left) In-house prototype of offline robotic programming software (Credits: Naveen); (Right) Digital twin of two robots performing a synchronous welding operation (Gan et al., 2013).

AM process used (e.g., powder bed fusion or material extrusion), the slicing software also automatically generates structures to act as temporary supports for cantilevered elements to be printed. These are usually printed at a lower resolution (i.e., much coarser) as they are removed after the printing. Further, these contours, toolpaths per contour, and transitions between each contour have to be converted into a machine-readable format called G-code. Additionally, a machine-code (M-code) is also generated, with which the manufacturing equipment is issued specific instructions such as the velocity of the nozzle, deposition temperature, material deposition cut-off times, bed positions, and robot arm positions. Both the G-code and the M-code together act as a machine-readable set of instructions for the manufacturing equipment (or a robot in terms of large-scale industrial manufacturing). When large-scale industrial robots are used for manufacturing, these codes are then subject to an inverse kinematic solver (or robotic motion solver), which simulates the robotic motions per the instructions to identify any self-collisions and singularities (a state in which the robot cannot execute a specified motion as it violates the degree of freedom of one or more of its axes). When the production system comprises multiple robots and associated manufacturing equipment, state-of-the-art industrial practices use offline robotic programming to synchronously simulate the sequence of robotic motions. For example, Figure 13.4 shows a sample of offline robot programming software in which a model is used to simulate the toolpath of an industrial robot executing a specific type of manufacturing or production activity.

Design for Additive Construction (DfAC)

Types of additive construction systems

The state-of-the-art developments in additive construction technologies leverage those in materials research and printing systems research. On the materials front, a growing body of work can be found on concrete 3D printing (additive concrete construction), clay 3D printing, and thermoplastic-based geo-polymer 3D printing, among other related developments (Rael & San Fratello, 2011). On the printing systems front, a variety of printing systems have been developed such as gantry, cable-suspended, small scale swarm robots, industrial robots, and foldable (in which 3D structures are designed as foldable 2D shell structures) (Labonnote et al., 2016) (Figure 13.5). The scope of this chapter is limited to additive concrete construction using industrial robots.

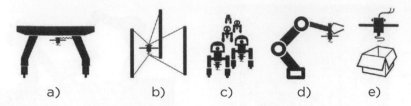

Figure 13.5 Types of additive construction systems. Adapted from Labonnote et al. (2016).

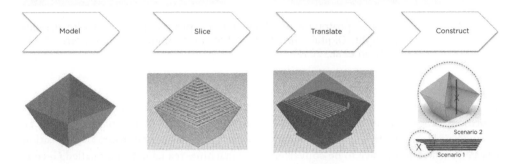

Figure 13.6 Conceptual framework for design for additive concrete construction (DfACC).

As a subset of the broader DfAM framework, a framework for design for additive concrete construction (DfACC) can be outlined (Figure 13.6). The process starts with the generation of a 3D model, followed by slicing the geometry and translating the contours, toolpath per contour, and transition between contours into a machine-readable code, which in turn is subject to an inverse kinematic solver for robot motion planning. However, the crucial difference here is with the material in use (concrete) and the slicing procedure. The material properties and behavior of concrete are starkly different from the materials traditionally used in AM such as polymers and metals. Such a scenario warrants specific treatment in the slicing of the geometry to be additively constructed to enable close-to-accurate realization of the envisioned geometry. For example, the diamond shape in Figure 13.6 has tapered (partially cantilevered) facets near the bottom of the geometry. Such tapered facets can be 3D printed successfully in the case of plastic or metal extrusions with additional temporary support structures generated during the slicing procedure. However, the same might not work for a concrete structure and might lead to potential failure of the part during printing (far right illustration in Figure 13.6 (Scenario1)—the left overhang exceeds the maximum inclination angle of a structure that permits printing without supports). Another instance that might cause similar type of failure in additive concrete construction is a scenario in which the interior portion of the diamond-shaped geometry might be hollow (Scenario 2 as indicated in Figure 13.6). To address such challenges, most of the additive concrete construction techniques developed to date discretize the overall structure into a kit of parts that can be printed in a convenient orientation to minimize the effects of gravity; allow the printed part to cure (hardening and setting of concrete); and then reorient them during assembly (van der Zee & Marijnissen, 2017). The scope of this study is to explore and demonstrate additive concrete construction techniques developed by a multidisciplinary team at Penn State as part of NASA's 3D-Printed Mars Habitat Centennial Challenge, which enables architectural scale concrete structures that do not require support structures or reorientation and assembly of printed components.

DESIGN OF TOOLPATH

Another important factor is the slicing procedure to develop the toolpath for additive concrete construction. Apart from the contours in the vertical direction, there are multiple possibilities to devise the toolpath per layer. Typically, in AM, the toolpath is divided into an outer wall (perimeter of the printed geometry) and an infill, which is the portion surrounded by the outer walls (Figure 13.7). The number of outer wall(s), infill pattern, infill pattern density (number of layers in horizontal direction), and bead shape and dimensions (dictated by the nozzle shape and size) can be customized pertaining to the design specifications. Beads are also represented as filaments elsewhere in the literature. We tend to use the term bead to represent individual concrete filaments due to the circular-shaped nozzle (Right side illustration in Figure 13.7) we use in our robotic setup.

To better understand the impact of these toolpath design variables on the overall performance of the 3D-printed geometry, let us assume the case of a simple concrete slab as an example (Figure 13.8). Here, as usual, the design process starts with a 3D model, which is then subject to the slicing procedure. As shown in Figure 13.8, two types of toolpath—A (continuous spiraling) and B (alternating zigzag)—were generated. Once these toolpaths were converted into machine-readable codes, a robotic setup was used to print the concrete slabs using both toolpath A and B. Based on physical testing, it was identified that a concrete slab

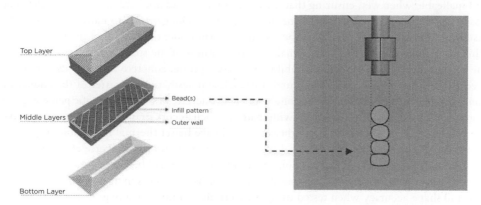

Figure 13.7 (Left) Toolpath simulation of a simple slab; (Right) Sectional view of concrete beads deforming under compressive load.

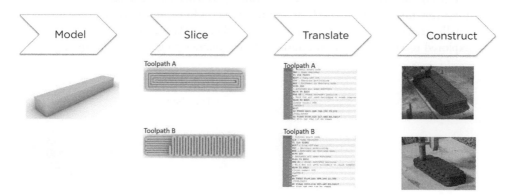

Figure 13.8 Tradeoffs in designing toolpath.

printed with toolpath B had better structural performance in terms of layer-to-layer adhesion than toolpath A (Ashrafi et al., 2019). However, it should also be noted that, due to the zig-zag nature of the toolpath, the robot had to perform complex maneuvers, which resulted in vibrations at each turn of the toolpath. Such vibrations, in turn, led to concrete deformations and hence a loss in shape accuracy. Trying to reduce the velocity of the robotic arm would be a straightforward answer to solve this issue. However, doing so affected the consistency of the concrete deposition (flowability), which caused concrete clogging at the nozzle head. Also, reducing the velocity increases the overall print time. Hence, there exists multiple such tradeoffs between various aspects of the toolpath design, which, in turn, affects the overall design performance. Moreover, it is essential to note that, as the scale and complexity of the geometry increases, the toolpath complexity also increases, thereby leading to multiple such tradeoffs.

DESIGN OF MATERIAL PROPERTIES

In addition to the toolpath design, it is equally important to develop concrete mixture(s) with the appropriate composition (cementitious material, aggregates, binders, and additives) to ensure successful 3D printing of concrete structures. While developing the material composition, it is essential to consider multiple rheological aspects such as flowability and setting time, among many other factors. In simple terms, a particular type of concrete mix might be plastic and malleable when wet, ensuring that the concrete mix does not harden within the delivery hose causing a clog. However, the same mix might take a longer time to harden once printed resulting in inadequate lower layers (beads) that deform under the weight of the upper layers. This potentially might result in anomalies in the flatness of the surface and, in turn, affects the shape accuracy. Apart from flowability and setting time, concrete mix can also be modified to fit other needs such as structural, thermal, and aesthetic properties of the additively constructed part. For example, functionally graded concrete, in which a specific percentage of aggregates in the concrete is replaced with materials such as cork granules can be used to make the 3D-printed concrete structure lightweight and have better thermal insulation properties. However, modifications to the material composition might also have adverse effects on other performance aspects. For example, toolpath A in Figure 13.8 had better shape accuracy when printed with a normal concrete mix but showed inconsistent results in terms of flatness of surface and shape accuracy when tested using initial trials of a functionally graded concrete mix (Figure 13.9). The functionally graded concrete–cork composition was perfected after many such trial 3D-printing tests and is covered in detail in Craveiro et al. (2017).

Apart from thermal insulation and structural performance, functionally graded concrete mixtures might also be used for aesthetic and architectural purposes. For example, functionally graded concrete mix with silica and other similar aggregate replacements have been explored to create a seamless transition from concrete to glass without the use of any

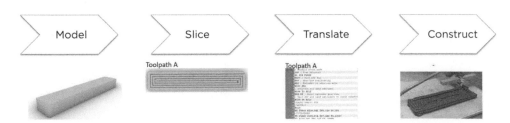

Figure 13.9 Tradeoffs in designing the material composition.

Figure 13.10   (Left) Conceptual render of shelter 3D printed using functionally graded material; (Right) Sample showing a block of functionally graded concrete seamlessly transitioning from 100% geopolymer concrete to 100% glass.

mechanical frame or bonding agent (Nazarian et al., 2015), and later incorporated into the design proposal developed by the Penn State team in the virtual design level of the final phase in NASA's 3D-Printed Mars Habitat Centennial Challenge Competition (Figure 13.10, Craveiro et al., 2020). However, this chapter does not delve into the details of functionally graded concrete–glass mixture.

DESIGN OF PRODUCTION SYSTEM AND LOGISTICS

Additive concrete construction is enabled through the synchronous sequence of activities of multiple pieces of equipment such as the material mixing, feeding, and deposition systems (Figure 13.11). Specifically, these systems include silos for raw material storage, concrete mixers, industrial robot(s), and robotic end effectors (nozzle, grippers, etc.), which are fitted to the end of the robot arm(s) to perform activities such as extruding material, picking and placing objects, feeding computer commands to the robot, and holding sensors for real-time feedback. Such equipment and systems, which must consider the conditions of the physical site on which they operate, impose certain production and logistical constraints. It is essential to consider these constraints during the design of the building to ensure its constructability. Particular to the 6-axis industrial robot (ABB IRB 6640) that was used by our team for NASA's 3D-Printed Mars Habitat Centennial Challenge, the robot's motion is constrained by the degrees of freedom of each axis of rotation and also has a limit on the maximum distance it can reach (2.8 m). In simple terms, an imaginary sphere of ~2.8-m radius is the maximum range that the robot arm can reach, limiting the size of the structure that can be additively constructed. Such constraints warrant the need for designing and installing end effectors (or extensions), which help to extend the capability of robots to exceed their limited reach and, in turn, allow the additive construction of larger structures (Watson et al., 2019). Additionally, raw materials (cement, water) are stored in silos and tanks and are connected to a mixer using hoses. Further, another hose delivers mixed concrete paste from the mixer to the nozzle attached to the robot end effector. It is essential to highlight the fact that even minor aspects such as the length of the hose connecting the material mixer to the robot end effector needs to be decided strategically in order to avoid any unnecessary slack in the hose, which might interfere with the toolpath and, in turn, affect the printing process. Hence, the positioning of these robots and other equipment requires strategic spatial and logistical planning and optimization in order to ensure efficient site preparation for safe printing of the envisioned structure without any hindrance.

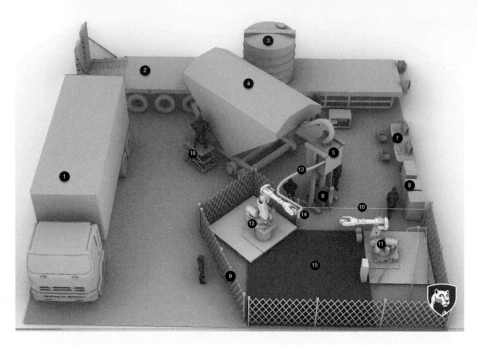

Figure 13.11   Rendered representation of the robotic construction setup: (1) Truck, (2) Cones-
toga trailer, (3) Water tank, (4) Large silo, (5) Small silo, (6) Mixer and pump,
(7) Computers, (8) Robot controllers, (9) Safety fence, (10) Safety laser,
(11) Opening-placement robot, (12) Printing robot, (13) Hose, (14) Nozzle,
(15) Printing area, and (16) Scissor jack for monitoring.

DESIGN OF OVERALL BUILDING

Apart from the design of toolpath, material, production, and logistics systems involved in
additively constructing the enclosure of the building (floor plates, walls, and roofs), the architectural design of the interior spatial layout and associated mechanical, electrical, and
plumbing (MEP) and safety systems adds another layer of complexity to the design. This
impacts many aspects of the building performance such as overall structural integrity, indoor spatial quality (accessibility, functionality, and aesthetics), indoor environmental quality
(IEQ) (heating, cooling, ventilation, and lighting), and sewage and sanitation. It also plays a
crucial role in dictating the overall geometry of the building, thereby impacting the sequence
of construction (and assembly), construction time, and cost. Traditionally, in building design
and construction projects, construction simulation is done only at later stages when the design
is much more detailed and specifically for construction management purposes. Conversely,
DfACC needs designers and engineers to account for constructability (in addition to other
performance factors) from the early design stages (Figure 13.12). Early stage construction
simulations are necessary to identify any potential robot–structure or robot–robot (if multiple robots are used) collisions downstream during the construction process, which might
lead to costly revisions. Additionally, there might be tradeoffs in deciding the geometry that
satisfies multiple performance requirements. For example, a particular design geometry that
has an optimal collision-free robotic motion plan might have poor compressive and lateral
load distribution or vice versa. Digital twins or close-to-accurate digital models of the setup
are necessary for efficient and meaningful 4D simulations.

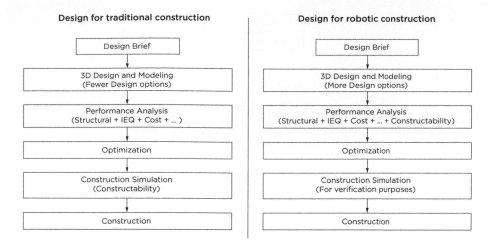

Figure 13.12 **Comparison highlighting differences in design process for traditional and robotic construction.**

Further, dealing with such a wide array of interconnected systems introduces multiple variations in how these systems can be configured with respect to the overall geometry of the building and vice versa. In such scenarios, it is essential to explore multiple design alternatives (or configurations) to make well informed design decisions. Technically, this requires generating/modeling multiple design configurations and analyzing them for multiple performance factors, such as structural, IEQ, energy, cost, and constructability. However, such concurrent-design-and-analysis approach requires a paradigm shift in the underlying design process as well as technological developments in terms of integrating the software and tools used by multidisciplinary stakeholders (Polit-Casillas & Howe, 2013). Multiple stakeholders dealing with various aspects such as toolpath design, material rheology, architectural systems, structural system, MEP system, environmental control and life support system (ECLSS), and robotic systems use a variety of software for modeling, analyses, and simulations. Few of these even involve setting up physical testing apparatus (such as compression tests, rheology tests, etc.) and data collection. Based on measurable observations and inferences from such physical tests, material design, toolpath design, or geometrical specifications of the design might need to be modified appropriately. It is vital to incorporate such modifications to an integrated building information model (BIM) to identify the impact of those changes in terms of other performance factors. In such cases, it is essential to develop parametric modeling capabilities, which allow rapid changes to the geometry of the structure based on the observations from these physical tests. State-of-the-art BIM environments support parametric modeling and rapid generation of multiple design options. Additionally, there has been a recent surge in the use of multi-objective optimization and search algorithms for structural, energy, and daylighting optimization in building design (Attia et al., 2013). However, these multi-objective optimization developments have been largely fragmented from advancements in BIM due to lack of integration between modeling and simulation environments (for multiple types of analyses) (Leicht et al., 2007; Haymaker et al., 2018). There is a need for an integrated BIM framework that can address and streamline the interoperability issues between multiple modeling, analysis, optimization, and construction simulation in the AEC field (Flager & Haymaker, 2009; Muthumanickam et al., 2020c) (Figure 13.13).

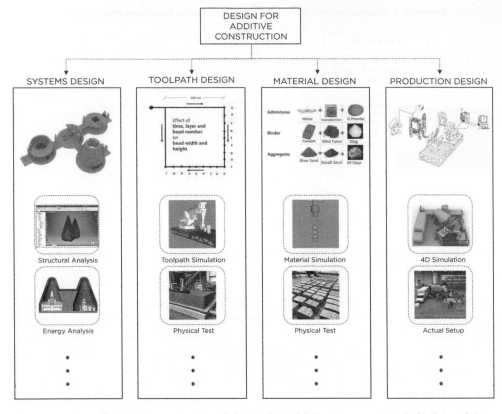

Figure 13.13 Multidisciplinary nature of design for additive construction (DfAC) involving a range of computational analyses and physical testing.

To address such technological gaps and streamline the additive construction design process, an end-to-end BIM framework was developed and used to design a Mars habitat from the conceptual design stages to additively constructing it using industrial robots in the final level of Phase 3 of NASA's 3D-Printed Mars Habitat Centennial Challenge. The next section presents a detailed overview of the various components of the integrated BIM framework for modeling, analysis, optimization, and simulation to support additive construction.

Design for additive construction of Mars habitat—NASA Centennial Challenge

An interdisciplinary team from Penn State participated in NASA's 3D-Printed Mars Habitat Centennial Challenge, in which multiple teams competed to push the state-of-the-art of additive construction technology to design and build sustainable habitats for humans to live in on Mars. The goal was to design a 3D-printable habitat that provided a pressure-retaining living area of at least 93 m² with a minimum ceiling height of 2.25 m, with the intent of supporting four astronauts for one year with sleeping, eating/meal preparation, sanitation, recreation, laboratory/work area, communication, as well as MEP, environmental control and life support systems (ECLSS), safety systems, and entry and exit hatch systems. The competition was hosted in multiple phases that included design (Phase 1), structural member (Phase 2), and on-site construction of a sub-scale habitat (Phase 3) with multiple levels under each phase. Phase 3 included two virtual construction levels and three actual construction levels. The virtual construction levels emphasized leveraging BIM to design the habitat (for simulated Martian conditions) as well as the underlying construction process and logistics involved in its additive construction. The actual construction levels emphasized leveraging autonomous robotic construction methods to additively construct parts of the habitat (in Earth-based conditions) with progressive complexity ranging from foundations at the initial level, construction of a cistern with two required pipes that penetrated its thick wall and performance of a hydrostatic test during the second level, and a 1:3 sub-scale habitat design (a simplified version of the full-scale habitat design submitted for the virtual construction level) during the third level of the competition.

End-to-end BIM framework

Building on the learning from the DfAM frameworks, challenges in streamlining and enhancing the DfAC framework were addressed by focusing on developing an end-to-end BIM framework that supported integrated modeling, analysis, optimization, and simulation (Figure 13.14) (Muthumanickam et al., 2020a, 2020b). A detailed overview of how the BIM framework was leveraged in DfAC of the Mars habitat for the NASA Challenge is outlined in the following section.

Model

As mentioned, the final phase of the NASA Challenge had two levels: a virtual construction level and an actual construction level. The virtual construction level required the design of a shelter that was to be optimized for Martian conditions, but for which a sub-scale version was to be 3D printed on Earth. Based on precedents and preliminary design charettes, the design concept took into account the maximum overhang angle that can be printed without formwork, which is ~60 degrees from horizontal; the minimum wall thickness required to provide protection from harmful cosmic radiation (on Mars), which varies between 2 and 3 feet (60 to 90 cm); and the maximum reach of a robotic arm. The resulting geometry

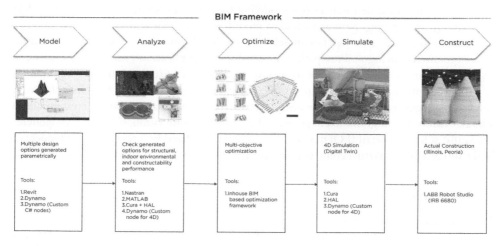

Figure 13.14 End-to-end BIM framework developed for DfAC of a Mars habitat for the NASA Challenge.

Figure 13.15   Design concept for a conical geometry along with variable configurations (tangential, overlapping, at a distance, and curvilinear arrangement).

included conical-shaped modules of varying sizes that could be connected and combined in different ways to obtain different shelter configurations and adjusted to different programmatic requirements and specific site conditions (Figure 13.15). The modular nature of the habitat guarantees expandability as it permits incremental construction of additional modules to host a growing human community on Mars. The same conical module concept was utilized for both the virtual and actual construction levels.

Each module was designed to cater to specific needs such as living area, working space, kitchen/dining, bed/bath, leisure area, and hydroponic food production module. The design for the virtual construction level had to include entry and exit hatch systems; MEP systems and ECLSS to enable indoor living and work activities of astronauts; safety systems to mitigate emergency situations; food production systems; and other interior elements (along with foundational structure and envelope) as discussed further below. On the other hand, the design for the actual construction level had to include only the entry and exit hatch systems, but not the MEP and safety systems. The services and systems were designed to be centralized for ease of access, assembly, and serviceability.

A procedural modeling algorithm was developed in Dynamo for Revit using node-based modeling in which several nodes execute geometrical manipulation tasks computationally to result in the overall habitat design. The algorithm consisted of various clusters of nodes responsible for different actions such as controlling input variables (for feeding input values); floor plan generator (for modeling floor plans with required rooms and interior spaces); interior systems modeler (for modeling MEP, ECLSS, and other service systems and components); conical module modeler (for modeling the conical enclosure); connector modeler (for solving intersections between adjacent modules); entry/exit and safety system modeler (for generating entry/exit hatches in selected modules); additive construction constraint solver (geometry slicing and toolpath related tasks); and application programming interfaces (APIs) (to connect the BIM model to various structural, environmental, toolpath analysis, and robotic simulation tools) (Figure 13.16). The parametric procedural modeling algorithm enabled rapid generation of multiple design alternatives with variable modular configurations. The algorithm was programmed to generate the enclosure (foundation, structural components, and walls) at level of detail (LOD) 300 & 400, and the MEP and ECLSS system components at LOD 100 & 200 (for virtual construction level 1 & 2, respectively) (Figure 13.17).

Analyze + optimize

The generated building design options were then tested for multiple performance factors such as structural, IEQ, construction time and cost, etc. using discipline-specific computational analysis software and physical tests. For sound structural performance of a building, it is crucial to ensure that the building can withstand compressive loads caused by gravity

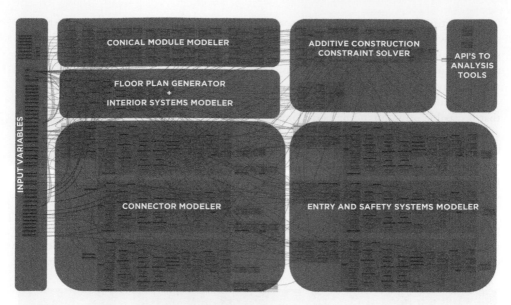

Figure 13.16 Parametric node based algorithm developed in Dynamo for Revit for procedural modeling of the Mars habitat.

Figure 13.17 (Left) Design options with variable module configurations and size and shapes and (Right) LOD 200 MEP, ECLSS, and interior systems generated by the parametric algorithm.

and vertical loads in the building and lateral loads due to multiple factors such as wind loads, seismic activity, pressure difference between interior and exterior, and so on. Martian conditions such as a reduced gravity (3.71 m/s², approximately one third that of Earth) and reduced atmospheric pressure (approx. 0.0006 MPa, Earth's atmospheric pressure is ~ 0.101 MPa, i.e., less than 1% that on Earth) create increased lateral loads on the walls of the building due to increased pressure difference between the interior and exterior of the building. This produces a condition in which buildings with walls at certain angles might fail due to the increased outward lateral load if not designed properly. Contrary to this, the primary reason behind the selection of a conical geometry (angular walls that meet at an apex point) was to enable a unified concrete structure that can be 3D printed continuously from floor to roof without the need for any assembly post print, the use of any prefabricated parts, or any temporary structural support during construction. It should be noted that most of the state-of-the-art concrete 3D printing of buildings involve printing of components as kit of parts and assembly using a gantry or crane mechanism. Our team focused on developing techniques that can enable 3D printing of tapered concrete structures without any formwork (or supporting structure) to avoid the complexity, cost, and logistics involved in setting up such formwork. The taper angle of the conical extrusion resulted in cantilevering of successive beads on top of each other. Due to the lack of external formwork, it is essential to design the taper in such a way that the center of gravity of each successive layer partially overlaps with the layer beneath it as a means to ensure continuous load transfer.

Given such complexities, it is essential to identify a conical structure with a taper angle that is capable of withstanding both compressive and lateral loads as well as ensuring shape accuracy when 3D printed without formwork. Detailed computational FEM was used to aid the selection of the structurally optimal design option (Figure 13.18). However, additional physical testing might be required as design options identified as optimal by the FEM might fail under real-time conditions. For example, computational FEM analysis of design options with taper angles of 60, 65, and 70 degrees seemed to yield optimal compressive strength.

Upon 3D printing small-scale samples to test the physical performance of these taper angles, it was identified that the 70-degree option performed well, whereas the other two angles (60 and 65 degrees) failed, as shown in Figure 13.19. However, a 70-degree taper angle of the conical extrusion resulted in an increased height of the overall building design, which would

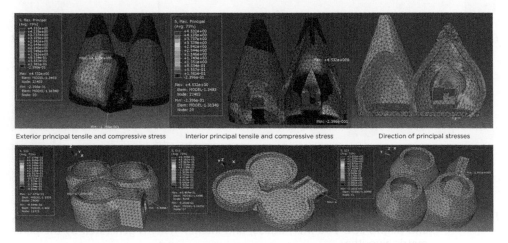

Figure 13.18 Sample of structural finite element model (FEM) of selective design options (Credits: Keunhyoung Park).

Figure 13.19 Failure of 65-degree taper angle due to material deformation caused by cantilevering of beads.

make it infeasible for the robot to print the top portion of the building without additional end effectors. Moreover, designing and fitting of an end effector to increase the range of the robot resulted in vibrations near the material delivery nozzle, thereby leading to over-extrusion of materials at some parts of the geometry (Figure 13.20). The increase in vibrations can be attributed to the shift in center of gravity of the end effector among other reasons and a lower stiffness when compared to the robot arm itself. Such issues can be addressed in several ways such as modifying the nozzle size or shape, robot speed, end-effector stiffness, or the overall geometry to avoid tight corners (to avoid kinks in toolpath). However, modifying these variables also impacts other aspects of the building design such as the overall structural performance, construction cost, material cost, and construction time. Hence, it is essential to capture such nuanced tradeoffs in additive construction in order to ensure successful printing.

Further, the taper angle also has an impact on the interior spatial planning, as a steep taper angle might result in reduced interior usable volume, essentially rendering the space near the wall–floor connection unusable. Hence it is also essential to incorporate the other elements of the buildings such as the interior furniture, MEP systems, and ECLSS, (Figure 13.21) and

Figure 13.20 Over-extrusion of material around corner profile due to vibrations caused by end effector.

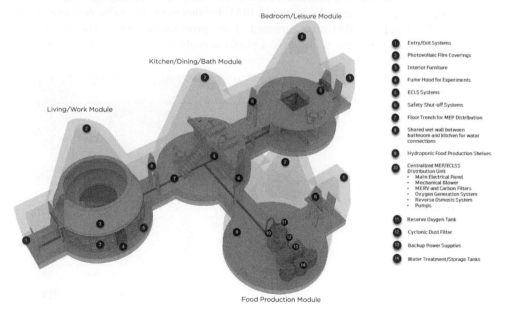

Figure 13.21 Schematic render of BIM showing multiple systems in the design selected for the virtual construction level.

also evaluate the overall spatial layout for accessibility and other spatial qualities. For the actual construction level, a minimum usable floor area (a_u) of 110 m² per the NASA habitability standards was prescribed as a requirement in the design brief (NASA and Bradley University, 2018). Incorporating other functional requirements—such as living and work areas, bedrooms, bathrooms, kitchen and dining area, leisure area and associated systems, services, and interior fixtures—introduces the need for interior walls and partitions. Such walls, partitions, and the intersections between the interior walls and the overall structure need to be designed within the constraints of the overall geometry. Subsequently, it is also equally important to design the MEP and ECLSS systems in such a manner that the routing of the service systems (pipes, cables, and ducts) do not have collision paths with other service elements and are easily serviceable. The design for the virtual construction level was envisioned to have a centralized MEP/ECLSS distribution system along with other water storage and treatment tanks. The positioning of these components involves identifying optimal routing paths for the floor trenches, which carry the ducts, pipes, and electrical cables. The route also had to be designed in such a manner that the number of kinks and the minimum distance between consecutive kinks in the pipe were to be optimized to avoid excessive internal pressure in the ducts and pipes. The wet wall that distributes the water and electricity outlets to the kitchen/dining and bath areas had to be positioned to align with the trench route. This, in turn, impacted the spatial planning of the room layout and other interior spaces.

In summary, there existed various tradeoffs while designing these interconnected systems and it was crucial to optimize the building design concurrently for multiple aspects (such as structural, IEQ, and constructability, i.e., toolpath and logistics) to ensure holistic performance of the additively constructed building (Figure 13.22). To enable such concurrent optimization for multiple design objectives (or goals), it is necessary to generate a large set of design options and concurrently analyze them for their performance factors. Since the building design process involves multidisciplinary stakeholders dealing with multiple domain-specific modeling, analysis, and simulation tools, it was necessary to integrate these federated BIMs into an integrated (or master) BIM. Furthermore, to enable concurrent optimization, the integrated BIM was connected to an optimization routine via Dynamo for Revit (Figure 13.23). Dynamo was used as a platform enabling common data exchange for

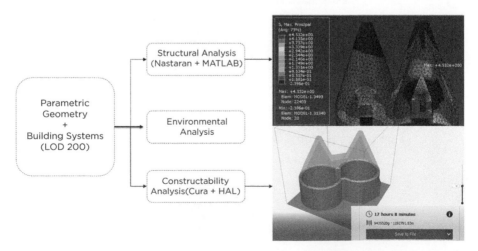

Figure 13.22 Conceptual representation of the data flow between the modeling and analysis tools (structural, environmental, and constructability tools).

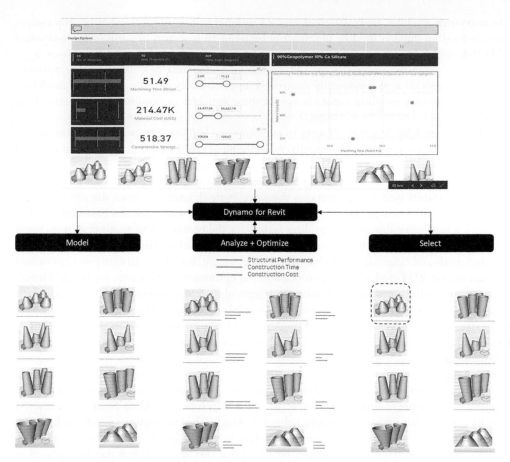

Figure 13.23 (Top) Interactive user interface for modifying high-level design goals and constraints; (Bottom) Conceptual representation of a connected BIM ecosystem for modeling, analysis, and optimization.

sharing information between the modeling, analyses, simulation, and optimization tools. It should be noted that, for the efficient use of such optimization algorithms, it is essential to define the quantitative design goals or objectives as a mathematical formulation.

First, the objective requirements and constraints were extracted from the design brief and encoded as rules in a procedural modeling algorithm (or generative algorithm) in Dynamo for Revit. Further, the minimum and maximum limits on usable living and functional area, access corridors, furniture spacing, and positioning per the habitability requirements from NASA-STD-3001, Volume 2 (NASA, 2019) were mathematically formulated into the procedural modeling algorithm as well. Design variables such as number of modules (n_m), radius of the base profile of the module(s) (r), connector type (tangential, overlapping, at a distance), distance between modules (d), angle between modules (α), height of straight walls (h_{msw}), overall height of the modules (h_{mo}), tapering angle of the conical extrusion (α_m), wall thickness (t_w), connector sectional profile manipulators, width of connector (w), height of straight walls in connector (h_{csw}), overall height of connector (h_{co}), tapering angle of connector (α_c), width (w_e) of entry/exit modules, height of straight walls in entry/exit modules (h_{esw}), overall height of entry/exit modules (h_{eo}), geometrical manipulators for openings and penetrations in entry/exit modules, floor slab thickness (t_f), number of floors (n_f), number of crop shelves inside food production module (n_s), spacing between crop shelves (h_s), minimum unkinked MEP duct/pipe length to maintain optimal pressure (l_{mep}), minimum room dimensions (r_{min}), maximum room dimensions (r_{max}), and minimum usable area (a_u), among other parameters were encoded as parametrically controlled input variables into the procedural modeling algorithm thereby enabling rapid change of these variables as required (Muthumanickam et al., 2020a).

The overarching design goals were to *maximize* usable floor area, *maximize* usable indoor volume, *maximize* compressive strength, *minimize* build cost based on construction material (concrete) quantity, and *minimize* overall 3D-printing time. The optimization routine aided in finding the combination of design variables that would satisfy the design goals. Additional constraints such as the limits on the taper angle determined from the physical tests, optimal wall thickness for Martian conditions, and optimal wall thickness based on material testing results were also used as guiding factors for the optimization routine. A web-based interactive user interface was developed that enabled multidisciplinary users to modify the design goals and constraints (Muthumanickam et al., 2020d). This, in turn, was connected to the master BIM model, analyses tools, and the optimizer via Dynamo for Revit. Hence, any change in the objectives or constraints triggered the optimizer to find a solution per the new inputs as well as update the master BIM model accordingly. The web-based interactive interface was hosted in Microsoft (MS) Azure and was connected to an optimizer utilizing nondominated sorting genetic algorithm II for searching the optimal design option. Whenever the design goals or constraints were modified on the interactive front end, the input values and the resultant optimal design option from the optimizer were appended to a database in MS Azure. This database of user inputs and optimal solutions were then used to train MS Azure's inbuilt supervised ML models (a subset of AI techniques). These AI techniques inbuilt within MS Azure helped build a predictive analytics model, which can identify optimal solutions based on input values more quickly as the size of the training database increases. However, it should be noted that this approach was purely explored to decrease the querying time and more research is necessary to validate the accuracy of the ML models used.

Using the above BIM-based optimization framework, two design options were selected: a three-module version for the virtual construction level and a two-module version for the actual construction level (Figure 13.24). The actual construction level had to be designed with interlocking mechanism to prevent lateral slip due to cold joints, where fresh concrete is deposited over cured concrete after an intermittent stop in 3D printing.

Figure 13.24 Design option selected for (Left) virtual construction level (Render credits: Eric Mainzer) and (Right) actual construction level. (Far Right) Design of interlocking geometries to address cold joints.

Digital twin-based 4D simulation

Once the design options were finalized, detailed digital twin models of the production setup were developed to perform detailed 4D simulations of the entire construction process. It should be noted with careful distinction that the constructability simulation (toolpath and robot motion planning) used as part of the analysis and optimization to arrive at a final geometry is different from the digital twin-based 4D simulation (outlined in this section). A digital twin-based 4D simulation includes of all the equipment used in the production process such as the material feeder system, material mixer system, storage silos, delivery truck, safety barricades, and enclosures, in addition to the robots. Ideally, such models can be used for analysis and optimization as well. But generating digital twin-based constructability simulations for multiple models as outlined in the previous section would be computationally expensive. Hence, a simplified toolpath simulation was used in the previous stage. The production system including the robots, equipment, and other logistics were modeled on top of the integrated BIM model in Revit. A custom node in Dynamo for Revit was used to stream this model into Grasshopper for Rhino, within which a HAL Robotics plugin was used to develop the 4D simulation. The toolpath of the sliced geometry was used as the G-code to guide the robotic motion in the 4D simulation. The order of execution of the other construction tasks and logistics were programmed sequentially using a custom-built timeline editor within Grasshopper for Rhino. Separate digital twin–based 4D simulations were generated for the virtual and actual construction levels of the NASA Challenge. The 4D simulation for the virtual construction level was developed to mimic a sequence of robotic construction tasks in the Martian environment (Figures 13.25 and 13.26), whereas the 4D simulation for the actual construction level was developed for conditions of the competition venue in Peoria, Illinois (Figure 13.27). To resist lateral loads on Mars, the base of the structure was envisioned to start from an excavated area. Furthermore, in order to protect the freshly printed wet concrete structure from extreme atmospheric conditions, a retractable enclosure would be deployed after which the steps 3–16 shown in Figure 13.25 would be executed in sequence.

The second digital twin–based 4D simulation model was developed using the same software framework as mentioned above, but this time for the actual construction level setup, which included a delivery truck, trailer, silo for feed stock material storage, water tank, mixer, pumps, two ABB IRB 6640 robots, computer stations, safety barricades, window fixtures, scissor jack for build space monitoring, and camera for visual feedback (Muthumanickam et al., 2020a) (Figure 13.27).

Based on multiple iterations of the simulations and learning from the production system setup at our Additive Construction Laboratory (AddCon Lab) at Penn State, the digital twin model of the production system to be deployed at the competition venue in Peoria, Illinois was refined and details prescribed per the NASA on-site safety standards prescribed in the competition brief. Figure 13.28 is an image comparing the digital twin model with the actual setup at the finals of the actual construction level of the NASA Challenge.

Construct

Finally, a sub-scale version (one-third scale) of the proposed design for the actual construction level was 3D printed on-site during the finale of the NASA 3D-Printed Mars Habitat Centennial Challenge held in Peoria, Illinois. The final print occurred over three days, during which each team was given ten hours a day to 3D print their proposed designs. The allocated ten hours per day was exclusive of the time for site preparation, production system setup, and daily

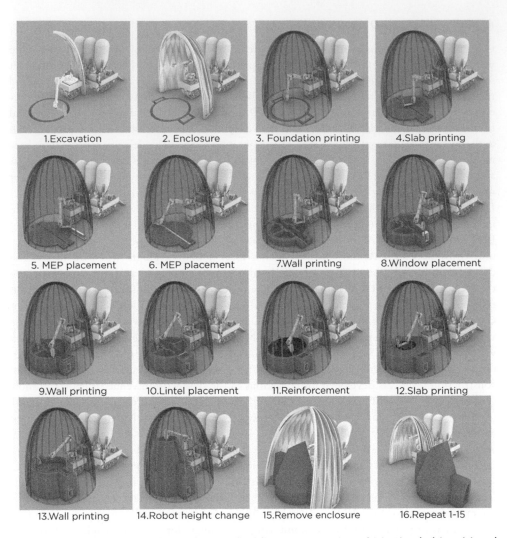

1.Excavation   2. Enclosure   3. Foundation printing   4.Slab printing

5. MEP placement   6. MEP placement   7.Wall printing   8.Window placement

9.Wall printing   10.Lintel placement   11.Reinforcement   12.Slab printing

13.Wall printing   14.Robot height change   15.Remove enclosure   16.Repeat 1-15

Figure 13.25   Digital twin 4D simulation of additive construction of Martian habitat (virtual construction level) (Simulation credits: Eduardo Castro e Costa and Negar Ashrafi).

equipment preparation and cleaning after stopping at the end of each day (one half hour was allotted in the morning and an additional half hour at day's end). Our proposed design was 3D printed in a cumulative time of 16.5 hours spanning three days with stops at the end of each day. Though most of the process was executed as per the digital twin–based 4D simulations, there were a few on-site anomalies in the robotic 3D printing process, which required manual intervention. Out of the three window fixtures that were programmed to be placed autonomously by a second ABB IRB 6640 robot, two windows were placed successfully, whereas the autonomous positioning of the third window failed. This was due to the over-extrusion of concrete at the edge surrounding the gap for the window, which made the gap smaller than the size of the window by a few millimeters. This prevented the window from sliding into the gap as planned and, hence, required manual scraping to remove the extra material deposited on the edge. Another challenge we faced during the competition was the failure of a few beads

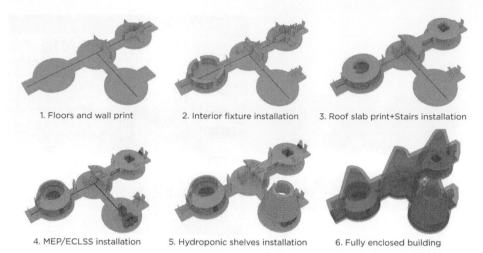

1. Floors and wall print 2. Interior fixture installation 3. Roof slab print+Stairs installation

4. MEP/ECLSS installation 5. Hydroponic shelves installation 6. Fully enclosed building

Figure 13.26 Sequence of printing of enclosure and assembly of interior components and systems (Enclosure will be printed right after Step, but not shown for visual clarity of interior elements).

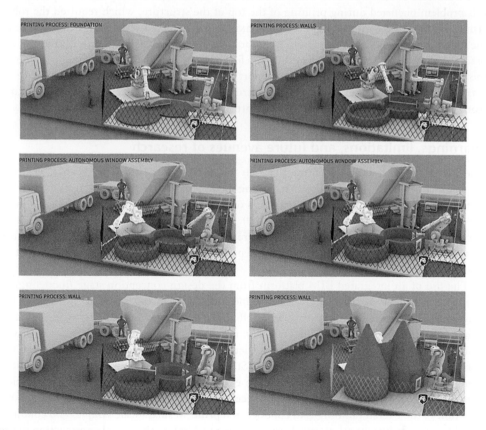

Figure 13.27 Digital twin 4D simulation of additive construction of one-third-scale habitat at competition venue (actual construction level) (Simulation credits: Naveen K. Muthumanickam and Eduardo Castro e Costa).

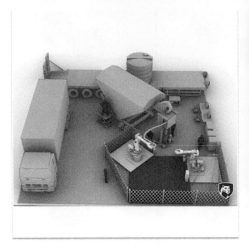

Figure 13.28 Comparison of BIM-based digital twin of the production setup and the actual setup at the competition venue during the finals.

on the interior of the walls at the location where the structure starts to taper. More specifically, this problem occurred during printing of the top of the structure, which required the robot arm to perform a 180-degree flip of its sixth axis (end effector) to reach such heights. Due to the flipping of the end effector, there was minor offset error in terms of the robot position calibration, which caused the toolpath to shift by a few millimeters, thereby resulting in the innermost beads falling without underneath support. However, despite such drawbacks, the team was able to complete 3D printing the entire structure as a unified tapering concrete structure from floor plate to the roof without any support structure or formwork (Figure 13.29).

Learnings, limitations, and future avenues of research

The unreinforced concrete structure that was 3D printed at the finals of the NASA Challenge was subject to a range of tests including a compressive strength test, during which a 90+ metric ton (MT) excavator pressed down on the top of the structure at the weakest location identified for the structure (Figure 13.30). The unreinforced concrete structure resisted the load until the tracks of the excavator were off the ground, at which time the structure partially failed. Even then, the structure only partially failed with one module staying intact showcasing significant structural strength.

The use of an integrated BIM platform from the design conception stage (modeling) to design development (analysis, optimization, and simulation) to the actual 3D printing of the structure using industrial robots, was as an efficient platform for multidisciplinary collaboration, design, and construction. Specifically, it helped the team in adopting a data-driven design approach, which helps minimize conflicts and costly revisions. However, based on the tests conducted in our AddCon Lab at Penn State as well as learning from the competition, there is room for improvement to make the existing BIM-based design and optimization framework more robust. Key to ensuring successful execution of the additive concrete construction of the overall building is to conduct trial prints of small-scale samples and conducting physical tests (structural, thermal, and leakage tests) before the actual construction of the full-scale structure. Often, there might be anomalies uncovered during the printing tests even when the robot strictly follows the 4D simulations, as it is difficult to construct a digital

Figure 13.29 Sequence of snapshots of additive construction of the sub-scale habitat at the finals.

| t seconds | t + 10 seconds | t + 20 seconds |
| t + 30 seconds | t + 42 seconds | t + 43 seconds |

Figure 13.30 Compression test showing raising of excavator trails (dotted white lines).

twin model that exactly mimics the instantaneous conditions (e.g., temperature changes, humidity, and air flow) on the printing site. Apart from the printing tests, rheological tests are crucial for predicting anomalies such as over-extrusion of materials. Though rheological experiments are predominantly physical experiments, detailed computational fluid dynamics (CFD) models can also be developed to virtually simulate the material flow for variable geometries. However, integrating such physics-based analysis tools with the BIM-based optimization framework would be difficult and, hence, is a potential area for future research.

Design of feedback mechanism

In case of geometrical errors due to material deformation or toolpath calibration error, some human intervention is necessary to handle such anomalies and avoid any potential failures or lapses in the additive construction process. To eliminate such human interventions, advanced computer vision sensors leveraging photogrammetric or LiDAR sensors can be used to collect real-time geometrical data about the printed geometry and deformations, if any. This can then be used for real-time corrective adjustment of motion-specific variables such as the toolpath and robot speed, or to control the material mixing ratio to avoid any potential failures. Such an effort requires creating a database for the storage of real-time computer vision data and sophisticated algorithms that can optimize the design in real time and update the BIM model and G-code according to these observations. Further, ML techniques (especially supervised reinforcement learning) can also be used to compare the predicted performance of the structure (from various performance analyses tools) and the actual performance of the structure (from the real time data collected via computer vision sensors) (Figure 13.31). Such an approach will help in increasing the accuracy of predicting the actual performance of the structure through simulations beforehand.

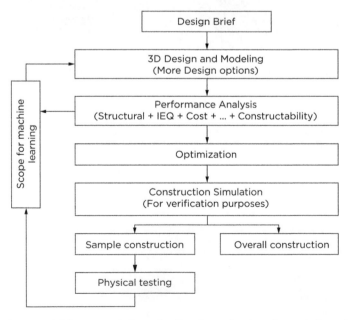

Figure 13.31 Conceptual framework for a feedback mechanism for real-time data collection from physical tests using computer vision sensors.

Conclusions

In summary, a novel connected software ecosystem utilizing state-of-the-art developments in BIM, parametric modeling, database management, and APIs was developed to support the design for additive concrete construction framework. Such a unified BIM platform allowed integration of multidisciplinary modeling, analysis, optimization, and simulation tools and enabled the consideration of manufacturability and constructability constraints in addition to other performance factors such as structural, indoor environmental performance, and cost. In addition to the BIM framework that allowed the concurrent design of the overall building, and along with the design of toolpath and robotic production system and logistics, the BIM-based digital twin models were highly imperative in simulating the entire sequence of robotic construction tasks. Utilizing such a framework, it was possible to construct the world's first fully enclosed concrete structure that was 3D printed from floor to roof, tapered toward its highest point, without any support structures/formwork at architectural scale. With promising trends yielded by the currently developed BIM framework, more robust and efficient designs can be developed by enhancing the BIM framework through its integration with real-time feedback systems and sophisticated CFD tools capable of simulating material flow.

Acknowledgments

This research was supported by prize money from NASA's 3D-Printed Mars Habitat Centennial Challenge and by grants from the College of Arts and Architecture and the College of Engineering, and developed at the Stuckeman Center for Design Computing (SCDC) and at the Additive Construction Laboratory, The Pennsylvania State University. The authors acknowledge the valuable contribution to the research and express their gratitude to the following members of the Penn State team: Nick Meisel, Aleksandra Radlińska, Randal|Bock, Maryam Hojati, Keunhyang Park, Negar Ashrafi, Eduardo Castro e Costa, Samuel Dzwill, Andrew Przyjemski, Flávio Craveiro, Joe Straka, Aiden Smith, and Zhanzhao Li.

References

Ashrafi, N., Duarte, J. P., Nazarian, S., & Meisel, N. A. (2019). Evaluating the relationship between deposition and layer quality in large-scale additive manufacturing of concrete. *Virtual Physical Prototyping*, 14, 135–140. https://doi.org/10.1080/17452759.2018.1532800

Attia, S., Hamdy, M., O'Brien, W., & Carlucci, S. (2013). Assessing gaps and needs for integrating building performance optimization tools in net zero energy buildings design. *Energy and Buildings*, 60, 110–124. https://doi.org/10.1016/j.enbuild.2013.01.016

Craveiro, F., Bártolo, H., Duarte, J., & Bártolo, P. J. (2017). Designing cork-based functionally-graded concrete walls. In F. Moreira da Silva, H. M. Bártolo, P. Bártolo, R. Almendra, F. Roseta, H. A. Almeida, A. C. Lemos (eds.), *Challenges for Technology Innovation: An Agenda for the Future* (pp. 431–434). London: CRC Press. https://doi.org/10.1201/9781315198101-86

Craveiro, F., Nazarian, S., Bartolo, H., Bartolo, P. J., & Duarte, J. P. (2020). An automated system for 3D printing functionally graded concrete-based materials. *Additive Manufacturing*, 33, 1–10. https://doi.org/10.1016/j.addma.2020.101146

Duarte, J. P. (2001). *Customizing Mass Housing: A Discursive Grammar for Siza's Malagueira Houses.* PhD. Thesis, Massachusetts Institute of Technology, Cambridge, MA. Retrieved from https://dspace.mit.edu/handle/1721.1/8189

Duarte, J. P. (2019). Customizing mass housing: Toward a formalized approach. In B. Kolarevic & J. P. Duarte (eds.), *Mass Customization and Design Democratization* (pp. 129–142). New York: Routledge.

Flager, F., & Haymaker, J. (2009). *A Comparison of Multidisciplinary Design, Analysis and Optimization Processes in the Building Construction and Aerospace Industries.* CIFE Technical Report. Stanford, CA: CIFE. Retrieved from https://purl.stanford.edu/mc198xh9178

Gan, Y., Dai, X., & Li, D. (2013). Off-line programming techniques for multirobot cooperation system. *International Journal of Advanced Robotic Systems,* 10(7), 282.

Haymaker, J., Bernal, M., Marshall, M. T., Okhoya, V., Szilasi, A., Rezaee, R., Chen, C., Salveson, A., Brechtel, J., Deckinga, L., Hasan, H., Ewing, P., & Welle, B., (2018). Design space construction: A framework to support collaborative, parametric decision making. *Journal of Information Technology in Construction,* 23(8), 157–178. Retrieved from http://www.itcon.org/2018/8

Labonnote, N., Rønnquist, A., Manum, B., & Rüther, P. (2016). Additive construction: State-of-the-art, challenges and opportunities. *Automation in Construction,* 72, 347–366. https://doi.org/10.1016/j.autcon.2016.08.026.

Leicht, R., Fox, S., Mäkelainen, T., & Messner, J. (2007). *Building Information Models, Display Media, and Team Performance: An Exploratory Study.* Espoo: VTT Technical Research Centre of Finland. VTT Working Papers, No. 88. Retrieved from http://www.vtt.fi/inf/pdf/workingpapers/2007/W88.pdf

Muthumanickam, N. K., Park, K., Duarte, J. P., Nazarian, S., Memari, A. M., & Bilén, S. (2020a). BIM for parametric problem formulation, optioneering and 4D simulation of a 3D-printed martian habitat: A case study of the NASA 3D-printed habitat challenge. In *Proceedings of the 5th Residential Building Design and Construction Conference.* March 4–6, 2020, State College, PA. Retrieved from https://www.researchgate.net/publication/341451080_BIM_for_parametric_problem_formulation_optioneering_and_4D_simulation_of_3D-printed_Martian_habitat_A_case_study_of_NASA's_3D_Printed_Habitat_Challenge

Muthumanickam, N. K., Duarte, J. P., Nazarian, S., Bilén, S. G. & Memari, A. M. (2020b). BIM for design generation, analysis, optimization and construction simulation of a Martian habitat. In *Proceedings of the ASCE (American Society of Civil Engineers) Earth & Space Conference 2021.* April 1–22, Seattle, WA. (Forthcoming)

Muthumanickam, N. K., Brown, N., Duarte, J. P., & Simpson, T. W. (2020c). Multidisciplinary analysis and optimization in architecture, engineering, and construction: A detailed review and call for collaboration. (Submitted to *Journal of Structural and Multidisciplinary Optimization*).

Muthumanickam. N. K., Duarte, J. P., & Simpson, T. W. (2020d). Multidisciplinary concurrent optimization framework for multi-phase building design processes. (In preparation).

NASA. (2019). *NASA-STD-3001: NASA spaceflight human-system standard, Volume 2: Human Factors, Habitability, and Environmental Health, Revision B.* Washington, DC: NASA. Retrieved from https://www.nasa.gov/sites/default/files/atoms/files/nasa-std-3001_vol_2_rev_b.pdf

NASA and Bradley University. (2018). *On-site Habitat Competition Rules,* NASA 3D-printed Mars habitat challenge - Phase 3. Retrieved from https://www.bradley.edu/sites/challenge/assets/documents/3DPH_Phase_3_Rules-v3.pdf

Nazarian, S., Pantano, C., Colombo, P., & Marangoni, M. "Ceramic glass joints: Transitioning interface from glass to geopolymer cement." [aka "Seamless architecture: Innovative material interfaces", US provisional patent application 62/322,864 filed on April 15, 2015; converted to a Patent Cooperation Treaty (PCT) application PCT/US2017/027976 on April 17, 2017; Published on October 19, 2017 as WO2017181191. Retrieved from https://patents.google.com/patent/WO2017181191A1/en

Polit-Casillas, R., & Howe, S. A. (2013). Virtual construction of space habitats: Connecting building information models (BIM) and SysML. In *AIAA Space 2013 Conference and Exposition,* pp. 1–19. San Diego, CA. Pasadena, CA: Jet Propulsion Laboratory, National Aeronautics and Space Administration. https://doi.org/10.2514/6.2013-5508

Rael, R., & San Fratello, V. (2011). *Developing Concrete Polymer Building Components for 3D Printing.* Retrieved from http://www.rael-sanfratello.com/media/emerging_objects/papers/243.pdf

Simon, H. (1969). *The Sciences of the Artificial* (1st ed.). Cambridge, MA: MIT Press.

Stiny, G. and Gips J. (1972) Shape grammars and the generative specification of painting and sculpture. In C. V. Freiman (Ed.), *Information Processing, 71* (pp. 1460–1465). Amsterdam: North-Holland. Retrieved from https://architecture.mit.edu/sites/architecture.mit.edu/files/attachments/publications/SGIFIPSubmitted.pdf

Sutherland, I. (1963) *Sketchpad: A Man-Machine Graphical Communication System.* PhD Thesis, Massachusetts Institute of Technology, Cambridge, MA. Retrieved from http://hdl.handle.net/1721.1/14979

Thompson, M. K., Moroni, G., Vaneker, T., Fadel, G., Campbell, R. I., Gibson, I., Bernard, A., Schulz, J., Graf, P., Ahujai B. and Martina, F. (2016). Design for additive manufacturing: Trends, opportunities, considerations, and constraints. *CIRP Annals*, 65(2), 737–760. https://doi.org/10.1016/j.cirp.2016.05.004

Turing, A. (1948). Machine intelligence. In B. J. Copeland (ed.), *The Essential Turing: The Ideas that Gave Birth to the Computer Age* (p. 412). Oxford: Oxford University Press.

van der Zee, A., & Marijnissen, M. (2017). 3D concrete printing in architecture: A research on the potential benefits of 3D printing in architecture. In A. Fioravanti, S. Cursi, S. Elahmar, S. Gargaro, G. Loffreda, G. Novembri, & A. Trento (Eds.), *ShoCK – Sharing of Computable Knowledge - Proceedings of the 35th International Conference on Education and Research in Computer Aided Architectural Design in Europe* (Vol. 2, pp. 299–308), Rome, Italy, 20–22 September 2017. Rome: eCAADe. Retrieved from http://papers.cumincad.org/cgi-bin/works/Show?ecaade2017_087

Watson, N. D., Meisel, N. A., Bilén, S. G., Duarte, J. P., & Nazarian, S. (2019). Large-scale additive manufacturing of concrete using a 6-axis robotic arm for autonomous habitat construction. *Solid Freeform Fabrication 2019*: Proceedings of the 30th Annual International Solid Freeform Fabrication Symposium, Austin, TX, 12–14 August 2019, pp. 1583–1595. Retrieved from http://utw10945.utweb.utexas.edu/sites/default/files/2019/134%20Large-Scale%20Additive%20Manufacturing%20of%20Concrete%20Usi.pdf

Winston, P. (1992). *Artificial intelligence* (3rd ed.). Reading, MA: Addison-Wesley.

14

Toward dynamic and explorative optimization for architectural design

David W. Newton

Design is an explorative process involved with exploring a space of possibilities. It can therefore be understood as a search process guided by goals, or objectives. In architectural design, these objectives can be quantitative in nature, such as energy performance, or qualitative, such as aesthetic goals. In design projects, there are often multiple and sometimes conflicting objectives that must be simultaneously satisfied. These multi-objective problems (MOPs) pose serious challenges to the allied design fields and developing methods to find optimum solutions has become an important area of research in the architectural discipline. Previous research on multi-objective optimization (MOO) in architecture, however, has focused exclusively on addressing static MOPs. Real-world architectural design problems, however, are often dynamic in nature (i.e., DMOPs) and involve balancing multiple quantitative and qualitative objectives; understanding the trade-offs between these objectives; and dynamically adjusting the direction of the design process when the goals, design parameters, and constraints of a project inevitably change. What algorithmic methods can be used to efficiently address the dynamic, multi-objective, and explorative nature of architectural design? How can computational MOO processes be developed to augment and engage the human imagination in order to efficiently explore a space of possible designs?

The conceptual design phase in architectural design involves the open-ended exploration of a design space (i.e., a space of all possible design solutions). The goal is to find a set of decision variables (i.e., input parameters) that map to a diverse but equivalent set of optimal performing solutions located within the objective space defined by the objectives (i.e., goals) of the optimization problem. This optimal set, referred to as the Pareto optimal set, is located on a multi-dimensional manifold referred to as the Pareto front. MOPs present several challenges for researchers developing algorithms to find optimum solutions to design problems, and these have been well documented by other researchers (Bechikh, Datta, & Gupta, 2016; Coello, Van Veldhuizen, & Lamont, 2002; Deb, 2014). Five challenges as following stand out:

Exploration. A significant stumbling block in developing algorithms to deal with MOPs is ensuring adequate exploration of an objective space as well as diversity in the solutions uncovered (Deb, Pratap, Agarwal, & Meyarivan, 2002). This is especially crucial for the conceptual design phase.

User preference-integration. Many algorithms used to solve MOPs require interaction with a decision-maker, but how and when the decision-maker should be involved in the process is an open problem (Bechikh, Kessentini, Said, & Ghédira, 2015).

Dimensionality. MOPs that have more than three objectives, known as many-objective MOPs can pose major challenges to the computability of the Pareto front due to the curse of dimensionality – once objectives increase past three, the size of the Pareto front can quickly become too large for many algorithms to cover effectively (Bechikh, Elarbi, & Said, 2017).

Dynamics. Many real-world MOPs involved in the conceptual design phase are dynamic and may have objectives, design parameters, and constraints that may change during the optimization process (Azzouz, Bechikh, & Said, 2017b).

Deception. A final complication is that MOPs and DMOPs can often be deceptive in nature— meaning they may be prone to leading decision-makers down the wrong path in a design space (Goldberg, 1987).

In the field of computer science, there has been significant research on optimization algorithms to address MOPs. Due to their adaptability, multi-objective evolutionary algorithms (MOEAs) have emerged as one of the most widely studied algorithmic approaches (Ashour & Kolarevic, 2015; Caldas, 2008; C. Mueller & Ochsendorf, 2011; Turrin, von Buelow, & Stouffs, 2011; Von Buelow, 2012). The field of MOEA research can be divided into six categories: aggregate; Pareto dominance-based; indicator-based; reference point-based; grid-based; and decomposition-based methods. Aggregate methods, in which all the objectives are combined into a single-objective function (e.g., effectively making the MOP a single-objective problem), have been shown to perform the most poorly, while Pareto-based methods have been the most popular, and decomposition-based approaches have been the highest performing (Zhang & Li, 2007). Furthermore, because MOEAs require feedback from a decision-maker, each of these categories can be divided into three subgroups based on whether a decision-maker's preferences are integrated before, during, or after the optimization process. These variants are referred to as: a priori; progressive; and a posteriori processes.

Progressive MOEAs demonstrate the best performance when dealing with optimization problems with more than three objectives (i.e., many-objective problems). Li, Deb, and Yao (2017) propose a progressive decomposition-based algorithm that requires the decision-maker to interactively define multiple regions of interest throughout the optimization process. These regions of interest then allow the optimization algorithm to focus on exploring a smaller volume of the objective space, making what would otherwise be a computationally expensive search less costly. Progressive Pareto dominance-based methods have shown significant effectiveness in addressing the challenges posed by many-objective problems as well (Bechikh, Said, & Ghédira, 2011; Deb & Kumar, 2007). Despite the promise of progressive techniques, there has been relatively little research on progressive MOEAs in comparison to nonprogressive variants.

In the discipline of architecture, standard Pareto-based a posteriori algorithms have been explored the most with little to no modifications for the specificities of architectural design. This cut-and-paste appropriation has limited the potential of MOEAs in the field of architecture by adopting the assumptions that the standard algorithms were developed under. Specifically, these algorithms assume that the objectives and decision variables of a design stay constant during the optimization process and that convergence to a particular set of solutions is preferred over the exploration of a space of possibility. In any real design process, the decision and objective spaces are never static. Instead, they are constantly being redefined to allow for more possibilities at certain moments and fewer possibilities at other moments.

This dynamic restructuring allows for an open-ended exploration of a design and requires an algorithmic approach that can deal with this dynamism.

Dynamic multi-objective evolutionary algorithms (DMOEAs) are currently being studied by researchers in the fields of optimization, operations research, and computer science to address DMOPs (Azzouz et al., 2017b). Previous research on DMOEAs has focused mostly on changes to a fixed number of objective functions, but previous work has not addressed situations where objectives and decision variables change simultaneously. Furthermore, much of this work does not explore the possibility of allowing the designer to interact progressively to guide the search process in an explorative manner.

This work addresses these understudied areas through the development and demonstration of a progressive DMOEA-based optimization tool called *Design Breeder*. The work demonstrates the potentials of optimization processes that endeavor to integrate both human and machine intelligence synergistically to solve problems neither could solve by themselves through their application on architectural design problems at the building and detail scale of design. Specifically, these processes are demonstrated through two case study projects. The first involves single family home design, and the second explores facade design.

Background

Multi-objective evolutionary algorithms in architectural optimization

Previous research related to building design has focused primarily on the application of a posteriori and progressive Pareto dominance-based MOEAs to address MOPs in the conceptual phase of design. Pareto-based MOEAs rank solutions using the concept of Pareto optimality (Censor, 1977), in which one design solution is said to dominate, or outperform another, if the value of at least one of its objectives is better than that of the other solution, while at the same time the values of its other objectives are equivalent to, or higher performing than, the other solution. Through Pareto ranking, a set of optimal solutions composed of different but equivalent solutions is discovered. As mentioned previously, this set is referred to as the Pareto front.

Pareto dominance-based approaches have been used on a variety of building design problems involving quantitative and aesthetic objectives. Turrin, von Buelow, Kilian, and Stouffs (2012) demonstrate their use in the design of roof structures that are optimized for daylighting, energy, and structural load. Aesthetic objectives are brought into the process through a progressive interactive user selection process. Hou, Liu, Zhang, Wang, and Dang (2017) use them to optimize building facades in relation to heating, cooling, lighting, and cost as objectives. In the field of structural engineering, C. T. Mueller and Ochsendorf (2015) apply them to evolve truss designs relative to mass, volume, and structural objective functions. Von Buelow (2012) uses a modified progressive Pareto-dominance MOEA that allows users to dynamically change the number of objectives, but no modifications are proposed to deal with the diversity and convergence issues that accompany such dynamic changes.

There are also several commercial computer aided design (CAD) packages that feature various a posteriori Pareto dominance-based MOEA implementations. Autodesk currently offers cloud-based optimization tools for their structural, mechanic, and architectural CAD products. ESTECO offers an optimization software called modeFrontier, which contains implementations of several standard MOEAs for design problems. Ansys's suite of engineering design software has a MOEA-based optimization platform as well as other optimization plugins like DesignXplorer are available. Bentley System's SITEOPS is a tool to explore the configuration possibilities of building sites optimized for geotechnical, hydrologic, topographic, legal, and architectural objectives. Dassault Systems offers several different parametric CAD packages (e.g., SolidWorks, Catia, and Digital Project) that feature MOEA-based optimization tools. Octopus (Vierlinger & Bollinger, 2014) is a MOEA plugin available for McNeel's parametric modeling plugin Grasshopper. All of these tools implement standard nondynamic MOEAs with little to no modification of their essential features for architectural design.

The previous research and commercial tools discussed share several drawbacks. The majority of MOEAs implemented do not allow for dynamic problems and none of these has design features that address the specific challenges posed by DMOPs. The vast majority of these approaches are also not designed with the goal of enabling a more explorative and open-ended user-guided search.

Progressive MOEAs in the design, engineering, and the arts

Progressive MOEAs allow the search and decision-making to occur simultaneously. These techniques use the decision-maker's preferences throughout the search process to help guide the MOEA through an objective space, therefore, offering the ability of navigating much more complex objective spaces than the other techniques mentioned. Research has also shown that progressive techniques can be more effective than a priori, or a posteriori, methods at solving deceptive design problems and problems with more than three objectives (Christman & Woolley, 2015).

In addition to the benefits offered by progressive MOEAs, there are also some important drawbacks that must be considered. According to Takagi (2001), user-fatigue is one major drawback. User fatigue begins to set-in at between 10 and 20 generations (assuming users are evaluating between 5 and 10 designs per generation). Another drawback is the lack of interactivity present in most progressive approaches. For example, in most implementations the decision-maker is relegated to only interacting with the search during the selection stage of the algorithm. This limited interactivity keeps the decision-maker only partially engaged and fails to make full use of their expertise to guide the search.

Progressive processes have been used extensively in problem domains involving MOPs and also those requiring qualitative assessments (e.g., aesthetics). They have been used in the arts (Sims, 1992), music (Marques, Reis, & Machado, 2010), fashion (Kim & Cho, 2000), and multiple design fields as shown by Takagi's comprehensive review (Takagi, 2001). In the design fields, they have been used for the conceptual design phase mostly. C. T. Mueller and Ochsendorf (2015) use a Pareto-based progressive MOEA to evolve truss designs and attempt to address the user-fatigue problem by showing only designs contained in the Pareto set to the decision-maker for selection. Mueller attempts to expand the interactivity of the MOEA by allowing the decision-maker to interactively change the population size and mutation rate. Von Buelow (2012) follows the same approach to reduce user-fatigue, but also includes an ability for multiple users to evaluate designs at the same time. Von Buelow attempts to address the interactivity problem by allowing users to interactively navigate and select designs for breeding from a database of all created solutions during the search.

This precedent research addresses user fatigue through a spectrum of approaches, but still offers a very limited set of possibilities for interaction with a decision-maker. In all these examples, the decision space being explored is fixed and the decision-maker is relegated to picking designs during the selection phase or changing evolutionary parameters (e.g., population, generation, or mutation) during the search. In contrast to these approaches, how can decision-makers be brought into the process in more interactive ways? How can processes be developed that allow for an open-ended search process guided by the creative imagination of the designer to occur?

Dynamic multi-objective evolutionary algorithms

DMOPs have objectives, design parameters, and constraints that change during the optimization process. When changes like these occur, traditional MOEAs perform poorly and are no longer able to converge to an optimal solution nor maintain a pool of diverse design solutions. For example, when the number of objectives increases, the problems posed to convergence and diversity can be clearly seen in Figure 14.1. After the change, the image on the right of the figure shows Pareto design solutions located only in a tiny area of the true Pareto front. The result is that both diversity and convergence are negatively affected.

When the number of objectives decreases, diversity becomes a major problem for MOEA optimization processes. Figure 14.2 shows an example of this situation. The left side of the figure shows the distribution found for three objectives and the right side of the figure shows how the distribution changes when the number of objectives decreases from three to two.

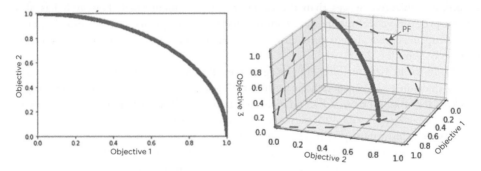

Figure 14.1 (Left) The image shows distribution of Pareto solutions for a benchmarking problem for two objectives. (Right) The image shows the distribution of solutions after an objective is added.

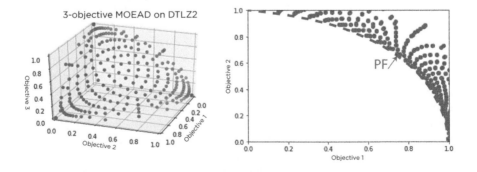

Figure 14.2 (Left) The image shows the distribution of Pareto solutions for a benchmarking problem for three objectives. (Right) The image shows the distribution of solutions after an objective has been subtracted.

After the change, solutions are very close to one another and there are many duplicates. This lack of diversity can cause the optimization process to converge prematurely and to miss optimal solutions.

In order to address these convergence and diversity problems, DMOEAs can be categorized by three types of approach: diversity; memory mechanism; and predictive approaches. Diversity approaches attempt to deal with this problem by adding diversity into a solution population when changes to the objective functions occur (Deb, Rao, & Karthik, 2007). Memory-based approaches use an archive to store useful solutions from the history of the search (Azzouz, Bechikh, & Said, 2017a). Predictive approaches use knowledge about the previous states of the Pareto front to predict the likely state of the new Pareto front (Hatzakis & Wallace, 2006).

Previous research on DMOEAs has focused on dynamic changes involving objective functions with time as an input variable (Azzouz et al., 2017b). Some examples include route optimization problems according to real-time traffic (Wahle, Annen, Schuster, Neubert, & Schreckenberg, 2001), scheduling of construction tasks for architectural projects, and control problems such as the optimization of indoor heating (Hämäläinen & Mäntysaari, 2002). Few researchers have looked at the problem of a changing number of objective functions (Chen, Li, & Yao, 2018; Von Buelow, 2012) and previous work has not addressed the situation where the number of decision variables is changing simultaneously with the number of objectives.

Toward explorative and dynamic optimization with design breeder

In order to address the dual problems of providing for an interactive–explorative search while providing efficient convergence to an optimal set of design solutions, this research proposes an interactive DMOEA-based design tool for the conceptual design phase called *Design Breeder*. Specifically, the research proposes a modification to the popular Pareto-based nondominated sorting genetic algorithm II (NSGA-II) (Deb et al., 2002) referred to here as the dynamic progressive NSGA-II (DP-NSGA-II). This algorithm makes up the core optimization engine of Design Breeder.

Figure 14.3 shows a comparison between a typical Pareto selection-based MOEA and the DP-NSGA-II algorithm at the core of Design Breeder. One important difference is that DP-NSGA-II is designed with unique procedures to deal with time-dependent changes in

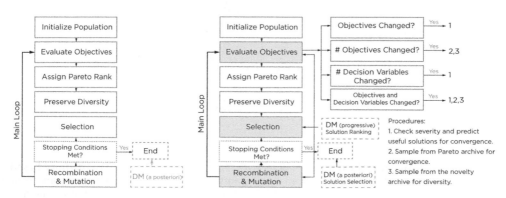

Figure 14.3   (Left) Diagram of a standard Pareto selection-based MOEA. (Right) Diagram of DP-NSGA-II.

David W. Newton

objective functions; changes in the number of objective functions; changes in the number of decision variables; and combinations of these changes that occur simultaneously. The dual problems of convergence and diversity are addressed through a combination of memory-based and prediction approaches as outlined in Figure 14.4. When the number of objectives changes DP-NSGA-II uses a memory-based approach and samples from novelty and Pareto archives to aid diversity and convergence respectively. To deal with changes in the number of decision variables, or time-dependent objective functions, the type and severity of the change is first computed. If the change is small, a prediction-based approach is applied in which already calculated objective values in the Pareto archive are scaled by a computed scale factor, sampled, and used to replace half of the current population. This aids convergence by using values that were known to have performed well before the change. The other half of

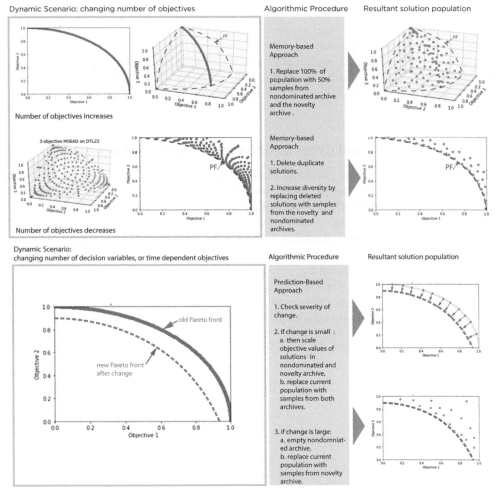

Figure 14.4 (Top) When the number of objectives changes DP-NSGA-II uses a memory-based approach and samples from novelty and Pareto archives to aid diversity and convergence respectively. (Bottom) To deal with changes in the number of decision variables, or time-dependent objective functions, a prediction-based approach is applied.

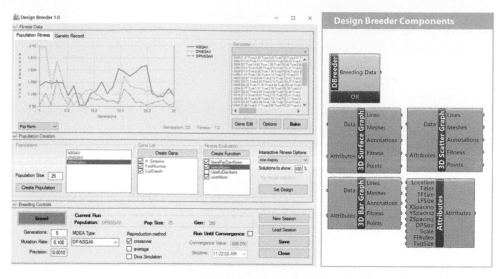

Figure 14.5 (Left) A screenshot of the Design Breeder interface. (Right) Images of the components that make up the Design Breeder Plugin for Grasshopper.

the population is then replaced with random samples from the novelty archive to aid diversity. If the change is big, the Pareto archive is completely emptied, and the current population
of solutions is repopulated with samples from the novelty archive.

Design Breeder was developed as a plug-in for the Grasshopper 3D parametric design
environment because of its popularity among multiple design fields for conceptual design
and because of its use of a visual programming environment. Figure 14.5 shows an image
of the Design Breeder graphical user interface within the Grasshopper environment. This
architecture allows users to interact with the optimization process in unique ways, because
the decision-maker can interactively change the decision and objective spaces in any of three
ways: existing decision variables and objective functions can be modified during the search
process; new decision variables and objectives can be added; or existing variables and objectives can be deleted. This allows users to continue to design as the optimization runs and to
steer the direction of the search.

Quantitative and qualitative objective functions can be interactively defined, added, and
subtracted on-the-fly to help steer the search. Figure 14.6 shows an example of a typical optimization run and the advantages that this type of interactivity can have in terms of allowing
for a more explorative search. The top left of the figure shows an objective space defined by
two objectives—minimizing cost and maximizing useful daylight. The top right shows the
objective space after a third objective (i.e., minimizing energy use) has been added by the
user and also shows how the search process is guided by the user as they add objectives and
design features to their design.

Qualitative objectives are defined by asking users to periodically rank solutions during the
search process. This solution ranking then guides the search toward a user-defined reference
direction in the objective space. Design Breeder allows users to define multiple reference
directions to guide the search. Figure 14.7 shows an example of two qualitative objectives
being combined to help guide the search.

User preferences are therefore integrated in a progressive fashion through the application of a hybrid method that incorporates the global structuring of a space of possibility

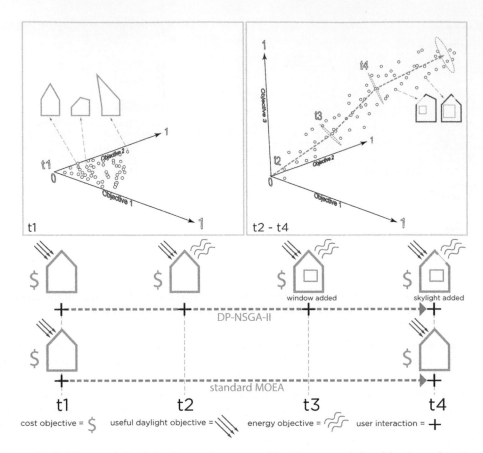

Figure 14.6 The top left of the figure shows an objective space defined by two objectives. The top right shows the objective space after a third objective has been added by the user and also shows how the search process is guided by the user as they add design features to their design at times $t = 3$ and $t = 4$.

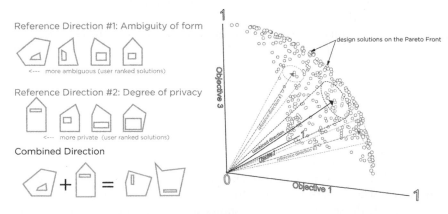

Figure 14.7 A diagram describing how qualitative objectives are combined to guide the optimization process through a space of possibility.

in combination with the ability to define and combine multiple search directions through solution ranking to guide the search at the local scale. This spectrum of interactions engages the decision-maker in a manner that requires a level of comparative thought that other approaches fall short of. Furthermore, it narrows the scope of the search in high-dimensional objective spaces and makes the optimization tractable, while engaging the user's abilities to help search a complex multi-dimensional space.

Case studies

In the conceptual, schematic, and design development phases of the design process, architects are faced with DMOPs at multiple scales. Developing an optimal design approach for the organization of a building on the site, the massing of the building, and a strategy for the building envelope in the early stages is especially crucial because they can have a large impact on the cost and energy performance of the building. The explorative capacity of Design Breeder is, therefore, demonstrated on two design problems at two different scales: one dealing with the generative design of a single family house that focuses on the building scale; and another generative task at the detail scale involved with the optimization of a facade.

Explorative search and optimization at the building scale

Residential design involves balancing multiple quantitative (e.g., energy efficiency, construction cost, daylight exposures, etc.) and qualitative objectives (e.g., aesthetic considerations, spatial quality, etc.). The number of different objectives involved can number in the dozens. This large number of objectives poses challenges for MOO processes. As discussed previously, when the number of objectives exceeds three, algorithmic optimization becomes computationally intractable without the incorporation of a human in the loop to guide the search process in specific directions. These types of many-objective problems, therefore, require computational optimization processes that are interactive and explorative—allowing the architect to engage with the optimization process as it unfolds and to direct the search process toward areas that exemplify a desired balance between objectives.

In order to address these issues, Design Breeder was used to find optimized design solutions for the design of two different single-family houses. The experiments were done as part of Chris Reeh's thesis work at the University of Nebraska-Lincoln's College of Architecture in 2019 (Reeh, 2019). Each house was located in a different geographic location and climate in the United States, and each had different occupant profiles reflecting different needs. The final optimized designs were then compared against normative residential construction in each geographic area in order to gauge the success of the optimization process.

Figure 14.8 describes the two optimization scenarios for the experiments. Scenario one involves the design of a single-family home in Lincoln, Nebraska located in climate zone 5; and scenario two the design of a home in Phoenix, Arizona located in climate zone 2. The objectives for the optimization are listed in the figure and include: home value (i.e., construction cost); leasing value; annual utility costs; and spatial quality. The last objective listed is qualitative in nature and is learned through intermittent interactions with the architect as the optimization process unfolds. Specifically, the architect is asked to rank solutions intermittently based on the degree to which they exhibit a chosen quality. The algorithm then uses this ranking to define a direction in the search space to explore further. As an example of this, Figure 14.9 shows an example in which two different qualities are defined by an architect. Those qualities are then combined to guide the search process.

David W. Newton

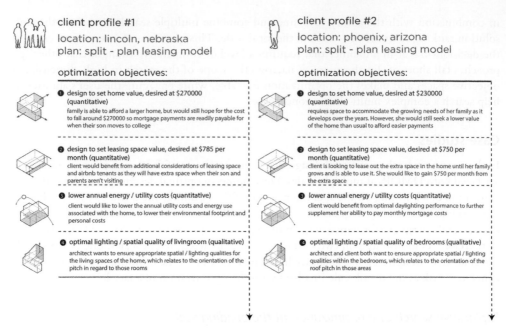

Figure 14.8 Shows the scenarios for the optimization of two different residences in different climate contexts: Lincoln, Nebraska in climate zone 5; and Phoenix, Arizona in climate zone 2 respectively.

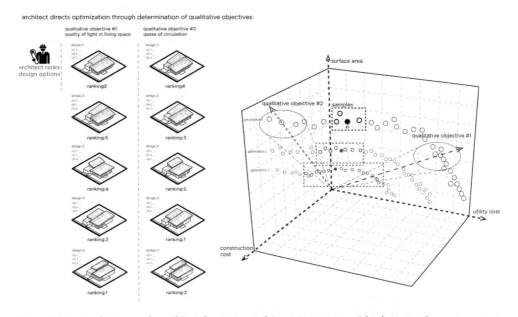

Figure 14.9 A diagram describing how an architect interacts with the search process to is shown. (Left) Two different qualitative objectives are defined by the architect to guide the search. (Right) The search space for the optimization is shown along with how the two qualitative objectives direct the search.

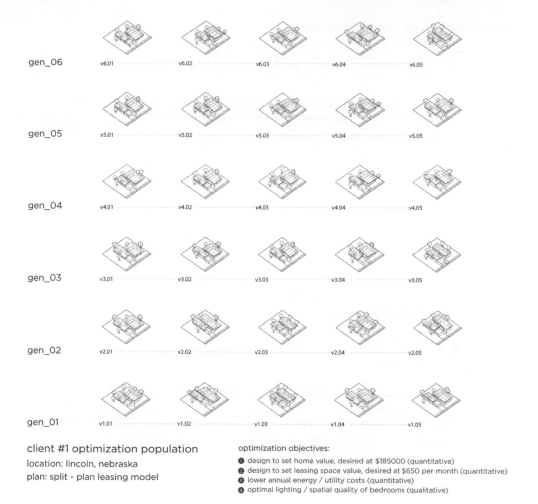

gen_06 v6.01 — v6.02 — v6.03 — v6.04 — v6.05

gen_05 v5.01 — v5.02 — v5.03 — v5.04 — v5.05

gen_04 v4.01 — v4.02 — v4.03 — v4.04 — v4.05

gen_03 v3.01 — v3.02 — v3.03 — v3.04 — v3.05

gen_02 v2.01 — v2.02 — v2.03 — v2.04 — v2.05

gen_01 v1.01 — v1.02 — v1.03 — v1.04 — v1.05

client #1 optimization population
location: lincoln, nebraska
plan: split - plan leasing model

optimization objectives:
❶ design to set home value, desired at $185000 (quantitative)
❷ design to set leasing space value, desired at $650 per month (quantitative)
❸ lower annual energy / utility costs (quantitative)
❹ optimal lighting / spatial quality of bedrooms (qualitative)

Figure 14.10 Generated design variations for the first optimization scenario are shown.

Figure 14.10 shows samples of generated residential designs for scenario one produced during the optimization process. Figure 14.11 shows optimization results and design samples from both scenarios compared against normative residential designs found in both geographical locations. The resulting optimized design solutions from both scenarios outperformed normative residential designs in relation to construction cost and energy efficiency. Specifically, the utility costs are almost half of what they are for common residential construction approaches. This can be attributed to the fact that these approaches do not typically optimize the building massing, position of windows, and position of vegetation relative to site orientation. This means most homes in a suburban development are not able to take advantage of passive strategies for heating and daylighting.

In addition to exploring the siting and massing of the building, the optimization process also took into account the materiality and construction methods of the houses in order to calculate the construction costs. Figure 14.12 shows a generated part list for one of the optimized designs along with the placement of hard and softscapes in the exterior spaces of the project. Exterior views of optimized examples from both scenarios are shown in Figures 14.13 and 14.14.

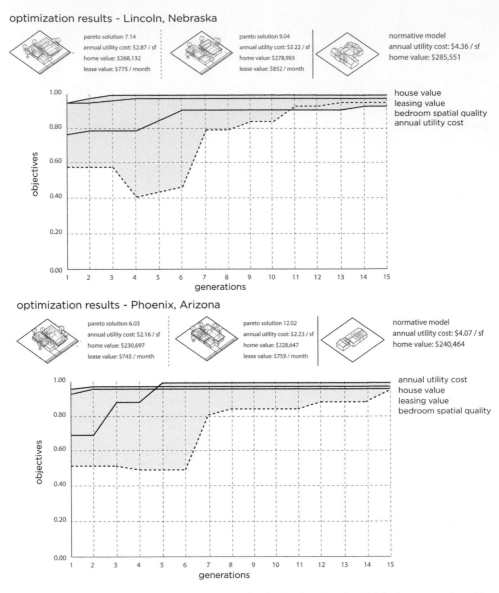

Figure 14.11 (Top) The final optimization results for the first residential design scenario in Lincoln, Nebraska are shown. (Bottom) The final optimization results for the second residential design scenario in Phoenix, Arizona are shown.

Explorative search and optimization at the detail scale

The second optimization task involves the optimization of an exterior solar shading facade system located in Kuwait city, Kuwait. For this task, the explorative and convergence capacities of Design Breeder are tested against competing MOO algorithms (e.g., NSGA-II and D-NSGA-II). For the optimization, a south facing 10′ × 10′ section of the facade is explored. The facade system is composed of computer numerically controlled (CNC) bent steel pipes connected into an assembly. Cool seawater is circulated in these pipes to collect condensation

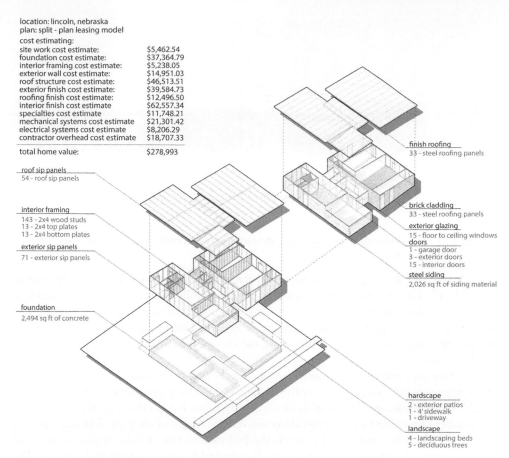

location: lincoln, nebraska
plan: split - plan leasing model

cost estimating:

site work cost estimate:	$5,462.54
foundation cost estimate:	$37,364.79
interior framing cost estimate:	$5,238.05
exterior wall cost estimate:	$14,951.03
roof structure cost estimate:	$46,513.51
exterior finish cost estimate:	$39,584.73
roofing finish cost estimate:	$12,496.50
interior finish cost estimate	$62,557.34
specialties cost estimate	$11,748.21
mechanical systems cost estimate	$21,301.42
electrical systems cost estimate	$8,206.29
contractor overhead cost estimate	$18,707.33
total home value:	$278,993

roof sip panels
54 - roof sip panels

interior framing
143 - 2x4 wood studs
13 - 2x4 top plates
13 - 2x4 bottom plates

exterior sip panels
71 - exterior sip panels

foundation
2,494 sq ft of concrete

finish roofing
33 - steel roofing panels

brick cladding
33 - steel roofing panels

exterior glazing
15 - floor to ceiling windows
doors
1 - garage door
3 - exterior doors
15 - interior doors

steel siding
2,026 sq ft of siding material

hardscape
2 - exterior patios
1 - 4' sidewalk
1 - driveway

landscape
4 - landscaping beds
5 - deciduous trees

Figure 14.12 A detailed view of the optimized design for the first residential design scenario in Lincoln, Nebraska.

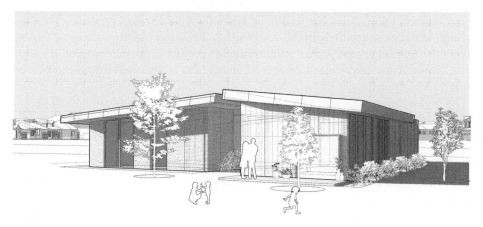

Figure 14.13 A rendering of an optimized design for the first design scenario in Lincoln, Nebraska.

Figure 14.14 A rendering of an optimized design for the second design scenario in Phoenix, Arizona.

from the air and also cool exterior spaces. A rendered image of the facade can be seen in Figure 14.15. The objectives for the optimization are as follows: maximizing the amount of condensation harvesting per year; maximizing useful daylighting levels on the interior of the facade; minimizing the temperature in the exterior balcony space between the facade and the building envelope; and minimizing the cost of the fabrication of the CNC folded facade modules.

The decision variables for the optimization process are based on the geometric parameters of the pipe assembly and are pictured in Figure 14.16. The pipe spacing and facade depth variables are continuous. The number of vertical divisions is a discrete variable that controls the number of possible fold locations along the vertical length of the pipe. The regional fold pattern is a discrete variable that controls the fold pattern that will be applied to the pipe given the vertical divisions. This variable is discrete and has four possible fold patterns. The global fold pattern variable has four discrete values and controls how regional patterns are combined to create a global pattern across a single facade panel.

Diva for Rhinoceros was used for daylight analysis. Autodesk's CFD was used for CFD and thermal analysis. The amount of condensation harvested was estimated following Bryant and Ahmed (2008). In order to speed-up the evaluation of designs, surrogate models for daylighting, thermal analysis, and fluid dynamics were developed by taking a number of sample simulations throughout the design space. These samples were then used to create polynomial regression models that could be used to predict performance values for illuminance, temperature, and airspeed. Images of some of the sample simulations can be seen in Figure 14.17.

The performance of Design Breeder is tested against static and dynamic versions of the NSGA-II algorithm for a number of dynamic test scenarios: test 1– the number of objectives change; test 2 – the number of decision variables change; test 3 – the objective function is time-dependent; and test 4—simultaneous changes in objective and decision variables. These tests are used to compare the ability of each algorithm to maintain diversity and provide efficient convergence when decision variables or objectives change during the optimization process.

The test results are summarized in Table 14.1. These results show that Design Breeder provides a better explorative capability under the majority of dynamic test scenarios than standard MOEAs equivalent in performance to static and dynamic versions of the NSGA-II

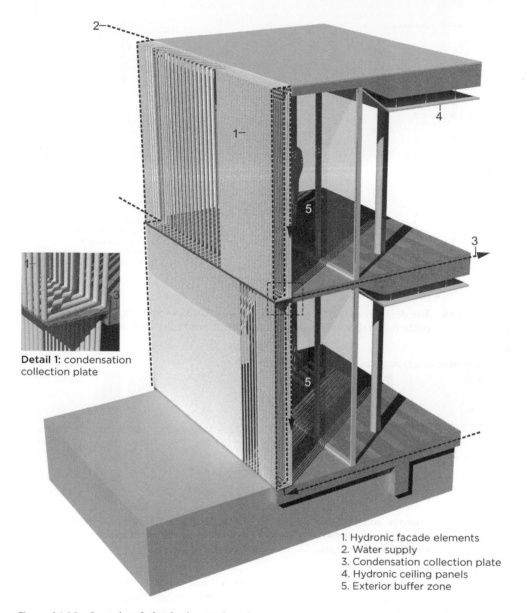

Detail 1: condensation collection plate

1. Hydronic facade elements
2. Water supply
3. Condensation collection plate
4. Hydronic ceiling panels
5. Exterior buffer zone

Figure 14.15 Sample of the hydronic facade system used for the dynamic multi-objective optimization tests.

algorithm. It performed less well, however, in the ability to converge to optimal solutions with the same pace of the competing algorithms. This trade-off is an important point of consideration for each discipline. In the engineering disciplines, optimization tools that perform well on convergence may be preferred over those that provide a better explorative capacity, but in the design disciplines, it is the reverse which is often more important (Benjamin, 2012). Figures 14.18 and 14.19 show diverse design examples found during the optimization process that demonstrate some of this explorative capacity.

David W. Newton

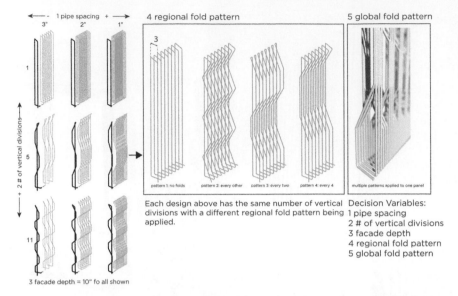

Figure 14.16   The decision variables for the optimization involve exploring the depth, the fold pattern, the spacing, and the regional pattern of the CNC assembly.

SUMMER: COLD PIPES IN HOTTER ENVIRONMENT

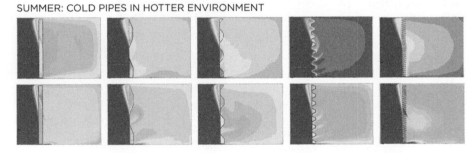

Figure 14.17   Thermal and CFD simulations for a select number of samples in the decision space. These samples were used to create a surrogate model to speed-up the evaluation of designs.

Table 14.1   Performance of Design Breeder against NSGA-II and D-NSGA-II for the four test cases: test 1—the number of objectives change; test 2—the number of decision variables change; test 3—the objective function is time-dependent; and test 4—simultaneous changes in objective and decision variables. Shows the percentage of times that DP-NSGA-II outperformed the other algorithms

	Against NSGA-II		Against D-NSGA-II	
	Novelty average (%)	Pareto rank average (%)	Novelty average (%)	Pareto rank average (%)
Test 1	80	67	65	49
Test 2	86	39	50	70
Test 3	47	49	35	31
Test 4	96	38	53	32

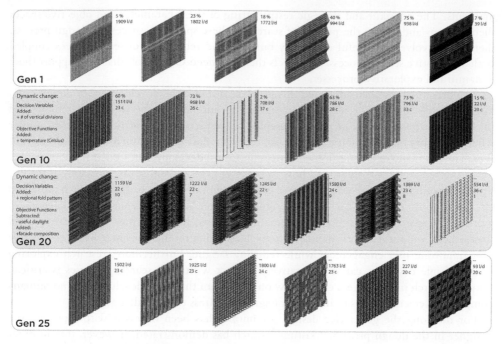

Figure 14.18 Samples of facade designs from test scenario 4 in which objectives and decision variables change simultaneously.

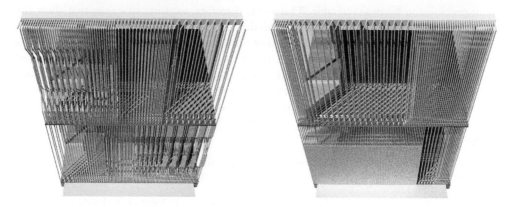

Figure 14.19 Sample designs generated during the optimization process.

Conclusions

The problem of architectural design is at its core a problem of search. It is a problem of first structuring a search space by defining the constraints and key parameters of a design problem and then exploring that space for an optimal set of design solutions. The design process can therefore be understood as a methodology that guides the structuring of this search space and also provides a way of efficiently navigating that space. In any real design process, the search space is never static, but is constantly being restructured on-the-fly to allow for more possibilities at certain moments in the design process and fewer possibilities at other moments. The constant and strategic restructuring of these parameter and objective spaces then informs and effects the process of searching these spaces. A successful design process, therefore, involves a graceful on-the-fly building and rebuilding of search spaces coupled with an adaptive search process. Architects therefore need CAD tools that can support these dynamic and explorative processes.

The presented research addressed this problem through the development of design optimization tools that support exploration and greater interactivity between the architect and the optimization process. The results presented suggest strategies researchers should consider when designing optimization tools that can accommodate exploration and interactivity, but there are still many open questions and areas for future development. One important avenue for future research revolves around how to better engage and enlist the capacities of the designer's imagination in the search process, while minimizing fatigue. The approach presented attempted to do this by allowing the designer a greater level of interactivity and agency in guiding the search process. Some of these interactions, however, may be more successful than others, and future work will need to explore which interactions may be most effective at maintaining user engagement while reducing fatigue. Furthermore, research exploring how multiple designers can collaboratively interact with such search processes is critical. Future research in these areas could draw on ideas from the game development and human-computer interaction fields to inform strategies to address these challenges.

For too long the generative design community has been obsessed with replacing the designer in the design process. Existing research has demonstrated, however, that in order to solve complex optimization problems, computational optimization processes must have a human in the loop to guide the search process. It is the intelligence that emerges from the collaboration between the human mind and a computational process, which allows these difficult problems to become tractable. This work, therefore, explores strategies that allow this collaboration to unfold. It represents a step in the direction toward the development of computational optimization processes that augment the human imagination instead of attempting to replace it. It is a call for a greater emphasis on the creation of computational design tools that foster a collaborative intelligence that is the result of the mixing of multiple thinking styles (e.g., linear and nonlinear; pragmatic and poetic; human and computer; etc.). It is a step toward generative design tools that are more inclusive, pluralistic, and explorative in nature.

References

Ashour, Y., & Kolarevic, B. (2015). *Optimizing creatively in multi-objective optimization*. Paper presented at the Proceedings of the Symposium on Simulation for Architecture & Urban Design, Alexandria, Virginia, 128–135.

Azzouz, R., Bechikh, S., & Said, L. B. (2017a). A dynamic multi-objective evolutionary algorithm using a change severity-based adaptive population management strategy. *Soft Computing*, 21(4), 885–906. DOI: 10.1007/s00500-015-1820-4

Azzouz, R., Bechikh, S., & Said, L. B. (2017b). Dynamic multi-objective optimization using evolutionary algorithms: A survey. In: S. Bechikh, R. Datta, & A. Gupta (eds.), *Recent Advances in Evolutionary Multi-Objective Optimization* (pp. 31–70). Springer, Cham. DOI: 10.1007/978-3-319-42978-6_2

Bechikh, S., Datta, R., & Gupta, A. (eds.). (2016). *Recent Advances in Evolutionary Multi-Objective Optimization* (Vol. 20). Springer, Cham. DOI: 10.1007/978-3-319-42978-6

Bechikh, S., Elarbi, M., & Said, L. B. (2017). Many-objective optimization using evolutionary algorithms. In: S. Bechikh, R. Datta, & A. Gupta (eds.), *A Survey Recent Advances in Evolutionary Multi-Objective Optimization* (pp. 105–137). Springer, Cham. DOI: 10.1145/2792984

Bechikh, S., Kessentini, M., Said, L. B., & Ghédira, K. (2015). Chapter four-preference incorporation in evolutionary multiobjective optimization: A survey of the state-of-the-art. *Advances in Computers*, 98, 141–207. DOI: 10.1016/bs.adcom.2015.03.001

Bechikh, S., Said, L. B., & Ghédira, K. (2011). *Negotiating decision makers' reference points for group preference-based Evolutionary Multi-objective Optimization*. Paper presented at the Hybrid Intelligent Systems (HIS), 2011 11th International Conference on, Melacca, Malaysia. DOI: 10.1109/HIS.2011.6122135

Benjamin, D. (2012). Beyond efficiency. In: S. Marble (ed.), *Digital Workflows in Architecture* (pp. 14–25). Basel: Birkhäuser.

Bryant, J. A.; Ahmed, T. (2008). *Condensate water collection for an institutional building in Doha, Qatar: An opportunity for water sustainability*. Energy Systems Laboratory (http://esl.tamu.edu). Available electronically from http: /hdl.handle.net/1969.1/90780.

Caldas, L. (2008). Generation of energy-efficient architecture solutions applying GENE_ARCH: An evolution-based generative design system. *Advanced Engineering Informatics*, 22(1), 59–70. DOI: 10.1016/j.aei.2007.08.012

Censor, Y. (1977). Pareto optimality in multiobjective problems. *Applied Mathematics and Optimization*, 4(1), 41–59. DOI: 10.1007/BF01442131

Chen, R. K. Li and X. Yao (2018). Dynamic multiobjectives optimization with a changing number of objectives. *IEEE Transactions on Evolutionary Computation*, 22(1), 157–171. DOI: 10.1109/TEVC.2017.2669638.

J. R. Christman and B. G. Woolley. (2015). Augmenting Interactive Evolution with Multi-objective Optimization. *2015 IEEE 14th International Conference on Machine Learning and Applications (ICMLA)* (pp. 973–980), Miami, FL. DOI: 10.1109/ICMLA.2015.139.

Coello, C. A. C., Van Veldhuizen, D. A., & Lamont, G. B. (2002). *Evolutionary algorithms for solving multi-objective problems* (Vol. 242), Springer, Boston, MA. DOI: 10.1007/978-1-4757-5184-0

Deb, K., & Jain, H. (2014). *An Evolutionary Many-Objective Optimization Algorithm Using Reference-Point-Based Nondominated Sorting Approach, Part I: Solving Problems With Box Constraints*. In IEEE Transactions on Evolutionary Computation (Vol. 18, No. 4, pp. 577–601). DOI: 10.1109/TEVC.2013.2281535

Deb, K., & Kumar, A. (2007). *Interactive evolutionary multi-objective optimization and decision-making using reference direction method*. In Proceedings of the 9th annual conference on Genetic and evolutionary computation (GECCO '07). Association for Computing Machinery, New York, NY, USA, 781–788. DOI: 10.1145/1276958.1277116

Deb, K., Pratap, A., Agarwal, S., & Meyarivan, T. (2002). A fast and elitist multiobjective genetic algorithm: NSGA-II. *IEEE Transactions on Evolutionary Computation*, 6(2), 182–197. DOI: 10.1109/4235.996017.

Deb, K., Rao N. U.B., Karthik S. (2007) Dynamic multi-objective optimization and decision-making using modified NSGA-II: A case study on hydro-thermal power scheduling. In: S. Obayashi, K. Deb, C. Poloni, T. Hiroyasu, & T. Murata (eds.), *Evolutionary Multi-Criterion Optimization*. EMO 2007. Lecture Notes in Computer Science, vol. 4403. Springer, Berlin, Heidelberg. DOI: 10.1007/978-3-540-70928-2_60

Goldberg, D. E. (1987). Simple genetic algorithms and the minimal, deceptive problem. *Genetic Algorithms and Simulated Annealing*, 74, 88.

Hämäläinen, R. P., & Mäntysaari, J. (2002). Dynamic multi-objective heating optimization. *European Journal of Operational Research*, 142(1), 1–15. DOI: 10.1016/S0377-2217(01)00282-X

Hatzakis, I., & Wallace, D. (2006). *Dynamic multi-objective optimization with evolutionary algorithms: A forward-looking approach*. In Proceedings of the 8th annual conference on Genetic and evolutionary computation (GECCO '06). Association for Computing Machinery, New York, NY, USA, 1201–1208. DOI: 10.1145/1143997.1144187

Hou, D., Liu, G., Zhang, Q., Wang, L., & Dang, R. (2017). Integrated building envelope design process combining parametric modelling and multi-objective optimization. *Transactions of Tianjin University*, 23(2), 138–146. DOI: 10.1007/s12209-016-0022-1

Kim, H.-S., & Cho, S.-B. (2000). Application of interactive genetic algorithm to fashion design. *Engineering Applications of Artificial Intelligence*, 13(6), 635–644. DOI: 10.1016/S0952-1976(00)00045-2

Li, K., Deb, K., & Yao, X. (2017). Integration of preferences in decomposition multi-objective optimization. *IEEE Transactions on Cybernetics*, 48(12), 3359–3370. DOI: 10.1109/TCYB.2018.2859363.

Marques, V. M., Reis, C., & Machado, J. T. (2010). *Interactive evolutionary computation in music*. In 2010 IEEE International Conference on Systems, Man and Cybernetics, Istanbul, pp. 3501–3507. DOI: 10.1109/ICSMC.2010.5642417.

Mueller, C., & Ochsendorf, J. (2011). *An interactive evolutionary framework for structural design*. In 7th International Seminar of the Structural Morphology Group (SMG), IASSWorkingGroup15 (pp. 1–6), London, UK.

Mueller, C. T., & Ochsendorf, J. A. (2015). Combining structural performance and designer preferences in evolutionary design space exploration. *Automation in Construction*, 52, 70–82. DOI:10.1016/j.autcon.2015.02.011

Reeh, C. (2019). *Generative suburban frameworks: Emerging architect-guided optimization workflows within suburban mass production*. (MArch), University of Nebraska-Lincoln, https://digitalcommons.unl.edu/marchthesis/2/.

Sims, K. (1992). *Interactive evolution of dynamical systems*. In Toward a Practice of Autonomous Systems: Proceedings of the First European Conference on Artificial Life (pp. 171–178), Paris, France.

Takagi, H. (2001). Interactive evolutionary computation: Fusion of the capabilities of EC optimization and human evaluation. *Proceedings of the IEEE*, 89(9), 1275–1296. DOI: 10.1109/5.949485

Turrin, M., von Buelow, P., Kilian, A., & Stouffs, R. (2012). Performative skins for passive climatic comfort. *Automation in Construction*, 22, 36–50. DOI: 10.1016/j.autcon.2011.08.001

Turrin, M., von Buelow, P., & Stouffs, R. (2011). Design explorations of performance driven geometry in architectural design using parametric modeling and genetic algorithms. *Advanced Engineering Informatics*, 25(4), 656–675. DOI: 10.1016/j.aei.2011.07.009

Vierlinger, R., & Bollinger, K. (2014). *Accommodating change in parametric design*. Paper presented at the Proceedings ACADIA: Association for Computer Aided Design in Architecture – Computational Ecologies: Design in the Anthropocene, Los Angeles, CA. DOI: 10.13140/RG.2.1.2827.5922

Von Buelow, P. (2012). ParaGen: Performative exploration of generative systems. *Journal of the International Association for Shell and Spatial Structures*, 53(4), 271–284.

Wahle, J., Annen, O., Schuster, C., Neubert, L., & Schreckenberg, M. (2001). A dynamic route guidance system based on real traffic data. *European Journal of Operational Research*, 131(2), 302–308. DOI: 10.1016/S0377-2217(00)00130-2

Zhang, Q., & Li, H. (2007). MOEA/D: A multiobjective evolutionary algorithm based on decomposition. *IEEE Transactions on Evolutionary Computation*, 11(6), 712–731. DOI: 10.1109/TEVC.2007.892759.

15
Synergizing smart building technologies with data analytics

Andrzej Zarzycki

As interconnected smart devices increasingly augment people's daily lives, the built environment—the human-made surroundings for people's lives, including buildings, green spaces, and infrastructure—remains relatively isolated from the pace and the intensity of this technological progress. The built environment is still heavily grounded in the mindset of industrialization, with a mechanical frame of reference, and without the benefits of modern sciences and information technologies. While smart technologies are increasingly adopted in cities and buildings (Achten, 2015; Decker, 2017; Zarzycki, 2016), there is still no comprehensive reconceptualization of what the built environment could and should be—rethinking of materiality, systems, and intellectual frameworks. Klaus Schwab points that the fourth industrial revolution—a concept introduced in 2012, characterized by the amplification of the technological progress by fusing the physical, biological, and digital—is a disruption that affects all aspects of our daily lives (Davis, 2016). This fusion is perhaps the best characterization of the future built environment. Schwab argues convincingly that "The question is not am I going to be disrupted but when is the disruption coming, what form will it take and how will it affect me and my organisation?" While these words may sound futuristic, they signal incoming changes to the way the built environment is constructed and used.

Some of these changes manifest themselves through embedded and interconnected devices facilitating new responsive buildings with adaptive assemblies and user-aware behaviors. These smart and autonomous environments are enhanced by the Internet of Things (IoT), a network of interconnected computing devices incorporating embedded systems, real-time analytics, and machine learning. Such environments engage users in an interactive dialogue and are critical for sustainable practices where buildings respond to environmental factors and monitor their own performance (Akkaya et al., 2015; Coen, 1998). Intelligent systems integrate information technologies with distributed sensing and actuating, raise users' expectations toward building behaviors, and increasingly address resiliency and zero-energy needs (Gorbil, Filippoupolitis & Gelenbe, 2011; Klippel, Freksa & Winter, 2006; Kobes, Helsloot, De Vries & Post, 2010). They also start to function as active co-participants within the built environment, facilitating occupants' comfort, safety, and well-being (Corna, Fontana, Nacci & Sciuto, 2015; Li, Calis & Becerik-Gerber, 2012; Schwartz, 2013). These emerging directions associated with information technologies and IoT frameworks not only point to new opportunities for the built environment but also set new research and design agendas for architects and construction professionals (Wurzer et al., 2011).

These new opportunities are associated with data collection and analysis as well as embedded intelligence that drives smart buildings. In the current state, many of the smart systems, devices, and appliances function as separate units. While they perform intended tasks well, these systems could also be scaled up and synergized to allow for creating new qualitative data sets and greater understanding of how buildings perform, and occupants behave.

Automated sliding doors in outside vestibules are a good example to illustrate this synergy or a "surplus value" associated with collection and analysis of data coming from this particular unit. While intended to facilitate building access, automated doors could also function as a counting sensor for the occupant movements and loads. This would require a small amount of intelligence added to the automated unit, with the ability to collect and process data as well as to distinguish between groups and individual. However, if the doors were integrated with other intelligent systems, generated data could enhance building operations and safety of its occupants. Knowing the number of people in a building or a space at any given time can facilitate a wide range of building functions and operations. This approach is also scalable and transferable to other similar situations. In the case of the auditorium doors, a counting ability could guard against maximum occupancy code violations or simply provide usage data for more efficient facility operations, such as adjustments to air exchanges or cooling loads due to an increased occupancy, before carbon dioxide (CO_2) or temperature sensors would register this change.

This chapter discusses the conceptual underpinnings of intelligence in buildings and construction, with a special focus on the opportunities associated with amplifying current smart technologies through increased interconnectivity with data collection and analysis. It points to the need for a close integration between smart devices, with the data their sensors produce, and artificial intelligence (AI) tools. Such integration could effectively synergize individual players into coherent and unified "conscious" environments: buildings that are aware of their performance and occupants. Furthermore, a number of case studies demonstrate how individual building components and assemblies can manifest new functional qualities once interconnected into a network of data-sharing agents. They also show how this qualitative and functional leap can be achieved with low-level building sensing and automation technologies while maintaining effective migration paths toward more intelligent buildings.

Smart building and device characteristics

While smart devices and assemblies can function autonomously when performing complex user tracking or performance optimizations, they do not necessarily need to exhibit the level of intelligence associated with AI algorithms. The term "smart device" is a rather inclusive category of objects, from those performing basic automation tasks, such as traditional (even mechanical) sensor-based thermostats or automated façade systems, to sophisticated predictive devices, such as the Nest thermostat utilizing supervised machine learning. There is little known about specific learning approaches in these commercial products. However, a number of researchers developed similar indoor temperature controlling systems utilizing a wide range of machine learning algorithms, such as a Bayesian-learning with a reinforcement-learning (Q-learning) method (Barrett & Linder, 2015) and the artificial neural network (ANN) (Kazarian et al., 2017).

The discussion and cited literature point to AI and machine learning playing a critical future role in developing high-level smart environments, particularly those utilizing diverse data sources and interfacing with complex human activities.

The IoT and smart building concepts continue to be a broad and semi-defined territory. Several classification approaches are useful when discussing smart device and smart building frameworks, particularly in the context of framing future developments. Independently of their level of autonomy and "smartness," smart objects (buildings, building components, and devices) commonly exhibit the following three typologies or design dimensions proposed by Kortuem et al. (2009):

> *Awareness* is the ability to understand—sense, interpret, and react to—events and human activities occurring in the physical world.
> *Representation* refers to a smart object's application and programming model—in particular, programming abstractions.
> *Interaction* signals the object's ability to communicate with the user in terms of control, input, output, and feedback.

The *awareness* of smart systems is often achieved through a conditional sequence of sensing (cause), logical processing of data (evaluation), and actuation (effect), diagrammed in Figure 15.1. While the Kortuem et al. classification is rather general, Das and Cook (2005) define smart environment with more granular detail and hierarchical structure, consisting of five layers corresponding to an increased smart object's intelligence. This classification not only accounts for real-time interactions between devices and users but also identifies the autonomy and decision-making and important features:

1   *Remote control of devices*: remote and automatic control of devices.
2   *Device communication*: devices' communication, data sharing, and information retrieval from outside sources over the internet or wireless infrastructure.
3   *Sensory information acquisition/dissemination*: information sharing by individual sensors and low-level decision-making.
4   *Enhanced services by intelligent devices*: includes location and context awareness.
5   *Predictive and decision-making capabilities*: full automation and adaptation that rely on the AI or information acquisition allowing the software to improve its performance.

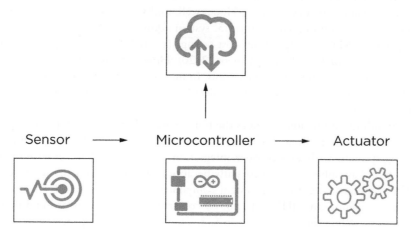

Figure 15.1   Smart objects combine sensing, data processing, and actuation abilities. The connectivity with other devices creates an opportunity for data sharing and interactions with artificial intelligence algorithms.

As with the classification by Kortuem et al., any of Das and Cook's categories could be achieved by individual smart devices or collectively by a group of interacting smart units when sharing and processing acquired data. Currently, only a small number of consumer-grade smart technologies demonstrate the predictive and decision-making capabilities postulated in point 5 above. These include the Nest thermostat with supervised learning and the Google Vision AIY kit utilizing neural networks. However, the direction of future developments points decidedly to the role of machine learning and AI in shaping smart building environments.

Building automation

The introduction of building environmental control systems gave an impulse for the development of early automation controls for indoor air quality (IAQ), temperature, and lighting levels. Though sometimes rudimentary, these controls not only provided increased comfort for living but also improved energy efficiency and reduced the environmental impact of buildings (Guillemin & Morel, 2001). However, automated controls were structured around a central, often isolated, control dashboard with limited sensing locations (e.g., thermostat), each delivering a single data point for a wide number of spatial conditions. This shows the need for more localized and fine-tuned approach to building controls that goes beyond the size of a single room into the scale of individual building components.

A broader building automation platform is needed to scale up data acquisition from sensors and to use these data for predictive scenarios and decision-making. Currently, building automation is implemented as centralized automatic controls for lighting, heating, and cooling, as well as other building systems including fire, security, and occupant safety. These software platforms are called a building automation system (BAS) and a building management system (BMS). The goals of building automation include improved efficient operation of building systems, such as reduction in operating costs and energy use as well as increased occupant comfort throughout the life cycle of the building. The majority of currently constructed buildings include BAS/BMS, and many older buildings are retrofitted with these systems. These systems include hardware and software frameworks that integrate controls for all or most building systems within a unified interface (dashboard). Such interfaces are offered by companies such as Siemens, Honeywell, and Cisco that are already involved in the manufacture of building environmental system equipment. These systems work effectively, capable of delivering significant cost savings (around 20%) as compared with buildings unequipped with BAS/BMS (Siemens, 2020). However, they usually do not include sophisticated autonomy and intelligence tools. In most cases, they follow a set of predefined explicit rules rather than respond to historical and real-time data for building occupancy and assembly conditions.

While building automation is seen as the framework behind intelligent buildings, it currently is limited to controlling mechanized and electric/electronic devices, such as cooling and heating systems, without a broader integration of sensors and actuators into building components and assemblies. This is partially because BMS/BAS platforms are developed by companies manufacturing building system components and their controls (heating, ventilating, and air conditioning [HVAC]), not by construction companies or building component fabricators. While these platforms do facilitate performance improvements of installed equipment, this does not address overall building operations or user experience.

This points to the need for a broader transformation of the building industry and buildings themselves to integrate technologies, possibly open-source, connecting embedded systems in building assemblies with machine learning tools. Windows, doors, floors, ceilings, and wall panels all could function as part of the building sensing interface interacting with users, collecting environmental inputs, and actuating desired spatial configurations. This would open the smart device ecosystem to machine learning.

A useful analogy to this approach is the European smart city initiative—SmartSantander—where the data from more than 12,000 sensors distributed throughout the city can be freely accessed. The general public is encouraged to use this open-source platform to develop the next level of tools and apps (UCityLabAdmin, 2019). Examples of such uses include a study that correlated traffic patterns with respect to air temperature (Jara, Genoud & Bocchi, 2014) and the use of machine learning and deep learning for parking availability predictions (Awan et al., 2020). While these examples demonstrate the applicability of machine learning techniques in the context of smart cities, a similar approach could be applied to smart buildings.

Internet of things and building automation

Mark Weiser proposes in the *Scientific American* article "The Computer for the Twenty-First Century" (Weiser, 1991), "When almost every object either contains a computer or can have a tab attached to it, obtaining information will be trivial." However, this statement does not consider the impediments coming from the overabundance of information and the limited ability to analyze and act on it. Dealing with large data sets requires robust communication and management systems. In the building context, the IoT can facilitate smart and embedded device communication, sensing, actuation, and interactions with the outside environment. Additionally, smart systems incorporate decision-making abilities by analyzing previously gathered data in a predictive or adaptive manner that often employs AI algorithms. BAS/BMS platforms benefit from collected building data. However, the IoT framework provides opportunities for greater resiliency and interoperability of the entire system, with data feeds to individual subcomponents—devices and assemblies—as compared to current BASs/BMSs.

While current BAS/BMS platforms follow preprogrammed sets of rules, the expectation is that the underlying reasoning (algorithm) for smart systems would evolve over time based on environmental and user feedback. This feedback could not only enhance smart building operations but also be shared with manufacturers, contractors, and architects. Data shared with clients (BAS/BMS) or interested third parties could be further combined with AI techniques for predictive decision-making regarding building occupancy and usage patterns (Zarzycki, 2018). Another direction for the enhanced data sharing involves connecting building automation and IoT with building information modeling (BIM) to improve operational and construction efficiencies (Marble, 2018; Shelden, 2018; Tang et al., 2019).

Enhanced living

Smart technologies not only address building performance and operations (Peña, Meek & Davis, 2017) but also increasingly focus on human interactions by tracking building occupants (Li, Calis & Becerik-Gerber, 2012) and considering their individual preferences. Through their user-centric focus, adaptable and embedded environments promote more inclusive and diverse groups of occupants by reducing physical accessibility barriers and facilitating independent living (Delnevo, Monti, Foschini & Santonastasi, 2018; Domingo, 2012). People with limited mobility or with visual impairments can greatly benefit from autonomous and smart buildings. For example, ambient assisted living (AAL) relies on smart technologies to support independent living for seniors in situations that would otherwise require traditional assisted living arrangements. These technologies can monitor seniors' activities to provide early warning signs and response to bodily activities. They can also facilitate interactions within the built environment, extend sensory perceptions, and simplify performance of daily tasks. As an area of early adoption for smart technologies and machine learning, AAL offers opportunities for a significant payback due to a natural fit between the technologies' capabilities and users' needs.

Monitoring and detection of daily activities in the context of AAL has been studied by a number of researchers. Chernbumroong et al. (2013) developed methods for daily activity recognition with a high classification rate exceeding 90% for elderly users utilizing a non-stigmatizing and nonintrusive (nonvisual) wrist sensor-based device. The study identified and tracked nine distinct activities, including eating with utensils, brushing teeth, dressing, walking, sleeping, watching TV, and ascending and descending stairs. In another study, Amoretti et al. (2013) adopted machine learning using classifiers based on a Bayesian network approach (Weka library) for sensor data synthesis, activity monitoring, and context reasoning. Their user activity monitoring system enabled machine learning to train for human posture detection, posture classification, and association of these postures with the activities being performed.

The above studies demonstrate how data generated by sensors and IoT devices can benefit from machine learning and AI techniques by facilitating an in-depth understanding of human activities. These examples indicate broader opportunities for using sensing and wireless communication to increase the built environment's responsiveness to its occupants. These studies also demonstrate strong benefits of AI tools when working with complex tasks and diverse user groups, particularly those who are physically disadvantaged. Smart technologies can facilitate the next level of accommodations toward people with disabilities and address their needs more directly and individually than is currently done through the Americans with Disabilities Act (ADA). The ADA, providing design guidelines for the static environment, relies on the statistical models of an average person and ergonomic needs associated with particular ailments. On the other hand, smart environments—sensing and adaptive— provide an opportunity to tailor spatial and accessibility requirements to individual users.

The future take on the ADA will require not only hardware solutions, both static and adaptive (e.g. ramps, stairs, areas of refuge, and adjustable sinks), but also embedded solutions (intelligence) where buildings are aware of their occupants and can effectively help them to use, navigate, access, and safely exit spaces (Nagy, Villaggi, Stoddart & Benjamin, 2017; Schwartz & Das, 2019; Simondetti & Birch, 2017). To achieve this, smart environments— building, assemblies, and appliances—should not only adapt in real time to user needs but also power AI frameworks to provide a better understanding of user needs and behavior. By doing so, they can also help to refine future buildings standards and regulations, such as the ADA.

Emerging synergies

A transition from the traditional and mechanical paradigm to electronic and digital presents us with new opportunities—synergies emerging from interconnectivity and a wide range of sensory inputs. It also puzzles us, not knowing how to make that step, how one technology can naturally transition into a new one in a natural, evolutionary way.

When replacing traditional tungsten with the LED light bulb, we not only save energy and have greater control of the light rendition but also open ourselves to new synergies. An LED light bulb no longer has the simplicity of the tungsten incandescent bulb and requires

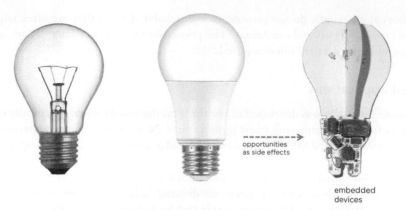

opportunities
as side effects

embedded
devices

Figure 15.2   The evolution of a light bulb from incandescent to the LED opens new opportunities for embedded devices. An introduction of the circuit boards packed with electronic components allows for additional sensors, actuators, and wireless communication.

a number of additional electronic components to operate (Figure 15.2). While this adds additional cost to the LED light bulb, the investment in the electronic board makes it easy to scale it up and add additional sensing and actuation capacities. This has resulted in various functional variations of a light bulb that emerged recently. From light bulbs controlled with embedded motion or light sensors to those with built-in Bluetooth speakers, these variations exemplify the concept that once even a simple device such as a light bulb gets embedded with a little electronics sensing, actuation, and wireless communication, its form and function open to a wide range of opportunities.

This story of the light bulb is not unique. It parallels similar evolutions of phones, and soon cars and buildings. However, this example points to synergistic opportunities associated with embedded technologies—sensor, actuation, and wireless communication. What is missing from these examples is the next step in integration of digital technologies— intelligence. While the embedded components expand the functionality of the original device or appliance and make them 'smart,' they still follow mechanical indiscriminate logic. While they provide an increased performance, often with reduced environmental impact, they cannot address individualized human needs. To realize a broader and more tailored impact, these devices need to be networked and to output data that can be further analyzed and synthesized.

A significant amount of research into smart environments, such as studies associated with AAL, relies on custom-developed sensing devices such as wearable electronics. However, another strategy utilizes existing appliances and sensor technologies. A number of studies use CO_2 sensors for measuring building occupancy (Pedersen, Nielsen & Petersen, 2017; Zuraimi et al., 2017). This is an example of synergies discussed earlier, when data acquired for one reason can be repurposed for another arena. CO_2 sensors are increasingly used on the smart and high-performance buildings with reduced HVAC loads that rely on natural ventilation, particularly associated with doors and operable windows (Peña, Meek & Davis, 2017). With tight building envelopes and reduced air exchanges, the accumulation of CO_2 could significantly impact the IAQ and the well-being of occupants. The doubling up on the use of sensors, such as using CO_2 for indicating IAQ or measuring occupancy loads, or using multiple sensors to capture complex conditions and human activities (Amoretti et al., 2013), brings to the forefront the need for intelligent data analysis—machine learning and other AI tools. Sensors alone usually do not provide enough reliable data, as they are often triggered by a broad range of inputs and conditions. The postsensing filtration, triangulation, and interpretation of sensor data are often required.

Extended applications

The following case study was developed to test the ideas discussed earlier, specifically emerging synergies from interconnected smart light fixtures. Noninvasive motion detection with the use of passive infrared (PIR) and microwave radar sensors is a common approach to lighting controls and energy savings in the built environment. It provides a high level of reliability with low initial cost and an easy integration with the existing fixtures. While the initial application of this technology was in on-demand lighting controls, mostly for safety and security reasons, they quickly became a standard for lighting controls in spaces with low or infrequent use. Currently, many office and residential spaces use them as the main lighting control approach. These motion sensors can be directly integrated with light fixtures, providing highly localized controls, or can be placed separately to control a group of fixtures. In the majority of current applications, motion-based lighting controls work autonomously and independent of each other, without data collections or sharing. Fixtures do not interface among each other, nor with a building automation system, since their primary function does not require a networked connection. However, this lack of interconnectivity can be seen as a missed opportunity if one considers possible synergies with other systems. If the wireless networking were implemented, the data could be collected and analyzed, which could facilitate qualitatively new applications.

Counting occupancy during emergencies

The idea behind this project was to channel unutilized sensor data from light controls to develop an occupancy load and space utilization framework that could be used not only for day-to-day facility management operations but also for emergencies. The knowledge of the state of occupancy—intensity and distribution—just before an emergency occurred (e.g., a fire or an earthquake) would allow more direct rescue operations. This sensor-derived knowledge could further facilitate egress by directing evacuees to fire-separated zones. Machine learning could also help predict possible exit paths utilizing sensor data on how individual users entered the building. Life safety research demonstrates that in case of emergencies, most people do not travel to the closest exit, but instead escape via familiar routes or try to retrace their original arrival sequence (Kobes et al., 2010). In residential and workplace building types, occupants may be familiar with floor layouts and have a good understanding of evacuation routes reinforced by periodic fire drills. By contrast, in buildings serving a large number of frequently changing occupants, such as medical facilities, stopping malls, or transportation hubs, users do not have preexisting knowledge of the building and its egress routes. Additionally, not all occupants are able to leave the building on their own during emergencies, since they would have to rely on elevators. The ability to correlate occupants' current location with their arrival route and to understand whether they were able to safely exit or reach an area of refuge could provide useful information to first responders. From the smart building perspective, the occupants' lack of the building layout and egress knowledge could be supplemented with the building's awareness of its occupants and the ability to guide them to a safe exit.

The project prototype used a web-based interface for occupancy visualization (Figure 15.3). Depending on the filter settings, one could see the most recent occupancy state

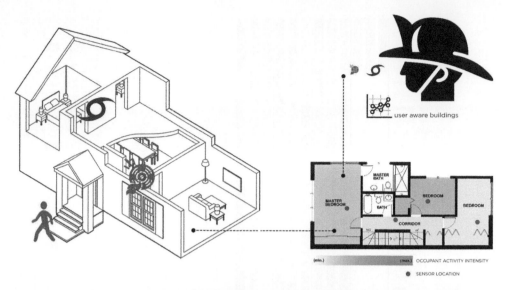

Figure 15.3 Building occupancy visualization in support of first responders. Tracking building occupants not only facilitates an understanding of the space utilizations but also can help first responders in directing their efforts during emergencies. This provides opportunities for data analytics and machine learning tools to enhance building services and occupant well-being.

or an occupancy average over a given period of time for each space. While the technological setup is rather simple, the ability to collect and analyze data provides new opportunities, such as life safety and first responder support, beyond the original intent of energy efficiency and lighting controls.

Window operation tracking

Similarly, to the light controls in the previous case study, security controls on doors and operable windows could be synergized to enable new understanding of building operations. The second project utilized magnetic switches, commonly used for monitoring doors, windows, and cabinetry to study user overrides of indoor air/climate controls. In the traditional HVAC approach, operable windows were seen as unnecessary feature, since their use interferes with centrally controlled air conditioning and ventilation. By contrast, many contemporary high-performance buildings rely on operable windows to provide required air exchanges and air conditioning while reducing the building's heating and cooling loads (Peña, Meek & Davis, 2017). However, the use of operable windows is not meant to eliminate the building's mechanical systems but rather to reduce the reliance on them. If not used properly, operable windows can negatively impact overall building performance. This is why window controls with user overrides need to be closely monitored to strike a balance between energy performance, user comfort, and the user's need to feel that they are in the control of their environment.

The study looked at the frequency with which operable windows are opened and closed by building occupants and the spatial distribution of these activities. It correlated these events with the temperature measurements inside and outside the building to look for patterns that would explain users' behavior (Figure 15.4). Since the space was semipublic (an architectural

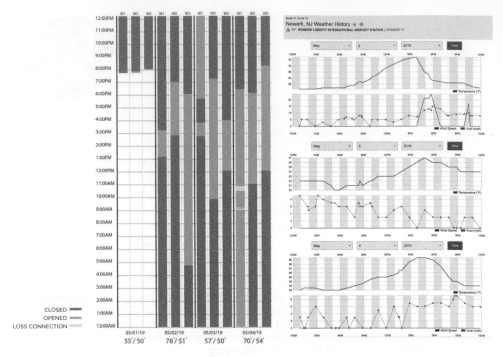

Figure 15.4 Opening and closure for three windows correlated to outdoor temperature. Tracking user actions against building environmental controls allows for an understanding of miscalibrations and can server as the postoccupancy evaluation. The study was developed by Evelin Taipe, Andrew Rivera, and Andrzej Zarzycki. The outside weather data was collected from Weather Underground repository (www.wunderground.com).

studio space shared by about 25–35 students), there was a certain inertia in students' responses to window operations. In most cases, users acted when the response was necessitated by one of the environmental factors. However, it was difficult to understand to what extent occupants used window controls to modify the quality of indoor air and to what extent these were habitual actions unrelated to the building's indoor environment. Sensors showed windows being opened during the middle of the day and closed from the evening till the following morning with the exception of one event. With the outside temperatures ranging from low 50's at night to the mid-70's during the day the window opening pattern would be consistent with maintaining a low temperature gradient between outside temperature and indoor set at around 70°–72° F. One event shows a window being left open for the entire night. Unfortunately, this study did not measure the occupancy levels, so it was difficult to see if there are other correlations. Studies like this one point to synergies between individual smart building monitoring and environmental control systems for real-time decision-making. They can also be used for qualitative postoccupancy evaluation (POE) of buildings, with findings informing future equipment commissioning and providing feedback to architecture, engineering, and construction teams (Council, 2002; Hardin, 2018; Hiromoto, 2015). An important part if this feedback loop involves sensor data set and machine learning models. For the building energy consumption, ANNs and support vector machines (SVMs) are the most commonly used machine learning methods (Zhao & Magoulès, 2012). For indoor thermal comfort predictions, a number of research projects use autoregressive models with exogenous inputs

(ARX), ARMAX and non-linear artificial neural network (ANN) models (Patil, Tantau & Salokhe, 2008; Thomas & Soleimani-Mohseni, 2007) and a back propagation neural network (BPNN) based on principal component analysis (PCA) (He & Ma, 2010).

Postoccupancy evaluation in smart buildings

When commissioning a building, initial equipment and system configurations—such as the calibration of user overrides in operable windows—are based on past, often uncodified, experiences. While these assumptions were informed by past projects, a new location, program type, or occupants often result in the need for a slight variation from the default configuration. An introduction of intelligence and machine learning allows for adaptive adjustment of the smart building's operational parameters to meet the evolving needs of its occupants—as habits change, building operations change. These adjustments could complement, or perhaps replace, traditional POE that is meant to provide validation for ordinal design and reinforce research feedback (knowledge loops) advocated by Thomas Fisher (2017) as part of architectural practice. Smart buildings, assemblies, and systems interfaced with AI and machine learning cannot only increase the fit between buildings and their occupants but also feedback this information to clients, architects, and contractors to inform their decision-making. This is evident in the WeWork's pioneering use of machine learning to evaluate its real estate holdings. The company deploys artificial neural networks to evaluate meeting room usage (Bailey, Phelan, Cosgrove, & Davis, 2018; Phelan, Davis & Anderson, 2017) and SVMs (scikit-learn toolkit) to predict marketability of offices (Fisher, 2017).

Conclusions

Smart buildings and autonomous spaces are at the forefront of the current architectural and design discourse (Park, 2017; Zarzycki & Decker, 2019). Future adaptive architecture will integrate AI with information technologies and distributed sensing to address emerging environmental and human needs. AI will also redefine the role autonomous spaces play as active co-participants in the built environment.

At the same time, smart environments are quickly becoming our social, cultural, and well-being sensors. Like mobile phones, smart buildings not only increase occupants' comfort and work efficiency but also function as monitoring devices. They collect location and activity data to facilitate better services. While listening to occupants' needs, they learn their personality, preferences, and daily routines. These data also tell the story of its users. The more individualized experience we expect, the deeper probe of sensors and data analysis we have to accept. While this may feel uncomfortable, how this data is used, sanitized, and shared to maintain integrity and privacy will speak to the success of these technologies.

References

Achten, H. (2015). Closing the Loop for Interactive Architecture-Internet of Things, Cloud Computing, and Wearables. In Martens, B., Wurzer, G., Grasl T., Lorenz, W. E. and Schaffranek, R. (eds.), *Real Time – Proceedings of the 33rd eCAADe Conference* (Vol. 2, pp. 623–632), Vienna, Austria.
Akkaya, K., Guvenc, I., Aygun, R., Pala, N., & Kadri, A. (2015, March). IoT-based occupancy monitoring techniques for energy-efficient smart buildings. In *2015 IEEE Wireless Communications and Networking Conference Workshops (WCNCW)* (pp. 58–63). IEEE. https://doi.org/10.1109/WCNCW.2015.7122529

Amoretti, M., Copelli, S., Wientapper, F., Furfari, F., Lenzi, S., & Chessa, S. (2013). Sensor data fusion for activity monitoring in the PERSONA ambient assisted living project. *Journal of Ambient Intelligence and Humanized Computing*, 4, 67–84. https://doi.org/10.1007/s12652-011-0095-6

Awan, F. M., Saleem, Y., Minerva, R., & Crespi, N. (2020). A comparative analysis of machine/deep learning models for parking space availability prediction. *Sensors*, 20(1), 322.

Bailey, C., Phelan, N., Cosgrove, A., & Davis, D. (2018). This room is too dark and the shape is too long: quantifying architectural design to predict successful spaces. In De Rycke, K., Gengnagel, C., Baverel, O., Burry, Mueller, C., Nguyen, M. M., Rahm, P., and Thomsen, M. R. (eds.), *Humanizing Digital Reality* (pp. 337–348). Springer, Singapore.

Barrett, E., & Linder, S. (2015) Autonomous HVAC control, a reinforcement learning approach. In Bifet A. et al. (eds.), *Machine Learning and Knowledge Discovery in Databases*. ECML PKDD 2015. Lecture Notes in Computer Science, vol. 9286 (pp. 3–19). Springer, Cham. https://doi.org/10.1007/978-3-319-23461-8_1

Chernbumroong, S., Cang, S, Atkins, A., & Yu, H. (2013, April). Elderly activities recognition and classification for applications in assisted living. *Expert System with Applications*, 40(5), 1662–1674, Apr. 2013. [Online], http://dx.doi.org/10.1016/j.eswa.2012.09.004

Coen, M. H. (1998). Design principles for intelligent environments. In C.R.A.J. Mostow, (ed.), *Proceedings of the Fifteenth National Conference on Artificial Intelligence (AAAI'98)* (pp. 547–554), AAAI Press / MIT Press, Madison, Wisconsin.

Corna, A., Fontana, L., Nacci, A. A., & Sciuto, D. (2015, March). Occupancy detection via iBeacon on Android devices for smart building management. In *2015 Design, Automation & Test in Europe Conference & Exhibition (DATE)* (pp. 629–632), IEEE. https://doi.org/10.7873/DATE.2015.0753

Council, F. F., & National Research Council. (2002). *Learning from Our Buildings: A State-of-the-Practice Summary of Post-Occupancy Evaluation* (Vol. 145). National Academies Press, Washington, DC.

Das, S. K., & Cook, D. J. (2005, December). Designing smart environments: A paradigm based on learning and prediction. In *International Conference on Pattern Recognition and Machine Intelligence* (pp. 80–90). Springer, Berlin, Heidelberg.

Davis, N. (2016) What is the fourth industrial revolution. *World Economic Forum*. https://www.weforum.org/agenda/2016/01/what-is-the-fourth-industrial-revolution/ (accessed July 30, 2020)

Decker, M. (2017). Soft human computer interfaces. In Fioravanti, A., Cursi, S., Elahmar, S., Gargaro, S., Loffreda, G., Novembri, G., Trento, A. (eds.), *ShoCK! Sharing Computational Knowledge! – Proceedings of the 35th eCAADe Conference* (Vol. 2, pp. 739–744), Rome, Italy.

Delnevo, G., Monti, L., Foschini, F., & Santonastasi, L. (2018, January). On enhancing accessible smart buildings using IoT. In *2018 15th IEEE Annual Consumer Communications & Networking Conference (CCNC)* (pp. 1–6). IEEE. https://doi.org/10.1109/CCNC.2018.8319275

Domingo, M. C. (2012). An overview of the Internet of Things for people with disabilities. *Journal of Network and Computer Applications*, 35(2), 584–596. https://doi.org/10.1016/j.jnca.2011.10.015

Fisher, T. (2017). Research and architecture's knowledge loop. *Technology| Architecture+ Design*, 1(2), 131–134. https://doi.org/10.1080/24751448.2017.1354601

Gorbil, G., Filippoupolitis, A., & Gelenbe, E. (2011). Intelligent navigation systems for building evacuation. In Erol Gelenbe, Ricardo Lent, and Georgia Sakellari (eds.), *Computer and Information Sciences II* (pp. 339–345). Springer, London.

Guillemin, A., & Morel, N. (2001). An innovative lighting controller integrated in a self-adaptive building control system. *Energy and Buildings*, 33(5), 477–487.

Hardin, M. (2018). Post-occupancy testing of thermal dynamics of design-build residences in Tucson, Arizona. *Technology| Architecture+ Design*, 2(2), 147–159. https://doi.org/10.1080/24751448.2018.1497361

He, F., & Ma, C. (2010). Modeling greenhouse air humidity by means of artificial neural network and principal component analysis. *Computers and Electronics in Agriculture*, 71, S19–S23. https://doi.org/10.1016/j.compag.2009.07.011

Hiromoto, J. (2015). *Architect & Design Sustainable Design Leaders*. Post Occupancy Evaluation Survey Report. SOM: New York. http://www.som.com/FILE/22966/post-occupancy-evaluation_survey-report_update_2.pdf

Jara, A. J., Genoud, D., & Bocchi, Y. (2014, May). Big data in smart cities: From poisson to human dynamics. In *2014 28th International Conference on Advanced Information Networking and Applications Workshops* (pp. 785–790). IEEE.

Kazarian, A., Teslyuk, V., Tsmots, I., & Mashevska, M. (2017, February). Units and structure of automated "smart" house control system using machine learning algorithms. In *2017 14th International*

Conference the Experience of Designing and Application of CAD Systems in Microelectronics (CADSM) (pp. 364–366). IEEE. https://doi.org/10.1109/CADSM.2017.7916151

Kortuem, G., Kawsar, F., Sundramoorthy, V., & Fitton, D. (2009). Smart objects as building blocks for the internet of things. *IEEE Internet Computing, 14*(1), 44–51.

Klippel, A., Freksa, C., & Winter, S. (2006). You-are-here maps in emergencies–the danger of getting lost. *Journal of Spatial Science, 51*(1), 117–131. https://doi.org/10.1080/14498596.2006.9635068

Kobes, M., Helsloot, I., De Vries, B., & Post, J. G. (2010). Building safety and human behaviour in fire: A literature review. *Fire Safety Journal, 45*(1), 1–11. https://doi.org/10.1016/j.firesaf.2009.08.005

Li, N., Calis, G., & Becerik-Gerber, B. (2012). Measuring and monitoring occupancy with an RFID based system for demand-driven HVAC operations. *Automation in Construction, 24*, 89–99.

Marble, S. (2018). Everything that can be measured will be measured. *Technology| Architecture+ Design, 2*(2), 127–129. doi.org/10.1080/24751448.2018.1497355

Nagy, D., Villaggi, L., Stoddart, J., & Benjamin, D. (2017). The buzz metric: A graph-based method for quantifying productive congestion in generative space planning for architecture. *Technology| Architecture+ Design, 1*(2), 186–195. doi.org/10.1080/24751448.2017.1354617

Park, D. (2017). Architecture from the bottom-up. *Technology| Architecture+ Design, 1*(2), 140–142. https://doi.org/10.1080/24751448.2017.1354603

Patil, S. L., Tantau, H. J., & Salokhe, V. M. (2008). Modelling of tropical greenhouse temperature by auto regressive and neural network models. *Biosystems Engineering, 99*(3), 423–431. https://doi.org/10.1016/j.biosystemseng.2007.11.009

Peña, R., Meek, C., & Davis, D. (2017). The Bullitt Center: A comparative analysis between simulated and operational performance. *Technology| Architecture+ Design, 1*(2), 163–173. https://doi.org/10.1080/24751448.2017.1354611

Pedersen, T. H., Nielsen, K. U., & Petersen, S. (2017). Method for room occupancy detection based on trajectory of indoor climate sensor data. *Building and Environment, 115*, 147–156. https://doi.org/10.1016/j.buildenv.2017.01.023

Phelan, N., Davis, D., & Anderson, C. (2017, May). Evaluating architectural layouts with neural networks. In *Proceedings of the Symposium on Simulation for Architecture and Urban Design* (pp. 1–7), Toronto, Canada.

Schwartz, M. (2013). Collaborative and human based performance analysis. In *eCAADe Proceedings of the 31st International Conference on Education and Research in Computer Aided Architectural Design in Europe* (pp. 365–373), Delft, The Netherlands.

Schwartz, M., & Das, S. (2019). Interpreting non-flat surfaces for walkability analysis. In *Proceedings of the Symposium on Simulation for Architecture & Urban Design, Society for Computer Simulation International* (pp. 287–294), Atlanta, Georgia.

Shelden, D. (2018). Cyber-physical systems and the built environment. *Technology| Architecture+ Design, 2*(2), 137–139. doi.org/10.1080/24751448.2018.1497358

Siemens, *Building Automation – Impact on Energy Efficiency* (p. 10), www.siemens.com/energyefficiency (accessed July 30, 2020)

Simondetti, A., & Birch, D. (2017). Computational design synergy: Stimulation through simulation. *Technology| Architecture+ Design, 1*(2), 143–145. doi.org/10.1080/24751448.2017.1354605

Tang, S., Shelden, D. R., Eastman, C. M., Pishdad-Bozorgi, P., & Gao, X. (2019). A review of building information modeling (BIM) and the internet of things (IoT) devices integration: Present status and future trends. *Automation in Construction, 101*, 127–139. https://doi.org/10.1016/j.autcon.2019.01.020

Thomas, B., & Soleimani-Mohseni, M. (2007). Artificial neural network models for indoor temperature prediction: Investigations in two buildings. *Neural Computing and Applications, 16*(1), 81–89. https://doi.org/10.1007/s00521-006-0047-9

UcityLabAdmin (2019) SmartSantander: An unique city-scale platform. *University Action Lab.* https://www.ucitylab.eu/index.php/2019/11/05/smartsantander-a-unique-city-scale-platform/ (accessed July 30, 2020)

Weiser, M. (1991). The computer for the twenty-first century. *Scientific American, 265*(3) September Issue, 94–100.

Wurzer, G., Ausserer M., Hinneberg H., Illera C., Rosic A. (2011) Sensitivity visualization of circulation under congestion and blockage. In Peacock, R., Kuligowski, E., & Averill, J. (eds.) *Pedestrian and Evacuation Dynamics.* Springer, Boston, MA. https://doi.org/10.1007/978-1-4419-9725-8_96

Zarzycki, A. (2016). Adaptive designs with distributed intelligent systems-building design applications. In Herneoja, A., Österlund, T., & Markkanen, P. (eds.), Complexity & Simplicity − *In Proceedings of the 34th eCAADe Conference* - Volume 1, University of Oulu, Oulu, Finland, 22–26 August 2016, pp. 681–690.

Zarzycki, A. (2018). Strategies for the integration of smart technologies into buildings and construction assemblies. In *Proceedings of eCAADe 2018 Conference* (pp. 631–640), Lodz, Poland.

Zarzycki, A., & Decker, M. (2019). Climate-adaptive buildings: Systems and materials. *International Journal of Architectural Computing*, *17*(2), 166–184. https://doi.org/10.1177/1478077119852707

Zhao, H. X., & Magoulès, F. (2012). A review on the prediction of building energy consumption. *Renewable and Sustainable Energy Reviews*, *16*(6), 3586–3592. https://doi.org/10.1016/j.rser.2012.02.049

Zuraimi, M. S., Pantazaras, A., Chaturvedi, K. A., Yang, J. J., Tham, K. W., & Lee, S. E. (2017). Predicting occupancy counts using physical and statistical Co2-based modeling methodologies. *Building and Environment*, *123*, 517–528.

16

Explainable ML

Augmenting the interpretability of numerical simulation using Bayesian networks

Zack Xuereb Conti and Sawako Kaijima

This chapter discusses a machine learning (ML) based approach to improve the interpretability of numerical simulation tools; a shift from utilizing numerical tools for validation toward generating and representing engineering intel for augmenting human intuition.

Numerical simulation, particularly finite element analysis (FEA) originated in the aerospace and aeronautics industry to validate the design of aircraft and spacecraft in terms of physical behavior, ahead of costly full-scale experiments. In subsequent decades, FEA became commercially available to the automotive and civil engineering industries. Today, FEA plays a critical role for informing decisions during the design and materialization of buildings. Research and advancements in numerical methods have facilitated engineers and architects to push geometric and engineering boundaries which were previously not feasible with analytical methods. Furthermore, the emergence of computational approaches to architectural design have facilitated the coupling of numerical simulation tools with computational representations of architectural geometry, to either navigate feasible design options or to drive the generation of design configurations, algorithmically. The latter has become a staple approach in so-called "performance-driven design."

This chapter highlights how despite the advancements in numerical simulation methods and applications, the involvement of human intelligence is easily bypassed, as it remains challenging to interpret and translate numeric simulation output into a usable insight. Human control is a much-desired attribute in architectural design. In this context, control is manifested as the understanding of *how* the simulation inputs influence the simulation output. In other words, interpretable intel about the relationship between architectural language and engineering behavior would facilitate the creative intuition to take lead in navigating the course of design. Augmenting numerical tools to translate and interpret engineering intel into architectural language would also benefit communication between an expert consultant and architecture teams during real project scenarios. In this context, this chapter aims to communicate that a successful human–computer relationship is one that does not bypass the designer's intellect, but augments it.

The task of learning about relationships between inputs and outputs of opaque systems such as a numerical simulation model, is a task for statistical modeling and statistical inference. The latter is a task of learning about relationships between variables. In fields such as mechanical engineering and aerospace engineering, statistical techniques have been used for decades, as a means to approximate the relationships between inputs and outputs of complex and computationally demanding numerical simulation models into simpler and more interpretable mathematical models, referred to as *metamodels* (also referred to as surrogate models). In recent times, ML techniques such as neural networks have become a popular approach to build even more accurate and more universal metamodels as very efficient substitutes for time-consuming numerical simulation codes such as FEA. Example applications include analysis of large-scale structures and simulation of fluid dynamics. However, despite their accurate representations, such ML-based metamodels are typically not interpretable in human-readable format and thus have limitations for supporting human intelligence in design.

This chapter presents Bayesian networks (BNs) as an approach to build interpretable simulation metamodels. BNs are a probabilistic technique that lie at the intersection of statistics and ML, where relationships are captured from data using ML techniques and subsequently represented in an interpretable form such that they can be explored intuitively using statistical techniques. A Bayesian network metamodel (BNM), can absorb the cognitive load to keep track of the intricate relationships between multiple variables, while facilitates to explore the cause and effect relationships comprehensively, in a bidirectional manner.

The remainder of the chapter opens with a discussion on applications and limitations of typical statistical and ML-based simulation metamodels, continues by introducing an interpretable metamodeling approach using BNs, and subsequently by will illustrate the interpretability of BNs as metamodels in a retrospective structural engineering case study application of the 2015 Serpentine Pavilion in London with the aim of revealing the relationship between global geometry and localized structural behavior.

Simulation metamodels: a statistical approach

What is a metamodel?

Numerical computer simulation models used to analyze proposed or existing real systems such as aircraft, spacecraft or buildings are often quite complex. Therefore, simpler approximations in the form of statistical models are often constructed. The approximate model serves as a simpler and computationally efficient "model of the model," more commonly referred to as a *metamodel* (Kleijnen, 1986). The process of formulating a metamodel is referred to as "metamodeling."

How to build a simulation metamodel

Formulating a metamodel involves the following four steps illustrated in Figure 16.1: (1) generate configurations of input values, (2) run the simulations to generate response output data, (3) use the input–output data to "fit" a statistical model to data points, and finally (4) validate the robustness of the model. Steps 1 and 2 deal with the design of a computer experiment, while steps 3 and 4 deal with the building of a reliable statistical approximation.

Metamodels are typically data-driven as they are formulated from data, which in turn is generated via a planned computer experiment. A computer experiment is very much like a physical experiment, only that the system under study is a numerical algorithm, rather than a physical system. This involves running a number of simulations at carefully selected input configurations (Sacks, Welch, Mitchell, & Wynn, 1989), whose values are determined through a so called "design of experiments" (DOE) approach (Fisher, 1935). It is

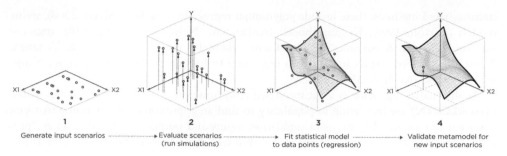

Figure 16.1 Typical metamodeling workflow.

well established that the selection of a DOE strategy has a direct impact on the quality and predictive accuracy of the resulting metamodel (Fang, Li, & Sudjianto, 2005). The selection of DOE strategy depends highly on the computational expense to run a simulation analysis. Popular types of DOE strategies used for metamodels include *classic factorial designs*, and *space-filling designs*. The latter are most popular with formulating simulation metamodels. For further literature regarding computer experiment strategies, see Simpson, Lin, & Chen (2001). Once the appropriate experimental design is selected and the necessary simulation runs are complete, the simulation response data is aggregated together with the generated input values to form an input–output dataset. With this dataset in hand, the next step is to build the actual metamodel.

Typical metamodels

In a general sense metamodeling is a task of *regression*, which is a statistical technique adopted to formulate a mathematical expression g that best describes the true relationship between the inputs X and output y of the numerical simulation code ff (Figure 16.2).

In more detail, regression involves (1) selecting an appropriate approximation function g from a family of techniques, that best describes the global trend of the data points, and subsequently (2) selecting a so-called "fitting" method to fine-tune the selected approximation model such that it fits tightly to the local characteristics of the data points. Typically, regression methods adopted for formulating simulation metamodels are associated with

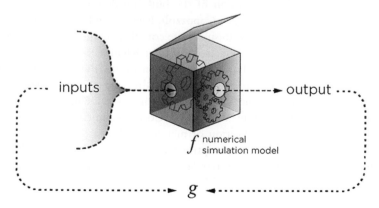

Figure 16.2 Simulation metamodel g built as an approximation from simulation inputs and output.

statistic-based methods; these include polynomial regression models (Kleijnen, 2008), spline models (Barton, 1998), Kriging models (Ankenman, Nelson, & Staum, 2010), response surfaces (Kleijnen & Sargent, 2000) and game-theoretic models (Poropudas & Virtanen, 2010a, 2010b). For further literature on regression techniques for metamodeling see Simpson, Poplinski, Koch, & Allen (2014).

Traditionally, regression is a statistic-based task, however, ML techniques such as neural networks (NN) are increasing in popularity to find an approximation function g that best describes the relationship between simulation inputs and outputs. NNs are good at "pretending" to be any type of regression model (Fonseca, Navaresse, & Moynihan, 2003). The advantage of NN as metamodels is that they can accommodate flexible types of relationships, varying from linear to very nonlinear relationships as is characteristic in scenarios with numerous inputs (Grossberg, 1988). In fact, they are considered powerful enough to build so-called "universal approximators," if their architecture is large enough (Funahashi, 1989; Hornik, Stinchcombe, & White, 1989). While more traditional statistics-based metamodels such as those mentioned above, are developed separately for each component of the output, ML-based metamodels can handle multiple outputs within the same model. It is important to note that ML-based approaches tend to need significantly more data than reasonably required in classic statistics (Brownlee, 2014).

Validating the metamodel

Once a metamodel is formulated, it is necessary to secure that the formulated metamodel captures the true input–output relationships underlying the numerical simulation code, as well as possible. The most typical validation technique is called cross-validation where the input–output dataset is split into so-called training set and testing set, prior to building the model. The model is then built from the training set and subsequently tested using the testing set. The prediction accuracy of the metamodel can be estimated statistically, by means of the root mean square error (RMSE). The RMSE is a widely accepted method to quantify the robustness of metamodels in general. Cross-validation and RMSE are used widely for both statistical and ML-based metamodels

Metamodels for building-design related applications

Metamodels have attracted the attention of the building-design community focusing on performance-based design. For example, Capozzoli, Mechri, and Corrado (2009) formulate a metamodel using regression analysis to substitute complex energy calculations and computationally demanding energy simulation, respectively; Klemm, Marks, and Klemm (2000) present a metamodel derived by polynomial regression from CFD simulation results to derive objective functions for faster optimization of building aerodynamics; Tresidder, Zhang, and Forrester (2012) use Kriging metamodels to optimize CO2 emissions and construction costs of buildings; and more recently, Wortmann, Costa, Nannicini, and Schroepfer (2015) demonstrate the advantageous application of metamodel-based optimization using radial-basis functions, for architectural daylight optimization problems. Brown and Mueller (2019) adopt metamodeling approaches to facilitate faster geometry manipulation and performance feedback during the exploratory stages of design.

The predominant application in the abovementioned metamodels is faster design, analysis, and optimization cycles. Nonetheless, these applications do not address the lack of interpretability in typical metamodels.

Discussion: interpretability of typical metamodels

The main difference between statistical models and ML models is their purpose. ML models, in general, are designed to make the most accurate predictions possible, whereas statistical models are more concerned with finding and understanding relationships between variables and their significance, whilst also catering for prediction. In other words, statistic-based metamodels can be considered interpretable while ML-based models are typically not suited for explaining underlying relationships. Nevertheless, once the number of inputs considered increases, the interpretability of statistic-based metamodels is rapidly compromised because the algebraic expressions required to mathematically describe relationships between multiple inputs and the output become unintelligible.

This challenge calls for a metamodeling approach that can (1) capture or "learn" input–output relationships between numerous variables from data and that can subsequently (2) represent these relationships in the form of a human–interpretable model. In response, the following sections will introduce BNs as a metamodeling approach that addresses (1) and (2). A BN is a type of probabilistic method that lies at the intersection of statistics and ML. BNs combine the power of ML to learn relationships over many variables directly from data using ML techniques, while facilitating statistical techniques to interpret and navigate such relationships.

Before diving into BNs, the next section provides a background explanation on how a probabilistic approach differs from typical metamodeling approaches mentioned above.

A probabilistic approach

Introduction: probabilistic representation

Unlike statistic-based and ML-based metamodels, a BNM is a type of probabilistic model where input and output variables are represented as random variables instead of scalar values. A random variable is a type of variable that takes on a probability distribution of possible values as opposed to a single point value. Furthermore, a probabilistic model does not assume a form and compress relationships into a "tightly fit" algebraic function, preselected from a family of possible functions (Figure 16.3, left). Instead, all data points are considered in what is referred to as a "joint probability distribution" (JPD), where relationships between random variables are represented probabilistically (Figure 16.3, right).

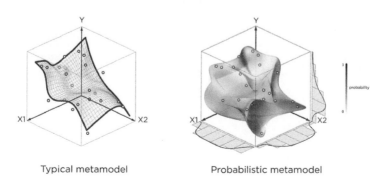

Typical metamodel · Probabilistic metamodel

Figure 16.3   Fitting a model to datapoints (left), encompassing all datapoints in a probabilistic model (right).

To illustrate a probabilistic approach in more detail, let us analogously visualize that predicting the output Y using a generic mathematical model is like "slicing" the function surface at the input values of interest. In typical metamodels such as those discussed previously, slicing the exact function at specific input values of $X1$ and $X2$, would result in a scalar singular point as illustrated in Figure 16.4 (top row); in other words, an exact scalar response Y. Such metamodels lack interpretability because the single point response value and the selected input values at $X1$ and $X2$ do not provide us with insight about their relationship. This lack of interpretability is emphasized further when the number of inputs considered are numerous.

On the other hand, slicing a probabilistic metamodel (Figure 16.4, bottom row) implies slicing a "probabilistic surface" (JPD) so to speak, that contains all datapoints rather than slicing an exact "surface" approximately fitted to a set of datapoints. In this context, slicing the probabilistic model at values of $X1$ and $X2$ will reveal which values along the range of Y are more probable than others to be outputted by the model. Note that, in the illustrative example in Figure 16.4 (bottom row) the resulting output Y distribution lies at the intersection between respective slices at $X1$ and $X2$.

In other words, the revealed probability distribution of Y, provides us with a view of how likely $X1$ and $X2$ values are likely to influence values along the range of Y. When

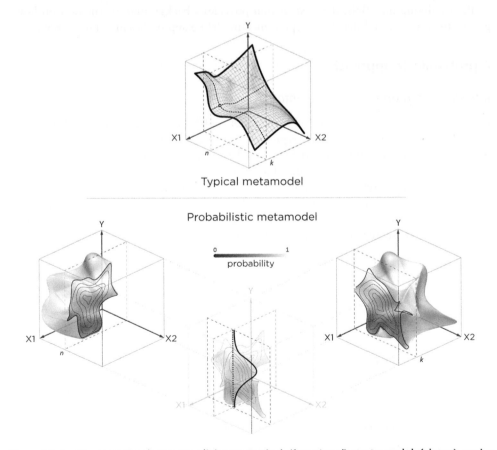

Figure 16.4 Comparative between slicing a typical (functional) metamodel (above) and a probabilistic metamodel (below).

accumulated, these slices provide a bigger picture of the relationships between the inputs (*X1*, *X2*) and the output (*Y2*). To summarize, slicing a probabilistic representation of a simulation input–output analysis provides us with a much richer insight into how *X1* and *X2* influence *Y*, in contrast to a singular input and output of a typical non-probabilistic representation.

Bidirectionality between multi-inputs and multi-outputs

The significant advantage of representing relationships probabilistically over typical approaches discussed above, is the mathematical indifference between inputs and outputs. The indifference facilitates (1) prediction of the simulation output and the inverse-inference of the inputs, and (2) multi-inputs and multi-simulation outputs. The result is a bidirectional multi-input, multi-output metamodel.

Therefore, in terms of our "slicing" analogy, the indifference implies that a probabilistic representation may be sliced in *any* direction, regardless of inputs or outputs. For example, we can slice the probabilistic model at an output at a value y of interest, and immediately reveal the likely joint distribution of *X1*, and *X2* to cause *Y*. This suggests a bidirectionality between inputs and outputs. More importantly, the inverse process reveals an insight into the relationship between the inputs and the output in terms of cause and effect (Figure 16.5).

Bayesian inference

In probability theory, the analogous act of "slicing" a probabilistic model, is a task of *inference*, where slicing the model at different intervals reveals probabilistic relationships between the random variables. More formally, these probabilistic relationships are referred to as *conditional* relationships and are described by conditional probabilities. For further literature on probability, see Subrahmaniam (1990).

Bayesian inference is a type of inference in which Bayes' theorem is used to "update" the probability distributions of a random variable under study when values of other variables are kept fixed. In other words, Bayes' theorem is used to navigate the probabilistic relationships composing the probabilistic model. Bayes' theorem, is named after its creator Rev. Bayes (1763), who was a famous mathematician.

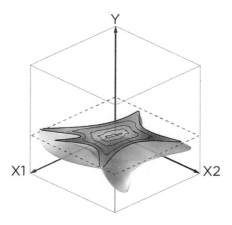

Figure 16.5   Slicing a probabilistic model at the output reveals the input distribution that "caused" it.

However, when the number of variables increase and hence, relationships become more difficult to interpret cognitively, the probabilistic model becomes exponentially tedious to compute and to store computationally (Karkera, 2014). To tackle this so-called curse of dimensionality, probabilistic graphic models (PGM) come into play because they can represent high-dimensional probabilistic representations very efficiently and very compactly. More specifically, BNs are a type of PGM that lie at the intersection of ML and statistics. BNs combine the power of ML algorithms to "learn" relationships over multiple dimensions directly from data while also taking advantage of classic probability theorems such as Bayesian inference to navigate/interpret relationships between numerous variables. The application of BN as metamodels for architectural design and engineering is a novel application (Xuereb Conti & Kaijima, 2018a, 2018b).

Bayesian network metamodel

Brief theory

BNs are a type of PGM. A PGM is a statistic model represented by a mathematical graph (Figure 16.6, right). In general, a graph is a representation of a mathematical structure using nodes and edges to model relations between objects. In PGMs, nodes represent random variables whose input is described by a probability distribution, while edges between the nodes represent probabilistic relationships. In the case of BNs, edges are directed and represent *causal* relationships between variables. In other words, the direction of the edge represents a dependence between two random variables due to their cause and effect relation. For example, in Figure 16.6, right, the edge going from $X1$ to Y implies that probability distribution of Y depends on its parent node $X1$. Therefore, when assembled, a BN is a network of probabilistic relationships between variables. All probabilities in a BN are discrete (Figure 16.6).

If knowledge about the problem domain is available, the probabilistic relationships can be specified manually, otherwise learned automatically from data using supervised learning algorithms such as expectation-maximization (EM) algorithm, borrowed form ML. On the other hand, the topology of the edges between nodes can also be encoded manually from knowledge or learned automatically from data. For detailed description regarding automatic learning of conditional probabilities, see Spiegelhalter (1998), while for structure topology, see Steck and Tresp (1999).

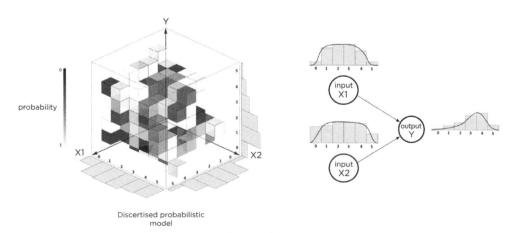

Discretised probabilistic model

Figure 16.6   Discrete Bayesian network metamodel.

Bayesian network metamodel

Adopting BNs as a metamodel implies a bidirectional multi-input multi-output metamodel, ergo the term, Bayesian network metamodel (BNM). This section provides a step-by-step guide to the formulation of a BNM as an approach for augmenting the interpretability of numerical simulation.

Simple case study

For illustrative purposes, let us assume an intuitive 2D structural frame analysis of a simple cantilever beam to motivate the formulation and use of a BNM. For this study, a parametric frame model of the beam is modeled in Grasshopper, a parametric modeling environment, while the analysis is done using "Millipede," a FEA solver in Grasshopper. Figure 16.7 illustrates the assumed parametric geometry where the span and depth of the beam can vary between 3 to 4 m and 0.2 to 1.2 m, respectively. The frame element is modeled as a hollow steel cross-section with a nonvariable thickness of 0.1 m and width at 0.5 m. The beam is fixed at one end in translation and rotation for all directions. Note that the selection of variables (to describe the geometry in this case), directly influences the quality of insight gained from the metamodel. The same applies to their selected ranges, if problem is unconstrained; For instance, in this case, selecting ranges that allow extreme geometries, allows us to capture and understand how depth and span influence the physical behavior of the beam under load.

Generating the data

Once the parametric analysis model is set up, the next step is to configure a computer experiment to generate simulation data, required for building the metamodel. In other words, to run simulations for different combinations of span and depth scenarios using the parametric analysis model. Despite the intuitiveness of this case study, let us assume that we know little to nothing about the relationship between the design variables (span and depth) and the simulation output (maximum deflection); in other words, we assume that interesting characteristics of the function are likely to be anywhere in the design space. Given this assumption, let us assume a quasi-random sequence algorithm; an algorithm used to sample pseudo-uniformly (random but everywhere) in the input domain bound by span and depth ranges (Figure 16.8, left). Inducing randomness is important to avoid any systematic correlations between the (independent) input variables.

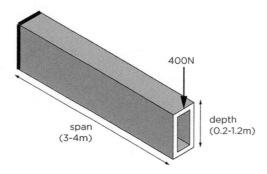

Figure 16.7   Parametric finite element model of the beam geometry in Grasshopper.

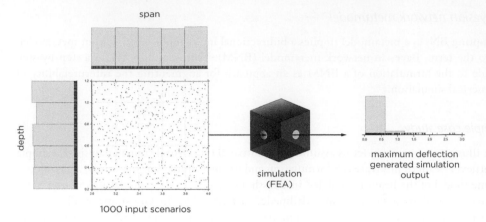

Figure 16.8 **Input and output probability distributions are frequency histograms of input samples and simulation outputs, respectively.**

For this study, we generate 1,000 input combinations of span and depth values, which is a benchmark size to secure a good model accuracy. Subsequently, the parametric simulation is run using the generated sequences of input values as simulation inputs, while recording the maximum deflection on each simulation run. Figure 16.8, right illustrates the maximum deflection probability distribution of generated outputs.

BNs take on only discrete distributions, therefore, once the simulation runs were complete and data was generated, both continuous inputs were discretized into five equally spaced bins/states, while the continuous output was discretized into five bins, spaced according to percentile. Binning according to percentile implies ensuring that each bin has the same number of data points. This safeguards situations where bins are dedicated to only a few points due to outlying datapoints, which is known to impact the accuracy of BNs.

Building the Bayesian network

The geometric variables *span* and *depth* are introduced as nodes in a BN, while the topology of the edges connecting the nodes is interpreted as a forward flow from inputs (span and depth) to output (maximum deflection) (Figure 16.9). The underlying probabilistic relationships composing the model were then learned automatically from the data using a supervised

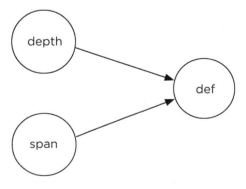

Figure 16.9 Bayesian network metamodel forward topology.

ML EM algorithm. The BN is validated using methods for measuring accuracy of classifier models to secure that the resulting model has captured the relationship between the inputs and the output as close to the (true) numerical simulation model as possible.

Interpretability via Bayesian inference

Once the BNM is built and validated, it can be used to navigate the input–output relationships bidirectionally using Bayesian inference in the background. To a user, it is as simple as assigning specific probability values of interest to any variable or set of variables; through inference, the remaining distributions are updated according to the network of relationships.

To illustrate how the BNM augments the interpretability of numerical simulation, let us navigate the model in either direction; forward direction (input–output) to predict the maximum deflection, and the inverse direction (input–output) to infer the input distributions for a specified deflection of interest.

Figure 16.10 illustrates how assigning 100% probability to the input bin ranges of interest (dashed outline), updates the maximum deflection probability distribution (solid outline) based on their relationship. The grey probability distribution in the background of each histogram represents the frequency distribution prior to updating. We can observe how beam geometries whose depth lies between 0.599 m and 0.797 m, and span between 3.597 m and 3.796 m, are likely to behave physically; in other words, yield maximum deflections within the red distribution. The likeliness depends on the assigned probability to that bin.

Given the mathematical indifference between inputs and outputs, the same BNM also facilitates the inverse operation. This is a significant advantage over typical statistic-based and ML-based metamodels discussed earlier. Therefore, assigning 100% probability to an output bin of interest; let's say feasible maximum deflections should lie between 3 cm and 6 cm; will update the span and depth probability distributions based on the entire network of relationship with the maximum deflection of the beam. Immediately, it becomes intuitive *how* to generate beam geometries whose deflection lies in the selected feasible range by observing the span and depth bin ranges with the highest probability. For instance, the first row in Figure 16.11, implies that spans between ~3 m and 3.2 m and depths between ~1 m and ~1.2 m are very likely to maintain the maximum deflection of the beam between 3 cm and 6 cm.

Furthermore, the spread of the updated distribution (variance) also serves as a sensitivity indicator; a widely spread input distribution implies a weaker sensitivity to reach the target output value because the 100% probability is distributed widely across the input range. For instance, in Figure 16.11 (first row) the wide spread of the span distribution implies that varying the span of the beam geometry is less influential than varying the depth of the beam cross section when yielding beam geometries whose maximum deflection falls within 3 cm and 6 cm. Subsequently, repeating the inverse (output-input) exercise for all bins in the output distribution provides a rich understanding of how span and depth influence the maximum deflection of the beam, as illustrated in Figure 16.11.

In general, the inverse operation described in this section is a difficult task to compute because there exists multiple possible combination of inputs that generate the same output, particularly when numerous inputs are being considered. This section has demonstrated how the probabilistic formulation of a BNM may overcome this difficulty.

To summarize, the above-simplified case scenario illustrated how a BNM facilitates to explore cause and effect relationships bi-directionally, while taking care of keeping track of the relationships between multiple variables. The next section introduces a retrospective study application on a built case project.

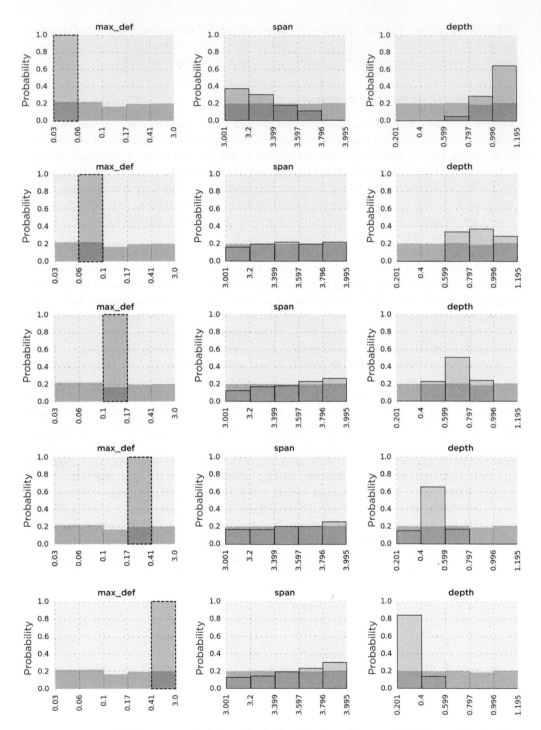

Figure 16.10 Updated output (solid outline) distributions for specified input distributions (dashed outline).

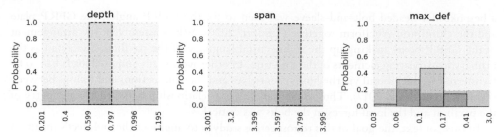

Figure 16.11 Inverse exploration: Updated input (solid outline) distributions for specified output target (dashed outline).

Case study: 2016 serpentine pavilion

This case study demonstrates the advantages of a bidirectional multi-input multi-output BNM in a realistic architectural design involving an intricate relationship between architecture and engineering.

Project background

The 2016 Serpentine Pavilion designed by Bjarke Ingels Group (BIG) and engineered by AKT-II (Adams Kara Taylor), consisted of two 30-m-long sinusoidal walls; one concave, and the other convex. The two walls undulate toward one another starting at the bottom until they merge into each other vertically, at the top. Each wall is composed of overlapping, open-ended boxes that vary in length depending on the sinusoidal geometry. The box pattern on either wall is set in an inverse checkerboard pattern to its neighbor, thus, allowing the cuboids from each wall to merge into a seamless grid at the top part of the pavilion (Figure 16.12).

Each of the boxes assembling the geometry of the pavilion is composed of four glass fiber-reinforced plastic (GFRP) plates with GFRP angles glued in each corner to increase lateral stability and vertical loading-bearing capacity (Figure 16.12). GFRP is a composite material formed of a glass fiber encapsulated within a plastic resin matrix that typically has strength comparable to that of steel but with only around a quarter of the weight (Kingman, Dudley, & Baptista, 2017). Neighboring GFRP boxes are connected by 10-mm thick cruciform-shaped aluminum that provided the necessary weight to strength ratio. Finally,

Figure 16.12 2016 serpentine pavilion in London (Bjarke Ingels Group) (left). Structural connection detail (source: Laurian Ghinitoiu) (right).

a bespoke flat-headed bolt-and-sleeve was used to fix the GFRP angles, the GFRP plate and the aluminum cruciform together (Tibuzzi, 2020). When assembled, the arrangement of the GFRP boxes making up the architectural language of the pavilion, also acted as the primary load-bearing elements of the structure. In other words, any imposed loads had to be transferred to the ground via the boxes themselves and the connections and fixings between them (Kara & Bosia, 2017). Thus, understanding the relationship between the geometry of the pavilion and the local forces in the bolts was critical.

In this context, the goal of this retrospective study is to augment the architect's intuition by communicating engineering feedback about structural behavior in an intuitive interpretation. More specifically, instead of analyzing only one scenario at a time in a lengthy back and forth communication, in this case study we illustrate how the engineering team may utilize the multi-input multi-output bidirectional inference capabilities of the BNMs to: (1) gain an understanding of the relationships between the architectural parameters controlling the global geometry and the local cross-sectional behavior of the pavilion, and (2) utilize the understanding of these relationships to communicate engineering feasibility constraints in the form of architectural constraints back to the architecture team, as an alternative to communicating isolated instances of feedback.

Generating simulation data

The parameters controlling the bulginess of each wall were identified by the engineering team as critical factors influencing the forces in the boxes. Therefore, for this case study we analogously describe the sinusoidal form of the walls by two parameters controlling the sinusoidal proportions of each respective wall. From here on, these parameters are labeled as *north wall scale factor* (*north wall sf*) and *south wall scale factor* (*south wall sf*) whose ranges vary from 0.75 to 1.3, and 0.85 to 1.3, respectively. Note that a value 1 implies the as-built geometry proportions (as indicated in Figure 16.13). The analysis model was composed of 2D cross-section FEM models along the axis of the West East axis, where cube cross-sections were represented by shell components and bolt connections by linear beam elements. For illustrative purposes, this section will discuss only two 2D cross-sections at extreme locations along the principal axis of the pavilion. For each cross-sectional analysis, total maximum deflection (*max_def*, mm) and the maximum resolved axial and shear forces in the bolts (*max_force*, kN)

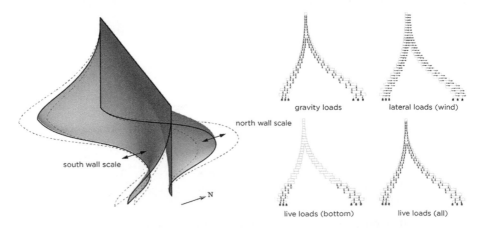

Figure 16.13 Parametric geometry (left), cross-sectional FEM model (right).

were recorded under four loading conditions as originally considered by the engineers, and as illustrated in Figure 16.13.

In the original project, the geometric parameters were continually tweaked by the architecture team based on the engineers' post-analysis feedback until reasonable forces in the bolts connecting the boxes were achieved. Instead, this study aims to capture the relationships between global geometry and local cross-sectional behavior into a BNM with which a global understanding can be inferred and communicated intuitively back to the architectural design team.

Building the Bayesian network metamodel

Figure 16.14 illustrates the BNM for exploring local behavior at different cross-sections of the pavilion. For this scenario, the *north wall sf* parameter and *south wall sf* parameters were introduced as BNM input distributions, while the FEA response outputs—total maximum deflection due to all four load cases, and maximum resolved axial and shear forces in the bolts due to all load cases—were respectively introduced as BNM output distributions.

For this study, we make use of "Inference Lab" (Xuereb Conti, 2020), a custom-designed plug-in for building BNM in Grasshopper (Rutten, 2012), and a by-product of this research. The plug-in is aimed at both expert and intuition-oriented users.

Interpreting input–output relationships

Once each of the sectional BNMs is built, we can manipulate their input and output probability distributions to explore the cause-effect relationships between the *north wall sf, south wall sf,* and cross-sectional maximum deflection and maximum forces in the bolt connections. For each scenario we keep in mind that the engineering goal is to avoid areas of extreme global forces by (1) maintaining maximum axial and shear forces in the connection bolts <= ~10 kN, and (2) keeping the maximum deflection at each section at a minimum.

The first cross-section under study is located close to the boundary of the pavilion's entrance, as illustrated in Figure 16.15. We begin this exercise by attempting to ask, which input settings are likely to maintain maximum axial and shear forces in the bolt connections below approximately 10 kN? We attempt to answer this question by setting the bins, whose range contains or falls below or equals to approximately 10 kN, to 100% probability (see Figure 16.16). The underlying BN automatically "updates" all other distributions in the network, based on the relationship between the *north wall sf* and *south wall sf* wall parameters and the *max_resolved_force.* The use of the word "updating" implies the computation of Bayesian inference. When observing the updated input probability distributions in Figure 16.16, one can immediately note a relationship trend, where decreasing the *south wall sf* while increasing the *north wall sf* can produce global geometries that maintain the maximum axial and shear force in the bolt connections of cross-section 1, below 10.94 kN. In other words, the *north*

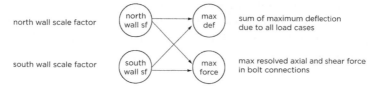

Figure 16.14   BNM used for each cross-section frame.

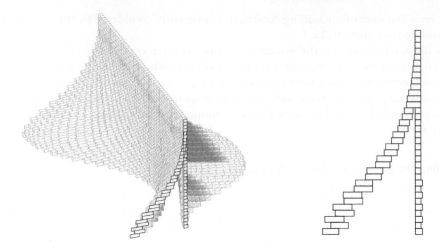

Figure 16.15   2D frame at cross-section 1.

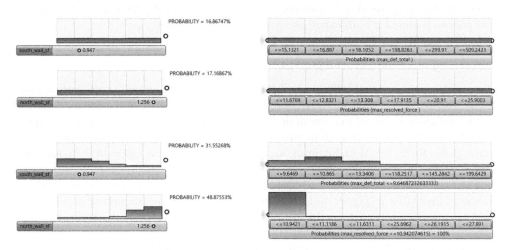

Figure 16.16   Top: Before updating. Bottom: Updated input distributions after specifying targets on force only.

wall sf, and south wall sf distributions in Figure 16.16 illustrate *how* to set geometric parameters to maintain axial and shear forces below 10.94 kN.

We can also note that after "updating" in Figure 16.16, the probability distributions of the other response was also updated because they share a common relationship with the inputs. Implicitly, these updated response distributions provide us with information about the trade-off relationships between the responses; reducing the maximum force seems to have an almost complementary relationship with reducing the maximum deflection at cross-section 1. For example, if we were to reset the distributions back to their preupdated state (see Figure 16.16, top), and this time set the smallest bin on the *max_def_total* distribution to 100% probability (Figure 16.17), we observe that updated *north wall sf* distribution illustrates a similar trend as the previous scenario in Figure 16.16, whereas *south wall sf* shows an almost inverse scenario.

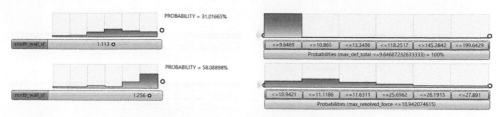

Figure 16.17   Updated input distributions after specifying target on deflection only.

The two goals of maintaining *max_resolved_force* below approximately 10 kN and maintaining a low maximum deflection seem to have a complementary relationship at section 1. Therefore, the natural next step would be to set the bins with the lowest bins in both *max_resolved_force* and *max_def_total* to 100% probability and to observe the updated input distributions (see Figure 16.18). The resulting updates immediately distribute the probability toward the regions of the input space that are likely to satisfy the "constraints" placed on the outputs. As expected, the probability distribution of the *north wall sf* is mostly distributed toward the maximum value (1.3 scale factor), while *south wall sf* probability distribution concentrates higher probability toward the center, the result of an overlap between the probability distributions in Figures 16.16 and 16.17.

Now, let us repeat the same exercise with the BNM built for cross-section 25, located toward the center of the pavilion geometry (Figure 16.19). Naturally, we can expect the engineering behavior to differ from cross-section 1 due to difference in geometry and location from the boundaries.

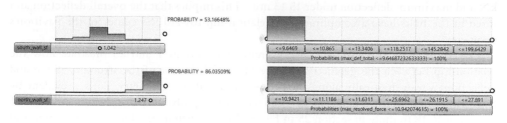

Figure 16.18   Updated input distributions after specifying targets on both deflection and force.

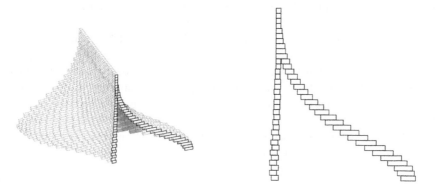

Figure 16.19   2D frame at cross-section 25.

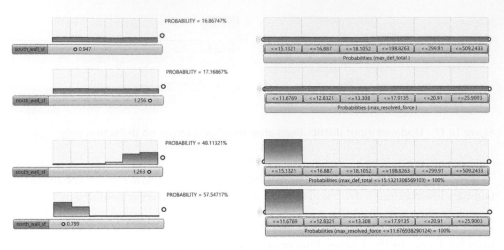

Figure 16.20   Before updating (above). Updated input distributions after specifying targets on both deflection and force (below).

Figure 16.20 (above) illustrates the discretized inputs and outputs probability distributions before updating. We make a double targeted query; what are the input distributions that are required to maintain a maximum resolved axial and shear force below ~10 kN, and the smallest maximum deflection? On updating all probability distributions in the network, we can immediately note (Figure 16.20, below) that scaling outward the south wall and scaling inward the north wall have a minimizing effect on both the forces in the bolt connections and the maximum deflection to guarantee maximum forces under 11.68 kN and maximum deflection under 15.13 mm. This implies that the overall deflection and force in the bolts have a complimentary relationship toward the center of the pavilion's geometry.

On comparison, the two inference exercises for sections 1 and 25 illustrate how the relationship between the geometry and the physical behavior of the structure (force and deflection) varies drastically along the cross-sections of the geometry. This is evident by comparing the difference in *north wall sf* and *south wall sf* probability distribution of section 1 in Figure 16.18 to those in section 25 in Figure 16.20, when queried for the same force and deflection-minimization goals. This difference also indicates to the architects, the need to have more localized control over the geometry, to secure structurally feasible cross-sections. Here, the BNM acts as a translational mechanism between engineering constraints and architectural language.

In a further step, we attempted to assemble a "global" BNM that considers the forces in more than two cross-sections across the pavilion geometry to get a more global picture and attempt to inverse infer global north wall and south wall geometry scale factors that secure forces below 10 kN across all cross-sections. As expected, the attempt was not successful due to competing relationships between cross-sections, as seen above with cross-sections 1 and 25. Nonetheless, the BNM was significantly useful to identify the smallest possible trade-off force of 13.4 kN between cross-sections suggesting to the engineers to redesign the bolts to handle capacity above 13.4 kN instead of the intended 10 kN (Figure 16.21).

It is worthy to note how the BNM can be utilized as a translational mechanism between engineering feasibility constraints and architectural language. In other words, the BNM may facilitate the architecture team to handover to the engineering team a parametric model and

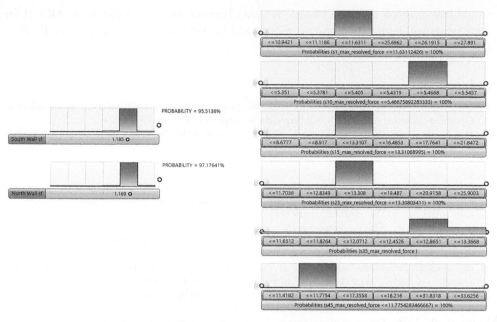

Figure 16.21 Multi-input multi-output BNM for trading off axial forces across multiple cross-sections.

in return, the engineers return the constrained version of the same parametric model. Thus, flexibility much desired by architects in the early stages, is not compromised when consulting engineering expertise, contrary to typical back and forth feedback communication loops.

Conclusion

This chapter discussed a bidirectional metamodeling approach using BNs to improve the interpretability of numerical simulation tools. A BNM facilitates an intuitive exploration of relationships, even in multi-simulation input and multi-simulation output scenarios. The BNM absorbs the cognitive load to keep track of relations to facilitate intuition-led decisions.

The application of a BNMs approach to hypothetical and realistic case studies, illustrated the significant benefits of interpretability in comparison to direct use of numerical simulation software and to typical metamodels. These included the following: (1) identifying feasible input regions to yield a target or targets of interest, (2) intuitive identification of sensitive input variables, and (3) exploration of trade-offs between simultaneous simulation responses. In particular, the latter can be interpreted as a significant contribution toward trade-off exploration in multi-objective optimization.

This chapter intended to emphasize that a successful human-computer relationship is one that augments the intuition, not bypasses it.

Acknowledgments

This research is an outcome of the first author's PhD thesis research conducted at the Singapore University of Technology and Design (SUTD) and supervised by Sawako Kaijima (Harvard Graduate School of Design) and Dr Shaowei Lin (SUTD). Additionally, the author would like to thank Edoardo Tibuzzi, Ricardo Baptista, and Jeg Dudley from AKT-II for their assistance in providing analysis models and insight regarding the Serpentine Pavilion case study.

References

Ankenman, B., Nelson, B. L., & Staum, J. (2010). Stochastic kriging for simulation metamodeling. *Operations Research, 58*(2), 371–382. http://dx.doi.org/10.1287/opre.1090.0754

Barton, R. R. (1998). *Simulation metamodels*. Paper presented at the Proceedings of the 30th conference on Winter simulation.

Bayes, T. (1763). A letter from the late Reverend Mr. Thomas Bayes, FRS to John Canton, MA and FRS. *Philosophical Transactions (1683–1775), 53*, 269–271.

Brown, N. C., & Mueller, C. T. (2019). Design variable analysis and generation for performance-based parametric modeling in architecture. *International Journal of Architectural Computing, 17*(1), 36–52. https://doi.org/10.1177/1478077118799491

Brownlee, J. (2014). *Machine learning mastery*. Retrieved from http://machinelearningmastery.com/discover-feature-engineering-howtoengineer-features-and-how-to-getgood-at-it

Capozzoli, A., Mechri, H. E., & Corrado, V. (2009). Impacts of architectural design choices on building energy performance applications of uncertainty and sensitivity techniques. IBPSA 2009 - *International Building Performance Simulation Association 2009*. 1000–1007

Fang, K.-T., Li, R., & Sudjianto, A. (2005). *Design and modeling for computer experiments*: New York: CRC Press. https://doi.org/10.1201/9781420034899

Fisher, R. A. (1935). *The design of experiments*. Edinburgh and London: Oliver & Boyd.

Fonseca, D., Navaresse, D., & Moynihan, G. (2003). Simulation metamodeling through artificial neural networks. *Engineering Applications of Artificial Intelligence, 16*(3), 177–183. https://doi.org/10.1016/S0952-1976(03)00043-5

Funahashi, K.-I. (1989). On the approximate realization of continuous mappings by neural networks. *Neural Networks, 2*(3), 183–192. https://doi.org/10.1016/0893-6080(89)90003-8

Grossberg, S. (1988). Nonlinear neural networks: Principles, mechanisms, and architectures. *Neural Networks, 1*(1), 17–61.

Hornik, K., Stinchcombe, M., & White, H. (1989). Multilayer feedforward networks are universal approximators. *Neural Networks, 2*(5), 359–366. https://doi.org/10.1016/0893-6080(89)90020-8

Kara, H., & Bosia, D. (2017). *Design engineering refocused*. London: John Wiley & Sons. https://doi.org/10.1002/9781119164838

Karkera, K. R. (2014). *Building probabilistic graphical models with python*. Birmingham: Packt Publishing.

Kingman, J., Dudley, J. E. G., & Baptista, R. (2017). The 2016 serpentine pavilion - A case study in large-scale GFRP structural design and assembly. In A. Menges, B. O. B. Sheil, R. Glynn, & M. Skavara (Eds.), *Fabricate 2017* (pp. 138–145). London: UCL Press. https://doi.org/10.2307/j.ctt1n7qkg7.22

Kleijnen, J. P. (2008). *Design and analysis of simulation experiments* (Vol. 20). Boston, MA: Springer. https://doi.org/10.1007/978-0-387-71813-2

Kleijnen, J. P. C. (1986). *Statistical tools for simulation practitioners*. New York: Marcel Dekker, Inc.

Kleijnen, J. P. C., & Sargent, R. G. (2000). A methodology for fitting and validating metamodels in simulation. *European Journal of Operational Research, 120*(1), 14–29.

Klemm, K., Marks, W., & Klemm, A. J. (2000). Multicriteria optimisation of the building arrangement with application of numerical simulation. *Building and Environment, 35*(6), 537–544.

Poropudas, J., & Virtanen, K. (2010a). Game-theoretic validation and analysis of air combat simulation models. *Systems, Man and Cybernetics, Part A: Systems and Humans, IEEE Transactions On, 40*(5), 1057–1070. https://doi.org/10.1109/TSMCA.2010.2044997

Poropudas, J., & Virtanen, K. (2010b). *Simulation metamodeling in continuous time using dynamic Bayesian networks*. Paper presented at the Proceedings of the Winter Simulation Conference. https://doi.org/10.1109/WSC.2010.5679098

Rutten, D. (2012). Grasshopper: Generative modeling for Rhino. *Computer software*, Retrieved April, 29, 2012.

Sacks, J., Welch, W. J., Mitchell, T. J., & Wynn, H. P. (1989). Design and analysis of computer experiments. *Statistical Science, 4*(4), 409–423. https://doi.org/10.1214/ss/1177012413

Simpson, T. W., Lin, D. K., & Chen, W. (2001). Sampling strategies for computer experiments: design and analysis. *International Journal of Reliability and Applications*, *2*(3), 209–240.

Simpson, T. W., Poplinski, J. D., Koch, N. P., & Allen, J. K. (2014). Metamodels for computer-based engineering design: Survey and recommendations. *Engineering with Computers*, *17*(2), 129–150. https://doi.org/10.1007/pl00007198

Spiegelhalter, D. J. (1998). Bayesian graphical modelling: A case-study in monitoring health outcomes. *Journal of the Royal Statistical Society: Series C (Applied Statistics)*, *47*(1), 115–133. https://doi.org/10.1111/1467-9876.00101

Steck, H., & Tresp, V. (1999). *Bayesian belief networks for data mining*. Paper presented at the Proceedings of the 2. Workshop on Data Mining und Data Warehousing als Grundlage moderner entscheidungsunterstützender Systeme.

Subrahmaniam, K. (1990). *A primer in probability*. Boca Raton: CRC Press. https://doi.org/10.1201/9781315273211

Tibuzzi, E. (2020). Rewired engineering: The impact of customisation and interoperability on design. In B. Sheil, M. R. Thomsen, M. Tamke, & S. Hanna (Eds.), *Design transactions. Rethinking Information Modelling for a New Material Age* (pp. 144–149). London: UCL Press.

Tresidder, E., Zhang, Y., & Forrester, A. I. (2012). Acceleration of building design optimisation through the use of kriging surrogate models. *Proceedings of building simulation and optimization*, 1–8.

Wortmann, T., Costa, A., Nannicini, G., & Schroepfer, T. (2015). Advantages of surrogate models for architectural design optimization. *Artificial Intelligence for Engineering Design, Analysis and Manufacturing*, *29*(4), 471–481. https://doi.org/10.1017/S0890060415000451

Xuereb Conti, Z. (2020). Inference Lab, Grasshopper plug-in (Version 1.0). Retrieved from http://www.xonti.co/

Xuereb Conti, Z., & Kaijima, S. (2018a). Enabling inference in performance-driven design exploration. In K. De Rycke, C. Gengnagel, O. Baverel, J. Burry, C. Mueller, M. M. Nguyen, P. Rahm, & M. R. Thomsen (Eds.), *Humanizing digital reality: Design modelling symposium Paris 2017* (pp. 177–188). Singapore: Springer. https://doi.org/10.1007/978-981-10-6611-5_16

Xuereb Conti, Z., & Kaijima, S. (2018b). A flexible simulation metamodel for exploring multiple design spaces. In *Proceedings of the IASS International Symposium on Shell and Spatial Structures 2018*, Boston, USA. https://doi.org/10.13140/RG.2.2.23313.53600

17

Image analytics for strategic planning

Aldo Sollazzo

The construction industry is a historically complex sector. In the late 20th century, the increasing difficulty to establish efficient practices became largely evident, indicating the need for a deep reassessment of its own foundation. The slow growth of the architecture, engineering, and construction (AEC) sector can easily be proved by means of comparison. In the United States, for instance, from 1947 to 2010, productivity in construction barely changed at all. Meanwhile, productivity increased by more than a factor of eight in manufacturing and by more than a factor of 16 in agriculture.

Such a slow evolution is mainly due to several factors such as the dependency of the construction industry on the public-sector demand, the fragmentation of the marketplace, and the consequential poor project management and execution as the lack of skills, inadequate design process, and underinvestments in research, development, and innovation. As a key aspect involving design and execution, it is equally relevant for the failure of planning mechanisms and the apparent inability of plans to represent the reality of on-site construction (Kamaruddin et al., 2016). In such a framework, a strong impact is foreseen in the next few years for companies introducing advanced automation systems. Indeed, automation—alongside the global need for new and updated infrastructure and better and more affordable housing—can help shape the direction of the industry. The key will be anticipating and preparing for the shift, in part by developing new skills in the current and future workforce. Behind the word automation, there is an essential factor enhancing the effective implementation of emerging solutions: data.

Data-driven practices are, indeed, triggering the introduction of novel applications bringing closer the different stakeholders in the AEC sector, from design to manufacturing to on-site operations. As an undeniable force capable of revamping the stagnant AEC sector of construction, data becomes central to redefine existing protocols and probably introduce new ones. From material properties informing design and fabrication protocols to performance-based simulations to on-site construction instructions and monitoring methods, data is stretching its roots in all principal stages of construction.

The implementation of data analytics in construction has been strongly promoted in the last decade by architects and engineers. As a result, the exponential growth of data used to create buildings is changing habits, enhancing novel communication protocols among actors involved in the construction. From ideation stage to manufacturing and on-site operations, data is offering companies the possibility to collect new inputs increasing understanding and control of the architectural artifact while optimizing timings, management, and logistics.

Construction firms are adopting data to take better decisions, increase productivity while improving job safety, and reduce risks (Jones, 2018). In this evolving panorama, data is produced at an unprecedented rate. Nonetheless the increasing capacity of data storage is not balanced by an equal ability to analyze its contents (Walker, 2015). In such an age of data expansion, novel extraction techniques must be introduced to describe spatial configurations. Emerging technologies offer tools to inform spatial strategies, unveiling dependencies, common patterns, and implications through a data-based protocol of observation and analysis.

The emerging field of visual analytics focuses on handling these massive, heterogeneous, and dynamic volumes of information by integrating human judgment by means of visual representations and interaction techniques in the analysis process. In particular, the practice of using new forms of data in combination with computational approaches and robotic perception can offer a clearer insight for strategic planning and spatial analytics with multiple applications on urban habitats, design to manufacturing protocols or on-site construction operations.

Multiple approaches for data collection have been implemented to provide datasets for data analytics. Data acquisition techniques rely on the integration of sensors capturing visible and invisible information from the environment using cameras equipped with multiple bands reading electromagnetic radiations such as radio waves, microwaves, infrared, (visible) light, ultraviolet, X-rays, and gamma rays. Remote sensing, a data collection technique used by satellites, paired with computer vision and predictive modeling, represents a valid operational approach to establish the criteria to study, observe, and analyze habitats, producing maps to enhance advanced planning strategies.

Introducing spatial metrics and advanced visualizations enables us to better understand complex spatial dynamics. In science, spatial data analysis can be defined as an extension of conventional statistics designed to support analysts to spatially describe how elements appear finding clusters, patterns, and correlations. Spatial and visual analytics have been implemented primarily in strategic spatial domain areas, including quantitative geography, public health, military, entertainment, and sport. Spatial analytics is the process of extracting or creating new information about a set of geographic features to perform routine examination, assessment, evaluation, analysis, or modeling of data in a geographic area. Visual analytics is concerned in creating graphic visual interfaces to complex datasets produced through optical data, tools underlying invisible data patterns to provide and reach strategic judgment.

Case study

The growth in spatial data, coupled with the fact that spatial queries can be computationally extensive, has attracted enormous interest from the research community to develop systems that can efficiently process and analyze this data. In recent years, a lot of spatial analytics systems have emerged.

In this chapter, will be introduced different methods of image-based processing applied to spatial analytics. The experience described will be part of two different environments, professional and academic, the first one oriented to urban analytics and the second, third, and fourth one associated to the AEC sector.

Aldo Sollazzo

Urban sensing unit

The first project described in this section is from Noumena, a Barcelona-based design and tech company implementing data-informed solutions for spatial analytics and strategic planning. Noumena is operating in the fields of robotics integrating spatial metrics and image analytics to decode complex spatial dynamics. Spatial analytics are intended as the process of extracting or creating new information about a set of geographic features to perform routine examination, assessment, evaluation, analysis, or data modeling in a specific area. In this context, Noumena is integrating robotics, computer vision, machine learning, and novel forms of data in combination with computational approaches to offer a clearer insight into urban habitats, on-site construction operations and precision agriculture for micro farming.

The project presented in this section is originally executed for the municipality of Barcelona, specifically for the department of urban development called Barcelona Regional. The primary objective of the operations described in this section aims at numerically and statistically expose the impact of urban greenery in the reduction of heating and pollution levels in the built environment, toward an informed and conscious organization of public street sections (Figure 17.1).

Existing cities demand solutions to improve energy efficiency while lowering the production of air pollution. According to WHO's most recent survey of 4,300+ cities worldwide, only 20% of the urban population surveyed live in areas that comply with WHO air quality guideline levels for PM2.5. In the case of Barcelona, air quality improvements stand as one of the major environmental policy challenges for the upcoming years. Aim of this project is to offer, through ground operations for data collection, three-dimensional reconstruction of urban spaces to evaluate and measure the impact of greenery in the reduction of the heat-island effect. The workflow proposed is based on the combination of hardware and software solutions. For hardware development, Noumena focused on developing an automated system for the collection of multispectral images through the implementation of a ground rover equipped with thermal and multispectral cameras (Figure 17.2).

Data processing has the precise scope of generating one single point cloud, storing visible RGB channels, multispectral channels to calculate the Normalized Difference Vegetation Index (NDVI), and thermal data over the same geometric organization. Using a custom python script is in fact possible to store in one single repository all RGB images

Figure 17.1   Point cloud view: a visualization of a point cloud reconstruction of Paseo de San Joan, Barcelona 2018.

Figure 17.2   Nero Rover: autonomous ground vehicle for data acquisition.

Figure 17.3   Bands + thermal overlap: the picture shows the match between the multispectral image in the background, and the thermal picture located in the center.

previously sorted in multiple folders. From this main folder, we perform the photogrammetry calculation in the open source software of Colmap, generating an RGB point cloud. To calculate the NDVI and thermal point clouds with the same geometric organization of the RGB one, we process the images generated from the parrot Sequoia associated with infrared and visible bands. Those images, with an identical resolution of the RGB one, are perfectly overlapped using computer vision image distortion called "homography". Planar homography relates the transformation between two planes and can be implemented for perspective removal or image correction and is based on common features extraction. As homography is performed, for each pixel, NDVI values are calculated using the python library of Geospatial Data Abstraction Library (GDAL) and rasterio. Output is a series of NDVI jpeg images (Figure 17.3).

Thanks to data interpolation, a direct correlation is determined between the facade partially covered by greenery and the one directly exposed to sunlight, where the tree's concentration is higher, and a bigger impact in terms of temperature reduction in the facade is observed (Figure 17.4). Through this method, we are able to prove that trees help in the reduction of the "heat island effect" lowering the temperature of facade and soil in a range from 11°C to 25°C. This approach has the potentiality to inform urban landscapes by introducing means of data evaluation for the application of urban forestry and calculation of its environmental and economic effect in energy saving and carbon adsorption.

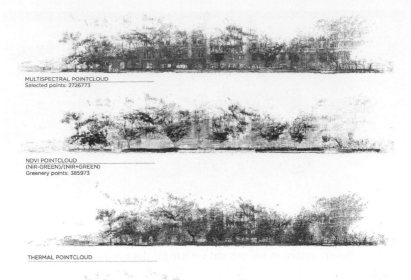

MULTISPECTRAL POINTCLOUD
Selected points: 2726773

NDVI POINTCLOUD
(NIR-GREEN)/(NIR+GREEN)
Greenery points: 385973

THERMAL POINTCLOUD

Figure 17.4　Data fusion: urban street elevation in point cloud RGB, NDVI and thermal point cloud of a street section.

Automating forestry survey for timber construction

This section focuses on projects developed in the framework of the master in robotics and advanced construction (MRAC), directed by Alexandre Dubor and Aldo Sollazzo at the Institute of Advanced Architecture of Catalonia (IAAC). The master is focused on the emerging design and market opportunities arising from novel robotic and advanced manufacturing systems. This transdisciplinary educational program focuses on expanding the application of automation and robotics in the AEC sectors. It is structured in three terms, each tailored to address emerging challenges: design to manufacturing, sensing and data analytics, and human-machine interactions.

Through seminars, workshops, and research studios, the Master seeks to investigate novel solutions involving students into hands-on research. In the two first editions of the Master program, several groups of students developed solutions integrating vision based systems to redefine management and logistic operations as part of the AEC sector.

The first case study of this section focuses on the optimization of material resources and the integration of aerial robotics as autonomous vehicles decoding physical variables into a digital data frame of geometries oriented to designing and manufacturing operations for timber construction and wood lamination.

Merging robotics for automated data acquisitions and image analytics with data processing, this project explores the impact of digitized forest surveying practices and the implementation of data-driven solutions informing design to production methods. A monocular drone is adopted to collect above and sub tree canopy information, with a precise focus on extracting tree geometries and branch deformations. The intention is to bridge design solutions with specific material resources adopting computer vision and point cloud segmentation to describe tree morphologies and lumber yield, and calculate carbon storage and land topography (Figure 17.5).

To define an autonomous path of navigation, a custom autonomous drone controller architecture has been introduced. The navigation system is structured in a ROS operative system capable of adjusting drone pose by means of estimation among target position and

Figure 17.5 Point cloud processing: extraction of plant robustness, species recognition, and lumber yield calculation from point cloud processing.

Figure 17.6 Navigation: implementation of simultaneous localization and mapping (SLAM) is also valid for real time 3D scene reconstruction.

on-board odometry metrics. The error estimation among the two datasets is used to adjust drone navigation path, controlling therefore actuators influencing velocity and consequentially drone autonomy.

Simultaneous localization and mapping (SLAM) algorithms are also introduced to evaluate drone positioning using a standard camera. This technology is implemented to construct maps of unknown operational environment, while determining the vehicle position in it. The implementation of SLAM is also valid for real time 3d scene reconstruction, bridging vehicle navigation with the description of its operational environment (Figure 17.6).

Means of computer vision are adopted to perform real time monocular depth segmentation, an existing technique operating over images or video frames, and capable of extracting objects from their background or analyzing sharp edges. This specific algorithm is introduced to enhance drone capacity to detect objects, avoid obstacles, and define objects' silhouette.

Other processes of digital representation are introduced to enhance the generation of a digital database describing each tree's geometric components. Photogrammetry is performed from the monocular drone camera, with the scope of generating a three-dimensional point cloud output. A segmentation is applied over the point cloud, adopting point cloud library to output point cloud clustering. This algorithm is suited to process a point cloud into a number of spatially isolated regions. A clustering operation is performed to split the original cloud into a series of discrete parts, which can be successively processed individually. This operation is necessary to separate trees from ground and leaves, outputting each separated tree trunk with its related branches. To finally estimate the orientation, torsion, and length of each component, a medial axis algorithm is applied to the original geometry. As a result, all three-dimensional elements are reduced to a set of splines from which curvature, torsion, and orientation are extrapolated and stored in a JavaScript Object Notation (JSON) format (Figure 17.7).

The resulting data frame composed of all JSON files is the key component connecting design and manufacturing operations for timber construction and lamination. Storing information on wood curvature directly connected to individual material resources can potentially improve all processes of wood bending. Through robotic fabrication, laminated timber strips are produced optimizing material consumption, thanks to custom sawing paths executed by the robot. This process allows to implement from each given curvature a specific material resource while introducing novel practice for forestry survey and material management (Figure 17.8).

Branches Catalogue

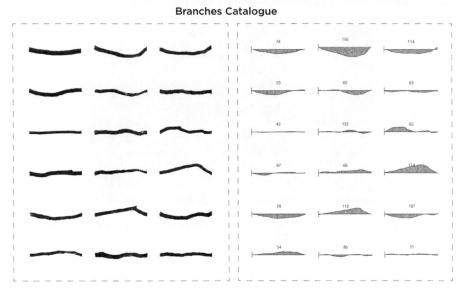

Figure 17.7 Database: storing information on wood curvature connected to individual material resources.

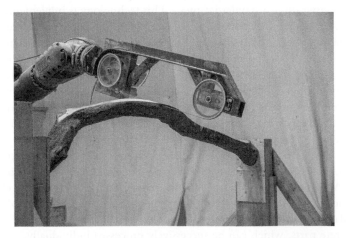

Figure 17.8 Database: storing information on wood curvature connected to individual material resources.

Digitizing material collation from demolition sites

The project described in this section focuses on the development of a digital tool for waste management and material sorting directly from pre-demolition sites.

Aim of this research, developed in the framework of the MRAC Research Studio II and III, is to support the utilization of waste materials by means of digital scanning and data-based infrastructure. The overall architecture is intended to introduce a data frame for waste management from demolition sites, integrating autonomous robots to perform operation of data acquisition, computer vision and machine learning methods for image processing, translating all processed data into a material platform accessible to different actors involved in the demolition process, and consequential design integrations.

The construction industry is one of the major waste generators. Existing practices for waste disposal are targeting landfills, aggravating the landfill shortage problem (Poon et al., 2001). Research interests in addressing construction and demolition waste management issues have resulted in a large amount of publications during the last decade. Previous research indicates that the majority of existing methods for data collection and data processing are mostly executed through descriptive analysis. The implementation of digital and automated methods for material sorting and classification can contribute to shift existing behaviors reducing material waste, while envisioning novel strategies for circular economy.

The data acquisition method introduced in this research relies on the integration of autonomous vehicles for image capture, specifically programmed to move and operate in unknown environments, thanks to the integration of a ROS infrastructure merging on-board sensors, SLAM algorithms, and autonomous navigation paths (Figure 17.9).

This research is relying on a bebop2 drone, compatible with ROS-robotic operating system. Data acquisition relies on visual sensors for drone navigation and image collection. The drone camera is associated with SLAM depth camera D435i, allowing the drone to perform operations of navigation, spatial explorations, and data acquisition. On-board optic sensors are responsible for the production of OctoMaps. These maps are capable of modeling

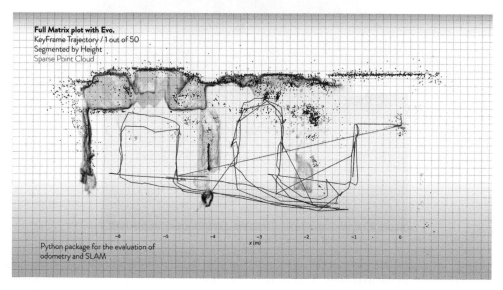

Figure 17.9 Data acquisition: ROS integration for data acquisition through UAS implementing SLAM algorithms.

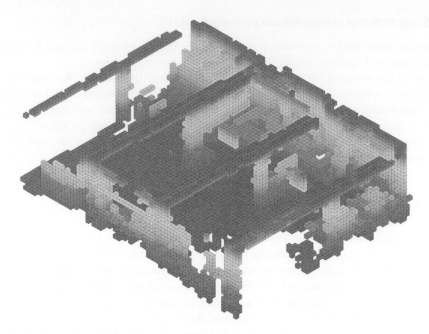

Figure 17.10   Point cloud depth map.

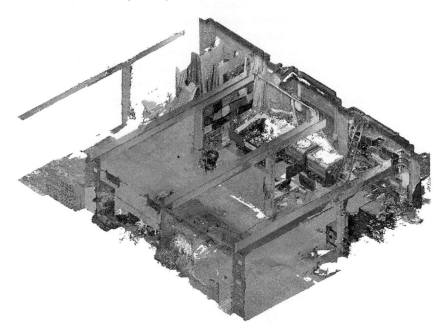

Figure 17.11   Point cloud reconstruction: OctoMap generation modeling arbitrary environments without prior assumptions.

arbitrary environments without prior assumptions of it, dynamically expanding in time and extension as the drone navigates along its trajectory (Figures 17.10 and 17.11).

Once data is collected, image processing methods are implemented to extract insights from frames and images, through means of computer vision and machine learning. Main image analytics methods are based on content-based image retrieval (CBIR) algorithms, built to extract features from images and then comparing the images for similarity based on the extracted feature vectors and distance metric. CBIR also includes methods combining techniques from computer vision, information retrieval, and databases to build real-world images search engines that can be deployed online.

Bag of visual words models are adopted to build scalable CBIR systems and classify image content. This method is valid to represent an image as a histogram counting the number of times each visual word appears based on feature extraction. Feature extraction methods can be accomplished detecting keypoints and extracting scale-invariant feature transform features from salient regions of the image.

As features are produced, clustering descriptors are generated in code words, and a model is trained to associate specific histogram-concentrations of these code words with each material reference categories. In this process, the image is subdivided according to a scalable kernel size, performing heuristics evaluation for material classification (Figure 17.12).

This overall method allows to retrieve material properties from built environments, as well as building shapes and physical morphologies, envisioning a novel automated protocol blending machine perception, image analytics, and machine learning into data infrastructures informing novel solutions for material and waste management (Figure 17.13).

Material Localization

Drone Capture Imagery

Analyze by sliding kernel of subpatches

Compile totals for each subpatch

Figure 17.12   Image processing: image subdivision to a scalable kernel size, performing heuristics evaluation for material classification.

Figure 17.13   Image processing: image subdivision to a scalable kernel size, performing heuristics evaluation for material classification.

Autonomous inspection system for building maintenance

Steel is one of the most abundant materials present in today's industry, in construction, machinery, and manufacturing. Reasons for its large implementation lie in its excellent mechanical resistance and structural applicability. However, steel and other alloys are known to react to oxygen and moisture due to their iron content, which forms a red oxide. The chemical composition of a rust is a compound named iron oxide (Diaz et al., 2017). For prevention and maintenance purposes, rust detection is significant, as it is a sign of material's deterioration. In the early days, detecting rust was done manually through a per piece or per section human inspection. That method is tedious and prone to human errors due to missed detection during inspection, which can lead to further damage of the material.

In the last decade, drone applications have expanded largely beyond military use. This shift toward public use of drones represent an opportunity to automate procedures that can disrupt a variety of built environments disciplines (Rakha, 2018). In this project, students introduced an unmanned aerial system for data acquisition operations paired with digital protocols for image analytics based on computer vision and machine learning. ROS based navigation methods are introduced to perform automated inspection. The monocular camera installed in the drone bebop2 is implemented to perform OctoMaps as described in the previous section. To explore all target geometries downsampled as mesh, the navigation algorithm is split into two steps: one looking for the least amount of points around the mesh as a view occlusion optimization based on the dynamic point of observation represented by the drone; two, generating a shortest navigation path through the selected points. These steps are based on two known mathematical problems: the art gallery problem and traveling salesman problem.

Hot spot areas are underlined integrating color-clustering algorithms. As a result a series of regions of interest are provided to the drone for its further detailed inspection. Those targeting regions are reached by aerial vehicle to capture static images for off-site analysis (Figure 17.14).

Convolutional neural networks are introduced to identify regions of each image associated with rust presence. Image segmentation, intended as the process of partitioning a digital image into sets of pixels, also known as image objects, is performed through Mask R-CNN algorithms, a conceptually simple, flexible, and general framework for object instance segmentation (He et al., 2017) (Figure 17.15).

Figure 17.14   Point cloud segmentation: color clustering over point cloud geometries for rust detection.

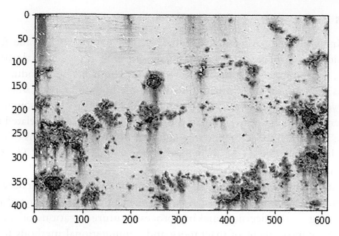

Figure 17.15   Image processing: edge detection segmentation to define area of rust through global thresholding.

The image dataset for this research is split into 600 rust images for training and 150 images for testing. The convolutional neural network is trained over 1.300 epochs, resulting in a detection performance of 94% accuracy level for tested operations. Segmentation algorithms are not only performing object detection, but as well computing the region of pixels associated to each specific component in a scene. This implies the capacity to estimate, through pixels, rust sizes, and therefore determine priorities for operations of intervention (Figure 17.16).

All data acquisition and image processing methods described are translated into operational maps to support strategic planning and maintenance operations, converting physical components into digital inputs providing databased methods for monitoring and intervention over architectural artefacts.

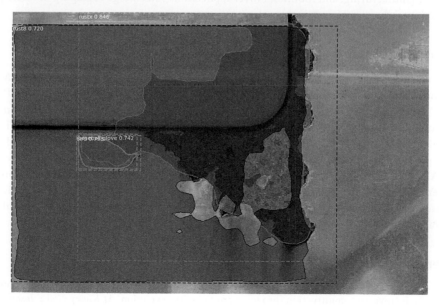

Figure 17.16   Semantic segmentation: applying Mask R-CNN semantic segmentation and rust detection.

Conclusions

In the increasingly complex AEC industry, data-driven workflows become fundamental to informed decision-making processes. Therefore, sensing emerges as a crucial variable to understand, evaluate, and project operations in our built environments by decoding physical components. In this scenario, the determination of digital methods supporting strategic planning is necessary to reveal associations among visible and phenomenal variables providing data-driven inputs to trigger novel applications in urban contexts and architecturally related operations.

Specifically, for the AEC sector, the introduction of automated means of evaluation will be crucial to address the digital transformation of this stagnant industry. The methodologies described in this article are envisioning a novel set of protocols to provide automated means for data acquisition, image processing through computer vision and machine learning, and finally translating into planning interfaces data-driven information directed to a variety of actors participating in the decision-making process. Future iterations of such applications will focus on the improvement of machinery and computational methods to sense, recognize, classify, and sort physical objects, with an increasing emphasis on the application of machine learning infrastructure oriented to image-based content processing.

A key aspect to introduce these methods will be the organization of data produced into compatible sets for training, testing, and improving existing algorithms. Providing scientific means of comparative advantages and disadvantages over the approaches introduced will assist and promote the effectiveness of novel applications, dispensing instruments to estimate holistic implications over novel technologies.

As a central figure dealing with heterogeneous actors, architects have the opportunity to take a leading role into a dynamic environment producing innovative solutions, although operating within an industry reticent in embracing much needed transformations. In conclusion, this chapter highlights the importance of a transdisciplinary approach toward innovative solutions for our built environments providing examples on how to blend data science, design, manufacturing, and robotics. Novel applications can emerge reshaping obsolete practice and introduce more sustainable solutions.

Acknowledgements

Robotic sensing unit, Noumena: Starsky Lara, Eugenio Bettucchi, Ardeshir Talei, Marco Sanalitro, and Marc Montlleo; automating forestry survey for timber construction, MRAC/IAAC, research studio I, II, and III, faculty: Alexandre Dubor, Starsky Lara, and Raimund; Krenmuller assistants: Kunal Chadda and Eugenio Bettucchi; students: Filip Biliecki, Jean Nicolas Dackiw, Soroush Garivani, and Andrzej Foltman. Digitalizing material collation from predemolition sites, MRAC/IAAC, research studio II and III faculty: Daniel Serrano and Alexandre Dubor; students: Anna Batallé, Irem Yagmur Cebeci, Matthew Gordon, and Roberto Vargas. Autonomous inspection system for building maintenance MRAC/IAAC, research studio II, faculty: Daniel Serrano and Alexandre Dubor, students: Abdelrahman Koura, Alexandros Varvantakis, Cedric Droogmans, and Luis Jayme Buerba.

References

Barbosa, F., Woetzel, J., Mischke, J., Ribeirinho, M. J., Sridhar, M., Parsons, M., ... & Brown, S. (2017). Reinventing construction through a productivity revolution. *McKinsey Global Institute*.

Diaz, J. A. I., Ligeralde, M. I., Jose, J. A. C., & Bandala, A. A. (2017, November). Rust detection using image processing via Matlab. In *TENCON 2017–2017 IEEE Region 10 Conference* (pp. 1327–1331). IEEE.

Froese, T. M. (2010). The impact of emerging information technology on project management for construction. *Automation in Construction, 19*(5), 531–538.

He, K., Gkioxari, G., Dollár, P., & Girshick, R. (2017). Mask r-cnn. In *Proceedings of the IEEE International Conference on Computer Vision* (pp. 2961–2969).

Hudjakov, R., & Tamre, M. (2012). Comparison of Aerial Imagery and Satellite Imagery for Autonomous Vehicle Path Planning. In *8th International DAAAM Baltic Conference* (pp. 19–21).

Itakura, K., & Hosoi, F. (2018). Automatic individual tree detection and canopy segmentation from three-dimensional point cloud images obtained from ground-based lidar. *Journal of Agricultural Meteorology, 74*(3), 109–113.

Jones, K. (2018, April 11). How big data can transform the construction industry. *ConstructConnect.*

Kamaruddin, S. S., Mohammad, M. F., & Mahbub, R. (2016). Barriers and impact of mechanisation and automation in construction to achieve better quality products. *Procedia-Social and Behavioral Sciences, 222*, 111–120.

Li, Y., & Liu, C. (2019). Applications of multirotor drone technologies in construction management. *International Journal of Construction Management, 19*(5), 401–412.

Poon, C. S., Ann, T. W., & Ng, L. H. (2001). On-site sorting of construction and demolition waste in Hong Kong. *Resources, Conservation and Recycling, 32*(2), 157–172.

Rakha, T., & Gorodetsky, A. (2018). Review of Unmanned Aerial System (UAS) applications in the built environment: Towards automated building inspection procedures using drones. *Automation in Construction, 93*, 252–264.

Seiferling, I., Naik, N., Ratti, C., & Proulx, R. (2017). Green streets− Quantifying and mapping urban trees with street-level imagery and computer vision. *Landscape and Urban Planning, 165*, 93–101.

Soto-Estrada, E., Correa-Echeveria, S., & Posada-Posada, M. I. (2017). Thermal analysis of urban environments in Medellin, Colombia, using an Unmanned Aerial Vehicle (UAV). *Journal of Urban and Environmental Engineering, 11*(2), 142–149.

The Impact and Opportunities of Automation in Construction. (2019, December) *Global Infrastructure Initiative.*

18

Urban development predictor

Using development pipeline data to predict San Francisco's growth

Skidmore, Owings & Merrill (SOM)

The advent of artificial intelligence and machine learning in the architecture, engineering, and construction industry brings with it the incredible potential for designers to navigate a vastly expanding landscape of architectural and infrastructural data with iterative predictions that can empower more meaningfully informed design decisions and improve the construction and maintenance of our infrastructure. For several years, Skidmore, Owings, & Merrill (SOM) has been exploring how machine learning could be harnessed to enhance the built environment in these ways. These explorations were expanded through research that was conducted as part of SOM's inaugural Year One accelerator program for recent graduates in 2018, which focused on the industry's most complex organism: the city.

Machine learning at an urban scale can be a powerful tool for architects and planners to diagnose complex issues and uncover the patterns that inform our city. It can also enable designers to make data-driven design decisions and provide a platform to intervene and adjust trends using our specialized knowledge and skills. In some cases, incorporating machine learning into the process could yield new design options that may not have been thought of otherwise (Figure 18.1).

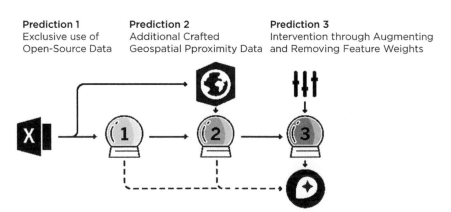

Prediction 1
Exclusive use of
Open-Source Data

Prediction 2
Additional Crafted
Geospatial Pproximity Data

Prediction 3
Intervention through Augmenting
and Removing Feature Weights

Figure 18.1 Development predictor workflow.

Machine learning at an urban scale

The great opportunity of urban-scale machine learning is the vast and endlessly expanding repository of open-source data available to designers from both private and public institutions. San Francisco is home to countless companies and organizations with proprietary urban datasets, including ridesharing, delivery services, location tracking, and many more. However, information from the private sector was difficult to incorporate due to the proprietary nature of these datasets. Of publicly available urban data cataloguing characteristics of San Francisco, SF OpenData (San Francisco Open Data, 2020) was the most robust and standardized public database and became the foundation for the project's machine learning models.

One critical lesson the research team uncovered through this project is the relationship between speculative machine learning questions of investigation and the appropriate datasets. Machine learning is heavily reliant on the quality of its data because of its built purpose: to form a prediction based on an analysis of existing information. When a machine learning model is built around a clean and robust dataset, there is a lot of information about each data point for the machine learning algorithm to grab onto, potentially discovering hidden patterns among features previously overlooked. In contrast, with an inconsistent and bare dataset, there is not much material for the machine learning algorithm to analyze, therefore leading to a model with poor performance and inaccurate results. Developing a machine learning model that benefits designers requires not only a meaningful design question, but also a relevant and complete set of data; the data and design question should be explored in tandem and inform one another.

The research team dedicated significant time to the analysis, selection, and cleaning of the pertinent data from SF OpenData (San Francisco Open Data, 2020). This portion of the research also encompassed the deliberation of datasets, which involved studying various case studies relevant to machine learning research at an urban scale, as well as the different lenses through which to analyze San Francisco—such as urban growth, sustainability, resiliency, and urban value. The question of growth and development in San Francisco was chosen as the research team's speculative design question as the subject is deeply pertinent to the ongoing urban discourse of the city's future and has a deep and foundational set of relevant data with which to train a machine learning model (Figure 18.2).

Making machine learning accessible

From the outset of the project, a critical goal for the research group was to facilitate a speculative machine learning research project that was intentionally open and accessible in both data and process to encourage its future use in SOM's city planning, architecture, and structure studios.

Open-source tools and workflows

Skidmore, Owings, & Merrill explored a wide range of tools and methods, including those commonly used for data science, spatial analysis, and data visualization. In an effort to democratize access to machine learning across SOM's many disciplines, the primary tool for building machine learning models in this study was Orange, an open-source visual programming software package with a variety of functions accessible to users with no programming experience (Demsar et al., 2013). The Orange model was organized into three different sections: training, validation, and prediction, where each group of widgets are customized components that the user can drag and drop in the Orange canvas to augment and generate

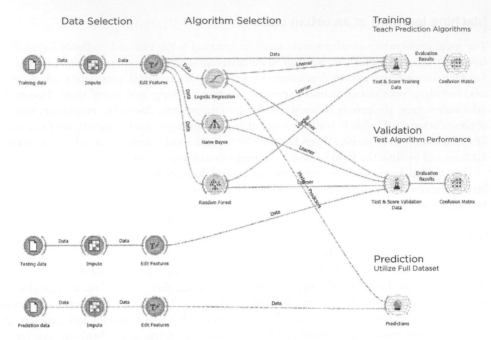

Figure 18.2 Sample visual programming machine learning model. SOM/Orange Visual Programming.

the predictive model. Visual programming software packages such as Grasshopper for Rhino are frequently used in SOM's city planning, architecture, and structural disciplines, and the utilization of Orange Visual Programming suits the wide-reaching digital and computational strength of the office's designers.

The resulting predictions from the models were formatted according to the geospatial characteristics of the data onto an interactive map using Mapbox as a tool for designers to visualize the evaluated urban patterns (Mapbox Inc., 2020).

Combining and cleaning relevant data

A critical step in curating an urban-scale machine learning-ready database, beyond cleaning and standardizing data, is building associations between tabular and geospatial data that fully describe the city. Massive amounts of data relevant to the cultural and infrastructural character of San Francisco are publicly available, but the process of standardizing and combining data of various types and from a variety of sources can be burdensome and prone to error. Moreover, finding a robust collection of data such as SF OpenData (San Francisco Open Data, 2020) can streamline the process of data consolidation but does not preclude a consistently identified set of data.

For the speculative design question, the research group consolidated all relevant data (including vector data such as lines, points, and polygons) into a tabular format. Most of the selected data were infrastructural in character, with the intent of providing a formatted framework that would allow for additional data from other sources to be added to the model that could provide more environmental, geological, or cultural insights. Standardizing the datasets in an accessible and legible way was also a critical step in making the research group's speculative models more easily integrated into the broader office's work and encouraging the use of machine learning in the evaluation of local projects (Figures 18.3 and 18.4).

EXLT	Latitude	Longitude	Year Property Built	Zoning Code	Construction Type	Property Area	Use Code	Property Class Code	Number of Stories	Number of Units	Supervisor District	Lot Area	Assessed Improvement Value	Assessed Land Value	Building Life	RPE
355004	37.8	-122.4	1923	SLR	C	7500	IRD	I	3	0	6	5000	204322	69455	88	Y
3730025	37.8	-122.4	1970	SLR	S	4200	IRD	I	0	0	3	4000	285821	191897	43	Y
319012	37.8	-122.4	1900	RC4	D	0	COMM	U	0	0	3	50425	141530	40191	114	Y
3753001	37.8	-122.4	1984	M1	D	180000	COMO	O	5	0	6	9600	2140213	260661	32	N
451203	37.7	-122.4	1928	RH3	D	4000	MRES	A5	2	8	2	3781.25	954518	927018	95	N
2998027	37.8	-122.4	1940	RH1	D	1450	SRES	O	3	1	7	2678	272263	636197	79	N
778002	37.8	-122.4	1934	RM1	D	13830	MRES	A15	1	18	5	5930	1437713	2119468	85	N
7161030	37.7	-122.5	1927	RH1	D	1100	SRES	D	1	1	11	2718	140102	129933	92	N
20080028	37.8	-122.5	1940	RH1	D	1125	SRES	D	1	1	4	2896	313772	73236	79	N
93011	37.8	-122.4	1927	RM1	D	1162	MRES	F	3	3	11	2466	39485	11494	69	N
1586012	37.8	-122.5	1941	RH1	D	975	SRES	D	1	1	2	2600	895309	695537	92	N
3600016	37.8	-122.4	1905	RH1	D	2266	SRES	D	1	2	1	1746	78527	160852	78	N
5730021	37.7	-122.4	1964	RH1	D	982	SRES	D	2	1	8	2316.94	749725	115459	114	N
21870006A	37.7	-122.5	1928	RH10	D	1054	SRES	D	1	1	9	1750	140768	122680	55	N
											7	4673	81342	150272	95	N

Figure 18.3   Excerpt of compiled dataset for training machine learning algorithms.

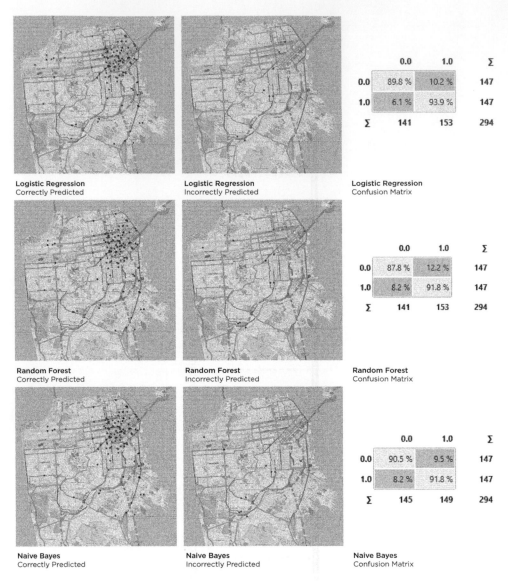

	0.0	1.0	Σ
0.0	89.8 %	10.2 %	147
1.0	6.1 %	93.9 %	147
Σ	141	153	294

Logistic Regression
Correctly Predicted

Logistic Regression
Incorrectly Predicted

Logistic Regression
Confusion Matrix

	0.0	1.0	Σ
0.0	87.8 %	12.2 %	147
1.0	8.2 %	91.8 %	147
Σ	141	153	294

Random Forest
Correctly Predicted

Random Forest
Incorrectly Predicted

Random Forest
Confusion Matrix

	0.0	1.0	Σ
0.0	90.5 %	9.5 %	147
1.0	8.2 %	91.8 %	147
Σ	145	149	294

Naive Bayes
Correctly Predicted

Naive Bayes
Incorrectly Predicted

Naive Bayes
Confusion Matrix

Figure 18.4 Training set performance of development pipeline dataset.

Predicting development in San Francisco

Ultimately, the research team wanted to predict the growth and development likely to occur in San Francisco—what the city could conceivably look like given the urban patterns evaluated by the selected algorithms. These predictions would allow an opportunity for designers and policymakers to understand how the city is likely to change given historic data and trends at a granular level. Such tools and findings can provoke future review and intervention by designers, city planners, and policymakers, becoming a powerful tool to visualize the likely impacts of legislation, rezoning, and construction on San Francisco's future.

This research project evaluates San Francisco's development pipeline database from SF OpenData as a foundational training dataset and the identifier of the types of properties that have been susceptible to construction and redevelopment from 2011 to 2019 (San Francisco Open Data, 2020). The aggregate features of ten thousand properties submitted for development became the lens through which, given the trends of the city's development, the machine learning model would predict which other properties were most likely to appear on the pipeline at some point in the future: this project's definition of development susceptibility.

The characteristics (features) of the development pipeline properties were further described by additional data from the city's assessor's block map. The assessor's block map, an open database of San Francisco's 200,000+ properties and their current (and historic) attributes, served as the base dataset for all properties in San Francisco (including those found in the development pipeline), and geospatial data from other datasets were combined in Orange using the city's unique MapBlockLotID to transform the tabular assessor's block map into a point-based and geospatial database. Furthermore, additional datasets relevant to the design question at hand were combined using this workflow. The compiled database included datasets related to zoning and district information, seismic and environmental hazards, crime and city operations metrics, census data, and historical property data. When combined, the machine learning model evaluated characteristics as granular as the size of the original construction and as broad as the property's district. Multiple individual machine learning models (logistic regression, random forest, and Naive Bayes) were trained on a randomly weighted selection of properties inside and outside of the development pipeline.

Furthermore, urban proximity data (proximity to urban amenities, etc.) generated by the research were incorporated into the database for a second model. A third set of models used the coefficients extracted from the logistic regression predictions of the second model to propose refinements to the weights of historical data, providing a means of design intervention that allows designers to prioritize certain features and iteratively evaluate alternative trajectories of development.

Training the model: supervised machine learning algorithms

The urban development machine learning model focused exclusively on supervised learning methods, where a base dataset acts as the teacher to train the model to make predictions. In order to train a machine learning model on the baseline data, the team explored three supervised machine learning algorithms: logistic regression, random forest, and Naive Bayes. The research team elected to focus on machine learning methods, but a subsequent phase of research could investigate the implementation of deep learning. Logistic regression was primarily chosen because of its parametric nature and ability to determine the influence (magnitude as well as direction in terms of the beta coefficients) of different features on the predictions. Random forest was chosen as it is a powerful nonparametric model that has been successfully used to determine complex decision boundaries in different problems. The Naive Bayes algorithm was selected because of its simplicity, and to provide a comparison against logistic regression and random forest. In this study, the logistic regression was implemented with Least Absolute Shrinkage and Selection Operator (LASSO) regularization with cost equal to unity, and the random forest was implemented with five trees and a number of attributes at each split equal to 5.80% of the data points were randomly selected from the baseline dataset and were used for training the three algorithms described above. The remaining 20% of the data points were used for validation and comparing the performance of different algorithms.

The confusion matrix calculated in terms of model prediction relative to actual classes in the validation set is a measure for studying the performance of different models. Refer to Figure 18.1 for the performance of the group's selected algorithms. The interpretation of the confusion matrix is as follows with respect to the logistic regression model: Out of the 100% of the data points that were designated category "0" in the validation set, the logistic regression model was able to successfully identify 89.8% data points in category "0" and misclassified 10.2% data points in category "1.0." Similarly, from the 100% data points in category "1.0," the model was able to successfully classify 93.9% data points in category "1.0"; however, it misclassified in 6.1% of cases (Figure 18.5).

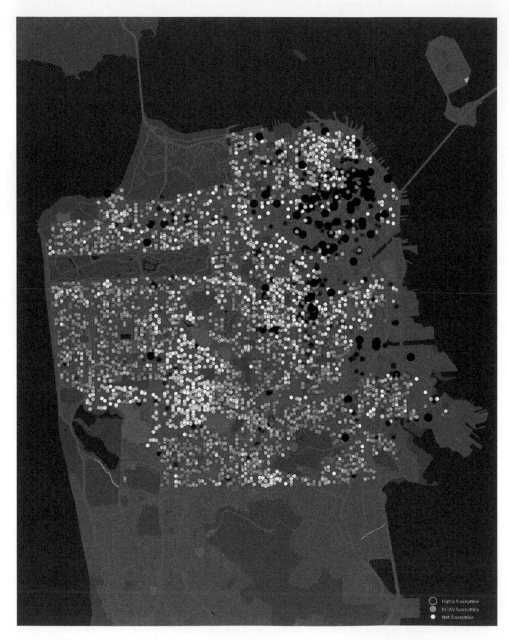

Figure 18.5 Prediction 1 results.

In other words, the false-positive rate was 10.2%, and the false-negative rate was 6.1%. Comparing all the three models, the false-positive rate was minimum for Naive Bayes, and the false-negative rate was minimum for logistic regression. Given the performance of these three algorithms, logistic regression was used for making predictions.

Prediction 1: an open-source process

The first (baseline) machine learning model predicted development susceptibility by aggregating characteristics (features) of properties found in the last decade's development pipeline and trained a set of algorithms to near-accurately predict whether an existing property is in the development pipeline. The performance of the algorithms was evaluated through a validation process, and the most successful (logistic regression in this case) was selected for prediction. The trained machine learning model was then used to predict the probability that any of San Francisco's 200,000+ properties not in the development pipeline would appear in the development pipeline in the future.

Figure 18.4 visualizes the parcel predictions of the trained logistic regression model that are more susceptible to redevelopment in the future. The strict decision boundary was constructed by indicating any parcel with a probability of redevelopment greater than 0.5 as susceptible and less than 0.5 as not susceptible. In this visualization, the predicted susceptibility percentage serves as a scaled weight to the property tags, showing a range of probabilities over a binary outcome.

The figure shows the parcels (in red) that share the attributes of the parcels that were already in the development pipeline. The geographical locations of the susceptible parcels resonated with the geographical locations of the parcels that were in the development pipeline as shown in the baseline data.

In order to study the influence of different features on the in-pipeline versus out-of-pipeline categorization, the features were ranked in Orange based on information gain, which distinguishes features that contribute less information to the final prediction (low gain) from those that contribute more information to the final prediction (high gain). Figure 18.10 shows the relative contribution of different features in terms of the information gain. In addition to the charts, property class, zoning code, and parcel area were discovered to have the strongest impact on a parcel's categorization. Other features that have a relatively strong impact are the assessed land value, construction type, number of units, and supervisory district.

Prediction 2: enhancing the baseline model

The baseline prediction model is an example of supervised machine learning that has trained associations between property features and its relationship to the target variable, susceptibility.

Although the baseline model produced a provocative and helpful map of how the city is likely to change, the open-source data did not include data that designers typically consider in the design of more safe, healthy, and equitable cities. In response, the research team crafted additional geospatial proximity data for each property to enable the machine learning model to describe and predict susceptibility based on a property's proximity toward amenities or hazards (proximity to transit, seismic hazard zones, parks, etc.). The model was retrained with these data, but these additional data did not dramatically alter the predictions. This was likely due to a saturation of location-based data in the first model.

Although the broader predictions were consistent between the two models, the additional geospatial and proximity-based data included in the "improved" model enable designers to better understand the correlations between the infrastructure of the city and its predicted development, such as a strong association between susceptible properties and seismic hazard zones (Figures 18.6–18.11).

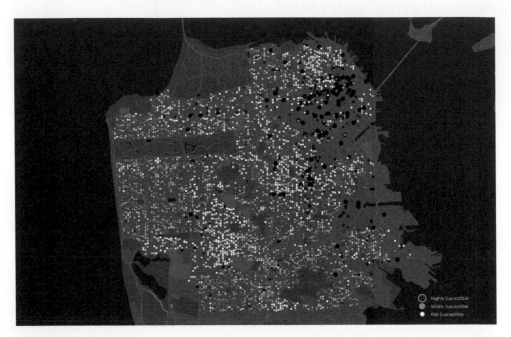

Figure 18.6   Prediction 2 with additional geospatial proximity data (below).

Figure 18.7   Euclidian distance to parks.

Figure 18.8 Euclidian distance to Bay Area Rapid Transit (BART) stations.

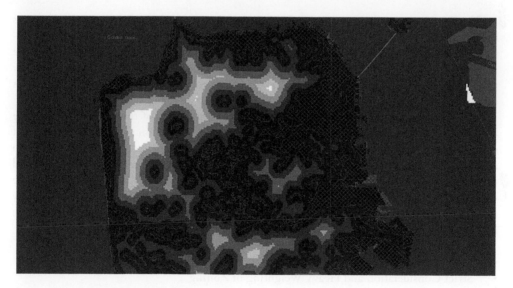

Figure 18.9 Seismic hazard (liquefaction) zone inclusion.

Prediction 3: intervening as designers

The first two models acted as a diagnosis for the existing conditions and patterns of San Francisco by predicting the likely growth and development of the city given its historical trends. However, designers, developers, and policymakers act as agents of urban change, and SOM was interested in the opportunity of leveraging the predictive model as a design tool for stakeholders to augment weights and features to understand the predicted impact of future development.

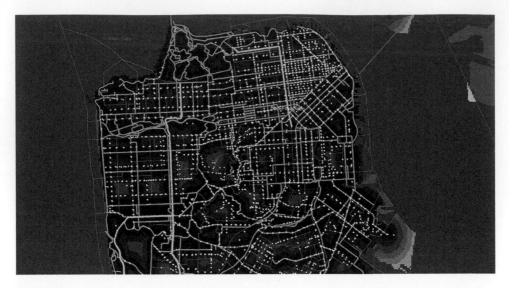

Figure 18.10 Euclidian distance to bikeways.

The third model used the weights of each feature from Model 2 and allowed the designers to augment coefficients and curate predictions according to specific values that are more desirable without compromising granular depth of the original model, such as maximizing the weight of proximity to parks to suggest a development pipeline that prioritizes accessibility to open space. For this exercise, a prediction equation from the logistic regression model was used to calculate the probability that a parcel will be redeveloped.

This was done so that the weight of the different categories of the continuous variable could be altered independently to study its impact on the prediction probabilities. Note that since the weights were manually augmented, they were no longer optimal with respect to any likelihood function based on a training dataset. Hence, the model cannot be referred to as a machine learning model. It is merely a prediction equation that is used to calculate class probabilities by using custom weights, and the intent of this study was to see how the class probabilities change once the weights are adjusted. The following scenarios were investigated:

- Increased Consideration of Properties Near Parks
- Strict Consideration and Heavy Weighting of Zoning
- Limits on Properties in Seismic Hazard Zones

After manually adjusting the weights of specific features, the research team retrained the predictive model. This allowed the designers to explore potential growth for San Francisco if the current trajectory of development was to be altered. For example, what would the city look like if zoning restrictions were lifted, or what if the policymakers considered limits on development within seismic hazard zones? These models deviated significantly from the two previous predictive models, and previously low-susceptibility corridors of the city became hot spots for development. This allowed the team to visualize the significant impact that city policies such as zoning regulations and supervisory districts have on the urban growth of San Francisco (Figures 18.12 and 18.13).

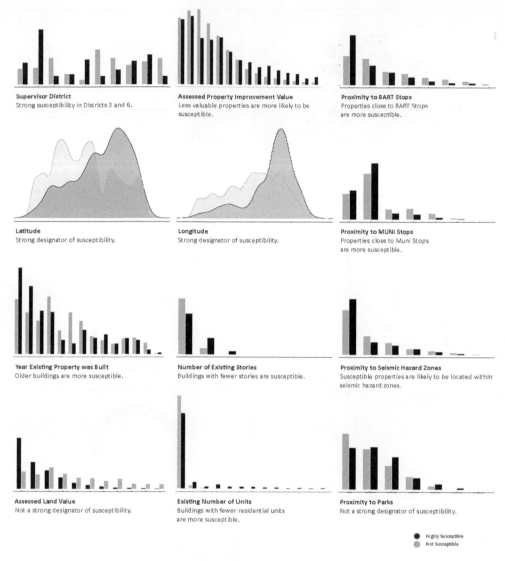

Figure 18.11 Prediction 1 and 2 distribution charts. The X-axis denotes categories (e.g., districts) or values (e.g., land value), and the Y-axis denotes the number of properties.

Findings and future opportunities

The predictive power unlocked by machine learning at an urban scale can enable designers to ask more meaningful questions about the existing conditions of our cities and pave the way for data-driven design solutions to be more acutely calibrated to increasingly robust and open-source datasets. In response to this opportunity, it is important that designers consider their role as navigators in an endless sea of data. The private technology sector has found great value in the use of machine learning at an urban scale, and designers, developers, and public officials should advocate for its use in the consideration, critique, and development of urban planning policy.

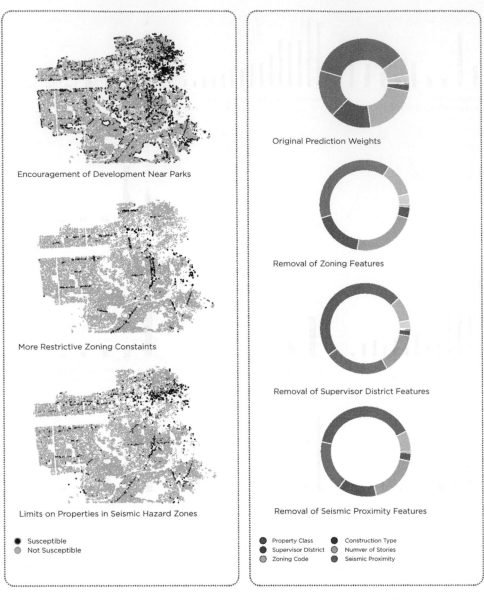

Figure 18.12 Prediction 3 (left) distribution charts. Manual weight overrides. By manually manipulating the predicted weight of each feature, designers can quickly visualize changes in susceptibility. (Right) Retrained model weights by percentage. In contrast, retraining a machine learning model results in a more accurate report of weighted values and features. The chart shows the relative retrained feature weights.

Where the traditional lexicon of city planning categorizes the urban fabric into broader-stroke districts and more easily defined groups of properties, the computational complexity managed by machine learning enables designers and planners to evaluate the impact of design and planning decisions at an incredibly granular, property-by-property scale. In many instances, the research team discovered properties flagged for susceptibility

Figure 18.13 Still from live Year One machine learning map with the GUI concept. This map visualizes properties predicted to be susceptible to future development in San Francisco, trained against the last decade of development pipeline data.

well outside of what one would consider an active area of construction and development in San Francisco; these properties should not be considered an exception but rather a provocation that the broad descriptors of our urban environment might not be the proper scale with which to address urban development. Although the resulting predictions and their perceived patterns of development reinforced the broader urban trajectory assumed by the research team, the presence of susceptible properties across the city asserts that the decisions that policymakers, designers, and developers make, however specific, have broad and unbounded ripple effects across the city.

The applications of urban machine learning can make the more organic patterns of our urban environment and the potential impacts we can have on our city more legible. How can SOM and the architecture, engineering, and construction industry further leverage these tools to transform how we think about, engage with, and design the city?

References

Demsar, J., Curk, T., Erjavec, A., Gorup, C., Hocevar, T., Milutinovic, M., Polajnar, M., Toplak, M., Staric, A., Stajdohar, M., Umek, L., Zagar, L., Zbontar, J., Zitnik, M., & Zupan, B. (2013). Orange: Data Mining Toolbox in Python. *Journal of Machine Learning Research*, 14, 2349–2353. http://jmlr.org/papers/v14/demsar13a.html

Mapbox Inc. (2020). Mapbox (Version 1.12.0). Mapbox, Inc. https://www.mapbox.com/

San Francisco Open Data. (2020). DataSF. https://datasf.org/opendata/

19

AI in crowdsourced design
Sourcing collective design intelligence

Imdat As, Prithwish Basu, and Sergey Burukin

In 1983, French President François Mitterrand launched an international competition for the Opera House Bastille in Paris as part of his monumental building program known as the *Grands Travaux*. The competition received 756 entries, and a 3-km-long stretch of drawing sheets was evaluated by the jury (De Haan, Frampton, Haagsma & Sharp, 1988). While one might question how such a large sum of design entries can be fairly evaluated, it is the fact that throughout history, seminal buildings were often acquired through competitions—from the Acropolis in Athens, to cathedrals in the Middle Ages, to the Duomo in the Renaissance. Just in England, 2,500 competitions were held in the 19th century alone (De Jong & Mattie, 1994). Nowadays, most European countries require the use of competitions in obtaining the design of public buildings. With the advent of the Internet and the World Wide Web, and online crowdsourcing platforms such as Arcbazar.com (Arcbazar), even smaller-scale projects, e.g., bathrooms and living rooms, can use the fair competition protocol in obtaining various design solutions. In this chapter, we briefly talk about the "competitions" model, discuss its translation into online crowdsourcing platforms, explore the integration of artificial intelligence (AI) in crowdsourcing processes, and demonstrate how AI—in particular, deep learning—can be used to produce conceptual designs potentially competing in future crowdsourced projects.

Competitions

Competitions are a popular way to acquire design solutions, because architecture is based on the logic of abductive reasoning (Steinfeld, 2017). That is, the solution space in design is not as clearly delineated as in engineering. Designers do not strive for a single correct answer, but instead try to solve the problem with a unique, original and idiosyncratic solution. No matter how good a design is, there is always room for a better solution. In other words, design can be iterated upon indefinitely. Therefore, competitions have been used throughout history to generate design options to compare, contrast, and choose from.

Nevertheless, one might find it surprising that architects submit to competitions at all, since the chance of winning and converting an idea into brick-and-mortar through this protocol is often lower than 1%. Thus, Louis Kahn argued that competitions are a free offering by architects to the larger community, because the majority of projects never get built and the architects do not get paid (Lipstadt & Bergdoll, 1989). And, not just in architecture, but also in other fields such as open-source software development, engineers work often for free on a given problem set for the good of the broader public. They get satisfaction if a user downloads their software, and obtain some fame in the community if it becomes more widely used. More recently, with the advent of big data, a more explicit competition model has permeated through software, thanks to well-publicized events such as the Netflix prize in 2006 and a plethora of Kaggle competitions.

Similarly, for most architects design is a passion, which can be explained by the concept of urges or drives in motivational psychology. Adolf Loos claimed that any creative act serves the sublimation of the creator's urges, and therefore performs functions beyond its apparent value proposition (Gleiter, 2008). Loos' argument, which was originally made against ornament in modernist architecture, may also explain why designers participate in design challenges at all: Competitions offer battlegrounds for "creative acts" to outshine.

Indeed, many architects made major breakthroughs in their careers and established their very name through competitions. For example, German architect Gunther Behnisch, who won the prestigious competition for the Munich Olympic Park in 1968, participated in more than 800 competitions over his career. Farshid Moussavi, a renowned contemporary architect, participated in more than 200 competitions, and values competitions for generating "creative leaps" (Moussavi, 2013). However, there are also well-known architects who avoided competitions altogether, such as Frank Lloyd Wright or Louis Kahn. According to Lipstadt and Bergdoll (1989), William Robert Ware in 1899 maintained that:

> Every competition … costs the profession hundreds of thousands of dollars, most of which falls upon men who can ill afford the loss. It is cruel and heartbreaking, when fifty or a hundred sets of drawings are submitted for judgement, to consider that… all but one… have labored in vain, and that out of all the schemes only half a dozen can possibly receive any serious consideration… Thus the profession grows and travails night and day, year in and year out, under the strain of sacrifices it can ill afford to make. No wonder that the system of competitions has come to be regarded as a sort of nightmare, as an incubus or vampire, stifling the breath of professional life, and draining its blood.
>
> *(p. 15)*

Despite such critique, the competition model is well accepted by the larger designer community and undoubtedly forms a major vehicle for the production of important edifices around the globe. A new embodiment of competitions—in the form of online *crowdsourcing models*—addresses the demand for even smaller-scale design projects and opens up the fair competition protocol to everyday design challenges.

Crowdsourcing

The architectural practice is constantly going through a transition of new technologies, e.g., novel graphic communication tools, new generative design, and construction software. New methods, techniques, and ideas are constantly tested out. This endless flux of changes coupled with the design talent available throughout the world makes crowdsourcing an attractive means for design acquisition. In general, crowdsourcing makes use of a swarm of experts around the globe to resolve a particular problem. This can range from aggregating and editing Wikipedia entries to solving wicked science problems (innocentive.com), or generating new logos (99designs.com), and many more. Crowds are solicited to "develop a new product

Figure 19.1 Cover image of Arcbazar, an online crowdsourcing platform for architectural design projects (arcbazar.com).

or service, refine a project, calculate or obtain different algorithms, or assist in providing, organizing, or evaluating significant amounts of information in viable data" (Bujor & Avasil-cai, 2018). In architecture, crowdsourcing opens up new opportunities to generate design options, and to facilitate collaboration among designers (Figure 19.1).

One such crowdsourcing platform is Arcbazar, a two-sided marketplace, with clients on the demand side and designers on the supply side. It enables clients to launch competitions, and designers to work on various types and scales of architectural challenges. Clients can onboard projects, i.e., provide a short description, upload images and dimensions, and set deadlines and monetary awards. During the competition process, they interact with designers via an anony-mous communication interface. On average, each competition receives about 12–13 design en-tries. All projects are viewable on the platform and can be rated by fellow designers. The ratings are based on the basis of idea, aesthetics, function, buildability, and graphic sophistication. Simi-lar to traditional competitions, projects are executed anonymously; i.e., the client does not know who the designers are and vice versa, in order to keep the evaluation process strictly fair and merit-based. However, every project contains an analytics page, which displays general real-time data about the location of designers, their education, gender, submissions, etc. (Figure 19.2).

Competing vs collaborating

Traditionally, competitions provide a level playing field where teams or individuals beat one another. The process is competitive and is based on prescribed rules and regulations that ide-ally facilitate a fair battleground. However, even in the best-case scenario, there is only one clear winner and all other participants are by definition on the losing end. In other words, all but one winner experience some sense of jealousy, disbelief, or disappointment. Therefore, the question is: Is there a possibility to have multiple winners in crowdsourcing models? Moreover, would it be possible for a designer to take a design from a competitor and iterate it further? What are the required intellectual protections?

Designers often build up teams to participate in competitions. Every team member brings preferably something complementary to the table. The team works together, shares the

Figure 19.2 Screenshots showing the cover images of design submissions to a competition (left), and the project analytics page (right).

burden, and eventually benefits or suffers equally from the success or demise. Is it possible to turn the competition model into a collaborative one, where participants do not compete but cooperate on projects? At Arcbazar, we explored the use of two promising models: (a) the exchange model and (b) the iterative model (Figure 19.3).

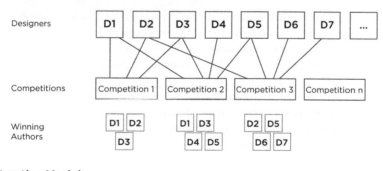

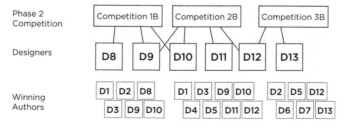

Figure 19.3 Two alternative collaborative models in crowdsourcing: the exchange model (top) and the iterative model (bottom).

Exchange model

This method of team building happens through direct complementary contributions; i.e., designer A produces a base drawing, and designer B uses the base drawing and takes designer A for an agreed-upon equity into the team. Complimentary work can range from drawings to environmental consulting, engineering input, partial design solutions, or any other project-related help. Designer A, in this way, can become part of multiple teams that agree on the terms put forth. Designers who do not have much time at their hands, or lack expertise in certain areas, can still add a "brick on the wall" and potentially become part of a winning team. It significantly lowers the barrier for designers to enter a competition.

Iterative model

This method is a two-staged crowdsourcing protocol. In the first phase, all designers submit their designs, and the projects are evaluated and ranked by the client. In the second phase, all designs are open for reuse by other designers. The knowledge produced in the first stage is not lost but developed further.

These models may sound counterintuitive, but by comparison, in the field of science, for example, a written article often has multiple authors, and the order of authors reveals the degree of each individual's contribution to the work. In a similar way, entries in crowdsourcing projects can be "authored" by multiple designers based on their level of contribution. When, and if, the entry wins a competition, the award is shared according to the set equity distribution. If the design gets built, a team of designers gets credited like its authors. The collaborative models put forth aim to facilitate a fair crediting mechanism for designers, in order to develop an objective framework that allows to harvest collective design intelligence built on aggregate design.

Evaluating design entries

One of the most controversial issues in competitions is the evaluation of design entries. According to Moussavi, the evaluation process in competitions has less to do with the merits than with the "theatre of unpredictability within which competitions unfold" (Moussavi, 2013). There is no particular framework that could be applied uniformly and objectively on each project. Therefore, evaluations in traditional competitions often follow the tournament model; i.e., designs get judged comparatively and eliminated one by one until a clear winner emerges. Or, projects are judged on an additive basis, i.e., adding virtues, experimental quality, and innovation, and the one with the most aggregated value gets selected. In either case, there are a limited number of possible outcomes for entries: (a) The design wins the competition, (b) the design loses it, (c) the design gets built through repurposing it for another project, or (d) the design becomes part of a new solution by another architect. All but one project will end up in the latter three categories.

In crowdsourcing projects, on the other hand, evaluations are based on quantitative and qualitative design criteria. Quantitative criteria involve voting procedures among designers, family, and friends of the client. Altogether, they provide a total score, which the system uses to rank the projects. This type of automation in evaluation is of essence, since the number of entries can often get overwhelming, like in the example mentioned above, where 756 entries were submitted to the Opera Bastille competition in Paris. It is literally impossible to have a fair evaluation through traditional juries with such a large number of entries, no matter how well the jury, regulations, intentions, and organization might be. Quasi-automated evaluation mechanisms can offer a solution for this type of problem. Qualitative criteria, on the other hand, are derived from the client's own critique, written feedback from experts, and opinions from family and friends. In this setting, the client is sanctioned to make an informed decision based on these data points. The evaluation process overall becomes transparent, and the competition outcome remains merit-based.

Tracking designer performance

Performing well in crowdsourcing projects does not always mean winning a contest. It can be more nuanced. For example, awards can be distributed in a more equitable way. Design entries can be evaluated, scored, and ranked automatically, and an award can be given not only to the top three designers, but distributed among all entrants based on relative scores. In this scenario, every qualified entry could get a share of the award. In other words, if there are, say, ten design submissions, each designer receives a proportional percentage of the total award—based on their final scores. In addition to monetary rewards, designers can also collect points for various acts, e.g., signing up for a competition, submitting their entry, making peer evaluations, sharing their work, and consulting project owners. At Arcbazar, these points define the history and ranking of designers on performance charts. They depict the history of designers and can be filtered by the location of designers, e.g., charts of top European designers, US designers, and landscape designers (Figure 19.4). Thus, architects can improve their standings by contributing to the larger community. In fact, it has been argued that "peer consumption and feedback are important motivators of participation in crowdsourcing operations and online communities in general" (Keslacy, 2018, p. 311).

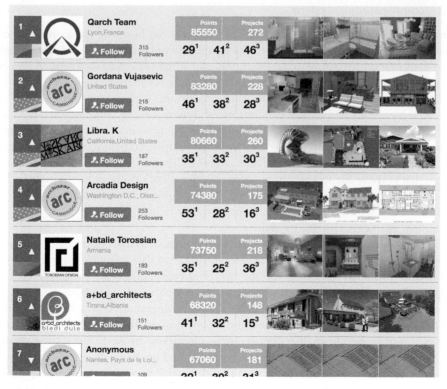

Figure 19.4   Screenshot of designer charts, showing the ranking of top designers on Arcbazar.

Arcbazar statistics

As of September 2020, Arcbazar gathered more than 30,000 projects worldwide and collected more than 300,000 renderings, drawings, videos, and millions of communication strings (see arcbazar.com/map). The types of competitions on the platform are distributed as follows: 40.6% remodeling, 16.4% landscape design, 15.7% interior design, 13.3% new residential, 12.5% commercial, and 1.5% institutional projects. 41.5% of projects were won by designers from Europe, 27.6% from the USA, and 21.2% from Asia, and the rest is shared among designers from Africa and Oceania (Figure 19.5).

About 15 million smaller-scale projects are remodeled each year in the USA alone. However, 89% of these projects are executed without an architect. Designs are either drafted by contractors or imagined by project owners themselves. Crowdsourcing is lowering the barriers for such projects to benefit from professional design help. It can become an important vehicle to spread competitive design to the wider segments of society and enlarge the potential design footprint of an architect all around the globe.

Artificial intelligence

Recent developments in AI offer exciting opportunities to improve the overall crowdsourcing experience. In particular, we present three use cases of AI below: first, in recommending award amounts; second, in surveying existing spaces; and third, in generating novel conceptual designs through deep learning.

Price recommendation system

One of the most common issues of clients on Arcbazar has been the question of the competition award. The problem is: What is an optimal award amount that is high enough to attract designers to participate in a competition, and at the same time low enough for clients to launch the project? We developed an AI-based pricing recommendation system that looks into 53 feature dimensions of previously run competitions, such as type, number of submissions, award amounts, honorable mentions issued, bonuses given, and the level of communication between clients and designers. In a nutshell, the system looks at the performance of previous projects in real time and suggests an award to upcoming new clients. However, the award suggestion is only a recommendation, and therefore, the client is free to set any award amount that is above the set minimum. Typically, the client's decision on the award is based on a combination of objectives: budget, mood, time limits, estimations, expectations, etc. The recommendation system has to take these objectives into account and output an award amount that satisfies both clients and designers.

The price recommendation system consists of (a) data analytics and (b) machine learning (ML) selection and evolution. We looked into quantitative data of high-performing projects on Arcbazar and discovered how various aspects of competitions are interconnected. The analysis gave us an idea about the type of data sources we should use to train the ML system. The accuracy of predictions, however, showed that the quantitative dataset was not entirely satisfactory in and of itself; therefore, we also looked into qualitative data, i.e., text description fields written by clients that contain latent objectives. At Arcbazar, a client describes their project quantitatively, e.g., scale, type, and size, and qualitatively, e.g., textual descriptions and comments. The full qualitative and quantitative portrayal of a project provided a more comprehensive representation of the competition performance and gave us a better

Figure 19.5   Screenshot of Arcbazar's general analytics page, showing the distribution of type and location of projects, location of designers, submission rates, etc. (arcbazar. com/map).

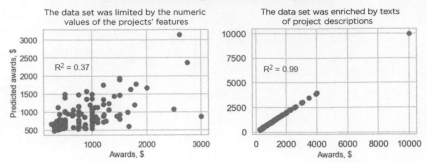

Figure 19.6 Graph comparing recommendation systems. The relationship of actual awards issued at Arcbazar and the predicted ones generated through the recommendation system is shown in the diagram. The left one was built using the random forest regressor algorithm that processed only numeric features from the dataset. The right one was built using the multilayer perceptron (DNN) regressor with the enriched dataset after adding natural language processing tools.

chance to find an optimal award amount range. Therefore, we applied natural language processing methods for the text fields, which increased the number of data fields used in training the ML system and improved the prediction accuracy overall (Figure 19.6). We went through some trial-and-error stages. Firstly, we only used numeric and numeric-like data and tested several ML algorithms on different splitting ratios for the training and validation datasets, ranging from 50/50 to 90/10, respectively. The random forest regressor gave us the best results. Secondly, we added preprocessed text values of the competition brief text fields and repeated testing several ML algorithms on different splitting ratios. This approach helps to reduce overfitting, and resulted in an optimal competition award recommendation system for Arcbazar.

Surveying existing spatial conditions

One of the bottlenecks in crowdsourcing is the need for accurate dimensions of the spaces in question. Clients do not only write their competition brief, upload images, and decide on a timeline and award amount, but also have to provide accurate dimensions of their existing spaces. Sometimes they have a blueprint of their home, and they take a picture of it and upload it. But often clients do not possess this piece of critical information, which leaves them with two options: Either they sketch the dimensions of the space(s) on a piece of paper and provide it to designers, or they have to hire an architectural surveyor to produce accurate dimensions of the space. This hurdle creates a barrier for many clients to launch a competition.

A simpler solution is to extract measurements straight from images. There are well-known companies working on solutions in photogrammetry in order to turn two-dimensional images into three-dimensional models, such as Autodesk ReCap or Rhino PhotoModeler. One has to provide a series of images covering the entire object or space and stitch them together manually. However, photogrammetry has been augmented with AI, for example, in aerial drone imagery to reconstruct larger urban areas or architectural heritage sites. Iconem—a French photogrammetry company—in collaboration with Microsoft AI is automatically stitching thousands of drone images together and thereby reconstructing accurate 3D digital models of entire historic heritage sites that are threatened by war—in order to record and

Figure 19.7 Artificial intelligence-based photogrammetry may identify dimensions and labels from single images (top left); and generate an orthographic drawing of the space (top right) (Courtesy: hostalabs.com).

archive edifices; for example, Iconem has digitized the ancient city of Palmyra, Syria, before it got destroyed during the ongoing conflicts in the Middle East.

The larger challenge is, however, to construct a 3D model from a single image, or few images that have been uploaded by a client and do not fully describe a space or object. It is a difficult task, because an image is a projection of a 3D space on a 2D picture plane, and a lot of spatial data are lost in such compression. An AI system can potentially assist in completing the 3D model with prior knowledge of similar spaces and furniture, fixture, and equipment and predict accurate measurements from a single picture. In an ideal scenario, the client uploads an image, and the system predicts, interpolates major dimensions, and generates a 3D model that designers can import into their software tools to jump-start the design process (Figure 19.7). We experimented with various emerging AI technologies, which at this point did not result in accurate enough dimensions to run a competition on Arcbazar. The goal however is to bring down the accuracy level to about +/−2 cm, at which point it will be feasible to onboard projects; or, alternatively, to develop a new interface for clients where they can upload a complete set of images to use current technologies to stitch together images and generate a 3D model.

Generating conceptual designs

In the late 19th century, the city of Quebec, Canada, organized a competition for the city hall. There were six design entries, none of which satisfied the jury. The city decided to produce a composite design made from bits and pieces of all entries. The final design by Georges-Émile Tanguay became a "Frankenstein" composition, incorporating Romanesque, neoclassical, and neo-Gothic-style features. Such a process was quite common in historical competitions. Today, stitching together a new design from various competition entries is certainly not considered acceptable or ethical. However, one could argue that decomposing projects and recombining the best aspects of each design entry into a new composition may offer the most ideal solution for a given design problem.

In 2017, we worked through a Defense Advanced Research Projects Agency (DARPA)-funded project, to use AI in order to generate conceptual design compositions. The goal of the research was to train deep neural networks (DNNs) with design data from Arcbazar, to compose new conceptual designs—by piecing together high-performing building blocks from past projects in the existing design database (Figure 19.8). There have been extensive developments in the field of deep learning over the last decade. Deep neural networks have been successfully used on a wide range of real-world applications. In contrast to rule-based systems, DNNs do not need to be programmed upfront, but can decipher rules through examining large amounts of data (Steinfeld, 2017). For example, one can train a DNN with millions of cat images and use it to label cats in new images. This is especially important for

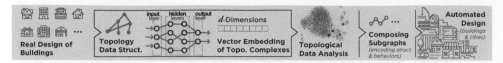

Figure 19.8   Diagram showing the workflow of discovering latent building blocks from home designs via deep learning.

self-driving cars, where the discrimination of objects, such as other cars, trucks, and walking/biking people, in real-time video feeds will make the difference between cars safely maneuvering through traffic or not.

Graph-based representation of architecture

Traditionally, architecture is represented through drawings, e.g., plans and sections, or through more sophisticated and information-rich building information models (BIMs). However, for this study, we represented architectural design using *attributed graphs*. We focused on the representation of essential elements of architecture, i.e., spaces (or rooms) of various types and their adjacency relationships that tend to occur in real conceptual design. We collected design data from BIMs and converted them into graphs in the following manner: (a) Nodes represent particular room types, e.g., bedroom and bathroom, with attributes such as area, volume, and perimeter; and (b) edges between nodes represent the connection type between rooms, e.g., a door connection, an open connection, and vertical connections, e.g., stairs, ramps, and elevators. We annotated type of rooms, type of relationship between rooms, and the evaluation scores based on various functional performance criteria, such as human-provided scores for *livability* (rating how well the living/family spaces were designed) or *sleepability* (rating how well the bedroom quarters were designed). Even though we limited our annotations to this narrow set of attributes, graph representations can be easily expanded with additional data, such as type of furniture, lighting fixtures, and color. In order to represent more detailed information, one would need to create auxiliary nodes that show the containment relationship within a subgraph. In short, graph representations can be expanded to contain more details, if those details are available. We used a novel application of graph-based DNNs, i.e., a supervised *graph convolutional neural network*, and trained DNNs to dissect home designs (graphs) into essential building blocks (subgraphs) and recompose them into new assemblies. Our early results revealed that DNNs are capable of extracting high-performing function-driven building blocks from design data (As, Pal & Basu, 2018).

Training DNNs

In order to set up the DNN, we divided home designs into two datasets, one for training and the other for testing. We trained the DNN with both design data on homes and their corresponding performance scores on *livability*. We then implemented a regression test on the remaining homes, which the DNN had not encountered before. For example, the original *livability* scores we gave of random three homes were 51, 32, and 67 (on a scale of 1–100). The DNN predicted them as 51.2, 24.5, and 67.2 in the test. The original scores provided were based on subjective evaluations given by reviewers, and therefore, it was astounding to see that the DNN was able to predict them with such close accuracy.

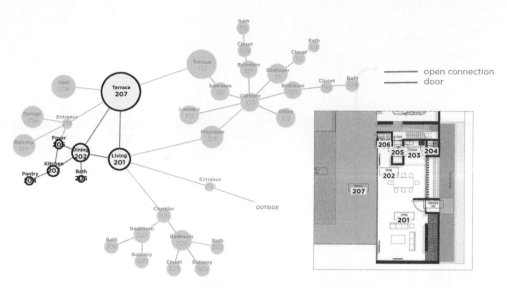

Figure 19.9 Discovering high-performing subgraphs, i.e., building blocks, in a graph representation of a house.

Identifying high-performing building blocks

Afterward, we used the DNN to identify subgraphs that responded well to the particular functional performance criteria, i.e., to detect essential function-driven building blocks. For example, the system detected the following building block as a high-performing subgraph responding to *livability*: ["2_Kitchen_82," "2_Foyer_39," "2_Pantry_26," "2_Terrace_1951," "2_Bath_26," "2_Living_479," "2_Dining_308"]. The string "2_Foyer_39" means a foyer on the second floor with an area of 39sf (Figure 19.9). We assume that the DNN classified this building block as high-performing due to the fact that it represents a living room that is quite spacious, 479sf large, is situated next to a dining room, and opens up to large terrace.

Merging building blocks into larger assemblies

Figure 19.10 shows two building blocks (left column) with high scores discovered for each of the two separate functional targets, i.e., *livability* and *sleepability*. To discover these building blocks, DNNs were trained separately on each functional target but with the same set of design samples. Next, we merged discovered building blocks into larger compositions. If, for example, someone wants to compose a new home that performs high on both *livability* and *sleepability*, the DNN simply discovers essential building blocks based on these function targets and merges them along edges via graph-merging algorithms (Ehrig & Kreowski, 1979). If there are nodes or edges that are typical in home designs but are missing in the discovered building blocks, we can add auxiliary ones to fill these gaps.

Vector embeddings

The process of adding auxiliary edges and nodes to new compositions in a mathematically principled manner is based on a method of embedding rooms in various design samples onto a latent vector space while preserving both the similarity of room types *across* the design

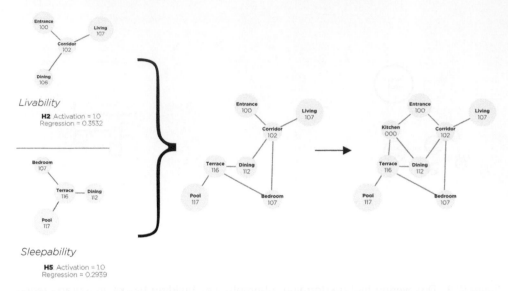

Figure 19.10   Discovered building blocks specific to the target functions of livability and sleepability, and merging discovered building blocks into larger design assemblies.

samples and the proximity of various types of rooms appearing *inside* each design. This was performed by a DNN-based method for *representation learning on attributed graphs*. All design graphs with annotated room attributes ("type" in this case) were merged into a single larger graph, and the latter was served as an input to a DNN. In this way, the DNN learned a multi-dimensional vector representation of each node (Figure 19.11). Vector representations of nodes depend on their type as well as their relative proximity to other types of nodes. As Figure 19.11 demonstrates, nodes corresponding to each type of room tend to cluster

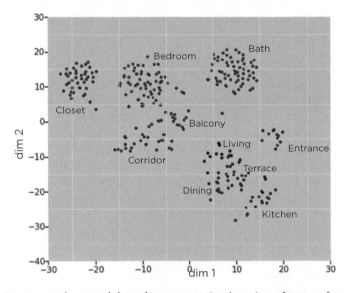

Figure 19.11   Deep neural network-based representation learning of types of rooms in a latent vector space while obeying proximities of types of rooms in design samples.

together since their types are identical. More interestingly, however, is that certain clusters of nodes, e.g., Bedrooms, tend to be closer to some clusters of nodes, e.g., Closets, Baths, Balcony, and Corridors, and not to other clusters, such as Entrance and Dining. Thus, the latent embedded vectors tend to reflect the average proximity of various types of rooms in design samples. Also note that the clusters corresponding to Living rooms, Dining rooms, and Terraces are very close to each other and overlapping at times. This is because most of the design samples had these types of rooms adjacent to each other. Vector embedding essentially exposes such latent design rules.

We used vector embedding to discover auxiliary edges or nodes that might be missing in new compositions. For example, building block H_2 for *livability* and H_5 for *sleepability* shown in Figure 19.10 (left column) have the Dining room node in common. We merged these two subgraphs along the Dining room node to form a larger graph. However, this procedure leaves the Bedroom reachable only through the Terrace, which is not ideal. To fix this problem, we computed the probability of connecting various types of rooms in H_2 to other types of rooms in H_5. Since the vector embedding reveals that the Bedroom cluster is close to the Corridor cluster, our composition algorithm added an auxiliary edge between Bedroom and Corridor with high probability (Figure 19.10, middle).

Note that in case there are no obvious candidate pairs of rooms to be connected by an auxiliary edge, we may need to add new nodes, e.g., rooms, into the composition. The rooms to be added can be determined by examining the vector embedding (Figure 19.11). For example, if the building blocks contain Bedrooms and Living rooms but not "connective" rooms such as Corridors, the latter type of room is needed to connect the former types. This can be seen as a problem of finding a *path* from the Bedroom cluster to the Living room cluster. Thus, an intermediate room of type "Corridor" can be added to the composed design in an algorithmic fashion. Or, for example, as seen in the composition of H_2 with H_5, the resulting graph has no kitchen; in such a situation, a Kitchen node can be added (Figure 19.10, right) through vector embedding—which depicts Kitchen spaces close to Dining, Terrace, and Entrance nodes.

Validating compositions

Afterward, we inspect whether new compositions break any geometric constraints. The subgraphs in themselves may work well, but when put together, they may form impossible assemblies. Therefore, we applied techniques to determine the fitness of generated designs, such as planarity constraints (Boyer, 2006). Once a solution has been validated, it can be converted into two-dimensional orthographic drawings or three-dimensional massing models through an algorithm that stacks nodes by obeying area and volume attributes, proximities, and connection types. The stacking can occur within a constrained building envelope, for example, as would be necessary if a new design had to fit into an existing building; or can be more loosely stacked, if there are no such spatial restrictions.

The long-term vision of this research is to develop an AI engine that can automate conceptual designs entirely. For example, a client defines a building program and provides the location of the project. The AI engine infers local climate data, lot boundaries, zoning regulations, building codes, etc., and generates a series of design options. If wanted, these designs can be wrapped with particular architectural style, e.g., classical, modern, or styles of renowned architects, and tailored to a unique massing model (Figure 19.12). The client can then pick one of the designs and hire a local contractor for implementation. Eventually, AI design bots may even participate in real-world crowdsourcing projects and become incorporeal competitors to corporeal designers.

| Deconstructivist | Greco-Roman | Gothic | Renaissance | Post-Modern | Art-Nouveau | Brutalist | Sustainable |

Figure 19.12 Empire State building in New York City, reimagined in different architectural styles (Courtesy: HomeAdvisor).

Conclusion

In this chapter, we discussed the reincarnation of traditional competitions in online crowd-sourcing platforms—taking the fair and open competition protocol to smaller-scale projects around the globe. We elaborated on competitive vs collaborative models of design acquisition and discussed the integration of various AI technologies into the crowdsourcing funnel, such as price recommendation and space-surveying systems. Furthermore, we elaborated on how AI—in particular, deep learning—can "read" architecture (through graph representations) and potentially generate conceptual designs.

Architects are increasingly relying on cloud services, advanced software tools, and ambient design knowledge provided by smart apps, which capture and process our surroundings, draft ideas, assist with design direction, and eventually may even design for us. Sooner or later, we will face the existential question: "What is our role as architects?" Anything that can be quantified somehow will be eventually performed better, faster, and more efficiently through automation. In the short term, designers may benefit from AI-driven software tools to jump-start their design process. In the long run, however, there may be consumer tools that are used directly by clients to generate and implement various design solutions. These developments will inevitably have significant bearings on the architectural profession. New practice models may emerge. In an interview with Crosbie (2018), we speculated that:

> … perhaps architectural practice could follow other creative fields, such as the music industry. For example, say, Frank Gehry develops a "style" and whoever uses his language through an AI-driven system pays him a royalty fee. Gehry in that way might "design" millions of structures all around the world…

New media, cutting-edge technologies, and novel forms of executing architecture do not necessarily have to be the demise of architects, but can cause quite the contrary and help magnify the potential design footprint of architects on many more projects all around the world.

Acknowledgments

This research was supported in part by the Defense Advanced Research Projects Agency (DARPA) under contract number HR001118C0039. Any opinions, findings, and conclusions or recommendations expressed in this material are those of the author(s) and do not necessarily reflect the views of Raytheon BBN and DARPA. This document does not contain technology or technical data controlled under either the US International Traffic in Arms Regulations or the US Export Administration Regulations.

References

As, I., Pal, S., & Basu, P. (2018). Artificial intelligence in architecture: Generating conceptual design via deep learning. *International Journal of Architectural Computing*, *16*(4), 306–327.

Boyer, J. M., & Myrvold, W. J. (2006). Simplified o (n) planarity by edge addition. *Graph Algorithms and Applications 5*, 241.

Bujor, A., & Avasilcai, S. (2018). Innovative architectural design development: The Arcbazar creative crowdsourcing contests perspective. In *MATEC Web of Conferences* (Vol. 184, p. 04002). EDP Sciences.

Crosbie, M., (2018, September 17). *Doom or Bloom: What Will Artificial Intelligence Mean for Architecture*. Retrieved from https://commonedge.org/doom-or-bloom-what-will-artificial-intelligence-mean-for-architecture/

De Haan, H., Frampton, K., Haagsma, I., & Sharp, D. (1988). *Architects in Competition: International Architectural Competitions: International Architectural Competitions of the Last 200 Years*. Thames and Hudson.

De Jong, C., & Mattie, E. (1994). *Architectural Competitions–Vol. 1–2*. Taschen.

Ehrig, H., & Kreowski, H. J. (1979). Pushout-Properties: An analysis of gluing constructions for graphs. *Mathematische Nachrichten*, *91*(1), 135–149.

Gleiter, J. H. (2008). Das neue Ornament-Zur Genealogie des neuen Ornaments im digitalen Zeitalter. *Arch Plus*, *189*, 78–83.

Keslacy, E. (2018). Arcbazar and the Ethics of Crowdsourcing Architecture. *Thresholds*, *46*, 300–317.

Lipstadt, H., & Bergdoll, B. (Eds.). (1989). *The Experimental Tradition: Essays on Competitions in Architecture*. Princeton Architectural Press.

Moussavi, F. (2013). Creative leaps in the arena of architectural competitions. *Architectural Review*, *233*(1392), 27–28.

Steinfeld, K. (2017). Dreams may come. In *ACADIA 2017: DISCIPLINES & DISRUPTION (Proceedings of the 37th Annual Conference of the Association for Computer Aided Design in Architecture)* (pp. 590–599), Cambridge, MA.

20

Interfacing architecture and artificial intelligence

Machine learning for architectural design and fabrication

Bastian Wibranek and Oliver Tessmann

Our society faces the global challenge of doubling the volume of our current built environment by 2060 (UN Environment 2017). This massive growth is to be achieved with the industry suffering from a shortage of skilled workers and a significant lack of productivity increase since the 1990s. The industry lacks innovation through digitalization, which results in an information gap between design and construction. The potential of digital modularization and prefabrication is not exploited (Melenbrink et al. 2020). Currently, productivity is even lowered through less qualified workforces and the need for simplified means of construction. The industry treats labor as one of the cheapest resources ignoring the economic downsides of this premise and its societal problems. To avoid this problem, architects need to increase intelligence (human and artificial), digitalization, and automation in all steps of architectural production.

To tackle the challenges mentioned above and increase productivity, construction companies have to move from a craft-based low-performance industry to a machine-based high-performance industry (Bock 2015). The architecture, engineering, and construction (AEC) industry needs a high degree of construction automation (Barbosa et al. 2017). Artificial intelligence (AI) is one promising revenue to improve the AEC industry.

The era of using the computer as merely a better, faster, and more precise version of the pencil has long been overcome. The computer-aided design replaced the drawing board in the 1980s. The concepts of algorithmic procedures, generating form, and space developed long before the hardware performance existed to make it possible to implement them. Interestingly, these early works by people such as Yona Friedmann, John Frazer, and Nicholas Negroponte on computer programs in design were not driven by the idea to establish a digital replica of the drawing process. Instead, these ideas dealt with questions of how to empower nonexperts to create their designs. Yona Friedmann's Flatwriter allows users to build a home to choose from a large variety of predefined options presented in a keyboard-like fashion. Flatwriter asks the user for their desires and uses this information to place the apartment within an empty infrastructure, negotiating the various lifestyles of multiple users. Architectural expert knowledge is encoded into a computer program that acts as mediators in the process of empowerment (Vardouli 2011).

Experts also benefited from algorithmic design in their search for novel formal expressions and the ambition to use calculus to explore larger solution spaces and the branching logic of combinatorial options. The far-reaching goal of computation in design has always been discovering novel territory in aesthetics and performance, unreachable through human intuition and tacit knowledge alone. The algorithmic tools developed to amplify human capacities of design exploration have been quickly applied for engineering-driven optimization tasks rather than searching for the unknown. Optimization is the low-hanging fruit of algorithmic design: The desired goal is already known, i.e., a maximum span of a bridge with the minimum consumption of material. It is only the shortest path toward that goal that needs to be found. Those well-defined problems served well to test and benchmark algorithms. However, finding answers for the unknown is still a challenging task for algorithmic design. AI might close this gap, away from optimization toward an understanding and exploration of the unknown.

This chapter regards the fusion of creative work, digital technology, and interdisciplinary research as the key to mastering the manifold challenges of our time. Architecture can benefit from applying AI at almost all stages. Therefore, we have to distribute human and AI smartly. We propose integrating machine intelligence at different stages of architectural production, shifting the designer's focus toward machine actions that have to be defined and rewarded to enable the machine to learn.

However, humans also have to learn: One of the biggest challenges in an AI-enhanced architecture is how we interfere with machine learning (ML) into the extensive body of processes. To make use of the tools provided by ML, we have to educate architects about the mechanisms of ML (Khean et al. 2018). Andong Lu (2017) pointed out that a high degree of autonomy of digital systems in the design process challenges the way humans are engaged in that process. With machines that outperform human abilities in dimensions such as accurate calculus or analyzing massive data sets, we have to invent effective forms of human engagement. The use of AI is the latest step in the development of algorithmic design procedures in architecture. We regard the process as an evolution that gradually shifts from intelligence amplification to AI.

Discrete design

An important element in mastering the productivity challenges is the closer linkage of the entire process chain from design to construction using prefabricated elements and automation. Notably, the implementation of prefabrication strategies and modularization can drastically improve productivity (Harvey et al. 2011). Design processes with fabrication and assembly procedures can solve later implementation problems for the use of prefabrication. The concept of Digital Materials (Gershenfeld et al. 2015) integrates ideas of modularity into the early stages of the design. It is extending the concept of the digital from the computer numerically controlled processes of manufacturing to the physical elements themselves (Gershenfeld 2012), focusing on discrete elements that can be combined and reassembled like the pixels on the computer screen. Thereby, repetitive elements can be serially fabricated and automatically assembled. The aim is a truly digital building system that translates digital properties into the physical world.

Recently, the discretization at the early stages of design has been addressed by architects and researchers (Retsin 2019). Beyond the formal definition of the concept of Digital Materials, there is also a flourishing ecosystem of digital design tools. In these tools, the designer starts the design with discrete elements and aggregates them into assemblies.

Discrete design tools

We link design to prefabrication through computational tools. Designers explore the manifold combinatorial possibilities of discrete elements with the help of the computer.

The examination of part-to-whole relationships is a continual process in architectural history. Computation fosters the use of discrete elements already during the design stage; they constrain design decisions, but also enlarge the designers' freedom within those boundaries. In architectural research, digital design tools have been explored for design in different environments such as game engines (Sanchez 2014), through agent-based modeling (Retsin 2016) and the use of voxel grammars (Tessmann & Savov 2016). All these approaches rely on custom-developed solutions and lack scalability or usability for users not trained in programming. To allow the exploration of such methodologies to designers with no prior programming knowledge, designers need versatile design tools and interfaces. Providing an accessible design tool—WASP by Andrea Rossi (2019)—an open-source plugin for Rhino/Grasshopper was developed at the Digital Design Unit at the Technical University of Darmstadt. It provides a set of tools to generate rule-based designs based on the paradigm of Digital Materials (Figure 20.1). In the software, designers define rules for aggregating repetitive units. These rules include connectivity and approximation of elements. Their aggregation is driven by external parameters such as force distribution (Rossi & Tessmann 2018). Fabrication constraints can already be checked during the aggregation process, allowing seamless integration between design and assembly. At the same time, elements can be integrated on different scales or resolutions within the same aggregation system (Rossi & Tessmann 2017a, 2017b).

The integration of fabrication constraints and the sequential nature of the processes contribute to an earlier binding between design and construction. Discrete design tools such as WASP are well suited for robotic manufacturing with regard to prefabricated elements following the paradigm of Digital Materials.

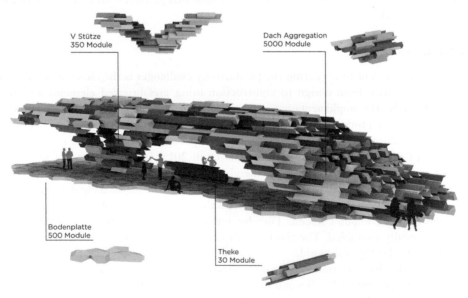

Figure 20.1 Assembly from discrete elements designed in a studio project at the Digital Design Unit at TU Darmstadt.

Design for robotic assembly

The complex arrangement of elements calls for a reconsideration of how to assemble them. The sequential nature of discrete structures is particularly interesting for robotic assembly. While previously, designers thought about production and assembly at later stages of the design, Digital Materials holds the promise of integrating the design for robotic processes already in the design stage (Figure 20.2). Robots offer great potential to cope with the rising complexity of the sequential assembly of discrete elements. Discreteness allows for circular reuse of building elements to extend their lifespan, but design for reassembly could also be regarded as a way to reconfigure inhabited spaces. We can see a significant effort in academic research to connect the material system with robot systems into the material–robot system (Jenett et al. 2019) or robot-oriented design (Bock & Linner 2015). Under such paradigms, the design of elements has to follow specific considerations of the robot's strengths and capabilities, including connections between elements and error-correction through self-alignment (Figure 20.3). An understanding of robotic processes allows us to address challenges in the assembly process. Therefore, different tools will enable the designer to simulate the robotic construction inside the digital design environment. Hence,

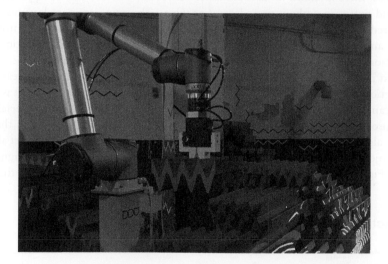

Figure 20.2   The robotic installation at the Luminale light festival 2018 places spectators in a space that is continuously reconfigured by a robot.

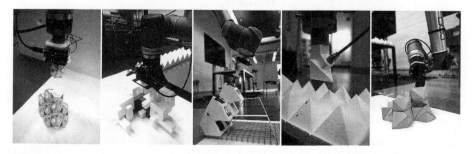

Figure 20.3   Different discrete elements designed for a robotic assembly.

workflows become integrated, and the classical separation between design and construction might dissolve.

Overall, Digital Materials will trigger a shift in the building culture created by algorithms and combinatorics and the usage of repetitive components designed for robotic assembly. The six-axis industrial robot arm is the common tool in research today but in the future, we will see robots especially appropriated for architectural assembly. These robots might not look anything like today's robots and work parallel in heterogeneous teams (Yablonina & Menges 2019). The underlying mechanisms of this shift have to follow a computational logic, offering great potential for the use of ML.

Reinforcement learning in architectural design

AI is a field almost as widespread as architecture. In our research, we focus on one field of AI called ML. Based on vast amounts of data, machines learn through supervised and unsupervised processes.

However, we are tackling the issue of innovative construction and technological futures that are unexplored. As a result of emerging design and construction concepts such as Digital Materials, there is almost no data available. Therefore, we need an ML approach that can explore and optimize without precedents. For these tasks, reinforcement learning (RL) is a well-tailored branch of ML. In the RL paradigm, an agent explores a given environment by observing and taking actions; a reward system guides the agent to take desired actions or punish bad actions. This environment can consist of discrete building elements, and the actions can be the next placement of an element. Instead of using precedents, the algorithm learns to take specific actions based on a reward. The RL algorithm aims to learn a policy that is a kind of rule that can be adapted to changing environments or tasks. The approach is especially promising for problems that consist of large sets of possibilities that change based on the actions. Thus, RL algorithms are well suited for combinatorial problems (Ruiz-Montiel et al. 2013).

The project Combinatorial Assemblies aims to formulate the aggregation design as an RL problem (Figure 20.4). The system is asked to aggregate elements into a predefined global

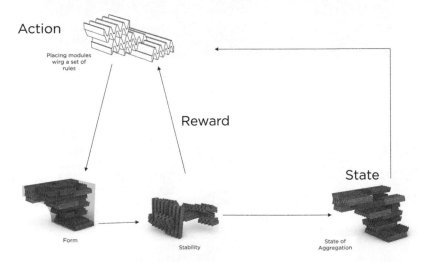

Figure 20.4   The framing of the RL approach in a discrete assembly project consists of action, reward, and observation of a state.

form described by a hull geometry. Actions were defined as the placement of single elements into an aggregation, subsequently building the final geometry. While the designer focuses on the global form and the shapes of the elements, the algorithmic system needs to find the best way to aggregate the building blocks. The observation of the environment consists of the current state of the aggregation and a reward. At each state, the current aggregation sequence is encoded, and the rewards are given by a function calculating the distance of the placed elements to the desired hull geometry. Additionally, the stability of aggregation becomes a reward. It is tested at the end of each learning episode using a physics simulation (e.g., CoppeliaSim) that becomes part of the environment, informing the physical process of aggregation. The role of the human designer is supplemented by another task: Understanding and designing the RL reward appropriate to the task.

Simulation as part of the prediction

Today, we can reproduce and abstract parts of the real world in simulation environments. Instead of representing merely geometry, we can simulate robot actions and physical behavior. Examples for physics simulation in Rhino/Grasshopper are Kangaroo (Piker 2020), Flexhoper (Felbrich 2019), or PhysX.GH (Kao et al. 2019). Moreover, Finite Element software, such as Karamba, analyzes material behavior and calculates deflections. Robot simulations (Kuka PRC, Robots, HAL Robots, Robot Components, etc.) are also implemented into design environments (Figure 20.5).

Simulation environments are especially crucial for the RL approach as it helps to map physical properties into the digital (Figure 20.6). Thereby, we can utilize computational power to learn inside the computer instead of the real world to speed up the learning process. These simulations serve as predictions of how a design will perform structurally or reveal

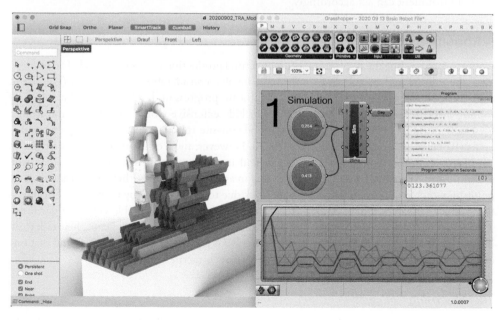

Figure 20.5 The plugin Robots by Vicente Soler simulate robot movements and check for collisions inside the design environment of Rhino/Grasshopper.

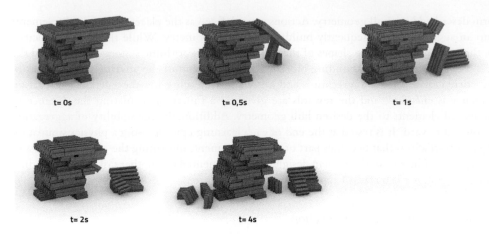

t= 0s   t= 0,5s   t= 1s

t= 2s   t= 4s

Figure 20.6   A cantilevering structure, assembled from discrete elements, collapsing based on physical simulation in PyBullet.

problems during assembly. Similar to a rendering that predicts the future appearance of a building, the simulation environments enable us to predict dynamic behavior.

Of course, simulations are abstractions and have to be tested against the material world. Accurate physical simulations of a structure that consists of discrete elements are still challenging due to the amount of contact between the elements. Moreover, simulations of robotic assembly tasks usually do not address the tolerances of building elements. Whereas in the digital, we are dealing with precision and accuracy; the material world comes with tolerances and unforeseen obstacles. One way of dealing with those differences between the digital and material realities is through sensors and adaptation; machines that can understand their environment can act accordingly.

Autonomous robots

Robots are extending the digitization of architectural production into the physical. Today, however, the joining and assembly of components involve considerable manual effort (Reinhardt et al. 2019). Academic research has shown significant progress in developing novel concepts of robotic manufacturing. These investigations include extensive work of Gramazio and Kohler Research at the ETH Zurich, researching mobile on-site robotics, and the joining of components (Robeller et al. 2017; Thoma et al. 2018). However, most of the investigations are set in lab-like conditions, need human supervision, and are preprogrammed, allowing no adaptation to unforeseen tolerances or obstacles. Especially in assembly processes, there are several delicate points in which preprogrammed robots get stuck due to issues caused by tolerances. To address those issues, researchers have equipped robots with sensors and adaptable control algorithms. Thereby, robots can acquire knowledge about the element being grasped, adapt their task to an obstacle, and apply necessary forces during assembly (Wibranek et al. 2019). We found that one crucial skill for building with prefabricated elements is tactile skills.

Tactile sensing

Construction workers can rely on a rich stream of sensual feedback—most importantly, the sense of touch—during assembly. Tactile capabilities offer the potential for construction scenarios in which contact is unavoidable or required. Roboticists are addressing the topic currently, and we see a growing variety of tactile sensors in academic research. Especially, force sensors estimate force and contact based on image data captured from a small camera sensor inside the fingers. Those visio-tactile sensors are progressing in academic research due to small and affordable camera sensors. Additionally, image processing is a quickly evolving field in the computer sciences and provides a variety of algorithms for analyzing the image data. We adopted such a sensor—the FingerVision sensor by A. Yamaguchi and C. G. Atkeson (2017)—to our gripper system (Figure 20.7). The sensor consists of a camera sensor that can capture black dots in soft transparent silicon bed that sits on a transparent rigid plate. Image-based algorithms can track the dots and predict forces based on their displacement. Additionally, the transparency enables to track objects between the fingers visually (Figure 20.8).

The sensor readings offer different modalities that can be combined and utilized to implement tactile skills (Figure 20.9). The information derived from the camera image can be feed as input to algorithms controlling the robot. These robot controllers use real-time feedback to calculate the robot's actions. Implemented correctly, the actions, together with the feedback, provide tactile skills for robotic construction.

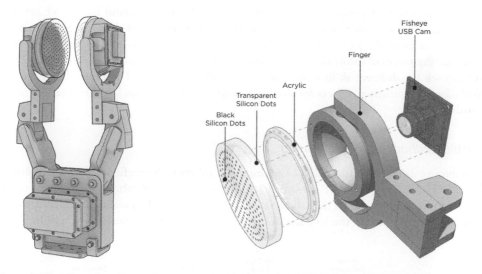

Figure 20.7   The sake gripper is equipped with the FingerVision sensor (left) and the separate components in order (right).

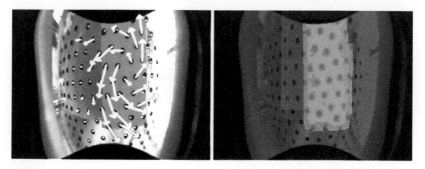

Figure 20.8   The two modalities offered by the FingerVision camera: blob deflection (left) and object recognition (right).

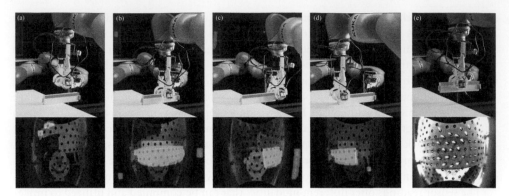

Figure 20.9 The robot slides along an object to determine the center for grasping (top row) and the image data from the FingerVision sensor (bottom row).

Library of tactile skills

Construction tasks depend on a variety of tactile skills, most of them in contact between the robot and one or more objects. Our current catalog consists of the most basic ones relevant for an assembly. Learning algorithms allow us to learn skills such as force estimation or acquiring pieces of information about the objects (Belousov et al. 2019). In Figure 20.10, we can see the different skills tested on our FingerVision sensor. The research aims to add skills for manipulating objects for assembly tasks and building an architectural library of tactile skills.

Tactile feedback for robotic joining

Combining different tactile skills is a necessity for robots to be useful on construction sites. We combined several robotic control strategies to test the applicability of different tactile skills in an assembly task. In the task, a vertical element had to be grasped and placed underneath a deformed slab at the location of the highest deformation, caused by a weight placed

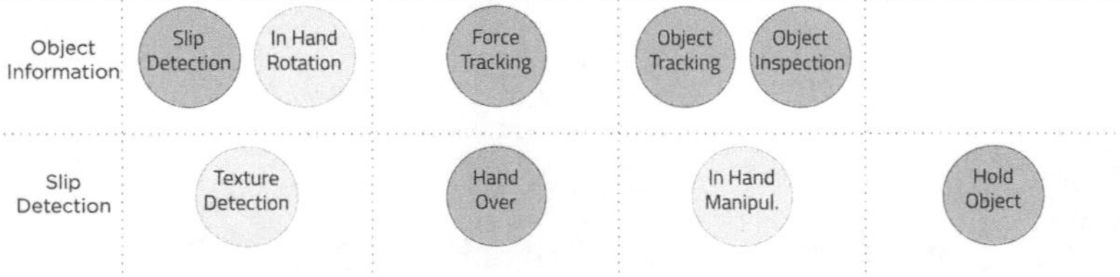

	Marker Detection	Average Force	Object Information	Slip Detection
Marker Detection	Arm Rotation			
Average Force	Force Learning, Collision Detection	Gentle Grasp		
Object Information	Slip Detection, In Hand Rotation	Force Tracking	Object Tracking, Object Inspection	
Slip Detection	Texture Detection	Hand Over	In Hand Manipul.	Hold Object

Figure 20.10 The library of tactile skills provided through algorithms based on the FingerVision sensor.

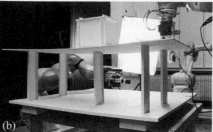

Figure 20.11 In the insertion task, the robot places the vertical element between the deformed slab directly underneath the weight.

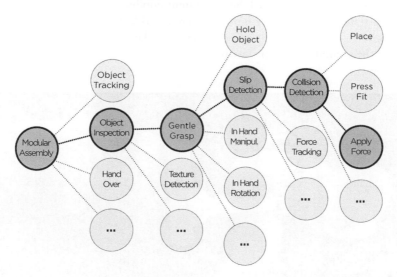

Figure 20.12 In an autonomous assembly process, the choice of the modalities can be optimized regarding the task.

on top of the slab (Figure 20.11). The robot had to locate an object and grasp it for transport and later placement. Therefore, a collision detection controller was implemented in combination with force detection. Additionally, the robot system can observe the scene actively and stream back actual build status into the digital model, forcing a stronger connection between digital representations and the built environment. The robot was able to place the element at the highest force. The assembly task was succeeded through a sequence of tactile skills (Figure 20.12), appropriately combining robot controllers to cope with uncertainties and unknown variables.

Man–machine collaboration

Humans can interfere with computers through interfacing devices such as mouse or keyboard. Construction workers do not commonly use those devices to maneuver their tools. The proposed tactile sensor enables future construction workers to interact with robots in ways similar to their human coworkers. The tactile sensor allows robots to participate in such interaction with human coworkers. For instance, it is possible to hand over building elements to the robot (Figure 20.13). Once the robot senses an element, placed between the fingers, the gripper closes. Combined with an active vision system that could track building element IDs, the robot would start a designated action with the grasped element. Another possibility is to guide the robot with an object inside the gripper. The human coworker can pull the object with the robot sensing a force in a specific direction and follow (Figure 20.14). In such a scenario, the human can use the robot's power to lift heavy elements while keeping control over building elements.

The proposed system furthermore establishes a knowledge base for robotic tactile skills applicable to assembly tasks and autonomous robotic construction. The number of components and information in this process are increasing and need proper orchestration in real-time (Figure 20.15). Moreover, an integrative approach that links the construction process strongly with the design model. Such a system implies a rethinking of the design and construction strategies. Intelligence is often referred to as learning based on the information and adapting to an environment; the presented project takes into account tactile information, thereby, lays the ground for robotic intelligence.

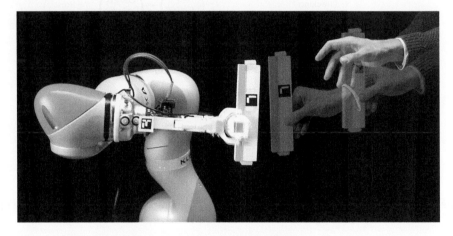

Figure 20.13   A human hands over an element to the robot.

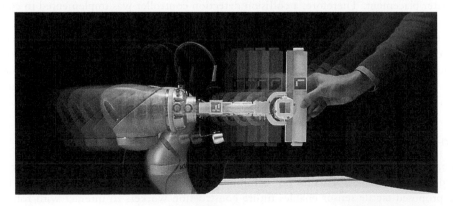

Figure 20.14   The human pulls the object into the desired direction with the robot following.

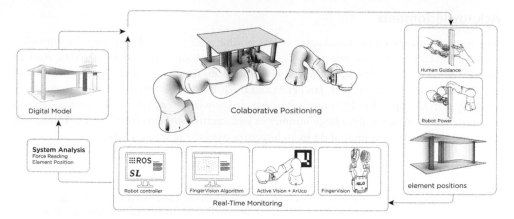

Figure 20.15 The software and machine components are contributing to the collaborative positioning of elements.

Conclusion

The presented projects prepare different stages of architectural production to be augmented with ML. Combining research on digital design tools for discrete elements with robotic autonomous assembly, it aims at continuous design-to-assembly procedures in the sense of Industry 4.0 (Braun et al. 2019). We propose algorithmic approaches for integrating the concept of Digital Materials at different stages, from design to assembly. We present a robotic system that can adapt to tactile inputs and facilitates skills necessary in autonomous assembly.

AI holds the promise of learning systems that can adapt to changing circumstances. As technologies such as robots and concepts such as Digital Materials come with little precedents in architecture, we have to develop approaches that explore this novel territory with appropriate tools, for instance, RL. At the same time, simulation environments are advancing and might further fuel ML in architecture. Similar to physical modeling, these simulation environments serve for testing and predicting the impact of architectural ideas, reaching from construction to usage.

The academic research still needs to be tested on an architectural scale and in real construction projects. One of the key challenges to bring these emerging technologies into practice is the highly unstructured environment of a construction site that is much more complex than off-site prefabrication. A further challenge is the lack of skilled labor at both ends, architects capable of integrating ML and robotic oriented design into their workflow as well as construction workers prepared for operating autonomous robots rather than outdated machines (Melenbrink et al. 2020). Universities are great places to prototype novel approaches in construction. Innovation, however, requires the overcoming of knowledge silos in disciplines such as architecture, engineering, computer science, and robotics.

ML and architecture will form a great alliance in extending the human set of skills to inform the production of space. Interfacing the two disciplines is just beginning. Future research has to focus on the development of interfaces between architecture and ML algorithms. The discipline of architecture has to embrace strategies of collaboration with AI that benefits from humans and machines, joining forces for a more versatile and intelligent built environment.

Acknowledgments

The research presented in this chapter would not have been possible without the curiosity, energy, creativity, and commitment of a large group of students and researchers. Andrea Rossi (DDU) not only developed WASP as a tool for discrete design but also supervised student work shown in this chapter. Jan Peters and Boris Belousov from the Intelligent Autonomous System Group at TU Darmstadt shared their knowledge on ML for autonomous robots in construction. And finally, a large number of architecture students from the TU Darmstadt explored the design potential of AI in architecture over the past five years.

References

Barbosa, F., Woetzel, J., Mischke, J., Ribeirinho, M.J., Sridhar, M., Parsons, M. et al., (Feb 2017). *Reinventing Construction: A Route to Higher Productivity*. Available at McKinsey Global Institute, Retrieved from https://www.mckinsey.com/industries/capital-projects-and-infrastructure/our-insights/reinventing-construction-through-a-productivity-revolution

Belousov, B., Sadybakasov, A., Wibranek, B., Veiga, F.F., Tessmann, O., & Peters, J. (2019). Building a library of tactile skills based on FingerVision. *Proceedings of the 2019 IEEE-RAS 19th International Conference on Humanoid Robots (Humanoids)*, IEEE.

Bock, T. (2015). Construction Robotics enabling innovative disruption and social supportability. *32nd International Symposium on Automation and Robotics in Construction and Mining: Connected to the Future, Proceedings* (pp. 1–11). https://doi.org/10.1016/j.autcon.2015.07.022

Bock, T., & Linner, T. (2015). Robot-oriented design: Design and management tools for the deployment of automation and robotics in construction. *In Robot-Oriented Design: Design and Management Tools for the Deployment of Automation and Robotics in Construction*. https://doi.org/10.1017/CBO9781139924146

Felbrich, B. (2019). HeinzBenjamin/FlexCLI: FlexCLI - FlexHopper (Version v1.1.2). Zenodo. http://doi.org/10.5281/zenodo.3355744

Gershenfeld, N. (2012). How to make almost anything: The digital fabrication revolution. *Foreign Affairs*, *91*(6), 43–57.

Gershenfeld, N., Carney, M., Jenett, B., Calisch, S., & Wilson, S. (2015). Macrofabrication with digital materials: Robotic assembly. *Architectural Design*, *85*(5), 122–127.

Harvey M. Bernstein, Gudgel, J. E., & Laquidara-Carr, D. (2011). Prefabrication and Modularization. In E. Fitch (Ed.), *SmartMarket Report*. McGraw-Hill Construction.

Jenett, B., Abdel-Rahman, A., Cheung, K., & Gershenfeld, N. (2019). Material–robot system for assembly of discrete cellular structures. *IEEE Robotics and Automation Letters*. https://doi.org/10.1109/lra.2019.2930486

Kao, G. T.-C., Nguyen, L., & The Asian Coders. (2021). PhysX.GH. Retrieved from https://github.com/TheAsianCoders/PhysX.GH

Khean, N., Fabbri, A., & Haeusler, M. H. (2018). Learning machine learning as an architect, how to? Presenting and evaluating a Grasshopper based platform to teach architecture students machine learning. In *Computing for a Better Tomorrow - Proceedings of the 36th ECAADe Conference - Volume 1* (pp. 95–102). Lodz University of Technology, Lodz. available at: http://ecaade.org/downloads/eCAADe-2018-Volume1.pdf

Lu, A. (2017). Autonomous assembly as the fourth approach to generic construction. *Architectural Design*. https://doi.org/10.1002/ad.2205

Melenbrink, N., Werfel, J., & Menges, A. (2020). On-site autonomous construction robots: Towards unsupervised building. *Automation in Construction*, *119*(June). https://doi.org/10.1016/j.autcon.2020.103312

Piker, Daniel. (2020) https://www.food4rhino.com/app/kangaroo-physics

Reinhardt, D., Haeusler, M. H., Loke, L., Barata, E. D. O., Firth, C., Khean, N., London, K., Feng, Y., Watt, R., Fabrication, R., Robots, C., Methodology, T., & Analysis, I. (2019). Towards a novel methodology for workflow capture and analysis of carpentry tasks for human-robot collaboration. In J. Sousa, J. Xavier, & G. Castro Henriques (Eds.), *Architecture in the Age of the 4th Industrial*

Revolution - Proceedings of the 37th eCAADe and 23rd SIGraDi Conference - Volume 3 (pp. 207–216). University of Porto. https://doi.org/10.5151/proceedings-ecaadesigradi2019_549

Retsin, G. (2016). Discrete Assembly and Digital Materials in Architecture. In A. Herneoja, T. Österlund, & P. Markkanen (Eds.), *Complexity & Simplicity - Proceedings of the 34th eCAADe Conference - Volume 1* (pp. 143–151). University of Oulu.

Retsin, G., ed. (2019). *Discrete: Reappraising the Digital in Architecture.* John Wiley & Sons.

Robeller, C., Helm, V., Thoma, A., Gramazio, F., Kohler, M., & Weinand, Y. (2017). Robotic Integral Attachment. *FABRICATE 2017.*

Rossi, A. (2019). Wasp - discrete design for grasshopper. https://github.com/ar0551/Wasp

Rossi, A. & Tessmann, O. (2017a). Collaborative assembly of digital materials. *In Acadia 2017 Disciplines & Disruption: Proceedings of the 37th Annual Conference of the Association for Computer Aided Design in Architecture*, Cambridge.

Rossi, A., & Tessmann, O. (2017b). Geometry as assembly. *Proceeding of 35th eCAADe Conference*, A. Fioravanti, G. Novembri, and A. Trento, eds., Rome, Sept. 20–22, pp. 201–210.

Rossi, A., & Tessmann, O. (2018). From voxels to parts: Hierarchical discrete modeling for design and assembly. *International Conference on Geometry and Graphics*, Milan, Aug. 3–7, Springer, Cham, pp. 1001–1012.

Ruiz-Montiel, M., Boned, J., Gavilanes, J., Jiménez, E., Mandow, L., & Pérez-De-La-Cruz, J. L. (2013). Design with shape grammars and reinforcement learning. *Advanced Engineering Informatics.* https://doi.org/10.1016/j.aei.2012.12.004

Sanchez, J. (2014). *ALIVE. Advancements in Adaptive Architecture.* M. Kretzer and L. Hovestadt, eds., Birkhaeuser, Basel, pp. 125–128.

Tessmann, O., & Savov, A. (2016). Modul und Fügung / module and jointing. *In GAM 12: Structural Affairs.* https://doi.org/10.1515/9783035609844-005

Thoma, A., Adel, A., Helmreich, M., Wehrle, T., Gramazio, F., & Kohler, M. (2019). Robotic Fabrication of Bespoke Timber Frame Modules. In Robotic Fabrication in Architecture, Art and Design 2018. https://doi.org/10.1007/978-3-319-92294-2_34

United Nations Environment Programme (2018). UN Environment Annual Report 2017. New York. available at: https://www.unenvironment.org/annualreport/2017/index.php

Vardouli, T. (2011). *Architecture by Yourself: Early Studies in Computer-Aided Participatory Design.* MIT, Cambridge.

Wang, S., Wan, J., Li, D., & Zhang, C. (2016). Implementing smart factory of industrie 4.0: an outlook. International journal of distributed sensor networks, 12(1), 3159805.

Wibranek, B., Belousov, B., Sadybakasov, A., Peters, J., & Tessmann, O. (2019). Interactive structure: Robotic repositioning of vertical elements in man-machine collaborative assembly through vision-based tactile sensing. *Proceedings of the 37th eCAADe and 23rd SIGraDi Conference - Volume 2* (pp. 705–713). University of Porto. https://doi.org/10.5151/proceedings-ecaadesigradi2019_387

Yablonina, M., & Menges, A. (2019). *Robotic Fabrication in Architecture, Art and Design 2018.* In Robotic Fabrication in Architecture, Art and Design 2018 (Issue October). Springer International Publishing. https://doi.org/10.1007/978-3-319-92294-2

Yamaguchi, A., & Atkeson, C. G. (2017). Implementing tactile behaviors using FingerVision. *IEEE-RAS International Conference on Humanoid Robots.* https://doi.org/10.1109/HUMANOIDS.2017.8246881

21

Machining and machine learning

Extending architectural digital fabrication through AI

Paul Nicholas

In 1959, the air force announced the invention of an intelligent computer numerically controlled (CNC) machine capable of receiving instructions in English, figuring out how to make what was wanted, and then teaching other machines how to make it. The potential of this new technology was demonstrated in a metal CNC milling ashtray—the world's first CAD/CAM object. While the delivery of this big idea is still in progress—the ambition of declarative design and complete automation found a recent echo in a prototype Siemans two-armed robot able to manufacture products without being programmed (Zistl, 2017)—digital fabrication foresaw the connection to artificial intelligence (AI) from the very start.

While the overarching question remains roughly the same—*could AI help in the translation between an element's description and its making?*—the underlying architectural drivers and technical approaches have radically changed from those of the late 1950s. Contemporary architecture operates highly digitized fabrication workflows in which architectural elements are designed and analyzed in 3D software, fabrication control code is generated automatically, and automated industrial robotics support both on- and off-site fabrication across varied methods and materials. Rather than automation leading to distancing, this digitization of architectural fabrication has drawn the designing and making processes closer together.

Emerging architectural research seeks to draw design and fabrication even closer through the application of machine learning (ML) models (Tamke et al 2018, Ramsgaard Thomsen et al. 2020), where deep neural nets are state of the art for prediction and classification. These algorithms, which optimize weight and bias values across a network to model a relationship between input and output data, are trained to perform highly specific tasks rather than for general intelligence. Their ability to find probabilistic patterns rests on brute force computing and abundant data: very large training datasets of 2D information, typically many thousands of images photographed from the real world. After training, they can predict, with greater or less error, new 2D datasets or classifications not part of their initial training data.

How can this 2D, probabilistic modeling approach be integrated into fabrication practice, which requires high precision to physically materialize 3D geometries? Here, the opportunity of AI is to open up new workflows, relations, and datasets that make fabrication more design-integrated and responsive by enabling architects to rethink how we make fabrication information, the materials that we fabricate with, and the relationship between humans and machines.

New opportunities for making fabrication information

Fabrication requires information as well as energy. The traditional relationship between the two has been sequential—all information required to make an element needs explicit specification in advance. Information is built sequentially and stepwise along a "digital chain"—a connecting series of geometric and calculative single-purpose models that end with a design-specific set of fabrication data. The inclusion of AI into the digital chain can introduce nonlinearity, flexibility, and simplicity in the creation of design information and the execution of machining tasks. Component models within the digital chain, or the results of fabrication, can become a source of training data for an AI model to feed back into other parts of the chain. AI models can also become "shortcuts" that replace more typical models completely, enabling faster and less complicated workflows to support versioning and customized designs, as well as new fabrication processes such as conformal printing where design modeling becomes interwoven with fabrication.

New opportunities for material complexity

Where digital fabrication initially required standardized materials with homogenous properties, the material models that underlie fabrication are being challenged to become more complex. There is a rising awareness that the material paradigms of modern architecture—well-known and highly engineered materials such as concrete, steel, glass, and plastic—are a source of substantial cost, waste, and detrimental environmental impact. The emerging shift to a more sustainable paradigm of biomaterials and optimized material deployment introduces materials with significantly more homogeneity (Ramsgaard Thomsen et al. 2020). Property variation can preexist within a material, occur between batches, or be induced through the actions of the fabrication process itself. Here, AI can capture complex interdependencies between fabrication parameters, as well as enable in-process material decision-making, replacing traditional and mechanistic models of material with highly specific models able to encode local and temporal changes.

New opportunities for interaction between humans and machines

Beyond the potential to make the fabrication process faster, more informed, and more responsive to material and contextual specifics, the integration of AI into fabrication enables a reconsideration of the relation between humans and machines. Where fabrication sometimes asks for a simple action but at speeds faster or with more accuracy than a human can achieve, other goals can include combining human–robot interaction to achieve a particular task or tune a generalist approach to a specific application.

The following cases undertaken at CITA—the Centre for Information Technology in Architecture—exemplify some specific opportunities within emerging robotic fabrication processes. These cases present a variety of models that learn from experience across very different stages of the fabrication process. The first case describes how ML can capture complex material behavior during a fabrication process, and the second case demonstrates how ML can help interweave design and fabrication workflows.

Robotic incremental metal forming

This section describes two case studies that apply ML to manage complex material behavior during a robotic incremental sheet forming (RISF) process. RISF is a mold-less, formative fabrication method for sheet metals. The process moves a highly localized mechanical force over the surface of an initially flat sheet to cause plastic deformation that over time forms the sheet into a desired 3D shape, following a spiraling toolpath generated in a CAD model. In these case studies, single-sided RISF is used to fabricate the structural arch "Stressed Skins," exhibited at the Design Museum Denmark in May 2015 (Nicholas et al., 2016). A double-sided approach was used to fabricate the bridge structure "A Bridge Too Far," exhibited at Meldahls Smedie, Copenhagen, in September 2016 (Nicholas et al., 2017, 2018). In this setup, an industrial robot works on each side of a moment frame, enabling forming out of the plane in opposed directions and significant freedom and complexity in the formed geometry. The structures have a material thickness of 1 mm mild steel and 0.5 mm prehardened aluminum. Both structures are frameless, with thin metal panels carrying all structural loads and containing all functional geometries, including connections and rigidization patterning. Their structural capacity is entirely dependent on the precise deformations and connections formed via RISF (Figures 21.1–21.3).

Fabrication and material behavior

Usually, in metal forming, the mold plays a key role in achieving precision. Because it is a freeform fabrication method, the positional accuracy of RISF is instead highly dependent upon a combination of material behavior and forming parameters. The forming velocity, toolpath, material type, and size, relation to support, and order of forming all affect springback—the movement of the sheet back toward its previous position after the tool head has moved on. Significant springback can impact and even halt the fabrication process, as the material is not where it is expected to be, and greatly reduce the geometric accuracy of the formed element.

Figure 21.1   Dual robotic incremental sheet forming setup at CITA, Copenhagen.

Figure 21.2   The research demonstrator *Stressed Skins*.

Figure 21.3   The research demonstrator *A Bridge Too Far*.

There are several current approaches to managing springback and improving geometric accuracy, the most direct of which is reforming. This approach simply reruns the original toolpath. It has been shown to achieve considerable improvement but doubles the length of fabrication time. The second approach is to try to calculate springback prior to fabrication by coupling a finite element model of the material with a model of the compliant robot structure. However, this approach is entirely dependent on simulation and risks that the reality of fabrication is not accurately represented.

AI provides a different approach to modeling complex springback behavior. We have explored and implemented two different ML-based approaches (Nicholas et al 2017, Nicholas et al 2018) that increase forming accuracy with only a minimal increase in fabrication time and are closely calibrated with actual fabrication through their inputs and training data (Zwierzycki et al. 2018).

Coupling ML to sensing for local learning

The first method has its basis in sensor feedback and adaptive control. To ensure geometric accuracy where it is most critical—the varying depths of the cones that connect the upper and lower skins together—the local position of each cone center point is measured prior to being formed using a single-point laser distance measure mounted to the robot arm. The cone is then formed, with the measured deviation between the actual position and ideal position automatically added to the target forming depth for that cone via a routine pre-programmed into the controller. To account for springback during this forming process, an overforming value is added to the target forming depth. As this value is not known before fabrication begins and varies according to the depth of forming, a regression-based curve fitting model is queried to determine the correct value. This model becomes more accurate as it collects more ongoing fabrication data. While not tested here, the larger potential for this model is to be redeployed and readjusted on other similar structures.

To collect data during the fabrication process, the depth of each cone is laser measured again after forming, and this data point (ideal depth/measured depth) is added to the curve-fitting model. There are continued remodeling and corresponding improvement in accuracy across the course of fabricating hundreds of cones (Figure 21.4). After the

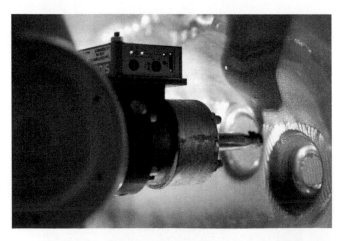

Figure 21.4   The forming depth of each connection cone is determined using a combination of laser distance sensing and a regression model.

initial forming and scanning, further automated correction methods can be triggered to bring any tolerances below 2 mm.

Coupling ML to 3D scanning for global learning

While the sensor-based learning process becomes more accurate over time, it is extremely limited spatially. To predict springback behavior over an entire panel, a complex undulating 3D landscape, requires a neural network, a more complex ML modeling approach that can be trained to capture spatial dependencies. For this case, we matched 3D models and 3D scans from five representative test panels. The neural network was trained on thousands of image samples of local geometric features—small 3D-scan fragments represented as a 2D heightmap, which encode local information about edges, ridge, and slope—as well as additional edge-distance information capturing local frame support. Each training sample has a real-world size of 5 × 5cm that is reduced to a 9 × 9-pixel grid using max pooling. The network consists of an input layer with 82 neurons (81 + 1 additional for the edge-proximity parameter), a hidden layer with 30 neurons, and an output layer with 1 neuron indicating the depth of the resulting point.

Using this neural network in CAD made it possible to predict the forming process result for an entire panel before beginning fabrication. As well as providing a check, the network's predictions can also be used to factor in springback in advance. This is achieved by simply increasing the input mesh heightmap values by the difference between the target and prediction heightmaps, and then generating toolpaths from this adjusted geometry. This approach was found to yield a substantial increase in geometric accuracy (Figure 21.5).

Conformal 3D printing

This section describes the application of ML within a conformal 3D-printing process to support an iterative and interwoven computational design and digital fabrication process. In contrast to the conventional approach of 3D printing, where horizontal layers are laid onto a flat plane of known position, conformal printing is the process of 3D printing onto existing 3D objects with nonplanar or uneven 3D-surface geometries. For architecture, conforming printing could enable the expanded and integrated use of 3D printing within renovation by printing new elements onto existing building structures, or the customization of generic prefabricated parts to make them nonstandard in a new build situation (Nicholas et al 2020).

In a typical fabrication workflow, design information is fully determined before the fabrication process begins. However, in conformal printing, the printing geometry can only be defined in response to the registration of an underlying surface. This couples design and fabrication processes tightly together. This case develops a workflow for the performance customization of architectural panels with unknown geometries. The workflow combines the registration of the unknown substrate geometry by scanning, the predicting of the structural performance of the panel using a deep neural network, and the use of the prediction to generate printing toolpaths (Nicholas et al 2020). The fabrication setup combines two UR10 robots working in collaboration over a geometrically unknown panel. One robot is fitted with a scanning head, and the other robot is fitted with a custom-built pellet extruder (Figure 21.6).

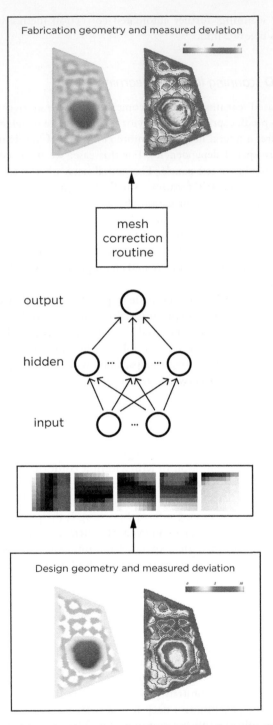

Figure 21.5 The network is trained on samples that pair data from the 3D model with a scan of the actually formed geometry. Once trained, predictions from the model can be used to adjust the underlying meshes and toolpaths so that they account for the predicted springback.

Figure 21.6 Two UR10 robots working collaboratively in a shared workspace. (Right) Scanner robot retreats after scanning, giving way for the printer robot (Left) to execute the material deposition.

Registering unknown geometries

The fabrication workflow uses a two-stage automated robotic scanning process. In the first stage, a low-resolution scan with a robot-mounted Intel RealSense camera registers the panel by scanning a set area. This scan is automatically clipped and oriented to identify the panel from any background features. Once the panel is identified, a scanning toolpath for the second high-resolution scan is generated automatically. This toolpath first follows the outline of the element, and then an infill path. The high-resolution scan is executed by the same robot but using an Artec3D EVA structured light scanner, producing a high-resolution point cloud.

Predicting performance

To enable the close coupling of registration, design, and fabrication, a Pix2Pix generative adversarial network (GAN) (Isola et al., 2017) is used to predict structural information directly from the unstructured point cloud captured in the previous step. This GAN learns to map from an input image to an output image, and its predictions become the input to a generative model that creates toolpaths for 3D printing.

ThePix2Pix GAN is trained using an entirely digitally generated dataset. To build the training data, 3,000 geometry examples are paired with finite element analysis results for normal displacement and von Mises stress under a wind loading of 1,500 Pa perpendicular to the panel plane. This information is remapped from a 3D domain to channels of an image that the network can train on. The results are mapped back onto the point cloud itself to visualize stress and deflection and are input to the automated generation of a reinforcement pattern that strategically stiffens the panel (Figures 21.7 and 21.8).

Generative reinforcement pattern design

The GAN model encodes its structural analysis prediction in the form of a false-color image. This prediction is directly read back into the CAD environment, where it drives a generative

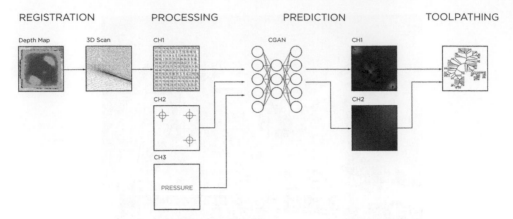

REGISTRATION   PROCESSING   PREDICTION   TOOLPATHING

Figure 21.7   Diagram of the developed 3D scan to the 3D print workflow: The point cloud from the dual-scanning process is encoded as an image and fed to the neural network to predict its structural performance under perpendicular load. The prediction is used to inform the generative reinforcement pattern to be printed. Gcode is then generated and sent to the robot for execution.

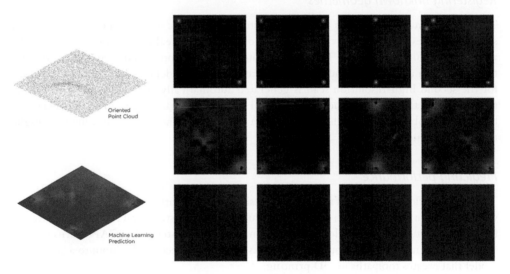

Figure 21.8   (Left) The workflow connects an unstructured scanned point cloud to a neural network–based prediction of stress and deflection, all parsed within the Grass-hopper environment. (Right) Image encoding geometry and support point information that is input to the cGAN (middle) von Mises stress map and (bottom) normal displacement maps predicted by the network.

reinforcement pattern that stiffens the panel against the wind load. Different reinforcement patterns are possible—here, we illustrate a recursive subdivision pattern where the number of iterations is informed by the stress state of the cell, a recursive branching pattern informed by the stress state, a reparameterized mesh based on the stress readings, and a pattern that creates a false-mesh topography based on stress readings from which flow lines can be extracted (Figures 21.9 and 21.10).

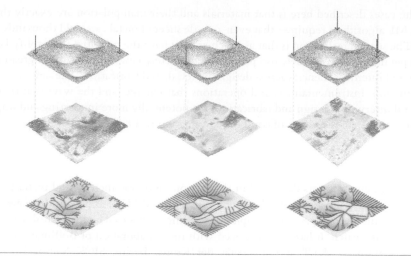

Figure 21.9 Pattern generation. (Top row) Point cloud of one 3D-scanned vacuum-formed panel with varying support points indicated in red, (middle row) predicted deformation and stress state based on neural network prediction, and (bottom) resulting recursive branching pattern reinforcement pattern reacting to the neural network input.

Figure 21.10 Conformal printing of differentiated pattern on the panel and details of 3D-printed panel.

Conclusion

AI will assume an increasingly important role in architectural fabrication as it continues to shift from centralized mass production to distributed, customized, and one-off making processes. The digital continuity between design and making provides many opportunities to implement AI along the frames outlined in the introduction and without doubt many others. While representational challenges—how material or fabrication information can be represented so that they are understood by an ML model—remain as hurdles, a key realization

403

across the cases described here is that materials and their manipulation are exactly the kind big data ML algorithms require—that even a single sheet of metal can yield thousands of data points. The second realization is that as much as they have the potential to simplify key fabrication parameters; ML models also provide a completely new way to capture greater complexities and interdependencies across design, material, and fabrication. The new associations of information, instrumentalities, and operations that emerge, and the ways that they short circuit and interweave design and fabrication, are potentially more interesting and impactful for architecture than the vision of complete automation in 1959.

Acknowledgments

The research demonstrators described in the section "Robotic incremental metal forming" were undertaken at the Centre for IT and Architecture, KADK, as part of the Sapere Aude Advanced Grant research project 'Complex Modelling', supported by the Danish Council for Independent Research. It has been achieved with the collaboration of Bollinger Grohmann consulting engineers, KET at Universität der Kunst, Berlin, SICK Sensor Intelligence Denmark, Monash University Materials Science and Engineering, and the robot command and control software HAL. The project team for *Stressed Skins* and *A Bridge Too Far* includes Paul Nicholas, Mateusz Zwierzycki, David Stasiuk, Esben Clausen Nørgaard, Scott Leinweber, Christopher Hutchinson, Riccardo La Magna, and Mette Ramsgaard Thomsen.

The research demonstrator described in the section "Conformal printing" was developed and funded in collaboration with University Technology Sydney and Arup Consulting Engineers as part of the Arup Global Research Challenge 2019. The project team includes Paul Nicholas, Gabriella Rossi, Tim Schork, Ella Williams, Michael Bennett, Tran Dang, Gwyn Jones, Tony Jones, Andrew Purnell, Stefan Lie, Teresa Vidal, Bree Trevana, Alessandro Liuti, Deepika Jaduram, Andrew Weetman, Haico Schepers, and Laura Craft.

References

Isola P., Zhu J. Y., Zhou T., Efros A. A. (2017). Image-to-image translation with conditional adversarial networks. https://arxiv.org/abs/1611.07004. doi: 10.1109/CVPR.2017.632

Nicholas P. (2018). Fabrication for differentiation: Towards an adaptive material practice. In M. Daas and A. J. Wit (Eds.) *Towards a Robotic Architecture*. 76–87. ORO Editions

Nicholas P., Rossi G., Williams E., Bennett M., Schork T. (2020). Integrating real-time multi-resolution scanning and machine learning for conformal robotic 3D printing in architecture. *International Journal of Architectural Computing*. doi: 10.1177/1478077120948203

Nicholas P., Zwierzycki M., Nørgaard E.C., Leinweber S., Stasiuk D., Ramsgaard Thomsen M., Hutchinson C. (2017). Adaptive robotic fabrication for conditions of material inconsistency: Increasing the geometric accuracy of incrementally formed metal panels. *Fabricate 2017*, 114–121. doi: 10.2307/j.ctt1n7qkg7.19

Ramsgaard Thomsen M., Nicholas P., Tamke M., Gatz S., Sinke Y., Rossi G. (2020). Towards machine learning for architectural fabrication in the age of industry 4.0. *International Journal of Architectural Computing*. doi: 10.1177/1478077120948000

Tamke M., Nicholas P., Zwierzycki M. (2018). Machine learning for architectural design: Practices and infrastructure. *International Journal of Architectural Computing* 16(2), 123–143. doi: 10.1177/1478077118778580

Zistl S. (2017). Retrieved from https://new.siemens.com/global/en/company/stories/research-technologies/artificial-intelligence/prototype-robot-solves-problems-without-programming.html

Zwierzycki M., Nicholas P., Ramsgaard Thomsen M. (2018). Localised and learnt applications of machine learning for robotic incremental sheet forming. *Proceedings of Design Modelling Symposium 2017*, 373–382. doi: 10.1007/978981106611532

22

Augmented intuition
Encoding ideas, matter, and why it matters

Mathias Bernhard, Maria Smigielska, and Benjamin Dillenburger

Artificial intelligence (AI) promises to support the production of architecture along the entire process chain. A common challenge of both computational design and AI is the question of *encoding*. How can a design idea be formalized? How can design problems and ideas be modeled so computers can process them? What is the minimum number of parameters needed for maximum freedom in design? Can these parameters be dimensions of a feature vector? What concepts of AI can address the challenges of generating and evaluating solutions? This challenge is present in various phases within a digital design to fabrication routine: starting with the first design sketches and ending with the robotic fabrication. Each of the steps requires different approaches to encoding. When successful, AI can become an active partner in the creative part of the design and allow for a new kind of intuitive fabrication.

This chapter discusses the meaning of intuition, creativity, and intelligence in the context of architecture and how information technology can potentially support designers and augment their intuition. It starts with looking at how technology has been employed to support the design process throughout history, even before computers were invented. The general introduction sheds light on different creative processes, asking what creativity is and how it can be classified. It is followed by a description of two case studies conducted by the authors. Although these projects are very diverse in type, application, and scale, they showcase the potential and promising applications of AI in architecture once the design is digitally encoded. The chapter reflects on the current and categorical limitations of AI and concludes with an optimistic outlook on various possible creative applications of AI in the domain of architecture.

Computational design in architecture

As architects and designers, we are driven to converge knowledge at different stages during the creative process from the design to its physical realization. Architecture fuses the imaginary with the rational, experimental with functional, art with science. It has always been embracing the state-of-the-art knowledge and technologies of its time. Therefore, there is no surprise in discussing machine learning (ML) applications in an architectural context. It seems to be the natural sequel as architecture got familiar with concepts of encoding of architectural knowledge already before the rise of digital technologies.

Computation itself dates back long before the modern electronic computer was invented: Leibniz introduced the first mechanical calculator in 1685. Ada Lovelace came up with the first idea of a programming language for the Difference Machine of Charles Babbage around 1840. Furthermore, the gesture of encoding architectural knowledge has existed in an analog format in each historical epoch. Compendiums store architectural data, examples, models, and protocols relevant for their time, in varied modes of representation, including texts, images, or drawings. Treaties of Palladio in the Renaissance proposed a "compositional machinery needed to design new buildings that are instances of the style" (Stiny & Mitchell, 1978), while Durand suggested the modular assembly of basic architectural elements that could be recombined in countless permutations with a system of universal principles.

Already in the early days when computers filled entire rooms, architects were curious about how this technology could actively support the design process, beyond being a mere digital drafting board (Steadman, 1976). This inevitably brings up the question, how project ideas can be quantified and made machine-readable. How can the design space be encoded (see Figure 22.1), and what forms of AI could help explore it (Bernhard, 2019)? Recent advancements in digital technologies continue to explore those methods but in a faster and automated manner. Automation enables the creation of entire populations of configurations. Instead of crafting a single idea, one can generate large amounts of solutions and select the preferred option. As such, the design process has been shifted from a deterministic format toward a more selective one.

The design space can be built in multiple ways, for instance, with a parametric modeling technique that allows us to manipulate any geometry with a few variables. We can call the collection of all parameters a feature vector, whose dimensions are indeed often directly linked to metric dimensions of the physical object. The design space, the set of potential solutions, is constrained by a predefined topology. With every additional parameter (read: dimension) and its corresponding range, the possible combinations grow exponentially.

Many disciplines draw inspiration from nature when looking for problem-solving strategies. Computer scientists borrowed ideas from evolution to find suitable candidates in large populations. Genetic algorithms (GAs) help explore promising design directions

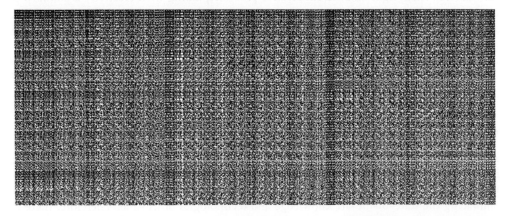

Figure 22.1 Part of the solution space of magnetic actuator combinations generating ferrofluid patterns in Proteus 2.0 project. Image: Maria Smigielska.

among numerous permutations using nature-inspired mechanisms of evolution, namely reproduction, mutation, and recombination. The jargon is borrowed from biology. The prototype model is called a genotype, and its instances with individual gene configurations are phenotypes. The difference lies in how the design space is traversed to find optimal solutions.

Instead of individually setting the parameter values, they are generated and evaluated through a fitness function widely explored in design and architecture (Frazer, 1995). GAs make use of the stochastic patterns of the fitness landscape—not a simple function but not entirely random either—to search for suitable solutions more efficiently.

ML in architecture

However, data-driven approaches advanced by ML algorithms seem to open new models for the encoding of architectural knowledge that reach out beyond purely formal, analytic, or classification models and promote human creativity and intuition. Besides quantifying human ideas, research in AI also investigates whether even ideas could be generated by computers, by a form of artificial creativity. Given the increasing amount and ubiquity of available data, designers embrace AI possibilities and merge it with all artistic forms from visual to performing arts, including speech, vision, and language. Now, it is easier than ever to become a music composer (Newton-Rex et al., n.d.), generate "The Next Rembrandt" portrait (Thompson et al., 2016), paint like van Gogh with style transfer (Gatys et al., 2015), generate a personalized web design (Tocchini, 2014), write the longest novel ever (Ross, 2018), or create an unprecedented strategic move in the game of Go (Silver et al., 2016).

According to DeepMind cofounder and CEO Demis Hassabis (Hassabis, 2018), most of the abovementioned generative acts would be categorized as *interpolation* based on the principle of averaging or generalizing training examples. While it might sound like an achievement for a computer to obtain such a degree of generative capacity, from a designer's perspective, it means filling the design space with large quantities of different variants of the same idea, extracted from the given examples. Those conventional methods of supervised ML—classification, regression, and clustering—could be perfect candidates to use any architectural compendium as their training data. The last example of AlphaGo represents the next level

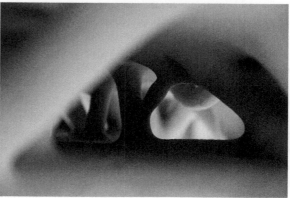

Figure 22.2 Concrete slab with optimized topology; left: view of the underside, right: close-up of the tubular structures. Photos: Andrei Jipa, DBT.

of the creative process described as *extrapolation*. It is characterized by extended boundaries within which AI finds new solutions, even though within the same context still.

What architecture and other creative industries strive for is to reach beyond replicating the existing ideas and create new original ones that allow rendering the impossible thought, think the unthinkable by "transforming the whole conceptual spaces and changing pre-existing assumptions," how cognitive scientist Margaret A. Boden formulates it (Boden, 2004). While this type of creativity, called *invention* by Hassabis, or *transformational creativity* by Boden, remains strictly a human domain, we firmly believe that the combination of human and machine intelligence can lead to unprecedented creative enhancement bringing alteration in overall architectural creation and production system.

How can we combine the two worlds, ML governed by statistics, combinatorics, and probabilities on the one hand and architecture driven by creativity, innovation, and surprise through the careful breaking of some rules on the other? How can architectural knowledge and ideas be quantified, formalized—encoded—for AI to be able to compute solutions and support the design process? And most importantly, how can this be achieved without losing the degrees of freedom for creative exploration needed by architecture? (Figure 22.2).

AI applications in the early design and robotic fabrication

The following two case studies demonstrate the potential applications of ML in architectural design. They are examples of how AI can assist the designer in different phases of the process—virtually in the design and tangibly in the production phase. They operate at different scales—from entire wall elements to filigree metal rods. The projects collect and generate different types of training data—digitally synthesized through simulation and collected in the real world from physical experiments and apply different algorithms to produce different outputs. They show how AI can be integrated into the design process already now. Both projects have very specific, relatively narrow, and well-defined tasks to be addressed by the AI, thereby augmenting the designer's creativity as smart assistants. Eventually, in the nearby future, more and more narrow tasks may be widened and connected. But we believe that it will always be a creative dialog and exchange of the designer interacting with various forms of smart assistants (see Figure 22.9).

The pursuit of integrating AI applications in architecture should not be to provide a one-button hands-off solution from sketch to fabrication. However, a fascinating and promising world opens up to architecture if various smart assistants augment and support each other. What solutions would become possible if the AI-assisted creativity in the early design phase was not limited by the constraints of conventional manufacturing methods? What creations could be realized if the AI-assisted fabrication and materialization would not have to rely on human's limited imagination only?

The two case studies have in common that they both encode the design-relevant aspects of the samples to allow the computer to extract hidden patterns and complex mathematical functions. They make the design space computable—arriving at solutions given a specific input situation. In both cases, the extracted patterns are used in the decision-making process but not for the automation of design or delegation of the creative process to mere statistics. Instead, ML models are trained to assist the architect by doing what computers do better than humans and provide guidance based on "knowledge" extracted from vast amounts of data.

The first case study is a research project entitled *TopoGAN* and was developed by Dr. Mathias Bernhard, Reza Kakooee, Patrick Bedarf, and Prof. Benjamin Dillenburger at Digital Building Technologies DBT, ETH Zurich in 2020. Further technical details on the project, the method, and results are described in the paper *TopoGAN—Topology Optimization with Generative Adversarial Networks* in the proceedings of the 2021 Advances in Architectural Geometry AAG, Paris (Bernhard et al., 2021).

The second case study is a research project carried out by Maria Smigielska with further collaborations with ABB Cergy France, Pierre Cutellic (*The Front Desk* project for Art[n+1] gallery in Paris, 2016), Mateusz Zwierzycki (*The Means* project for Tallinn Architecture Biennale, 2017), and through educative workshops held internationally (Digital Knowledge at ENSA Paris Malaquais 2018, FHNW HGK Institute Industrial Design, Basel 2018) with a diversified robotic infrastructure at hand.

Case study 1: TopoGAN—topology optimization with generative adversarial networks

The strive for spanning large distances with slender beams has always also been an aesthetic one. The great master builders of gothic cathedrals demonstrated the elegance of artful force redirection through a highly performant use of materials. Increasing awareness of the devastating consequences of the construction industry's waste production calls for efficient deployment of natural resources. For structural design, topology optimization (TO) is a way to run finite element analysis (FEA) in a loop, converging the design to a target value. For example, this target can be the maximum stiffness of an element with a specified fraction of material (Bendsøe & Kikuchi, 1988; Bendsøe & Sigmund, 2003). The intricately branching lattices resulting from TO have typically been challenging to produce with conventional methods. Advances in digital fabrication—specifically additive manufacturing at large scales—have brought the use of TO as a design instrument for architectural components into the realms of possibility, as shown in Figure 22.2 (Aghaei Meibodi et al., 2017; Jipa et al., 2016).

However, setting up all the necessary boundary conditions for TO (such as loads, supports, voids, or fixed elements) and finally running multiple FEA solver epochs is very laborious, time-consuming, and requires advanced expert knowledge and specialized software. TO is, therefore, often performed once as an input for further refinement in the design process. It assumes a static set of constraints, and changing boundary conditions require a complete recalculation of the TO from scratch as if no solution had been computed before. The project *TopoGAN* addresses this dilemma (Bernhard et al., 2021). TopoGAN investigates the applicability of ML to the structural design of optimized topologies in an early design phase.

The trained model learns some kind of artificial intuition about the distribution of material. The model's suggestions are not numerically precise enough to replace an accurate simulation, but fast enough for an interactive working mode in an early design phase, where qualitative concepts are more important than quantitative precision. Because the ground truth—the real solution the ML model is supposed to predict or generate—can be simulated virtually, there is no need to collect training data in the wild and manually label it. Instead, an arbitrary number of synthetic training samples can be generated.

While the method is scale-independent, TopoGAN is applied to a building element, a three-by-three-meter wall. The walls are assumed to be loaded along the top edge and supported along the bottom edge. What varies among all the samples is the size, shape, position, and rotation of the openings. A total of approximately three thousand sample inputs in three different datasets are thus randomly generated (see Figure 22.3).

Besides the input, the training data also requires the ground truth, the actual result of the TO for a given wall layout. Each sample takes approximately one minute to run 50 epochs of TO on a 128 × 128-pixel input image. This number was identified to be sufficient in most cases to have the changes below a certain threshold per additional epoch. The TO on the inputs is batch processed using a Python implementation of the algorithm (Aage & Johansen, 2013), and its result is concatenated with the input to one training pair image. As the TO algorithm is deterministic, it is run once per randomly generated wall scheme only.

As its name suggests, TopoGAN uses a generative adversarial network (Goodfellow et al., 2014), where two neural networks compete and mutually improve each other's performance. The generator network tries and learns to produce output images that pass as real, while the discriminator network tries and learns to distinguish between real and fake. Instead of generating output from normally distributed random noise, the generator learns a conditional function to translate from an input to an output image, as shown in Figure 22.4 (Isola et al., 2016). The number of possible outputs for TopoGAN, grayscale images of 128 × 128 pixels, is gigantic. Even for a tiny thumbnail of 5 × 6 pixels with only black or white colors allowed, the number of possible images is 230=1'073'741'824, over 1 billion solutions.

For what is known as the curse of dimensionality (Bellman, 1957), an exhaustive enumeration to find the best solution is impractical or impossible. Hence, encoding on a higher, more abstract level has to be found. This is where the specific ML model architecture—multilayer convolutional neural networks (CNNs), the building blocks of all computer vision nowadays—unfold its real strength (Krizhevsky et al., 2012). In stacked levels, they extract simple gradients first, edges or textures next, and then ever more complex features such as patterns, parts, and finally objects further up the hierarchy to compress the essence of an image to a reduced number of dimensions. In TopoGAN, the number of dimensions in the last layer is 524'288. On the one hand, half a million values are still too much to control manually, like in a parametric design setup. On the other hand, these numbers are also meaningless

Figure 22.3 Three training samples from each of the data sets with rectangular, elliptic, and rotated linear openings. Image: Mathias Bernhard, DBT.

as they are abstractions. They do not represent the length of an edge or the diameter of a hole. They are coordinates in a project-specific metric space, where redundancies are out of the equation and only relative differences count. Similar topologies are close to each other, dissimilar ones are further apart.

Obviously, to only simulate one solution does not justify the effort of generating 1'000 samples (1 minute each is more than 16 hours of calculation time), and then training a model for another few hours. But once the model is trained, being able to generate an output in a tenth of a second is a game-changer. It is not only about eventually winning time in the long run, but the fast response makes ML-based TO a suitable candidate to be integrated into a computer-aided design (CAD) environment.

Whenever the design changes, whenever windows are moved around or scaled, Topo-GAN can display these changes' structural implications in real-time by running interactively alongside the design software. Instead of being a separate process disconnected from the CAD environment, it can be integrated, immediate, and responsive. TopoGAN does not pursue the unique goal of performance by speeding up one instance of TO. Instead, with immediate feedback provided within the CAD environment, architectural and structural design can be evolved in parallel, without one of them being set first and the other suffering from the inherited consequences. Aesthetics and efficiency become the tandem they always deserved to be.

Is TopoGAN creative? Maybe not, as it learns a mapping function for a clearly defined and very constrained engineering problem. As long as the windows in the input do not span the entire width of the wall—preventing the loads from being redirected to the supports—there *is* one and only solution the TO algorithm will output. This cannot be said for the plethora of architectural challenges where genuine creativity is needed—not for *finding* a solution in proximity to other solutions for similar problems, but for *inventing* a suitable response to an unseen question. Is TopoGAN artificially intelligent? Maybe, as its accomplishments are still surprising and astonishing. It was able to learn and apply hard numerical constraints without being explicitly programmed. For example, it learned to avoid the openings by distributing

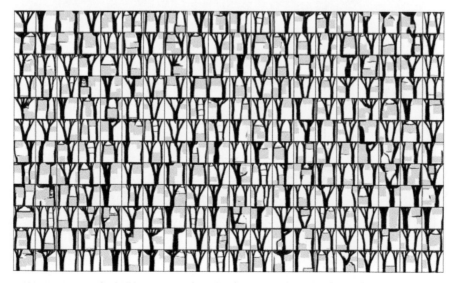

Figure 22.4 The 240 outputs of the TopoGAN generator network for previously unseen inputs (dotted surfaces). Image: Mathias Bernhard, DBT.

material and hence deviating forces around them, but also a more complex constraint like the desired volume fraction within a few percent of error from the target value. TopoGAN may not invent original solutions itself, but it can stimulate the architects' creativity. Playing with the constraints and discovering the consequences in real-time, the resulting material distribution becomes a design choice rather than an irrevocable law to obey.

This behavior awakens the interest and provides confidence that ML models such as TopoGAN can help beyond the very constrained setting of the described case study. Given the right amount and diversity of training data, it may learn to generalize, extract patterns, and applicable rules for more complex or dynamically changing boundary conditions. The concept can be transferred from structural design to other engineering problems, such as fluid dynamics or thermal insulation.

Case study 2: Robotic rod bending technology

While there is more and more attention given to ML applications in architectural design, the topic of fabrication remains a bottleneck on the way to physically evaluate or materialize new ideas. The industrial revolution has divided the field of manufacturing into the standardized industrial production in large quantities that is generally slow in embracing new technologies (Hossain & Nadeem, 2019) or artisanal hand-making with unique solutions beyond financial reach for most of the architectural projects. The first promise of individualized production appeared with the introduction of digitization to manufacturing and early concepts of mass customization (Toffler, 1970). However, it did not allow for much of a formal design differentiation as the system was dedicated to one specific fabrication process. It did not help in the areas where human knowledge cannot be replaced with a versatile machine, including dealing with complex materials (Figure 22.5).

Figure 22.5 The Front Desk project at Art[n+1] gallery, Paris 2016. Photo: Leslie Ware.

The *Bendilicious* research project (Smigielska, 2018) tries to bridge this gap by proposing a simple, yet versatile, open, but automated fabrication solution with the example of metal-work. Metals as architectural material have celebrated the progress of both technology and civilization for centuries. It has traditionally occupied an ambivalent place of wonder and fear due to its mysterious, both solid and liquid properties requiring high skills and knowledge of specialized craftsmen. A cold-forming bending process with manual table benders has not changed until the mid-90s, when the first conceptual schemes of computer integration shifted this technology from a labor-intensive and hazardous process to a safer, faster, and almost fully automated one (Dunston & Bernold, 2000).

However, the problem of the dependency on human expertise was only addressed in early 2000 when ML was integrated to help adaptively compensate for the variable springback effect. Unequally distributed internal compression and tension forces make the material want to return to its initial shape (Dunston & Bernold, 2000). This technology was incorporated and black-boxed by heavy industry, leaving little space for custom or one-off projects.

Bendilicious also utilizes ML algorithms to encode and predict the material's deformation behavior but in a simplified and open format. We developed a simplified fabrication model consisting of a single robotic arm with a custom end effector (see Figure 22.6) and a portable rod–holding station. The robotic system serves a function of both a gripper and a bender (as opposed to standard computer numerically controlled bending machines). Along with the hardware development, the digital workflow was entirely embedded in Grasshopper—the visual programming environment of the CAD software Rhinoceros—to provide continuity of the information flow between different phases of project development: from concept design iteration, FEA, geometry rationalization, and generation of production data informed by material behavior. The software containing design-to-fabrication processes is based on both existing plugins and custom-made tools that do not require any intermediate conversion to external software or machine code.

The data representing the nonlinear material behavior were collected from physical experiments and then encoded in a regression model. The third polynomial function stems from data points of desired angle and their respective resulting springback value, which was harvested with the photo average-angle readout. While this method could be easily automated with available computer vision, adaptive threshold, and line recognition algorithms, our simple photo readouts of only 120 data points guaranteed the prediction precise enough

Figure 22.6   A simplified robotic bending hardware setup. Photo: Maria Smigielska.

for fabrication and assembly of two large space-frame projects. *The Front Desk* of the size 550 × 140 × 75 cm consisted of linearly assembled 800 unique elements, each between 12 and 100 cm long, with the number of bends ranging between 2 and 7 and with a total amount of 2'400 unique bending values (see Figure 22.5). The other project *The Means* was of the size 50 × 50 × 220 cm consisted of more complicated 3D elements with an increased length of 60–120 cm, and twice the number of bends, ranging between 6 and 14 each (see Figure 22.7).

Is the ML methods directly creative? No, but the project brings a change on many other levels. First, it aims to finally develop a simplified, versatile, and decentralized mode for the future building industry. It promotes diversified over standardized solutions, as the robotic arm, once trained, performs the same marginal cost of production for identical or unique items. Such a model is applicable off-site as a flexible alternative to overconstrained, centralized industrial systems, and routine and hazardous manual work. An additional benefit lies in its potential for on-site fabrication. The springback value is dependent on many of the chart factors, such as changing room temperature, metal thickness, type, quality, etc. By coupling robotic systems with visual and environment probing sensors, the trained model of, e.g., the neural network could predict according to those changing conditions. Additionally, with an online ML strategy, the data can be progressively gathered during production, grow bigger, and more varied over time with each new project, which significantly improves the precision of prediction, as well as the flexibility of the system that can be used in various site and daily conditions.

Such a fabrication method occurs to be far from a hardcoded industrial system and reminds more of a craftsmen's work, who develop their skill and build necessary tacit knowledge over time through experience and practice. With those amplified cognitive abilities, the robotic system gains a material intuition that allows for a more intricate and meaningful communication with the physical world. Shifting the long process of material knowledge acquisition to the machine is the key to successful automation for both encapsulation of complex material behavior and sophisticated artisanal and autographic fabrication requiring higher cognitive processes. Such an approach pushes the concept of digital fabrication beyond mass customization or "nonstandard seriality" introduced by Mario Carpo (Carpo, 2011)

Figure 22.7 View of The Means project during Tallinn Architecture Biennale 2017. Photo: Maria Smigielska.

Figure 22.8 Gugelmann Galaxy: A browser application for exploring a large image collection in 3D, with a detailed view of the selected item. Images can be arranged by four different custom criteria. Image: Mathias Bernhard.

toward automated digital crafts for both existing and future materials such as complex, synthetic, and graded composites.

While the material encoding is not strictly an architectural question, it does change how the knowledge circulates in the design-to-production workflow. During a standard architectural workflow, design intention is being crafted with the knowledge of engineering, structure, material, and fabrication in a unidirectional and sequential manner. Digital data helps to bridge design with fabrication in a seamless way, but it is the material encoding that tightens this relationship, understood not only as a continuous but more importantly, bidirectional, fully informed, and negotiable workflow.

Johan Östling, Professor for the history of knowledge, describes such a model of knowledge exchange as circular (Östling et al., 2018). It assumes the movement of information in both directions. Such reciprocity not only allows to transmit the information from A to B but also assumes the transformation of the information during those passages. This assumption allows for a more vibrant and reciprocal relationship between architecture, construction, and material engineering by offering a powerful holistic system over a compartmentalized and discontinuous disciplinary approach.

It also actively changes the role of the architect who retrieves the control over the fabrication process, which was ubiquitous before the historical Albertian cutoff that separated conception and construction through the introduction of notational architecture. Whether the motivation was to maintain the intellectual and artisanal authorship as for Brunelleschi, who built his dome in Florence, or mainly because there is no means to notate and translate the design intention to fabrication language as with the example of Antoni Gaudí, who himself built parts of the Sagrada Familia (Carpo, 2011). This gesture opens up a vast field of experimentation for architectural design research, which might reshape the roles and capacities of architects and other practitioners.

As Roberto Bottazzi puts it, "the means of expression available at any given time determine the bounds of architectural imagination" (Bottazzi, 2018). Through expression, we understand what is possible to be constructed both virtually and physically. Therefore, we

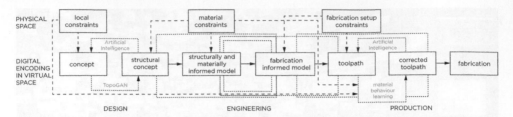

Figure 22.9 Human intelligence augmented by AI in different phases of an architectural project. Image: Authors.

try to highlight the importance of AI explorations in both design and fabrication to amplify and augment architectural creation with those two case studies.

AI in design opens up what can be imagined, while AI applied in the robotic fabrication and material domains not only facilitates the materialization of innovative ideas but also has a chance to drive them. We tend toward design innovation, understood broader than geometrical diversity within standard solutions, but more importantly, as a creation of new, particular architectural systems that incorporate new materials, requiring custom production chains (Figure 22.9).

Conclusion

The encoding scheme is of utmost importance, as its number and type of dimensions directly translate into the design space—the number and diversity of possible solutions. Any design can be reduced and compressed to the chosen number of features. Conversely, the reduction in encoding also means that any design can be recovered by decoding the latent vector into a full solution. This assumes that all designs are instances of the same building plan, or to express it in evolutionary design jargon, phenotypes with a common genotype.

However, correlation does not imply causation. The ability to encode two designs in a custom metric space does not permit the reverse conclusion that these metrics were the driving parameters generating the design. A model where the control points of building outlines are encoded in polar coordinates—distance from centroid and angle from X-axis—excludes a courtyard house by design. Given a large enough corpus of raw material, ML can extract common denominators and measure similarities among the individual samples. This allows the training of a classification system to detect architectural styles in photographs (Shalunts et al., 2011; Zhao et al., 2018). It works in hindsight, for buildings that already exist. But even the most elaborate model trained on the most extensive collection of Baroque architecture will only be able to generate more Baroque architecture. The results may well be impressive, and maybe even fool historians, as richly orchestrated compositions arranged in the style of Johann Sebastian Bach do with experts of classical music.

ML models have become stunningly good at discovering patterns to not only classify but also synthesize new instances based on probability distributions—talented forgers able to create credible shams. Are AI-assisted CAD tools a modern version of Sebastiano Serlio's Regole Generali (Serlio, 1537)—crutches enabling the mediocre architect to produce more of the same? Is a masterpiece one that artfully breaks with conventions? Philosopher Sean Dorrance Kelly calls artificial Bach compositions "mimicry," excluding "by design" a new Schönberg who fundamentally changed what music is, creating pieces different in kind and not just variations on existing ones (Kelly, 2019). The outliers, the nonconformists, often brought a culture forward by shifting the gravity center in the encoded space.

This anthropomorphic understanding of technologies in which we perceive AI as the one to directly mimic the human brain and machine that directly replaces human muscle might trigger the competitive dichotomy of a man versus machine. However, technologies are indeed unlike us, even if they can automate and replicate almost anything, we create that can be measured or quantitatively described. AI can process more information and faster than us, machines construct larger or significantly smaller elements with much higher precision than us, but they lack human intuition and radical creativity.

AI calculates solutions to quantifiable problems in no time, but it does not make sense of the problem itself. Therefore, AI for architectural design should neither be about replacing the designer by a competing automated building synthesizer nor about lights-out factories. Instead, the computer can become a powerful assistant in a cocreative process, like in the idea of Centaur—a mythological hybrid of two species that complete and empower traits of their individuals in such a symbiotic scenario.

AI can act as a smart librarian, providing previous answers to similar questions drawn in fractions of seconds from extensive collections, eventually proposing required adjustments (Yoo et al., 2020). It can act as a curator, helping to sort and cluster collections along custom dimensions defined by the user (Bernhard, 2016; Bernhard et al., 2015). These can be dimensions not previously available in the data but extracted, encoded, and eventually unveiling unexpected neighborhoods and providing new insights. The project *Gugelmann Galaxy* demonstrates this use of ML in a browser application (see Figure 22.8). It allows building new models for more meaningful interaction (Smigielska, 2020), where the computer can even disappear entirely and learn the designer's preferences by correlating brain activity with changing patterns the designer is exposed to during the training phase, as shown in Figure 22.10 (Smigielska & Cutellic, 2018). Elaborate ML models using multiple layers of convolutions (CNNs) can learn very intricate qualitative patterns in high-dimensional spaces, beyond quantitative parameters. What may appear as mere collections of meaningless numbers becomes very informative and unveiling when being visualized (Olah et al., 2017).

AI has the potential to enhance architects' creativity by speeding up tedious processes and providing immediate responses by providing a trigger for a new idea to be developed or by tightening the design-to-production process. It tries to bridge the gap between human and machine intelligence by developing models that encode higher cognitive capacities, like intuition, required in architecture and other creative industries. It also allows the architect

Figure 22.10   Ferrofluid patterns in Proteus 2.0 project. Photo: Maria Smigielska.

for more intricate communication with the physical world by opening and diversifying possible modes of production. While former developments in digital technologies addressed mainly geometrical complexity and design freedom, AI has the chance to affect architecture at multiple scales and dimensions. Thus, it requires a massive leap of experimentation and imagination, which might remain the biggest challenge for designers on the way to build architectural scenarios through AI models and methods.

As theorist Stephan Trüby has stated, architecture is "perhaps the most complex cultural technology that humanity has produced" (Trüby, 2017), and therefore its quality is difficult to measure. It is not about maximizing a target value of a function such as stress or compliance. Instead, it is arguable and uncertain if a function to measure quality even exists. If so, its parameters are unknown, more complex, impossible to be evaluated from the perspective of a single discipline, and far less intuitive to describe than most conventional features extracted for image classification. While it is impossible to encode all the architectural interests at once, we can progressively harness the AI models' powerful ability to find hidden and often inexplicable connections in vast amounts of data, to guide our decision-making among myriads of options.

References

Aage, N., & Johansen, V. E. (2013). Topology Optimization Codes Written in Python. http://www.topopt.mek.dtu.dk/Apps-and-software/Topology-optimization-codes-written-in-Python

Aghaei Meibodi, M., Bernhard, M., Jipa, A., & Dillenburger, B. (2017). The Smart Takes from the Strong: 3D Printing Stay-in-Place Formwork for Concrete Slab Construction. In A. Menges, B. Sheil, R. Glynn, & M. Skavara (Eds.), *Fabricate* (Vol. 3, pp. 210–217). UCL Press.

Bellman, R. (1957). *Dynamic Programming.* Princeton University Press.

Bendsøe, M. P., & Kikuchi, N. (1988). Generating Optimal Topologies in Structural Design Using a Homogenization Method. *Computer Methods in Applied Mechanics and Engineering,* 71, 197–224.

Bendsøe, M. P., & Sigmund, O. (2003). *Topology Optimization: Theory, Methods, and Applications. In Engineering* (2nd ed.). Springer Berlin Heidelberg. https://doi.org/10.1063/1.3278595

Bernhard, M. (2016). Gugelmann Galaxy: An Unexpected Journey through a collection of Schweizer Kleinmeister. *International Journal for Digital Art History, Visualizing Big Image Data,* Vol. 2 (2016), 95–113. https://doi.org/10.11588/dah.2016.2.23250

Bernhard, M. (2019). Domain Transforms in Architecture—Encoding and Decoding of Cultural Artefacts [Doctoral thesis, ETH Zurich]. https://doi.org/10.3929/ethz-b-000381227

Bernhard, M., Kakooee, R., Bedarf, P., & Dillenburger, B. (2021). TopoGAN - Topology Optimization with Generative Adversarial Networks. AAG - Advances in Architectural Geometry, unpublished.

Bernhard, M., Marinčić, N., & Orozco, J. (2015). ANY-FOLD: On Curation, Literacy & Space. *Trans, curated* Vol.27 (September 2015), 84–87.

Boden, M. A. (2004). *The Creative Mind: Myths and Mechanisms* (2nd ed). Routledge.

Bottazzi, R. (2018). *Digital Architecture beyond Computers: Fragments of a Cultural History of Computational Design.* Bloomsbury Visual Arts.

Carpo, M. (2011). *The Alphabet and the Algorithm.* MIT Press.

Dunston, P., & Bernold, L. (2000). Adaptive Control for Safe and Quality Rebar Fabrication. *Journal of Construction Engineering and Management,* Vol. 126, Issue 2 (March 2000) 122–129. https://doi.org/10.1061/(ASCE)0733-9364(2000)126:2(122)

Frazer, J. (1995). *An Evolutionary Architecture* (P. Johnston, D. Crompton, J. McIvor, & M. Sparrow, Eds.; Themes VII). Architectural Association AA Publications. https://issuu.com/aaschool/docs/an-evolutionary-architecture-webocr

Gatys, L. A., Ecker, A. S., & Bethge, M. (2015). *A Neural Algorithm of Artistic Style.* ArXiv:1508.06576 [Cs, q-Bio]. http://arxiv.org/abs/1508.06576

Goodfellow, I. J., Pouget-Abadie, J., Mirza, M., Xu, B., Warde-Farley, D., Ozair, S., Courville, A., & Bengio, Y. (2014). *Generative Adversarial Networks.* http://arxiv.org/abs/1406.2661

Hassabis, D. (2018). Creativity and AI. www.youtube.com/watch?v=d-bvsJWmqlc

Hossain, M. A., & Nadeem, A. (2019). Towards digitizing the construction industry: State of the art of construction 4.0. *ISEC 2019 - 10th International Structural Engineering and Construction Conference*. https://doi.org/10.14455/isec.res.2019.184

Isola, P., Zhu, J.-Y., Zhou, T., & Efros, A. A. (2016). *Image-to-Image Translation with Conditional Adversarial Networks*. http://arxiv.org/abs/1611.07004

Jipa, A., Bernhard, M., Dillenburger, B., & Aghaei-Meibodi, M. (2016). 3D-Printed Stay-in-Place Formwork for Topologically Optimized Concrete Slabs. In *Proceedings of the 2016 TxA Emerging Design + Technology Conference* Texas Society of Architects (pp. 96–107). https://doi.org/10.3929/ETHZ-B-000237082

Kelly, S. D. (2019). A Philosopher Argues That An AI Can't Be an Artist. In *MIT Technology Review*. https://www.technologyreview.com/s/612913/a-philosopher-argues-that-an-ai-can-never-be-an-artist/

Krizhevsky, A., Sutskever, I., & Hinton, G. E. (2012). ImageNet Classification with Deep Convolutional Neural Networks. In F. Pereira, C. J. C. Burges, L. Bottou, & K. Q. Weinberger (Eds.), *Advances in Neural Information Processing Systems* (Vol. 25, pp. 1097–1105). http://papers.nips.cc/paper/4824-imagenet-classification-with-deep-convolutional-neural-networks.pdf

Newton-Rex, E., Trevelyan, D., Chanquion, P., Kosta, K., Medeot, G., & Selvi, M. (n.d.). Jukedeck. TikTok. www.jukedeck.com

Olah, C., Mordvintsev, A., & Schubert, L. (2017). Feature Visualization. *Distill*, 2(11), 10.23915/distill.00007. https://doi.org/10.23915/distill.00007

Östling, J., Sandmo, E., Larsson Heidenblad, D., Nilsson Hammar, A., & Hernæs Nordberg, K. (Eds.) (2018). The History of Knowledge and the Circulation of Knowledge: An Introduction. In *Circulation of Knowledge: Explorations in the History of Knowledge* (pp. 9–33), Nordic Academic Press. https://lup.lub.lu.se/search/ws/files/36167357/Circulation_of_Knowledge.pdf

Ross, G. (2018). *Automatic on the Road*. https://www.youtube.com/watch?v=TqsW0PMd8R0

Serlio, S. (1537). *Regole generali di architettura sopra le cinque maniere de gli edifici*. Francesco Marcolini Da Forli.

Shalunts, G., Haxhimusa, Y., & Sablatnig, R. (2011). Architectural Style Classification of Building Facade Windows. In G. Bebis, R. Boyle, B. Parvin, D. Koracin, S. Wang, K. Kyungnam, B. Benes, K. Moreland, C. Borst, S. DiVerdi, C. Yi-Jen, & J. Ming (Eds.), *Advances in Visual Computing* (Vol. 6939, pp. 280–289). Springer Berlin Heidelberg. https://doi.org/10.1007/978-3-642-24031-7_28

Silver, D., Huang, A., Maddison, C. J., Guez, A., Sifre, L., Driessche, G. van den, Schrittwieser, J., Antonoglou, I., Panneershelvam, V., Lanctot, M., Dieleman, S., Grewe, D., Nham, J., Kalchbrenner, N., Sutskever, I., Lillicrap, T., Leach, M., Kavukcuoglu, K., Graepel, T., & Hassabis, D. (2016). Mastering the Game of Go with Deep Neural Networks and Tree Search. *Nature*, 529, 484–503.

Smigielska, M. (2018). Application of Machine Learning Within the Integrative Design and Fabrication of Robotic Rod Bending Processes. In De Rycke K. et al. (Eds.), *Humanizing Digital Reality*, pp. 523–536. Singapore: Springer. https://doi.org/10.1007/978-981-10-6611-5_44

Smigielska, M. (2020). *Proteus. Architecture and Naturing Affairs: Media and Architectonic Concepts*. An M., Hovestadt, L., & Bühlmann, V. (Eds.), pp. 90–95, Berlin, Basel: Birkhäuser. https://doi.org/10.1515/9783035622164

Smigielska, M., & Cutellic, P. (2018). *Proteus Project [Installation]*. https://mariasni.com/project/proteus/

Steadman, P. (1976). Graph-Theoretic Representation of Architectural Arrangement. In L. March (Ed.), *The Architecture of Form* (pp. 94–115). Cambridge University Press.

Stiny, G., & Mitchell, W. J. (1978). The Palladian Grammar. *Environment and Planning B: Planning and Design*, 5, 5–18. https://doi.org/10.1068/b050005

Thompson, W., Flores, E., Franken, M., & Haanstra, B. (2016). *The Next Rembrandt*. www.nextrembrandt.com

Tocchini, D. (2014). *The Grid*. https://thegrid.io/

Toffler, A. (1970). *Future Shock. The Third Wave*. Random House.

Trüby, S. (2017). Positioning Architecture. *E-Flux Architecture*. https://www.e-flux.com/architecture/history-theory/159235/positioning-architecture-theory/

Yoo, A., Shammas, D., Akizuki, Y., Bernhard, M., & Dillenburger, B. (2020). *OpenPlans [Innov3dum]*. Digital Building Technologies, ETH Zurich.

Zhao, P., Miao, Q., Song, J., Qi, Y., Liu, R., & Ge, D. (2018). Architectural Style Classification based on Feature Extraction Module. *IEEE Access*, 6, 52598–52606.

23

AI and architecture

An experimental perspective

Stanislas Chaillou

Artificial intelligence (AI), as a discipline, has already been permeating countless fields, bringing means and methods to previously unresolved challenges, across industries. The advent of AI in architecture is still in its early days but offers promising results. More than a mere opportunity, such potential represents for us a major step ahead, about to reshape the architectural discipline.

Our work proposes to evidence this promise when applied to the built environment. Specifically, we offer to apply AI to floor plan analysis and generation. Our ultimate goal is threefold: (1) to generate floor plans, i.e., optimize the generation of a large and highly diverse quantity of floor plan designs, (2) to qualify floor plans, i.e., offer a proper classification methodology, and (3) to allow users to "browse" through generated design options.

Our methodology follows two main intuitions: (1) the creation of building plans is a nontrivial technical challenge, although encompassing standard optimization technics and (2) the design of space is a sequential process, requiring successive design steps across different

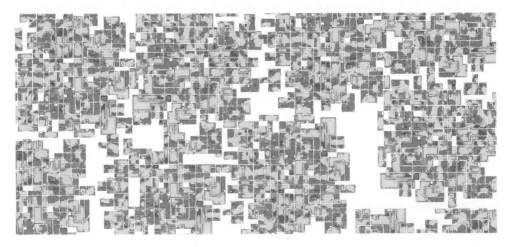

Figure 23.1 GAN-generated masterplan.

scales (urban scale, building scale, and unit scale). Then, to harness these two realities, we have chosen nested generative adversarial neural networks or GANs. Such models enable us to capture more complexity across encountered floor plans and break down the complexity by tackling problems through successive steps. Each step corresponding to a given model, specifically trained for this particular task, the process can eventually evidence the possible back and forth between humans and machines.

Plans are indeed a high-dimensional problem, at the crossroad of quantifiable technics, and more qualitative properties. The study of architectural precedent remains too often a hazardous process that negates the richness of the number of existing resources while lacking in analytical rigor. Our methodology, inspired by current data science methodologies, aims at qualifying floor plans. Through the creation of six metrics, we propose a framework that captures architecturally relevant parameters of floor plans. On the one hand, footprint shape, orientation, and thickness and texture are three metrics capturing the essence of a given floor plan's style. On the other hand, program, connectivity, and circulation are meant to depict the essence of any floor plan organization.

In a nutshell, the machine, once the extension of our pencil, can today be leveraged to map architectural knowledge and trained to assist us in creating viable design options.

Framework

Our work finds itself at the intersection of architecture and AI. The former is the topic, and the latter is the method. Both have been simplified into clear and actionable categories.

Architecture is, here, understood as the intersection between style and organization. On the one hand, we consider buildings as vectors of a cultural significance, which express a certain style through their geometry, taxonomy, typology, and decoration. Baroque, Roman, Gothic, modern, and contemporary: as many architectural styles that can be found through a careful study of floor plans. On the other hand, buildings are the product of engineering and science, answering to strict frameworks and rule-building codes, ergonomics, energetic efficiency, egress, program, etc.—that can be found as we read a floor plan. This organizational imperative will complete our definition of architecture and drive our investigation (Figure 23.2).

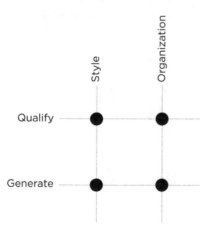

Figure 23.2 Framework matrix.

AI will be employed, using two of its main fields of investigation—analytics and GANs—as an investigative tool. At first, we dive into the topic of generation. Using GANs, we offer to educate our own AI systems to architectural design. We postulate that its utilization can enhance the practice of the architectural discipline. This field is as recent as it is experimental and yields to this day surprising results. We hope to be able to train it to draw actual building floor plans. Then, we come up with a robust analytical framework to qualify and classify the generated floor plans. Ultimately, our goal is to organize the results of our GANs to offer the possibility for the user to browse seamlessly through the variety of created design options. To that end, the quantity and ubiquity of tools offered by data science will prove to be valuable to our investigation. Through this dual-lens, at the crossroad of style and organization, qualification and generation, we lay down a framework that organizes the encounter of architecture and AI.

Generation

The design of architectural floor plans is at the core of the architecture practice. Its mastery stands as the gold standard of the discipline. It is an exercise that practitioners have tried over-time relentlessly to improve through technology. In this first part, we dive into the potential of AI applied to floor plan generation, as a mean to push the envelope even further.

Using our framework, to tackle floor plans' style and organization, we lay down in the following chapter the potential of AI-enabled space planning. Our objective is to offer a set of reliable and robust tools to both evidence the potential of our approach and test our assumptions. The challenge is threefold: (1) choosing the right toolset, (2) isolating the right phenomena to be shown to the machine, and (3) ensuring that the machine "learns" properly.

AI and GANs

GANs are here our weapon of choice. Within the field of AI, neural networks stand as a key field of investigation. The creative ability of such models has been recently evidenced, through the advent of GANs. As with any machine-learning model, GANs learn statistically significant phenomena among data presented to them. Their structure (Figure 23.3), however, represents a breakthrough: made of two key models, the generator and the discriminator, GANs leverage a feedback loop between both models to refine their ability to generate

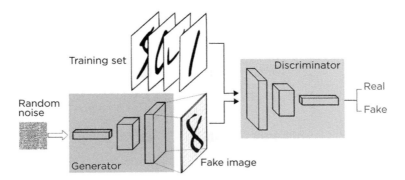

Figure 23.3 GAN's architecture.

relevant images. The discriminator is trained to recognize images from a set of data. Properly trained, this model can distinguish between a real example, taken out of the dataset, and a "fake" image, foreign to the dataset. The generator, however, synthesizes images, while receiving some feedback from the discriminator. The discriminator will in fact penalize the generator, based on its outputs' resemblance to the images from the dataset. That way, the generator will gradually tune its weights to receive better grades from the discriminator. Through this feedback loop, a GAN slowly builds up its ability to create relevant synthetic images, factoring in phenomena found among observed data.

Representation and learning

If GANs represent a tremendous opportunity for us, knowing what to show them is crucial. We have, here, the opportunity to let the model learn directly from floor plan images. By formatting images, we can control the type of information that the model will learn. As an example, by simply showing our model the shape of a parcel and associated building footprint will yield a model able to create typical building footprints given a parcel's shape. To ensure the quality of the outputs, we will use our own architectural "sense" to curate the content of our training sets: a model will only be as good as the data we give to the machines, as architects.

In Figure 23.4, we illustrate a typical training sequence: this sequence, realized over a day and half of training, displays how one of our GAN models progressively learns how to layout rooms and fenestration for a housing unit. Although the initial attempts are imprecise and confusing, after 250 iterations, the machine builds for itself some form of intuition.

Figure 23.4 Training sequence.

Precedents

If GANs' application to architectural design is still in its infancy, a handful of precedents inspired our work and drove our intuition. Hao Zheng and Weixin Huang offered an initial publication at the ACADIA conference in 2018, demonstrating the potential of GAN for floor plan recognition and furniture layout generation. Using patches of color, their model would draw the infill of rooms, based on the room program, and its opening position. The same year, Nathan Peters in his thesis, at the Harvard GSD, proposed to use GANs (pix2pix) to tackle program repartition in single-family modular homes, based on the house footprint.

Regarding GANs as design assistants, Hao Zheng's conference paper (Drawing with Bots: Human–Computer Collaborative Drawing Experiments, 2018) and Nono Martinez's thesis at the GSD (2017) inspired our investigations. Both authors tackled the idea of a loop between the machine and the designer to refine the very notion of "design process."

Our work expands on these precedents and offers to nest three models (footprint, program, and furnishing) to create a full "generation stack" while improving results' quality at each step. By automating multiunit processing, our work then scales to entire building generation and masterplan layouts. We further offer an array of models dealing with style transfer. Finally, our contribution adds a rigorous framework to parse and classify resulting outputs, enabling users to "browse" consistently through generated options (Figure 23.5).

Style transfer

Within a floor plan, "style" can be observed by studying the geometry and figure plane of its walls. Typical baroque churches will display bulky columns with multiple round indents. A modern villa by Mies van der Rohe will show thin flat walls. This "crenellation" of the wall surface is a feature that a GAN can appreciate. By showing its pair of images, with one image being a segmented version of a plan and the other one the original wall structure, we can then build a certain amount of machine intuition with regard to architectural style.

Figure 23.6 shows the results of a model, trained to learn the Baroque style. Then, we proceed to a style transfer, where a given floor plan is manually segmented (A) and dressed back with a stylistic new wall (B).

Layout assistant

In this section, we offer a multistep pipeline (Figure 23.8), integrating all the necessary steps to draw a floor plan. Jumping across scales, it emulates the process taken by an architect and tries to encapsulate each step into one specific model, trained to perform a given operation.

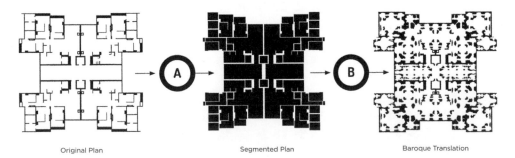

Original Plan   Segmented Plan   Baroque Translation

Figure 23.5 Modern-to-Baroque floor plan translation.

Figure 23.6 Style transfer results: apartment units modern-to-Baroque style transfer.

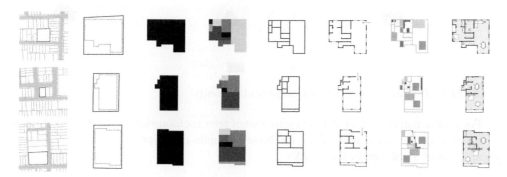

Figure 23.7 Layout assistant, a step-by-step pipeline.

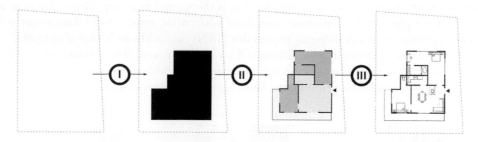

Figure 23.8 Generation pipeline (models I to III).

From the parcel to the building footprint (I), from the footprint to a room split with walls and fenestration (II), and from a fenestrated floor plan to a furnished one (III): each step has been carefully engineered, trained, and tested.

At the same time, by dividing the pipeline into discrete steps, the system allows for the user's intervention between each model. By selecting the output of a model, and editing it, before giving it to the next model, the user stays in control of the design process. Its input shapes the decisions made by the model, therefore achieving the human–machine interaction expected.

Footprint

The first step in our pipeline tackles the challenge of creating an appropriate building footprint for a given parcel geometry. To train this model, we used an extensive database of Boston's building footprints and were able to create an array of models, each tailored for a specific property type: commercial, residential (house), residential (condo), industrial, etc.

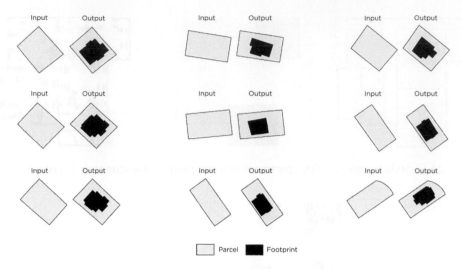

Figure 23.9   The results of generated footprints (housing).

For a given parcel, each model can create a set of relevant footprints, resembling in dimension and style the type it was trained for. Nine examples of footprints using the residential (house) model are shown in Figure 23.9.

Room split and fenestration

The layout of rooms across a building footprint is the natural next step. Being able to split a given floor plan, while respecting meaningful adjacencies, typical room dimensions and proper fenestrations is a challenging process that GANs can tackle with surprising results.

Using a dataset of around 700+ annotated floor plans, we were able to train a broad array of models. Each is geared toward a specific room count and yields surprisingly relevant results once used on empty building footprints. Some typical results are displayed in Figure 23.10.

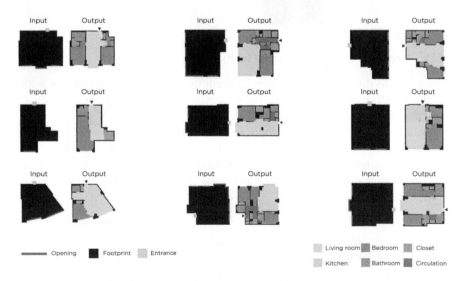

Figure 23.10   The results of the generated program and fenestration.

Furnishing

This last step brings the principle of generation to its most granular level: the addition of furniture across space. To that end, first, we trained a model to furnish the entire apartment all at once. The network was able to learn, based on each room program, the relative disposition of furniture across space and the dimensions of each element. The results are displayed in Figure 23.11.

If these results can give a rough idea of potential furniture layouts, the quality of the resulting drawings is still too fuzzy. To further refine the output quality, we have trained an array of additional models for each room type (living room, bedroom, kitchen, etc.). Each model is only in charge of translating a color patch added onto the plan into a properly drawn piece of furniture. Furniture types are encoded using a color code. The results of each model are displayed in Figure 23.12.

Figure 23.11   **The results of furnished units.**

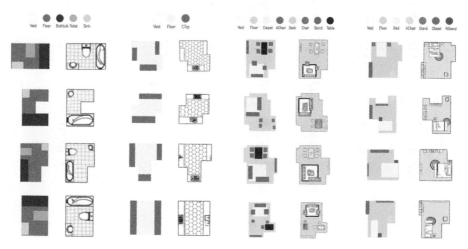

Figure 23.12   **The results of room furnishing models—bathroom, kitchen, living room, and bedroom.**

Going further

If generating standard apartments can be achieved using our technic, pushing the boundaries of our models is the natural next step. GANs can offer quite remarkable flexibility to solve seemingly highly constrained problems. In the case of the floor plan layout, as the footprint changes in dimension and shape, partitioning and furnishing the space by hand can be a challenging process. Our models prove here to be quite "smart" in their ability to adapt to changing constraints, as evidenced in Figure 23.13.

Our ability to control the units' entrance door and windows position, coupled with the flexibility of our models, allows us to tackle space planning at a larger scale, beyond the logic of a single unit. In the examples shown in Figures 23.14 and 23.15, we scale our technic to entire buildings.

Qualify

> Failing to name things adds to the World's disarray.
> Albert Camus

To balance out our ability to generate floor plans, finding the proper framework to organize, sort, and classify the wealth of generated design options is more than crucial. The floor plans we offer will only be as good as our ability to navigate across our database of generated options. By borrowing concepts from architecture, we hope to transform common architectural adjectives into quantifiable metrics. To that end, we have isolated six key metrics, describing six essential aspects of floor plan design: footprint, program, orientation, thickness and texture, connectivity, and circulation.

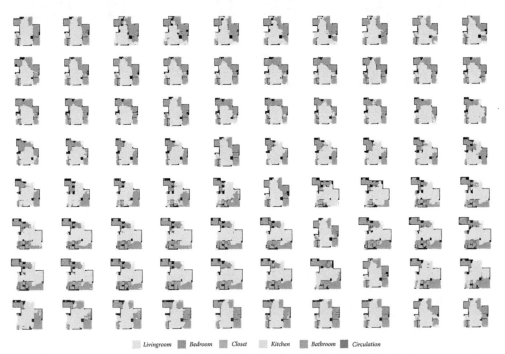

Livingroom Bedroom Closet Kitchen Bathroom Circulation

Figure 23.13 GAN-enabled space layout under morphing footprint.

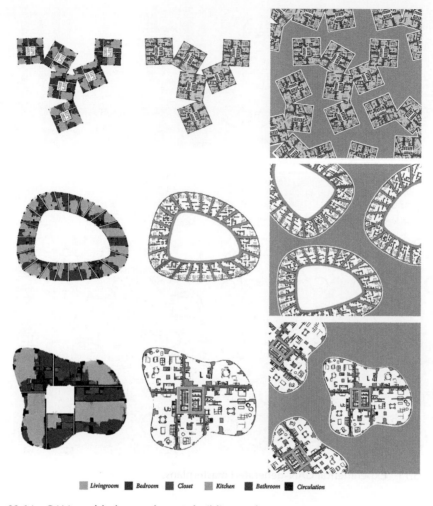

Livingroom ■ Bedroom ■ Closet ■ Kitchen ■ Bathroom ■ Circulation

Figure 23.14 GAN-enabled space layout, building scale.

These metrics work together as a comprehensive framework, addressing both the stylistic and organizational dimensions of floor plans. Each one has been developed as an algorithm and tested thoroughly.

Footprint

The shape of a building is the simplest and most intuitive proxy to qualify its style. The "footprint" metric analyzes the shape of the floor plan perimeter and translates it into a histogram, as shown in Figure 23.16.

This descriptor, while encoding the shape of a building, can translate common adjectives—"thin," "bulky," "symmetrical," etc.—used by architects into numerical information to communicate with a computer about building shapes.

From a technical standpoint, this metric uses polar convexity to turn a given outline into a list of discrete values (vector) that can then be compared to other floor plans. We use a polar

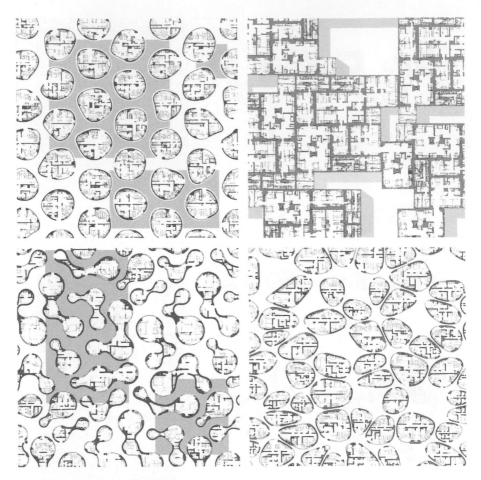

Figure 23.15 **Experimental GAN-generated masterplans.**

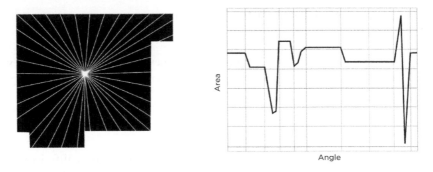

Figure 23.16 **Footprint polar diagram.**

array of lines, stemming from the center of the plan, to extract the area of the plan captured by each slice of space obtained. This methodology has proven to yield satisfactory results, as shown in the queries in Figure 23.17. This technic can also be employed to qualify indoor spaces' shape as well as building perimeter's geometry.

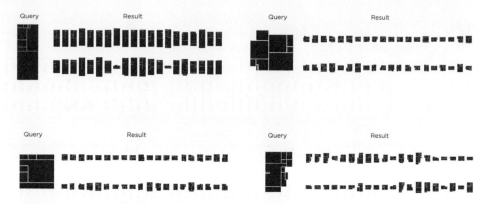

Figure 23.17 Typical floor plan retrieval using the footprint metric (left: query; right: results).

Program

The program of a building, or in other words, the type of rooms it contains, is a major driver of its internal organization. Capturing this reality is central to our approach. To describe the "mix" of rooms, we represent through a color code the list of rooms contained in any given floor plan. This colored band becomes the proxy to describe the program. It acts as a template, aggregating both the quantity and the programmatic quality of the rooms within the floor plan. It is an intuitive visual description for humans, which can translate into a reliable encoding technic for machines (Figure 23.18).

From a technical standpoint, by using this colored band, we can compute the programmatic similarities and dissimilarities between any given pair of floor plans. To visualize results, each plan is reported as both a colored floor plan and a one-dimensional color vector of its program. We display in Figure 23.19 some typical results of this metric, where for a given floor plan, the algorithm returns a list of alike plans and their programmatic "band."

Orientation

The orientation of walls in a plan is a valuable source of information. It can describe both the enclosure (how secluded spaces are due to the presence of walls) and the style of a plan. Using

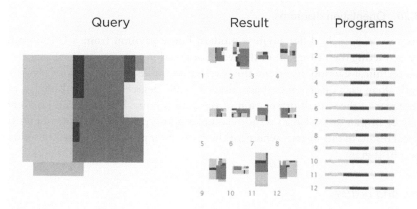

Figure 23.18 Typical floor plan retrieval using the program metric (left: query; right: results).

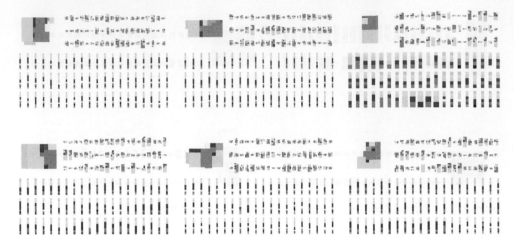

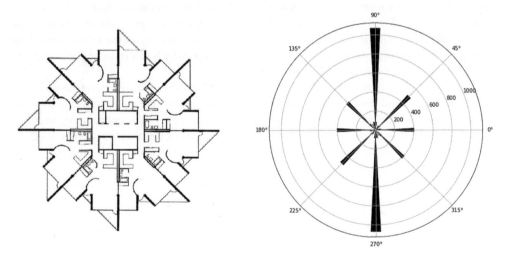

Figure 23.19 Typical floor plan retrieval using the program metric (left: query; right: results; bottom: program's results).

Figure 23.20 Orientation diagrams.

this metric, we can easily differentiate a modern house pavilion from a Gothic cathedral, simply by extracting the histogram of the walls' orientation.

From a technical standpoint, orientation extracts the walls of a given floor plan and sums their length along each direction of space, from 0 to 360 degrees. The resulting list of values is an assessment of the overall orientation of the plan (Figure 23.20). It can be averaged to get a single descriptor or used as a vector to compare across plans. We display in Figure 23.21 some typical results of this metric, where for the given floor plans, the algorithm returns their orientation histogram.

Thickness and texture

The thickness and texture metric qualifies the "fat" of a plan: its wall thickness and the variation of this thickness. The thickness of walls across a plan, as well as the geometry of

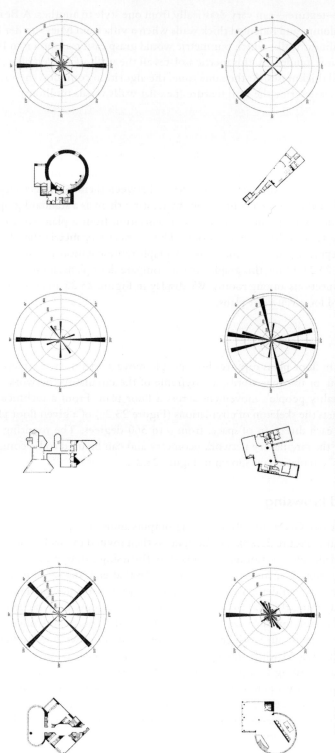

Figure 23.21 Typical floor plan analysis using the orientation metric (left: plan; right: orientation diagram).

the wall surface—texture—can vary drastically from one style to another. A Beaux-Arts hall would display columns and indented thick walls when a villa from Mies van der Rohe would display thin rectilinear walls, which our metric would grasp easily, as shown in Figure 23.22.

From a technical standpoint, this metric isolates all the walls of a given plan and outputs a histogram of wall thicknesses. At the same time, the algorithm computes the variation of the thickness, to better describe the wall texture (i.e., flat walls versus mullions).

Connectivity

The connectivity metric tackles the question of room adjacencies. The proximity of rooms to one another is a key dimension of a floor plan. Moreover, their connection through doors and corridors defines the existence of connections between them. Connectivity investigates the quantity and quality of such connections by treating them as a standard graph.

From a technical standpoint, by using the fenestration from a plan, we can deduce the graph of existing relationships among rooms. The connectivity metric then builds an adjacency matrix, reporting these connections. A graph representation is finally generated, as shown in Figure 23.24. Using this graph, we can compare floor plans, taking into account the similarity of connections among rooms. We display in Figure 23.25 an array of connectivity graphs, generated for given floor plans.

Circulation

The circulation in floor plans captures how people move across it. By extracting a skeleton of the circulation, or in other words, a wireframe of the circulatory network, we can both quantify and qualify people's movement across a floor plan. From a technical standpoint, circulation extracts the skeleton of circulations (Figure 23.26) of a given floor plan and sums its length along each direction of space, from 0 to 360 degrees. The resulting histogram is an assessment of the circulatory network geometry and can be used to be compared against other floor plans' circulation, as shown in Figure 23.27.

Mapping and browsing

Looking back at our GAN models, each one outputs multiple options at each step of our generation pipeline (Figure 23.28). The designer is then invited to "pick" a preferred option, modify it if needed, before actioning the next step. Browsing through the generated options, however, can be frustrating and time-consuming. To that end, the set of metrics defined in the "Qualify" section can demonstrate their full potential here and complement our generation pipeline. By using them as filters, the user can narrow down the range of options and find the relevant option for its design in a matter of seconds. This duality of generation filtering is where the value of our work gets all the more evidenced: we provide here a complete framework, leveraging AI while staying within reach of a standard user.

Once filtered according to a given criterion (footprint, program, orientation, thickness and texture, connectivity, or circulation), we provide the users with a tree-like representation of their choice. The selected option is at the center, and around it, its nearest neighbors are classified according to a user-selected criterion. The user can then narrow down the search and find its ideal design option, or select another option within the tree, to recompute the graph. Figure 23.29 displays a typical similarity tree, computed using the program metric.

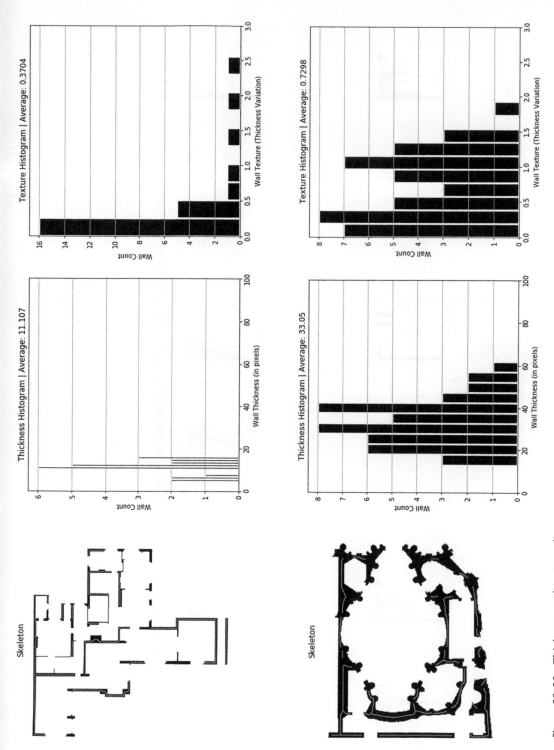

Figure 23.22 Thickness and texture diagrams.

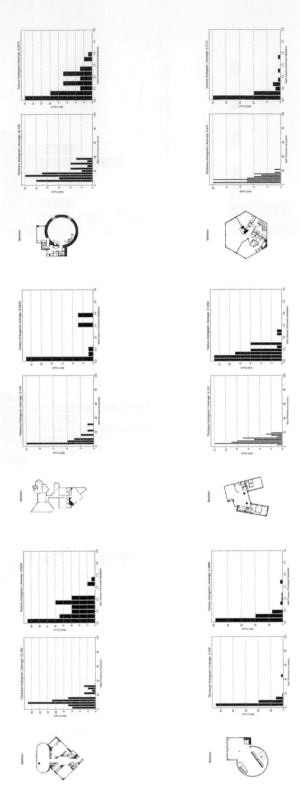

Figure 23.23   Typical floor plan analysis using the thickness and texture metric (left: plan; right: resulting diagrams).

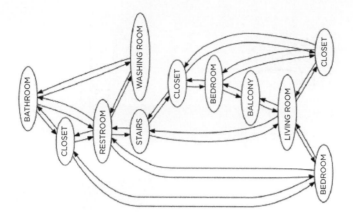

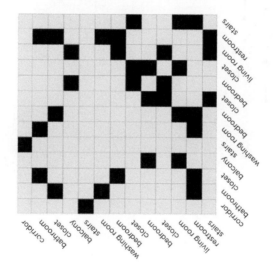

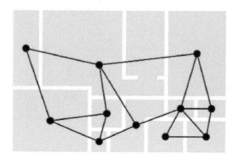

Figure 23.24 Connectivity diagram and adjacency matrix.

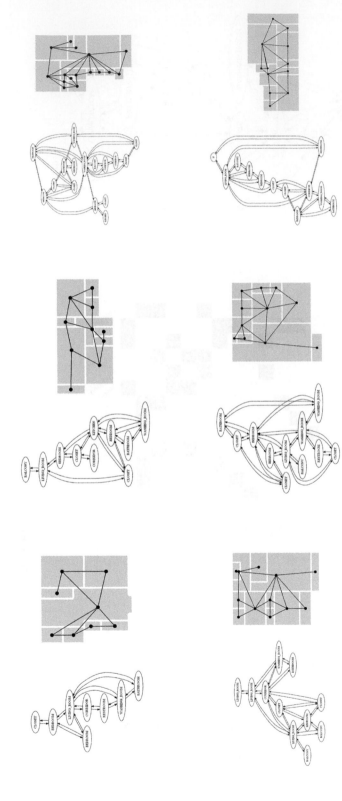

Figure 23.25 Typical floor plan analysis using the connectivity metric (left: connectivity graph; right: plan adjacencies).

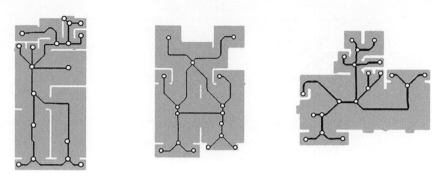

Figure 23.26   Circulation diagram.

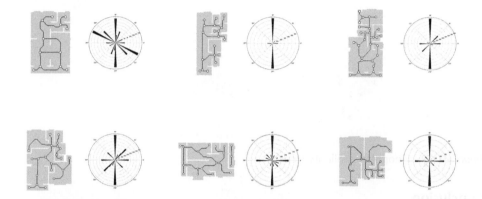

Figure 23.27   Typical floor plan analysis using the circulation metric (left: circulation graph; right: diagram).

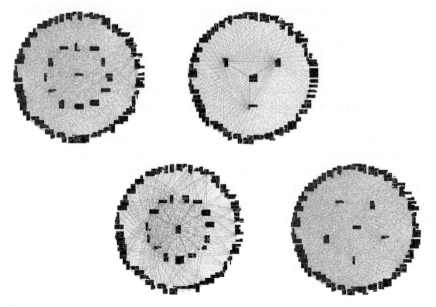

Figure 23.28   Similarity graphs, comparing one plan to many.

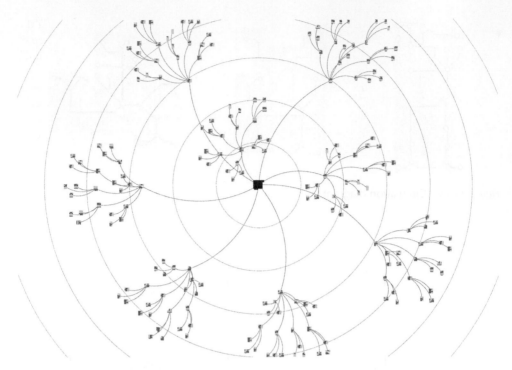

Figure 23.29 Floor plan similarity trees.

Conclusion

AI will soon massively empower architects in their day-to-day practice. As such, potential is about to be demonstrated, our work participates to the proof of concept while our framework offers a springboard for discussion, inviting architects to start engaging with AI, and data scientists to consider architecture as a field of investigation. However, today, our manifesto could be summarized in four major points.

Conceptually first, we believe that a statistical approach to design conception shapes AI's potential for architecture. Its less-deterministic and more-holistic character is undoubtedly a chance for our field. Rather than using machines to optimize a set of variables, relying on them to extract significant qualities and mimicking them all along the design process are a paradigm shift.

Second, we are directionally convinced that our ability to design the right pipeline will condition AI's success as a new architectural toolset. Our choice for the "grey boxing" approach, as introduced by Prof. Andrew Witt in Log, will likely secure the best potential results. This method contrasts with the "black box" approach, which only allows users to input information upfront and to get finished design options at the end of the process, without any control over the successive generation steps. On the contrary, by breaking out our pipeline into discrete steps, "grey boxing" permits the user to intervene all along the way. His tight control over the machine is his ultimate guarantee of the design process quality.

Third, we technically believe that the sequential nature of the application will facilitate its manageability and foster its development. The ability to intervene throughout the generating process is a fundamental dimension: as each step of the pipeline represents a distinct portion of architectural expertise, each model can be trained independently, opening the way to significant improvements and experimentation in the near future. Indeed, improving this entire pipeline end-to-end could be a long and cumbersome task, while amending it step by step remains a manageable process, within the reach of most architects and engineers in the industry.

Finally, we hope our framework will help to address the endless breadth and complexity of the models to be trained and those used in any generation pipeline. Tackling parcels-footprint-room split-etc., as we do is one possible approach among, we believe, a large set of options. To encapsulate the necessary steps of space planning, the key is more the principle than the method. And, with the growing availability of architectural data, we encourage further work and open-minded experimentation.

Far from thinking about AI as the new dogma in architecture, we conceive this field as a new challenge, full of potential, and promises. We see here the possibility for rich results that will complement our practice and address some blind spots of our discipline.

24

An anonymous composition

A case study of form-finding optimization through a machine learning algorithm

Akshay Srivastava, Longtai Liao, and Henan Liu

With the technological transformations taking place every day, machine learning (ML) is gradually becoming an inevitable apparatus in almost every discipline, including architecture. An intrinsic advantage of ML is its innovative mechanism of processing a colossal amount of data at a "relatively" fast speed. As Mario Carpo states, instead of compressing data into simple rules and patterns, scientists and designers are trying to straightforwardly handle and utilize all the discrete data by using the almost unlimited power of computation (Carpo, 2014). Such a trending mindset provokes us to delve into understanding how ML algorithms could be integrated into digital design and utilizing the ability of a machine to learn and process a huge amount of data in a short period of time.

Background

Throughout the development of artificial intelligence, machines have been more successful in analytical and cogent skills than design generation or composition. Traditional algorithm's deductive nature makes it extremely hard to mimic the seemingly random process of humans' creative thinking. However, Parag Mittal, a computational artist, proposed a provoking approach to such an issue (Mital, 2013a). Instead of training a machine to create a design from scratch, he trains the machine to start by subtracting existing video clips as elements, which he then uses to recreate a new animation as a whole in real time. The traditional process of creative design is thus decomposed into several phases during which the machine is only trained to perform in the specific phases that it is good at. In this case, the trained machine develops its way to select video clips from the source pool and then creatively arranges them with no absolute (Figure 24.1). Following this logic, the question for us becomes which phases during a creative design process are the ones that need a machine with learning abilities the most and how ML could be integrated into design processes.

In most cases of digital design, the phases involving repetitive tasks and intensive labor are done by scripting. Such phases usually have predetermined goals, and the script simply functions by following basic human logical steps using computational power. The script essentially consists of two different components that make up the body for the language to perform the task by the computer. The first one is functions, which can be defined as a set of instructions

Figure 24.1 Visual synthesis demonstration (Mital, 2013b).

predetermined and packaged in a box that when executed carries out the needful. Functions usually appear as Grasshopper (grasshopper3d.com) components or Python (python.org) definitions depending on which scripting platform is employed. The other one is input variables, which can be considered as the ingredients for a recipe; the ingredients are provided to be altered by the function (steps involved in the recipe) to achieve the desired output. They often appear as number sliders or floats, still, depending on which scripting platform is employed. Although these two components relieve designers from repetitive labors, they are still created by humans and sometimes even in an extremely time-consuming way. Because writing functions involves highly complex skills and thinking processes, training a machine to write functions independently is hard to achieve at this moment. However, the phase of adjusting input variables (or adjusting the quantity of each ingredient of a recipe) is relatively simple but repetitive. After developing an entire script and achieving an outcome, designers would still need to look at the generated configurations, then, manually adjust every input variable accordingly, and repeat this process until it meets their desired goals. In the scenarios of having more than ten variables to generate a configuration, manually adjusting every variable is extremely time-consuming and practically almost impossible to find an ideal combination. Greg Lynn even calls it a "happy accident" that designers can only wait and pray for a result to be satisfying (Lynn, 2008). Therefore, the most technically essential part of this experiment is to train a machine to "understand" the designer's predisposition and adjust every variable value based on its understanding.

Methods

Form-finding scripting

To start with, a form-finding script is created in Grasshopper to generate 3D configurations automatically. The idea is to tell a 3D modeling software (Rhino in our case) to randomly select 3D elements from the already-built source pool and compose them as a whole in a specific manner. A pool of elements is manually created to include as many varieties of shapes and sizes as possible. Some of these elements have architectural influences, such as traditional Chinese details, Mies van der Rohe's cross-column, and Frank Gehry's sculptural geometries; some of them have references outside the realm of architecture, including shapes inspired by Japanese comic novels and movies (Figure 24.2).

To control the generation of these "whole" shapes, 12 variables or control attributes were introduced that steer the output configurations, including "size" that controls the size of each element, "dance" that controls the degree of random movement of each control point, and "index" that determines which elements from the source pool are being selected to compose the configuration (Figure 24.3). The above elements, variables, and a set of morphology functions together perform as a generative script that can create a 3D configuration.

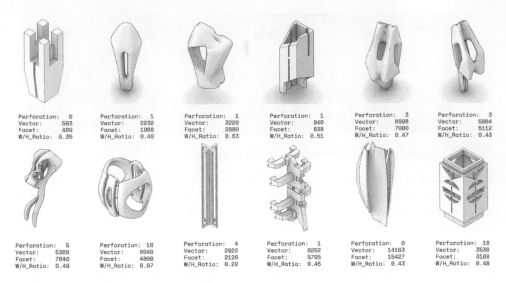

Figure 24.2 3D elements source pool.

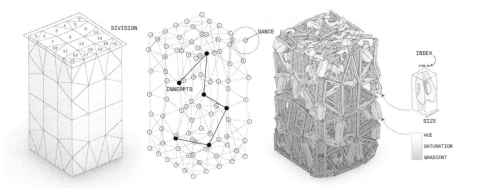

Figure 24.3 Effects of variables.

Library creating and labeling

To generate enough configurations and corresponding data (which is the value of each control attribute) for ML, a mechanism is inserted to automatically generate unbiased random variables to provide controlling attributes and, therefore, generate corresponding configurations. Each set of 12 variables is recorded in an Excel file as numeric data while every configuration generated is recorded as an image simultaneously.

The above portion of library creating and form finding are combined in one single grasshopper script (Figure 24.4). Most of the components used in the script are built-in ones except a spreadsheet writer and a few simple Python definitions that generate and organize data for simpler manipulation and reading.

To train the machine to understand designers' preferences, all the output configurations from the generated library are then labeled by each designer as a simple binary determination of good or bad, which could be understood by the machine as desired or undesired.

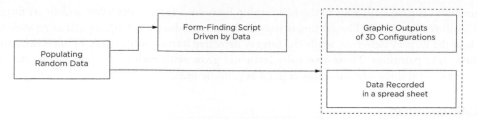

Figure 24.4 Library creating, form finding, and data recording.

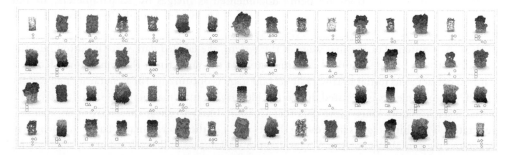

Figure 24.5 A small portion of the library created.

The labels are then recorded into the Excel file aligned with corresponding data. In our experiment, 8,000 configurations and 96,000 variables are created and recorded accordingly (Figure 24.5).

ML operation

To set up a system that can produce configurations that match a designer's preference, an ML system based on the TensorFlow library is introduced in the analysis process. Generative adversarial networks (GANs) are the key strategy applied in the ML system to generate preferred variables in this experiment (Zhu, 2020). ML is employed to supply desired and undesired configuration data to the machine with the intent of receiving a set of data to generate a configuration that the machine believes to be the user's desired result.

Introduction of GAN

GAN is a type of generative model system. Its function is grabbing the training data from a given library and learning the probability distribution from those data (Goodfellow et al., 2014). The system consists of two basic modules. One is a generator, which is used for generating variables based on certain logic and, in this experiment, each set of 12 variables can construct a corresponding configuration. Another module is the discriminator, which is used to identify the variables of configurations trained by generator network or human designers.

The goal of the generator network is to try and generate data as close to the input data as possible that are not able to be identified by the discriminator network, whereas the discriminator network's goal is to try and identify the data that are not similar to the input data. The key working strategy of GAN is letting those two modules compete and iterate with each other and optimizing those two modules. The final output of the GAN system can be as similar as possible to the designer's preference. The relationship between discriminator and generator can be analogous to the relationship between a forgery detective and an art forger (Cahill & Her, 2019). The art forger tries his best to produce paintings as real as possible to cheat the forgery detective, while the forgery detective learns continuously by authenticating those fake paintings. Those two roles learn and grow with each other, and finally, the art forger can produce fake paintings as good as genuine ones.

GAN operation

The ML GAN system was set up in Jupyter Notebook with the ML library TensorFlow. As the labeled configurations are being documented as images by 12 parameters, all and only the numeric information is inputted into the GAN system as multidimensional data. A fully connected neural network (FCNN) is applied in both the discriminator and generator of the GAN system. For the first stage of the system, the labeled data were inputted into the discriminator to set up the initial discriminator. At the same time, the generator is fed by a random dataset as its initial setting. The second stage is optimizing the generator. The weight of different parameters is adjusted due to the identifying information that is produced by the initial discriminator. Thus, more data that are more likely to cheat the discriminator can be generated. The third stage is improving the accuracy of the discriminator based on the newly generated data by the generator. Stages 2 and 3 will iterate with each other repeatedly, and finally, the system trains a generator that can generate data that meet the criteria of what the designer labeled as the desired configuration. These three stages of GAN are all processed within the training box of the operation flow (Figure 24.6).

Training process

The form-finding script based on Grasshopper generates unbiased random variables, and every 12 variables constructs a configuration. In this experiment, the form-finding script generates 2,000 groups of random variables that provide data for 2,000 configurations. These configurations are regarded as the library. The initial library is manually labeled as good or bad ("good" is labeled as "1," and "bad" is labeled as "0"). The configurations labeled as "1" account for around 20% of the total library, and the "good" configurations are defined as the target. The manual labeling process is performed by analyzing images of those configurations through visual impressions rather than abstract data ideologies. When it comes to the

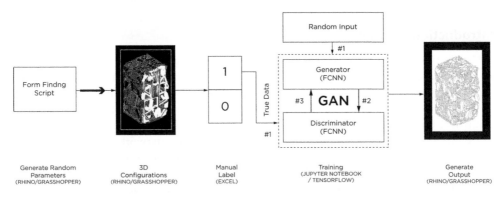

Figure 24.6   ML operation flow chart.

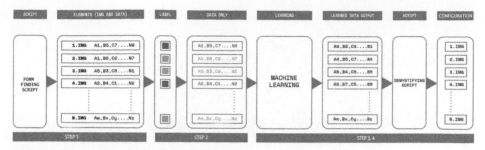

Figure 24.7 Simplified experiment flow chart.

subsequent ML operation, configurations are analyzed based on their 12 variables, and those operations are purely numeric.

To better understand the whole experiment, the ML process can be regarded as a black box, and the whole process is shown below (Figure 24.7):

1 Generate unbiased random configurations from the form-finding script.
2 Manually label the configurations based on a certain criterion by a human designer.
3 Input the labeled data into the black box (ML).
4 The black box is trained by the labeled data and iterates itself, and finally outputs configurations that match the designer's preference.

Results and evaluation

To further evaluate the effectiveness of the system, terms with abstract architectural connotations are selected for both labeling and evaluation criteria to be tested. Simple and straightforward criteria, including "big," "thin," "tall," "blue," "red," which all have clear definitions that could be either perfectly transferred to numbers or verbally articulated without ambiguity, are employed to test the system's ability to understand simple notions and achieving straightforward goals. For the sake of testing, the term "thin" was taken as a term for selection criterion. According to the distribution maps (Figure 24.9), the trained machine has a clear understanding of such a term and possesses the ability to create configurations that precisely meet the criterion (Figure 24.8). In this case, "thin" was considered as something

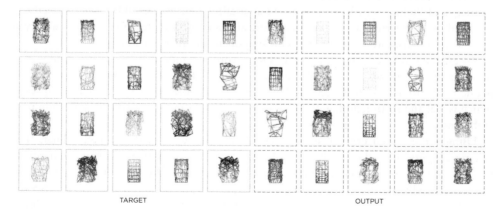

TARGET   OUTPUT

Figure 24.8 Comparison between the target (a small portion of the pool) and the output, using "thin" as the criteria.

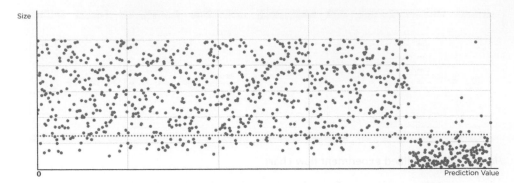

Size

0

Prediction Value

Figure 24.9 The "size" value distribution of the output meets the "thin" criteria.

that comprises slim elements and thus creates a frail and delicate composition. As seen in the figure, the target objects are in close resemblance to the output ones making the test a success. This shows that the algorithm can read the user's sensibility ("thin") and help in creating more iterations based on the same ideology.

During fine-tuning our network, we were lucky to find that a simplified nonadversarial network is also able to carry out the task properly when dealing with comparably easy tasks of simple criteria. Instead of a combination of generator and discriminator, we built up a classifier that works similarly to a discriminator. Like the discriminator, it has an FCNN structure and is fed with a true/false-labeled database. After "learning" the pattern of the input data, it generates a large set of purely random data and "picks" the preferred ones based on what it has learned. Compared to the GAN, the simplified network is easier to build and is generic in terms of potential application as far as we know.

The preferred scenario of the simplified nonadversarial network is one with only a few dimensions/variables having clear patterns (the pattern that can be easily distinguished both from analyzing data variables and looking at corresponding images) such as "big" or "solid," which sometimes has only two or three variables changing that have a significant impact on the result and therefore exhibits less convoluted distribution patterns, whereas the rest of variables are distributed almost randomly. It may be hard to compete with the precision and sophistication of GAN, but it certainly is an effective approach to start with.

On the other hand, sophisticated criteria, including "delicate," "monumental," "dynamic," and "solid," which are abstract to a certain extent that could not be perfectly articulated or transferred to a simple number, are employed to test the system's ability to understand sophisticated notions and achieving open and unarticulated goals.

To expound on the ambiguity of choosing a word like monumentality, the word is more of an emotion "evokes an aura of greatness, a sense of power and gravity that demands public recognition" (G, 2018), so it follows more of a nontraditional approach of semantics, which is feel and sentiment than that of a dictionary. This tends to make its definition more ambiguous.

Using sophisticated criteria, in this case, brings up two essential benefits. First, these criteria are judged based on multiple attributes (variables) and dimensions that can hardly be processed by any traditional algorithm, which could better test the machine's advantages. For instance, a traditional algorithm could easily "understand" the notion of "big" by detecting the range of the variable "size," which perhaps is bigger than 0.5, but a notion like "monumental" does not give a similar distribution as more than one variable would be affecting its production that may or may not be correlated to one another. The GAN system, on the contrary, could handle the job without any obstacle by treating the variables multidimensionally. Second, such criteria could better test the method's advantage of treating human vision and computer vision correspondingly. Sophisticated criteria are hard to be verbally articulated or defined but could be well judged by visual representations. For instance, it is hard for a human being to quantify the notion of "monumentality" into computer-readable variables, but it is easy for one to judge whether a certain 3D configuration conveys the sense of "monumentality" or not by simply looking at its image while at the same time let the machine read its corresponding data, leaving each player of the game only focuses on what it is good at.

Comparison between each target and output configuration shows three interesting facts. First, the output configurations are visually similar to the target ones as is expected—the higher the prediction value is, the stronger the similarity becomes. Second, within a certain range of prediction value, the machine can output surprising and criteria-meeting configurations with fewer similarities but architecturally more provoking moments with the targets. The serendipitous creations are what makes the algorithm worthwhile as those unconscious outputs are what a designer looks for which they would have not been able to achieve with a very calculated and conscious effort. Last, the outputs, based on the same criteria, could vary dramatically among different individuals who label the data, which shows the machine's ability to understand the architectural notions of each designers' subjectivities and sensibilities (Figure 24.10).

The idea behind the postproduced render (Figure 24.11) of an output configuration is to provide a possibility of the scenario of the functionality of the outputs in an imaginary scenario. These are abstract notions of imagination shown in the four images where the background or environment of the images are manually created or selected. As a designer or an architect, it becomes easier to visualize objects in some real-time (virtual real time) settings to understand the real emotion around the space created.

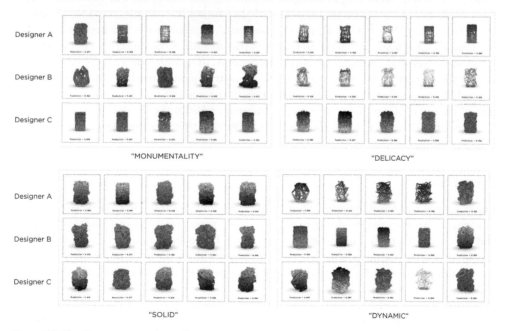

Figure 24.10 Cross-comparisons between outputs of different criteria and designers.

"MONUMENTALITY" (Designer B) "DELICACY" (Designer A)

"SOLID" (Designer C) "DYNAMIC" (Designer B)

Figure 24.11   The postproduction of the four output configurations with the highest prediction values. Render background is downloaded from https://wall.alphacoders.com.

In this case, whoever labels and trains the machine gets to render the raw geometric output in his or her way that reinforces or even enhances the concept in mind. For instance, the concept of "solid," according to Designer C, reminds him of a castle-like structure, with its thick enclosure and a glance of shimmering light coming from inside, standing against the cold. To express Designer B's notion of "dynamic," he renders the geometry using colors without any clear boundary between them and tries to address the object's mysterious uncertainty and its tendency to move or morph. Designer A, to reinforce the concept of "delicacy," sets up an extreme contrast by putting the geometry against rough-textured rocks and a single-light source from the back that articulates the geometry's fine details. For "monumentality," the sense of symmetry, apocalypse, infinity, and even the loneliness of the person in the background are all parts of the visual representation that manifests Designer B's unique understanding of such a term.

Discussion

Judging from the results mentioned above, the proposed methodology processes data in a new aggressive way and by doing so eliminates the repetitive labor of manual adjustments and selections of a traditional generative algorithm. Designers do not need to wait and pray for their preferred results anymore, they could simply skim through an automatically generated library and then let the machine generate a pool of customized outcomes that meets their goal.

Such a system could be employed in design collaboration between humans with varying design ideologies. In this globalized world, people are coming from different backgrounds and experiences that shape how one thinks and functions in the present. Though English seems to be the language that unites us all but is also a big misnomer for people. To give an example, in American English, a cheeseburger means a beef patty with cheese, but in a different country in the world, it may mean as simple as a slice of cheese between two pieces of bun. It should not be judged based on the language a person speaks but the emotion he or she wants to convey with those words projected. Similarly, the connotation of the word "monumentality" may vary for different people, which was evident in this research as the three authors had different notions of it. The algorithm intends to go beyond the language conformities and as designers just focus on the sentiment of the form and space. The conversation should be regarding what a space makes one feel but not how it is explained in the semantics of a language. Designing in a cooperative alliance facilitates the interaction of designers in the most amicable form and helps generate a common design solution by making designers contribute judgments equally during the supervising process without requiring an alpha dog who makes every final decision.

As a design decrypter, the system could be an executant that helps understand the sensibility of an untrained person, such as a client, who may lack the architectural jargon or vocabulary to fully present his or her thoughts. The system could act similarly to what a google translator does, but instead of converting spoken languages, it would interpret a client's philosophy into a format that is easily legible to the designer.

Another utility of this system could be seen in a novel geometric generation, which eliminates the necessity for preexisting precedence to start the design process, as well as unexpected repetition, unintentional plagiarism, and situations where designers fall into their mindsets and narrow down their scopes. However, with that said, it is noticed that the methodology could be further improved in several aspects.

Under the current labeling process, designers might find gray areas where a certain configuration neither meets the criteria sufficiently nor fails to meet the criteria entirely. Such ambiguity may result in inconsistent judgments in the labeling process and disproportionate data, which would be impossible to be used to train any network. Improvements could be made by adding a typical rating mechanism that provides designers with a scale, for example, from 0 to 5. Such a rating mechanism would ideally eliminate the gray areas and make the target data more precisely reflect the designers' preference.

Moreover, the experiment brings up a question that needs to be further discussed. It is apparent from the results that subjectivity and sensibility vary between each designer. However, is it possible to merge two supervised learning data from two different designers into a shared one? Answers to such a question would open up new possibilities of merging two different aesthetic styles or sensibilities into one surprising and even uncanny result.

Acknowledgments

This chapter is based on the thesis work of Henan Liu, Longtai Liao, and Akshay Srivastava in Taubman College, University of Michigan. Thanks to the instruction of Matias del Campo and Sandra Manninger and the technical support from Alexandra Carlson and Feifan Liao.

References

Cahill, J., & Her, S. (2019, February 24). *GANs and Art Forgery.* Retrieved September 9, 2020, from http://thephilosophersmeme.com/2019/02/24/gans-and-art-forgery/

Carpo, M. (2014). Breaking the Curve: Big Data and Design. *ArtForum International*, 52(6), 168–173.

G. (n.d.). (2018). *MONUMENTality.* Retrieved September 14, 2020, from http://www.getty.edu/research/exhibitions_events/exhibitions/monumentality/?hp-main-carousel=1

Goodfellow, I., Abadie, J. P., Mirza, M., Xu, B., Farley, D. W., Ozair, S., . . . Bengio, Y. (2014). Generative Adversarial Nets. *Advances in Neural Information Processing Systems*, 2672–2680. Retrieved from https://arxiv.org/pdf/1406.2661.pdf

Lynn, G. (2008). Beautiful Monsters. *Perspecta*, 40, 176–179. Retrieved September 14, 2020, from http://www.jstor.org/stable/40482296

Mital, P. (Director). (2013a, April 05). *Synthesis of Akira Kurosawa's Dreams using Van Gogh* [Video file]. Retrieved September 14, 2020, from https://vimeo.com/63410890

Mital, P. K., Grierson, M., & Smith, T. J. (2013b). Corpus-based Visual Synthesis. *Proceedings of the ACM Symposium on Applied Perception - SAP '13*, 51–58. doi:10.1145/2492494.2492505

Mirza, M., & Osindero, S. (2014). *Conditional Generative Adversarial Nets*. Retrieved from https://arxiv.org/pdf/1411.1784.pdf

Zhu, L. (2020, February 02). *Implementation of GAN by Pytorch* [Web log post]. Retrieved September 13, 2020, from https://blog.csdn.net/OpenSceneGraph/article/details/104148018

Index

Note: Page numbers in *italics* and **bold** refer to figures and tables; Page numbers followed by "n" refer to notes.

Printed and bound by CPI Group (UK) Ltd, Croydon, CR0 4YY

23/10/2024

01778258-0001